History of the Second World War

'It is a work of great length and great learning, illuminated by flashes of insight . . . full of brilliant strategic analysis.'

A. J. P. TAYLOR

'It is a work of art, deceptively simple and plain. It is a work of many years of mature consideration. It will become a standard text. Its perspectives will be inescapable. It is full of "Liddell Hartisms" – the expanding torrent of armoured warfare, elastic defence in depth, the indirect approach, logistic "overstretch", twin objectives and so on . . . Liddell Hart is not simply a prophet and a critic but a historian of great rank.'   *Economist*

One of the world's outstanding teacher-historians, Sir Basil Liddell Hart was born in Paris in 1895 and educated at St Paul's and Corpus Christi College, Cambridge. He joined the Army (King's Own Yorkshire Light Infantry) and served in the First World War; in 1924 he was invalided and three years later retired with the rank of Captain. He evolved several military tactical developments including the Battle Drill system and was an early advocate of airpower and armoured forces. In 1937 he became personal adviser to the War Minister, but reorganization of the Army was so slow that he resigned a year later to press the need publicly.

Liddell Hart was military correspondent to the *Daily Telegraph* from 1925–35 and to *The Times* until the outbreak of the Second World War. He lectured on strategy and tactics at staff colleges in numerous countries and wrote more than thirty books. He died in 1970.

Also by B. H. Liddell Hart in Papermac
History of the First World War

History of the Second World War

B. H. Liddell Hart

PAPERMAC

First published 1970 by Cassell and Co Ltd

This edition published 1997 by Papermac
a imprint of Macmillan Publishers Ltd
25 Eccleston Place, London SW1W 9NF
Basingstoke and Oxford

Associated companies throughout the world

ISBN 0 333 58262 4

7 9 8 6

A CIP catalogue record for this book is available from
the British Library.

Printed and bound in Great Britain by
Mackays of Chatham plc, Chatham, Kent

FOREWORD

by

Lady Liddell Hart

When Desmond Flower, the chairman of Cassell's, asked me to write the Foreword to my husband's *History of the Second World War*, I very soon realized that to thank all those who have helped in its preparation, acknowledgements should properly be given to hundreds of people, from field-marshals to privates, professors, students, and friends, with whom Basil had had contact during his active, inquiring life. In the Foreword to his *Memoirs*, he wrote that 'Memoirs are, on their happiest side, a record of friendships – and in these I have been very fortunate.' This *History* has also benefited from such friendships.

As a small boy Basil developed a love of games and the tactics of games, and he kept records and newspaper cuttings about them, as he did about the early days of aviation, when pilots were his schoolboy heroes. This habit he kept throughout his life and for all his ever-widening interests, so that at the time of his death he left hundreds of thousands of cuttings, letters, memoranda, pamphlets and the like on subjects which ranged from armoured warfare to fashions in clothes. Later, in diary form, or what he called 'Talk Notes', he recorded discussions he had about subjects that especially interested him, as soon as possible after they had taken place.

His first postwar book was *The Other Side of the Hill*, the record of his talks with a number of the German generals who were prisoners-of-war in England. Many had been readers of his prewar books and were eager to discuss their campaigns with him. In December 1963, looking back, he wrote 'A note on why and how I wrote this book' which explains why he attached so much value to this kind of record:

When exploring the events of the First World War, in the 1920s and 1930s, I came to realize how much history was handicapped because no independent and historically minded inquirer had been able to ascertain and record what the military chiefs were actually thinking at the time – as a check on their subsequent recollections. For it became very evident that the memories of the participants in dramatic events are apt to become coloured or twisted in retrospect, and increasingly as the years pass. Moreover official documents often fail to reveal their real views and aims, while sometimes even drafted to conceal them.

So during the Second World War, when visiting the British and Allied commanders, I made extensive 'notes for history' of the discussions I had with them, recording particularly their current views – as a supplement to the documentary records and a means of checking memories and accounts written in later years.

At the end of the war I was given an early opportunity of interrogating the German commanders who were then prisoners-of-war, and had many long discussions with them about the operations in which they were concerned and about wider matters. While this investigation naturally could not be quite so contemporaneous, as a light on what they had been thinking before a particular event or decision, it came at any rate *before* memories had become hazy with the passage of time, while their accounts could be cross-checked with those of other witnesses, as well as by the documentary records.

Readers of this *History* will see from the footnote references to these talks how they have stood up to the test of the 'passing of time' – and to Basil's continued cross-checking over the years.

Early in 1946 the Colonels-Commandant of the Royal Tank Regiment asked Basil to write the history of the Regiment and its predecessors, covering the two World Wars and the years between the wars. It was an immense task which took many years, and the book was not published by Cassell until 1958. But the research needed for *The Tanks* was a great help when Basil came to write this *History*, for he had come to know personally many of the younger commanders who had fought on both sides, while he had also had many long discussions with such old and valued friends as Field-Marshal Montgomery, Field-Marshal Alexander, and Field-Marshal Auchinleck, as well as his 'tank people' and many of the German Generals 'on the other side of the hill'.

After the 1946 War of Independence, Israeli officers of all ranks came to see Basil to consult him about the formation of their Army. Among them was Yigal Allon, who became a close friend – and it was Yigal who inscribed his photograph in the library at States House with the now much-quoted words 'To the Captain who teaches Generals'. In 1961 Basil was asked to visit Israel and lecture to the armed forces and universities. Many tributes have been paid to Basil's teachings by the

Israelis, and Basil often said, somewhat ruefully, that rather than his own countrymen, the Germans and the Israelis were his 'best pupils'.

In 1951 Frau Rommel asked him if he would edit her husband's papers. He agreed and a warm relationship developed between us and Field-Marshal Rommel's widow, his son Manfred, and with General Bayerlein, who had been Rommel's Chief of Staff; and also with Mark Bonham Carter of Collins, who was the very able publisher's editor.

In 1952 Basil lectured at War Colleges in Canada and the United States. These were exhausting months, but rewarding, and he was able to meet wartime friends from both countries and to make new ones. Among the honours he received that gave him most pleasure was his honorary membership of the US Marine Corps, and until he died he daily wore the gold tie clip presented to him on that occasion.

In 1965 he was asked to be Visiting Professor of History at the University of California, Davis: so at the age of seventy he became a Professor and lectured and taught on the two World Wars. This was a stimulating experience which he thoroughly enjoyed, but unfortunately our stay was cut short by several months as he had to return to England for a major operation. At the time of his death he was looking forward – against his doctor's advice – to returning to America in April 1970 at the invitation of the US Naval War College to give a series of lectures on strategy.

Travel was an essential part of Basil's life, and he accepted many invitations to visit European countries and to lecture at Staff Colleges. He was a brilliant map reader and his vivid accounts of Sherman's battles in the American Civil War were written with the aid of an intensive study of large-scale maps, long before he visited the battle-fields of the Southern States. After the last war we made almost yearly visits to Western Europe to study battlefields and landing beaches, to visit old friends, and, maps in hand, to check data for this *History*. He loved beautiful country, cathedrals, and good food, so for our tours the *Guide Michelin*, battlefield maps and tourists' guides were always put in the car together, and careful daily notes about terrain, food, and church architecture were dictated to me for subsequent filing in the ever-grow-ing records at home.

Basil had been critical of the Official Historians of the First World War, saying that sometimes the word 'Official' cancelled out the word 'History', but he had a high opinion of most of those who wrote about the Second World War, and his files are full of correspondence with many of them in this country, the Commonwealth, and America. Friendships with historians – the younger historians particularly – and students from all over the world enriched his life and he spent a great deal of time reading and criticizing the drafts of their theses and books, to the neglect of his own work but to his infinite pleasure. As one of them, Ronald Lewin, wrote: '... he praised only where on his terms praise was due, and [gave] you hell if he thought you were wrong in fact or opinion.' Young scholars, academics, authors, journalists – and older ones – came to work in the library and to examine the books and papers which were all made available to them. 'Tutorials' would be given at any time of the day or night, over meals and during walks in the garden. Correlli Barnett, General André Beaufre, Colonel Henri Bernard, Brian Bond, Alan Clark, Colonel A. Goutard, Alastair Horne, Michael Howard, Robert O'Neill, Peter Paret, Barrie Pitt, W. R. Thompson, Michael Williams, are but some of the best known among the many contemporary historians who came first for discussion and work, became regular correspondents, and to our great happiness returned again and again as our friends. Many others, such as Jay Luvaas and Don Schurman, who with their families became our devoted friends, came from America and Canada.

To all these people therefore, and to the hundreds in all those many spheres other than strategy and defence in which Basil's far-ranging interests lay whose names I have not given and who will, I trust, forgive me for that, this *History* owes much. Nobody believed more than did Basil that a teacher will be 'taught by his pupils', and his pupils and friends were among the most stimulating it was possible to have. While writing the *History*, Basil had some very able assistants. Christopher Hart, then Peter Simkins, now at the Imperial War Museum, Paul Kennedy who did some valuable work on the Pacific Campaign, and Peter Bradley who helped with the chapters on Air.

Many secretaries worked with great efficiency over the years and their interest and patience in typing and re-typing the successive drafts of the *History* made the task easier for Basil. Miss Myra Thomson (now Mrs Slater) was with us for eight years during the time we lived at Wolverton Park. Later, here at States House, Mrs Daphne Bosanquet and Mrs Edna Robinson were helpful in every possible way, and in the last stages of the preparation of the *History*, Mrs Wendy Smith, Mrs Pamela Byrnes and Mrs Margaret Haws did valuable work.

Among the countless other people to be thanked are the directors and staff of Cassell's, the publishers of the British edition of the *History*. Desmond Flower commissioned the book in 1947 and has waited patiently for it to be finished. Thanks are also due to David Higham, not only as the literary agent for many of Basil's books, but for his friendship over the years.

I would also like to thank the directors and staff of Clowes, the printers, and particularly Bill Raine at their Beccles works, for their interest in the book and the fine quality of the printing, and for producing it to schedule in spite of many difficulties. I am glad that Clowes have printed this *History*, Basil's last book, since it was they whom he approached to print one of his first, *Science of Infantry Tactics*, in 1921.

The publishers and I are especially grateful to the following who so generously read various chapters or the whole of the *History* before or after Basil's death and gave him the benefit of their criticisms: G. R. Atkinson, Brian Bond, Dr Noble Frankland, Vice-Admiral Sir Peter Gretton, Adrian Liddell Hart, Malcolm Mackintosh, Captain Stephen Roskill, Vice-Admiral Brian Schofield, Lieut-Colonel Albert Seaton, Major-General Sir Kenneth Strong, and Dr M. J. Williams. Some of them have generously allowed Basil to make quotations from their own books – Colonel Seaton before his was even published.

We would like also to thank Ann Fern and Richard Natkiel for their work in respectively researching and drawing the maps; and once again thanks are due to Miss Hebe Jerrold, who has produced a first-class index, though having to work under much pressure.

Of the many people who have helped, I know that we all are most indebted to Kenneth Parker of Cassell's, Basil's editor and friend, who has had the heavy task of organizing the *History* for publication after Basil's death. Without him, the book would have been delayed even longer. Basil said, in the Foreword to his *Memoirs*, that he had 'been blessed ... with a most stimulating, knowledgeable and exacting editor with whom it has been a delight to work'. To those words I would like to add my special gratitude for his work on the *History*.

Basil had small private means, so research for the *History* was always slowed down as he had to earn a living by his journalism and by writing other, more quickly produced books. He was helped during the years 1965–7 by a grant from the Wolfson Foundation and he appreciated the special interest that Mr Leonard Wolfson showed in the *History*. Help came from another direction in 1961, when King's College, London, where Michael Howard was then Director of Military Studies, generously made possible the conversion of the stables of States House into a Library, and a small flat was built in the barn for the use of visiting historians. This greatly added to our working space and to the comfort of the scholars. Also the Inland Revenue authorities in the three different districts where we lived during these years, by their understanding of the nature and the problems of Basil's work, made it possible for us to live and work in England. Without this, we would have been forced to live abroad and the *History*, as well as much else of Basil's writing and teaching, would have suffered.

To 'all who helped', therefore, named and unnamed in this Foreword, I would like to dedicate this book.

KATHLEEN LIDDELL HART

States House,
Medmenham,
Bucks, England
July 1970

CONTENTS

PART V

THE TURN
(1942)

PART VI

THE EBB
(1943)

PART VII

FULL EBB
(1944)

PART VIII

FINALE
(1945)

Part IX
EPILOGUE
(*page* 731)

MAPS

DRAWN BY

Richard Natkiel, FRGS

Map Research by Ann Fern

PART I

THE PRELUDE

CHAPTER ONE

How War was Precipitated

On April 1st, 1939, the world's Press carried the news that Mr Neville Chamberlain's Cabinet, reversing its policy of appeasement and detachment, had pledged Britain to defend Poland against any threat from Germany, with the aim of ensuring peace in Europe.

On September 1st, however, Hitler marched across the Polish frontier. Two days later, after vainly demanding his withdrawal, Britain and France entered the fight. Another European War had started – and it developed into a second World War.

The Western Allies entered that war with a two-fold object. The immediate purpose was to fulfil their promise to preserve the independence of Poland. The ultimate purpose was to remove a potential menace to themselves, and thus ensure their own security. In the outcome, they failed in both purposes. Not only did they fail to prevent Poland from being overcome in the first place, and partitioned between Germany and Russia, but after six years of war which ended in apparent victory they were forced to acquiesce in Russia's domination of Poland – abandoning their pledges to the Poles who had fought on their side.

At the same time all the effort that was put into the destruction of Hitlerite Germany resulted in a Europe so devastated and weakened in the process that its power of resistance was much reduced in the face of a fresh and greater menace – and Britain, in common with her European neighbours had become a poor dependant of the United States.

These are the hard facts underlying the victory that was so hopefully pursued and so painfully achieved – after the colossal weight of both Russia and America had been drawn into the scales against Germany. The outcome dispelled the persistent popular illusion that 'victory' spelt peace. It confirmed the warning of past experience that victory is a 'mirage in the desert' – the desert that a long war creates, when waged with modern weapons and unlimited methods.

It is worthwhile to take stock of the consequences of the war before dealing with its causation. A realization of what the war brought may

Europe at the Outbreak of War

0 Miles   200   400
0 Km.   200   400   600

NOR...
Os...

NORTH SEA

IRELAND
Dublin

GREAT
BRITAIN

DENM

HOLLAND
Amsterdam

ATLANTIC

London

The Hague

OCEAN

Brussels
BELGIUM

B

Cologne

GER

Paris

LUX.

SUDET
LAN

Seine

MAGINOT
LINE

SIEGFRIED
LINE

FRANCE

Munich

Bern
SWITZ.

Geneva

Milan

Marseilles

PORTUGAL
Lisbon

Madrid

SPAIN

Corsica

ITA

R...

Sardinia

Tangier   Gibraltar

MEDITERRANEAN   SEA

S...

SPAN
MOROCCO

ALGERIA

clear the way for a more realistic examination of how the war was produced. It sufficed for the purposes of the Nuremberg Trials to assume that the outbreak of war, and all its extensions, were purely due to Hitler's aggression. But that is too simple and shallow an explanation.

The last thing that Hitler wanted to produce was another great war. His people, and particularly his generals, were profoundly fearful of any such risk – the experiences of World War I had scarred their minds. To emphasize the basic facts is not to whitewash Hitler's inherent aggressiveness, nor that of many Germans who eagerly followed his lead. But Hitler, though utterly unscrupulous, was for long cautious in pursuing his aims. The military chiefs were still more cautious and anxious about any step that might provoke a general conflict.

A large part of the German archives were captured after the war, and have thus been available for examination. They reveal an extraordinary degree of trepidation and deep-seated distrust of Germany's capacity to wage a great war.

When, in 1936, Hitler moved to re-occupy the demilitarized zone of the Rhineland, his generals were alarmed at his decision and the reactions it might provoke from the French. As a result of their protests only a few token units were sent in at first, as 'straws in the wind'. When he wished to send troops to help Franco in the Spanish Civil War they made fresh protests about the risks involved, and he agreed to restrict his aid. But he disregarded their apprehensions about the march into Austria, in March 1938.

When, shortly afterwards, Hitler disclosed his intention of putting the screw on Czecho-Slovakia for the return of the Sudetenland, the Chief of the General Staff, General Beck, drafted a memorandum in which he argued that Hitler's aggressively expansionist programme was bound to produce a world-wide catastrophe and Germany's ruin. This was read out at a conference of the leading generals, and, with their general approval, sent to Hitler. As Hitler showed no sign of changing his policy, the Chief of the General Staff resigned from office. Hitler assured the other generals that France and Britain would not fight for Czecho-Slovakia, but they were so far from being reassured that they plotted a military revolt, to avert the risk of war by arresting Hitler and the other Nazi leaders.

The bottom was knocked out of their counter-plan, however, when Chamberlain acceded to Hitler's crippling demands upon Czecho-Slovakia, and in concert with the French agreed to stand aside while that unhappy country was stripped of both territory and defences.

For Chamberlain, the Munich Agreement spelt 'peace for our time'.

For Hitler, it spelt a further and greater triumph not only over his foreign opponents but also over his generals. After their warnings had been so repeatedly refuted by his unchallenged and bloodless successes, they naturally lost confidence, and influence. Naturally, too, Hitler himself became overweeningly confident of a continued run of easy success. Even when he came to see that further ventures might entail a war he felt that it would be only a small one, and a short one. His moments of doubt were drowned by the cumulative effect of intoxicating success.

If he had really contemplated a general war, involving Britain, he would have put every possible effort into building a Navy capable of challenging Britain's command of the sea. But, in fact, he did not even build up his Navy to the limited scale visualized in the Anglo-German Naval Treaty of 1935. He constantly assured his admirals that they could discount any risk of war with Britain. After Munich he told them that they need not anticipate a conflict with Britain within the next six years at least. Even in the summer of 1939, and as late as August 22nd, he repeated such assurances – if with waning conviction.

How, then, did it come about that he became involved in the major war that he had been so anxious to avoid? The answer is to be found not merely, nor most, in Hitler's aggressiveness, but in the encouragement he had long received from the complaisant attitude of the Western Powers coupled with their sudden turn-about in the spring of 1939. That reversal was so abrupt and unexpected as to make war inevitable.

If you allow anyone to stoke up a boiler until the steam-pressure rises beyond danger-point, the real responsibility for any resultant explosion will lie with you. That truth of physical science applies equally to political science – especially to the conduct of international affairs.

Ever since Hitler's entry into power, in 1933, the British and French Governments had conceded to this dangerous autocrat immeasurably more than they had been willing to concede to Germany's previous democratic Governments. At every turn they showed a disposition to avoid trouble and shelve awkward problems – to preserve their present comfort at the expense of the future.

Hitler, on the other hand, was thinking out his problems all too logically. The course of his policy came to be guided by the ideas formulated in a 'testament' which he expounded in November 1937 – a version of which has been preserved in the so-called 'Hossbach Memorandum'. It was based on the conviction of Germany's vital need for more *lebensraum* – living space – for her expanding population if there was to be any chance of maintaining their living standards. In his view

Germany could not hope to make herself self-sufficient, especially in food-supply. Nor by buying it abroad could she obtain what was needed, since that meant spending more foreign exchange than she could afford. The prospects of her obtaining an increased share in world trade and industry were too limited, because of other nations' tariff walls and her own financial stringency. Moreover the method of indirect supply would make her dependent on foreign nations, and liable to starvation in case of war.

His conclusion was that Germany must obtain more 'agriculturally useful space' – in the thinly populated areas of Eastern Europe. It would be vain to hope that this would be willingly conceded her. 'The history of all times – Roman Empire, British Empire – has proved that every space expansion can be effected only by breaking resistance and taking risks ... Neither in former times nor today has space been found without an owner.' The problem would have to be solved by 1945 at the latest – 'after this we can only expect a change for the worse'. Possible outlets would be blocked while a food crisis would be imminent.

While these ideas went much farther than Hitler's initial desire to recover the territory that had been taken from Germany after World War I, it is not true that Western statesmen were as unaware of them as they later pretended. In 1937–8 many of them were frankly realistic in private discussion, though not on public platforms, and many arguments were set forth in British governing circles for allowing Germany to expand eastwards, and thus divert danger from the West. They showed much sympathy with Hitler's desire for *lebensraum* – and let him know it. But they shirked thinking out the problem of how the owners could be induced to yield it except to threat of superior force.

The German documents reveal that Hitler derived special encouragement from Lord Halifax's visit in November 1937. Halifax was then Lord President of the Council, ranking second in the Cabinet to the Prime Minister. According to the documentary record of the interview, he gave Hitler to understand that Britain would allow him a free hand in Eastern Europe. Halifax may not have meant as much, but that was the impression he conveyed – and it proved of crucial importance.

Then, in February 1938, Mr Anthony Eden was driven to resign as Foreign Minister after repeated disagreements with Chamberlain – who in response to one of his protests had told him to 'go home and take an aspirin'. Halifax was appointed to succeed him at the Foreign Office. A few days later the British Ambassador in Berlin, Sir Nevile Henderson, called on Hitler for a confidential talk, in continuation of Halifax's November conversation, and conveyed that the British Government was much in sympathy with Hitler's desire for 'changes in Europe' to Germany's benefit – 'the present British Government had a keen sense of reality'.

As the documents show, these events precipitated Hitler's action. He thought that the lights had changed to green, allowing him to proceed eastward. It was a very natural conclusion.

Hitler was further encouraged by the accommodating way that the British and French Governments accepted his march into Austria and incorporation of that country in the German Reich. (The only hitch in that easy coup was the way many of his tanks broke down on the road to Vienna.) Still more encouragement came when he heard that Chamberlain and Halifax had rejected Russian proposals, after that coup, to confer on a collective insurance plan against the German advance.

Here it should be added that when the threat to the Czechs came to a head in September 1938, the Russian Government again made known, publicly and privately, its willingness to combine with France and Britain in measures to defend Czecho-Slovakia. That offer was ignored. Moreover, Russia was ostentatiously excluded from the Munich conference at which Czecho-Slovakia's fate was settled. This 'cold-shouldering' had fatal consequences the following year.

After the way that the British Government had appeared to acquiesce in his eastward move, Hitler was unpleasantly surprised by their strong reaction, and the partial mobilization, which developed when he 'put the heat' on Czecho-Slovakia in September. But when Chamberlain yielded to his demands, and actively helped him to impose his terms on Czecho-Slovakia, he felt that the momentary threat of resistance had been in the nature of a face-saving operation – to meet the objections of the large body of British opinion, headed by Mr Winston Churchill, which opposed the governmental policy of conciliation and concession. He was no less encouraged by the passivity of the French. As they had so readily abandoned their Czech ally, which had possessed the most efficient Army of all the smaller Powers, it seemed unlikely that they would go to war in defence of any remnant of their former chain of allies in East and Central Europe.

Thus Hitler felt that he could safely complete the elimination of Czecho-Slovakia at an early moment, and then expand his eastward advance.

At first he did not think of moving against Poland – even though she possessed the largest stretch of territory carved out of Germany after World War I. Poland, like Hungary, had been helpful to him in threatening Czecho-Slovakia's rear, and thus inducing her to surrender to his demands – Poland, incidentally, had exploited the chance to seize a slice of Czech territory. Hitler was inclined to accept Poland as a junior partner for the time being, on condition that she handed back the German port of Danzig and granted Germany a free route to East Prussia through the Polish 'Corridor'. On Hitler's part, it was a remarkably moderate demand in the circumstances. But in successive discussions that winter, Hitler found that the Poles were obstinately disinclined to make any such concession, and also had an inflated idea of their own strength. Even so, he continued to hope that they would come round after further negotiation. As late as March 25th he told his Army Commander-in-Chief that he 'did not wish to solve the Danzig problem by the use of force'. But a change of mind was produced by an unexpected British step that followed on a fresh step on his part in a different direction.

In the early months of 1939, the heads of the British Government were feeling happier than they had for a long time past. They lulled themselves into the belief that their accelerated rearmament measures, America's rearmament programme and Germany's economic difficulties were diminishing the danger of the situation. On March 10th Chamberlain privately expressed the view that the prospects of peace were better than ever, and spoke of his hopes that a new disarmament conference would be arranged before the end of the year. Next day Sir Samuel Hoare – Eden's predecessor as Foreign Secretary and now Home Secretary – hopefully suggested in a speech that the world was entering 'a Golden Age'. Ministers assured friends and critics that Germany's economic plight made her incapable of going to war, and that she was bound to comply with the British Government's conditions in return for the help that it was offering her in the form of a commercial treaty. Two ministers, Mr Oliver Stanley and Mr Robert Hudson, were going to Berlin to arrange it.

That same week *Punch* came out with a cartoon which showed 'John Bull' awaking with relief from a nightmare, while the recent 'war scare' was flying out of the window. Never was there such a spell of absurdly optimistic illusions as during the week leading up to the 'Ides of March', 1939.

Meantime the Nazis had been fostering separatist movements in Czecho-Slovakia, to produce its breakdown from within. On March 12th the Slovaks declared their independence, after their leader, Father Tiso, had visited Hitler in Berlin. More blindly, Poland's Foreign Minister, Colonel Beck, publicly expressed his full sympathy with the Slovaks. On the 15th, German troops marched into Prague, after the

Czech President had yielded to Hitler's demand to establish a 'Protectorate' over Bohemia and to occupy the country accordingly.

The previous autumn, when the Munich agreement was made, the British Government had pledged itself to guarantee Czecho-Slovakia against aggression. But Chamberlain told the House of Commons that he considered that Slovakia's break-away had annulled the guarantee, and that he did not feel bound by this obligation. While expressing regret at what had happened, he conveyed to the House that he saw no reason why it should 'deflect' British policy.

Within a few days, however, Chamberlain made a complete 'about-turn' – so sudden and far-reaching that it amazed the world. He jumped to a decision to block any following move of Hitler's and on March 29th sent Poland an offer to support her against 'any action which threatened Polish independence, and which the Polish Government accordingly considered it vital to resist'.

It is impossible to gauge what was the predominant influence on his impulse – the pressure of public indignation, or his own indignation, or his anger at having been fooled by Hitler, or his humiliation at having been made to look a fool in the eyes of his own people.

Most of those in Britain who had supported and applauded his previous appeasement policy underwent a similarly violent reaction – sharpened by the reproaches of the 'other half' of the nation, which had distrusted the policy. The breach was cemented, and the nation reunited, by a general surge of exasperation.

The unqualified terms of the guarantee placed Britain's destiny in the hands of Poland's rulers, men of very dubious and unstable judgement. Moreover, the guarantee was impossible to fulfil except with Russia's help, yet no preliminary steps were taken to find out whether Russia would give, or Poland would accept, such aid.

The Cabinet, when asked to approve the guarantee, was not even shown the actual report of the Chiefs of Staff Committee – which would have made clear how impossible it was, in a practical sense, to give any effective protection to Poland.* It is doubtful, however, whether this would have made any difference in face of the prevailing mood.

When the guarantee was discussed in Parliament it was welcomed on all sides. Mr Lloyd George's was a solitary voice when he warned the House that it was suicidal folly to undertake such a far-stretched

---

* I was told this soon afterwards by Mr Hore-Belisha, then Secretary of State for War, and also by Lord Beaverbrook, who had heard about the matter from other members of the Government.

commitment without first making sure of Russia's backing. The Polish Guarantee was the surest way to produce an early explosion, and a world war. It combined the maximum temptation with manifest provocation. It incited Hitler to demonstrate the futility of such a guarantee to a country out of reach from the West, while making the stiff-necked Poles even less inclined to consider any concession to him, and at the same time making it impossible for him to draw back without 'losing face'.

Why did Poland's rulers accept such a fatal offer? Partly because they had an absurdly exaggerated idea of the power of their out of date forces – they boastfully talked of a 'cavalry ride to Berlin'. Partly because of personal factors: Colonel Beck, shortly afterwards, said that he made up his mind to accept the British offer between 'two flicks of the ash' off the cigarette he was smoking. He went on to explain that at his meeting with Hitler in January he had found it hard to swallow Hitler's remark that Danzig '*must*' be handed back, and that when the British offer was communicated to him he saw it, and seized it, as a chance to give Hitler a slap in the face. This impulse was only too typical of the ways in which the fate of peoples is often decided.

The only chance of avoiding war now lay in securing the support of Russia – the only power that could give Poland direct support and thus provide a deterrent to Hitler. But, despite the urgency of the situation, the British Government's steps were dilatory and half-hearted. Chamberlain had a strong dislike of Soviet Russia and Halifax an intense religious antipathy, while both underrated her strength as much as they overrated Poland's. If they now recognized the desirability of a defensive arrangement with Russia they wanted it on their own terms, and failed to realize that by their precipitate guarantee to Poland they had placed themselves in a position where they would have to sue for it on her terms – as was obvious to Stalin, if not to them.

But beyond their own hesitations were the objections of the Polish Government, and the other small powers in eastern Europe, to accepting military support from Russia – since these feared that reinforcement by her armies would be equivalent to invasion. So the pace of the Anglo-Russian negotiations became as slow as a funeral march.

Very different was Hitler's response to the new situation. Britain's violent reaction and redoubled armament measures shook him, but the effect was opposite to that intended. Feeling that the British were becoming opposed to German expansion eastward, and fearful of being blocked if he tarried, he drew the conclusion that he must accelerate his steps towards *lebensraum*. But how could he do it without bringing on a general war? His solution was coloured by his historically derived picture of the British. Regarding them as cool-headed and rational, with their emotions controlled by their head, he felt that they would not dream of entering a war on behalf of Poland unless they could obtain Russia's support. So, swallowing his hatred and fear of 'Bolshevism', he bent his efforts and energies towards conciliating Russia and securing her abstention. It was a turn-about even more startling than Chamberlain's – and as fatal in its consequences.

Hitler's courting approach to Russia was eased because Stalin was already looking on the West from a new slant. The Russians' natural resentment of the way they had been cold-shouldered by Chamberlain and Halifax in 1938 was increased when, after Hitler's march into Prague, their fresh proposal for a joint defensive alliance had a tepid reception, while the British Government rushed into an independent arrangement with Poland. Nothing could have been more certain to deepen doubt and heighten suspicion.

On May 3rd a warning, unmistakable except to the blind, was conveyed in the news that Litvinov, Russia's Foreign Commissar, had been 'released' from office. He had long been the chief advocate of cooperation with the Western Powers in resistance to Nazi Germany. To his post was appointed Molotov, who was reported to prefer dealing with dictators to dealing with liberal democracies.

Tentative moves towards a Soviet-Nazi *entente* began in April, but were conducted on both sides with extreme wariness – for mutual distrust was profound, and each side suspected that the other might be merely trying to hinder it reaching an agreement with the Western Powers. But the slow progress of the Anglo-Russian negotiations encouraged the Germans to exploit the opportunity, quicken their pace, and press their suit. Molotov remained non-committal, however, until the middle of August. Then a decisive change took place. It may have been prompted by the Germans' willingness, in contrast to British hesitations and reservations, to concede Stalin's exacting conditions, especially a free hand with the Baltic States. It may also have been connected with the obvious fact that Hitler could not afford to postpone action in Poland beyond early September, lest the weather might bog him down, so that the postponement of the Soviet-German agreement until late in August ensured that there would not be time for Hitler and the Western Powers to reach another 'Munich agreement' – which might spell danger for Russia.

On August 23rd Ribbentrop flew to Moscow, and the pact was signed. It was accompanied by a secret agreement under which Poland was to be partitioned between Germany and Russia.

This pact made war certain, and all the more so because of the lateness of the timing. Hitler could not draw back on the Polish issue without serious loss of face in Moscow. Moreover, his belief that the British Government would not venture on an obviously futile struggle to preserve Poland, and did not really wish to bring in Russia, had been freshly fostered by the way that Chamberlain had, in late July, started private negotiations with him through his trusted adviser, Sir Horace Wilson, for an Anglo-German pact.

But the Soviet-German Pact, coming so late, did not have the effect on the British that Hitler had reckoned. On the contrary, it aroused the 'bulldog' spirit – of blind determination, regardless of the consequences. In that state of feeling, Chamberlain could not stand aside without both loss of face and breach of promise.

Stalin had been only too well aware that the Western Powers had long been disposed to let Hitler expand eastward – in Russia's direction. It is probable that he saw the Soviet-German Pact as a convenient device by which he could divert Hitler's aggressive dynamism in the opposite direction. In other words, by this nimble side-step he would let his immediate and potential opponents crash into one another. At the least this should produce a diminution of the threat to Soviet Russia, and might well result in such common exhaustion on their part as to ensure Russia's postwar ascendancy.

The Pact meant the removal of Poland as a buffer between Germany and Russia – but the Russians had always felt that the Poles were more likely to serve as a spearhead for a German invasion of Russia than as a barricade against it. By collaborating in Hitler's conquest of Poland, and dividing it with him, they would not only be taking an easy way of regaining their pre-1914 property but be able to convert eastern Poland into a barrier space which, though narrower, would be held by their own forces. That seemed a more reliable buffer than an independent Poland. The Pact also paved the way for Russia's occupation of the Baltic States and Bessarabia, as a wider extension of the buffer.

In 1941, after Hitler had swept into Russia, Stalin's 1939 side-step looked a fatally short-sighted shift. It is likely that Stalin overestimated the Western nations' capacity for resisting, and thus exhausting, Germany's power. It is likely, too, that he also overestimated the initial resisting power of his own forces. Nevertheless, surveying the European situation in later years, it does not seem so certain as in 1941 that his side-step proved to Soviet Russia's disadvantage.

For the West, on the other hand, it brought immeasurable harm. The primary blame for that lies with those who were responsible for the successive policies of procrastination and precipitation – in face of a palpably explosive situation.

Dealing with Britain's entry into the war – after describing how she allowed Germany to re-arm and then to swallow Austria and Czecho-Slovakia, while at the same time spurning Russia's proposals for joint action – Churchill says:

... when every one of these aids and advantages has been squandered and thrown away, Great Britain advances, leading France by the hand, to guarantee the integrity of Poland – of that very Poland which with hyena appetite had only six months before joined in the pillage and destruction of the Czechoslovak State. There was sense in fighting for Czechoslovakia in 1938, when the German Army could scarcely put half a dozen trained divisions on the Western Front, when the French with nearly sixty or seventy divisions could most certainly have rolled forward across the Rhine or into the Ruhr. But this had been judged unreasonable, rash, below the level of modern intellectual thought and morality. Yet now at last the two Western democracies declared themselves ready to stake their lives upon the territorial integrity of Poland. History, which, we are told, is mainly the record of the crimes, follies, and miseries of mankind, may be scoured and ransacked to find a parallel to this sudden and complete reversal of five or six years' policy of easy-going placatory appeasement, and its transformation almost overnight into a readiness to accept an obviously imminent war on far worse conditions and on the greatest scale ...

Here was decision at last, taken at the worst possible moment and on the least satisfactory ground, which must surely lead to the slaughter of tens of millions of people.*

It is a striking verdict on Chamberlain's folly, written in hindsight. For Churchill himself had, in the heat of the moment, supported Chamberlain's pressing offer of Britain's guarantee to Poland. It is only too evident that in 1939 he, like most of Britain's leaders, acted on a hot-headed impulse – instead of with the cool-headed judgement that was once characteristic of British statesmanship.

* Churchill: *The Second World War*, vol I, pp 311–12. Full bibliographical details of all books referred to in the text can be found on p. 747.

CHAPTER TWO

The Opposing Forces at the Outbreak

On Friday September 1st, 1939, the German armies invaded Poland. On Sunday, the 3rd, the British Government declared war on Germany, in fulfilment of the guarantee it had earlier given to Poland. Six hours later the French Government, more hesitantly, followed the British lead.

In making his fateful announcement to the British Parliament the seventy-year old Prime Minister, Mr Chamberlain, finished by saying: 'I trust I may live to see the day when Hitlerism has been destroyed and a liberated Europe has been re-established.' Within less than a month Poland had been overrun. Within nine months most of Western Europe had been submerged by the spreading flood of war. And although Hitler was ultimately overthrown, a liberated Europe was not re-established.

In welcoming the declaration of war, Mr Arthur Greenwood, speaking for the Labour Party, expressed his relief that 'the intolerable agony of suspense from which all of us have suffered is over. We now know the worst.' From the volume of cheers it was clear that he was expressing the general feeling of the House. He ended: 'May the war be swift and short, and may the peace which follows stand proudly for ever on the shattered ruin of an evil name.'

No reasonable calculation of the respective forces and resources provided any ground for believing that the war could be 'swift and short', or even for hoping that France and Britain alone would be able to overcome Germany – however long the war continued. Even more foolish was the assumption that 'We now know the worst'.

There were illusions about the strength of Poland. Lord Halifax – who, as Foreign Minister, ought to have been well-informed – believed that Poland was of more military value than Russia, and preferred to secure her as an ally. That was what he conveyed to the American Ambassador on March 24th, a few days before the sudden decision to offer the British guarantee to Poland. In July, the Inspector-General of the Forces, General Ironside, visited the Polish Army and on his return gave what Mr Churchill described as 'most favourable' reports.*

There were still greater illusions about the French Army. Churchill himself had described it as 'the most perfectly trained and faithful mobile force in Europe'.† When he saw General Georges, the Commander-in-Chief of the French field armies, a few days before the war, and saw the comparative figures of French and German strength, he was so favourably impressed as to say: 'But you are the masters.'**

This may have increased the eagerness with which he joined in pressing the French to hasten to declare war in support of Poland – the French Ambassador's dispatch said: 'One of the most excited was Mr Winston Churchill; bursts of his voice made the telephone vibrate.' In March, too, Churchill had declared himself 'in the most complete agreement with the Prime Minister' over the offer to guarantee Poland. Along with almost all Britain's political leaders he had dwelt on its value as a means of preserving peace. Mr Lloyd George had been alone in pointing out its impracticability and danger – and his warning was described by *The Times* as 'an outburst of inconsolable pessimism from Mr Lloyd George, who now seems to inhabit an odd and remote world of his own.'

For balance, it should be mentioned that these illusions about the prospects were not shared in the more sober military circles.†† But in general the prevailing mood of the moment was supercharged with emotions that drowned the sense of immediate realities, and obscured the long view.

Could Poland have held out longer? Could France and Britain have done more than they did to take the German pressure off Poland? On the face of the figures of armed strength, as now known, the answer to both questions would at first sight seem to be 'Yes'. In *numbers* of men Poland had sufficient to check the German forces on her front, and at the least impose a long delay on their advance. It is equally apparent, on the figures, that the French should have been able to defeat the German forces left to oppose them in the West.

The Polish Army consisted of thirty active divisions and ten reserve divisions. It had also no less than twelve large cavalry brigades – al-

* Churchill: *The Second World War*, vol I, p 357.
† April 14th, 1938.
** Churchill: *The Second World War*, vol I, p 357.
†† My own strategic appreciation written at the outbreak of war, forecasting the early defeat of Poland and the likelihood that France would not long continue the fight, epitomized the situation in its conclusion: 'In sum, by making our stand on ground that was strategically unsound we have got into a very bad hole – perhaps the worst in our history.'

though only one of them was motorized. Its potential strength in numbers was even larger than the total figure of divisions conveys – for Poland had nearly 2,500,000 'trained men' available to mobilize.

France mobilized the equivalent of 110 divisions, of which no less than sixty-five were active divisions. They included five cavalry divisions, two mechanized divisions, and one armoured division that was in process of being formed – the rest being infantry. Of the grand total, even after providing for the defence of southern France and North Africa against a possible threat from Italy, the French Command were able to concentrate eighty-five divisions on their northern front facing Germany. Moreover, they could mobilize 5,000,000 trained men.

Britain had promised to send four Regular divisions to France at the outset of war – besides providing for the defence of the Middle East and the Far East – and actually sent the equivalent of five divisions. Because of the problem of sea transport, however, and the circuitous route considered necessary to avoid air attack, this initial contingent could not arrive until late in September.

Besides her small but high quality Regular Army, Britain was just in the process of forming and equipping a Territorial field army of twenty-six divisions, and on the outbreak of war the Government had made plans for expanding the total to fifty-five divisions. But the first contingent of this new force would not be ready to enter the field until 1940. Meantime, Britain's main contribution could only be in the traditional form of naval power exercising a sea blockade – a form of pressure that was inherently slow to take effect.

Britain had a bomber force of just over 600 – double that of France, though considerably less than half that of Germany – but in view of the limited size and range of the machines then in service, it could exert no serious effect by direct attack on Germany.

Germany mobilized ninety-eight divisions, of which fifty-two were active divisions (including six Austrian). Of the remaining forty-six divisions, however, only ten were fit for action on mobilization and even in these the bulk of the men were recruits who had only been serving about a month. The other thirty-six divisions consisted mainly of veterans of World War I, forty-year-olds who had little acquaintance with modern weapons and tactics. They were very short of artillery and other weapons. It took a long time to get these divisions organized and trained collectively to operate as such – longer even than had been reckoned by the German Command, which was much alarmed at the slowness of the process.

The German Army was not ready for war in 1939 – a war which its chiefs did not expect, relying on Hitler's assurance. They had consented unwillingly to Hitler's desire to expand the army quickly, as they preferred a gradual process of building up thoroughly trained cadres, but Hitler had repeatedly told them that there would be plenty of time for such training, as he had no intention of risking a major war before 1944 at the earliest. Equipment, too, was still very short compared with the scale of the army.

Yet after the event it came to be assumed generally that Germany's sweeping victories in the early stages of the war were due to an overwhelming superiority of weapons, as well as of numbers.

The second illusion was slow to fade. Even in his war memoirs, Churchill said that the Germans had at least a thousand 'heavy tanks' in 1940. The fact is that they had then no heavy tanks at all. At the start of the war they had only a handful of medium tanks, weighing barely 20 tons. Most of the tanks they used in Poland were of very light weight and thin armour.*

Casting up the balance sheet, it can be seen that the Poles and French together had the equivalent of 130 divisions against a German total of ninety-eight divisions, of which thirty-six were virtually untrained, and unorganized. In numbers of 'trained soldiers' the balance against the Germans was much larger still. What could be weighed against this adverse numerical balance was that the weightier combination was widely separated – divided into two parts by Germany's central position. The Germans were able to attack the weaker of the two partners, while the French had to attack the Germans' prepared defence if they were to bring relief to their ally.

Even so, on a quantitative reckoning, the Poles had large enough forces to *hold up* the striking force launched against them – which consisted of forty-eight active divisions. These were followed up by some half dozen of the reserve divisions that were mobilized, but the campaign ended before they came into action.

On the surface, it would appear that the French had ample superiority to crush the German forces in the West, and break through to the Rhine. The German generals were astonished, and relieved, that they did not do so. For most of them still tended to think in 1918 terms, while overrating the French Army as much as the British did.

But whether Poland could have held out, and France been more effective in helping her, looks very different when examined more closely – with clearer understanding of the inherent handicaps and of the new technique of warfare that was first put into practice in 1939.

* Liddell Hart: *The Tanks*, vol II, Appendix V.

From this modern viewpoint it seemed impossible, even before the event, that the course of events could be altered.

Describing the collapse of Poland in his war memoirs, Churchill said:

Neither in France nor in Britain had there been any effective comprehension of the consequences of the new fact that armoured vehicles could be made capable of withstanding artillery fire, and could advance a hundred miles a day.*

That statement is only too true, in so far as it applies to the bulk of the senior soldiers and statesmen of both countries. But it was in Britain, first of all, that these new potentialities had been visualized and explained, publicly and unceasingly, by a small band of progressive military thinkers.

In his second volume, dealing with the collapse of France in 1940, Churchill made the notable, if qualified, admission:

Not having had access to official information for so many years, I did not comprehend the violence of the revolution effected since the last war by the incursion of a mass of fast-moving heavy armour. I knew about it, but it had not altered my inward convictions as it should have done.†

It was a remarkable statement, coming from the man who had played so great a part in sponsoring the tank in World War I. The admission was honourable in its frankness. But he had been Chancellor of the Exchequer up to 1929, while the Experimental Armoured Force, the first in the world, had been formed on Salisbury Plain in 1927 to try out the new theories which the exponents of high speed tank warfare had been preaching for several years. He was fully acquainted with their ideas, and had visited the Experimental Force at work, while he continued to meet them in subsequent years.

The incomprehension of the new idea of warfare, and official resistance to it, was even greater in France than in England. And greater in Poland than in France. That incomprehension was the root of the failure of both armies in 1939, and of the French again, more disastrously, in 1940.

The Poles were antiquated in their ruling military ideas, and also to a large extent in the pattern of their forces. They had no armoured or

* Churchill: *The Second World War*, vol I, p 425.
† Ibid, p 39.

motorized divisions, and their old-type formations were very short of anti-tank and anti-aircraft guns. Moreover, Poland's leaders still pinned their trust to the value of a large mass of horsed cavalry, and cherished a pathetic belief in the possibility of carrying out cavalry charges.* In that respect, it might truly be said that their ideas were eighty years out of date, since the futility of cavalry charges had been shown as far back as the American Civil War – although horse-minded soldiers continued to shut their eyes to the lesson. The maintenance of great masses of horsed cavalry by all armies during World War I, in the hope of the opening that never came, had been the supreme farce of that static war.

The French, on the other hand, had many of the ingredients of an up-to-date army, but they had not organized them into such – because their military ideas at the top were twenty years out of date. Contrary to the legends that arose after their defeat, they had more tanks than the Germans had built by the time the war came – many of them bigger and more thickly armoured than any of the German tanks, though rather slower.† But the French High Command still regarded tanks through 1918 eyes – as servants of the infantry, or else as reconnaissance troops to supplement cavalry. Under the spell of this old-fashioned way of thought they had delayed organizing their tanks in armoured divisions – unlike the Germans – and were still inclined to employ them in penny packets.

The weakness of the French, and still more of the Poles, in new-style ground forces was made all the worse by their lack of air power to cover and support their armies. With the Poles that was due partly to lack of manufacturing resources, but the French had no such excuse. In both cases the needs of air power had been subordinated to the building up of large armies – because the voice of the generals was dominant in the distribution of the military budget, and the generals naturally tended to favour the kind of force with which they were familiar. They were far from realizing the extent to which the effectiveness of ground forces was now dependent on adequate air cover.

The downfall of both armies may be traced to a fatal degree of self-satisfaction at the top. In the case of the French it had been fostered by

* It is grimly ironical to recall that when, in my book *The Defence of Britain*, published shortly before the war, I expressed anxiety about the way that the Polish military chiefs continued to put faith in cavalry charges against modern arms (pp 95–7), the Polish Foreign Office was spurred by them to make an official protest against such a reflection on their judgement.

† Liddell Hart: *The Tanks*, vol II, pp 5–6.

the victory of World War I and the way that their partners had always
deferred to their assumption of superior military knowledge. In the case
of the Poles it had been nourished by their defeat of the Russians in
1920. The military leaders in both cases had long shown themselves
arrogantly complacent about their armies and military technique. It is
only fair to say that some of the younger French soldiers, such as
Colonel de Gaulle, showed a keen interest in the new ideas of tank
warfare that were being preached in England. But the higher French
generals paid little attention to these British-born 'theories' – in marked
contrast to the way the new school of German generals studied them.*

Even so, the German Army was still far from being a really efficient
and modernly designed force. Not only was it unready for war as a
whole, but the bulk of the active divisions were out of date in pattern,
while the conceptions of the higher command still tended to run in old
grooves. But it had created a small number of new-type formations by
the time war broke out – six armoured and four 'light' (mechanized)
divisions, as well as four motorized infantry divisions to back them up.
It was a small proportion of the total, but it counted for more than all
the rest of the German Army.

At the same time the German High Command had, rather hesitat-
ingly, recognized the new theory of high-speed warfare, and was willing
to give it a trial. That was due, above all, to the enthusiastic advocacy
of General Heinz Guderian and a few others, and the way that their
arguments appealed to Hitler – who favoured any idea that promised a
quick solution. In sum, the German Army achieved its amazing run of
victories, not because it was overwhelming in strength or thoroughly
modern in form, but because it was a few vital degrees more advanced
than its opponents.

The European situation in 1939 gave fresh emphasis, and a new turn, to
that much quoted remark of Clemenceau's in the last great conflict of
nations: 'War is too serious a business to be left to soldiers.' For it
could not now be left to soldiers even if there had been the most complete trust in their judgement. The power to maintain war, if not to
launch it, had passed out of the military sphere of the soldier into that
of economics. As machine-power gained a growing domination over
manpower on the battlefield, so, in a realistic view, did industry and
economic resources push the armies at the front into the background of
grand strategy. Unless the supplies from the factories and oilfields

* Liddell Hart: *The Tanks*, vol II, pp 5–6.

could be maintained without interruption they would be no more than inert masses. Impressive as the marching columns might look to the awed civilian spectator, in the eyes of the modern war scientist they were but marionettes on a conveyor-belt. And in that aspect was presented the potential factor that could save civilization.

If existing armies and armaments alone counted, the picture would have been much more gloomy. The Munich settlement had changed the strategic balance of Europe, and for a time at least made it heavily adverse to France and Britain. No acceleration of their armament programmes could be expected to offset for a long time the removal from the scales of Czecho-Slovakia's thirty-five well-armed divisions, and the accompanying release of the German divisions which they could have held in balance.

Such increase of their armaments as France and Britain had achieved by March was then more than counterbalanced by what Germany gained through her swoop into helpless Czecho-Slovakia, whose munition factories as well as military equipment she took over. In heavy artillery alone, Germany doubled her resources at a stroke. To make the prospect worse, German and Italian help had enabled Franco to complete the overthrow of Republican Spain, thereby raising the spectre of an additional menace to the frontiers of France, and to the sea communications of both France and Britain.

Strategically, nothing save the assurance of Russia's support could promise to redress the balance within a measurable time. Strategically, too, no time was likely to be so favourable for joining issue with the Western Powers. But the strategic scales rested on an economic base, and it was doubtful whether under the pressure of war this would long support the weight of Germany's forces.

There were some twenty basic products essential for war. Coal for general production. Petroleum for motive power. Cotton for explosives. Wool. Iron. Rubber for transport. Copper for general armament and all electrical equipment. Nickel for steel-making and ammunition. Lead for ammunition. Glycerine for dynamite. Cellulose for smokeless powders. Mercury for detonators. Aluminium for aircraft. Platinum for chemical apparatus. Antimony, manganese, etc., for steel-making and metallurgy in general. Asbestos for munitions and machinery. Mica as an insulator. Nitric acid and sulphur for explosives.

Except for coal, Britain herself lacked most of the products which were required in quantity. But so long as the use of the sea was ensured, most of them were available in the British Empire. In the case of nickel about 90 per cent of the world's supply came from Canada, and most of the remainder from the French colony of New Caledonia. The main deficiencies were in antimony, mercury, and sulphur, while the petroleum resources were insufficient for war needs.

The French Empire could not supply these particular deficiencies, and was in addition short of cotton, wool, copper, lead, manganese, rubber, and several smaller needs.

Russia had an abundant supply of most of the products; she lacked antimony, nickel, and rubber, while the supply of copper and sulphur was inadequate.

The best placed of all the powers was the United States which produced two-thirds of the world's total petroleum supply, about half the world's cotton, and nearly half the copper, while being itself dependent on outside sources only for antimony, nickel, rubber, tin and, partially, for manganese.

In striking contrast was the situation of the Berlin–Rome–Tokyo triangle. Italy had to import the bulk of her needs in nearly every product, even to coal. Japan was almost as dependent on foreign sources. Germany had no home production of cotton, rubber, tin, platinum, bauxite, mercury, and mica, while her supplies of iron-ore, copper, antimony, manganese, nickel, sulphur, wool, and petroleum were quite inadequate. By the seizure of Czecho-Slovakia she had gone some way to reduce her deficiency of iron-ore, while by her intervention in Spain she had been able to secure a further supply of it on favourable terms, and also of mercury – although its continuance depended on her use of the sea. Again, she had succeeded in meeting part of her need for wool by a new wood substitute. Likewise, though at much greater cost than the natural product, she had provided about a fifth of her rubber requirements from 'buna', and a third of her petrol needs from home-produced fuel.

Here lay the greatest weakness of all in the war-making capacity of the Axis, in times when armies had come increasingly to depend on motor-movement, and air forces had become a vital element in military power. Apart from coal-derivatives Germany obtained about half a million tons of oil from her own wells, and a trifling amount from Austria and Czecho-Slovakia. To make up her peacetime needs she had to import nearly five million tons, the main sources being Venezuela, Mexico, the Dutch Indies, the United States, Russia, and Rumania. Access to any of the first four would be impossible in wartime, and to the last two only by conquest. Moreover, it was estimated that Germany's wartime requirements would exceed twelve million tons a year. In the light of this it was hard to expect that any increase in artificial fuel could suffice. Only the capture of Rumania's oil-wells – which produced seven million tons – in an undamaged state could offer a promise of meeting the deficiency.

Italy's requirements, if she entered the war, would increase the drag, since of the probable four million tons a year which she would require in war, she could only count on providing about 2 per cent, from Albania, even in the case of her ships being willing to cross the Adriatic.

To put oneself in a possible opponent's shoes is a good check on shaking in one's own. Gloomy as the military outlook had become, there was reason for comfort in the inadequacy of German and Italian resources for sustaining a long war – if the powers opposed to them at the outbreak could withstand the early shocks and strains until help came. In any such conflict as was now on the horizon the fortunes of the Axis would turn on the chance that the war could be settled quickly.

PART II

THE OUTBREAK
1939–40

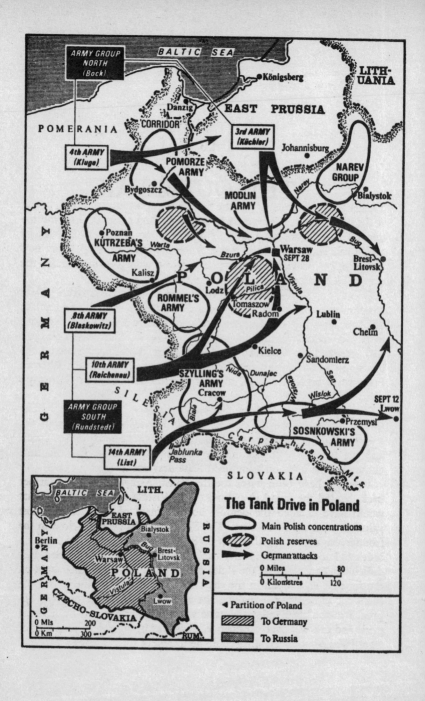

The Tank Drive in Poland

CHAPTER THREE

The Overrunning of Poland

The campaign in Poland was the first demonstration, and proof, in war of the theory of mobile warfare by armoured and air forces in combination. When the theory had been originally developed, in Britain, its action had been depicted in terms of the play of 'lightning'. From now on, aptly but ironically, it came into world-wide currency under the title of 'Blitzkrieg' – the German rendering.

Poland was all too well suited for a demonstration of Blitzkrieg. Her frontiers were immensely wide – some 3,500 miles in all. The stretch of 1,250 miles adjoining German territory had recently been extended to 1,750 miles by the occupation of Czecho-Slovakia. This had also resulted in Poland's southern flank becoming exposed to invasion – as the north flank, facing East Prussia, was already. Western Poland had become a huge salient that projected between Germany's jaws.

The Polish plain offered flat and fairly easy going for a mobile invader – though not so easy as France would offer, because of the scarcity of good roads in Poland, the deep sand often met off the roads, and the frequency of lakes and forests in some areas. But the time chosen for the invasion minimized these drawbacks.

It would have been wiser for the Polish Army to assemble farther back, behind the broad river-lines of the Vistula and the San, but that would have entailed the definite abandonment of some of the most valuable parts of the country. The Silesian coalfields were close to the frontier, having belonged to pre-1918 Germany, while most of the main industrial zone, though farther back, lay west of the river-barrier. It is difficult to conceive that the Poles could have maintained their hold on the forward areas even in the most favourable circumstances. But the economic argument for making the attempt to delay the enemy's approach to the main industrial zone was heavily reinforced by national pride and military over-confidence, as well as by an exaggerated idea of what Poland's Western allies could do to relieve the pressure.

The unrealism of such an attitude was repeated in the Polish dispositions. Approximately a third of the forces were concentrated in or near
the Corridor, where they were perilously exposed to a double envelopment – from East Prussia and the west combined. This indulgence of
national pride – in opposing Germany's re-entry into the piece of her
pre-1918 territory for which she had been agitating – was inevitably at
the expense of the forces available to cover the areas more vital to
Poland's defence. For in the south, facing the main avenues of approach, the forces were thinly spread. At the same time nearly another
third of Poland's forces were massed in reserve north of the central
axis, between Lodz and Warsaw, under the Commander-in-Chief,
Marshal Smigly-Rydz. This grouping embodied the offensive spirit,
but its aim of intervening with a counterattack did not correspond to
the Polish Army's limited capacity for manoeuvre, even if this had not
been cramped by German air attack on the rail and road routes of
movement.

The Poles' forward concentration in general forfeited their chance of
fighting a series of delaying actions, since their foot-marching army was
unable to get back to the positions in rear, and man them, before they
were overrun by the invader's mechanized columns. In the wide spaces
of Poland the unmechanized state of her forces was a heavier handicap
than the fact that she was caught by surprise before all her reserves had
been called up. Lack of mobility was more fatal than incomplete mobilization.

By the same token, the forty odd infantry divisions of normal pattern
which the Germans employed in the invasion counted for much less
than their fourteen mechanized or partially mechanized divisions made
up of six armoured divisions, four light divisions (motorized infantry
with two armoured units), and four motorized divisions. It was their
deep and rapid thrusts that decided the issue, in conjunction with the
overhead pressure of the Luftwaffe which wrecked the Polish railway
system, and destroyed much of the Polish air force in the early stages of
the invasion. The Luftwaffe operated in a very dispersed way, instead
of in large formations, but it thereby spread a creeping paralysis over
the widest possible area. Another weighty factor was the German radio
bombardment, disguised as Polish transmissions, which did much to
increase the confusion and demoralization of the Polish rear. All these
factors were given a multiplied effect by the way that Polish over-
confidence in the power of their men to defeat machines led, on the
rebound, to a disintegrating disillusionment.

The German forces had crossed the Polish frontier shortly before 6

AM on September 1st; air attacks had begun an hour earlier. In the north, the invasion was carried out by Bock's Army Group, which comprised the 3rd Army (under Küchler) and the 4th Army (under Kluge). The former thrust southward from its flanking position in East Prussia, while the latter pushed eastward across the Polish Corridor to join it in enveloping the Poles' right flank.

The greater role was given to Rundstedt's Army Group in the south. This was nearly twice as strong in infantry, and more in armour. It comprised the 8th Army (under Blaskowitz), the 10th (under Reichenau), and the 14th (under List). Blaskowitz, on the left wing, was to push towards the great manufacturing centre of Lodz, and help to isolate the Polish forces in the Poznan salient, while covering Reichenau's flank. On the right wing, List was to push for Cracow and simultaneously turn the Poles' Carpathian flank, using Kleist's armoured corps to drive through the mountain passes. The decisive stroke, however, was to be delivered by Reichenau, in the centre, and for that purpose he was given the bulk of the armoured forces.

The success of the invasion was helped by the way that the Polish leaders, despising the defensive, had devoted little effort to the construction of defences, preferring to rely on counterattacks – which they believed that their army, despite its lack of machines, could effectively execute. Thus the mechanized invaders had little difficulty in finding and penetrating open avenues of advance, while most of the Polish counterattacks broke down under the combined effect of a repulse to their forward movement and a deepening German threat to their own rear.

By September 3rd – when Britain and France entered the war – Kluge's advance had cut the Corridor and reached the Lower Vistula, while Küchler's pressure from East Prussia towards the Narev was developing. What was more important, Reichenau's armoured forces had penetrated to the Warta, and forced the crossings. Meanwhile List's army was converging from both flanks on Cracow, forcing Szylling's army in that sector to abandon the city and fall back to the line of the Nida and the Dunajec.

By the 4th Reichenau's spearheads had reached and crossed the Pilica, 50 miles beyond the frontier. Two days later his left wing was well in rear of Lodz, after capturing Tomaszow, and his right wing had driven into Kielce. Thus the Polish Rommel's army covering the Lodz sector was outflanked, while Kutrzeba's army was still far forward near Poznan, and in danger of being isolated. The other German armies had all made progress in fulfilling their part in the great enveloping manoeuvre planned by Halder, the Chief of the General Staff, and directed by Brauchitsch, the Commander-in-Chief. The Polish armies were splitting up into uncoordinated fractions, some of which were retreating while others were delivering disjointed attacks on the nearest enemy columns.

The German advance might have travelled still faster but for a lingering conventional tendency to check the mobile forces from driving far ahead of the infantry masses that were backing them up. But as newly gained experience showed that such a risk was offset by the opponents' confusion, a bolder course was pursued. Exploiting an open gap between Lodz and the Pilica, one of Reichenau's armoured corps raced through to the ourskirts of Warsaw on the 8th – it had covered 140 miles in the first week. By the following day the light divisions on his right wing reached the Vistula farther south, between Warsaw and Sandomierz. They then turned northward.

Meanwhile, near the Carpathians, List's mobile forces had swept across the Dunajec, Biala, Wisloka, and Wislok in turn, to the San on either flank of the famous fortress of Przemysl. In the north Guderian's armoured corps (the spearhead of Küchler's army) had pushed across the Narev and was attacking the line of the Bug, in rear of Warsaw. Thus a wider pincer movement was strongly developing outside the inner pincers that were closing on the Polish forces in the bend of the Vistula west of Warsaw.

This stage of the invasion had seen an important variation of plan on the Germans' side. Their view of the situation was momentarily confused by the extraordinary state of confusion on the Poles' side, where columns appeared to be moving in many different directions, raising clouds of dust that befogged the aerial view. In this state of obscurity the German Supreme Command inclined to the belief that the bulk of the Polish forces in the north had already escaped across the Vistula. On that assumption, they gave orders that Reichenau's army was to cross the Vistula between Warsaw and Sandomierz, with the aim of intercepting the Poles' anticipated withdrawal into south-eastern Poland. But Rundstedt demurred, being convinced that the bulk of the Polish forces were still west of the Vistula. After some argument his view prevailed, and Reichenau's army was wheeled north to establish a blocking position along the Bzura west of Warsaw.

As a result the largest remaining part of the Polish forces was trapped before it could withdraw over the Vistula. To the advantage which the Germans had gained by their strategic penetration along the line of least resistance was now added the advantage of tactical defence. To complete their victory they had merely to hold their ground – in face of the hurried assaults of an army which was fighting in reverse, cut off from its bases, with its supplies running short, and increasingly pressed from the flank and behind by the converging eastward advance of Blaskowitz's and Kluge's armies. Although the Poles fought fiercely, with a bravery that greatly impressed their opponents, only a small proportion ultimately managed to break out, by night, and join the garrison of Warsaw.

On the 10th Marshal Smigly-Rydz had issued orders for a general retreat into south-eastern Poland, where General Sosnkowski was placed in charge, with the idea of organizing a defensive position on a relatively narrow front for prolonged resistance. But this was now a vain hope. While the big encirclement west of the Vistula was being tightened the Germans were now penetrating deeply into the area east of the Vistula. Moreover, they had turned both the line of the Bug in the north and the line of the San in the south. On Küchler's front, Guderian's armoured corps drove southward in a wide outflanking thrust to Brest-Litovsk. On List's front, Kleist's armoured corps reached the city of Lwow on the 12th. Here the Germans were checked, but they spread northwards to meet Küchler's forces.

Although the invading columns were feeling the strain of their deep advances, and were running short of fuel, the Polish command system was so badly dislocated that it could not profit either by the enemy's temporary slackening or by the stubbornness that many isolated bodies of Polish troops still showed. These dissipated their energy in random efforts while the Germans were closing up to complete the encirclement.

On September 17th the armies of Soviet Russia crossed Poland's eastern frontier. That blow in the back sealed her fate, for there were scarcely any troops left to oppose this second invasion. Next day the Polish Government and High Command crossed the Rumanian frontier – the Commander-in-Chief sending back a message to tell his troops to fight on. Perhaps it was as well that it did not reach most of them, but many gallantly fulfilled its intention in the days that followed, although their resistance collapsed bit by bit. The garrison of Warsaw held out until the 28th, despite heavy bombardment from the air and the ground, and the last considerable Polish fragment did not surrender until October 5th, while guerrilla resistance continued into the winter. Some 80,000 escaped over neutral frontiers.

The German and Russian forces had met and greeted each other, as partners, on a line running south from East Prussia past Bialystok,

Brest-Litovsk, and Lwow to the Carpathians. That partnership was sealed, but not cemented, by a mutual partition of Poland.

Meantime the French had merely made a small dent in Germany's western front. It looked, and was, a feeble effort to relieve the pressure on their ally. In view of the weakness of the German forces and defences it was natural to feel that they could have done more. But, here again, deeper analysis tends to correct the obvious conclusion suggested by the comparative figures of the opposing forces.

Although the French northern frontier was 500 miles long, in attempting an offensive the French were confined to the narrow ninety-mile sector from the Rhine to the Moselle – unless they violated the neutrality of Belgium and Luxembourg. The Germans were able to concentrate the best part of their available forces on this narrow sector, and they sowed the approaches to their Siegfried Line with a thick belt of minefields, thus imposing delay on the attackers.

Worse still, the French were unable to start their offensive action until about September 17th – except for some preliminary probing attacks. By that date, Poland was so obviously collapsing that they had a good excuse for countermanding it. Their incapacity to strike earlier arose from their mobilization system, which was inherently out of date. It was the fatal product of their reliance on a conscript army – which could not come effectively into action until the mass of 'trained reserves' had been called up from their civil jobs, and the formations had been made ready to operate. But the delay was increased by the French Command's persistence in old tactical ideas – particularly their view that any offensive must be prepared by a massive artillery bombardment on the lines of World War I. They still regarded heavy artillery as the essential 'tin-opener' in dealing with any defended position. But the bulk of their heavy artillery had to be brought out of storage, and could not be available until the last stage of mobilization, the sixteenth day. That condition governed their preparations to deliver an offensive.

For several years past one of France's political leaders, Paul Reynaud, had constantly argued that these conceptions were out of date, and had urged the necessity of creating a mechanized force of professional soldiers ready for instant action, instead of relying on the old and slow-mobilizing conscript mass. But his had been a voice crying in the wilderness. French statesmen, like most French soldiers, placed their trust in conscription, and numbers.

The military issue in 1939 can be summed up in two sentences. In the East a hopelessly out-of-date army was quickly disintegrated by a small tank force, in combination with a superior air force, which put into practice a novel technique. At the same time, in the West, a slow-motion army could not develop any effective pressure before it was too late.

CHAPTER FOUR

'The Phoney War'

'The Phoney War' was a phrase coined by the American Press. Like so many vivid Americanisms it soon came to be adopted on both sides of the Atlantic. It has become firmly established as a name for the period of the war from the collapse of Poland in September, 1939, until the opening of Hitler's Western offensive in the following spring.

Those who coined the phrase meant to convey that the war was spurious – because no great battles were being fought between the Franco-British and German forces. In reality, it was a period of ominous activity – behind the curtain. In the midst of it all a strange accident befell a German staff officer. The incident gave Hitler a fright, and in the following weeks the German military plan was completely changed. The old one would have had nothing like the same chance of success as the new one attained.

But all this was unknown to the world. The people everywhere could only see that the battlefronts remained quiet, and concluded that Mars had fallen into a slumber.

Popular explanations of this outwardly passive state differed. One was that Britain and France were not really serious in their war-making intentions, despite their declaration of war on behalf of Poland, and were waiting to negotiate peace. The other popular explanation was that they were being cunning. The American Press contained many 'reports' that the Allied High Command had deliberately adopted a subtly conceived scheme of defensive strategy, and was preparing a trap for the Germans.

There was no foundation for either of these explanations. During that autumn and winter the Allied Governments and High Command spent much time in discussing offensive plans against Germany or Germany's flanks – which they had no possibility of achieving with their resources – instead of concentrating on the preparation of an effective defence against Hitler's coming attack.

After the fall of France, the Germans captured the files of the French High Command – and published a collection of sensational documents from them. These showed how the Allied chiefs had spent the winter in contemplating offensive plans all round the circle – for striking at Germany's rear flank through Norway, Sweden, and Finland; for striking at the Ruhr through Belgium; for striking at her remote eastern flank through Greece and the Balkans; for cutting off her lone source of petrol supply by striking at Russia's great oilfields in the Caucasus. It was a wonderful collection of fantasies – the vain imaginings of Allied leaders, living in a dream-world until the cold douche of Hitler's own offensive awoke them.

Hitler, whose mind was always moving ahead of events, began to think of taking the offensive in the West while the Polish campaign was drawing to a close, and before he made his public proposal for a general peace conference. It is evident that he had already come to realize that any such proposal was unlikely to receive consideration by the Western Allies. For the moment, however, he allowed only his immediate entourage to know how his mind was turning. He kept the General Staff in the dark until after he had publicly made his peace offer, on October 6th, and it had been publicly rebuffed.

Three days later he set out his views in a long directive* for the German Army chiefs, giving the reasons for his conviction that an offensive in the West was the only possible course left to Germany. It is a most illuminating document. In it he set forth his conclusion that a prolonged war with France and Britain would exhaust Germany's resources, and expose her to a deadly attack in the back from Russia. He feared that his pact with Russia would not ensure her neutrality a moment longer than suited her purpose. His fear urged him to force peace on France by an early offensive. He believed that once France fell out Britain would come to terms.

He reckoned that for the moment he had the strength and equipment to beat France – because Germany possessed a superiority in the new arms that mattered most:

The tank-arm and air force have, at the present time, attained technical heights – not only as weapons of attack but also for defence – that no other power has reached. Their strategic potential for operations is ensured by their organization and well-practised leadership, which is better than in any other country.

* Nuremberg Documents C–62.

While recognizing that the French had a superiority in the older weapons, particularly heavy artillery, he argued that 'these weapons are of no decisive significance whatsoever in mobile warfare'. With his technical superiority in the newer arms he could also discount the French superiority in the number of trained soldiers.

He went on to argue that if he waited, in the hope that the French would get tired of war, 'the development of British fighting power would bring to France a new fighting element that would be of great value to her, both psychologically and materially' – to buttress her defence.

What must be prevented above all is that the enemy should make good the weakness of his own armaments, particularly in anti-tank and anti-aircraft weapons – thereby creating a balance of power. In this respect the passing of every further month represents a loss of time unfavourable to the German power of attack.

He showed anxiety about the 'will to war' of the German soldier once the exhilarating effect of the easy conquest of Poland wore off. 'His respect for himself is as great as the respect he commands from others, at present. But six months of delaying warfare and effective propaganda on the part of the enemy might cause these important qualities to weaken once more.'* Hitler felt that he must strike soon, before it was too late, saying: 'In the present situation, time may be reckoned an ally of the Western powers rather than of ours.' His memorandum wound up with the conclusion that: 'The attack is to be launched this autumn, if conditions are at all possible.'

He insisted that Belgium must be included in the area of attack, not only to obtain room for manoeuvre to outflank the French Maginot Line, but also to forestall the danger of the Anglo-French forces entering Belgium and deploying on the frontier close to the Ruhr, 'thereby bringing the war near to the heart of our armaments industry'. (As the

---

* Events showed that Hitler's anxiety was misplaced. French morale declined more than the German in the seven months' delay that actually occurred. Allied propaganda was not effective – there was far too much talk of overthrowing Germany, and far too little attempt to distinguish between the ordinary German and the Nazi chiefs. Worse still, scant encouragement was given by the British Government to several secret approaches made by groups in Germany who wanted to overthrow Hitler and make peace if they could get satisfactory assurance as to the peace conditions that the Allies had in mind.

French archives reveal, that was exactly what Gamelin, the French Commander-in-Chief, had been advocating.)

The disclosure of Hitler's intentions came as a shock to Brauchitsch, the Commander-in-Chief of the Army, and Halder, the Chief of the General Staff. In common with most of the senior German generals, they did not share Hitler's belief in the power of the new arms to overcome the opponents' superiority in military trained manpower. Reckoning on customary lines in numbers of divisions, they argued that the German Army had not nearly enough strength to defeat the Western armies. They pointed out that the ninety-eight divisions which Germany had managed to mobilize were considerably fewer than the total on the other side, and that thirty-six of these divisions were badly armed and barely trained. They were apprehensive, too, that the war would spread into another world war, fearing that it would have a fatal ending for Germany.

They were so disturbed that they contemplated desperate remedies. Just as at the time of the Munich crisis, a year before, they started to consider taking action to overthrow Hitler. The idea was to dispatch a picked force from the front to march on Berlin. But General Friedrich Fromm, the Commander-in-Chief of the Home Forces, declined to co-operate – and his help was essential. Fromm argued that if the troops were ordered to turn against Hitler they would not obey – because most of the ordinary soldiers put their trust in Hitler. Fromm's judgement about the troops' reaction was probably correct. It is corroborated by most of the officers who were in touch with troops and did not know what was being discussed in higher headquarters.

The mass of the troops and people, if not intoxicated by triumph, were doped by Dr Goebbels's propaganda about Hitler desiring peace while the Allies were determined on the destruction of Germany. Unfortunately, the Allied statesmen and Press furnished Goebbels with all too many quotable morsels of this kind that he could use to support his picture of the Allied wolf wanting to devour the German lamb.

While this first wartime plot against Hitler was stillborn, he did not succeed in launching his offensive in the autumn as he had hoped. Ironically, that proved fortunate for him and unfortunate for the rest of the world – including the German people.

The date provisionally fixed for the offensive was November 12th. On the 5th Brauchitsch made a fresh attempt to dissuade Hitler from invading France, setting forth at much length the reasons against it. But Hitler rebuffed his arguments and rebuked him severely, while insisting that the attack must start on the 12th. On the 7th, however, the order was cancelled – when meteorologists forecast bad weather. The date was put off three days, and then postponed again and again.

While the bad and bitter weather that set in was an obvious ground for postponement, Hitler was furious at having to acquiesce, and far from satisfied that it was the only cause. He summoned all the high commanders to a conference, on November 23rd. Here he set out to dispel their doubts about the necessity of taking the offensive – expressing anxiety about the looming menace of Russia, while emphasizing that the Western Allies would not consider his peace offers and were multiplying their armaments. 'Time is working for our adversary.' 'We have an Achilles' Heel – the Ruhr ... If Britain and France push through Belgium and Holland into the Ruhr, we shall be in the greatest danger.'

He went on to reproach them with faint-heartedness, and let them know that he suspected them of trying to sabotage his plans. He pointed out that they had opposed each of his steps from the re-occupation of the Rhineland onwards, that he had been justified by success each time, and that he now expected them to follow his ideas unconditionally. Brauchitsch's attempt to point out the differences and greater risks in the new venture merely drew down on his head a harder rebuke. That evening Hitler saw Brauchitsch privately and gave him a further 'dressing down'. Brauchitsch thereupon tendered his resignation, but Hitler brushed it aside, and told him to obey orders.

However, the weather proved a better saboteur than the generals, and led to a fresh series of postponements during the first half of December. Then Hitler decided to wait until the New Year, and grant Christmas leave. The weather was again bad just after Christmas but on January 10th Hitler fixed the start of the offensive for the 17th.

But the very day he took that decision the most dramatic 'intervention' took place. The story of it has been mentioned in numerous accounts, but was most succinctly put in that of General Student, the Commander-in-Chief of the German Airborne Forces:

On January 10 a major detailed by me as liaison officer to the 2nd Air Fleet flew from Munster to Bonn to discuss some unimportant details of the plan with the Air Force. He carried with him, however, *the complete operational plan for the attack in the West.*

In icy weather and a strong wind he lost his way over the frozen and snow-covered Rhine, and flew into Belgium, where he had to make a forced landing. He was unable to burn completely the vital document. Important parts of it fell into the hands of the Belgians, and consequently the outline of the German plan for the Western offensive. The German Air Attaché in The Hague reported that on the same evening the King of the Belgians had a long telephone conversation with the Queen of Holland.*

Of course, the Germans did not know at the time exactly what had happened to the papers, but they naturally feared the worst, and had to reckon with it. In that crisis Hitler kept a cool head, in contrast to others:

It was interesting to watch the reactions of this incident on Germany's leading men. While Goering was in a rage, Hitler remained quite calm and self-possessed ... At first he wanted to strike immediately, but fortunately refrained – and decided to drop the original operational plan entire. This was replaced by the Manstein plan.*

General Walter Warlimont, who held a key post† in the Supreme Command headquarters, recorded that Hitler made up his mind on January 16th to change the plan, and that 'this was chiefly due to the air accident'.**

That proved very unfortunate for the Allies, even though they were given a further four months' grace for preparation – since the German offensive was now put off indefinitely while the plan was being completely recast, and did not come until May 10th. When it was launched, it threw the Allies completely off their balance and led to the speedy collapse of the French armies, while the British barely escaped by sea, from Dunkirk.

It is natural to ask whether the major's forced-landing really was an accident. It might be expected that any of the German generals involved would after the war be only too glad to put himself in a favourable light with his captors by claiming that he had arranged this warning to the Allies. Yet, in fact, none did so – and all seemed convinced that the accident was quite genuine. But we know that Admiral Canaris, the head of the German Secret Service – who was later executed – took many hidden steps to thwart Hitler's aims, and that just prior to the attacks in the spring on Norway, Holland, and Belgium, warnings were conveyed to the threatened countries – though they were not prop-

* Liddell Hart: *The Other Side of the Hill*, p 149.
† He was Deputy Chief of the OKW Operations Staff, under General Jodl.
** Liddell Hart: *The Other Side of the Hill*, p 155.

erly heeded. We know, too, that Canaris worked in mysterious ways, and was skilled in covering up his tracks. So the fateful accident of January 10th is bound to remain an open question.

No such doubt surrounds the origination of the new plan. It forms another strange episode – though strange in a different way.

The old plan, worked out by the General Staff under Halder, had been to make the main attack through central Belgium – as in 1914. It was to be carried out by Army Group 'B' under Bock, while Army Group 'A' under Rundstedt delivered a secondary attack, on the left, through the hilly and wooded Ardennes. No big results were expected here, and all the armoured divisions were allotted to Bock, as the General Staff regarded the Ardennes as far too difficult country for a tank drive.*

The Chief of Staff of Rundstedt's Army Group was Erich von Manstein – regarded by his fellows as the ablest strategist among the younger generals. He felt that the first plan was too obvious, and too much a repetition of the Schlieffen plan of 1914 – so that it was just the kind of stroke for which the Allied High Command would be prepared. Another drawback, Manstein argued, was that it would meet the British Army, which was likely to be a tougher opponent than the French. Moreover, it would not lead to a decisive result. To quote his own words:

> We could perhaps defeat the Allied forces in Belgium. We could conquer the Channel coast. But it was probable that our offensive would be definitely stopped on the Somme. Then there would grow up a situation like 1914 ... there would be no chance of reaching a peace.†

Reflecting on the problem, Manstein had already conceived the bold solution of shifting the main stroke to the Ardennes, feeling that this would be the line of least expectation. But there was one big question

---

* The French General Staff took exactly the same view. So had the British General Staff. When in November, 1933, I was consulted as to how our fast tank formations – which the War Office was just beginning to form – could best be used in a future war I had suggested that, in the event of a German invasion of France, we should deliver a tank counterstroke through the Ardennes. I was thereupon told that 'the Ardennes were impassable to tanks', to which I replied that, from personal study of the terrain, I regarded such a view as a delusion – as I had emphasized in several books between the wars.

† Liddell Hart: *The Other Side of the Hill*, p 152.

in his mind, about which he had consulted Guderian in November 1939.

Here is Guderian's own account:

Manstein asked me if tank movements would be possible through the Ardennes in the direction of Sedan. He explained his plan of breaking through the extension of the Maginot Line near Sedan, in order to avoid the old-fashioned Schlieffen plan, familiar to the enemy and likely to be expected once more. I knew the terrain from World War I, and, after studying the map, confirmed his view. Manstein then convinced General von Rundstedt, and a memorandum was sent to OKH [Supreme Headquarters of the Army, headed by Brauchitsch and Halder]. OKH refused to accept Manstein's idea. But the latter succeeded in bringing his idea to Hitler's knowledge.*

Warlimont brought Manstein's idea to the notice of Hitler's headquarters, after a talk he had with Manstein in mid-December. He mentioned it to General Alfred Jodl, Chief of OKW Operations Staff, who passed it on to Hitler. But it was only after the air accident of January 10th, when Hitler was looking for a new plan, that Manstein's proposal, thus brought back into his mind, began to get a hold. Even then a month passed before he swung definitely in favour of it.

The final decision was clinched in a curious way. Brauchitsch and Halder had not liked the manner in which Manstein had pressed his 'brain-wave' in opposition to their plan. So it was decided to remove him from his post, and send him to command an infantry corps – where he would be out of the main channel and not so well placed to push his ideas. But following this transfer he was summoned to see Hitler, and thus had an opportunity to explain his idea in full. This interview was arranged on the initiative of General Schmundt, Hitler's chief aide-de-camp, who was a fervent admirer of Manstein and felt he had been badly treated.

After that, Hitler pressed the idea on Brauchitsch and Halder so hard that they gave way, and remodelled the plan on Manstein's lines. While Halder was a reluctant convert, he was an extremely able staff officer and the detailed drafting of the plan was a remarkable piece of logistical planning.

A characteristic sequel was that Hitler, once he had swung in favour of the new key-idea, was quick to assume that he had himself conceived it. All he gave Manstein was the credit of having agreed with him:

* Liddell Hart: *The Other Side of the Hill*, pp 153–4.

'Among all the generals I talked to about the new plan in the West, Manstein was the only one who understood me.'

If we analyse the course of events when the offensive was launched, in May, it becomes clear that the old plan would almost certainly have failed to produce the fall of France. Indeed, it might have done no more than push the Allied Armies back to the French frontier, even if it did that. For the main German advance would have run head-on into the strongest and best-equipped of the Franco-British forces, and would have had to fight its way forward through a stretch of country filled with obstacles – rivers, canals and large towns. The Ardennes might seem more difficult still, but if the Germans could race through that wooded hill-belt of southern Belgium before the French High Command awoke to the danger, the rolling plains of France would lie open to them – ideal country for a great tank drive.

Had the old plan been maintained, and come to an impasse as was probable, the whole outlook of the war would have been very different. While it is unlikely that France and Britain could ever have defeated Germany on their own, a definite check to the German offensive would have given them time to develop their armaments, particularly in air-craft and tanks, and thus establish a balance of power in these new arms. The unconcealable failure of Hitler's bid for victory would in time also have undermined the confidence of his troops and people. Thus a stalemate in the West would have given Hitler's strong group of opponents at home a good chance to gain increasing support and de-velop their plans for overthrowing him, as a preliminary to peace. How-ever things had turned out after the check, it is likely that Europe would have been saved much of the ruin and misery that befell her peoples as the result of the chain of events that ensued from the collapse of France.

While Hitler benefited so much from the air accident that led him to change the plan, the Allies suffered much from it. One of the strangest features of the whole story is that they did so little to profit by the warning that had fallen into their lap. For the documents which the German staff officer was carrying were not badly burned, and copies of them were promptly passed on by the Belgians to the French and Bri-tish Governments. But their military advisers were inclined to regard the documents as having been planted on them as a deception. That view hardly made sense, for it would have been a foolish kind of decep-tion to risk putting the Belgians on their guard and driving them into closer collaboration with the French and British. They might easily have decided to open their frontier and let the Franco-British armies come in, to reinforce their defences, before the blow fell.

Even stranger was that the Allied High Command made no change in its own plans, nor took any precautions to meet the probability that if the captured plan were genuine the German High Command would almost certainly shift the weight of their attack elsewhere.

In mid-November the Allied Supreme Council had endorsed Gamelin's Plan 'D', a hazardous development – which the British Staff had at first questioned – of an earlier plan. Under Plan 'D' the reinforced left wing of the Allied Armies was to rush into Belgium as soon as Hitler started to move, and push as far eastward as possible. That played straight into Hitler's hands, as it fitted perfectly into his new plan. The farther the Allied left wing pushed into central Belgium the easier it would be for his tank drive through the Ardennes to get round behind it and cut it off.

The outcome was made all the more certain because the Allied High Command employed the bulk of its mobile forces in the advance into Belgium, and left only a thin screen of second-rate divisions to guard the hinge of its advance – facing the exits from the 'impassable Ardennes'. To make it all the worse, the defences which they had to hold were particularly weak – in the gap between the end of the Maginot Line and the beginning of the British fortified front.

Mr Churchill mentions in his memoirs that anxiety had been felt in British quarters during the autumn about the gap and says: 'Mr Hore-Belisha, the Secretary of State for War, raised the point in the War Cabinet on several occasions ... The Cabinet and our military leaders however were naturally shy of criticizing those whose armies were ten times as strong as our own.'* After Hore-Belisha's departure early in January, following the storm which his criticisms had aroused, there was still less inclination to press the point. There was also a dangerous growth of false confidence, in Britain as well as in France. Churchill declared, in a speech on January 27th, that 'Hitler has lost his best chance'. That comforting assertion was headlined in the newspapers next day. It was the very time when the new plan was fermenting in Hitler's mind.

* Churchill: *The Second World War*, vol II, p 33.

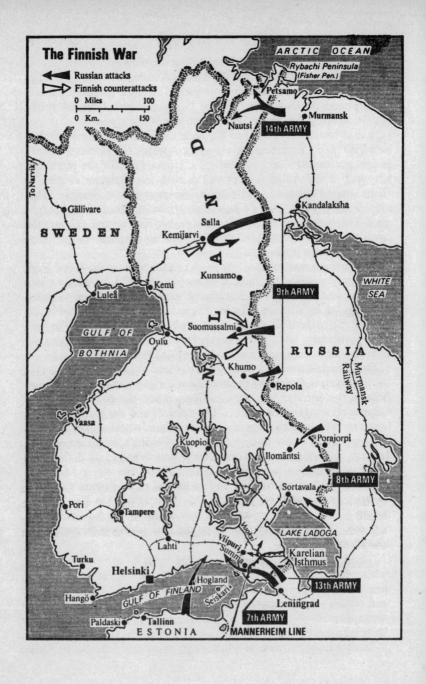

The Finnish War

Russian attacks
Finnish counterattacks

0   Miles   100
0   Km.   150

ARCTIC OCEAN

Rybachi Peninsula
(Fisher Pen.)

Petsamo

Murmansk

Nautsi

14th ARMY

To Narvik

Kandalaksha

Gällivare

Salla

SWEDEN

Kemijarvi

WHITE SEA

Kunsamo

Kemi

9th ARMY

Luleå

RUSSIA

Suomussalmi

Murmansk Railway

Oulu

GULF OF BOTHNIA

Khumo

Repola

Vaasa

Kuopio

Porajorpi

Ilomäntsi

Pori

Sortavala

8th ARMY

Tampere

LAKE LADOGA

Lahti

Turku

Vuoksi

Viipuri

Summa

Karelian Isthmus

Helsinki

13th ARMY

Hogland

Hangö

GULF OF FINLAND

Seiskari

Leningrad

Paldaski

Tallinn

7th ARMY

ESTONIA

MANNERHEIM LINE

FINLAND

CHAPTER FIVE

The Finnish War

Following the partition of Poland, Stalin was anxious to safeguard Russia's Baltic flank against a future threat from his temporary colleague, Hitler. Accordingly, the Soviet Government lost no time in securing strategic control of Russia's old-time buffer-territories in the Baltic. By October 10th it had concluded pacts with Estonia, Latvia, and Lithuania which enabled its forces to garrison key-points in those countries. On the 9th conversations began with Finland. On the 14th the Soviet Government formulated its demands. These were defined as having three main purposes.

First, to cover the sea approach to Leningrad, by (a) 'making it possible to block the Gulf of Finland by artillery from both coasts, to prevent enemy warships or transports entering the Gulf'; (b) 'making it possible to prevent any enemy gaining access to the islands in the Gulf of Finland situated west and north-west of the entrance to Leningrad'. For this purpose the Finns were asked to cede the islands of Hogland, Seiskari, Lavanskari, Tytarskari, and Loivisto, in exchange for other territories; also to lease the port of Hangö for thirty years so that the Russians might there establish a naval base with coastal artillery, capable, in conjunction with the naval base at Paldaski on the opposite coast, of blocking access to the Gulf of Finland.

Second, to provide better cover on the land approach to Leningrad by moving back the Finnish frontier in the Karelian Isthmus, to a line which would be out of heavy artillery range of Leningrad. The readjustments of the frontier would still leave intact the main defences on the Mannerheim Line.

Third, to adjust the frontier in the far north 'in the Petsamo region, where the frontier was badly and artificially drawn'. It was a straight line running through the narrow isthmus of the Rybachi peninsula and cutting off the western end of that peninsula. This re-adjustment was apparently designed to safeguard the sea approach to Murmansk by preventing an enemy establishing himself on the Rybachi peninsula.

In exchange for these re-adjustments of territory the Soviet Union offered to cede to Finland the districts of Repola and Porajorpi – an exchange which, even according to the Finnish White Book, would have given Finland an additional 2,134 square miles in compensation for the cession to Russia of areas totalling 1,066 square miles.

An objective examination of these terms suggests that they were framed on a rational basis, to provide a greater security to Russian territory without serious detriment to the security of Finland. They would, clearly, have hindered the use of Finland as a jumping-off point for any German attack on Russia. But they would not have given Russia any appreciable advantage for an attack on Finland. Indeed, the territory which Russia offered to cede to Finland would have widened Finland's uncomfortably narrow waistline.

National sentiment, however, made it hard for the Finns to agree to a settlement on these lines. While they expressed willingness to cede all the islands except Hogland, they were adamant about leaving the port of Hangö on the mainland – contending that this would be inconsistent with their policy of strict neutrality. The Russians then offered to buy this piece of territory, arguing that such a purchase would be in accord with Finland's neutrality obligations. The Finns, however, refused this offer. The discussions became acrimonious, the tone of Russian Press comment became threatening, and on November 28th the Soviet Government cancelled the non-aggression treaty of 1932. On the 30th the Russian invasion began.

The original advance ended in a check that astonished the world. A direct push from Leningrad up the Karelian Isthmus came to a halt in the forward layers of the Mannerheim Line. An advance near Lake Ladoga did not make progress. At the other end of the front the Russians cut off the small port of Petsamo on the Arctic Ocean, as a means of blocking the entry of help to Finland by that route.

Two more immediately menacing thrusts were delivered across the waist of Finland. The more northerly thrust penetrated past Salla to Kemijarvi, halfway to the Gulf of Bothnia, before it was driven back by the counterattack of a Finnish division which had been switched up by rail from the south. The southerly thrust, past Suomussalmi, was interrupted in turn by a counterstroke, early in January 1940. Circling round the invaders' flank, the Finns blocked their line of supply and retreat, waited until their troops were exhausted by cold and hunger, then attacked and broke them up.

In the West, sympathy with Finland as a fresh victim of aggression had rapidly developed into enthusiasm at the apparent success of the weak in repulsing the strong. This impression had far-reaching repercussions. It prompted the French and British Governments to consider the dispatch of an expeditionary force to this new theatre of war with the object not only of aiding Finland but also of securing the Swedish iron mines at Gällivare from which Germany drew supplies, while establishing a position that threatened Germany's Baltic flank. Partly because of the objections raised by Norway and Sweden, this project did not materialize before Finland collapsed. France and Britain were thus spared entanglement in war with the USSR as well as with Germany at a time when their own powers of defence were perilously weak. But the obvious threat of an Allied move into Scandinavia precipitated Hitler's decision to forestall it by occupying Norway.

Another effect of Finland's early successes was that it reinforced the general tendency to underrate the Soviet military strength. This view was epitomized in Winston Churchill's broadcast assertion of January 20th, 1940, that Finland 'had exposed, for the world to see, the military incapacity of the Red Army'. His misjudgement was to some extent shared by Hitler – with momentous consequences the following year.

More dispassionate examination of the campaign, however, provided better reasons for the ineffectiveness of the original advance. There was no sign of proper preparations to mount a powerful offensive, furnished with large stocks of munitions and equipment from Russia's vast resources. There were clear signs that the Soviet authorities had been misled by their sources of information about the situation in Finland, and that, instead of reckoning on serious resistance, they imagined that they might have to do no more than back up a rising of the Finnish people against an unpopular Government. The country cramped an invader at every turn, being full of natural obstacles that narrowed the avenues of approach and helped the defence. Between Lake Ladoga and the Arctic Ocean the frontier appeared very wide on the map but in reality was a tangle of lakes and forests, ideal for laying traps as well as for stubborn resistance. Moreover, on the Soviet side of the frontier the rail communications consisted of the solitary line from Leningrad to Murmansk, which in its 800-mile stretch had only one branch leading to the Finnish frontier. This limitation was reflected in the fact that the 'waistline' thrusts which sounded so formidable in the highly coloured reports from Finland were made with only three divisions apiece, while four were employed in the outflanking manoeuvre north of Ladoga.

Much the best approach to Finland was through the Karelian Isthmus between Lake Ladoga and the Gulf of Finland, but this was blocked by the Mannerheim Line and the Finns' six active divisions, which were concentrated there at the outset. The Russian thrusts farther north, though they fared badly, served the purpose of drawing part of the Finnish reserves thither while thorough preparations were being made, and fourteen divisions brought up, for a serious attack on the Mannerheim Line. This was launched on February 1st, under the direction of General Meretskov. Its weight was concentrated on a ten-mile sector near Summa, which was pounded by a tremendous artillery bombardment. As the fortifications were pulverized, tanks and sledge-carried infantry advanced to occupy the ground, while the Soviet air force broke up attempted countermoves. After little more than a fort-night of this methodical process a breach was made through the whole depth of the Mannerheim Line. The attackers then wheeled outward to corner Finnish forces on either flank, before pushing on to Viipuri (Viborg). A wider flanking operation was carried out across the frozen Gulf of Finland by troops who advanced from the ice-bound island of Hogland and landed well in the rear of Viipuri. Although an obstinate defence was still maintained for several weeks in front of Viipuri, Finland's limited forces had been worn down in the effort to hold the Karelian Isthmus. Once a passage was forced, and their communications menaced, eventual collapse was certain. Capitulation was the only way in which it could be averted, since the proffered Franco-British expeditionary force had not arrived, though almost ready to sail.

On March 6th, 1940, the Finnish Government sent a delegation to negotiate peace. Beyond the earlier Soviet conditions, Finland was now asked to cede areas in the communes of Salla and Kunsamo, the whole of the Karelian Isthmus, including Viipuri, and also the Finnish part of the Fisher Peninsula. They were also asked to build a railroad from Kemijarvi to the frontier (which was not yet established) to link up to the Russian spur. On March 13th it was announced that the Soviet terms had been accepted.

In the radically changed circumstances, particularly after the disastrous collapse in the Summa sector of the Mannerheim Line on February 12th, the new Soviet terms were remarkably moderate. But Field-Marshal Mannerheim, who was more of a realist than most statesmen, and rightly dubious about the pressing Franco-British offers of help, urged acceptance of the Soviet terms. In raising his requirements so little, Stalin too showed statesmanship, while evidently anxious to be quit of a commitment which had occupied more than a million of Russia's troops, as well as a high proportion of her tanks and aircraft, at a time when the crucial spring of 1940 was looming near.

Whereas conditions in Poland were more favourable to a Blitz-krieg offensive than anywhere else in Europe, Finland offered a most unsuitable theatre for such a performance, especially at the time of the year when the invasion was staged.

The geographical encirclement of the Polish frontier was intensified by the ampleness of the German communications and the scarcity of the Polish. The open nature of the country offered scope for the thrusts of mechanized forces that was guaranteed by the dry September weather. The Polish Army was even more wedded to the offensive tradition than most armies, and thus all the weaker in utilizing its sparse means of defensive action.

In Finland, by contrast, the defender profited by having a much better system of internal communications, both rail and road, than the attacker possessed on his side of the frontier. The Finns had several lines of railway parallel to the frontier for the rapid lateral switching of their reserves; the Russians had only the solitary line from Leningrad to Murmansk, with its one branch to the Finnish frontier. Elsewhere, the Russians would have to advance anything from 50 to 150 miles from the railway before crossing the frontier, and considerably farther before they could threaten any point of strategic importance. That advance, moreover, had to be made through a country of lakes and forests, and over poor roads that were now deep in snow.

These difficulties set a narrow limit to the forces which the Soviet Union could move and maintain, except in a direct advance through the Karelian Isthmus against the strongly defended Mannerheim Line. This neck of land, seventy miles wide on the map, is much less in strategic reality. Half of it is barred by the broad Vuoksi River, while much of the remainder is covered by a series of lakes, with forests between them. Only near Summa is there room for deploying any considerable force.

Moreover, beyond the strategic difficulties of assembling any large forces on the apparently exposed parts of the Finnish frontier and pushing them deep into the enemy's country, lay the tactical difficulty of overcoming the resistance of defenders who knew the ground and were able to exploit its advantages. Lakes and forests tend to shepherd an invading force into narrow channels of advance where it can be swept by machine-gun fire; they offer innumerable opportunities for concealed flanking manoeuvres as well as for guerrilla harassing. To penetrate into such a country in face of a skilful foe is hazardous enough in summer; it is much more difficult to attempt in the Arctic winter, when heavy columns are as clumsy as a man in clogs trying to grapple with an opponent in gym-shoes.

If Field-Marshal Mannerheim obviously took risks in keeping all his reserves in the extreme south until the Russians had shown their hand, his strategy was justified on the whole by the opportunities which the enemy's initial penetrations offered to subsequent counterstrokes – especially in that kind of country under winter conditions.

As for the Russians, it is only to be expected that plans which have been based on a false assumption should break down when put to the test of reality. But that is not of itself proof of military inefficiency throughout the army concerned. While authoritarian régimes are particularly susceptible to the kind of reports on the situation which accord with their wishes, no type of government is immune from such risks. It is wise to remember that perhaps the greatest of all false assumptions in modern history were those on which the French plans in 1914 and 1940 were based.

PART III

THE SURGE
1940

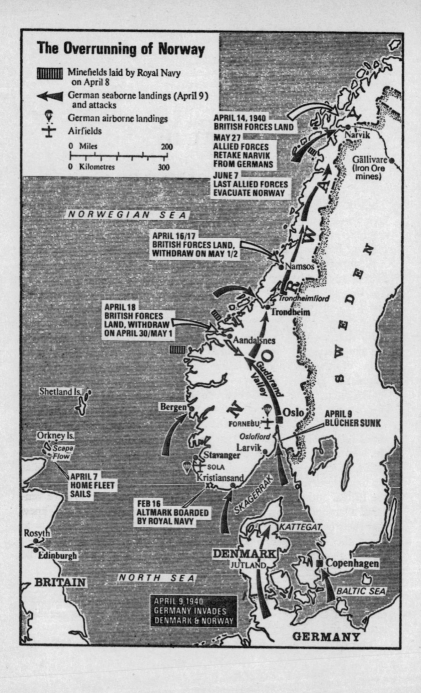

The Overrunning of Norway

Minefields laid by Royal Navy on April 8

German seaborne landings (April 9) and attacks

German airborne landings

Airfields

0 Miles 200

0 Kilometres 300

APRIL 14, 1940 BRITISH FORCES LAND

MAY 27 ALLIED FORCES RETAKE NARVIK FROM GERMANS

JUNE 7 LAST ALLIED FORCES EVACUATE NORWAY

Narvik

Gällivare (Iron Ore mines)

NORWEGIAN SEA

APRIL 16/17 BRITISH FORCES LAND, WITHDRAW ON MAY 1/2

Namsos

Trondheimfjord

Trondheim

APRIL 18 BRITISH FORCES LAND, WITHDRAW ON APRIL 30/MAY 1

Aandalsnes

Gudbrand Valley

N O R W A Y

S W E D E N

Bergen

FORNEBU

Oslo

APRIL 9 BLÜCHER SUNK

Oslofiord

Larvik

Shetland Is.

Stavanger

SOLA

Kristiansand

Orkney Is.

Scapa Flow

APRIL 7 HOME FLEET SAILS

FEB 16 ALTMARK BOARDED BY ROYAL NAVY

SKAGERRAK

KATTEGAT

Rosyth

Edinburgh

NORTH SEA

BRITAIN

DENMARK

JUTLAND

Copenhagen

BALTIC SEA

APRIL 9, 1940 GERMANY INVADES DENMARK & NORWAY

GERMANY

CHAPTER SIX

The Overrunning of Norway

The six months' deceptive lull that followed the conquest of Poland ended with a sudden thunderclap. It came, not where the storm-clouds centred, but on the Scandinavian fringe. The peaceful countries of Norway and Denmark were struck by a flash of Hitlerian lightning.

Newspapers on April 9th featured the news that on the previous day, British and French naval forces had entered Norwegian waters and laid minefields there – to block them to any ships trading with Germany. Congratulatory comment on this initiative was mingled with justificatory arguments for the breach of Norway's neutrality. But the radio that morning put the newspapers out of date – for it carried the far more startling news that German forces were landing at a series of points along the coast of Norway, and had also entered Denmark.

The audacity of these German moves, in defiance of Britain's superiority in seapower, staggered the Allied leaders. When the British Prime Minister, Mr Chamberlain, made a statement in the House of Commons that afternoon he said that there had been German landings up the west coast of Norway, at Bergen and Trondheim, as well as on the south coast, and added: 'There have been some reports about a similar landing at Narvik, but I am very doubtful whether they are correct.' To the British authorities it seemed incredible that Hitler could have ventured a landing so far north, and all the more incredible since they knew that their own naval forces were present on the scene in strength – to cover the mine-laying operations and other intended steps. They thought that 'Narvik' must be a misspelling of 'Larvik', a place on the south coast.

Before the end of the day, however, it became clear that the Germans had gained possession of the capital of Norway, Oslo, and all the main ports including Narvik. Every one of their simultaneous seaborne strokes had been successful.

The British Government's quick disillusionment on this score was followed by a fresh illusion. Mr Churchill, then First Lord of the Admiralty, told the House of Commons two days later:

> In my view, which is shared by my skilled advisers, Herr Hitler has committed a grave strategic error ... we have greatly gained by what has occurred in Scandinavia ... He has made a whole series of commitments upon the Norwegian coast for which he will now have to fight, if necessary, during the whole summer, against Powers possessing vastly superior naval forces and able to transport them to the scenes of action more easily than he can. I cannot see any counter-advantage which he has gained ... I feel that we are greatly advantaged by ... the strategic blunder into which our mortal enemy has been provoked.*

These fine words were not followed up by deeds to match. The British countermoves were slow, hesitant, and bungled. When it came to the point of action the Admiralty, despite its prewar disdain for airpower, became extremely cautious and shrank from risking ships at the places where their intervention could have been decisive. The troop-moves were still feebler. Although forces were landed at several places with the aim of ejecting the German invader, they were all re-embarked in barely a fortnight, except from one foothold at Narvik - and that was abandoned a month later, following the main German offensive in the West.

The dream-castles raised by Churchill had come tumbling down. They had been built on a basic misconception of the situation, and of the changes in modern warfare - particularly the effect of airpower on seapower.

There had been more reality and significance in his closing words when, after depicting Norway as a trap for Hitler, he spoke of the German invasion as a step into which Hitler had 'been provoked'. For the most startling of all postwar discoveries about the campaign has been the fact that Hitler, despite all his unscrupulousness, would have preferred to keep Norway neutral, and did not plan to invade her until he was provoked to do so by palpable signs that the Allies were planning a hostile move in that quarter.

It is fascinating to trace the sequence of events behind the scene on either side - though tragic and horrifying to see how violently offensive-minded statesmen tend to react on one another to produce explosions of destructive force. The first clear step on either side was on September

* Churchill: *War Speeches*, vol I, pp 169–70.

19th, 1939, when Churchill (as his memoirs record) pressed on the British Cabinet the project of laying a minefield 'in Norwegian territorial waters' and thus 'stopping the Norwegian transportation of Swedish iron-ore from Narvik' to Germany. He argued that such a step would be 'of the highest importance in crippling the enemy's war industry'. According to his subsequent note to the First Sea Lord: 'The Cabinet, including the Foreign Secretary [Lord Halifax], appeared strongly favourable to this action.'

This is rather surprising to learn, and suggests that the Cabinet were inclined to favour the end without carefully considering the means – or where they might lead. A similar project had been discussed in 1918, but on that occasion, as is stated in the Official Naval History:

> ... the Commander-in-Chief [Lord Beatty] said it would be most repugnant to the officers and men in the Grand Fleet to steam in overwhelming strength into the waters of a small but high-spirited people and coerce them. If the Norwegians resisted, as they probably would, blood would be shed; this, said the Commander-in-Chief, 'would constitute a crime as bad as any that the Germans had committed elsewhere.'

It is evident that the sailors were more scrupulous than the statesmen, or that the British Government was in a more reckless mood at the opening of war in 1939 than at the end of World War I.

The Foreign Office staff exerted a restraining influence, however, and made the Cabinet see the objections to violating Norway's neutrality as proposed. Churchill mournfully records: 'The Foreign Office arguments about neutrality were weighty, and I could not prevail. I continued ... to press my point by every means and on all occasions.'* It became a subject of discussion in widening circles, and arguments in its favour were even canvassed in the Press. That was just the way to arouse German anxiety and countermeasures.

On the German side the first point of any significance to be found in the captured records comes in early October, when the Commander-in-Chief of the Navy, Admiral Raeder, expressed fears that the Norwegians might open their ports to the British and reported to Hitler on the strategic disadvantages that a British occupation might bring. He also suggested that it would be advantageous to the German submarine campaign 'to obtain bases on the Norwegian coast – eg Trondheim – with the help of Russian pressure'.

* Churchill: *The Second World War*, vol I, p 483.

But Hitler put the suggestion aside. His mind was focused on plans for an attack in the West, to compel France to make peace, and he did not want to be drawn into any extraneous operations or diversion of resources.

A fresh and much stronger incitement, to both sides, arose out of the Russian invasion of Finland at the end of November. Churchill saw in it a new possibility of striking at Germany's flank under the cloak of aid to Finland: 'I welcomed this new and favourable breeze as a means of achieving the major strategic advantage of cutting off the vital iron-ore supplies of Germany.'*

In a note of December 16th he marshalled all his arguments for this step, which he described as 'a major offensive operation'. He recognized that it was likely to drive the Germans to invade Scandinavia for, as he said: 'If you fire at the enemy he will fire back.' But he went on to assert 'we have more to gain than to lose by a German attack upon Norway and Sweden'. (He omitted any consideration of what the Scandinavian peoples would suffer from having their countries thus turned into a battleground.)

Most of the Cabinet, however, still had qualms about violating Norway's neutrality. Despite Churchill's powerful pleading they refrained from sanctioning the immediate execution of his project. But they authorized the Chiefs of Staff to 'plan for landing a force at Narvik' – which was the terminus of the railway leading to the Gällivare ironfields in Sweden, and thence into Finland. While aid to Finland was the ostensible purpose of such an expedition, the underlying and major purpose would be the domination of the Swedish iron-fields.

In the same month an important visitor came to Berlin from Norway. This was Vidkun Quisling, a former Minister of Defence, who was head of a small party of Nazi type that was strongly sympathetic to Germany. He saw Admiral Raeder on arrival, and impressed on him the danger that Britain would soon occupy Norway. He asked for money and underground help for his own plans of organizing a coup to turn out the existing Norwegian Government. He said that a number of leading Norwegian officers were ready to back him – including, he alleged, Colonel Sundlo, the commander at Narvik. Once he had gained power he would invite the Germans in to protect Norway, and thus forestall a British entry.

Raeder persuaded Hitler to see Quisling personally, and they met on December 16th and 18th. The record of their talk shows that Hitler said 'he would prefer Norway, as well as the rest of Scandinavia, to

* Churchill: *The Second World War*, vol I, p 489.

remain completely neutral', as he did not want to 'enlarge the theatre of war'. But 'if the enemy were preparing to spread the war he would take steps to guard himself against the threat'. Meantime Quisling was promised a subsidy and given an assurance that the problem of giving him military support would be studied.

Even so, the War Diary of the German Naval Staff shows that on January 13th, a month later, they were still of the opinion that 'the most favourable solution would be the maintenance of Norway's neutrality', although they were becoming anxious that 'England intended to occupy Norway with the tacit agreement of the Norwegian Government'.

What was happening on the other side of the hill? On January 15th General Gamelin, the French Commander-in-Chief, addressed a note to Daladier, the Prime Minister, on the importance of opening a new theatre of war in Scandinavia. He also produced a plan for landing an Allied force at Petsamo, in the north of Finland, together with the precautionary 'seizure of ports and airfields on the west coast of Norway'. The plan further envisaged the possibility of 'extending the operation into Sweden and occupying the iron-ore mines at Gällivare'.

A broadcast by Churchill, who addressed the neutrals on their duty to join in the fight against Hitler, naturally fanned German fears.* There were all too many public hints of Allied action.

On the 27th Hitler gave explicit orders to his military advisers to prepare comprehensive plans for an invasion of Norway if necessary. The special staff formed for the purpose met for the first time on February 5th.

That day the Allied Supreme War Council met in Paris, and Chamberlain took Churchill with him. At this meeting plans were approved for preparing a force of two British divisions and a slightly smaller French contingent as 'Aid to Finland' – they were to be 'camouflaged as

* On January 20th Mr Churchill, in a broadcast address, claimed success for the Allied navies at sea, and contrasted the losses of neutral ships to U-boat attack with the safety of Allied ships in convoy. Then, after a brief *tour d'horizon*, he asked: 'But what would happen if all these neutral nations I have mentioned – and some others I have not mentioned – were with one spontaneous impulse to do their duty in accordance with the Covenant of the League, and were to stand together with the British and French Empires against aggression and wrong?' (Churchill: *War Speeches*, vol I, p 137). The suggestion caused a stir, and the Belgian, Dutch, Danish, Norwegian, and Swiss Presses hastened to reject it, while in London it was announced, with some reversion to the days of appeasement, that the broadcast only represented Churchill's personal views.

volunteers' in an endeavour to diminish the chances of an open war with Russia. But an argument developed over the route of their dispatch. The British Prime Minister emphasized the difficulties of landing at Petsamo, and the advantages of landing at Narvik – particularly 'to get control of the Gällivare ore-field'. That was to be the main object, and only a part of the force was to push on to Finland's aid. The British arguments prevailed, and it was arranged that the force should sail early in March.

A fateful incident occurred on February 16th. A German vessel, the *Altmark*, which was carrying British prisoners back from the South Atlantic, was chased by British destroyers and took refuge in a Norwegian fiord. Churchill sent a direct order to Captain Vian of HMS *Cossack* to push into Norwegian waters, board the *Altmark* and rescue the prisoners. Two Norwegian gunboats were on the scene, but they were overawed and the subsequent protest of the Norwegian Government about the intrusion into their waters was rebuffed.

Hitler regarded the protest as merely a gesture to hoodwink him, and was convinced that the Norwegian Government was England's willing accomplice. That belief was nourished by the passivity of the two gunboats and by the reports of Quisling that the action of the *Cossack* had been a 'pre-arranged' affair. According to the German admirals, the *Altmark* affair was decisive in swinging Hitler in favour of intervention in Norway. It was the spark that set fire to the powder trail.

Hitler felt that he could not wait for Quisling's plan to develop, especially as German observers in Norway reported that Quisling's party was making little progress, while reports from England indicated that some action in the Norwegian area was being planned, together with the assembly of troops and transports.

On the 20th Hitler sent for General von Falkenhorst and appointed him to command and prepare an expeditionary force for Norway, saying, 'I am informed that the English intend to land there, and I want to be there before them. The occupation of Norway by the British would be a strategic turning movement which would lead them into the Baltic, where we have neither troops nor coastal fortifications ... the enemy would find himself in a position to advance on Berlin and break the backbone of our two fronts.'

On March 1st, Hitler issued his directive for the complete preparation for the invasion. Denmark was to be occupied, too, as a necessary strategic stepping-stone and safeguard to his lines of communication.

But even now it was not a definite decision to strike. The records of Raeder's conferences with Hitler show that Hitler was still torn between his conviction that 'the maintenance of Norway's neutrality is the best thing' for Germany and his fear of an imminent British landing there. In presenting the naval plans on March 9th he dwelt on the hazards of undertaking an operation 'contrary to all the principles of naval warfare', while at the same time saying that it was 'urgent'.

In the following week the state of anxiety on the German side became more feverish. On the 13th it was reported that British submarines were concentrated off the south cost of Norway; on the 14th the Germans intercepted a radio message which ordered Allied transports to be ready to move; on the 15th a number of French officers arrived at Bergen. The Germans felt that they were certain to be forestalled as their own expeditionary force was not yet ready.

How were things actually going on the Allied side? On February 21st Daladier urged that the *Altmark* affair should be used as a pretext for the 'immediate seizure' of the Norwegian ports 'by a sudden stroke'. Daladier argued: 'It's justification in the eyes of world opinion will be the more easy the more rapidly the operation is carried out and the more our propaganda is able to exploit the memory of the recent complicity of Norway in the *Altmark* incident' – a way of talking which was remarkably like Hitler's. The French Government's proposal was viewed with some doubt in London, as the expeditionary forces were not ready and Chamberlain still hoped that the Norwegian and Swedish Governments would agree to the entry of Allied troops.

At the meeting of the War Cabinet on March 8th, however, Churchill unfolded a scheme of arriving in force off Narvik and throwing a detachment of troops ashore immediately – on the principle of 'displaying strength in order to avoid having to use it'. At a further meeting on the 12th the Cabinet 'decided to revive the plans' for landings at Trondheim, Stavanger, and Bergen as well as at Narvik.

The force landed at Narvik was to push rapidly inland and over the Swedish frontier to the Gällivare iron-field. Everything was to be ready for putting the plans into execution on March 20th.

But then the plans were upset by Finland's military collapse and her capitulation to Russia on March 13th – which deprived the Allies of the primary pretext for going into Norway. In the first reaction to the cold douche, two divisions which had been allotted for the Norway force were sent to France, though the equivalent of one division remained available. Another sequel was the fall of Daladier, and his replacement as Prime Minister of France by Paul Reynaud – who came into power on the surge of a demand for a more offensive policy and quicker action. Reynaud went to London for a meeting of the Allied Supreme

War Council, on March 28th, determined to press for the immediate execution of the Norwegian project that Churchill had so long been urging.

But there was no need now for any such pressure – for, as Churchill has related, Chamberlain had become 'much inclined to aggressive action of some kind at this stage'. As in the spring of 1939, once he had taken his resolve he jumped in with both feet. Opening the Council, he not only argued strongly for action in Norway but also urged the adoption of Churchill's other favourite project – that of dropping by air a continuous stream of mines into the Rhine and other rivers of Germany. Reynaud expressed some doubt about the latter operation, and said he would have to obtain the agreement of the French War Committee. But he eagerly embraced the Norwegian operation.

It was settled that the mining of Norwegian waters should be carried out on April 5th, and be backed by the landing of forces at Narvik, Trondheim, Bergen, and Stavanger. The first contingent of troops was to sail, for Narvik, on the 8th. But then a fresh delay arose. The French War Committee would not agree to the dropping of mines in the Rhine lest it should bring German retaliation 'which would fall upon France'. They showed no such concern about the retaliation that would fall on Norway from the other operation – and Gamelin had even emphasized that one of its aims was 'to draw the enemy into a trap by provoking him to land in Norway'. Chamberlain, however, tried to insist that both operations should be carried out, and arranged with Churchill that the latter should go over to Paris on the 4th and make a fresh effort – which did not succeed – to persuade the French to adopt his Rhine plan.

That meant a short deferment of 'Wilfred', the Norwegian plan. It is strange that Churchill was agreeable to it, for at the War Cabinet meeting the day before, reports had been presented from the War Office and Foreign Office showing that large numbers of German ships were concentrated, with troops on board, at the ports nearest to Norway. Rather absurdly it was suggested – and astonishingly, believed – that these forces were waiting in readiness to deliver a counterstroke to a British descent on Norway.

The start of the Norwegian operations was postponed three days, until the 8th. That further delay proved fatal to its prospects of success. It enabled the Germans to get into Norway just ahead of the Allies.

On April 1st Hitler had finally made up his mind and ordered the invasion of Norway and Denmark to begin at 5.15 AM on the 9th. His decision followed a disturbing report that Norwegian anti-aircraft and coastal batteries had been given permission to open fire without awaiting higher orders – which suggested that the Norwegian forces were being made ready for action and that if Hitler waited any longer his chances of surprise, and success, would vanish.

In the dark hours of April 9th advance detachments of German troops, mostly in warships, arrived in the chief ports of Norway, from Oslo right up to Narvik – and captured them with little difficulty. Their commanders announced to the local authorities that they had come to take Norway under German protection against an Allied invasion that was imminent – a statement that the Allied spokesmen promptly denied, and continued to deny.

As Lord Hankey, a member of the War Cabinet at the time, stated:

> ...from the start of planning to the German invasion, both Great Britain and Germany were keeping more or less level in their plans and preparations. Britain actually started planning a little earlier ... both plans were executed almost simultaneously, Britain being twenty-four hours ahead in the so-called act of aggression, if the term is really applicable to either side.

But Germany's final spurt was faster and more forceful. She won the race by a very short head – it was almost a 'photo-finish'.

One of the most questionable points of the Nuremberg Trials was that the planning and execution of aggression against Norway was put among the major charges against the Germans. It is hard to understand how the British and French Governments had the face to approve the inclusion of this charge, or how the official prosecutors could press for a conviction on this score. Such a course was one of the most palpable cases of hypocrisy in history.

Passing now to the course of the campaign, a surprising revelation is the smallness of the force which captured the capital and chief ports of Norway in the opening coup. It comprised two battlecruisers, a pocket battleship, seven cruisers, fourteen destroyers, twenty-eight U-boats, a number of auxiliary ships, and some 10,000 troops – the advance elements of three divisions that were used for the invasion. At no place was the initial landing made by more than 2,000 men. One parachute battalion was also employed – to seize the airfields at Oslo and Stavanger. This was the first time that parachute troops had been used in war and they proved very valuable. But the most decisive factor in the German success was the Luftwaffe; the actual strength employed in the campaign was about 800 operational planes and 250 transport planes. It overawed the Norwegian people in the first phase, and later paralysed the Allies' countermoves.

How was it that the British naval forces failed to intercept and sink the much weaker German naval forces that carried the invading detachments? The extent of the sea-space, the nature of the Norwegian coast, and the hazy weather were important handicaps. But there were other factors, and more avoidable handicaps. Gamelin records that when, on April 2nd, he urged Ironside, the Chief of the Imperial General Staff, to hasten the dispatch of the expeditionary force, the latter replied: 'With us the Admiralty is all-powerful; it likes to organize everything methodically. It is convinced that it can prevent any German landing on the west coast of Norway.'

At 1.25 PM on the 7th British aircraft actually spotted 'strong German naval forces moving swiftly northward' across the mouth of the Skaggerak, towards the Norwegian coast. Churchill says: 'We found it hard at the Admiralty to believe that this force was going to Narvik' – in spite of a 'report from Copenhagen that Hitler meant to seize that port'. The British Home Fleet sailed at 7.30 PM from Scapa Flow, but it would seem that both the Admiralty and the admirals at sea were filled with the thought of catching the German battlecruisers. In their efforts to bring these to battle they tended to lose sight of the possibility that the enemy had a landward intention, and lost a chance of intercepting the smaller troop-carrying warships.

Since an expeditionary force was already embarked and ready to sail, why was it so slow to land and eject the German detachments before they had time to establish their grip on the Norwegian ports? The prime reason is contained in the last paragraph. When the Admiralty heard that the German battlecruisers had been spotted, they ordered the cruiser squadron at Rosyth 'to march her soldiers ashore, even without their equipment, and join the Fleet at sea'. Similar orders were sent to the ships in the Clyde that were loaded up with troops.

Why did not the Norwegians put up a better resistance against such a small invading force? Primarily, because their forces were not even mobilized. Despite warnings from their Minister in Berlin and urgings from the Chief of their General Staff, the order for mobilization was not given until the night of April 8th–9th, a few hours before the invasion. That was too late, and the swift-moving invaders disrupted the process.

Moreover, as Churchill remarks, the Norwegian Government at the time was 'chiefly concerned with the activities of the British'. It was unfortunate, and also ironical, that the British mine-laying operation should have absorbed and distracted the Norwegians' attention during the crucial twenty-four hours before the Germans landed.

As for the Norwegians' chance of rallying from the opening blow, this was diminished by their lack of fighting experience and an out-of-date military organization. In no way were they fitted to cope with a modern Blitzkrieg, even on the small scale applied to their case. The weakness of the resistance was all too clearly shown by the speed with which the invaders raced along the deep valleys to overrun the country. If the resistance had been tougher, the melting snow on the valley-sides – which hampered outflanking manoeuvre – would have been a more serious impediment to the German prospects of success.

The most astonishing of the opening series of coups was that at Narvik, for this far northern port was some 1,200 miles distant from the German naval bases. Two Norwegian coast-defence ships gallantly met the attacking German destroyers, but were quickly sunk. The shore defences made no attempt at resistance – more by incompetence than treachery. Next day a British destroyer flotilla steamed up the fiord and fought a mutually damaging action with the Germans, which on the 13th were finished off by the inroad of a stronger flotilla supported by the battleship *Warspite*. But by this time the German troops were established in and around Narvik.

Farther south, Trondheim was captured with ease after the German ships had run the gauntlet of the batteries dominating the fiord – a hazard that had dismayed Allied experts who had considered the problem. By securing Trondheim, the Germans had possessed themselves of the strategic key to central Norway, though the question remained whether their handful of troops there could be reinforced from the south.

At Bergen, the Germans suffered some damage from the Norwegian warships and batteries, but had little trouble once they were ashore.

In the approach to Oslo, however, the main invading force suffered a jolt. For the cruiser *Blücher*, carrying many of the military staff, was sunk by torpedoes from the Oscarborg fortress, and the attempt to force the passage was then given up until this fortress surrendered in the afternoon, after heavy air attack. Thus the capture of Norway's capital devolved on the parachute troops who had landed on the Fornebu airfield; in the afternoon this token force staged a parade march into the city, and its bluff succeeded. But the delay at least enabled the King and Government to escape northward with a view to rallying resistance.

The capture of Copenhagen was timed to coincide with the intended arrival at Oslo. The Danish capital was easy of access from the sea, and shortly before 5 AM three small transports steamed into the harbour, covered by aircraft overhead. The Germans met no resistance on landing, and a battalion marched off to take the barracks by surprise. At the same time Denmark's land frontier in Jutland was invaded, but after a brief exchange of fire resistance was abandoned. The occupation of Denmark went far to ensure the Germans' control of a sheltered sea-corridor from their own ports to southern Norway, and also gave them advanced airfields from which they could support the troops there. While the Danes might have fought longer, their country was so vulnerable as to be hardly defensible against a powerful attack with modern weapons.

More prompt and resolute action might have recovered two of the key points in Norway which the Germans captured that morning. For at the time they landed, the main British fleet under Admiral Forbes was abreast of Bergen, and he thought of sending a force in to attack the German ships there. The Admiralty agreed, and suggested that a similar attack should be made at Trondheim. A little later, however, it was decided to postpone the Trondheim attack until the German battlecruisers were tracked down. Meanwhile a force of four cruisers and seven destroyers headed for Bergen, but when aircraft reported that two German cruisers were there, instead of one as earlier reported, the Admiralty was overcome with caution and cancelled the attack.

Once the Germans had established a lodgment in Norway, the best way of loosening it would have been to cut them off from supply and reinforcements. That could only be done by barring the passage of the Skaggerak, between Denmark and Norway. But it soon became clear that the Admiralty - from fear of German air attack - was not willing to send anything except submarines into the Skaggerak. Such caution revealed a realization of the effect of airpower on seapower that the Admiralty had never shown before the war. But it reflected badly on Churchill's judgement in seeking to spread the war to Scandinavia - for unless the Germans' route of reinforcements could be effectively blocked nothing could stop them building up their strength in southern Norway, and they were bound to gain a growing advantage.

There still appeared to be a chance of preserving central Norway if the two long mountain defiles leading north from Oslo were firmly held, and the small German Force at Trondheim was quickly overcome. To this aim British efforts were now bent. A week after the German coup, British landings were made north and south of Trondheim, at Namsos and Aandalsnes respectively, as a preliminary to the main and direct attack on Trondheim.

But a strange chain of mishaps followed the decision. General Hotblack, an able soldier with modern ideas, was appointed as the military commander; but after being briefed for his task he left the Admiralty about midnight to walk back to his club, and some hours later was found unconscious on the Duke of York's Steps, having apparently had a sudden seizure. A successor was appointed next day and set off by air for Scapa but the plane suddenly dived into the ground when circling the airfield there.

Meantime a sudden change took place in the views of the Chiefs of Staff, and the Admiralty. On the 17th they had approved the plan but the next day swung round in opposition to it. The risks of the operation filled their minds. Although Churchill would have preferred to concentrate on Narvik, he was much upset at the way they had turned round.

The Chiefs of Staff now recommended, instead, that the landings at Namsos and Aandalsnes should be reinforced and developed into a pincer-move against Trondheim. On paper the chances looked good, for there were less than 2,000 German troops in that area, whereas the Allies landed 13,000. But the distance to be covered was long, the snow clogged movement, and the Allied troops proved much less capable than the Germans of overcoming the difficulties. The advance south from Namsos was upset by the threat to its rear produced by the landing of several small German parties near the top of the Trondheim fiord, supported by the one German destroyer in the area. The advance from Aandalsnes, instead of being able to swing north on Trondheim, soon turned into a defensive action against the German troops who were pushing from Oslo up the Gudbrand Valley and brushing aside the Norwegians. As the Allied troops were badly harried by air attack, and lacked air support themselves, the commanders on the spot recommended evacuation. The re-embarkation of the two forces was completed on May 1st and 2nd – thus leaving the Germans in complete control of both southern and central Norway.

The Allies now concentrated on gaining Narvik – more for 'facesaving' purposes than from any continued hope of reaching the Swedish iron-mines. The original British landing in this area had been made on April 14th, but the extreme caution of General Mackesy hindered any speedy attack on Narvik – despite the ardent promptings of Admiral Lord Cork and Orrery, who was put in charge of the combined force in this area. Even when the land forces had been built up to 20,000 troops, their progress was still slow. On the other side 2,000 Austrian Alpine troops reinforced by as many sailors from the German destroyers, and skilfully handled by General Dietl, made the most of the defensive advantages of the difficult country. Not until May 27th were they pushed out of Narvik town. By this time the German offensive in the West had bitten deep into France, which was on the verge of collapse. So on June 7th the Allied forces at Narvik were evacuated. The King and the Government left Norway at the same time.

Over the whole Scandinavian issue the Allied Governments had shown an excessive spirit of aggressiveness coupled with a deficient sense of time – with results that brought misery on the Norwegian people. By contrast Hitler had, for once, shown a prolonged reluctance to strike. But when he eventually made up his mind to forestall the Western powers he lost no more time – and his forces operated with a swiftness and audacity that amply offset the smallness of their numbers during the critical stage.

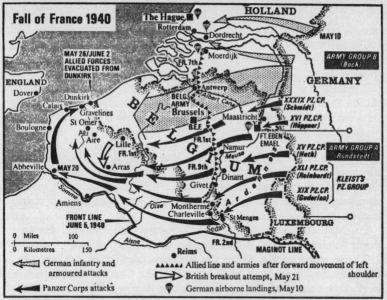

Fall of France 1940

MAY 26/JUNE 2
ALLIED FORCES
EVACUATED FROM
DUNKIRK

HOLLAND
The Hague
Rotterdam
Dordrecht
Moerdijk
FR. 7th
MAY 10
ARMY GROUP B
(Bock)
GERMANY

ENGLAND
Dover
Dunkirk
Calais
Gravelines
St Omer
Boulogne
Aa
Aire
Lille
FR. 1st
Abbeville
MAY 20
Arras
Somme
Amiens

BELGIUM
Antwerp
Albert Canal
BELG. ARMY
Brussels
B.E.F.
Maastricht
FR. 1st
Namur
Meuse
FT. EBEN EMAEL
FR. 9th
Givet
Dinant
Oise
Montherme
Charleville
St Menges
Sedan
Aisne

XXXIX PZ.CP. (Schmidt)
XVI PZ.CP. (Höppner)
XV PZ.CP. (Hoth)
ARMY GROUP A (Rundstedt)
XLI PZ.CP. (Reinhardt)
XIX PZ.CP. (Guderian)
KLEIST'S PZ.GROUP

Ardennes
LUXEMBOURG
FR. 2nd
Reims
MAGINOT LINE

FRONT LINE
JUNE 5, 1940

0 Miles 100
0 Kilometres

◁ German infantry and armoured attacks
◀ Panzer Corps attacks
▲▲▲▲▲ Allied line and armies after forward movement of left shoulder
British breakout attempt, May 21
German airborne landings, May 10

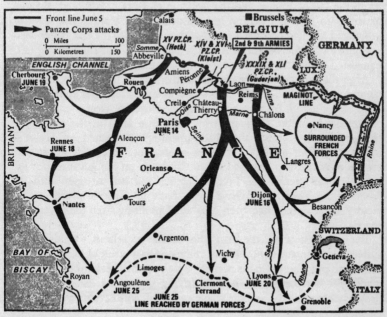

Front line June 5
Panzer Corps attacks

0 Miles 100
0 Kilometres 150

Calais
Brussels
BELGIUM
GERMANY

ENGLISH CHANNEL
Cherbourg
JUNE 19
Somme
Abbeville
XV PZ.CP. (Hoth)
Rouen
Amiens
Péronne
XIV & XVI PZ.CP. (Kleist)
2nd & 9th ARMIES
XXXIX & XLI PZ.CP. (Guderian)
LUX
Laon
Compiègne
Creil
Oise
Château-Thierry
Reims
Aisne
MAGINOT LINE
BRITTANY
Rennes
JUNE 18
Paris
JUNE 14
Marne
Châlons
Alençon
Seine
Nancy
SURROUNDED FRENCH FORCES
F R A N C E
Orleans
Langres
Loire
Nantes
Tours
Dijon
JUNE 16
Besançon
Argenton
SWITZERLAND
BAY OF BISCAY
Vichy
Saône
Geneva
Limoges
Lyons
JUNE 20
Royan
Angoulême
JUNE 25
Clermont Ferrand
JUNE 25
LINE REACHED BY GERMAN FORCES
Grenoble
ITALY
Rhine
Rhine

CHAPTER SEVEN

The Overrunning of the West

The course of the world in our time was changed, with far-reaching effects on the future of all peoples, when Hitler's forces broke through the defence of the West on May 10th, 1940. The decisive act of the world-shaking drama began on the 13th, when Guderian's panzer corps crossed the Meuse at Sedan.

On May 10th also, Mr Churchill, restless and dynamic, became Prime Minister of Great Britain in place of Mr Chamberlain.

The narrow breach at Sedan was soon expanded into a vast gap. The German tanks, pouring through it, reached the Channel coast within a week, thus cutting off the Allied armies in Belgium. That disaster led on to the fall of France and the isolation of Britain. Although Britain managed to hold out behind her sea-ditch, rescue only came after a prolonged war had become a world-wide struggle. In the end Hitler was overthrown by the weight of America and Russia, but Europe was left exhausted and under the shadow of Communist domination.

After the catastrophe, the rupture of the French front was commonly viewed as inevitable, and Hitler's attack as irresistible. But appearances were very different from reality – as has now become clear.

The heads of the German Army had little faith in the prospects of the offensive, which they had unwillingly launched on Hitler's insistence. Hitler himself suffered a sudden loss of confidence at the crucial moment, and imposed a two days' halt on the advance just as his spearhead pierced the French defence and had an open path in front of it. That would have been fatal to Hitler's prospects of victory if the French had been capable of profiting from the breathing space.

But strangest of all, the man who led the spearhead – Guderian – suffered momentary removal from command as a result of his superiors' anxiety to put a brake on his pace in exploiting the breakthrough he had made. Yet but for his 'offence' in driving so fast the invasion would probably have failed – and the whole course of world events would have been different from what it has been.

Far from having the overwhelming superiority with which they were credited, Hitler's armies were actually inferior in numbers to those opposing them. Although his tank drives proved decisive, he had fewer and less powerful tanks than his opponents possessed. Only in airpower, the most vital factor, had he a superiority.

Moreover, the issue was virtually decided by a small fraction of his forces before the bulk came into action. That decisive fraction comprised ten armoured divisions, one parachute division, and one air-portable division – besides the air force – out of a total of some 135 divisions which he had assembled.

The dazzling effect of what the new elements achieved has obscured not only their relatively small scale but the narrow margin by which success was gained. Their success could easily have been prevented but for the opportunities presented to them by the Allied blunders – blunders that were largely due to the prevalence of out-of-date ideas. Even as it was, with such help from the purblind leaders on the other side, the success of the invasion turned on a lucky series of long-odds chances – and on the readiness of one man, Guderian, to make the most of those which came his way.

The Battle of France is one of history's most striking examples of the decisive effect of a new idea, carried out by a dynamic executant. Guderian has related how, before the war, his imagination was fired by the idea of deep strategic penetration by independent armoured forces – a long-range tank drive to cut the main arteries of the opposing army far back behind its front. A tank enthusiast, he grasped the potentialities of this idea, arising from that new current of military thought in Britain after the First World War, which the Royal Tank Corps had been the first to demonstrate in training practice. Most of the higher German generals were as dubious of the idea as the British and French authorities had been – regarding it as impracticable in war. But when war came Guderian seized the chance to carry it out despite the doubts of his superiors. The effect proved as decisive as other new ideas had been in earlier history – the use of the horse, the long spear, the phalanx, the flexible legion, the 'oblique order', the horse-archer, the longbow, the musket, the gun, the organization of armies in separate and manoeuvrable divisions. Indeed, it proved more immediately decisive.

The German invasion of the West opened with dramatic successes on the right flank, against key points in the defence of neutral Holland and Belgium. These strokes spearheaded by airborne troops focused the

Allies' attention there in such a way as to distract them for several days from the main thrust – which was being delivered in the centre, through the hilly and wooded country of the Ardennes, towards the heart of France.

The capital of Holland, The Hague, and the hub of its communications at Rotterdam, were attacked in the early hours of May 10th by airborne forces, simultaneously with the assault on its frontier defences a hundred miles to the east. The confusion and alarm created by this double blow, in front and rear, were increased by the widespread menace of the Luftwaffe. Exploiting the disorder, German armoured forces raced through a gap in the southern flank and joined up with the airborne forces at Rotterdam on the third day. They cut through to their objective under the nose of the French Seventh Army which was just arriving to the aid of the Dutch. On the fifth day the Dutch capitulated, although their main front was still unbroken. Their surrender was accelerated by the threat of further close-quarter air attack on their crowded cities.

The German forces here were much smaller than those opposing them. Moreover the decisive thrust was delivered by merely one panzer division, the 9th – the only one that could be spared for the attack on the Dutch front. Its path of advance was intersected by canals and broad rivers that should have been easy to defend. Its chances of success depended on the effect of the airborne coup.

But this new arm was also very small – and amazingly small compared with what it achieved. In May 1940, Germany had only 4,500 trained parachute troops. Of this meagre total, 4,000 were used in the attack on Holland. They formed five battalions, and were backed up by a light infantry division, of 12,000 men, that was carried in transport aircraft.

The main points of the plan are best summarized in the words of Student, the Commander-in-Chief of the airborne forces:

The limitations of our strength compelled us to concentrate on two objectives – the points which seemed the most essential to the success of the invasion. The main effort, under my own control, was directed against the bridges at Rotterdam, Dordrecht, and Moerdijk by which the main route from the south was carried across the mouths of the Rhine. Our task was to capture the bridges before the Dutch could blow them up, and keep them open until the arrival of our mobile ground forces. My force comprised four parachute battalions and one air-transported regiment (of three battalions). We achieved complete success, at a cost of only 180 casualties. We dared not fail, for if we did the whole invasion would have failed.*

Student himself was one of the casualties, being wounded in the head, and he was out of action for eight months.

A secondary attack was made on the Dutch capital, The Hague. Its aim was to capture the heads of the Government and the Services in their offices, and disrupt the whole machinery of control. The force employed at The Hague was one parachute battalion and two air-transported regiments, under General Graf Sponeck. This attack was foiled, though it caused much confusion.

The invasion of Belgium also had a sensational opening. Here the ground attack was carried out by the powerful 6th Army under Reichenau (which included Höppner's 16th Panzer Corps). It had to overcome a formidable barrier before it could effectively deploy. Only 500 airborne troops were left to help this attack. They were used to capture the two bridges over the Albert Canal and the fort of Eben Emael, Belgium's most modern fort, which flanked this waterline-frontier.

That tiny detachment, however, made all the difference to the issue. For the approach to the Belgian frontier here lay across the southerly projection of Dutch territory known as the 'Maastricht Appendix', and once the German Army crossed the Dutch frontier the Belgian frontier guards on the Albert Canal would have had ample warning to blow the bridges before any invading ground forces could cross that fifteen-mile strip. Airborne troops dropping silently out of the night sky offered a new way, and the only way, of securing the key bridges intact.

The very limited scale of airborne forces used in Belgium was in extraordinary contrast to the reports at the time that German parachutists were dropping at scores of places, in numbers that cumulatively ran into thousands. Student provided the explanation – to compensate the scantiness of actual resources, and create as much confusion as possible, dummy parachutists were scattered widely over the country. This ruse certainly proved most effective, helped by the natural tendency of heated imaginations to multiply all figures.

According to Student:

The Albert Canal venture was also Hitler's own idea. It was perhaps the most original idea of this man of many brain-waves. He sent for me and asked my opinion. After a day's consideration I affirmed the

* Liddell Hart: *The Other Side of the Hill*, pp 160–1. Other extracts in this chapter from same source.

possibility of such an enterprise, and was ordered to make the preparations. I used 500 men under Captain Koch. The Commander of the Sixth Army, General von Reichenau and his chief of staff General von Paulus, both capable generals, regarded the undertaking as an adventure in which they had no faith.

The surprise attack on Fort Eben Emael was carried out by a Lilliputian detachment of 78 parachute-engineers commanded by Lieutenant Witzig. Of these, only 6 men were killed. This small detachment made a completely unexpected landing on the roof of the fort, overcame the anti-aircraft personnel there, and blew up the armoured cupolas and casemates of all the guns with a new highly intensive explosive – previously kept secret ... The surprise attack on Eben Emael was based on the use of this new weapon, which was silently transported to the objective by another new weapon – a freight-carrying glider.*

The fort was well-designed to meet every menace except the possibility of enemy troops dropping on top of it. From the roof of the fort Witzig's handful of 'sky-troopers' kept the garrison of 1,200 men in check until twenty-four hours later when the Germans' ground forces arrived on the scene.

The Belgian guards on the two key bridges were likewise taken by surprise. At one bridge they actually lit the fuse to blow up the bridge – but the crew of a glider got into the blockhouse on the heels of the sentries to extinguish it in the nick of time.

It is notable that on the whole front of the invasion the bridges were blown up everywhere by the defenders, according to plan, except where airborne attackers were used. That shows how small was the margin between success and failure on the German side – since the prospect of the invasion turned on the time-factor.

By the second morning sufficient German troops had arrived over the canal to burst through the shallow Belgian line of defence behind. Then Höppner's two panzer divisions (the 3rd and 4th) drove over the undemolished bridges and spread over the plains beyond. Their onsweeping drive caused the Belgian forces to start a general retreat – just as the French and British were arriving to support them.

This breakthrough in Belgium was not the decisive stroke in the invasion of the West, but it had a vital effect on the issue. It not only drew the Allies' attention in the wrong direction but absorbed the most mobile part of the Allied forces in the battle that developed there, so

* ibid, pp 163–4.

that these mobile divisions could not be pulled out and switched south to meet the greater menace that on May 13th suddenly loomed up on the French frontier – at its weakest part, beyond the western end of the incomplete Maginot Line.

For the mechanized spearheads of Rundstedt's Army Group had meantime been driving through Luxembourg and Belgian Luxembourg towards France. After traversing that seventy-mile stretch of the Ardennes, and brushing aside weak opposition, they crossed the French frontier and emerged on the banks of the Meuse early on the fourth day of the offensive.

It had been a bold venture to send a mass of tanks and motor-vehicles through such difficult country, which had long been regarded by conventional strategists as 'impassable' for a large-scale offensive, let alone for a tank operation. But that increased the chances of surprise, while the thick woods helped to cloak the advance and conceal the strength of the blow.

It was the French High Command, however, which contributed most to Hitler's success. The shattering effect of the Ardennes stroke owed much to the design of the French plan – which fitted perfectly, from the Germans' point of view, into their own remodelled plan. What proved fatal to the French was not, as is commonly imagined, their defensive attitude or 'Maginot Line complex', but the more offensive side of their plan. By pushing into Belgium with their left shoulder forward they played into the hands of their enemy, and wedged themselves in a trap – just as had happened with their near-fatal Plan XVII of 1914. It was the more perilous this time because the opponent was more mobile, manoeuvring at motor-pace instead of at foot-pace. The penalty, too, was the greater because the left shoulder push – made by three French armies and the British – comprised the most modernly equipped and mobile part of the Allied forces as a whole.

With every step forward that these armies took in their rush into Belgium, their rear became more exposed to Rundstedt's flanking drive through the Ardennes. Worse still, the hinge of the Allied advance was guarded by a few low-grade French divisions, composed of older men and scantily equipped in anti-tank and anti-aircraft guns, the two vital needs. To leave the hinge so poorly covered was the crowning blunder of the French High Command, under Gamelin and Georges.

The German advance through the Ardennes was a tricky operation, and an extraordinary feat of staffwork. Before dawn of May 10th the greatest concentration of tanks yet seen in war was massed opposite the frontier of Luxembourg. Made up of three panzer corps, these were arrayed in three blocks, or layers, with armoured divisions in the first two, and motorized infantry divisions in the third. The van was led by General Guderian, and the whole was commanded by General von Kleist.

To the right of Kleist's group lay a separate panzer corps, the 15th, under Hoth, which was to dash through the northern part of the Ardennes, to the Meuse between Givet and Dinant.

The seven armoured divisions, however, formed only a fraction of the armed mass that was drawn up along the German frontier ready to plunge into the Ardennes. Some fifty divisions were closely packed on a narrow but very deep front.

The chances of success essentially depended on the quickness with which the German panzer forces could push through the Ardennes and cross the Meuse. Only when they were across that river-barrier would the tanks have room for manoeuvre. They needed to get across before the French High Command realized what was happening and collected reserves to stop them.

The race was won, though with little margin. The result might have been different if the defending forces had been capable of profiting from the partial checks caused by demolitions that were carried out according to previous plan. It was unfortunate for the security of France that these were not backed by adequate defenders. The French had been foolish to rely on cavalry divisions to delay the invaders.

By contrast, an armoured counterstroke against the flank of the German advance at this stage would probably have paralysed that advance – by its effect on the higher commanders. Even as it was, they were momentarily shaken by the shadow of a stroke towards their left flank.

Seeing how well the advance was going, Kleist had already, on the 12th, endorsed Guderian's view that the crossing of the Meuse should be tackled without waiting for the infantry corps to arrive. But arrangements had been made for a heavy air concentration, including twelve squadrons of dive-bombers, to help in forcing a passage. These appeared on the scene early in the afternoon of the 13th, and maintained such a hail of bombs as to keep most of the French gunners down in their dug-outs until nightfall.

Guderian's attack was concentrated on a one-and-a-half-mile stretch of the river just west of Sedan. The chosen sector provided a perfect setting for forcing a passage. The river bends sharply north towards St Menges and then south again, forming a pocket-like salient. The surrounding heights on the north bank are wooded, thus providing cover for attack preparations and gun-positions as well as fine artillery observation. From near St Menges there was a wonderful panoramic view over this river-salient, and across to the wooded heights of the Bois de Marfée which form the back-curtain on the far side.

The assault was launched at 4 PM, led by the panzer infantry in rubber boats and on rafts. Ferries were soon in operation, bringing light vehicles across. The river-salient was quickly overrun, and the attackers pressed on to capture the Bois de Marfée and the southern heights. By midnight the wedge was driven nearly five miles deep, while a bridge was completed at Glaire (between Sedan and St Menges) over which the tanks began to pour.

Even so, the German foothold was still precarious on the 14th – with only one division yet across the river, and only one bridge by which reinforcements and supplies could reach it. The bridge was heavily attacked by the Allied air forces, which enjoyed a temporary advantage as the weight of the Luftwaffe had been switched elsewhere. But the anti-aircraft artillery regiment of Guderian's corps kept a thick canopy of fire over the vital bridge, and Allied air attacks were beaten off with heavy loss.

By the afternoon all three of his panzer divisions were over the river. After beating off a belated French counterattack, he made a sudden turn westward. By the following evening he had broken through the last line of defence, and the roads to the west – to the Channel coast – lay open to him.

Yet that night was a trying one for Guderian – though not owing to the enemy:

An order came from Panzer Group Headquarters to halt the advance and confine the troops to the bridgehead gained. I would not and could not put up with this order, as it meant forfeiting surprise and all our initial success.*

After a lively argument on the telephone with Kleist, the latter agreed 'to permit the continuation of the advance for another twenty-four hours – in order to widen the bridgehead'.

The utmost advantage was taken of this cautious permission, and full rein was given to the panzer divisions. The westward drive of Guderian's three panzer divisions converged with that of Reinhardt's two divisions from the Monthermé crossing, and also with those of Hoth's two divisions from the crossings near Dinant. It produced a spreading collapse of French resistance, and swept through an empty space.

* ibid, p 177.

By the night of the 16th the westward drive had gone more than fifty miles farther, towards the Channel, and reached the Oise. Yet once again the brake was applied, not by the enemy, but from above.

The higher commanders on the German side were amazed at the ease with which the Meuse had been overcome, and could hardly believe their luck. They still expected a heavy French counterstroke against their flank. Hitler shared these apprehensions. In consequence he put a curb on the advance – halting it for two days, so that the infantry corps could come up and form a flank shield along the Aisne.

After the matter had been referred to higher quarters, Guderian was reinstated, and given qualified permission to carry on strong reconnaissance. 'Strong reconnaissance' as interpreted by Guderian had an elastic meaning and enabled him to maintain a considerable degree of offensive pressure during the two days' interval before the infantry corps of the 12th Army had begun to form a strong flank shield on the Aisne and he was allowed to race all out for the Channel coast.

So much time had been gained in the preceding stages and so much dislocation had been caused on the opposing side, that the pause on the Oise had no serious effect on the German prospects. Even so, it revealed a significant difference of time-sense on the German side. The gap between the new school and old school there was greater than that between the Germans and the French.

Gamelin, writing at the end of the war, said of the Germans' strategic exploitation of the Meuse crossing:

It was a remarkable manoeuvre. But had it been entirely foreseen in advance? I do not believe it – any more than that Napoleon had foreseen the manoeuvre of Jena, or Moltke that of Sedan [in 1870]. It was a perfect utilization of circumstances. It showed troops and a command who knew how to manoeuvre, who were organized to operate quickly – as tanks, aircraft, and wireless permitted them to do. It is perhaps the first time that a battle has been won, which became decisive, without having had to engage the bulk of the forces.*

According to General Georges, who was the executive Commander-in-Chief of the battlefront, it was reckoned that the planned obstructions in Belgian Luxembourg were likely 'to retard for at least four days' the Germans' arrival on the Meuse. General Doumenc, the Chief of Staff, said:

* ibid, p 181.

Crediting our enemies with our own procedure, we had imagined that they would not attempt the passage of the Meuse until after they had brought up ample artillery: the five or six days necessary for that would have easily given us time to reinforce our own dispositions.*

It is remarkable how closely these French calculations corresponded to those made in the higher quarters on 'the other side of the hill'. It can be seen that the French military chiefs had justification – more justification than was apparent immediately after the event – for their basic assumptions about the German offensive. But they had left out of the reckoning an individual factor – Guderian. His adoption of the theory of deep strategic penetration by armoured forces operating independently, his fervent conviction of its practicability, and his consequent impulsion in stretching subordination upset the calculations of the French High Command to an extent that the German High Command would never have done of its own volition. It is clear that Guderian and his tankmen pulled the German Army along after them, and thereby produced the most sweeping victory in modern history.

The issue turned on the time-factor at stage after stage. French counter-movements were repeatedly thrown out of gear because their timing was too slow to catch up with the changing situations, and that was due to the fact that the German van kept on moving faster than the German High Command had contemplated.

The French had based their plans on the assumption that an assault on the Meuse would not come before the ninth day. That was the same time-scale the German chiefs had in mind originally, before Guderian intervened. When it was upset, worse was to follow. The French commanders, trained in the slow-motion methods of 1918, were mentally unfitted to cope with panzer pace, and it produced a spreading paralysis among them.

One of the few men on the Allied side who realized the danger in time was the new French Prime Minister, M. Paul Reynaud. As an outside critic before the war, he had urged his countrymen to develop armoured forces. Understanding their effect all too clearly, he telephoned Mr Churchill early on the 15th, to say: 'We have lost the battle.'

Churchill's reply was: 'All experience shows that the offensive will come to an end after a while. I remember the 21st of March, 1918. After five or six days they have to halt for supplies and the opportunity for counterattack is presented. I learned all this at the time from the

* ibid, p 181.

lips of Marshal Foch himself.'* Next day he flew over to Paris, and there argued against any withdrawal of the Allied armies in Belgium. Even as it was, Gamelin was too slow in pulling them back. He now planned a deliberate counter-offensive in the 1918 way – with massed infantry divisions. Churchill continued to pin his faith to this. It was unfortunate that Gamelin's mind remained in an out-of-date groove, as he had more capacity for action than anyone in France.

That day, too, Reynaud made a move to replace Gamelin – summoning Weygand, Foch's old assistant, from Syria. Weygand did not arrive until the 19th, so that for three days the Supreme Command was in a state of suspense. On the 20th Guderian reached the Channel, cutting the communications of the Allied armies in Belgium. Moreover, Weygand was even more out-of-date than Gamelin, and continued to plan on 1918 lines. So hope of recovery faded.

In sum, the Allied leaders did things too late or did the wrong thing, and in the end did nothing effective to avert disaster.

The escape of the British Expeditionary Force in 1940 was largely due to Hitler's personal intervention. After his tanks had overrun the north of France and cut off the British Army from its base, Hitler held them up just as they were about to sweep into Dunkirk – which was the last remaining port of escape left open to the British. At that moment the bulk of the BEF was still many miles distant from the port. But Hitler kept his tanks halted for three days.

His action preserved the British forces when nothing else could have saved them. By making it possible for them to escape he enabled them to rally in England, continue the war, and man the coasts to defy the threat of invasion. Thereby he produced his own ultimate downfall, and Germany's, five years later. Acutely aware of the narrowness of the escape, but ignorant of its cause, the British people spoke of 'the miracle of Dunkirk'.

How did he come to give the fateful halt order, and why? It remained a puzzle in many respects to the German generals themselves, and it will never be possible to learn for certain how he came to his decision and what his motives were. Even if Hitler had given an explanation it would hardly be reliable. Men in high position who make a fatal mistake rarely tell the truth about it afterwards, and Hitler was not one of the most truth-loving of great men. It is more likely that his evidence would confuse the trail. It is also quite likely that he could not

* Churchill: *The Second World War*, vol II, pp 38–9.

have given a true explanation even if he had wished, because his motives were apt to be so mixed and his impulses so changeable. Moreover, all men's recollection tends to be coloured by what happens later.

In prolonged exploration of this critical event, sufficient evidence has emerged for the historian to be able to piece together not only the chain of events but what seems a reasonably probable chain of causation leading up to the fateful decision.

After cutting the lines of supply to the Allied left wing in Belgium, Guderian's panzer corps had reached the sea near Abbeville on the 20th. Then he wheeled north, heading for the Channel ports and the rear of the British Army – which was still in Belgium, facing the frontal advance of Bock's infantry forces. On Guderian's right in this northward drive was Reinhardt's panzer corps, which was also part of Kleist's group.

On the 22nd, Boulogne was isolated by his advance, and on the next day Calais. This stride brought him to Gravelines, barely ten miles from Dunkirk – the British Expeditionary Force's last remaining port of escape. Reinhardt's panzer corps also arrived on the canal line Aire–St Omer–Gravelines. But there the continuation of the drive was stopped by orders from above. The panzer leaders were told to hold their forces back behind the line of the canal. They bombarded their superiors with urgent queries and protests, but were told that it was 'the Führer's personal order'.

Before probing deeper into the roots of that saving intervention let us see what was happening on the British side, and follow the course of that grand-scale escape.

On the 16th General Lord Gort, the Commander-in-Chief, brought the BEF a step back from its advanced line in front of Brussels. But before it arrived in its new position on the Scheldt, that position had been undermined by Guderian cutting the BEF's communications far to the south. On the 19th the Cabinet heard that Gort was 'examining a possible withdrawal towards Dunkirk if that were forced upon him'. The Cabinet, however, sent him orders to march south into France and force his way through the German net that had been flung across his rear – though they were told that he had only four days' supplies and ammunition sufficient for one battle.

These instructions accorded with the new plan which Gamelin, the French Commander-in-Chief, had belatedly made and issued that morning. In the evening Gamelin was sacked and replaced by Weygand, whose first act was to cancel Gamelin's order, while he studied the situation. After three days' further delay he produced a plan similar to his predecessor's. It proved no more than a paper plan.

Meanwhile Gort, though arguing that the Cabinet's instructions were impracticable, had tried an attack southward from Arras with two of his thirteen divisions and the only tank brigade that had been sent to France. When this counterstroke was launched on the 21st it had boiled down to an advance by two weak tank battalions followed by two infantry battalions. The tanks made some progress but were not backed up, the infantry being shaken by dive-bombing. The neighbouring French First Army was to have cooperated, with two of its thirteen divisions, but its actual contribution was slight. During these days the French were repeatedly paralysed by the moral effect of the German dive-bombers and the swift manoeuvring tanks.

It is remarkable, however, what a disturbing effect this little armoured counterstroke had on some of the German higher commanders. For a moment it led them to think of stopping the advance of their own tank spearheads. Rundstedt himself described it as 'a critical moment', saying: 'For a short time it was feared that our armoured divisions would be cut off before the infantry divisions could come up to support them.'* Such an effect showed what a vital difference to the issue might have been made if this British riposte had been made with two armoured divisions instead of merely two tank battalions.

After the flash-in-the-pan at Arras the Allied armies in the north made no further effort to break out of the trap, while the belated relief offensive from the south that Weygand planned was so feeble as to be almost farcical. It was easily baulked by the barricade which the German motorized divisions had quickly built up along the Somme, to keep out interference while the panzer divisions drove northward to close the trap. With such slow-motion forces as Weygand commanded, his grandiloquent orders had no more chance of practical effect than Chur-

* Forecasting the very situation that arose in 1940, it had been urged from 1935 on in *The Times*, and other quarters, that Britain's military effort should be concentrated on providing a stronger air force and two to three armoured divisions for a counterstroke against any German breakthrough in France, instead of sending an expeditionary force composed of infantry divisions – of which the French had plenty. This principle was accepted by the Cabinet at the end of 1937, but discarded early in 1939 in favour of building an expeditionary force of the familiar pattern. By May 1940, thirteen infantry divisions (including three 'labour' divisions) in all had been sent to France, without a single armoured division, but proved unable to do anything to save the situation.

chill's adjurations to the armies to 'cast away the idea of resisting attack behind concrete lines or natural obstacles' and regain the mastery 'by furious, unrelenting assault'.

While the highest circles continued to debate impracticable plans, the cut-off armies in the north were falling back on a slant closer to the coast. They were under increasing frontal pressure from Bock's infantry armies – though they were spared a deadly stab in the back from the panzer forces.

On the 24th Weygand bitterly complained that 'the British Army had carried out, on its own initiative, a retreat of twenty-five miles towards the ports at a time when our troops moving up from the south are gaining ground towards the north, where they were to meet their allies'. In fact, the French troops from the south had made no perceptible progress and the British were not yet retreating – Weygand's words merely showed the state of unreality in which he was living.

But on the evening of the 25th Gort took the definite decision to retreat to the sea, at Dunkirk. Forty-eight hours earlier, the German panzer forces had already arrived, on the canal line only ten miles from the port. On the 26th the British Cabinet allowed the War Office to send him a telegram approving his step and 'authorized' him to carry out such a retirement. Next day a further telegram told him to evacuate his force by sea.

That same day the Belgian Army's line cracked in the centre under Bock's attack, and no reserves were left at hand to fill the gap. King Leopold had already sent repeated warnings to Churchill, through Admiral Keyes, that the situation was becoming hopeless. Now, at a stroke, it was so. Most of Belgium had already been overrun and the army had its back close to the sea, penned in a narrow strip of land that was packed with civilian refugees. So in the late afternoon the King decided to sue for an armistice – and the 'cease fire' was sounded early the next morning.

The Belgians' surrender increased the danger that the BEF would be cut off before it could reach Dunkirk. Churchill had just sent King Leopold an appeal to hold on, which he privately described to Gort as 'asking them to sacrifice themselves for us'. It is understandable that the encircled Belgians, already aware that the BEF was preparing to evacuate, did not see that appeal in the same light as Churchill. Nor was King Leopold willing to follow Churchill's advice that he should himself 'escape by aeroplane before too late'. The King felt that he 'must stay with his Army and people'. His decision may have been unwise in the long view, but in the circumstances of the time it was an honourable choice. Churchill's subsequent criticisms of it were hardly fair, while the violent denunciations made by the French Prime Minister and press were grossly unjust – considering the way that the Belgian downfall had been produced by the collapse of the French defence on the Meuse.

The British retreat to the coast now became a race to re-embark before the German trap closed – notwithstanding bitter French protests and reproaches. It was fortunate that preparatory measures had begun in England a week before – although on a different assumption. On the 20th Churchill had approved steps 'to assemble a large number of small vessels in readiness to proceed to ports and inlets on the French coast', with the idea that they might help in rescuing bits of the BEF that might be cut off as it tried to push south into France, under the existing plan. The Admiralty lost no time in making preparations. Admiral Ramsay, commanding at Dover, had been placed in operational control on the previous day, the 19th. A number of ferry-craft, naval drifters and small coasters were at once collected for what was called 'Operation Dynamo'. From Harwich round to Weymouth sea-transport officers were directed to list all ships up to a thousand tons.

In the days that followed the situation became rapidly worse, and it was soon clear to the Admiralty that Dunkirk would be the only possible route of evacuation. 'Dynamo' was put into operation on the afternoon of the 26th – twenty-four hours before the Belgian appeal for an armistice, and also before the Cabinet had authorized the evacuation.

At first it was not expected that more than a small fraction of the BEF could be saved. The Admiralty told Ramsay to aim at bringing away 45,000 within two days and that it was probable the enemy would by then have made further evacuation impossible. Actually, only 25,000 were landed in England by the night of the 28th. It was fortunate that the period of grace proved considerably longer.

For the first five days the rate of evacuation was restricted by an insufficiency of small boats to carry troops from the beaches to the ships waiting offshore. This need, though pointed out by Ramsay originally, had not been adequately met. But the Admiralty now made more extensive efforts to provide them and to man them, the naval personnel being reinforced by a host of civilian volunteers – fishermen, lifeboatmen, yachtsmen, and others who had some experience in handling boats. Ramsay recorded that one of the best performances was that of the crew of the fire-float *Massey Shaw* from the London Fire Brigade.

At first, too, there was much confusion on the beaches, owing to the disorganized state of the troops waiting to embark – at that time largely base personnel. Ramsey considered that it was aggravated 'by the fact that Army officers' uniform is indistinguishable from that of other ranks', and found that 'the appearance of Naval officers, in their unmistakable uniforms, helped to restore order ... Later on, when troops of fighting formations reached the beaches these difficulties disappeared.'

The first heavy air attack came on the evening of the 29th and 'it was only by good fortune that the vital Dunkirk Harbour channel was not blocked by sinking ships at this early date'. Its preservation was the more important because the majority of the troops were embarked from the harbour and less than one-third from the beaches.

In the next three days the air attacks increased, and on June 2nd daylight evacuation had to be suspended. The fighters of the RAF, from airfields in southern England, did their utmost to keep the Luftwaffe at bay, but, being outnumbered and unable to stay long over the area because of the distance, they could not maintain anything like adequate air cover. The oft-repeated bombing attacks were a severe strain on the troops waiting on the beaches, though the soft sand blanketed the effects. Far more material damage was done over the sea where the losses included six destroyers, eight personnel ships, and over 200 small craft – out of a total of 860 British and Allied vessels of all sizes employed in the evacuation. It was very lucky that the German Navy made very little attempt to interfere, either with U-boats or E-boats. Happily, too, the evacuation was favoured by extremely good weather.

By May 30th, 126,000 troops had been evacuated, while all the rest of the BEF had arrived in the Dunkirk bridgehead – except for fragments that were cut off during the retreat. The defence of the bridgehead against the enemy's encircling advance on land now became much firmer in consequence. The Germans had missed their opportunity.

Unhappily the French higher commanders in Belgium, still conforming to Weygand's impossible plan, had hesitated to retreat to the sea and to do so as quickly as possible along with the British. As a result of that delay nearly half of what was left of the French First Army had been cut off on the 28th near Lille, and were forced to surrender on the 31st. Their gallant three-day stand, however, helped the escape of the remainder, as well as the British.

By midnight on June 2nd the British rearguard embarked and the evacuation of the BEF was complete – 224,000 men had been safely brought away, and only some 2,000 were lost in ships sunk en route to England. Some 95,000 Allied troops, mainly French, had also been evacuated. On the next night every effort was made to bring away the remaining Frenchmen, despite increasing difficulties, and 26,000 more were saved. Unfortunately a few thousand of the rearguard were left – and this left sore feelings in France.

By the morning of the 4th, when the operation was broken off, a total of 338,000 British and Allied troops had been landed in England. It was an amazing result compared with earlier expectations, and a grand performance on the part of the Navy.

At the same time it is evident that the preservation of the BEF 'to fight another day' would have been impossible without Hitler's action in halting Kleist's panzer forces outside Dunkirk twelve days before, on May 24th.

At that moment there was only one British battalion covering the twenty-mile stretch of the Aa between Gravelines and St Omer, and for a further sixty miles inland the canal line was little better defended. Many of the bridges were not yet blown up, or even prepared for demolition. Thus the German panzer troops had no difficulty in gaining bridgeheads over the canal at a number of places on May 23rd – and it was as Gort said in his Dispatch, 'the only anti-tank obstacle on this flank'. Having crossed it, there was nothing to hold them up – and stop them establishing themselves astride the BEF's lines of retreat to Dunkirk – except the halt that Hitler imposed.

It is clear, however, that Hitler had been in a highly strung and jumpy state ever since the breakthrough into France. The extraordinary easiness of the advance, the lack of resistance his armies had met, had made him uneasy – it seemed too good to be true. The effects can be followed in the diary that was kept by Halder, the Chief of the General Staff. On the 17th, the day after the French defence behind the Meuse had dramatically collapsed, Halder noted: 'Rather unpleasant day. The Führer is terribly nervous. Frightened by his own success, he is afraid to take any chance and so would rather pull the reins on us.'

That was the day when Guderian was suddenly pulled up when in full stride for the sea. Next day, noted Halder: 'Every hour is precious ... Führer HQ sees it quite differently ... unaccountably keeps worrying about the south flank. He rages and screams that we are on the best way to ruin the whole campaign.' Not until late that evening, when Halder was able to assure him that the follow-up infantry army was wheeling into line along the Aisne as a flank shield, did Hitler agree to let the panzer forces sweep on.

Two days later these reached the coast, cutting the communications of the Allied armies in Belgium. That brilliant success seems to have temporarily drowned Hitler's doubts. But they revived as his panzer forces swung northward, especially after the momentary alarm caused by the British tank counterattack from Arras, slight as this was. His panzer forces, which he regarded as so precious, were now heading towards the zone occupied by the British, whom he looked on as particularly tough opponents. At the same time he was uneasy as to what the French in the south might be planning.

On the surface it appears to have been unlucky for Hitler that he chose to visit Rundstedt's headquarters on the morning of May 24th, a crucial moment. For Rundstedt was a wary strategist, careful to take full account of unfavourable factors and avoid erring on the side of optimism. For that reason he was often a good corrective to Hitler, by providing a coolly balanced estimate – but it did not benefit German chances on this occasion. In his review of the situation he dwelt on the way that the tank strength had been reduced in the long and rapid drive, and pointed out the possibility of having to meet attacks from the north and south, particularly the latter.

Since he had, the night before, received orders from Brauchitsch, the Army Commander-in-Chief, that the completion of the encirclement in the north was to be handed over to Bock, it was the more natural that he should be thinking of the next phase in the south.

Moreover, Rundstedt's headquarters were still at Charleville, near Sedan – close behind the Aisne, and in the centre of the German front facing south. That location fostered a tendency to focus on what was in front and give less attention to what was happening on the extreme right flank, where victory seemed to be assured. Dunkirk only came into the corner of his eye.

Hitler 'agreed entirely' with Rundstedt's reservations, and went on to emphasize the paramount necessity of conserving the panzer force for future operations.

On his return to his own headquarters in the afternoon, he sent for the Commander-in-Chief. It was 'a very unpleasant interview', and ended in Hitler giving a definite halt order – Halder that evening mournfully summarized its effect in his diary:

The left wing, consisting of armoured and motorized forces, which has no enemy before it, will thus be stopped in its tracks upon direct orders of the Führer. Finishing off the encircled enemy army is to be left to the Luftwaffe!

Was Hitler's halt order inspired by Rundstedt? If Hitler had felt that his halt order was due to Rundstedt's influence, he would almost certainly have mentioned it, after the British escape, among the excuses he gave for his decision, for he was very apt to blame others for any mistakes. Yet in this case there is no trace of his ever having mentioned, in the course of his subsequent explanations, Rundstedt's opinion as a factor. Such negative evidence is as significant as any.

It seems more likely that Hitler went to Rundstedt's headquarters in the hope of finding further justification for his own doubts and for the change of plan he wanted to impose on Brauchitsch and Halder. In so far as it was prompted by anyone else, the initial influence probably came from Keitel and Jodl, the two chief military members of his own staff. There is particular significance in the evidence of General Warlimont, who was in close touch with Jodl at the time. Astonished on hearing a rumour of the halt order, he went to ask Jodl about it:

> Jodl confirmed that the order had been given, showing himself rather impatient about my inquiries. He himself took the same stand as Hitler, emphasizing that the personal experience that not only Hitler but also Keitel and himself had in Flanders during the First World War proved beyond any doubt that armour could not operate in the Flanders marshes, or at any rate not without heavy losses – and such losses could not be borne in view of the already reduced strength of the panzer corps and their tasks in the impending second stage of the offensive in France.*

Warlimont added that if the initiative for the halt order had come from Rundstedt, he and the others at OKW would have heard of it; and that Jodl, who was on the defensive about the decision, 'certainly would not have failed to point to Field-Marshal von Rundstedt as the one who had initiated or at least supported that order' – as that would have silenced criticism, because of Rundstedt's 'undisputed authority in operational matters among all senior general staff officers':

> One other reason, however, for the halt order was revealed to me at the time – that Göring appeared and reassured the Führer that his air force would accomplish the rest of the encirclement by closing the sea side of the pocket from the air. He certainly overrated the effectiveness of his own branch.*

This statement of Warlimont's gains significance when related to the last sentence in Halder's diary note of the 24th, already quoted. More-

* Liddell Hart: *The Other Side of the Hill*, p 197.

over, Guderian stated that the order came down to him from Kleist, with the words: 'Dunkirk is to be left to the Luftwaffe. If the conquest of Calais should raise difficulties that fortress likewise is to be left to the Luftwaffe.' Guderian remarked: 'I think that it was the vanity of Göring which caused that fateful decision of Hitler's.'

At the same time there is evidence that even the Luftwaffe was not used as fully or as vigorously as it could have been – and some of the air chiefs say that Hitler put the brake on again here.

All this caused the higher circles to suspect a political motive behind Hitler's military reasons. Blumentritt, who was Rundstedt's operational planner, connected it with the surprising way that Hitler had talked when visiting their headquarters:

> Hitler was in very good humour, he admitted that the course of the campaign had been 'a decided miracle', and gave us the opinion that the war would be finished in six weeks. After that he wished to conclude a reasonable peace with France, and then the way would be free for an agreement with Britain.
>
> He then astonished us by speaking with admiration of the British Empire, of the necessity for its existence, and of the civilization that Britain had brought into the world. He remarked, with a shrug of the shoulders, that the creation of its Empire had been achieved by means that were often harsh, but 'where there is planing, there are shavings flying'. He compared the British Empire with the Catholic Church – saying they were both essential elements of stability in the world. He said that all he wanted from Britain was that she should acknowledge Germany's position on the Continent. The return of Germany's lost colonies would be desirable but not essential, and he would even offer to support Britain with troops if she should be involved in any difficulties anywhere. He remarked that the colonies were primarily a matter of prestige, since they could not be held in war, and few Germans could settle in the tropics.
>
> He concluded by saying that his aim was to make peace with Britain on a basis that she would regard as compatible with her honour to accept.*

In subsequent reflection on the course of events, Blumentritt's thoughts often reverted to this conversation. He felt that the 'halt' had been called for more than military reasons, and that it was part of a political scheme to make peace easier to reach. If the BEF had been

* ibid, pp 200–01.

captured at Dunkirk, the British might have felt that their honour had
suffered a stain which they must wipe out. By letting it escape Hitler
hoped to conciliate them.

Since this account comes from generals who were highly critical of
Hitler, and admit that they themselves wanted to finish off the British
Army, it is of the more significance. Their account of Hitler's talks at
the time of Dunkirk fits in with much that he himself wrote earlier in
Mein Kampf – and it is remarkable how closely he followed his own
testament in other respects. There were elements in his make-up which
suggest that he had a mixed love-hate feeling towards Britain. The
trend of his talk about Britain at this time is also recorded in the diaries
of Ciano and Halder.

Hitler's character was of such complexity that no simple explanation
is likely to be true. It is far more probable that his decision was woven
of several threads. Three are visible – his desire to conserve tank
strength for the next stroke; his long-standing fear of marshy Flanders;
and Göring's claims for the Luftwaffe. But it is quite likely that some
political thread was interwoven with these military ones in the mind of
a man who had a bent for political strategy and so many twists in his
thought.

The new French front along the Somme and the Aisne was longer
than the original one, while the forces available to hold it were much
diminished. The French had lost thirty of their own divisions in the
first stage of the campaign, besides the help of their allies. (Only two
British divisions remained in France, though two more that were not
fully trained were now sent over.) In all, Weygand had collected forty-
nine divisions to cover the new front, leaving seventeen to hold the
Maginot Line. Not much could be done to fortify the front in the short
time available, and the shortage of forces counteracted the belated attempt to apply the method of defence in depth. As most of the mechanized divisions had been lost or badly depleted there was also a lack of
mobile reserves.

The Germans, by contrast, had brought their ten panzer divisions up
to strength again with relays of fresh tanks, while their 130 infantry
divisions were almost untouched. For the new offensive the forces were
redistributed, two fresh armies (the 2nd and 9th) being inserted to
increase the weight along the Aisne sector (between the Oise and the
Meuse), and Guderian was given command of a group of two panzer
corps that was moved to lie up in readiness there. Kleist was left with

two panzer corps, to strike from the bridgeheads over the Somme at Amiens and Péronne respectively, in a pincer-move aimed to converge on the lower reach of the Oise near Creil. The remaining armoured corps, under Hoth, was to advance between Amiens and the sea.

The offensive was launched on June 5th, initially on the western stretch between Laon and the sea. Resistance was stiff for the first two days, but on the 7th the most westerly armoured corps broke through on the roads to Rouen. The defence then collapsed in confusion, and the Germans met no serious resistance in crossing the Seine on the 9th. But it was not here that they intended their decisive manoeuvre, so they paused, which was fortunate for the small British force, under General Alan Brooke, most of which was thus enabled to achieve a second evacuation when the French capitulated.

Kleist's pincer-stroke did not, however, go according to plan. The right pincer eventually broke through on the 8th but the left pincer, from Péronne, was hung up by tough opposition north of Compiègne. The German Supreme Command then decided to pull back Kleist's group and switch it east to back up the breakthrough that had been made in Champagne.

The offensive there did not open until the 9th, but then the collapse came quickly. As soon as the infantry masses had forced the crossings, Guderian's tanks swept through the breach towards Châlons-sur-Marne, and then eastward. By the 11th Kleist was widening the sweep and crossed the Marne at Château-Thierry. The drive continued at racing pace, over the Plateau de Langres to Besançon and the Swiss frontier – cutting off all the French forces in the Maginot Line.

As early as the 7th Weygand advised the Government to ask for an armistice without delay, and next day he announced that 'the Battle of the Somme is lost'. The Government, though divided in opinion, hesitated to yield, but on the 9th decided to leave Paris. It wavered between a choice of Brittany and Bordeaux, and then went to Tours as a compromise. At the same time Reynaud sent off an appeal to President Roosevelt for support, in which he declared: 'We shall fight in front of Paris; we shall fight behind Paris; we shall shut ourselves up in one of our provinces, and, if we should be driven out, we shall go to North Africa . . .'

On the 10th Italy declared war. Mussolini had been belatedly offered various colonial concessions, but spurned them in the hope of improving his position with Hitler. An Italian offensive, however, was not launched until ten days later, and was then easily held in check by the weak French forces.

On the 11th Churchill flew to Tours in a vain effort to encourage the French leaders. Next day Weygand addressed the Cabinet, told them the battle was lost, blamed the British for both defeats, and then declared: 'I am obliged to say clearly that a cessation of hostilities is compulsory.' There is little doubt that he was correct in this estimate of the military situation, for the French armies were now splitting up into fragments, and most of these made little attempt to stand, but merely dissolved in a southerly flow. The Cabinet was now divided between capitulation and a continuance of the war from North Africa, but only decided to move itself to Bordeaux, while instructing Weygand to attempt a stand on the Loire.

The Germans entered Paris on the 14th and were driving deeper on the flanks. On the 16th they reached the Rhône valley. Meanwhile Weygand had continued his pressure for an armistice, backed by all the principal commanders. In a last-hour effort to avert this decision, and ensure a stand in Africa, Churchill made a far-reaching proposal for a Franco-British Union. It made little impression, except to produce irritation. A vote was taken upon it, a majority of the French Cabinet rejected it, and it turned into a decision for capitulation. Reynaud resigned, whereupon a new Cabinet was formed by Marshal Pétain, and the request for the armistice was transmitted to Hitler on the night of the 16th.

Hitler's terms were delivered to the French envoys on the 20th - in the same railway coach in the forest of Compiègne wherein the German envoys had signed the armistice of 1918. The German advance proceeded beyond the Loire while discussion continued, but on the 22nd the German terms were accepted. The armistice became effective at 1.35 AM on June 25th, after an accompanying armistice with Italy had been arranged.

CHAPTER EIGHT

The Battle of Britain

Although the war started on September 1st, 1939, with the German invasion of Poland, and this was followed two days later by the successive British and French declarations of war on Germany, it is one of the most extraordinary features of history that Hitler and the German Supreme Command had made no plans or preparations to deal with Britain's opposition. Stranger still, nothing was done during the long interval, of nearly nine months, before the great German offensive in the West was launched in May 1940. Nor were any plans made even after France was obviously crumbling and its collapse assured.

It thus becomes very clear that Hitler was counting on the British Government's agreement to a compromise peace on the favourable terms he was disposed to grant, and that for all his high ambitions he had no wish to press the conflict with Britain to a decisive conclusion. Indeed, the German generals were given to understand by Hitler that the war was over, while leave was granted and part of the Luftwaffe was shifted to other potential fronts. Moreover, on June 22nd Hitler ordered the demobilization of thirty-five divisions.

Even when Churchill's rejection of any compromise was made emphatic, and his determination to pursue the war was manifest, Hitler still clung to the belief that it was a bluff, and felt that Britain was bound to recognize 'her militarily hopeless situation'. That hope was slow to fade. It was not until July 2nd that he even ordered a study of the problem of overcoming Britain by invasion, and he still sounded a note of doubt about the need when at last on July 16th, two weeks later, he ordered preparation of such an invasion, christened 'Operation Sealion'. He did say, however, that the expedition must be ready by mid-August.

Even then Hitler's underlying reservations – or, at the least, his split mind – were shown in the fact that he told Halder on July 21st that he intended to turn and tackle the problem of Russia, if possible launching an attack on her that autumn. On the 29th, at OKW, Jodl told Warlimont that Hitler was determined on war against Russia. Several days

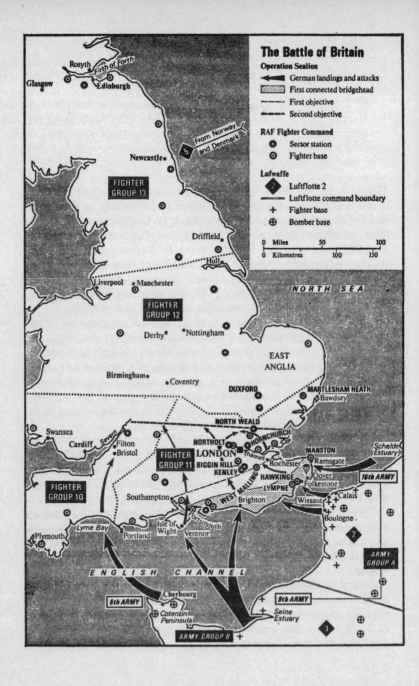

The Battle of Britain

Operation Sealion

➤ German landings and attacks
▨ First connected bridgehead
--- First objective
-·-·- Second objective

RAF Fighter Command

⦿ Sector station
◉ Fighter base

Luftwaffe

◆ Luftflotte 2
━━ Luftflotte command boundary
+ Fighter base
⊕ Bomber base

Miles	0		50		100
Kilometres	0	50	100	150	

Glasgow
Rosyth
Firth of Forth
Edinburgh

From Norway and Denmark
5

Newcastle

FIGHTER GROUP 13

Driffield

Hull
Liverpool
Manchester

FIGHTER GROUP 12

Derby
Nottingham

NORTH SEA

Birmingham
Coventry

EAST ANGLIA

DUXFORD
MARTLESHAM HEATH
Bawdsey

NORTH WEALD

Swansea
Cardiff
Severn
Filton
Bristol

NORTHOLT
HORNCHURCH
LONDON
BIGGIN HILL
KENLEY
Thames
Rochester

MANSTON
Ramsgate
Schelde Estuary

16th ARMY

FIGHTER GROUP 11

HAWKINGE
WEST MALLING
LYMPNE
Brighton

Dover
Folkestone
Wissant
Calais

FIGHTER GROUP 10

Southampton

Boulogne

ARMY GROUP A

Plymouth
Lyme Bay
Portland
Isle of Wight
Portsmouth
Ventnor

2

ENGLISH CHANNEL

6th ARMY
Cherbourg

9th ARMY

Cotentin Peninsula

Seine Estuary

ARMY GROUP B

3

earlier, the operational staff of Guderian's panzer group had been sent back to Berlin to prepare plans for the employment of the panzer forces in such a campaign.

When France collapsed the German Army was in no way prepared for such an undertaking as the invasion of England. The staff had not contemplated it, let alone studied it; the troops had been given no training for seaborne and landing operations; and nothing had been done to build landing-craft for the purpose. So all that could be attempted was a hurried effort to collect shipping, bring barges from Germany and the Netherlands to the Channel ports, and give the troops some practice in embarking and disembarking. It was only the temporary 'nakedness' of the British forces, after losing most of their arms and equipment in France, that offered such a hasty improvisation the possibility of success.

The main part in the operation was given to Field-Marshal von Rundstedt and his Army Group A, which was to employ the 16th Army (General Busch) on the right and the 9th Army (General Strauss) on the left. Embarking in the various harbours between the estuaries of the Scheldt and the Seine, seaborne forces were to converge on the southeast coast of England between Folkestone and Brighton, while an airborne division was to capture the cliff-covered Dover–Folkestone area. Under this 'Sealion' plan, ten divisions would be landed in the first wave over a period of four days to establish a wide bridgehead. After about a week the main advance inland would begin, its first objective being to gain the high ground along an arc from the Thames estuary to Portsmouth. In the next stage, London was to be cut off from the west.

A subsidiary operation was to be mounted by the 6th Army (Field-Marshal von Reichenau) of Army Group B, with three divisions in the first wave, to sail from Cherbourg and land in Lyme Bay west of Portland Bill for a push northward to the Severn estuary.

The second wave of the invasion would be an exploiting mobile force composed of six armoured and three motorized divisions in three corps, and this would be followed by a third wave of nine infantry divisions and a fourth wave of eight infantry divisions. Although there were no armoured divisions in the first wave, it was allotted approximately 650 tanks, all to be carried in the first of its two echelons (the leading echelon amounted to just over a third of its total strength of 250,000 troops). The cross-Channel conveyance of this two-piece first wave called for 155 transports, totalling some 700,000 tons, besides over 3,000 smaller craft – 1,720 barges, 470 tugs, and 1,160 motorboats.

Preparations were only set going late in July, and the German Naval Staff declared that such a large quantity of shipping could not be assembled ready to launch 'Sealion' before the middle of September at the earliest – whereas Hitler had ordered preparations to be completed by mid-August. (Indeed, at the end of July the Naval Staff recommended that the operation should be postponed until the spring of 1941.)

But that was not the only check. The German generals were very apprehensive of the risks that their forces would run in crossing the sea. They had little confidence in the capacity of either their own navy or their air force to keep the passage clear, and urged that the invasion should be on a wide enough front (from Ramsgate to Lyme Bay) to stretch and distract the defending forces. The German admirals were even more apprehensive of what would happen when the British fleet arrived on the scene. They had little or no confidence in their own power to prevent its interference, while at the outset insisting that the Army plan for a wide front of invasion would be impossible to protect, and that the crossing must be confined to a relatively narrow mine-covered corridor, with army forces of smaller size – limitations that deepened the generals' doubts. Above all, Admiral Raeder emphasized, air superiority over the crossing area was essential.

After a discussion with Raeder on July 31st, Hitler accepted the naval view that 'Sealion' could not be launched before the middle of September. But the operation was not yet definitely postponed until 1941, as Göring assured him that the Luftwaffe could check the British Navy's interference as well as drive the British out of the sky. The Navy and Army chiefs were quite willing to let him try his preliminary air offensive, which did not commit them to anything definite unless and until it proved successful.

In the event, it did not succeed, and so the struggle in the air became the principal feature – indeed, the only feature – of the decisive Battle of Britain.

The superiority of the Luftwaffe over the Royal Air Force was not so great as was generally imagined at the time. It was unable to maintain a continuous attack by wave after wave of massed bombers as the British public had feared, and the number of its fighters was not much more than that of the British.

The offensive was mainly conducted by Air Fleets (Luftflotten) 2 and 3, under Field-Marshals Albert Kesselring and Hugo Sperrle – the former based on north-east France and the Low Countries, and the latter on north and north-west France. Each air fleet was a self-contained force of all components – an integration which had been advantageous when cooperating with the Army's advances in Poland and the West, but was less so in an all-air campaign. Each air fleet produced its own plans and submitted them separately; there was no overall plan.

On August 10th, when the offensive was about to start in earnest, Air Fleets 2 and 3 had a total of 875 normal (high-level) bombers, and 316 dive-bombers. (The dive-bombers proved so vulnerable to the British fighters that they were withdrawn from the battle after August 18th, and reserved for the invasion.)

In addition, Luftflotte 5 in Norway and Denmark, under General Stumpff, had 123 high-level bombers, but it took part in the battle on one day only, August 15th, and its losses then proved too heavy for the distant excursion to be repeated. By its presence off stage, however, it did have a distracting effect in keeping part of the British Fighter Command's forces in the north-east of Engand. It also provided about a hundred bombers in the later part of August to replace losses in Luftflotten 2 and 3.

These had started the battle on August 10th with 929 fighters available. They were mostly single-engined Messerschmitt 109s, but had 227 twin-engined and relatively long-range Me 110s. The Me 109, of which the prototype had appeared in 1936, had a top speed of over 350 mph, and its high rate of climb gave it a further advantage over the British fighters. But in turning and manoeuvring it was at a disadvantage in combat with them. Moreover, unlike them, most had at the outset of the battle no armour protection for the pilot, although they did have bullet-proof fuel tanks, which the British lacked.

Limited range was a decisive factor for the German single-engined fighters in this battle. The Me 109's official cruising range of 412 miles was very misleading. Its real radius of action, out and back, was little more than 100 miles, and from the Pas de Calais or the Cotentin Peninsula that could take it only just to London, allowing it scant time for fighting there. Put in another way, it had a total flight duration of barely 95 minutes, which gave it only 75–80 minutes tactical flying time. When the heavy loss in bombers, and their very palpable vulnerability, made it necessary to provide them with fighter escorts, no more than 300–400 bombers could be used on any one day even against objectives in the south of England – allowing two fighters to escort a bomber.

The Me 109, too, was difficult to handle at take-off and landing, while its undercarriage was weak, and this trouble was accentuated by the hastily improvised airfields on the French coast.

The twin-engined Me 110, despite its nominal top speed of 340 mph, proved considerably slower – often barely 300 mph or even less – and was thus easily outpaced by the Spitfire, while it was sluggish in acceleration and difficult to manoeuvre. It had been intended as 'the operational flower of the Luftwaffe's fighters' but it proved the worst technical disappointment of all – and eventually had to be escorted by Me 109s for its own protection.

But the German fighters' greatest handicap was the primitiveness of their radio equipment. Although they had radio-telephony for inter-communication during flight, theirs was poor compared with the British – and they could not be controlled from the ground.

The RAF fighter strength had been rebuilt, after its loss of more than 400 in France, to a figure of some 650 by mid-July – its strength when the German offensive was launched in May. They were mostly Hurricanes and Spitfires, although still including nearly a hundred of other and older types.

That remarkable recovery owed much to the efforts of Lord Beaverbrook, who had been appointed to the new office of Minister of Aircraft Production in May on the formation of Mr Churchill's Government. His critics complained that his energetic interference had an upsetting effect on long-term progress. But Air Chief Marshal Sir Hugh Dowding, the Commander-in-Chief of Fighter Command, went on record in declaring that 'the effect of the appointment can only be described as magical'. By mid-summer even, the production of fighters had increased two and a half times, and during the whole year Britain produced 4,283 fighters compared with just over 3,000 single- and twin-engined fighters produced by Germany.

The relative situation in armament is more difficult to determine. The Hurricanes and Spitfires were armed solely with machine-guns; they had eight apiece, fixed forward in the wings. These were American Browning machine-guns – a weapon which had been chosen because it was reliable enough to be remotely controlled, while its rate of fire was high, 1,260 rounds a minute. The Me 109 fighters in general were armed with two fixed machine-guns in the cowlings and two 20-mm cannon in the wings – a weapon developed as a result of experience in the Spanish Civil War, which had been utilized as a testing ground for the Luftwaffe – the Me 109 had been tried out there, as well as earlier types of fighters now replaced.

Adolf Galland, the German ace, had no doubt, in retrospect, that the

Me 109's armament was the better. British opinion was divided, as it was considered that the high firing rate of the Brownings carried the advantage in short bursts of fire. But it was recognized that half a dozen cannon shells could do far more damage than the equivalent length of Browning bursts – and some of the British fighter pilots complained bitterly that even when sure that they were hitting an opponent 'nothing happened'. Significantly, some thirty Spitfires were equipped with two 20-mm Hispano (Oerlikon) cannon during the course of the battle, and Hurricanes fitted with four cannon came into use from October on.

What is quite clear, and became evident at the start, was that the German bombers were too poorly armed – with a few free-traversing machine-guns – to be able to beat off the British fighters without a fighter escort of their own.

The respective situation in regard to fighter pilots was more complex, and in the earlier phases of the battle far from favourable to the British. While trained to a high standard, their shortage in number was serious. The RAF flying training schools were slow in expanding, and their shortcomings largely determined the conduct of the battle. Wastage had to be kept to a minimum even if it meant some raids getting through. Men, not planes, were Dowding's main worry.

By husbanding his resources in July, Dowding managed to increase his pilot strength to 1,434 at the beginning of August – helped by a contribution, on 'loan', of sixty-eight from the Fleet Air Arm. But a month later the number was down to 840, and losses were averaging 120 a week. By contrast, no more than 260 fighter pilots were turned out by the RAF's Operational Training Units during the whole month. In September the scarcity became worse, as the number of highly skilled pilots shrank, while the hurriedly trained new arrivals were more vulnerable through inexperience. Fresh squadrons brought in to relieve tired ones often lost more than those they replaced. Tiredness was in numerous cases accompanied by declining morale and increasing 'nerviness'.

The Germans had no such heavy initial handicap in numbers. Despite their heavy losses on the Continent in May and June, the flying schools were turning out more pilots than could be absorbed into front-line squadrons. But morale was affected insidiously by the way Göring and others at the head of the Luftwaffe looked on, and treated, the fighter arm as merely 'defensive' and of secondary importance. Moreover it was drained of many of its best pilots to make up losses in the bomber and dive-bomber arms, while Göring kept on criticizing it for lack of aggressiveness, and blamed it for the Luftwaffe's failures – largely due to his own lack of foresight and mistakes in planning. By contrast, the morale of the British fighter pilots was fortified by knowing that they were regarded and acclaimed during these critical months as Churchill's 'Few', the flower of the Royal Air Force and the heroes of the nation.

The strain on the German fighters, both pilots and planes, was multiplied by the way they were increasingly used for, and tied to, escort duties – two or three sorties a day, and sometimes as many as five. Göring would not allow rest days, or the rotation of front-line units. Thus sheer tiredness was added to the sense, and strain, of their heavy losses. Morale was becoming low by the time September came. It was deepened by a sense of doubt whether invasion was really intended, in view of the slightness, and amateurishness, of the preparations the pilots saw, so that they began more and more to wonder whether they were merely being sacrificed to maintain a façade, for an operation that was being abandoned.

The bomber crews were suffering from heavy losses, and from a sense of their vulnerability to RAF fighter attack. Thus their decline in morale tended to become even more marked, gallantly as they continued to carry out orders.

In sum, while both sides were closely matched in skill and courage during the early phases of the battle, the British were helped in gaining the upper hand as it wore on by the fact, and still more the feeling, that the enemy were suffering a worse loss, and strain, than they themselves were – heavy though their own was on both counts.

A constant German handicap throughout the battle was poor Intelligence. The Luftwaffe's basic guide in conducting the offensive was a prewar handbook, known as the 'Blue Study', which set out the available data about the situation and lay-out of industrial plant in Britain and the results of comprehensive photographic reconnaissance carried out on 'civil route proving flights'. This was inadequately supplemented by the Luftwaffe's own Intelligence department – which was headed only by a major. In a survey of the RAF which this Major Schmid made in July 1940, he greatly underestimated British fighter production, allowing for only 180–300 a month – whereas it actually rose to 460–500 Hurricanes and Spitfires alone in August and September, the period of the battle, following Beaverbrook's efforts to speed up the programme. (The false impression caused by that big error was increased by reports from General Udet's production department which dwelt on the drawbacks of the Hurricane and Spitfire without pointing out their advantages.)

In Major Schmid's survey report there was no mention of the RAF's well-knit defence system, with its radar stations, operations rooms, and high-frequency radio network. Yet the British radar research station at Bawdsey on the Suffolk coast and the lofty lattice masts going up round the coast had been wide open to intelligent observation well before the war, and by 1939 it seemed hardly possible that the Germans could lack information of the key features in the British warning system. Although the Germans knew in 1938 that the British were experimenting with radar, and even captured a mobile radar station on the beach at Boulogne in May 1940, their scientists considered the set crude. Much fuller information about the British radar was freely available in France, owing to French carelessness over security, when the Germans overran the major part of that country, but the Germans do not seem to have profited by it. Göring himself took little account of its potential effect on the battle.

Indeed, it was not until the Germans had set up their monitoring stations along the coast of France in July that they came to realize, from the stream of signals radiating from the radar masts along the English coast, that they were faced with something new and of vital importance. Even the range and effectiveness of British radar were underrated by the Luftwaffe chiefs, and little effort was made to jam it or destroy it. Nor did the discovery that the British fighters operated under close radio control dismay them as it might have – they drew the conclusion that the system made Fighter Command inflexible, and that mass attacks would swamp the system.

The tendency to exaggerate the opponent's losses during intense air fighting was a fault common to both sides, but became more of a handicap on the German side. Initially Luftwaffe Intelligence assessed Dowding's resources, correctly, as totalling about fifty squadrons of Hurricanes and Spitfires, with an operational strength of approximately 600 aircraft, of which 400–500 at the most were in the southern part of England. But after the battle started, miscalculation and confusion developed from the combined effect of overestimated British losses and underestimating British aircraft production, so that Luftwaffe pilots became puzzled, and then depressed, by the way the number of British fighters was maintained. Many more were reported shot down than actually existed.

Another cause of miscalculation was the habit of the Luftwaffe chiefs, when they bombed a Fighter Command base, of striking off, in red pencil, the number of the RAF squadron there. That was partly due to poor photo-reconnaissance, and partly to unduly optimistic analysis of the results. For example, the Luftwaffe estimated that up to August 17th no less than eleven airfields had been 'permanently destroyed' – whereas, in fact, only one, Manston, was put out of action for any appreciable time. Moreover, effort was wasted in attacking airfields in the south-east that were not part of Fighter Command's organization. At the same time the Luftwaffe chiefs failed to realize the vital importance of the sector stations – such as Biggin Hill, Kenley, Hornchurch – in the Fighter Command organization, and were unaware that their operations rooms were above ground – dangerously exposed. Thus the devastating attacks on sector stations that the Luftwaffe delivered at the end of August were not followed up.

Another German handicap was the weather, and that in a double sense: the weather over the English Channel was often unfavourable for the attacking side, and as it usually came from the west, the British usually knew about it first. The Germans had broken the cipher of the British radio meteorological reports from the Atlantic, but they profited little from it, and were often caught out. In particular, the timing of the rendezvous between their bombers and the fighter escorts was repeatedly upset by unexpected cloud and poor visibility. Banks of cloud over northern France and Belgium would delay the bombers, whose crews had little experience of 'blind' navigation, with the result that they arrived late at their rendezvous, and the fighters, who could not afford to waste fuel, would attach themselves to other bombers, so that one bomber formation would fly out with doubled protection and another without any escort – and suffer heavy loss. When the autumn approached, and the weather worsened, such hitches increased, with catastrophic effects.

In one respect, however, the Germans benefited by better planning. The British air-sea rescue service was at first very haphazard, and pilots who came down in the sea had to depend largely on luck for their chances of being picked up. That was the more serious because in mid-August nearly two-thirds of the air fights that had a definite issue were taking place over the sea. The Germans were better organized. They used some thirty Heinkel sea-planes for rescue work, while their fighter pilots and bomber crews were equipped with inflatable rubber dinghies, a life-jacket, a light-pistol, and a chemical that made a bright green stain on the sea round them. A fighter pilot who 'ditched' could reckon on having 40 to 60 seconds to get out before the plane sank. Without the reassurance given by these sea-rescue precautions the Luftwaffe's morale might have declined quicker than it did.

The Luftwaffe's offensive had also to face formidable opposition beyond that of the RAF's fighters, the anti-aircraft guns assigned for the Air Defence of Great Britain. These were provided by, and belonged to, the Army (like those which had accompanied the Expeditionary Force) although operationally linked with, and subordinate to, RAF Fighter Command. If they brought down relatively few German bombers in the Battle of Britain they added much to the strain on the attackers by their upsetting effect in general, and on bombing accuracy in particular.

The GOC-in-C Anti-Aircraft Command was Lieutenant-General Sir Frederick Pile. Originally a gunner, he had transferred to the Royal Tank Corps on its permanent formation in 1923, and soon became one of the most dynamic exponents and advocates of mobile armoured forces. But in 1937, after promotion to major-general, the Army Council had appointed him to the command of the 1st Anti-Aircraft Division, which covered London and the south of England. The next year the two existing AA divisions were expanded into five, and then into seven. At the end of July 1939, just before the war, 'Tim' Pile was promoted to overall command of the whole, including the light batteries that were being formed for the defence of airfields and other vital points against low-flying attack.

Another valuable element in meeting that kind of attack was the balloon barrage – a string of sausage-shape balloons anchored, at heights up to 5,000 feet, by steel cables. This was provided by the RAF itself, and was under separate control, although under Fighter Command.

Throughout these prewar years, the expansion of the anti-aircraft forces for home defence had been grudgingly agreed at the best, and often strongly opposed, by the Army Council – which tended to regard them as a regrettable subtraction from the strength of the Army. So Pile's efforts to develop these anti-aircraft forces and their effectiveness met with much obstruction in the War Office, and brought him into disfavour there – with adverse effects on his prospects of re-entry, and further advancement, in the main stream of the Army. Fortunately for the country, however, he had succeeded in establishing close and harmonious relations with Dowding, a difficult personality, and they worked together remarkably well.

By the outbreak of war, at the beginning of September 1939, the approved establishment of Anti-Aircraft Command had been raised, successively, to a scale of 2,232 heavy AA guns – nearly double the so-called 'Ideal' plan rejected two years before – as well as 1,860 light AA guns, and 4,128 searchlights. But, as a result of the hesitations and delays, only 695 heavy guns and 253 light guns could be deployed when the war started - approximately one-third of the heavy guns and one-eighth of the light guns by then authorized. (That was at any rate a great improvement on the Munich Crisis a year earlier, when only 126 heavy AA guns were ready for action.) The searchlight situation was relatively good, as 2,700 were deployed out of an authorized scale of 4,128 - more than two-thirds.

After the war began a fresh complication came from the Admiralty's demand for 255 heavy guns to defend its six Fleet anchorages - a demand that had not been made before the war when the Admiralty had shown great confidence in the unaided power of its ships to beat off air attack with their own AA armament. It now wanted no less than ninety-six guns to protect the anchorage at Rosyth in the Firth of Forth - as many as were then available for the whole of London, and four times as many as protected the Derby area where the vital Rolls-Royce engine works were situated.

The expedition to Norway in April 1940 brought a further large demand for, and drain upon, both heavy and light AA guns.

Then, after the fall of France in June, the situation of the Air Defence of Great Britain itself was changed radically for the worse, as Britain became enveloped by a ring of enemy air bases from Norway round to Brittany.

At that time, AA Command's available strength had risen to 1,204 heavy guns and 581 light guns - respectively nearly double the number and over double the number at the outbreak of war. It would have been better but for the various drains upon it. During the next five weeks the fresh intake was 124 heavy and 182 light guns, but nearly half the former and a quarter of the latter had to be allocated for training purposes and for places overseas that were now endangered by Italy's entry into the war on Germany's side. At the end of July the Air Defence of Great Britain still had little more than half the scale of heavy AA guns, and barely one-third of the light AA guns, that had been considered necessary at the outbreak of war - when the strategic circumstances were far more favourable than they had become. Searchlights were more plentiful, nearly 4,000 being now available, almost up to the level of the establishment - although the changed circumstances now called for a large increase in the scale.

The preliminary phase of the Battle of Britain saw the gradual development of German air operations against British shipping and ports in the Channel, along with spasmodic efforts to lure out the British fighters. Until August 6th no precise instructions for the conduct of the offensive were sent to the chief Luftwaffe commanders, Kesselring and Sperrle – which serves to explain why the pattern of these early operations was so puzzling.*

Regular attacks on shipping started on July 3rd, while next day a force of eighty-seven dive-bombers, escorted by Me 109s, attacked the Naval harbour at Portland, but without much effect. On the 10th a small force of bombers, with a large escort of fighters, attacked a convoy off Dover, and the Me 110s, significantly, fared badly against the Hurricanes sent out to defend the convoy. After a heavier attack on a convoy in the same area on July 25th the Admiralty decided to send convoys through the straits by night, and some successful attacks on destroyers led it to the decision that those stationed at Dover should withdraw to Portsmouth. The passage of another convoy in the night of August 7th was spotted by German radar from the cliffs near Wissant, and the next day it was assailed by escorted waves of dive-bombers, up to eighty at a time. They sank nearly 70,000 tons of shipping at a cost of thirty-one aircraft.

On the 11th, in confused combats, the RAF lost thirty-two fighters. Even so, during this phase from July 3rd to August 11th, the Germans lost 364 bombers and fighters, while the RAF lost 203 fighters – a loss nearly replaced by a week's output from the factories.

Following Hitler's belated order of August 1st – for the Luftwaffe to 'destroy the enemy air force as soon as possible' – and Göring's discussions with his chief executives, the opening of the grand offensive was fixed for August 13th. This was christened *Adlertag* – 'Eagle Day'. Over-optimistic reports of Luftwaffe successes in the preliminary phase had convinced Göring that he could achieve air superiority in four days of good weather. By August 13th, however, the weather had become less favourable than earlier.

Nevertheless on Eagle Day itself, the Luftwaffe launched its initial bombing attacks on British fighter airfields and radar stations in the south-east of England. The forward airfields at Manston, Hawkinge, and Lympne were badly damaged, while some of the radar stations were put out of action for several hours. The one at Ventnor in the Isle of Wight was put completely out of action, but the fact was concealed from the Germans by signals from another transmitter. The radar

---

* I was sent daily charts of the raids by General Pile in the hope that I might be able to find a clue, but could perceive no clear indication of pattern or purpose.

towers themselves tended to keep the dive-bombers away from the operations rooms at their base, and in any case the Germans mistakenly assumed that these would be safely placed underground. In this connexion, tribute is due to the women radar plotters of the WAAF, the Women's Auxiliary Air Force, who went on reporting raids until their own station was bombed.

The thick layer of cloud lying over south-east England caused Göring to postpone the main attack until the afternoon – but several formations failed to get the deferment signal and wasted their effort in disjointed raids. When the big attack was delivered in the afternoon it was too scattered, and its results disappointing. During that day the Luftwaffe flew 1,485 sorties, double the number of the RAF. For a cost of forty-five German aircraft, bombers and fighters, it only shot down thirteen RAF fighters – although claiming to have destroyed seventy.

In this opening stage of the main offensive, much of the Luftwaffe effort was wasted in attacking airfields that were not those of Fighter Command – which should have been their key target and objective. It also suffered from poor coordination between bomber formations and their fighter escorts.

The next day, August 14th, clouds helped to reduce the attack to about a third of its weight on the opening day, but when the weather cleared on the morning of the 15th, the Luftwaffe launched its biggest effort of the whole battle – a total of 1,786 sorties, in which over 500 bombers were employed. The first attacks were against the airfields at Hawkinge and Lympne, and although the former, the more important, escaped serious damage, the latter was put out of action for two days.

Then in the early afternoon over a hundred bombers of Luftflotte 5, in two formations, flew in over the North Sea to attack airfields near Newcastle and in Yorkshire. The larger one, of some sixty-five bombers from Stavanger in Norway, was escorted by about thirty-five Me 110s, but these proved of little protective value, and the force met such stiff resistance from the RAF fighters of No 13 Group and from anti-aircraft guns that it caused no serious damage anywhere, and had fifteen planes shot down while the RAF lost none. The other attacking force, of some fifty bombers from Aalborg in Denmark, had no escort, but although No. 12 Group put up three squadrons to meet it, a large part of it succeeded in getting through to the RAF bomber base at Driffield in Yorkshire, where it caused a lot of damage – although it lost seven of its bombers over England and three more on the flight back.

In the south, the British defence was less successful – under a heavier and more varied series of attacks, at shorter range. Early in the afternoon a raid by thirty bombers, heavily escorted, got through to Rochester and bombed the Short aircraft factory there, while about the same time a raid by twenty-four fighter-bombers did severe damage to the RAF fighter airfield at Martlesham Heath in Suffolk. The multiplicity of raids confused the radar picture, and British fighter squadrons, sent out individually, were chasing to and fro. Fortunately for the defence, Luftflotten 2 and 3 did not effectively coordinate their attacks, and thus lost the advantage of keeping the RAF on the run. It was not until 6 PM that a mass of about 200 aircraft from Luftflotte 3 streamed over the Channel to attack airfields in the south-centre of England. Helped by good radar warning, Fighter Groups No. 10 and 11 – the two covering the southern part of the country – put up no less than fourteen squadrons, a total of about 170 fighters, to meet this massive attack, and it achieved little. Soon afterward Luftflotte 2 attacked afresh in the southeast, with about 100 aircraft, but this likewise met prompt resistance and had little effect. Even when attacks reached their objective, they found the British fighters well dispersed and well camouflaged.

On this day, perhaps the most decisive of the battle, the actual German loss over the whole country was seventy-five aircraft, compared with thirty-four British fighters. Significantly, the Luftwaffe had employed less than half its bomber strength – a recognition, and indirect admission, of its dependence on the escort of its own fighters, almost all of which had been used. Moreover the day's operations had clearly shown the unsuitability of the German dive-bombers, the hitherto alarming Stukas, for the tasks they were now attempting – as well as of the Me 110 fighters, on which such great hopes had been built.

It was this day which inspired Churchill to say: 'Never in the field of human conflict was so much owed by so many to so few'.

Next day however, the 16th, the Luftwaffe made another strong effort – under the delusion that the RAF had lost over 100 aircraft on the 15th, and had only 300 fighters left. But although the attacks were damaging in several places, they were disappointing on the whole. On the 17th no major attacks were made despite quite good weather. On the 18th a fresh and stronger effort resulted in the German loss of seventy-one aircraft (half of them bombers) compared with an RAF loss of twenty-seven fighters. From then on the attacks dwindled. In fact, hedge-hopping raids on Kenley and Biggin Hill had done considerable damage, and been difficult to counter, as they came in below the level of the radar screen. But the Germans did not realize this, and felt that their losses had been too great to continue. Bad weather then brought a lull in the battle.

Göring had called another conference of his chief executives on the 19th, and after discussion it was decided to pursue the air offensive – with a fresh effort to knock out the British fighter force.

During the two weeks following August 10th the Luftwaffe lost 167 bombers (including forty dive-bombers), and the bomber chiefs in consequence were calling for stronger and stronger fighter escorts. Tension, and friction, between the two arms was increased by Göring's tendency to side with the bombers and blame the fighters.

But there was friction also on the British side, especially between Air Vice-Marshal Keith Park, commanding No. 11 Fighter Group in the crucial south-east of England, and Air Vice-Marshal Trafford Leigh-Mallory, commanding No. 12 Fighter Group in the Midlands. Park emphasized the importance of meeting the Germans forward of their objectives and shooting down their bombers, thus driving them to use more and more of their Me 109 fighters in a close escort role for which they were not fitted. Leigh-Mallory considered that this policy put too great a strain on the RAF fighter pilots, who were apt to be caught on the ground, often when refuelling, or before they could gain sufficient height.

There were differences as well over the tactics to be used, the 'Leigh-Mallory faction' advocating the 'big wing' theory of massive, concentrated intercepting forces, while Park held to what he believed was the more flexible policy afforded the British by their radar, feeding in interceptors as the German forces arrived – the 'diluted concentration' policy.

It was also argued that Dowding, in accord with Park, was too intent to maintain the forward airfields in the south-east, for the sake of civilian morale, when it would have been wiser to withdraw behind London, out of range of the Me 109s and their escorted bombers.

Fighter Command had lost ninety-four pilots in the period August 8th–18th, and sixty wounded. But there was as yet no shortage of aircraft, despite the loss of 175 fighters during the period, a further sixty-five severely damaged, and thirty aircraft destroyed on the ground.

When the weather improved on the 24th Göring launched his second bid for command of the air. This time it was better planned. Luftflotte 2, under Kesselring, usually kept some planes in the air on the French side of the Channel, and that kept Park guessing, as radar could not differentiate between bombers and fighters, or tell when aircraft would suddenly dash across the Channel. In this new phase No. 11 Group's forward airfields suffered more severely than before, and Manston had to be abandoned.

Another feature of the new plan was an intensive attack on RAF stations and installations around London – and this led to the unintended dropping of bombs on London. On the night of the 24th some ten German bombers, which had lost their way *en route* to targets at Rochester and Thameshaven, dropped their loads in central London. That mistake led to an immediate reprisal raid on Berlin the next night by some eighty British bombers, and this raid was followed up by several more – leading Hitler, after threats that were ignored, to order reprisal raids on London.

Prior to the new offensive most of the Me 109 fighters with Luftflotte 3 were transferred to Luftflotte 2, so as to increase the strength of the escorts in the Pas de Calais area. That policy paid. The RAF's fighters had more difficulty, and lost more heavily, in penetrating the German fighter screen, while the German bombers were better able to get through to their targets. Moreover the Germans developed a new tactic of splitting up into separate raids once the mass formations had passed through the radar screen.

On the opening day, August 24th, the sector stations at North Weald and Hornchurch were only saved by their AA gun defence. That also saved Portsmouth Dockyard in a heavy attack by Luftflotte 3, although the city itself suffered badly from the resultant scatter of bombs. After this effort Luftflotte 3 turned to night bombing, and attacked Liverpool on four successive nights from the 28th on, but many of the bombers failed to find the Merseyside area owing to their inadequate training and to British interference with German navigational beams. These raids, however, also brought out the shortcomings of British defence against night attack.

The last two days of August proved particularly bad for Fighter Command. Significantly, small formations of bombers, fifteen to twenty, had fighter escorts three times as many as themselves. On the 31st the RAF suffered its heaviest loss of the whole battle, having thirty-nine fighters shot down against a German loss of forty-one aircraft. The rate of loss was more than the RAF could afford on its limited strength, and it was failing to deter the attackers. Most of the airfields in the south-west were by now seriously damaged, and some were so wrecked as to be unusable.

Even Dowding was considering the withdrawal of his fighting line in the south-east and bringing it back out of range of the Me109s. He was also becoming more strongly criticized for keeping twenty fighter squadrons to protect the north, which had only been attacked once in daylight – an attack which had not been repeated. Moreover those of

No. 12 Group, in East Anglia and the Midlands, were clamouring to take a more direct part in the battle – while Park complained that they did not cooperate in the way he wanted. Strained relations between Park and Leigh-Mallory, and between Dowding and Newall, the Chief of the Air Staff, did not aid a smooth solution of the problem.

During the month of August, Fighter Command lost in combat 338 Hurricanes and Spitfires, as well as having 104 badly damaged, compared with a German loss of 177 Me 109s, with twenty-four badly damaged. That was a loss of 2 for 1 in fighters. Other causes accounted for forty-two RAF fighters and fifty-four Me 109s.

Thus at the beginning of September there was all too much reason for Göring to feel that he was within reach of his goal – the destruction of Britain's fighter strength and of its installations in the south-east. But he did not grasp the importance of following up the advantage he had gained.

On September 4th, the Luftwaffe's concentration on Fighter Command's airfields was varied, and diluted, by a series of attacks on British aircraft factories – the Short factory at Rochester and the Vickers-Armstrong works at Brooklands. The variation was quite effective in itself, but carried with it a lowering of pressure on Fighter Command. That was the more valuable because the endurance and the nerves of pilots were strained to breaking point, and their performance had been showing a marked decline.

Dowding, with a sense of essentials, ordered maximum fighter cover for the fighter factories in the south; a fresh attack on Brooklands two days later was headed off – as well as attacks on five sector stations around London.

During the whole two weeks' period August 24th to September 6th, 295 British fighters had been destroyed and 171 badly damaged – compared with a total output of 269 new and repaired fighters. The Luftwaffe's loss in Me 109s was barely half the number – although it had also lost more than a hundred bombers.

The Luftwaffe's losses, along with the call for much stronger escort of the bombers, was now seriously affecting the effort it made, or could make. Whereas it had flown about 1,500 sorties a day, and momentarily rose again to a figure of 1,300–1,400 in the last two days of August, it never reached 1,000 sorties during the first week of September. During the first two months of the battle – which had become a battle of attrition – the Luftwaffe had lost more than 800 aircraft. Kesselring's Luftflotte 2, carrying the main burden of the offensive, was now down to about 450 serviceable bombers and 530 Me 109 fighters. So at the end of this third phase of the battle the scales were at last beginning to tilt in Britain's favour. They were to do so more definitely in the fourth phase, helped by the Luftwaffe's switch of effort.

On September 3rd Göring had held, at The Hague, another conference of his chief executives and this had confirmed the fateful decision to switch the daylight bombing offensive to London – as Kesselring had urged from the outset, and Hitler had now agreed. The starting date was fixed for September 7th.

At the same time the 300 bombers available in Luftflotte 3 would be used for a night bombing offensive. That suited Sperrle, who had always favoured the bombing of shipping and ports, and had become increasingly sceptical about the prospect of crushing the British fighter force and knocking out its airfields.

On the afternoon of the 7th an air armada of about a thousand aircraft of Luftflotte 2 – over 300 bombers escorted by 648 fighters – set out for London, watched by Göring and Kesselring from the cliffs at Cap Blanc Nez, between Calais and Wissant. It was echeloned upwards in solid layers at between 13,500 and 19,500 feet, flying in close-knit formations and in two waves. The German fighter screen adopted new tactics, one escort flying well ahead at a height of 24,000–30,000 feet, while another escort gave the bombers close cover, and on all sides, at a distance of only about 300 yards.

This new technique proved difficult to counter, but on this first occasion it was hardly needed. For at No. 11 Group Headquarters, the Controller had been expecting another attack on the inner sector stations, and such of the fighter squadrons as were airborne, four in number, were mostly concentrated north of the Thames. So the path to London was clear. The first wave flew straight to the London docks; the second flew over central London and then back over the East End and the docks. The bombing was not so accurate as the Germans thought, many of the bombers aiming short, but in the densely crowded area of the East End, that resulted in all the more loss among the population. In this first mass daylight attack on London – which was also the last – over 300 civilians were killed, and over 1,300 seriously injured.

It had been a frustrating evening for Fighter Command. But although its squadrons were mostly late on the scene, and then baffled by the new German tactics, it managed to inflict a loss of forty-one aircraft for its own loss of twenty-eight. The biggest shock to the Germans came from a particularly fierce attack by No. 303 (Polish) Squadron from Northolt.

The fires raging in the East End served as a guiding beacon for the night attack that followed, and continued from 8 PM until nearly 5 AM. Göring telephoned his wife, telling her triumphantly 'London is in flames'. The lack of opposition led him, and many of his subordinates, to believe that the British fighter force was near to being exhausted. So next day he ordered an extension of the area of London that was to be bombed.

Meanwhile the assembly of invasion barges in the Channel had been growing larger day by day, and on the morning of the 7th the British Government had issued a precautionary invasion warning. After the air attack that followed so closely, the warning was inflated, with the result that a number of auxiliary units were called out and some church bells, which were to signal the invasion, were rung.

Because of the lack of suitable night fighters the defence of London, as of other cities, depended at this crucial time mainly on anti-aircraft guns and searchlights. On the night of the 7th there were only 264 guns on the spot to defend London, but thanks to Pile's prompt measures the number was doubled in the next forty-eight hours. Moreover he laid on 'the barrage' from the night of the 10th onward, telling every gun to fire as much as it could, on whatever information it had. Although the number of hits was slight, the sound of the barrage had a great tonic effect on the morale of the population, while it also had an important material effect by driving the bombers higher.

Kesselring launched his second daylight attack against London on the afternoon of the 9th. No. 11 Group was ready for it this time, with nine fighter squadrons in position, while others from No. 10 and 12 Groups cooperated. Interceptions were so successful that most of the German formations were broken up long before they reached London. Less than half the bombers got through, and hardly any of them succeeded in hitting their targets.

Much the most important effect of this new German offensive was the way it eased the strain on Fighter Command, which had been suffering so badly from the Germans' concentration on it, and was close to breaking point when the Germans switched their effort to the attack on London. The punishment that the capital and its people suffered was to be the saving factor in the preservation of the country's defence.

Moreover, the disappointing result of September 9th led Hitler once again to postpone his ten-day warning period for the invasion – this time to the 14th, for invasion on the 24th.

Deteriorating weather provided some respite for the London defences, but on the 11th and 14th a number of bombers got through, and fighter interception was so scrappy that the Luftwaffe optimistically reported that Fighter Command's resistance was beginning to collapse. So Hitler, although putting off the warning date again, postponed it only three days, to the 17th.

Kesselring launched a big new attack in the morning of Sunday the 15th. This time the fighter defence against it was better planned and timed. Although the air armada was assailed all the way from the coast by a series of single or paired squadrons, twenty-two in all, 148 bombers got through to the London area – but they were prevented from dropping their bombs accurately, and most were widely scattered. Then as the Germans wheeled for home, No. 12 Group's Duxford wing of some sixty fighters swept down from East Anglia, and although losing some of its effect through not yet having gained sufficient height, its massiveness gave the German airmen a shock. In the afternoon, cloud helped the attackers, and a large number had a clear run to London, where their bombs inflicted much damage, especially in the crowded houses of the East End. But during the day as a whole about a quarter of the bombers were put out of action and many more damaged, often with one or more of the crew being killed or wounded, to be carried back to their base, with a consequent effect on morale at those airfields.

The actual German loss that day, as established in later checking, was sixty aircraft. That was much less than one-third of the figure of 185 triumphantly announced by the British Air Ministry at the time – but it compared very well with the RAF loss of twenty-six fighters (of which half the pilots were saved) and was a much more favourable balance than in recent weeks. Göring, still blaming his fighters, continued to talk optimistically, and estimated that the British fighter force would be finished off in four or five days. But neither his subordinates nor his superiors continued to share his optimism.

On the 17th Hitler, agreeing with his Naval Staff that the RAF was still by no means defeated, and emphasizing that a period of turbulent weather was due, postponed the invasion 'until further notice'. The following day he ordered that no more shipping was to be assembled in the Channel ports, and agreed that its dispersal might begin – 12 per cent of the transports (21 out of 170), and 10 per cent of the barges (214 out of 1,918) had been sunk or damaged by British air attacks. On October 12th, 'Sealion' was definitely postponed until the spring of 1941 – and in January Hitler ruled that all preparations should be stopped except for a few long-term measures. His mind had now turned definitely to the East.

Göring still persisted with his daylight attacks, but the results were increasingly disappointing, despite occasional successes at out-of-the-way ports. The aircraft works at Filton, near Bristol, were severely hit on September 25th, and next day the Spitfire factory near Southampton was temporarily wrecked. But a big raid on the 27th against London was a bad failure, and in the last big daylight attack on September 30th only a fraction of the aircraft reached London, while forty-seven aircraft were lost compared with twenty fighters lost by the RAF.

After the disappointing results in the second half of September, and his heavy bomber losses, Göring turned to the use of fighter-bombers operating at high altitude. About mid-September the German fighter formations engaged in the battle had been ordered to give up a third of their strength for conversion into fighter-bombers, and a total of about 250 was thus produced. But insufficient time was allowed to retrain the pilots and the bomb-load they could carry was not enough to do much damage, while they were instinctively inclined to jettison their bombs as soon as they were engaged.

The best that could be said for them was that their use temporarily brought a diminution of German losses while keeping up strain on the RAF. But by the end of October, German losses were rising again to the old ratio, while the worsening weather was multiplying the strain on the fighter-bombers' crews, who were operating from improvised and swamp-like airfields. In the month of October the Germans lost 325 aircraft, much in excess of the British loss.

The only serious harassment of Britain was now coming from night bombing by 'normal' bombers. From September 9th the 300 bombers of Sperrle's Luftflotte 3 settled down to a standard pattern, and for fifty-seven nights London was attacked, by an average force of 160 bombers.

Early in November Göring issued new orders that marked a clear change of policy. The air offensive was to be entirely concentrated on night bombing – of cities, industrial centres, and ports. With the release of Luftflotte 2's bombers, up to 750 bombers became available, although only about a third of the total were employed at a time. As they could afford to fly at a slower speed, and at a lower height, they could carry heavier bomb-loads than in daylight, and as much as 1,000 tons were dropped in a night. But the accuracy was poor.

The new offensive was launched on the night of November 14th with the attack on Coventry. It was helped by bright moonlight as well as by a special 'pathfinder' force. But its effectiveness was not equalled in the big attacks that followed on other cities – such as those on Birmingham, Southampton, Bristol, Plymouth, and Liverpool. On December 29th much damage was caused in London, particularly the centre of the City, but attacks then eased off until the weather improved in March. A series of heavy attacks culminated in a very damaging raid against London on the night of May 10th, the anniversary of the launching of the 1940 Blitzkreig in the West. But in the sky over Britain the 'Blitz', as it was called, came to an end on May 16th after which the bulk of the Luftwaffe was sent eastward for the coming invasion of Russia.

The German air offensive from July until the end of October, 1940, had caused much more damage and disruption than was admitted, and the effects would have been even more serious had there been greater persistency in pressing, and repeating, attacks on the main industrial centres. But it had not succeeded in·its object of destroying the RAF's fighter strength and the British people's morale.

In the course of the Battle of Britain, from July until the end of October, the Germans had lost 1,733 aircraft – not the 2,698 claimed by the British – while the RAF lost 915 fighters – not the 3,058 claimed by the enemy.

CHAPTER NINE

Counterstroke from Egypt

When Hitler's attack on the West reached a point – with the breach of the improvised Somme–Aisne front – where the defeat of France became certain, Mussolini brought Italy into the war, on June 10th, 1940, in the hope of gaining some of the spoils of victory. It appeared to be an almost completely safe decision from his point of view and fatal to Britain's position in the Mediterranean and Africa. This was the darkest hour in her history. For although a large proportion of her army in France had escaped by sea, it had been forced to leave most of its weapons and equipment behind, and in that unarmed state faced an imminent threat of invasion by the victorious Germans. There was nothing available to reinforce the small fraction of the British Army that guarded Egypt and the Sudan against the imminent threat of invasion from the Italian armies in Libya and Italian East Africa.

The situation was all the worse because Italy's entry into the war had made the sea-route through the Mediterranean too precarious to use, and reinforcements had to come by the roundabout Cape route – down the west coast of the African continent and up the east coast into the Red Sea. A small instalment of 7,000 troops, which had been ready for dispatch in May 1940, did not reach Egypt until the end of August.

Numerically, the Italian armies were overwhelmingly superior to the scanty British forces opposing them, under General Sir Archibald Wavell who, on Mr Hore-Belisha's proposal, had been appointed in July 1939 to the newly created post of Commander-in-Chief, Middle East, when the first steps were taken to strengthen the forces there. But even now there were barely 50,000 British troops facing a total of half a million Italian and Italian colonial troops.

On the southerly fronts, the Italian forces in Eritrea and Abyssinia mustered more than 200,000 men, and could have pushed westwards into the Sudan – which was defended by a mere 9,000 British and Sudanese troops – or southwards into Kenya, where the garrison was no larger. Rugged country and distance, together with Italian difficulties in holding down the recently conquered Ethiopians and their own inefficiency, formed the main protection of the Sudan during this perilous period. Except for two small frontier encroachments, at Kassala and Gallabat, no offensive move developed on the Italians' part.

On the North African front a still larger force in Cyrenaica under Marshal Graziani faced the 36,000 British, New Zealand, and Indian troops who guarded Egypt. The Western Desert, inside the Egyptian frontier, separated the two sides on this front. The foremost British position was at Mersa Matruh, 120 miles inside the frontier and some 200 miles west of the Nile Delta.

Instead of remaining passive, however, Wavell used part of his one incomplete armoured division as an offensive covering force right forward in the desert. It was very offensive, keeping up a continual series of raids over the frontier to harass the Italian posts. Thus at the outset of the campaign General Creagh's 7th Armoured Division – the soon-to-be famous 'Desert Rats' – gained a moral ascendency over the enemy. Wavell paid special tribute to the 11th Hussars (the armoured-car regiment) under Lieutenant-Colonel J. F. B. Combe, saying that it 'was continuously in the front line, and usually behind that of the enemy, during the whole period'.

On June 14th a mobile column under Brigadier J. A. C. Caunter made a surprise stroke against Fort Capuzzo, and captured this important frontier stronghold, though the British did not try to hold it permanently, as their strategy was to keep mobile – 'masters of the desert' – while inducing the Italians to concentrate and provide targets. The published list of Italian casualties for the three months until mid-September amounted to 3,500, while the British were only just over 150 – despite being often bombed and machine-gunned from the air, where the relatively numerous Italian aircraft met little interference at that time.

It was not until September 13th that the Italians, after massing more than six divisions, began a cautious move forward into the Western Desert. After advancing fifty miles, less than half way to the British position at Mersa Matruh, they sat down at Sidi Barrani, and there established themselves in a chain of fortified camps – which were too widely separated to support one another. Week after week then passed without any attempt to move on. Meanwhile further reinforcements reached Wavell, including three armoured regiments rushed out from England in three fast merchant ships, on Churchill's bold initiative.

Wavell now decided that, as the Italians did not come on, he would sally forth and strike at them. That stroke was to have an astonishing

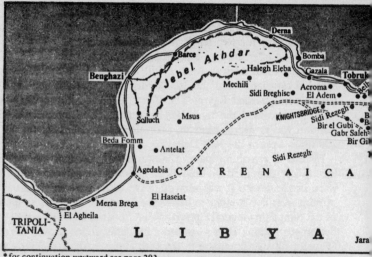

* for continuation westward see page 292

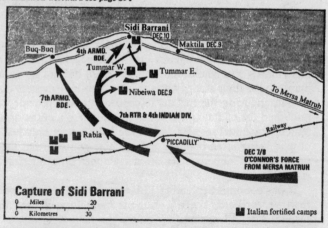

Capture of Sidi Barrani

| | Miles | 20 |
| 0 | Kilometres | 30 |

Italian fortified camps

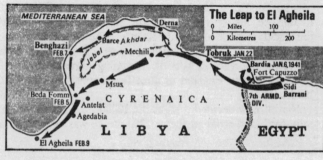

The Leap to El Agheila

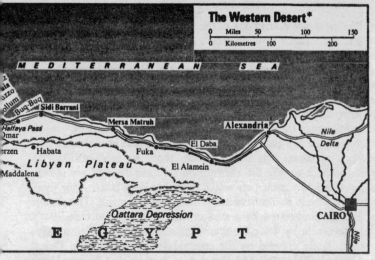

The Western Desert*

M E D I T E R R A N E A N   S E A

Sidi Barrani

Buq Buq

Halfaya Pass
Omar

Habata

Fuka

Mersa Matruh

El Daba

Alexandria

Nile Delta

El Alamein

Libyan Plateau

Maddalena

Qattara Depression

E G Y P T

CAIRO

Nile

Miles 50 100 150

Kilometres 100 200

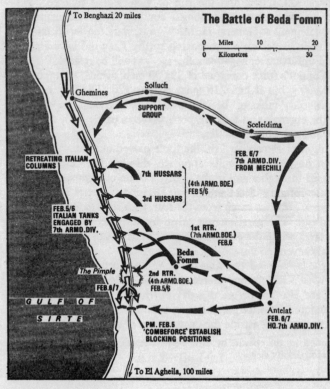

The Battle of Beda Fomm

To Benghazi 20 miles

Miles 10 20

Kilometres 30

Ghemines

Solluch

SUPPORT GROUP

Sceleidima

RETREATING ITALIAN COLUMNS

7th HUSSARS

(4th ARMD. BDE.)
FEB 5/6

3rd HUSSARS

FEB. 6/7
7th ARMD. DIV.
FROM MECHILI

FEB.5/6
ITALIAN TANKS
ENGAGED BY
7th ARMD. DIV.

1st RTR.
(7th ARMD. BDE.)
FEB.6

Beda Fomm

The Pimple

FEB. 6/7

2nd RTR.
(4th ARMD. BDE.)
FEB.5/6

GULF OF

SIRTE

Antelat
FEB. 6/7
HQ.7th ARMD. DIV.

PM. FEB. 5
'COMBEFORCE' ESTABLISH
BLOCKING POSITIONS

To El Agheila, 100 miles

effect, leading to the destruction of the whole Italian army and the near-collapse of the Italians' hold on North Africa.

But such a dramatic result was unforeseen. The stroke was planned, not as a sustained offensive, but rather as a large-scale raid. Wavell thought of it as a sharp punch to stun the invaders temporarily while he diverted part of his strength down to the Sudan, to push back the other Italian army there. Thus, unfortunately, no adequate preparations were made to follow-up the overwhelming victory that was actually gained.

Much was due to a radical change which was made in the attack plan following a rehearsal that raised doubts about its practicability. An indirect approach to take the enemy's camps from the rear was substituted for a frontal assault that would probably have failed – the more probably because it would have had a minefield in its path. The change of method was suggested by a staff officer, Brigadier Dorman-Smith, who had been sent by Wavell to attend the rehearsal. But its advantages were immediately grasped by the commander of the Western Desert force, General O'Connor, and the run of victory that followed was mainly due to his executive handling – for the higher commanders, Wavell and Lieutenant-General H. M. Wilson, were too far distant to exert positive influence on a fast-moving battle. They did have an important, and unfortunate, negative influence – as will be related.

Dick O'Connor's force consisted of 30,000 men, against an opposing force of 80,000 – but it had 275 tanks against 120. The fifty heavily armoured 'Matilda' tanks of the 7th Royal Tank Regiment, impervious to most of the enemy's anti-tank weapons, played a particularly decisive role in this and subsequent battles.

On the night of December 7th, the force moved out from the Matruh position on its seventy-mile approach through the desert. Next night it passed through a gap in the enemy's chain of camps, and early on the 9th the infantry of the 4th Indian Division (General Beresford-Peirse) stormed Nibeiwa camp from the rear, with the 7th Royal Tanks as its spearhead. The garrison was taken by surprise, and 4,000 prisoners captured, while the attackers' casualties were small – among the tankmen only seven.

The Matildas then led the way northward against the camp called 'Tummar West', which was stormed in the early afternoon, while 'Tummar East' also fell before this day of triumph ended. Meanwhile the 7th Armoured Division* had driven on westward and reached the coast road, thus getting astride the enemy's line of retreat.

---

* Commanded in this battle by Brigadier J. A. C. Caunter, as General Creagh was temporarily sick.

On the next day the 4th Indian Division moved north against the cluster of Italian camps close around Sidi Barrani. The enemy were now on the alert, while violent sandstorms were also a hindrance to the advance. But, after an initial check, a converging assault from both flanks – with two additional tank regiments sent back by the 7th Armoured Division – was launched in the afternoon, and the greater part of the Sidi Barrani position was overrun before the day ended.

On the third day the reserve brigade of the 7th Armoured Division was brought up for a further enveloping bound to the westward, and arrived on the coast beyond Buq-Buq to intercept a large column of retreating Italians. The capture here of a further 14,000 Italians and eighty-eight guns brought the total bag to nearly 40,000 prisoners, and 400 guns.

The remnants of the invading Italian army, after recrossing their own frontier, took refuge in the coast-fortress of Bardia. There they were speedily isolated by the encircling sweep of the 7th Armoured Division. Unfortunately, there was no backing-up infantry division at hand to take advantage of their demoralization, for the British higher commanders had planned to take away the 4th Indian Division as soon as Sidi Barrani was captured and to bring it back to Egypt for dispatch to the Sudan. Their remoteness from the battlefield made it hard for them to realize what a decisive victory O'Connor had won, or what an immense opportunity it offered, and they persisted in the order for the recall of the 4th Indian Division.

Thus on December 11th, the third day of battle, the routed Italians were running westwards in panic while half the victor's force was marching eastwards – back to back! It was a strange spectacle, and entailed a fateful delay. For three weeks elapsed before the 6th Australian Division arrived from Palestine to aid in continuing the British advance.

On January 3rd, 1941, the assault on Bardia was at last launched, with twenty-two Matildas of the 7th Royal Tank Regiment leading the way as 'tin-openers'. The defence quickly collapsed, and by the third day the whole garrison had surrendered – 45,000 prisoners, with 462 guns and 129 tanks. The Australian divisional commander (Major-General I. G. Mackay) said that each Matilda tank was worth a whole infantry battalion to him.

Immediately after the capture of Bardia, the 7th Armoured Division drove westward to isolate Tobruk until the Australians could come up to mount an assault on the coastal fortress. Tobruk was attacked on January 21st and fell next day – yielding a bag of 30,000 prisoners, 236 guns and eighty-seven tanks. Only sixteen Matildas were left for use in this assault, but once again they made the decisive penetration. That night some of the men of the RTR listened in to a news broadcast, and heard the commentator say: 'We suspect that the assault was led by a famous cavalry regiment.' One tankman was so incensed that he gave the box a hearty kick, exclaiming: 'You have to be colonial, black, or cavalry, to get any credit in this — war.' It was a justifiable reaction. For never in the history of warfare has a single fighting unit played such a decisive part in the issue of a series of battles as the 7th RTR did at Sidi Barrani, Bardia, and Tobruk in turn.

The rapid progress of the British advance into Cyrenaica was the more remarkable since it was made under a fresh handicap. Reinforcements, transport, and aircraft that should have been sent to O'Connor were held back in Egypt, and a number of units were even taken away from him. For Mr Churchill's imagination was now chasing a different hare. Following the scent of his old venture in the First World War, and stimulated by the way that the Greeks were standing up to the Italians, he pictured the possibility of creating a powerful combination of the Balkan countries against Germany. It was an attractive picture, but unrealistic, for the primitive Balkan armies had no power to withstand Germany's air and tank forces, while Britain could send them very little help.

Early in January Churchill decided to press the Greeks to accept a contingent of British tank and artillery units, to be landed at Salonika, and ordered Wavell to make immediate preparations for dispatching such a force – although it meant weakening O'Connor's small strength.

But General Metaxas, who was then head of the Greek Government, declined the proposal, saying that the force offered would be likely to provoke the German invasion without being nearly strong enough to counter it. Moreover the Commander-in-Chief, General Papagos, expressed the view that the British would be wiser to complete their conquest of Africa before attempting anything fresh, and splitting the effort.

This polite rebuff from the Greek Government coincided with O'Connor's capture of Tobruk, so the British Government now decided to allow him to push on another step and capture the port of Benghazi. That would complete the conquest of Cyrenaica, the eastern half of Italian North Africa. But the British Prime Minister continued to cherish his Balkan project, and Wavell was told not to give O'Connor any reinforcements that might subtract from the building up of a force for that theatre.

On receiving permission to push on, O'Connor once again achieved much more than could be expected from his meagre resources. (His mobile arm, the 7th Armoured Division, had shrunk to only fifty cruiser tanks, with ninety-five light tanks – which had very thin armour and no effective armour-piercing gun.) Finding the enemy in a strong position at Derna on the coast road, he planned to lever them out of it by a flanking move as soon as further supplies and cruiser tanks reached him. These were expected in time for him to resume the advance on February 12th.

But on the 3rd, air reconnaissance showed that the enemy was preparing to abandon the Benghazi corner, and to retreat to the Agheila bottleneck, where they could block the route from Cyrenaica into Tripolitania. Large columns were seen to be already on the way.

O'Connor immediately planned a bold stroke to intercept the enemy's withdrawal, employing only the depleted 7th Armoured Division under General Creagh, and dispatching it across the desert interior with the aim of reaching the coast road well beyond Benghazi. It had about 150 miles to go, from its position at Mechili – the first long stretch being across extremely rough country. It moved off with only two days' rations and a bare sufficiency of petrol – on one of the most daring ventures and breathless races in military history.

Caunter's 4th Armoured Brigade started at 8.30 AM on the 4th, preceded by the 11th Hussars' armoured-cars. (The other armoured brigade, the 7th, had been reduced to one unit only, the 1st Royal Tanks.) At midday an air report brought the disconcerting news that the retreating enemy were already south of Benghazi. In an attempt to hasten the interception, Creagh ordered Caunter to organize an entirely wheeled force of motor infantry and artillery, and send it ahead with the 11th Hussars under Colonel Combe. Caunter's objections to this were borne out by the confusion and delay caused in pulling out these units from the rear of the column, and in organizing special transport and signals for them. Moreover, on the terribly rough ground that was met in the afternoon, the tanks almost overtook the wheeled force. Caunter pushed on until after midnight, by moonlight, before pausing to allow his tank crews a few hours' rest.

In the morning (of the 5th), with easier ground, 'Combeforce' made faster progress. By the afternoon it had established a blocking position south of Beda Fomm across the enemy's two routes of retreat. That evening it trapped a very surprised column of Italian artillery and civilian evacuees.

Meanwhile Caunter's tanks, closely following up, had arrived at about 5 PM on the enemy's line of retreat past Beda Fomm. They broke up two columns of artillery and transport before dark. That action fittingly capped an advance in which they had actually covered 170 miles in thirty-three hours – a record in armoured mobility that has never been equalled. The roadlessness and ruggedness of the country made the feat all the more astonishing.

Next morning, the 6th, the enemy's main columns began to appear on the scene, escorted by tanks. There were over 100 new Italian cruiser tanks in all, whereas Caunter had only twenty-nine cruiser tanks. Fortunately, the Italian tanks came along in packets, instead of in a concentrated body, and kept near the road, whereas the British tanks skilfully manoeuvred to gain fire-positions where their hulls were concealed and protected by folds in the ground. A series of these tank battles went on all day, the brunt being borne by the nineteen cruiser tanks of the 2nd RTR, which were reduced to seven by the afternoon – when the 1st RTR of the other brigade arrived, with ten more cruisers. The 3rd and 7th Hussars, using their light tanks boldly, did much to distract and harass the enemy.

When night fell on the battlefield, sixty of the Italian tanks had been crippled, and a further forty were found abandoned in the morning, while only three of the British tanks had actually been knocked out. The Italian infantry and other troops surrendered in crowds when their protecting tanks were destroyed and they were left exposed.

Combe's force, acting as a back-stop, caught such fractions as managed to evade the 4th Armoured Brigade. The Italians' last effort to break out was made against this rear position soon after daylight, and headed by sixteen tanks, but was checked by the 2nd Battalion, Rifle Brigade.

Altogether 20,000 prisoners were taken in this battle of Beda Fomm, as well as 216 guns and 120 tanks. The total British strength, in both Caunter's and Combe's forces was only 3,000 men. When Bardia and its garrison fell on January 4th, Anthony Eden, who had just returned to the Foreign Office as Secretary of State after seven months at the War Office, had coined a new version of Churchill's famous phrase, saying 'never has so much been surrendered by so many to so few'. That was even more true of the crowning victory at Beda Fomm.*

* Much of the credit was due to a man who took no part in the campaign – Major-General P. C. S. Hobart, who had been appointed to command the armoured division in Egypt when it was originally formed in 1938, and had developed its high pitch of manoeuvring ability. But his ideas of how an

The radiance of victory, however, was soon dimmed. The complete extinction of Graziani's army had left the British with a clear passage through the Agheila bottleneck to Tripoli. But just as O'Connor and his troops were hoping to race on there – and throw the enemy out of his last foothold in North Africa – they were finally stopped by order of the British Cabinet.

On February 12th Churchill sent Wavell a long telegram which, after expressing delight that Benghazi had been captured 'three weeks ahead of expectation', directed him to halt the advance, leave only a minimum force to hold Cyrenaica, and prepare to send the largest possible force to Greece. Almost the whole of O'Connor's air force was removed immediately, leaving only one squadron of fighters.

What had produced this somersault? General Metaxas had died suddenly, on January 29th, and the new Greek Prime Minister was a man of less formidable character. Churchill saw an opportunity of reviving his cherished Balkan project, and was prompt to seize it. He again pressed his offer on the Greek Government – and this time they were persuaded. On March 7th, with Wavell's agreement and the approval of the Chiefs of Staff and the three Commanders-in-Chief, Middle East, the first contingent of a British force of 50,000 troops landed in Greece.

On April 6th the Germans invaded Greece, and the British were quickly driven to a second 'Dunkirk'. They narrowly escaped complete disaster, being evacuated by sea with great difficulty, leaving all their tanks, most of their other equipment, and 12,000 men behind in German hands.

O'Connor and his staff were confident that they could have captured Tripoli. Such an advance required the use of Benghazi as a base-port and some of the transport there had been reserved for the gamble in Greece. But all this had been worked out. General de Guingand, who later became Montgomery's Chief of Staff, has revealed that the Joint Planning Staff in the Middle East were convinced that Tripoli could be captured and the Italians swept out of Africa before the spring.

---

armoured force should be handled, and what it could achieve when operating in strategical independence of orthodox forces, had been contrary to the views of more conservative superiors. His 'heresy', coupled with an uncompromising attitude, had led to his removal from command in the autumn of 1939 – six months before the German panzer forces, applying the same ideas, proved their practicability.

General Warlimont, a leading member of Hitler's staff, has revealed that the German Supreme Command took the same view:

> We could not understand at the time why the British did not exploit the difficulties of the Italians in Cyrenaica by pushing on to Tripoli. There was nothing to check them.* The few Italian troops who remained there were panic-stricken, and expected the British tanks to appear at any moment.

On February 6th, the very day that Graziani's army was being finally wiped out at Beda Fomm, a young German general, Erwin Rommel – who had brilliantly led the 7th Panzer Division in the French campaign – was summoned to see Hitler and told to take command of a small German mechanized force that was to be sent to the Italians' rescue. It would consist of two small-scale divisions, the 5th Light and the 15th Panzer. But the transportation of the first could not be completed until mid-April, and that of the second not until the end of May. It was a slow programme – and the British had an open path.

On the 12th Rommel flew to Tripoli. Two days later a German transport arrived, carrying a reconnaissance battalion and an anti-tank battalion, as a first instalment. Rommel rushed them up to the front, and backed up this handful with dummy tanks that he quickly got built, in the hope of creating an air of strength. These dummies were mounted on Volkswagens, the 'people's motor-car' that was cheaply mass-produced in Germany. It was not until March 11th that the tank regiment of the 5th Light Division arrived in Tripoli.

Finding the British did not come on, Rommel thought he would try an offensive move with what he had. His first aim was merely to occupy the Agheila bottleneck. This succeeded so easily, on March 31st, that he decided to push on. It was evident to him that the British much overestimated his strength – perhaps deceived by his dummy tanks. Moreover the Germans had the balance of strength in the air, which helped to conceal from the British command their weakness on the ground, and led also to some of the misleading reports rendered by the RAF during the subsequent battles.

Rommel was lucky, too, in his timing. The 7th Armoured Division had been sent back to Egypt at the end of February to rest and refit. Its place was taken by part of the newly arrived and inexperienced 2nd Armoured Division – the other part had gone to Greece. The 6th Australian Division had been sent to Greece, and the 9th which replaced it

* Liddell Hart: *The Other Side of the Hill*, p 250n.

was short of both equipment and training. O'Connor too had been given a rest, and had been relieved by Neame, an untried commander. Moreover Wavell, as he later admitted, did not credit reports of an impending German attack. The figures justified his view, and he can hardly be blamed for not making allowance for a Rommel.

Disregarding higher orders to wait until the end of May, Rommel resumed his advance on April 2nd, with fifty tanks, followed up more slowly by two new Italian divisions. By mobility and ruse he sought to magnify his slight strength. Following the shock of Rommel's initial assault, his shadow loomed so large that his two slim fingers, nearly a hundred miles apart, became magnified into encircling horns.

The effect of this audacious thrust was magical. The British forces hastily fell back in confusion, and on April 3rd evacuated Benghazi. In this emergency O'Connor was sent up to advise Neame, but in the retreat their unescorted car ran into the back of a German spearhead group, on the night of the 6th, and both were taken prisoner. Meanwhile the one British armoured brigade had lost almost all its tanks in the long and hasty retreat, while the next day the commander of the 2nd Armoured Division, with a newly arrived motor brigade and other units, was surrounded at Mechili and had to surrender – the strength of the encircling force being magnified by the dust-clouds that Rommel's men raised, with lines of trucks, to disguise their weakness in tanks. The Italians were still lagging behind.

By April 11th the British were swept out of Cyrenaica and over the Egyptian frontier, except for a small force shut up in Tobruk. This was in its way as astonishing a feat as the earlier conquest of Cyrenaica, and had been even quicker.

The British had now to begin all over again their efforts to clear North Africa, and under much heavier handicaps than before – above all, the presence of Rommel. The price to be paid for forfeiting the golden opportunity of February 1941 was heavy.

CHAPTER TEN

The Conquest of Italian East Africa

When Fascist Italy entered the war in June 1940 on Mussolini's instigation, her forces in Italian East Africa – which since 1936 had included conquered Ethiopia – immensely outnumbered the British, as they did in North Africa. According to the Italian records the forces in that area amounted to some 91,000 white troops and close on 200,000 native troops – although the latter seems to have been largely on paper, and might more reasonably be estimated as about half the claimed number. In the early months of 1940, preceding Italy's entry into the war, the British strength was only some 9,000 British and native troops in the Sudan, and 8,500 British East African troops in Kenya.

In this vast theatre of war, a double theatre, the Italians were almost as slow to take the initiative as they were in North Africa. A prime reason was their awareness that they were unlikely to get further supplies of motor fuel and munitions through the British blockade. But that was hardly a good reason since it made it more important to exploit their great superiority of strength before the British forces in Africa could be adequately reinforced.

Early in July the Italians moved hesitantly forward from Eritrea, in the north-west, and occupied the town of Kassala, a dozen miles inside the Sudanese frontier, employing a force of two brigades, four cavalry regiments, and two dozen tanks – some 6,500 men – against an outpost held by a company, of about 300 men, of the Sudan Defence Force. Major-General William Platt, commanding in the Sudan, had then only three British infantry battalions for the whole of that large area, posted respectively at Khartoum, Atbara, and Port Sudan. Wisely, he did not throw them into the fight until he could see how the Italian invasion developed. Instead of pushing on, it stopped – after occupying a few other frontier posts such as Gallabat, just over the north-west frontier of Ethiopia, and Moyale, on the northern frontier of Kenya.

It was not until early in August that the Italians started a more serious offensive move, and that was launched against the easiest possible target – British Somaliland, the strip of coastal territory on the

African shore of the Gulf of Aden. Even that very limited move was defensive in motive. Indeed, Mussolini had ordered the Italians to stay on the defence. But the Duke of Aosta, who was Viceroy of Ethiopia, and supreme commander in that area, felt that the French Somaliland port of Djibouti offered an easy entry for the British into Ethiopia, and did not trust the armistice agreement with the French. So he decided to occupy the adjoining and larger area of British Somaliland.

The British garrison there, under Brigadier A. R. Chater, consisted of only four African and Indian battalions, with a British battalion, the 2nd Black Watch, on the way. The Italian invading force comprised twenty-six battalions provided with artillery and tanks. But the small Somaliland Camel Corps effectively delayed its advance, and Major-General A. R. Godwin-Austen arrived on the scene to take over just as the invaders reached the Tug Argan Pass on the approaches to Berbera, the seaport capital. Here the defenders put up such a tough defence that the attackers were kept at bay in a four-day battle, but in default of further reinforcements or defensive positions, the British force was evacuated by sea from Berbera – most of it being shipped to augment the British build-up now taking place in Kenya. It had inflicted over 2,000 casualties at a cost to itself of barely 250, and left an impression on the Italians that had a far-reaching strategic effect on their future action.

The British forces in Kenya, under Lieutenant-General Sir Alan Cunningham, who took over in November 1940, comprised the 12th African Division under Godwin-Austen (1st South African, 22nd East African, and 24th Gold Coast Brigades), shortly reinforced by the 11th African Division.

By the autumn the forces in Kenya had been raised to about 75,000 men – 27,000 South Africans, 33,000 East Africans, 9,000 West Africans, and about 6,000 British. Three divisions had been formed – the 1st South African, and the 11th and 12th African. In the Sudan there was now a total of 28,000 troops, including the 5th Indian Division, while the 4th Indian was to move there after taking part in the initial stage of the brilliant counterstroke against the Italians in North Africa. A squadron of tanks had been sent there from the 4th Royal Tanks. There was also the Sudan Defence Force.

Mr Churchill felt that such large British forces demanded more activity than had been shown, and he repeatedly pressed for more aggressive action than had yet been taken, or contemplated. Wavell, who was Commander-in-Chief of the Middle East, proposed in agreement with Cunningham that an advance from Kenya into Italian Somaliland

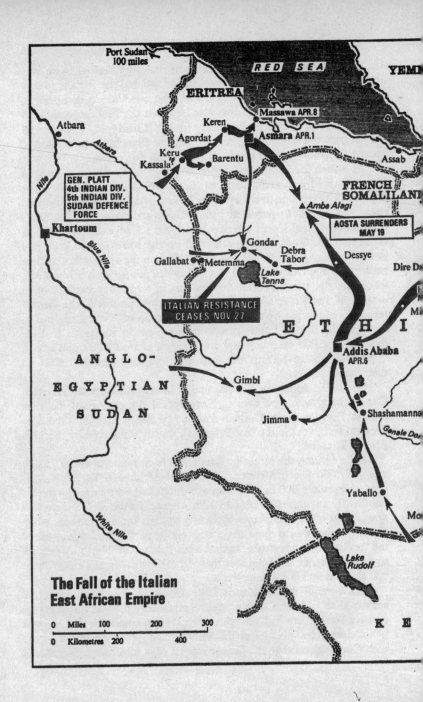

The Fall of the Italian East African Empire

Port Sudan
100 miles

RED SEA

YEMEN

ERITREA

Massawa APR.8

Keren

Agordat

Asmara APR.1

Assab

Atbara

Keru

Kassala

Barentu

FRENCH
SOMALILAND

GEN. PLATT
4th INDIAN DIV.
5th INDIAN DIV.
SUDAN DEFENCE
FORCE

Amba Alagi

AOSTA SURRENDERS
MAY 19

Khartoum

Gondar

Debra
Tabor

Dessye

Dire Da

Gallabat

Metemma

Lake
Tanna

ITALIAN RESISTANCE
CEASES NOV 27

E   T   H   I

Mi

Addis Ababa
APR.6

ANGLO-
EGYPTIAN
SUDAN

Gimbi

Jimma

Shashamanne

Genale Do

Yaballo

Mo

White Nile

Lake
Rudolf

K E

0   Miles   100   200   300

0   Kilometres   200   400

should begin in May or June after the spring rains. Wavell's doubts were increased by the tough resistance which Platt's first advance on the northern front had met in November, when launched against Gallabat by the 10th Indian Brigade under Brigadier W. J. Slim, a resolute leader who later became one of the most illustrious high commanders in the war. The initial attack on Gallabat succeeded, but the follow-up attack on the neighbouring post of Metemma suffered a check against an Italian colonial brigade of almost equal strength. That was largely due to the unexpected failure of a British battalion which had just been inserted in this Indian brigade, contrary to Slim's advice, for supposed stiffening. As later events showed, the Italian forces in this northern sector were much tougher than those elsewhere.

The only hopeful episodes of the winter were the activities of Brigadier D. A. Sandford, a retired officer who had been recalled to service on the outbreak of war, and subsequently sent into Ethiopia to raise revolt among the highland chiefs around Gondar, activities that were supported and extended during the winter by the still more unorthodox Captain Orde Wingate with a Sudanese battalion and his elusive 'Gideon Force'. The exiled Emperor Haile Selassie was brought back, by air, to Ethiopia on January 20th, 1941 – and barely three months later, on May 5th, he re-entered his capital, Addis Ababa, in company with Wingate – far earlier than even Churchill had imagined possible.

For under continued pressure from Churchill, and from Smuts in South Africa, Wavell and Cunningham had been spurred to open the invasion of Italian Somaliland from Kenya in February 1941. The port of Kismayu was captured with unexpected ease, thus simplifying the supply problem, whereupon Cunningham's forces crossed the Juba River, and pushed on some 250 miles to Mogadishu, the capital and larger port, which they occupied barely a week later, on February 25th. Here they captured an immense quantity of motor and air fuel, the speed of the advance having forestalled the planned demolitions, as at Kismayu. Good air support was another important factor in the rapid advance.

Cunningham's forces then turned inland, into Southern Ethiopia, and by March 17th the 11th African Division occupied Jijiga, close to the provincial capital of Harar, after a 400 mile advance. That brought them close to the frontier of former British Somaliland, where a small force from Aden had re-landed on the 16th. By March 29th, after some tougher resistance, Harar was occupied, and Cunningham's forces then swung westward towards the Ethiopian capital, Addis Ababa, 300 miles distant in the west centre of Ethiopia. Cunningham's forces occupied it barely a week later, on April 6th – a month before the Emperor Haile Selassie returned to his capital, escorted by Wingate. The remarkably ready surrender of the Italians was hastened by reports of the atrocities committed by Ethiopian irregulars among Italian women.

In the north, however, the opposition was much stiffer, as it had been from the outset. Here General Frusci, who was in command, had about 17,000 well-equipped Italian troops in the front in the area of Eritrea, with over three divisions farther back. General Platt's advance, starting in the third week of January, was carried out by the powerful 4th and 5th Indian Divisions. The Duke of Aosta had ordered the Italian forces in Eritrea to fall back before the British advance developed, and as a result the first serious stand was made at Keru, sixty miles east of Kassala and forty miles inside the Eritrean frontier.

Harder resistance was met by the two Indian columns in mountain-ous positions at Barentu and Agordat, respectively forty-five and seventy miles east of Keru. Fortunately the 4th Indian, under General Beresford-Peirse, reached the more distant objective first, and that eased the 5th Indian's advance on Barentu.

Wavell then realized the possibility of extending his objective, to the conquest of Eritrea as a whole, and gave fresh orders to General Platt accordingly. But the capital, Asmara, was more than 100 miles beyond Agordat (and the port of Massawa further still), while almost midway between lay the mountainous position of Keren, one of the strongest defensive positions in East Africa, and the only gateway to Asmara and Massawa, the Italian naval base.

The first attempts to force a passage, starting early on February 3rd, were a failure, and suffered repeated repulses in the following days. The Italian commander on the spot, General Carnimeo, showed splen-did fighting spirit and tactical skill. After more than a week of effort the attack was abandoned, and a long lull followed. Not until mid-March was the offensive resumed, when the 5th Indian Division was brought up and ready to join in. Once again the struggle was a pro-longed one, and a series of Italian counter-attacks threw back the at-tackers, but at last on March 27th a squadron of heavily armoured 'infantry' tanks of the 4th RTR broke through the block and pierced the Italian front – the same factor that in the hands of the 7th RTR had been decisive in the successive North African battles from Sidi Barrani to Tobruk.

That finished the battle of Keren, after fifty-three days. General Frusci's forces fell back southward into Ethiopia, and on April 1st the British occupied Asmara. Then they pushed on eastward to Massawa, fifty miles beyond, and produced its surrender, after a fight, on April 8th. That ended the Eritrean campaign.

Meanwhile the remaining Italian forces, under the Duke of Aosta, had withdrawn southward into Ethiopia, planning a final stand in a mountain position at Amba Alagi, some eighty miles south of Asmara. He had only 7,000 troops left, with forty guns, and barely three months' supplies. Moreover Italian morale was dwindling as a result of reports about the Ethiopian treatment of prisoners. So the Duke, though a gallant soldier, was more than willing to agree to surrender on 'honourable terms', which took place on May 19th – and brought the total of Italian prisoners to 230,000. There still remained isolated Italian forces under General Gazzera in the south-west of Ethiopia and in the north-west under General Nasi near Gondar, but these were rounded up in the summer and autumn respectively. That was the end of Mussolini's short-lived African Empire.

PART IV

THE SPREAD
1941

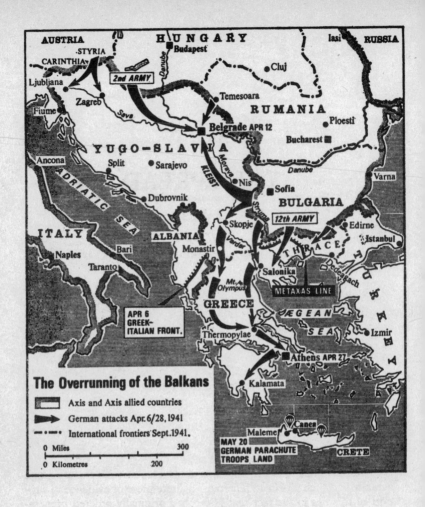

The Overrunning of the Balkans

CHAPTER ELEVEN

The Overrunning of the Balkans and Crete

Some claim that the dispatch of General Wilson's force to Greece, though it ended in a hurried evacuation, was justified because it produced six weeks' postponement of the invasion of Russia. This claim has been challenged, and the venture condemned as a political gamble, by a number of soldiers who were well acquainted with the Mediterranean situation – notably General de Guingand, later Montgomery's Chief of Staff, who was on the Joint Planning Staff in Cairo. They argue that a golden opportunity of exploiting the defeat of the Italians in Cyrenaica, and capturing Tripoli before German help arrived, was sacrificed in order to switch inadequate forces to Greece that had no real chance of saving her from a German invasion.

This latter view was confirmed by events. In three weeks, Greece was overrun and the British thrown out of the Balkans, while the reduced British force in Cyrenaica was also driven out by the German Afrika Korps, which had been enabled to land at Tripoli. These defeats meant a damaging loss of prestige and prospect for Britain, and only hastened the misery that was brought on the Greek people. Even if the Greek campaign was found to have retarded the invasion of Russia, that fact would not justify the British Government's decision, for such an object was not in their minds at the time.

It is of historical interest, however, to discover whether the campaign actually had such an effect. The most definite piece of evidence in support of this lies in the fact that Hitler had originally ordered preparations for the attack on Russia to be completed by May 15th, whereas at the end of March the tentative date was deferred about a month, and then fixed for June 22nd. Field-Marshal von Rundstedt said that the preparations of his Army Group had been hampered by the late arrival of the armoured divisions which had been employed in the Balkan campaign, and that this was the key-factor in the delay, in combination with the weather.

Field-Marshal von Kleist, who commanded the armoured forces under Rundstedt, was still more explicit. 'It is true', he said, 'that the forces employed in the Balkans were not large compared with our total strength, but the proportion of tanks employed there was high. The bulk of the tanks that came under me for the offensive against the Russian front in southern Poland had taken part in the Balkan offensive, and needed overhaul, while their crews needed a rest. A large number of them had driven as far south as the Peloponnese, and had to be brought back all that way.'*

The views of Field-Marshals von Rundstedt and von Kleist were naturally conditioned by the extent to which the offensive on their front was dependent on the return of these armoured divisions. Other generals attached less importance to the effect of the Balkan campaign. They emphasized that the main role in the offensive against Russia was allotted to Field-Marshal von Bock's Central Army Group in northern Poland, and that the chances of victory principally turned on its progress. A diminution of Rundstedt's forces, for the secondary role of his Army Group, might not have affected the decisive issue, as the Russian forces could not be easily switched. It might even have checked Hitler's inclination to switch his effort southward in the second stage of the invasion – an inclination that, as we shall see, had a fatally retarding effect on the prospects of reaching Moscow before the winter. The invasion, at a pinch, could have been launched without awaiting the reinforcement of Rundstedt's Army Group by the arrival of the divisions from the Balkans. But, in the event, that argument for delay was reinforced by doubts whether the ground was dry enough to attempt an earlier start. General Halder's view was that the weather conditions were not in fact suitable before the time when the invasion was actually launched.

The retrospective views of generals are not, however, a sure guide as to what might have been decided if there had been no Balkan complications. Once the tentative date had been postponed on that account the scales were weighted against any idea of striking before the extra divisions had returned from the quarter.

But it was not the Greek campaign that caused the postponement. Hitler had already reckoned with that commitment when the invasion of Greece was inserted in the 1941 programme, as a preliminary to the invasion of Russia. The decisive factor in the change of timing was the unexpected coup d'état in Yugo-Slavia that took place on March 27th, when General Simovich and his confederates overthrew the Government which had just previously committed Yugo-Slavia to a pact with the Axis. Hitler was so incensed by the upsetting news as to decide, that

* Liddell Hart: *The Other Side of the Hill*, p 251.

same day, to stage an overwhelming offensive against Yugo-Slavia. The additional forces, land and air, required for such a stroke involved a greater commitment than the Greek campaign alone would have done, and thus impelled Hitler to take his fuller and more fateful decision to put off the intended start of the attack on Russia.

It was the fear, not the fact, of a British landing that had prompted Hitler to move into Greece, and the outcome set his mind at rest. The landing did not even check the existing Government of Yugo-Slavia from making terms with Hitler. On the other hand, it may have encouraged Simovich in making his successful bid to overthrow the Government and defy Hitler – less successfully.

Still more illuminating was the summary of the operations in the Balkan campaign given by General von Greiffenberg, who was Chief of Staff of Field-Marshal List's 12th Army which conducted the Balkan campaign.

Greiffenberg's account emphasized, remembering the Allied lodgement at Salonika in 1915 which ultimately developed into a decisive strategic thrust in September 1918, that Hitler feared in 1941 that the British would again land in Salonika or on the southern coast of Thrace. This would place them in the rear of Army Group South when it advanced eastward into southern Russia. Hitler assumed that the British would try to advance into the Balkans as before – and recalled how at the end of World War I the Allied Balkan Army had materially contributed to the decision.

He therefore resolved, as a precautionary measure before beginning operations against Russia, to occupy the coast of Southern Thrace between Salonika and Dedeagach (Alexandropolis). The 12th Army (List) was earmarked for this operation, and included Kleist's Panzer Group. The army assembled in Rumania, crossed the Danube into Bulgaria, and from there was to pierce the Metaxas Line – advancing with its right wing on Salonika and its left wing on Dedeagach. Once the coast was reached, the Bulgarians were to take over the main protection of the coast, where only a few German troops were to remain. The mass of the 12th Army, especially Kleist's Panzer Group, was then to turn about and be sent northward via Rumania, to go into action on the southern sector of the Eastern Front. The original plan did not envisage the occupation of the main part of Greece.

When this plan was shown to King Boris of Bulgaria, he said that he did not trust Yugo-Slavia, which might threaten the right flank of the 12th Army. German representatives, however, assured King Boris that in view of the 1939 pact between Yugo-Slavia and Germany they anticipated no danger from that quarter. They had the impression that King Boris was not quite convinced.

He was proved right. When the 12th Army was about to begin operations from Bulgaria according to plan, the coup which led to the abdication of the Regent, Prince Paul, was suddenly launched in Belgrade, just before the movement of the troops began.

> It appeared that certain Belgrade circles disagreed with Prince Paul's pro-German policy and wanted to side with the Western powers. Whether the Western powers or the USSR backed the coup beforehand, we as soldiers cannot gauge. But at any rate it was not staged by Hitler! On the contrary it came as a very unpleasant surprise, and nearly upset the whole plan of operations of the 12th Army in Bulgaria.*

For example, Kleist's panzer divisions had to proceed immediately from Bulgaria north-westward against Belgrade. Another improvisation was an operation by the 2nd Army (Weichs), with quickly gathered formations based on Carinthia and Styria, southward into Yugo-Slavia. The flare-up in the Balkans compelled a postponement of the Russian campaign, from May to June. To this extent, therefore, the Belgrade coup materially influenced the start of Hitler's attack on Russia.

But the weather also played an important part in 1941, and that was accidental. East of the Bug–San line in Poland, ground operations are very restricted until May, because most roads are muddy and the country generally is a morass. The many unregulated rivers cause widespread flooding. The farther one goes east the more pronounced do these disadvantages become, particularly in the boggy forest regions of the Rokitno (Pripet) and Beresina. Even in normal times movement is very restricted before mid-May, but 1941 was an exceptional year. The winter had lasted longer. As late as the beginning of June the Bug was over its banks for miles.

Similar conditions prevailed farther north. General von Manstein, who was then commanding a spearhead panzer corps in East Prussia, said that heavy rain fell there during late May and early June. It is evident that if the invasion had been launched earlier the prospect would have been poor, and as Halder said, it is very doubtful whether an earlier date would have been practicable, quite apart from the Balkan hindrance. The weather of 1940 had been all too favourable to the invasion of the West, but the weather of 1941 operated against the invasion of the East.

* Blumentritt in Liddell Hart: *The Other Side of the Hill*, p 254.

When the Germans invaded Greece in April 1941, following the landing of a small British army of reinforcement at Salonika, the Greek Army was mainly aligned to cover the passages through the mountains from Bulgaria, where the German forces had assembled. But the expected advance down the Struma Valley masked a less direct move. German mechanized columns swerved westward from the Struma up the Strumitza Valley parallel with the frontier, and over the mountain passes into the Yugo-Slav end of the Vardar Valley. Thereby they pierced the joint between the Greek and Yugo-Slav armies, and exploited the penetration by a rapid thrust down the Vardar to Salonika. This cut off a large part of the Greek Army, anchored in Thrace.

The Germans followed up this stroke, not by a direct advance southward from Salonika past Mount Olympus, where the British army had taken up its position, but by another swerving thrust down through the Monastir Gap, farther west. The exploitation of this advance towards the west coast of Greece cut off the Greek divisions in Albania, turned the flank of the British and, by its threatened swerve back on to the line of retreat of the surviving Allied forces, produced the speedy collapse of all resistance in Greece. The bulk of the British and Allied forces were evacuated by sea to Crete.

The capture of Crete by an invasion delivered purely by air was one of the most astonishing and audacious feats of the war. It was, also, the most striking airborne operation of the war. It was performed at Britain's expense – and should remain a warning not to discount the risk of similar surprise strokes 'out of the blue' in the future.

At eight o'clock on the morning of May 20th, 1941, some 3,000 German parachute troops dropped out of the sky upon Crete. The island was held by 28,600 British, Australian, and New Zealand troops, along with two Greek divisions amounting in numbers to almost as many.

The attack had been expected, as a follow-up to the German conquest of the Balkans, and good information about the preparations had been provided by British agents in Greece. But the airborne threat was not regarded as seriously as it should have been. Churchill has revealed that General Freyberg, VC, who had been appointed to command in Crete on his suggestion, reported on May 5th: 'Cannot understand nervousness; am not in the least anxious about airborne attack.'* He

* Churchill: *The Second World War*, vol III, p 246.

showed more concern about seaborne invasion – a danger which was, in the event, dispelled by the Royal Navy.

Churchill felt anxious about the threat, 'especially from the air'. He urged that 'at least another dozen "I" [Infantry] tanks' should be sent to reinforce the mere half dozen that were there.* An even more fundamental weakness was the complete lack of air support – to combat the German dive-bombers and intercept the airborne troops. Even the provision of anti-aircraft guns was scanty.

By the first evening, the number of Germans on the island had been more than doubled, and was progressively reinforced – by parachute drop, by glider, and from the second evening onwards by troop-carriers. These began landing on the captured Maleme airfield while it was still swept by the defenders' artillery and mortar-fire. The final total of German troops brought by air was about 22,000. Many were killed and injured by crashes on landing, but those that survived were the toughest of fighters, whereas their numerically superior opponents were not so highly trained and some were still suffering from the shock of being driven out of Greece. More important were their deficiencies in equipment, and especially the lack of short-range wireless equipment. Nevertheless, many of these troops fought hard, and their stiff resistance had important effects that only became known later.

Optimism continued to prevail for a time in British high quarters. In the light of reports received, Churchill told the House of Commons on the second day that 'the greater part' of the airborne invaders had been wiped out. Middle East Headquarters went on for two more days talking about the Germans being 'mopped up'.

But on the seventh day, the 26th, the British commander in Crete reported: 'In my opinion the limit of endurance has been reached by the troops under my command ... our position here is hopeless.' Coming from such a stout-hearted soldier as Freyberg, this verdict was not questioned. Evacuation began on the night of the 28th, and ended on the night of the 31st – the Royal Navy suffering heavy losses from the enemy's dominant air force in its persistent efforts to bring away as many troops as possible. A total of 16,500 were rescued, including about 2,000 Greeks, but the rest were left dead or prisoner in German hands. The Navy had well over 2,000 dead. Three cruisers and six destroyers were sunk. Thirteen other ships were badly damaged, including two battleships and the only aircraft-carrier then in the Mediterranean Fleet.

The Germans had some 4,000 men killed, and about half as many

* Churchill: *The Second World War*, vol III, p 249.

wounded. Thus their permanent loss was less than a third of what the British had suffered, apart from the Greeks and local Cretan levies. But as the loss fell mostly on the picked troops of Germany's one existing parachute division, it had an unforeseen effect on Hitler that turned out to Britain's benefit.

At the moment, however, the collapse in Crete looked disastrous. It hit the British peoples all the harder because it followed hard on the heels of two other disasters. For in April the British forces had been swept out of Cyrenaica in ten days, by Rommel, and out of Greece within three weeks from the start of the German invasion. Wavell's winter success in capturing Cyrenaica from the Italians came to appear no more than a delusory break in the clouds. With this fresh run of defeats at German hands, and the spring renewal of the air 'Blitz' on England, the prospect was darker even than in 1940.

But Hitler did not follow up his third Mediterranean victory in any of the ways expected on the British side – a pounce upon Cyprus, Syria, Suez, or Malta. A month later he launched the invasion of Russia, and from that time on neglected the opportunities that lay open for driving the British out of the Mediterranean and the Middle East. If his forfeit was mainly due to his absorption in the Russian venture, it was also due to his reaction after the victory in Crete. The cost depressed him more than the conquest exhilarated him. It was such a contrast to the cheapness of his previous successes and far larger captures.

In Yugo-Slavia and Greece his new armoured forces had been as irresistible as in the plains of Poland and France, despite the mountain obstacles they met. They had swept through both countries like a whirlwind and knocked over the opposing armies like ninepins.

Field-Marshal List's army captured 90,000 Yugo-Slavs, 270,000 Greeks, and 13,000 British – at a cost to itself of barely 5,000 men killed and wounded, as later records showed. At the time British newspapers estimated the German loss as over a quarter of a million, and even a British official statement put them as 'probably 75,000'.

The blemish on Hitler's Cretan victory was not only the higher loss but the fact that it temporarily weakened the one new kind of landfighting force he had which could reach out and seize places over the sea without risking interception by the British Navy – which still dominated the seascape, despite its heavy losses. In effect, Hitler had sprained his wrist in Crete.

After the war General Student, the Commander-in-Chief of the German Airborne Forces, revealed, surprisingly, that Hitler was a reluctant convert to the scheme of attacking Crete:

He wanted to break off the Balkan campaign after reaching the south of Greece. When I heard this, I flew to see Göring and proposed the plan of capturing Crete by airborne forces alone. Göring – who was always easy to enthuse – was quick to see the possibilities of the idea, and sent me on to Hitler. I saw him on April 21. When I first explained the project Hitler said: 'It sounds all right, but I don't think it's practicable.' But I managed to convince him in the end.

In the operation we used our one Parachute Division, our one Glider Regiment and the 5th Mountain Division, which had no previous experience of being transported by air.*

The air support was provided by the dive-bombers and fighters of Richtofen's 8th Air Corps, which had been a decisive instrument in forcing the gate into Belgium and France successively in 1940.

No troops came by sea. Such a reinforcement had been intended originally, but the only sea transport available was a number of Greek caiques. It was then arranged that a convoy of these small vessels was to carry the heavier arms for the expedition – anti-aircraft and anti-tank guns, the artillery and some tanks – together with two battalions of the 5th Mountain Division ... they were told that the British Fleet was still at Alexandria – whereas it was actually on the way to Crete. The convoy sailed for Crete, ran into the fleet, and was scattered. The Luftwaffe avenged this setback by 'pulling a lot of hair' out of the British Navy's scalp. But our operations on land, in Crete, were much handicapped by the absence of the heavier weapons on which we had reckoned ...

At no point on May 20 did we succeed completely in occupying an airfield. The greatest degree of progress was achieved on Maleme airfield, where the valuable Assault Regiment fought against picked New Zealand troops. The night of May 20–21 was critical for the German Command. I had to make a momentous decision. I decided to use the mass of the parachute-reserves, still at my disposal, for the final capture of Maleme airfield. If the enemy had made an organized counterattack during this night or the morning of May 21, he would probably have succeeded in routing the much battered and

* This and the extracts on pages 144 and 145, from Student in Liddell Hart: *The Other Side of the Hill*, pp 238–43.

exhausted remnants of the Assault Regiment – especially as these were badly handicapped by shortage of ammunition.

But the New Zealanders made only isolated counterattacks. I heard later that the British Command expected, besides the airborne venture, the arrival of the main German forces by sea on the coast between Maleme and Canea, and consequently maintained their forces in occupation of the coast. At this decisive period the British Command did not take the risk of sending these forces to Maleme. On the 21st the German reserves succeeded in capturing the airfield and village of Maleme. In the evening the 1st Mountain Battalion could be landed, as the first air-transported troops – and so the battle for Crete was won by Germany.

But the price of victory was much heavier than had been reckoned by the advocates of the plan – partly because the British forces on the island were three times as large as had been assumed, but also from other causes.

Much of the loss was due to bad landings – there were very few suitable spots in Crete, and the prevailing wind blew from the interior towards the sea. For fear of dropping the troops in the sea, the pilots tended to drop them too far inland – some of them actually in the British lines. The weapon-containers often fell wide of the troops, which was another handicap that contributed to our excessive casualties. The few British tanks that were there shook us badly at the start – it was lucky there were not more than two dozen. The infantry, mostly New Zealanders, put up a stiff fight, though taken by surprise.

The Führer was very upset by the heavy losses suffered by the parachute units, and came to the conclusion that their surprise value had passed. After that he often said to me: 'The day of parachute troops is over.' . . .

When I got Hitler to accept the Crete plan, I also proposed that we should follow it up by capturing Cyprus from the air, and then a further jump from Cyprus to capture the Suez Canal. Hitler did not seem averse to the idea, but would not commit himself definitely to the project – his mind was so occupied with the coming invasion of Russia. After the shock of the heavy losses in Crete, he refused to attempt another big airborne effort. I pressed the idea on him repeatedly, but without avail.

So the British, Australian, and New Zealand losses in Crete were not without compensating profit. Student's project of capturing the Suez Canal may have been beyond attainment, unless Rommel's panzer forces in Africa had also been strongly reinforced, but the capture of Malta would have been an easier task. Hitler was persuaded to undertake it a year later, but then changed his mind and cancelled it. Student said: 'He felt that if the British Fleet appeared on the scene, all the Italian ships would bolt for their home ports and leave the German airborne forces stranded.'

CHAPTER TWELVE

Hitler Turns against Russia

The whole outlook of the war was revolutionized when Hitler invaded Russia on June 22nd, 1941 – a day before the anniversary of Napoleon's invasion of 1812. That step proved as fatal to Hitler as it had to his forerunner, though the end did not come so quickly.

Napoleon was forced to retreat from Russia before the end of the year, and the Russians entered *his* capital in April of the second year following his invasion. Hitler was not driven out of Russia until three years had passed, and the Russians did not enter *his* capital until April of the fourth year. He had pentrated twice as far into Russia as Napoleon had done, though failing to repeat Napoleon's illusory success in entering Moscow. His deeper penetration was due to superior means of mobility. But this was not adequate for the fulfilment of his purpose. Space spelt first his frustration, and then his defeat.

History repeated itself also in the auxiliary effects of the aggressor's suicidal step. It brought Britain reprieve from a situation that appeared hopeless in the eyes of most people outside her own insular boundaries. It was obvious to them how desperate was the position of a small island on the edge of a hostile continent, which enveloped it more closely than in Napoleonic times. The value of the sea-moat was diminished by the development of airpower. The industrialization of the island had made it dependent on imports, and thus multiplied the menace of submarine power. By refusing to consider any peace offer the British Government had committed the country to a course that under such conditions was bound, logically, to lead through growing exhaustion to eventual collapse – even if Hitler abstained from attempting its quick conquest by invasion. The course of no compromise was equivalent to slow suicide.

The United States might pump in 'air' to keep Britain afloat, but that would merely suffice to prolong the process, not to avert the end. Moreover the measure of this respite was offset by Churchill's mid-summer decision to pursue the bombing of Germany with all Britain's

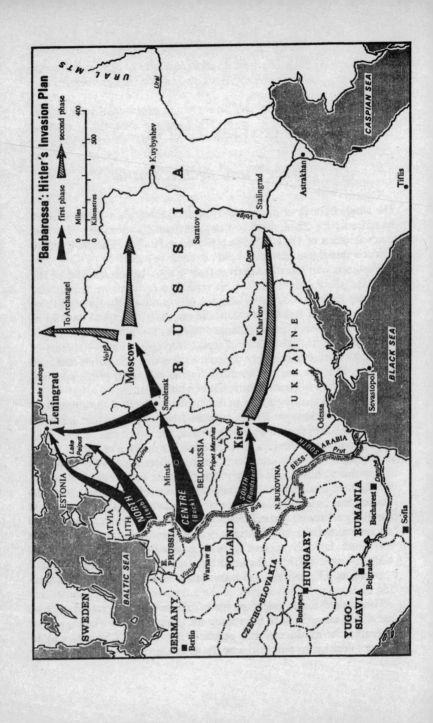

'Barbarossa': Hitler's Invasion Plan

puny strength. Such bombing attacks could amount to no more than pin-pricks, but they inherently tended to hinder Hitler's inclination to turn his attention elsewhere.

But the British people took little account of the hard facts of their situation. They were instinctively stubborn and strategically ignorant. Churchill's inspiring speeches helped to correct the depression of Dunkirk, and supplied the tonic the islanders wanted. They were exhilarated by his challenging note, and did not pause to ask whether it was strategically warranted.

Deeper than the influence of Churchill was the effect of Hitler. His conquest of France and near approach to their shores aroused them as no earlier evidence of his tyranny and aggressiveness had done. They reacted once again in their long-bred way – intent to keep their teeth in Hitler's skin at any cost. Never was their collective characterization as a bulldog so clearly demonstrated, and justified, in all its sublime stupidity.

Once again a conqueror of the West was confounded by a people who 'did not see that they were beaten'. Hitler understood them better than Napoleon, as *Mein Kampf* shows, and he had thus taken unusual pains to avoid wounding their pride. But he had reckoned on their practical sense, and was baffled that they could not see the hopelessness of the outlook nor recognize that the conditions framed in his peace offer were extraordinarily easy considering the circumstances. In that state of confusion he hesitated as to what he should do next, and then turned in the same direction as Napoleon – to the conquest of Russia as the preliminary to a final settlement with Britain.

It was not a sudden turn of his mind, but made by degrees. It was also complex in causation – more complex than Napoleon's turn – and cannot be explained simply by any single factor or reason.

The heavy losses of the Luftwaffe over southern England were less decisive strategically, though more decisive tactically, than the check to the French fleet off Cape Finisterre in 1805. For Göring's defeat had no such instantaneous effect on Hitler's mind as Villeneuve's retreat had produced on Napoleon's. For the time being, Hitler persevered with his efforts to bend the British people's will, and merely changed the form of his pressure – from an attempted destruction of the defending air force to night bombing of the industrial cities. The intermittent relaxation of pressure was due, apart from weather, to a wavering of his mind. He seems to have been reluctant to proceed to extremes against Britain if he could possibly persuade her to accept peace, and he clung to the hope while pursuing the aim clumsily.

Meanwhile his mind was moving with increasing momentum in another direction, under the influence of his economic needs and fears, multiplied by his prejudices. Although his pact with Stalin had paved the way for his victory in the West, his conquests there had been largely the product of circumstances, whereas he had always contemplated the overthrow of Soviet Russia. For him that idea was more than a matter of expediency in pursuit of ambition; anti-Bolshevism was his most profound emotional conviction.

This eastward impulse was strongly influenced by Britain's resistance, but its revival had begun before Britain's rejection of his peace offer.

Early in June 1940, while Hitler was still engaged in the French campaign, Stalin had seized the opportunity to occupy Lithuania, Estonia, and Latvia. Hitler had agreed that the Baltic States should be within the Soviet Union's sphere of influence, not to their actual occupation, and he felt that he had been tricked by his partner, although most of his advisers realistically considered the Russian move into the Baltic States to be a natural precaution, inspired by fear of what Hitler might attempt after his victory in the West. Hitler's deep distrust of Russia had been shown in the way he worried throughout the campaign in the West at having left only ten divisions in the East, facing a hundred Russian divisions.

Then on June 26th, again without notice to her partner, Russia addressed an ultimatum to Rumania, demanding the immediate restoration of Bessarabia, and the surrender of northern Bukovina in addition – as a 'small compensation' for the way that Russia had been 'robbed' of the former province in 1918. The Rumanian Government was allowed only 24 hours for its answer, and when it yielded to the threat the Russian troops swarmed in at once, by air as well as overland.

That was worse than a 'slap in the face' for Hitler, since it placed the Russians ominously close to the Rumanian oilfields on which he counted for his own supply, now that he was cut off from overseas sources. In the following weeks he became increasingly nervous about that risk, and anxious about its bearing on the air offensive against England. He became correspondingly suspicious of Stalin's intentions. On July 29th he spoke to Jodl about the possibility of having to fight Russia if she tried to seize the Rumanian oilfields. A few weeks later, as a countermove, he began the transfer of two armoured and ten infantry divisions to Poland. A directive of September 6th to the Counter-Intelligence Service, said: 'The Eastern territory will be manned more strongly in the weeks to come. These regroupings must not create the impression in Russia that we are preparing for an offensive in the East.' The strength of the German forces was to be camouflaged by frequent changes of area:

On the other hand, Russia will realize that strong and highly-trained German troops are stationed in the Government-General, in the Eastern provinces, and in the Protectorate. She should draw the conclusion that we are ready to protect our interests, particularly in the Balkans, with strong forces against Russian seizure.

This directive had a predominantly defensive note. It showed concern to provide a deterrent to Russian aggression rather than foreshadowing German aggression. But because of the distance that separated his front from the oilfields he had to safeguard, he could not count on being able to give them direct protection, and was prompted to consider an offensive diversion on the Polish front. The idea of such a diversion soon developed into that of a major invasion – to forestall the particular risk by excising the whole danger.

In mid-September reports came that the Russian propaganda service had switched to a line of anti-German talk within the Red Army. This showed the Russians' suspicious reaction to the first increase of the German forces in the East, and their promptness to prepare their troops for a Russo-German conflict. But to Hitler's mind it was evidence of their offensive designs. He began to feel that he could not afford to wait – until he had completed and consolidated his victory in the West – before dealing with Russia. His fears, ambitions, and prejudices reacted on one another, giving impetus to the fresh turn of his thought. In that state of mind his suspicions were easily quickened. Puzzled by the way that the British did not seem to realize their hopeless situation, he looked to Russia for the explanation. Over and over again as the months went on he said, to Jodl and others, that Britain must be hoping for Russian intervention, or she would have given in. Already there must be some secret agreement. The dispatch of Sir Stafford Cripps to Moscow, and his conversations with Stalin, were confirmation of it. Germany must strike soon, or she would be strangled. Hitler could not see that the Russians, likewise, might have fears of his aggression.

The plan for an offensive against Russia had already been sketched out when General Paulus (later to become famous as commander of the army that was trapped by the Russians at Stalingrad) became Deputy

Chief of the General Staff at the beginning of September. He was instructed 'to examine its possibilities'. The objectives defined were, first, the destruction of the Russian armies in western Russia; and then an advance into Russia deep enough to secure Germany against the risk of air attack from the east, carried as far as a line from Archangel to the Volga.

By the beginning of November the plan was completed in detail, and then tested in a couple of war games. Hitler had now become less anxious about a Russian offensive – yet more inclined to take the offensive against Russia. The preparation and contemplation of vast strategic plans always intoxicated him. The doubts which his generals expressed, when he disclosed the trend of his mind, merely served to make it more definite. Had he not proved right on each issue where they had doubted his capacity to succeed? He must prove them wrong again, and more strikingly – their doubts showed that for all their subservience, they still had an underlying distrust of him as an amateur. Moreover, his admirals and his generals were apprehensive about an oversea move against England – and he could not remain passive. He had set on foot plans for a move through Spain against Gibraltar, to close the western end of the Mediterranean, but that was too small an operation to satisfy his gigantic ambition.

A fresh development at the end of October had an influence on his decision – and a greater one ultimately on its outcome. This was Mussolini's invasion of Greece, launched without reference to Hitler, who was incensed by his junior partner's disregard for his guidance, by the way it upset his own programme, and by the possibility that the Italians might establish themselves in his intended sphere. Although the last risk soon waned with the Italian reverses, Mussolini's independent initiative led Hitler to expedite his own Balkan moves. It formed a fresh reason for deferring the completion of his western programme, and accentuated the easterly turn of his mind. As he had to outstrip his associates in a race for control of the Balkans, he would settle with Russia next, and leave the British problem until later. It was not a clearcut decision even yet, but it was the thought uppermost in his mind.

On November 10th Molotov arrived in Berlin to discuss a wide range of questions, including the German suggestion that Russia should definitely join the Axis. At the end of the conversations an agreed communiqué was issued, saying: 'The exchange of ideas took place in an atmosphere of mutual trust, and led to a mutual understanding on all important questions interesting Germany and the Soviet Union.' Privately, too, the German participants were fairly well satisfied with the results, which were summed up thus on the 16th.

> For the time being there will be no fixed treaty. Russia appears willing to join the Three Power Pact after several further questions have been clarified ... Molotov is notified of contemplated German action in the Balkans in support of Italy and raises no objection. He suggests the creation of conditions suitable for Russian influence in Bulgaria, similar to German influence in Rumania, but this suggestion is not entered into by the Germans. Germany, however, expresses her disinterestedness in Turkey's domination of the Dardanelles and sympathy with Russian desires for bases there ...

But 'mutual trust' was entirely lacking, and the diplomatic phrase never had a more hollow ring. On the 12th Hitler's War Directive No. 18 had said:

> Political discussions have been initiated with the aim of clarifying Russia's attitude for the time being. Irrespective of the results of these discussions, all preparations for the East which have already been verbally ordered will be continued.

While the diplomats were talking the military plans were progressing. Hitler himself did not find the result of the conversations as satisfactory as others did, regarded Russia's further questions about the Three Power Pact as pure evasion, and was dominated by his growing desire to take the offensive. Raeder, who saw him on the 14th, noted that 'the Leader is still inclined to instigate the conflict with Russia'. After Molotov left, Hitler saw a number of his executives and made it plain to them that he was going to invade Russia. Their attempts to dissuade him from the venture were in vain. When they argued that it meant war on two fronts – a situation which had proved fatal to Germany in the First World War – he retorted that it was impossible to rely on Russia remaining quiet until Britain's resistance was broken. To overcome Britain required an expansion of the air force and navy, which meant reducing the army, but no such reduction was feasible while Russia remained a menace. The situation had been changed by 'Russia's unreliability, as evident in the Balkan States'. So 'Operation Sealion' would have to be postponed.

On December 5th Hitler received Halder's report on the eastern plan, and on the 18th issued 'Directive No. 21 – Case Barbarossa.' It opened with the decisive statement: 'The German armed forces must be prepared to crush Soviet Russia in a quick campaign before the end of the war against England.'

For this purpose the Army will have to employ all available units, with the reservation that the occupied countries will have to be safe-guarded against surprise attacks. The concentration of the main effort of the Navy remains unequivocally against England!

If the occasion arises, I shall order the concentration of troops for action against Soviet Russia eight weeks before the intended begin-ning of operations. Preparations requiring more time are - if this has not already been done - to begin immediately, and are to be com-pleted by May 15, 1941. [This was considered the earliest possible date for suitable weather conditions.] Great caution has to be exer-cised so that the intention to attack will not be recognized . . .

The mass of the Russian Army in Western Russia is to be des-troyed in daring operations by driving four deep wedges with tanks, and the retreat of the enemy's battle-ready forces into the wide spaces of Russia is to be prevented.

The directive went on to say that if these results did not suffice to cripple Russia, her last industrial area in the Urals could be eliminated by the Luftwaffe. The Red Fleet would be paralysed by the capture of the Baltic bases. Rumania would help by pinning down the Russian forces in the south and by providing auxiliary service in the rear - Hitler had sounded the new Rumanian dictator, General Antonescu, in November about participating in an attack on Russia.

The phrase 'if occasion arises' has an indefinite sound, but there seems little doubt that Hitler's intention was fixed. The qualification may be explained by a later passage in the directive: 'All orders which shall be issued by the High Commanders in accordance with this in-struction have to be clothed in such terms that they may be taken as measures of precaution in case Russia should change her present atti-tude towards ourselves.' The plan was to be cloaked by an elaborate deception programme, and it came naturally to Hitler to take the lead in this respect.

Moreover, deception had to be practised on his own people as well as on the enemy. So many of those to whom he broached the project were troubled about the risks of invading Russia, especially as it meant a two-front war, that he thought it wise to wear the appearance of reserving a final decision. This would give them time to become acclimatized to the change of wind, while giving him time to produce more persuasive evidence of Russia's hostile intentions. His generals, in particular, expressed such doubts that he was anxious about the effect of their half-heartedness. Although he could command obedience under the oath they had given him, that would not suffice to produce in their minds the determination required for success. As he had to make use of them as professional instruments it was necessary to convince them.

On January 10th a fresh treaty was signed with Russia that embodied the results of the November conversations with Molotov on frontier and economic questions. The surface was thus made to look smoother. But Hitler's private view was expressed in his comment that Stalin was an 'ice-cold blackmailer'. At the same time disquieting reports came from Rumania and Bulgaria about Russian activity there.

On the 19th Hitler was visited by Mussolini, and at this meeting spoke of his difficulties with Russia. He did not reveal his own offensive plans, but significantly mentioned that he had received a strong protest from Russia about the concentration of German troops in Rumania. An important sidelight on his own thought was contained in his remark: 'Formerly Russia would have been no danger at all, for she cannot imperil us in the least; but now in the age of airpower, the Rumanian oilfields can be turned into an expanse of smoking debris, by air attack from Russia and the Mediterranean, and the life of the Axis depends on these oilfields.' That was also his argument to his own generals who suggested that, even if the Russians were intending an invasion, the risk could be adequately met by increasing the defensive strength of the German forces behind the frontier, instead of launching an offensive into Russia.

On February 3rd Hitler approved the final text of the 'Barbarossa' plan, following a conference of his military chiefs at Berchtesgaden, in which the points of the plan were unfolded. Keitel gave an estimate of the enemy's strength in western Russia as approximately 100 infantry divisions, twenty-five cavalry divisions, and the equivalent of thirty mechanized divisions. This was close to the mark, for when the invasion was launched the Russians had available in the west 88 infantry divisions, seven cavalry divisions, and fifty-four tank and motorized divisions. Keitel then said that the German strength would be not quite so large, 'but far superior in quality'. Actually the invading armies comprised 116 infantry divisions (of which fourteen were motorized), a cavalry division, and nineteen armoured divisions – besides nine lines-of-communication divisions. The enumeration of strength was not calculated to allay the disquiet of the generals, for it showed they were

GERMAN ARMY GROUPS IN THE EAST*
Showing Changes of Designation and Commanders
June 1941 – May 1945

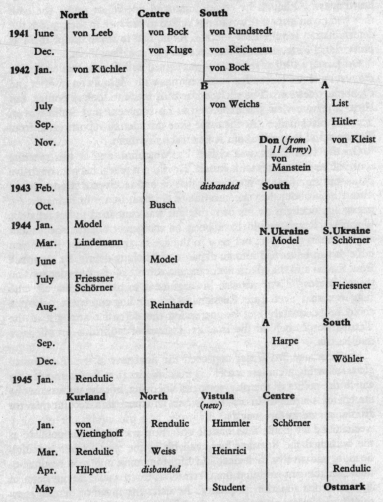

	North	**Centre**	**South**	
1941 June	von Leeb	von Bock	von Rundstedt	
Dec.		von Kluge	von Reichenau	
1942 Jan.	von Küchler		von Bock	
		B		**A**
July		von Weichs		List
Sep.				Hitler
Nov.			**Don** (*from 11 Army*) von Manstein	von Kleist
1943 Feb.		*disbanded*	**South**	
Oct.		Busch		
1944 Jan.	Model		**N. Ukraine** Model	**S. Ukraine** Schörner
Mar.	Lindemann			
June		Model		
July	Friessner Schörner			Friessner
Aug.		Reinhardt	**A**	**South**
Sep.			Harpe	
Dec.				Wöhler
1945 Jan.	Rendulic			
	Kurland	**North**	**Vistula** (*new*)	**Centre**
Jan.	von Vietinghoff	Rendulic	Himmler	Schörner
Mar.	Rendulic	Weiss	Heinrici	
Apr.	Hilpert	*disbanded*		Rendulic
May			Student	**Ostmark**

* Reproduced by kind permission of Lieutenant-Colonel Albert Seaton from Appendix B of his book *The Russo-German War, 1941–1945* (London: Arthur Barker, 1970).

embarking on a great offensive without any odds in their favour, and with marked adverse odds in the decisive element – the armoured forces. It was clear that the planners were gambling heavily on the superiority of quality.

Keitel continued: 'Russian operational intentions are unknown. There are no strong forces at the frontier. Any retreat could only be of small extent, since the Baltic States and the Ukraine are vital to the Russians for supply reasons.' That seemed reasonable at the time, but proved an over-optimistic assumption.

The invading forces were to be divided into three army groups, and their operational tasks were outlined. The northern one (under Leeb) was to attack from East Prussia through the Baltic states towards Leningrad. The central one (under Bock) was to strike from the Warsaw area towards Minsk and Smolensk, along the Moscow highway. The southern one (under Rundstedt) was to attack south of the Pripet Marshes, extending down to Rumania, with the Dnieper and Kiev as its objectives. The main weight was to be concentrated in the central group, to give it a superiority of strength. It was reckoned that there would be bare equality in the north, and an inferiority of strength in the southern sector.

In his survey, Keitel remarked that Hungary's attitude was still doubtful, and emphasized that arrangements with those countries that might cooperate with Germany could be made only at the eleventh hour, for reasons of secrecy. Rumania, however, had to be an exception to this rule, because her cooperation was 'vital'. (Hitler had just previously seen Antonescu again, and asked him to permit German troops to pass through Rumania to support the Italians in Greece, but Antonescu had hesitated, arguing that such a step might precipitate a Russian invasion of Rumania. At a third meeting Hitler promised him not only the return of Bessarabia and northern Bukovina, but the possession of a stretch of southern Russia 'up to the Dnieper' as a recompense for Rumanian aid in the attack.)

Keitel added that the Gibraltar operation was no longer possible as the bulk of the German artillery had been sent east. While 'Operation Sealion' had also been shelved, 'everything possible should be done to maintain the impression among our own troops that the invasion of Britain is being further prepared'. To spread the idea certain areas on the Channel coast and in Norway were to be suddenly closed, while as a double bluff the eastward concentration was to be represented as a deception exercise for the landing in England.

The military plan was coupled with a large-scale economic 'Plan

Oldenburg' for the exploitation of the conquered Soviet territory. An Economic Staff was created, entirely separate from the General Staff. A report of May 2nd, on its examination of the problem, opened with the statements : 'The war can only be continued if all armed forces are fed by Russia in the third year of the war. There is no doubt that many millions of people will starve to death in Russia if we take out of the country the things necessary for us.' It is not clear whether this was simply a cold-blooded scientific statement or intended as a warning against excessive aims and demands. The report went on to say : 'The seizure and transfer of oil seeds and oil cakes are of prime importance; grain is only secondary.' An earlier report by General Thomas, Chief of the War Economy Department of the OKW (Armed Forces General Staff), had pointed out that the conquest of all European Russia might relieve Germany's food problem, if the transport problem could be solved, but would not meet other important parts of her economic problem – the supply of 'india rubber, tungsten, copper, platinum, tin, asbestos, and manila hemp would remain unsolved until communication with the Far East can be assured'. Such warnings had no effect in restraining Hitler. But another conclusion, that 'the Caucasian fuel supply is indispensable for the exploitation of the occupied territories', was to have a very important effect in spurring him to extend his advance to the point of losing his balance.

The 'Barbarossa' plan suffered even worse from a preliminary upset that had far-reaching delayed effect. This was due to the psychological effect, on Hitler, of the double diplomatic rebuff he received from Greece and Yugo-Slavia, with British backing.

Before striking at Russia Hitler wanted to have his right shoulder free – from British interference. He had hoped to secure control of the Balkans without serious fighting – by practising armed diplomacy. He felt that after his victories in the West it ought to succeed more easily than ever. Russia had smoothed his way into Rumania by her push into Bessarabia; Rumania had fallen into his arms on the recoil. The next step also proved easy. On March 1st the Bulgarian Government swallowed his bribe and committed itself to a pact whereby the German forces were allowed to move through its territory and take up positions on the Greek frontier. The Soviet Government broadcast its disapproval of this departure from neutrality, but its abstention from anything more forcible made Hitler more sure that Russia was not ready for war.

The Greek Government was less responsive to Hitler's diplomatic approaches, as was natural after the way Greece had been invaded by his Axis partner. Nor did the Greek Government wilt at his threats. The spirit of the Greek people had been aroused and was heightened by their success in repelling Mussolini's invasion. In February arrangements had been made for their reinforcement by British troops, and these began to land a few days after the Germans' entry into Bulgaria.

The challenge provoked Hitler to put under way his attack on Greece – which was launched a month later. This was a needless diversion from his main path. For the force that Britain could furnish was not large enough to be capable of doing more than cause a slight irritation to his right shoulder, and the Greeks were fully occupied in dealing with the Italians.

The adverse effect on his Russian plan was intensified by the events in Yugo-Slavia. Here his approach had a favourable start. Under German pressure the Yugo-Slav Government agreed to link itself to the Axis on a compromise basis of being released from military obligations, but with the secret condition that the Belgrade–Nish rail line towards the Greek frontier was to be available for German troops. The Yugo-Slav representatives signed the Pact on March 25th. Two days later a military coup d'état was carried out in Belgrade by General Simovich, the Chief of the Yugo-Slav Air Force, and a group of young officers. They seized control of the radio station and the telephone centre, turned out the Government, established a new one under Simovich's leadership, and then defied the German demands. British agents had helped to foster the plot, and when the news of its success reached London Churchill announced in a speech: 'I have great news for you and the whole country. Early this morning Yugo-Slavia found its soul.' He went on to declare that the new Government would receive 'all possible aid and succour' from Britain.

The coup revolutionized the Balkan situation. Hitler could not tolerate such an affront, and Churchill's glee infuriated him. He at once decided to invade Yugo-Slavia as well as Greece. The necessary moves were made so swiftly that he was able to launch the blow ten days later, on April 6th.

The direct results of this Balkan defiance were pitiful. Yugo-Slavia was overrun within a week, and her capital devastated by the opening air attack. Greece was overrun in just over three weeks, and the British force hustled back into its ships, after a long retreat with little fighting. It had been out-manoeuvred at each stage. The outcome reflected on Churchill's judgement, and on that of those who supported him by declaring the feasibility of a successful military intervention – in view not merely of Britain's loss of credit but of the vast burden of misery that was cast on the people of Yugo-Slavia and Greece. The sense of being let down had lasting effects. Moreover, it is one of the ironies of history that the ultimate issue of Churchill's initiative was the resurrection of Yugo-Slavia in the form of a state hostile to all he represented.

But the indirect results of the episode were vital, and they reflected on Hitler's judgement. Operating with such a small margin of force – even when reckoned as quantity × quality – he could not afford to conduct a campaign in Yugo-Slavia and Greece at the same time as his invasion of Russia. A particular handicap was his numerical disadvantage in tanks compared with the Russians. A quick conquest of the Balkans depended on employing panzer divisions, and he would need every one of them that could be collected before he could venture to launch the offensive in Russia. So on April 1st 'Barbarossa' was postponed – from the middle of May to the second half of June.

It remains an amazing military achievement that Hitler was able to conquer two countries so quickly that he could keep the new date of entry into Russia. Indeed, his generals considered that if the British had succeeded in holding Greece 'Barbarossa' could not have been carried out. In the event, the delay was only five weeks. But it was a factor in forfeiting his chance of victory over Russia, which can be coupled with the Yugo-Slav coup d'état, a fortuitous delay in August – from indecision of mind – and with the early coming of winter that year.

By May 1st the British had re-embarked from the southern beaches of Greece, save for those who were cut off and captured. That same day Hitler fixed the date of 'Barbarossa'. His directive summarized the respective strengths and then added:

Estimate of the course of operations – Presumably violent battles on the frontiers, lasting up to four weeks. In the course of the further development weaker resistance is expected. A Russian will fight on an appointed spot to his last breath.

On June 6th Keitel issued the detailed timetable for the venture. Besides enumerating the forces to be employed in the invasion, it showed that forty-six infantry divisions had been left in the West facing Britain, though no more than one was motorized, and only one armoured brigade had been left there. Operations 'Attila' (the seizure of French North Africa) and 'Isabella' (the counter to a possible British move in Portugal) could 'still be executed at ten days' notice, but not simultaneously'. 'Luftflotte 2 has been withdrawn from action and transferred to the East, while Luftflotte 3 has taken over sole command in the conduct of air warfare against Britain.'

These orders intimated that negotiations with the Finnish General Staff, to secure their cooperation in the attack, had begun on May 25th. The Rumanians, already secured, were to be informed of the final arrangements on June 15th. On the 16th the Hungarians were to be given a hint to guard their frontier more strongly. On the following day all schools in eastern Germany were to be closed. German merchant ships were to leave Russia without attracting notice, and outward sailings were to cease. As from the 18th 'the intention to attack need no longer be camouflaged'. It would then be too late for the Russians to carry out any large-scale reinforcement measures. The latest possible time for the cancellation of the offensive was given as 1300 hours on the 21st, and the codeword in that contingency would be 'Altona' – for starting the attack it would be 'Dortmund'. The hour fixed for crossing the frontier was 0330 on the 22nd.

Despite German precautions, the British Intelligence Service obtained remarkably good information of Hitler's intentions long in advance, and conveyed it to the Russians. It even accurately predicted the exact date of the invasion – a week before it was finally fixed. But its repeated warnings were received with an attitude of disbelief, and of continued trust in the Soviet–German Pact, which the British found as baffling as it was exasperating. They felt that the Russian disbelief was genuine – that feeling was reflected in Churchill's broadcast when the news of Hitler's attack came – and when the Red Army suffered initial disasters they ascribed these partly to the results of it being taken by surprise.

A study of the Russian press and broadcasts would hardly have supported that impression. From April onwards they contained significant indications of precautionary measures, while showing an awareness of German troop movements. At the same time there were much more prominent references to Germany's strict observance of the Pact, combined with denunciations of British and American attempts to sow discord between Russia and Germany, especially by spreading rumours of German preparations to strike at Russia. A broadcast of this nature on June 13th, in Stalin's distinctive style, remarked that 'the dispatch of German troops into the east and north-east areas of Germany must be assumed to be due to motives which have no connexion with Russia' – a remark that might well encourage Hitler to assume that his deception programme had here succeeded in making the desired impression. Double bluff can be met by redoubling. The same broadcast answered foreign reports of the call-up of Russian reservists by explaining that this was merely for training prior to the usual summer manoeuvres. On the 20th Moscow wireless gave a glowing account of the military exercises that were in progress, near the Pripet Marshes – which may have been calculated to fortify confidence at home. It also announced that the civil air raid defences of Moscow were to be tested 'under realistic conditions' on Sunday, the 22nd. Even so, foreign reports of a coming German invasion were once again described as 'delirious fabrications by forces hostile to Russia'.

The Germans were informed of the British efforts to warn the Russians. Indeed, on April 24th their naval attaché in Moscow reported: 'The British Ambassador predicts June 22nd as the day of the outbreak of war.' But this did not lead Hitler to vary the date. He may have reckoned on the Russians' discounting any report from British quarters, or have felt that the actual day did not matter.

It is difficult to gauge how far Hitler believed that the Russians were unprepared for his blow. For he often veiled his thoughts from his own circle. Reports from his observers in Moscow had been telling him since the spring that the Soviet Government was apprehensively passive and anxious to appease him; that there was no danger of Russia attacking Germany as long as Stalin lived. As late as June 7th the German Ambassador there reported: 'All observations show that Stalin and Molotov, who alone are responsible for Russian foreign policy, are doing everything to avoid a conflict with Germany.' Confirmation of this seemed to come not only from the way the Russians were keeping their deliveries under the trade agreement, but by their sops to Hitler of withdrawing diplomatic recognition of Yugo-Slavia, Belgium, and Norway.

On the other hand, Hitler often declared that Nazi diplomats in Moscow were the worst informed in the world. He also furnished his generals with reports of an opposite nature – that the Russians were preparing an offensive, which it was urgent to forestall. Here he may have been deliberately deceiving them, rather than believing the reports himself, for he was having continued difficulty with his generals, who were still putting up arguments for abstaining from the invasion. Or a belated realization that the Russians were not so unready as he had hoped may have led him, on the rebound, to assume that their intentions were similar to his own. After crossing the frontier the generals found little sign of Russian offensive preparations near the front, and thus saw that Hitler had misled them.

CHAPTER THIRTEEN

The Invasion of Russia

The issue in Russia depended less on strategy and tactics than on space, logistics, and mechanics. Although some of the operational decisions were of great importance they did not count so much as mechanical deficiency in conjunction with excess of space, and their effect has to be measured in relation to these basic factors. The space factor can be easily grasped by looking at the map of Russia, but the mechanical factor requires more explanation. A preliminary analysis of it is essential to the understanding of events.

As in Hitler's previous invasions everything turned on the mechanized forces, though they formed only a small fraction of the total forces. The nineteen panzer divisions available amounted to barely one tenth of the total number of divisions, German and satellite. The vast residue included only fourteen that were motorized and thus able to keep up with the armoured spearheads.

Altogether the German Army possessed twenty-one panzer divisions in 1941 compared with ten in 1940. But that apparent doubling of its armoured strength was an illusion. It had been achieved mainly by dilution. In the Western campaign the core of each division was a tank brigade of two regiments – each comprising 160 fighting tanks. Before the invasion of Russia a tank regiment was removed from each division, and on each 'rib' a fresh division was formed.

Some of the best qualified tank experts argued against the decision, pointing out that its real effect was to multiply the number of staffs and of unarmoured auxiliary troops in the so-called armoured forces while leaving the scale of armoured troops unchanged, and thus diminishing the punch that each division could deliver. Of its 17,000 men, only some 2,600 would now be 'tank men'. But Hitler was obdurate. Seeing the vastness of Russia's spaces he wanted to feel that he had a larger number of divisions that could strike deep, and he reckoned that the technical inferiority of the Russian forces would compensate the dilution of his own. He could also stress the fact that owing to the increasing output of the later Mark III and Mark IV types, two-thirds of the armoured strength of each division would now consist of medium tanks – with larger guns and doubled thickness of armour – whereas in the Western campaign two-thirds had been light tanks. The power of its punch would thus be increased even though the scale was halved. That was a good argument up to a point, and for the moment.

The reduction in the scale of tanks, however, emphasized the fundamental flaw in the German 'armoured division' – that the bulk of its elements were unarmoured and lacked cross-country mobility. The

The Initial Onslaught on Russia

greatest development which the tank had produced in warfare – more important even than its revival of the use of armour – was its ability to move off the road, to be free from dependence on the smooth and hard surface of a prepared track. Whereas the wheeled motor-vehicle merely accelerated the pace of marching, and reproduced the effect of the railway in a rather more flexible form, the tank had revolutionized mobility. By laying its own track as it moved it dispensed with the need to follow a fixed route along a prefabricated track, and thus superseded one-dimensional by two-dimensional movement.

The significance of that potentiality had been realized by the original British exponents of mechanized warfare. In the pattern of armoured force they had proposed at the end of World War I all the vehicles, including those which carried supplies, were to be of the tracked cross-country trype. Their vision had not been fulfilled even in the German Army, which had done more than any other to make use of it.

In the reorganized panzer division of 1941 there were less than 300 tracked vehicles in all, while there were nearly 3,000 wheeled vehicles, mostly of a road-bound type. The superabundance of such vehicles had not mattered in the Western campaign, when a badly disposed defence suffered a far-reaching collapse and the attacker could profit by a network of well-paved roads in exploiting his opportunity. But in the East, where proper roads were scarce, it proved a decisive brake in the long run. The Germans here paid the penalty for being, in practice, twenty years behind the theory which they had adopted as their key to success.

That they succeeded as far as they did was due to their opponents being still more backward in equipment. For although the Russians possessed a large numerical superiority in tanks, their total quantity of motor vehicles was so limited that even their armoured forces did not have a full scale of motor transport. That proved a vital handicap in manoeuvring to meet the German panzer drives.

The Germans' armoured strength in this offensive totalled 3,550 tanks, which was only eight hundred more than in the invasion of the West. (The Russians, however, claimed in August that they had destroyed 8,000.) The total Red Army tank strength, according to Stalin's dispatch to Roosevelt of July 30th, 1941, amounted to 24,000, of which more than half were in Western Russia.

Early on Sunday morning, June 22nd, the German flood poured across the frontier, in three great parallel surges between the Baltic Sea and the Carpathian Mountains.

On the left, the Northern Army Group under Leeb crossed the East Prussian frontier into Russian-occupied Lithuania. On the left centre, east of Warsaw, the Central Army Group under Bock started a massive advance against both flanks of the bulge that the Russian front formed in northern Poland. On the right centre there was a sixty-mile stretch of calm, where the German flood was diverted by the western end of the Pripet marshland area. On the right, the Southern Army Group under Rundstedt surged forward on the north side of the Lwow bulge formed by the Russian front in Galicia, near the Carpathians.

The gap between Bock's right and Rundstedt's left was deliberately left to gain concentration of force and the clearest possible run. The speed of the German advance was thereby increased in the first stage. But since this Pripet sector was left untouched, the Russians were granted a sheltered area where their reserves could assemble under cover, and from which, at a later stage, they could develop a series of flank counterattacks southward which put a brake on Rundstedt's advance on Kiev. This would have mattered less if Bock's advance north of the Pripet Marshes had succeeded in its aim of trapping the Russian armies around Minsk.

The German offensive had its centre of gravity on the left centre. Here Bock was entrusted with the leading role for which he had been originally cast in the invasion of the West, only to see it transferred from his army group to Rundstedt's. For his decisive mission he was given the larger part of the armoured forces, two panzer groups under Guderian and Hoth, while the other army groups had one apiece. Bock also had the 4th and 9th Armies, each of three infantry corps.

The panzer groups (later redesignated panzer armies) each comprised four to five panzer divisions, and three motorized divisions.

While all the German leaders agreed that the issue would turn on the use of these panzer groups, a conflict of opinion arose as to the best way of using them. This 'battle of theories' was of far-reaching importance. Some senior commanders wanted to destroy the Russian armies in a decisive battle of the classic encirclement pattern, to be brought off as soon as possible after crossing the frontier. In framing such a plan they adhered to the orthodox theory of strategy that had been formulated by Clausewitz, established by Moltke, and developed by Schlieffen. They favoured it all the more strongly because of their anxiety over the risk of pushing far into Russia before the main Russian armies were beaten. To ensure the success of the plan they insisted that the panzer groups must cooperate with the infantry corps in the battle by wheeling inwards from either flank, as pincers, and closing round the rear of the enemy forces to complete the ring.

The tank experts, headed by Guderian, had a different idea. They wanted the panzer groups to drive as deep as they could as fast as they could – following the course that had proved so decisive in France. Guderian argued that his group and Hoth's should lose no time in exploiting their cut-through in the direction of Moscow, and at the least reach the Dnieper before wheeling in. The sooner they gained that line the more likely that the Russians' resistance would be dislocated as that of the French had been, and the more chance that the Dnieper might serve the same anvil purpose that the English Channel had fulfilled in 1940. In Guderian's view, the encirclement of the Russian forces in the space between the two panzer thrusts should be left to the infantry corps, helped by relatively small detachments which the panzer groups might switch inward as they raced onward.

The 'battle of theories' was decided in favour of orthodoxy – by the decision of Hitler. For all his boldness he was not bold enough to stake his fortunes on the card to which he owed his previous coups. His compromise with conservatism turned out more adversely than in 1940. Although the tank experts themselves were given a higher place than in 1940, they were refused the chance of fulfilling it in the way they considered best. Hitler's decision was influenced not only by his doubts of their way but by his vivid imagination – his mind was filled by a vision of rounding up the bulk of the Red Army in one gigantic ring.

That vision became a will-o'-the-wisp, luring him deeper and deeper into Russia. For the first two attempts did not succeed. The third brought a bigger bag of prisoners, but carried him beyond the Dnieper. At the fourth attempt over half a million Russians were trapped, but winter weather intervened to check the Germans' exploitation of the yawning gap in the front. Each of the staged battles had consumed time in the process of opening and closing the pincers, with the result that the strategical object was missed in trying to complete the tactical design.

Whether Guderian's method would have proved more successful remains an open question. But it was supported even at the time by some of the ablest members of the German General Staff who did not belong to the tank school of thought, and in retrospect their judgement was still more definitely in its favour. While recognizing the difficulties of reinforcement and supply to such a deep-thrusting advance they felt that these could have been overcome by making full use of the available air transport and by stripping the panzer forces of impedimenta – pushing forward their fighting elements, and concentrating on the maintenance of these, while leaving the accessory motorized columns to follow on. But that idea of moving light in Sherman style was too contrary to the convention of European warfare to gain general acceptance at this stage.

The 'battle of theories' having been settled in favour of orthodox strategy, the plan was designed to produce a vast encirclement that should net, and ensure the annihilation of, the main Russian forces before the Dnieper was reached. To increase the chances, the plan for Bock's front embraced a short-range encircling manoeuvre by the infantry corps of the 4th and 9th Armies and a longer-range manoeuvre outside it by the panzer groups, which were to drive deeper than the former before wheeling inwards. That telescopic pattern went some way, though not far enough, to meet the views of Guderian, Bock and Hoth.

The axis of the advance was along the great motor-road to Minsk, and Moscow. This ran through the sector of the 4th Army, under Kluge, to which Guderian's panzer group was attached. The entry was barred by the fortress of Brest-Litovsk, which itself was covered by the River Bug. Thus the initial problem was to secure a bridgehead over the river and clear away the fortress obstacle, so that the subsequent advance could gain momentum from the use of the motor-road.

In weighing the problem, the question arose whether the panzer divisions should wait until the infantry divisions had made a gap, or whether they should cooperate in the breakthrough, alongside the infantry divisions. The second course was adopted, to help in saving time. While infantry divisions were used to capture the fortress, they were flanked by a couple of panzer divisions on either side. After forcing the passage of the Bug, these swept round Brest-Litovsk and converged on the stretch of the motor-road beyond it. As another aid to celerity all the forces engaged in the breakthrough were temporarily placed under Guderian's executive control. And when the breakthrough was achieved the panzer group sped forward independently – like a shell from a gun.

Through the wideness of the front and their by-passing tactics, as well as the suddenness of the attack, Bock's armies made a deep penetration at many points. On the second day the armoured forces on his right wing reached Kobryn, forty miles beyond Brest-Litovsk, while his left wing captured the fortress and rail-centre of Grodno. The Russian salient in northern Poland – the Bialystok salient – was visibly changing 'ts shape and being pinched into a wasp-waist. The pinch became more severe in the following days as the wings converged on Baranovichi threatening to cut off all the Russian forces in the forward zone. The progress of the manoeuvre was helped by the ineffectiveness of the Russians' numerically strong tank forces.

But the Germans' progress was retarded by the extremely tough resistance of the Russians. The Germans usually out-manoeuvred their opponents but they could not outfight them. Surrounded forces were sometimes compelled to surrender, but this often came only at the end of prolonged resistance – and their stubbornly slow reaction to a strategically hopeless situation and the delay put a serious brake on the attacker's plans. It counted all the more in a country where communications were sparse.

The effect was first seen in the opening attack at Brest-Litovsk. Here, the garrison of the old citadel held out for a week in spite of intense bombardment from massed artillery and from the air, exacting a heavy price from the assaulting troops before it was at last overwhelmed. That initial experience, repeated at other points, opened the Germans' eyes to what was in store for them, while the stiff opposition that was met at many road-centres put a brake on their by-passing movements by blocking the routes needed by their road-bound supply columns.

The dawning sense of frustration was deepened by the character of the country that their invasion traversed. The impression it made was aptly expressed by one of the German generals:

The spaces seemed endless, the horizons nebulous. We were depressed by the monotony of the landscape, and the immensity of the stretches of forest, marsh and plain. Good roads were so few, and bad tracks so numerous, while rain quickly turned the sand or loam into a morass. The villages looked wretched and melancholy, with their straw-thatched wooden houses. Nature was hard, and in her midst were human beings just as hard and insensitive – indifferent to weather, hunger, and thirst, and almost as indifferent to life and losses, pestilence, and famine. The Russian civilian was tough, and the Russian soldier still tougher. He seemed to have an illimitable capacity for obedience and endurance.

The first attempted encirclement reached a climax around Slonim, a hundred miles beyond the original front, where the inner pincers almost closed round the two Russian armies that had been assembled in the Bialystok salient. But the Germans were not quick enough in completing the encirclement, and about half of the enveloped forces managed to escape, though in small and uncoordinated groups. The preponderance of unmechanized troops in the German 4th and 9th Armies was a handicap on the fulfilment of the design.

The main armoured forces on the wings drove more than a hundred miles deeper, crossed the 1939 Russian frontier, and then wheeled inwards beyond Minsk – which was captured on June 30th, the ninth day. That night one of Guderian's wide-flung spearheads reached the historic Beresina river near Bobruisk – ninety miles south-east of Minsk, and less than forty miles from the Dnieper. But the effort to close the ring failed, and with the failure of their grand encirclement Hitler's dream of a quickly decisive victory faded. Sudden rain – for which the French had prayed in vain the previous summer – came to the rescue of the hard-pressed Russians. It turned the sandy soil into mud.

That was far worse a handicap in Russia than it would have been in France, since it not only cramped tactical manoeuvring across country but held up strategic road movements. For the one good tarred road in the whole area was the new highway that ran past Minsk direct to Moscow, and that was only of partial service to Hitler's plan – which contemplated, not a race for Moscow, but a widecast encircling manoeuvre that had to use the soft-surfaced roads on either flank. Following the rainstorms of early July, these 'quicksands' sucked down the invader's mobility, and multiplied the effect of the stubborn resistance offered by many isolated pockets of Russian troops within the area that the Germans had overrun. Although over 300,000 prisoners were taken in the double battle of encirclement around Bialystok and Minsk, roughly the same number was able to slip out before the net was drawn tight. Their extrication was of importance in providing a means of stiffening the next defensive line – which ran in front and behind the Dnieper.

The nature of the country also became an increasing brake in this crucial stage. South-east of Minsk lies a vast stretch of forest and swamp, while the Beresina is not a clear-cut river-line but a bunch of streams winding through a black peat marsh. The Germans found that only on two roads – the main highway through Orsha, and the one to Mogilev – were the bridges built to carry heavy loads. On the other roads they were rickety wooden structures. Although the Germans had moved fast, they found that the Russians had blown up the bridges that mattered most. The invaders also began to come upon minefields for the first time, and suffered the more delay from these because of the way the advance was confined to the roads. The Beresina was almost as effective in checking Hitler's advance as in wrecking Napoleon's retreat.

All these factors multiplied the impediment to the intended process of closing the trap round the Russians in the area west of the Dnieper.

The frustration of the grand encirclement now drew the German Command into that advance beyond the Dnieper which they had hoped to avoid. They were already over 300 miles deep into Russia. The pincers opened out again to execute the design of a fresh encirclement, aimed to close in behind the Russians on the line of the Dnieper, beyond Smolensk. But the first two days of July had passed in the process of trying to close the Minsk trap and in bringing up the infantry corps of the 4th and 9th Armies – some of which marched twenty miles a day for two and a half weeks in coming up to help in breaking through the Stalin line.

This assault proved easier than the German Command had anticipated, as the retreating Russians had not time to reorganize for a proper stand nor to improve the defences, which were far from complete. The Dnieper itself was the biggest obstacle, but Guderian's armoured divisions overcame this by swift surprise attacks at a number of points away from the main crossings. By the 12th the Germans had breached the Stalin line over a wide front between Rogachev and Vitebsk, and were racing for Smolensk. The ease of the breakthrough suggested that there would have been more gain than risk in allowing an armoured force to push ahead in the first place, as Guderian had wished.

The difficulties of the country, as increased by the bursts of rain, were a greater check than the disorganized opposition. In these circumstances a heavy forfeit was paid for the time lost in the pause. For each heavy shower temporarily reduced the invaders' mobility to stagnation. From the air, it was a strange spectacle – stationary 'panzer' blobs strung out across the landscape for a distance of a hundred miles and more.

The tanks might have continued to advance, but these and the other tracked vehicles formed only a small part of each so-called armoured division. Their supplies and their massive infantry element were carried in wheeled vehicles of a large and heavy type, which could not move off the road, nor move on it if the surface turned into mud. When the sun came out again, the sandy roads dried quickly – and the procession then moved on. But the cumulative delay was a serious handicap on the strategic plan.

This was not outwardly apparent because of the relatively rapid advance by Guderian's panzer group along the main highway to Smolensk

– which was entered on the 16th. The stretch of over a hundred miles between the Dnieper and the Desna was covered within a week. But Hoth's panzer group on the northern wing was delayed by the swamps as well as the rainstorms, on its course. Its slow progress naturally affected the fulfilment of Hitler's encirclement plan, and gave the Russians more time to rally their forces around Smolensk. Stiffer resistance on both flanks was met in the final stage of the effort. Indeed, the resistance was almost too stubborn, for the pincers came within ten miles of closing, and the Germans reckoned that half a million Russians were caught in the trap. Although a large part were extricated, a further 300,000 nevertheless went into captivity by August 5th.

That incomplete victory left the Germans with an unsolved problem. It meant that their path to Moscow, a further 200 miles ahead, was still blocked by considerable forces – which were being continuously increased by newly mobilized reinforcements. At the same time the Germans' capacity to mount a fresh effort was cramped by the difficulty of bringing up reinforcements on their side over the bad roads.

That spelt an inevitable delay, but nothing like the length of the delay that now occurred. For October came before the advance on Moscow was resumed. The best two months of the summer were allowed to pass while Bock's armies were halted on the Desna. The causes are to be found in Hitler's uncertainty of mind, coupled with the progress of Rundstedt's armies south of the Pripet marshes.

On that southern front the Germans had enjoyed no initial superiority of force. Indeed, they had started with odds against them that on paper looked formidable. The Russians' South-western Army Group under Marshal Budenny comprised thirty tank and motorized divisions, five cavalry divisions, and forty-five infantry divisions in southern Poland and the Ukraine; of these, six tank and motorized divisions, three cavalry divisions, and thirteen infantry divisions were in Bessarabia, facing the Rumanians. In armour it had nearly twice the strength of Marshal Timoshenko's Western Army Group which had faced the main German drive. Altogether, Budenny had about 5,000 tanks, of various types, whereas Kleist's panzer group – which formed Rundstedt's armoured punch – consisted of only 600 tanks. Moreover, a large proportion of the latter had been engaged in the Greek campaign, and been allowed little time for overhaul before they were launched into this greater venture.

Rundstedt had to depend for an advantage on surprise, speed, space – and the opposing commanders. Budenny, the famous old cavalry hero of the Civil War, was most aptly described by one of his own officers as 'a man with an immense moustache but a very small brain'. Some of the best Russian commanders had been eliminated in the prewar purges, and those who had survived as politically safe were often militarily unsafe. It was only after these too solid seniors had been weeded out under the test of war that the pick of a younger generation came to the top.

Rundstedt's main effort was concentrated on his left wing, along the Bug. The plan made the most of his limited strength, while profiting by the fact that his starting line lay well behind the flank of the Lwow salient formed by the Russian zone in Galicia. The attack was thus delivered from a natural wedge, which had only to be driven in a little further before it began to threaten the communications of all the Russian forces near the Carpathians. After Reichenau's 6th Army had forced the crossings of the Bug, Kleist's armoured forces were launched in a drive through the breach towards Luck and Brody.

Surprise helped not only to facilitate his initial breakthrough, but to nullify the potentially dangerous countermove which the Russians might otherwise have made. Knowing that they had twenty-five divisions facing Hungary's Carpathian frontier, Rundstedt had anticipated that these might swing round and strike at his right flank as he advanced towards Luck. Instead, they retreated. (That reaction, coupled with the lack of preparedness found in the Russians' forward zone, led Rundstedt and other German commanders to doubt whether there had been any justification for Hitler's argument that the Russians were about to take the offensive.)

Even with this flying start, Rundstedt's forces were not able to make such rapid progress as Bock's in the left centre. Guderian urged the importance of keeping the Russians on the run, and allowing them no time to rally. He was convinced that he could reach Moscow if no time was wasted, and that such a thrust at the nerve-centre of Stalin's power might paralyse Russia's resistance. Hoth shared his views and Bock endorsed them. But Hitler reverted to his own original idea in a directive of July 19th for the next stage of operations. The panzer forces were to be taken away from Bock, in the centre, and sent to the wings – Guderian's panzer group was to wheel southward to help in overcoming the Russian armies facing Rundstedt in the Ukraine, while Hoth's panzer group was to turn northward to aid Leeb's attack on Leningrad.

Once again Brauchitsch temporized, instead of at once pressing for a different plan. He argued that before any further operations were started, the panzer forces must have a rest to overhaul their machines and get up replacements. Hitler agreed the necessity for such a pause.

Meanwhile the high-level discussion about the course to be followed went on, and it continued even after the panzer forces could have resumed their drive.

After several weeks had slipped away in such discussions, the Chief of the General Staff, Halder, spurred Brauchitsch to put forward proposals for a speedy advance on Moscow. Hitler retorted with a new and more definite directive on August 21st, which began:

> I am not in agreement with the proposals submitted by the Army, on August 18, for the prosecution of the war in the East. Of primary importance before the outbreak of winter is not the capture of Moscow, but rather the occupation of the Crimea, of the industrial and coal-mining area of the Donetz basin, the cutting of the Russian supply routes from the Caucasian oil-fields...

Accordingly, he gave orders that to clear the way to these southern objectives, part of Bock's army group (including Guderian's panzer forces) was to turn south and help to overcome the Russian armies around Kiev that were opposing Rundstedt.

When these orders were received, Halder tried to get Brauchitsch to tender their joint resignation. But Brauchitsch said it would be a useless gesture, as Hitler would simply reject their resignation. As for arguments, Hitler brushed these aside with the remark, which he often repeated: 'My generals know nothing about the economic aspects of war.' All that he would concede was that after the Russian armies in the Kiev area had been wiped out, Bock should be allowed to resume his advance on Moscow, and Guderian's panzer forces be returned to him for the purpose.

The Kiev encirclement was in itself a great success, and raised rosy expectations. Guderian thrust downward across the Russians' rear while Kleist's panzer group thrust upward. The two pincers met 150 miles east of Kiev, closing a trap in which over 600,000 Russians were caught, according to the German claim. But it was late in September before the battle ended as poor roads and rainy weather had slowed down the pace of the encircling manoeuvre. The brightness of victory was darkened by the shadow of winter, carrying its historic menace to an invader of Russia. The two wasted months of the summer proved fatal to the prospects of reaching Moscow.

The renewed advance began on September 30th. Its prospects looked bright when Bock's armies brought off a great encirclement round Vyasma, where a further 600,000 Russians were captured. That left the

Germans momentarily with an almost clear path to Moscow. But the Vyasma battle had not been completed until the end of October, the German troops were tired, the country became a morass as the weather got worse, and fresh Russian forces appeared in front of Moscow.

Most of the German generals wanted to break off the offensive and take up a suitable winter-line. They remembered what had happened to Napoleon's army. Many of them began to re-read Caulaincourt's grim account of 1812. But on the higher levels a different view prevailed. This time it was not entirely due to Hitler, who was becoming impressed, and depressed, both by the increasing difficulties and by the wintry conditions. On November 9th he sombrely remarked: 'The recognition that neither force is capable of annihilating the other will lead to a compromise peace.' But Bock urged that the German offensive must be continued. Brauchitsch and Halder agreed with him – Halder telling a conference of the higher staff on November 12th that there was good reason to believe that Russian resistance was on the verge of collapse.

Brauchitsch and Halder, as well as Bock, were naturally the more reluctant to call a halt because of their earlier struggle in getting Hitler to accept their arguments for capturing Moscow rather than pursuing objectives in the south. So the push for Moscow was resumed on November 15th, when there was a momentary improvement in the weather. But after two weeks' struggle in mud and snow, it was brought to a halt twenty miles short of Moscow.

Even Bock came to doubt the value of trying to push on, although he had just previously been declaring: 'The last battalion will decide the issue.' But Brauchitsch, from far in the rear, continued to insist that the offensive must be continued at all costs. He was a sick man, and desperately worried by Hitler's anger about the poor results achieved.

On December 2nd a further effort was launched, and some detachments penetrated into the suburbs of Moscow, but the advance as a whole was held up in the forests covering the capital.

This was the signal for a Russian counteroffensive of large scale, prepared and directed by Zhukov. It tumbled back the exhausted Germans, lapped round their flanks, and produced a critical situation. From generals downwards, the invaders were filled with ghastly thoughts of Napoleon's retreat from Moscow. In that emergency Hitler forbade any retreat beyond the shortest possible local withdrawals, and in this situation he was right. His decision exposed his troops to awful sufferings in their advanced positions facing Moscow – for they had neither the clothing nor equipment for a Russian winter campaign – but if they had once started a general retreat it might easily have degenerated into a panic-stricken rout.

Hitler had lost his chance of capturing Moscow by his August decision to halt the advance in that direction, ånd turn aside to clear a path into southern Russia. The forfeit of Moscow was not compensated by what his armies attained in the south. After the great round-up at Kiev, Rundstedt overran the Crimea and the Donetz basin, but without Guderian's tanks was frustrated in his drive for the Caucasian oilfields. His troops succeeded in reaching Rostov on the Don, but in an exhausted state, and were soon pushed out by the Russians. He then wanted to fall back to a good defensive line on the Mius River, but Hitler forbade such a withdrawal. Rundstedt replied that he could not comply with such an order, and asked to be relieved of his command. Hitler promptly replaced him, but immediately after this the front was broken and Hitler was forced to accept the necessity of a retreat. That was in the first week of December – simultaneously with the repulse at Moscow.

That same week Brauchitsch asked to be relieved on the grounds of sickness, the next week Bock did likewise, and a little later Leeb resigned when Hitler rejected his proposal for a withdrawal on the northern front near Leningrad. So all the four top commanders departed.

Hitler appointed no successor to Brauchitsch, but took the opportunity to make himself the direct Commander-in-Chief of the Army. By Christmas he had got rid of Guderian, the principal agent of his earlier victories, who had withdrawn his exhausted troops without Hitler's permission.

A fundamental factor in the failure of the invasion was the invaders' miscalculation of the reserves that Stalin could bring up from the depths of Russia. In that respect the General Staff and its Intelligence Service were as much deceived as Hitler. The fatal error is epitomized in one pregnant sentence of Halder's diary in mid-August: 'We underestimated Russia: we reckoned with 200 divisions, but now we have already identified 360.'

That largely cancelled out the wonderful success of the start. Instead of having a path swept clean of defenders, the Germans had now to deal with fresh armies that had arrived on the scene. The massive Soviet mobilization system succeeded in getting under way well out of the reach of the German armies, and from the winter of 1941 onwards the Germans were always to be outnumbered on the Russian front. Thanks to their own superior technique and training, they eventually succeeded in destroying these armies in successive battles of encirclement – but then became bogged in the autumn mud. By the time that the winter frost had hardened the ground, they again found fresh armies blocking the route, and they themselves were too exhausted to struggle on to their goal.

Next to their miscalculation of Russia's resources, the most fatal factor had been the way that Hitler and his top generals had wasted the month of August in arguing as to what should be their next move – there was an amazing state of mental haziness on the topmost level of the German Command.

Lower down, Guderian in particular had a clear idea of what he wanted to do – to drive for Moscow as fast as he could, leaving the infantry armies to mop up the disorganized bodies that he had cut through. In 1940 he had won the Battle of France in that way. It would have meant running big risks, but might have captured Moscow before the Russian second-line armies were ready to cover it. Far greater risks developed, and fatally, from the course that was followed.

As it was, Russia owed her survival more to her continued primitiveness than to all the technical development achieved since the Soviet revolution. That reflection applies not only to the toughness of her people and soldiers – their capacity to endure hardships and carry on under shortages that would have been paralysing to Western peoples and Western armies. A greater asset still was the primitiveness of the Russian roads. Most of them were no better than sandy tracks. The way that they dissolved into bottomless mud, when it rained, did more to check the German invasion than all the Red Army's heroic sacrifices. If the Soviet régime had given Russia a road system comparable to that of Western countries, she would have been overrun almost as quickly as France.

But this conclusion has a converse. Hitler lost his chance of victory because the mobility of his army was based on wheels instead of on tracks. On Russia's mud-roads its wheeled transport was bogged when the tanks could move on. If the panzer forces had been provided with *tracked* transport they could have reached Russia's vital centres by the autumn in spite of the mud.

CHAPTER FOURTEEN

Rommel's Entry into Africa

In 1941 the course of the war in Africa went through a series of startling changes that upset expectation on either side in turn but had no conclusive issue. It was a war of swift movement – but see-saw movement, repeatedly tilting up and down. The year had begun with the British throwing the Italians out of Cyrenaica, but then a German force arrived on the scene under the leadership of General Erwin Rommel, and barely two months later the British were thrown out of Cyrenaica except for a foothold which they retained at the small port of Tobruk. Rommel in turn was repulsed in two successive attacks on Tobruk, but then the British suffered reverses in two successive attempts to relieve the besieged garrison. After five months' pause to build up strength, they made a bigger effort in November that produced a see-saw battle of a month's duration, with repeated changes of fortune before the exhausted remains of the opposing army was forced to withdraw once again to the western border of Cyrenaica. But even then Rommel delivered a frontier riposte in the last week of the year, which proved a foreshadowing of another dramatic reversal of the British advance.*

Rommel's opening thrust at the end of March 1941, and its far-reaching exploitation, created all the greater shock because the possibility of an early advance by the enemy had been discounted on the British side. In an appreciation of the situation that Wavell sent to the Chiefs of Staff in London on March 2nd, after a warning report that German troops had begun to arrive in Tripoli, he emphasized that they would need to build up their strength to two divisions or more before attempting a serious attack, and concluded that the difficulties 'make it unlikely that such an attack could develop before the end of the summer'. In contrast, Churchill's messages showed apprehension that the Germans would not wait to complete an orthodox build-up, and a strong sense of the need for offensive counteraction, although over-optimistic about the

* For maps, see pp 118–19.

capacity of the actual British forces. On March 26th he telegraphed to Wavell:

> We are naturally concerned at rapid German advance to Agheila. It is their habit to push on wherever they are not resisted. I presume you are only waiting for the tortoise to stick his head out far enough before chopping it off. It seems extremely important to give them an early taste of our quality.*

But quality was lacking, both technically and tactically. Although the depleted 2nd Armoured Division that was posted in the forward area still had three armoured units to Rommel's two, and a numerically favourable balance of gun-armed tanks, a large proportion of these were captured Italian M13s that had been taken over by British crews to compensate the shortage of British cruiser tanks, while almost all were in badly worn condition. The prospects of such a scratch force were diminished by Wavell's instructions that 'if attacked' it was to fall back and 'fight a delaying action'. For by abandoning the bottleneck position east of Agheila at Rommel's initial onset, on March 31st, it opened the way for him to enter a desert expanse where he could exploit a wide choice of alternative routes and alternative objectives to its own confusion, while being itself in no fit state for such strenuous manoeuvring. In the days that followed, Rommel allowed it no respite. Most of its tanks were lost, not in fighting, but through breaking down or running out of fuel in a prolonged and disjointed series of withdrawals.

In less than a week the British had fallen back more than 200 miles from their position on the western border of Cyrenaica. In less than a fortnight they were 400 miles back, on the eastern border of Cyrenaica – and western frontier of Egypt – except for a force invested at Tobruk. The decision to hold on to this small port, and the retention of that position as a 'thorn in the enemy's side', had a far-reaching influence on the course of the African campaign during the next twelve months.

The swiftly spreading collapse had naturally tended to shake the confidence of commanders and troops on the British side, while leading them to magnify the strength of the attackers. At a distance it was easier to keep account of the enemy's limited strength and strategic handicaps. Churchill in London, duly weighing them, telegraphed to Wavell on April 7th:

> You should surely be able to hold Tobruk, with its permanent Italian defences, at least until or unless the enemy brings up strong artillery

* Churchill: *The Second World War*, vol III, p 178.

forces. It seems difficult to believe that he can do this for some weeks. He would run great risks in masking Tobruk and advancing upon Egypt, observing that we can reinforce from the sea and would menace his communications. Tobruk therefore seems to be a place to be held to the death without thought of retirement. I should be glad to hear of your intentions.*

Wavell had already decided to hold Tobruk if possible, but when he flew there from Cairo on the 8th he reported that the situation had greatly deteriorated, and sounded so dubious about the prospects of defending the place that Churchill, in conclave with the Chiefs of Staff, drafted a still more emphatic message saying that 'it seems unthinkable that the fortress of Tobruk should be abandoned'. Before the message was dispatched, however, word came from Wavell that he had made up his mind to hold on there for a time, and assemble a mobile force on the frontier to divert the enemy and ease the pressure, while striving 'to build up old plan of defence in Mersa Matruh area' – 200 miles farther back. In the event there was no further withdrawal, thanks to the stubborn defence of Tobruk, though nearly eight months passed before it was relieved.

The main part of the garrison was provided by the 9th Australian Division under General Morshead, which had got back safely from the Benghazi area. In addition the 18th Infantry Brigade (of the 7th Australian Division) had arrived by sea, and was followed by detachments of the 1st and 7th Royal Tank Regiment with which a small armoured force of fifty odd tanks was built up.

Rommel's attack opened on Good Friday, April 11th, with probing thrusts. The main attack was launched early on Easter Monday, against the middle stretch of the southern face of the thirty-mile perimeter, some nine miles from the port. It broke through the thin defences, and the leading panzer battalion drove on two miles northward, but was there checked by the defender's artillery, and then squeezed out of the narrow pocket it had made, losing sixteen tanks out of the thirty-eight engaged – a total that revealed the slenderness of Rommel's strength. The Italians attempted an attack on the 16th, but their effort quickly collapsed, and nearly a thousand surrendered when counterattacked by an Australian battalion.

The Italian Supreme Command in Rome, already uneasy about Rommel's deep advance, now begged the German Supreme Command to restrain his adventurous initiative and reported intention of thrusting

* Churchill: *The Second World War*, vol III, p 183.

into Egypt. Halder, the Chief of the German General Staff, was equally anxious to curb any action overseas that might require reinforcement at the expense of the German forces in the main theatre that were now preparing to invade Russia. He also had an instinctive dislike of Hitler's inclination to back dynamic leaders, such as Rommel, who did not conform to General Staff pattern. So Halder's deputy, General Paulus, was sent on a visit to Africa 'to head off this soldier gone stark mad', as Halder bitingly wrote in his diary. Paulus came, saw, and checked – but after administering an admonition, he sanctioned a fresh assault on Tobruk.

The assault was launched on April 30th, by which time some advance elements of the 15th Panzer Division – though not its tank regiment – had arrived from Europe to reinforce the 5th Light Division. This time the blow was aimed at the south-western corner of the defences, and delivered under cover of darkness. By daylight on May 1st the German infantry had made a breach more than a mile wide, and the leading wave of tanks then started an exploiting drive towards Tobruk, ten miles away. But after advancing a mile they ran unsuspectingly on a minefield that had been newly laid, as a trap, and seventeen tanks out of forty were disabled – though all except five got back safely, after their tracks had been repaired under fire. The second wave of tanks and infantry wheeled south-eastward along the back of the perimeter to roll up the defences. But after a lateral advance of nearly three miles they were finally checked by the combination of fire from artillery deployed behind the minefield, a counterattack by twenty British tanks, and the continued resistance of several Australian posts which they had failed to subdue. As for the Italian supporting troops, they were slow in backing up and quick in backing out.

Next day only thirty-five German tanks out of the initial 70-odd remained fit for action, and the attack was suspended. On the night of the 3rd, Morshead launched a counterattack with his reserve infantry brigade, but this in turn failed, and the situation became one of mutual frustration. The south-western corner of the perimeter remained in Rommel's grip, but it was evident that his strength was not adequate for the capture of Tobruk, and Paulus, before returning home, imposed a veto on any attempt to renew the attack. So a state of seige developed, which lasted until late in the year – after the failure of two early efforts by Wavell to drive Rommel back and bring relief to the garrison.

The first of these, in mid-May, had a tentativeness that was expressed in its code-name, 'Operation Brevity', but greater weight was given and much greater hopes attached to its mid-June successor,

'Operation Battleaxe'. The outcome was poor compensation for the heavy risks that had been taken, on Churchill's initiative, to ensure its success – the risk of providing a large reinforcement of tanks for Egypt at a time when the forces defending England were still ill-equipped, and when Hitler had not yet turned away to attack Russia; also, the further risk of dispatching this reinforcement by the Mediterranean route, 'running the gauntlet' of the enemy's air forces.

Churchill's bold readiness to run such double risks, in the endeavour to gain success in Africa and preserve the British position in Egypt, was in striking contrast to the attitude of Hitler and Halder, who were agreed in trying to curtail the German commitment in the Mediterranean theatre. In October, when General von Thoma had been sent on an exploratory visit to Cyrenaica, he had reported that a force of four panzer divisions would be needed, and should suffice, to ensure success in the invasion of Egypt, but Mussolini had been as unwilling to accept such a scale of German help as Hitler was to provide it. Rommel's small force of two divisions had only been dispatched there after the Italian defeat, in an effort to preserve Tripoli. Even when he had shown how far he could go with such a small panzer force, Hitler and Halder remained unwilling to provide the relatively small reinforcement that would in all probability have decided the issue. By that refusal they forfeited the chance of conquering Egypt and ousting the British from the Mediterranean area at a time when the British were still weak – while they were led to make a much greater commitment, and sacrifice, in the long run.

But in Britain, despite her still scanty resources, a convoy with large armoured reinforcements had already been assembled in April for dispatch to Egypt. It was about to sail when a telegram came from Wavell, on April 20th, emphasizing the gravity of the situation and the urgency of his need for more armour. Churchill immediately proposed,* and got the Chiefs of Staff to agree, that the five fast ships carrying the tanks should turn east at Gibraltar and take the short cut through the Mediterranean – which would save nearly six weeks in time of arrival. He

* In a personal minute that day for the Chiefs of Staff, he pungently wrote: 'The fate of the war in the Middle East, the loss of the Suez Canal, the frustration or confusion of the enormous forces we have built up in Egypt, the closing of all prospects of American cooperation through the Red Sea – all may turn on a few hundred armoured vehicles. They must if possible be carried there at all costs.' (*The Second World War*, vol III, p 218.)

also insisted that the scale of the reinforcement should be increased and a hundred of the latest cruiser tanks included, although the Chief of the Imperial General Staff, General Dill, opposed such a subtraction from the slender strength available at home to meet a possible spring invasion.

This 'Operation Tiger' was the first attempt to pass a convoy through the Mediterranean since the Luftwaffe had made its appearance there in January. Helped by misty weather, the convoy was successfully taken through without suffering damage from the air, though one of the ships, with fifty-seven tanks, was sunk by a mine in passing through the Sicilian Narrows. The other four ships reached Alexandria safely on May 12th, with 238 tanks (135 Matildas, eighty-two cruiser, and twenty-one lights) – which was four times as many as those which Wavell had been able to scrape together for the defence of Egypt.

Without waiting for this large reinforcement, however, Wavell had decided to take advantage of Rommel's rebuff at Tobruk, and reported acute shortage of supplies, by trying an offensive stroke with the scratch force assembled near the frontier, under Brigadier Gott. This was 'Operation Brevity'. Wavell's initial aim was to recapture the frontier positions near the coast – which he knew were lightly held – and scupper their garrisons before the enemy reinforced them. He hoped to do more than that, as he told Churchill in a telegram on May 13th: 'If successful will consider immediate combined action by Gott's force and Tobruk garrison to drive enemy west of Tobruk.'

Two tank units were brought up to provide the punch for Gott's force – the 2nd RTR, equipped with twenty-nine old-type cruisers which had been reconditioned, and the 4th RTR with twenty-six Matildas, heavily armoured, relatively slow, and officially classified as 'infantry tanks'. The 2nd RTR with a support group of motorized infantry and artillery was to move round the desert flank of the fortified positions to Sidi Azeiz, and block the enemy's route of reinforcement and retreat. The 4th RTR was to lead the motorized 22nd Guards Brigade in the direct assault.

After a thirty-mile approach march by night, the Italian-held post at the top of the Halfaya Pass was stormed by surprise early on May 15th and several hundred prisoners taken, though seven Matildas were knocked out by the defenders' artillery as they closed in. Two other posts, Bir Waid and Musaid, were quickly taken, but surprise had passed before Fort Capuzzo was reached, and when a German battlegroup intervened by flank action the attack became disjointed. Although the fort was eventually captured, it was later evacuated. Meanwhile the flanking move to Sidi Azeiz had been broken off under threat of a counterattack. On the other hand, the enemy commander on the frontier had been so impressed by the apparent strength of the attack that he was led to start withdrawing.

Thus by nightfall both sides were in process of falling back. But while the German–Italian withdrawal was promptly countermanded by Rommel, who was rushing a panzer battalion to the scene from Tobruk, Gott had decided on a retirement to Halfaya, and the troops were already on the move, before a stand fast order reached him from the distant higher command. When daylight came the Germans found the battlefield empty – much to their relief, as the reinforcing panzer battalion had run out of petrol, and was immobilized until a refill arrived late that day.

The British withdrawal did not stop at Halfaya, but left a small garrison there. The Germans were quick to take advantage of its exposed position, and recaptured the Pass on the 27th by a sudden converging stroke from several directions. Its recapture was a valuable gain to them, as it seriously hampered the next and heavier British offensive, 'Battleaxe'. Moreover, during the interval Rommel laid traps for the British tanks at Halfaya as well as at other forward posts by digging in batteries of 88-mm guns, converted most effectively from an anti-aircraft to an anti-tank role.

That emergency step proved of great importance for the issue of the coming battle. At this time nearly two-thirds of the German anti-tank guns were still the old 37-mm, developed five years before the war, and much inferior to the British 2-pounder tank and anti-tank gun. They could do little against the British cruiser tanks and were helpless against the Matildas. Even the new 50-mm anti-tank gun, of which Rommel now had fifty odd, could only pierce the Matilda's thick armour at very close range. But the wheeled 88-mm was capable of penetrating the Matilda's frontal armour (77 mm thick) at a range of 2,000 yards. Rommel had only twelve of these guns, but one battery (of four) was posted at Halfaya and another at Hafid Ridge – two points which the British aimed to capture at the outset of their attack.

That was fortunate for Rommel, for in many respects he stood at a serious disadvantage when the attack was launched, particularly in the number of tanks – the prime arm in these desert battles. No further reinforcements had arrived from Germany, and he had barely a hundred gun-armed tanks available when the battle opened, more than half of which were with the force investing Tobruk, eighty miles back. On the other side, the arrival of the 'Tiger' convoy enabled the British to deploy some 200 gun-armed tanks – which gave them a 4 to 1 advantage in the opening stage. Much depended on whether they could exploit this advantage to smash the enemy forces in the frontier area before Rommel could bring up the rest of his tanks (5th Panzer Regiment) from distant Tobruk.

Unfortunately for the British, the chances were diminished by an 'infantry-minded' planning of the offensive. This trend was fostered by the mixture of tank types and, in the event, led to a dissipation of the numerical advantage.

The arrival of the 'Tiger' convoy had enabled Wavell to reconstitute two armoured brigades for the new offensive, but so few tanks were left after the abortive 'Brevity' attack in mid-May that the total was only enough to equip two of the three regiments in each brigade.* Moreover the number of new cruiser tanks that had arrived sufficed only to equip one regiment, and of the earlier cruisers only enough remained for a second regiment. The two regiments of the other brigade were equipped with Matildas, 'infantry tanks' – which strongly influenced the Command decision to use this brigade at the outset to assist the infantry in a direct assault on the enemy's fortified position, instead of concentrating all available tank strength to crush the enemy's panzer forces in the forward area. The consequences of that decision proved fatally frustrating to the development of the offensive.

The aims of 'Operation Battleaxe' were ambitious – as set by Churchill, they were to gain a 'decisive' victory in North Africa and 'destroy' Rommel's forces. Wavell expressed a cautious doubt about the possibility of such complete success, but said that he hoped the attack would 'succeed in driving the enemy back west of Tobruk'. That was the object defined in the operation instructions he gave to General Beresford-Peirse who, as commander of the Western Desert Force, was to conduct the offensive.

The plan of attack comprised three stages, opening with an assault on the fortified area Halfaya–Sollum–Capuzzo by the 4th Indian Division,

* Churchill urged that a further hundred tanks – the number required to equip a third regiment for each brigade – should be sent out by the Mediterranean route, but the Admiralty were reluctant to run the risk again. Churchill bitterly remarks in his memoirs: 'I should not have been deterred from seeking and obtaining a Cabinet decision upon the issue but for the fact that General Wavell himself did not press the point, and indeed took the other side. This cut the ground from under my feet.' (*The Second World War*, vol III, p 223.) So the convoy went round the Cape and did not reach Suez until mid-July.

aided by the 4th Armoured Brigade (which was equipped with Matilda tanks), while the rest of the 7th Armoured Division covered the desert flank. In the second stage, the 7th Armoured Division was to make an exploiting drive for Tobruk, with both its armoured brigades. In the third stage, this division together with the Tobruk garrison was to push on westwards. It was a plan that contained the seeds of its own frustration. For by detaching half the armour to help the infantry in the first stage, it more than halved the chances of defeating the enemy's panzer regiment in the forward area before this could be reinforced by the other panzer regiment from Tobruk, and thus greatly diminished the chances of achieving the second and third stages of the British plan.

To reach the enemy's frontier positions the attacking force had to make a thirty-mile approach march, which started in the afternoon of June 14th. The final bound, of eight miles, was made by moonlight in the early hours of the 15th, and the battle opened with the right wing's attack on the enemy's outlying position at the Halfaya Pass. But the defenders were better prepared than in May, while the chance of surprise was forfeited by the planning decision that the tanks should not deliver the assault until the artillery had sufficient light for shooting. That decision proved the worse because the one battery allotted to support the Halfaya assault became stuck in the sand. It was broad daylight when the squadron of Matildas leading this attack started on the last lap of the advance, and the first news that came back was from its commander's voice on the radio: 'They are tearing my tanks to bits.' That was his last message. Of the thirteen Matildas, only one survived the 'tank trap' of four 88s that Rommel had placed at what the British troops aptly called 'Hellfire pass'.

Meanwhile the centre column had been pushing on across the desert plateau towards Fort Capuzzo, spearheaded by a whole regiment of Matildas. There were no 88s in the path, and the garrison's resistance crumbled in face of this massed menace. The fort was captured, and two counterattacks repulsed later in the day.

But the brigade of cruiser tanks leading the left column, which was intended to turn the enemy's flank, had run into Rommel's tank trap on the Hafid Ridge, and there been checked. Renewing the attack in the late afternoon, it only pushed deeper into the trap, with heavier loss. By that time the bulk of the forward panzer regiment had come on the scene, and it developed a counter flank threat which caused the remaining British tanks to fall back slowly to the frontier wire.

By nightfall on the first day, the British had lost more than half their tanks, mainly in the two anti-tank traps, whereas Rommel's tank strength was almost intact, and with the arrival of his other panzer regiment from Tobruk the balance shifted in his favour.

On the second day Rommel seized the initiative by using the whole of his 5th Light Division from Tobruk to envelop the British left flank in the desert in conjunction with a strong counterattack at Capuzzo by the 15th Panzer Division. This counterattack at Capuzzo was repulsed – the British here enjoying the advantage of the defensive in well-chosen and concealed positions. But the combined effect of the frontal and flank threats disjointed the British plan for a renewed offensive effort that day, and by nightfall the Germans' enveloping move had made ominous progress.

Pressing this advantage, Rommel switched the whole of his mobile forces to the desert flank in the early hours of the third day, with the aim of making a scythe-like sweep to the Halfaya Pass and cutting the British lines of retreat. When the menace became manifest in mid-morning, the British higher commanders issued orders, after hasty consultation, for a precipitate retreat of their disjointed forces. The advanced portion at Capuzzo had a very narrow escape, but the stubborn resistance of the remaining British tanks there gained time for the extrication of the lorry-borne infantry, and by the fourth morning the British forces were back on the line – thirty miles back – from which they had started.

The human losses in the three days' 'Battleaxe' battle were slight – less than a thousand killed, wounded and missing on the British side, and about the same on the other side. But the British lost ninety-one tanks and the Germans only 12. Being left in possession of the battlefield they were able to recover and repair most of their damaged tanks, whereas the British in their hasty retreat had to abandon many which were merely disabled by mechanical troubles, and could have been repaired if time had been allowed. The disproportionate tank losses emphasized the failure of this offensive to fulfil the high hopes, and far-reaching aims, with which it had been launched.

Tobruk, 'Brevity' and 'Battleaxe' marked a fresh turn in the tactical trend of the war. Hitherto, it had been an almost complete reversal of the ascendancy of the defensive that had prevailed during World War I and the previous half-century. Since September 1939 the offensive had been so repeatedly and sweepingly successful in every theatre, when carried out by fast-moving armoured forces, that both public and military opinion had come to regard the defensive as inherently weak, and to believe that any attack was bound to prevail. But 'Battleaxe' showed, as Tobruk and 'Brevity' had foreshadowed, how effective defence could be – even in such open country as the North African desert – if conducted with skill and based on an understanding of the properties of modern instruments. From this time onwards, as the war continued and experience grew, it became increasingly evident that defence, in a more mobile form, had regained the advantage it held in World War I, and could only be overcome by a great superiority of strength or a very high degree of skill – in upsetting the opponent's balance.

Unfortunately for the prospects of the next British attempt to crush Rommel and clear North Africa, the lessons of 'Battleaxe' were either missed or misunderstood. The most important point missed by the British higher headquarters in their conclusions was the part that the 88s had played in the defence. They discounted reports that this heavy anti-aircraft gun was being used as an anti-tank gun. When they came belatedly to realize that fact in the autumn, after further heavy tank losses from its fire, they remained obstinately sure that such a bulky weapon could only be used from a dug-in position. Thus they failed to foresee and evolve tactics to counter the next advance in Rommel's defensive tactics – that of using the 88s in a mobile role.

Another important development missed, by the British fighting troops as well as by their higher commanders, was the enemy's increasingly bold use of his normal anti-tank guns in close combination with his tanks – not only in defence but also in attack. In the coming battles that combination became a dominant factor, exerting an even greater influence on the issue than the 88s. Indeed, the principal cause of the disproportionately heavy loss of tanks on the British side appears, in analysis, to have been the way the German 50-mm anti-tank guns, comparatively small and handy, were pushed out ahead of their own tanks to concealed positions in hollows. That was not realized by the British tank crews, who could not know whether an armour-piercing shot that penetrated their armour had been fired by a tank or anti-tank gun – and naturally tended to ascribe it to the most visible opponent. That mistaken deduction led, in the aftermath, to a mistaken belief that their own tanks and tank-guns were inferior to the enemy's – and thereby to a spreading loss of confidence.

Besides the points that were missed in reviewing the course of the summer campaign, there was also an important one which was misunderstood, with serious effect on the British plan for the next offensive. Wavell in his Dispatch, drafted nearly three months after 'Battleaxe', reached the conclusion that the prime 'cause of our failure was undoubtedly the difficulty of combining the action of cruiser and "I" [Infantry] tanks ...' But in fact the combination had not been tried, nor its possibility tested. The two regiments of Matildas had been detached from the armoured division and placed under the commander of the infantry division at the outset, and he had clung on to them throughout the battle, instead of releasing them after the first phase as intended in the plan. With intelligent combination the 'I' tanks could have played a valuable part in the armoured battle, operating as a strong offensive pivot of manoeuvre for the cruiser tanks. There was only a slight difference of speed between the Matildas and the A10 cruisers, which had effectively cooperated with the faster cruisers in the first Libyan campaign and in 'Battleaxe' itself. The Germans, both at this time and later, proved capable of combining tank types with as large a difference of speed as that between the faster British cruisers and the Matildas.

Unfortunately, the untested assumption that the combination was too difficult led to a complete division between the cruiser and 'I' tank brigades in the next British offensive – which became a battle waged, on the British side, in two separate compartments.

CHAPTER FIFTEEN

'Crusader'

The frustration of the mid-summer effort of 1941 to gain a decisive victory in Africa, and sweep the enemy out of that continent, made Churchill more intent than ever to achieve that aim. He was determined to renew the effort as soon as possible, with stronger forces. To this end, he poured reinforcements into Egypt and brushed aside his military advisers' reminders about the longstanding decision that the defence of the Far East, and particularly of Singapore, was the second priority after the defence of Britain itself, and before the Middle East. The Chief of the Imperial General Staff, Sir John Dill, tried to remind Churchill of the carefully weighed decision, as between the two regions and risks, but was too gentle a personality and too deferential by habit to maintain it in face of Churchill's force of personality, argument, and position.

Yet the danger in the Far East had now become acute, while the British forces there remained pitifully weak. Although Japan had stayed out of the war hitherto, the steps which Roosevelt and Churchill took in July to cut off her economic resources were bound to make her strike back in the only way possible for her – by force of arms. Her hesitancy allowed America and Britain more than four months' grace for developing their defence in the Pacific, but they failed to profit by it – and in Britain's case that neglect was largely due to the way that Churchill's interest and efforts had become focussed on North Africa. Thus Rommel indirectly produced the fall of Singapore – and as much by the personal impression he made on a personality-minded Prime Minister as by his potential threat to the Nile Valley and the Suez Canal.*

For the renewed offensive in Africa, code-named 'Operation Crusader', the British forces were much increased and also re-equipped. The four tank units were increased to fourteen, so that four complete armoured brigades (each of three units) were provided for the striking force, while the Tobruk garrison was given one brigade (of two tank

* For maps, see pp 118–19.

units and an additional squadron), sent in by sea, for use in the breakout to meet the striking force. (For the main part the brigades were equipped with the new Crusader cruiser tanks or with the new American Stuart tanks, the fastest of any in the field, but there were four units of 'I' tanks, Matildas or Valentines.) Three more motorized infantry divisions were brought up, making a total of four, besides a fresh division in Tobruk – where the British 70th relieved the 9th Australian that had borne the brunt of the siege.

By contrast, Rommel received very few reinforcements from Germany, and no additional tank units to augment his original four. The 5th Light Division was rechristened the 21st Panzer Division, but was not given an increased scale of tanks, and all that he could manage in the way of enlarging his force was to improvise an unmotorized infantry division (at first called the Afrika Division, and later the 90th Light) out of some extra artillery and infantry battalions. The Italian force of three divisions (one armoured) was augmented by three more small infantry divisions – but their value was much diminished by their obsolete equipment and lack of motor transport, so that they could only be used in a static role, and were an awkward handicap on Rommel's strategic freedom of manoeuvre.

In the air, also, the British now had a big advantage. Their strength was built up to a total of nearly 700 aircraft immediately available for the support of the offensive, against a total of 120 German aircraft and 200 Italian.

In armour, the British superiority was even greater. When the offensive was launched the British had more than 710 gun armed tanks (of which some 200 were 'I' tanks), while the enemy had only 174 German gun-armed tanks and 146 Italian – which were of obsolete type, and little value. Thus the British had a superiority well exceeding 2 to 1 over the enemy as a whole, and more than 4 to 1 over the Germans – whose two panzer divisions, with their two tank units apiece, were regarded by the British Commander-in-Chief as 'the backbone of the enemy's army'. Moreover, Rommel had no tanks in reserve, other than a few under repair, whereas the British had some 500 in reserve or in shipment on the way – so that they were much more capable of maintaining a prolonged fight. In the outcome, that reserve eventually turned the scales of the battle.*

* The figures of the comparative tank strengths and resources are those tabulated in the British Official History, pp 30–31. The figures given for the British operational strength – a total of 713 (including 201 'I' tanks) were arrived at by deduction from a number of differing records, differently com-

Rommel's chief asset, in countering the heavy odds against him in tanks, was that by the autumn two-thirds of his ordinary anti-tank guns were of the new long-barrelled 50-mm type – which was about 70 per cent superior in penetration to his old 37-mm gun, and 25 per cent superior to the British 2-pounder gun. Thus his defence was no longer so dependent on his handful of 88s as it had been in the summer.

Besides dispatching large reinforcements to Egypt, and most of Britain's newly manufactured equipment, Churchill also provided the striking force there with a new set of commanders. Four days after the failure of 'Battleaxe', Wavell was removed from command and replaced by Sir Claude Auchinleck, the Commander-in-Chief in India, while the force commander and the armoured division commander were replaced soon afterwards. Churchill had become increasingly impatient with Wavell's cautiousness, and the disappointing result of 'Battleaxe' clinched his decision to appoint a new commander-in-chief. But he found, to his renewed irritation, that Auchinleck was firm in resisting his pressure for an early renewal of the offensive and insisted on waiting until fully prepared and strong enough to ensure a good chance of decisive success. So the next offensive, 'Operation Crusader', was not launched until mid-November, five months after 'Battleaxe'. Meanwhile the greatly enlarged force was renamed Eighth Army, and command given to Lieutenant-General Sir Alan Cunningham – who had conducted the clearance of Italian Somaliland and the subsequent advance from the south into Ethiopia which led to the ejection of the Italians. The new army was divided into the 13th Corps under Lieutenant-General A. R. Godwin-Austen, and the 30th (armoured) Corps under Lieutenant-General C. W. M. Norrie. But with the exception of Norrie, a cavalryman, none of the new commanders had experience in handling tanks and in operating against armoured forces, and he was brought in as a substitute when the expert tankman originally chosen to command the armoured corps was killed in an air crash shortly before the offensive opened.

The 13th Corps included the New Zealand and 4th Indian Divisions, with a brigade of infantry tanks. The 30th Corps included the 7th Armoured Division with two armoured brigades (the 7th and 22nd), the 4th Armoured Brigade Group, the 22nd Guards (Motor) Brigade, and the 1st South African Division. The 2nd South African Division was in reserve.

---

piled. On another calculation from the records, the total comes to 756 (including 225 'I' tanks).

The basis of the offensive plan was that the 13th Corps would pin down the enemy troops who were holding the frontier positions, while the 30th Corps swept round the flank of these fortified positions 'to seek out and destroy' Rommel's armoured force – and then link up with the Tobruk garrison, seventy miles beyond the frontier, which was to break out to meet the 30th Corps. Thus the two corps, and their respective armour, would be operating in widely separated areas – rather than with combined effect. The most formidable part of the British armour, the brigade of Matildas and Valentines, would make no contribution to the armoured battle but merely be employed in small packets with the infantry. And when the advance developed this separated distribution soon spread into dispersion, with consequent weakness everywhere.

Thereby the British forfeited the opening advantage gained by their strategic outflanking move, which had taken the enemy by surprise and temporarily confused him. The British attack became disjointed – and to a large extent had disjointed itself. As Rommel caustically said: 'What difference does it make if you have two tanks to my one, when you spread them out and let me smash them in detail? You presented me with three brigades in succession.'

The source of the trouble lay in the hoary maxim, long inculcated in every official military manual and at Staff College, that 'the destruction of the enemy's main armed forces on the battlefield' is the prime objective, and the only sound one for a military commander. Between the wars that maxim came to be applied even more fervently by infantry-minded commanders when considering how they should use the tanks placed at their disposal, and they were apt to say: 'Kill off the enemy's tanks, and then we can get on with the battle.' The persistence of that habit of thought was all too manifest in the instructions given to the Eighth Army, and its armoured corps: 'Your immediate objective is the destruction of the enemy's armoured forces.' But an armoured force is not in itself suited to be an immediate objective. For it is a fluid force, not easily fixed – as infantry formations can be. The aim of destroying it is more likely to be attained indirectly, by drawing it to cover or retrieve some point of key importance. In trying to 'kill' Rommel's elusive panzer forces in a too direct way, the British armour not only became stretched and scattered but let itself be drawn all too easily into his gun-lined tank traps.

The British 30th Corps crossed the frontier early on November 18th and then began a right wheel towards Tobruk ninety miles distant. The advance was covered by an 'air umbrella', but this protection against discovery and interference was not immediately needed, as a heavy storm in the night had swamped the enemy's airfields and his aircraft were grounded. Nor, for the same reason, did it matter that the advance was slowed down by the bad going. Rommel had no inkling of the 'storm of steel' that was about to burst upon him. His mind was focused on the preparation for his own intended assault on Tobruk, and his striking force had moved thither in readiness to deliver it, although he had placed a strong covering force in the desert to the south as a check on interference.

By nightfall on the 18th the British armoured columns were astride the Trigh el Abd, and next morning pushed on northward – their thirty-mile frontage becoming stretched to fifty miles in the course of driving back Rommel's screen. The ill-effects of that overstretch were not long in developing.

In the centre, the two leading regiments of the 7th Armoured Brigade reached and captured the enemy airfield on top of the escarpment at Sidi Rezegh – only twelve miles from the Tobruk perimeter. But the rest of the brigade and the division's Support Group did not come up until next morning, the 20th, and by then Rommel had rushed up part of the Afrika Division, with a large number of anti-tank guns, to hold the top edge of the escarpment and block the path. No reinforcements arrived to build up the British force there. For the two other armoured brigades had run into trouble, one far to the west and the other far to the east, while the 1st South African Division had also been diverted westward.

What had happened on the western flank was that the 22nd Armoured Brigade had run into Italian tanks, and in driving them back had been led to attack the Italians' fortified position near Bir el Gubi. The 22nd was a brigade composed of yeomanry regiments which had not long been mounted in tanks and also came fresh to the desert war. In a too gallant assault – carried out in the immortal spirit of the 'Charge of the Light Brigade' at Balaclava – they were heavily hammered by the Italians' dug-in guns, and lost more than forty of their 160 tanks. Under the impression that the attack was going well, the corps commander diverted the South Africans thither to occupy Bir el Gubi.

On the eastern flank the 4th Armoured Brigade Group, which had become strung out over a twenty-five-mile stretch in chasing a German reconnaissance unit, had been suddenly taken aback by the appearance of a strong German armoured force near its rear – and its rearmost unit was badly mauled before one of the other two units returned to help in checking the enemy. This blow was the sequel to Rommel's first countermove and was delivered by a strong battle-group (including the two tank units of the 21st Panzer Division) which had been sent southward to explore the situation.

It was lucky for the British armour on this flank that it did not have to meet a concentrated blow by the whole Afrika Korps next morning. That respite was due to a misleading report received by its commander, Cruewell, which led him to imagine that the most dangerous British advance was coming along the northerly route, the Trigh Capuzzo. So he moved both his panzer divisions thither, towards Capuzzo – and found the area empty. Blinded by lack of air reconnaissance, the Germans were still groping in the 'fog of war'. Worse still, the 21st Panzer Division ran out of fuel on this eastward excursion, and was temporarily stranded. Only the 15th Panzer Division was able to return that day, and in the afternoon it struck the still isolated 4th Armoured Brigade at Gabr Saleh – so that this brigade for the second day in succession bore the brunt of the German counterblow, and suffered another mauling. Although the British higher commanders had good information about the enemy's movements they were slow to take advantage of the respite, and opportunity, provided by the Afrika Korps' temporary departure from the scene. No immediate step was taken to concentrate the three widely scattered armoured brigades. But towards midday, when the danger to the 4th Armoured Brigade became manifest, the 22nd was sent eastward to reinforce it, instead of moving up to join the 7th at Sidi Rezegh as previously intended. But the 22nd had a long way to go, on this switch from one flank to the other, and did not arrive until nightfall. It was thus too late to help in the fight.

Yet all this time the New Zealand Division and the 'I' tank brigade of the 13th Corps had been lying only seven miles away, at Bir Gibni – panting to advance and eager to help. But it was not called on to take a hand in the armoured battle, and its offers to help were declined. It is an extraordinary revelation of how far the 'two-compartment' idea was carried in conducting this battle.

When morning came, on November 21st, the British armoured brigades at Gabr Saleh found that the enemy had vanished from their front. This time it was not for a blow in the air – for Rommel had by now gained a clear picture of the British lay-out, and had ordered Cruewell to strike a concentrated blow, with both panzer divisions, against the British advanced force at Sidi Rezegh.

Norrie had just told this force to drive on towards Tobruk, and ordered the Tobruk garrison to start its breakout attack. But before the drive got going it was thrown out of gear. At 8 AM two German armoured columns were seen approaching from south and east. Two of the three British armoured units at Sidi Rezegh were hurriedly diverted to meet them. Thus only one (the 6th Royal Tanks) was left to lead the drive for Tobruk, and was soon shattered by the enemy's well-posted guns, which were able to concentrate on this single unit. It was another 'Charge of the Light Brigade' – a too light brigade in this case. Meanwhile the other two armoured units were assailed by the full weight of the Afrika Korps. One of them, the 7th Hussars, was overrun and almost wiped out by the 21st Panzer Division. The other, the 2nd Royal Tank Regiment, attacked the 15th Panzer Division so boldly and with such effect, thanks to its superior skill in firing on the move, that the enemy turned away. But the Germans attacked afresh in the afternoon, and cleverly employed their new tactics of pushing forward anti-tank guns unobtrusively ahead of their tanks and round the opponent's flanks. In this way they took such heavy toll that the rapidly dwindling remnant of the 7th Armoured Brigade was only saved from annihilation by the long-awaited and belated arrival of the 22nd Armoured Brigade from Gabr Saleh – the 4th did not come up until next day. As for the breakout attack from Tobruk, this drove four miles deep into the German–Italian investing position, but was then suspended in view of the setback which the 30th Corps had suffered – and the breakout force was thus left in an awkwardly deep and narrow salient.

When dawn broke on the fifth day the Africa Korps had again disappeared – but this time only to replenish its fuel and ammunition. Even that short lull was not to Rommel's liking, and about midday he arrived at the headquarters of the 21st Panzer Division, which had stayed near the battlefield, and launched it on an indirect approach and attack. Driving westward through the valley north of Sidi Rezegh, the panzer regiment wheeled round and struck at the western flank of the British position there. Sweeping up the slope, it overran the airfield and overwhelmed part of the Support Group before the two remaining British armoured brigades were able to intervene. Their belated counterattacks were not coordinated, and ended in a state of confusion as darkness fell. But that was not the end of a bad day. For the 15th Panzer Division, returning to the battle area at dusk after its 'day off', hit the rear of the 4th Armoured Brigade and surrounded the leaguer in which its headquarters and reserve, the 8th Hussars, were lying. Taken by surprise, most of the personnel, tanks, and wireless links were captured. The brigade commander had been directing the counterattack at Sidi Rezegh, and thus escaped capture – but when dawn came on the 23rd he found himself left with a mutilated and scattered brigade while short of the means to direct and reassemble its fragments. That plight paralysed his action on what proved a still more critical day.

It was a compensation, though not immediately, that the headquarters of the Afrika Korps suffered a similar fate early on the 23rd. This came about because Cunningham had at last given the order for the 13th Corps to start advancing – although only in a limited way. The New Zealanders took Capuzzo on the 22nd, and one brigade (the 6th) was then told to push on towards Sidi Rezegh. Soon after dawn on the 23rd it bumped into and overran the Afrika Korps HQ. Cruewell only escaped capture because he had just gone off to conduct the next phase of the battle. But his loss of operational staff and wireless links became a serious handicap in the days that followed – more of a handicap than was realized by the British, who were concerned with their own troubles and growing afflictions.

November 23rd was a Sunday – in England the 'Sunday next before Advent' and in Germany 'Totensonntag', the 'Sunday of the Dead'. In the light of what happened in the desert that day it was grimly apt that the battle was subsequently given that name by the Germans.

During the night the British force at Sidi Rezegh had withdrawn a short step southward, to await reinforcement by the 1st South African Division, which was now being brought up. But the junction was never achieved. For a concentrated thrust by the two panzer divisions, emerging from the early morning mist, took the British and South Africans by surprise and split them apart, as well as sweeping through their transport leaguers and producing a stampede. The disaster would have been greater if the panzer divisions had not been called off at this moment by a signal from Cruewell, who had not got a clear picture of the situation, and wanted to link up with the Italian Ariete Division before attempting a decisive blow. But the Italians were cautiously slow in advancing, and it was not until the afternoon that Cruewell launched his attack, from the south, against the major portion of Norrie's advanced forces, the now isolated 5th South African Brigade and 22nd Armoured Brigade – some of the smaller fragments had managed to slip out of the trap in the interval. By the time he struck, a good defence had been organized. His concentrated attack eventually succeeded in bursting into the position and overwhelming the defenders – of whom some 3,000 were captured or killed. But the Afrika Korps lost over seventy of its remaining 160 tanks.

The tank losses suffered in this one direct attack on a defensive position largely offset the material profit gained by skilful manoeuvre during the previous days. Indeed the crippling cost of this tactical success was strategically more damaging to the Germans than anything else in the course of 'Operation Crusader'. While the 30th Corps had suffered much heavier losses – and had only some seventy tanks left fit for action out of the 500 with which it had started – the British had a large reserve from which to restore their tank strength, whereas Rommel had no such reserve.

On November 24th the battle took another dramatic turn. For Rommel now sought to exploit his success by a deep thrust to, and over, the frontier – into the rear area of the Eighth Army – with all his mobile forces. Rather than lose time while they were assembling, he set off with the 21st Panzer Division as soon as it was ready to move, and himself took the lead – telling the 15th to follow, and being promised that the Italian Mobile Corps (Ariete armoured and Trieste motor divisions) would back up the panzer divisions, to close the ring round the British forces.

His initial intention, as indicated by his overnight report to Berlin and Rome, was to take advantage of the splintered state of the British forces and relieve the German–Italian frontier garrisons. But during the night his aim expanded, according to the evidence of his principal staff officers, and their statements are borne out by the headquarters war diary, which recorded that: 'The Commander-in-Chief decided to pursue the enemy with his armoured divisions, to restore the situation on the Sollum front, and at the same time advance against rearward communications of the British in the area of Sidi Omar ... This would mean that they would soon be compelled to give up the struggle.'

Rommel was striking at the mind of the opposing commander, as well as against the rear of the opposing forces and their supplies. At that moment such a stroke had greater promise than Rommel knew. For on the previous day, following the disastrous outcome of the armoured battle, Cunningham had thought of retreating over the frontier, and had only been stopped by the arrival of Auchinleck – who flew up from Cairo and insisted on a continuance of the struggle. Rommel's dash for the frontier, however, then caused a stampede among those who were in its path, and naturally produced still greater alarm at Eighth Army Headquarters.

By four o'clock in the afternoon, Rommel reached the frontier at Bir Sheferzen – having covered sixty miles in five hours' drive through the desert. On arrival, he immediately sent a battle-group through the frontier wire on a north-eastward drive to the Halfaya Pass, to dominate the Eighth Army's coastward route of retreat and supply, while extending the threat to its rear. After leading the battle-group some distance on its way, Rommel turned back, but was stranded in the desert by engine trouble. Luckily for him, Cruewell happened to pass the spot in his own command vehicle, and picked him up. But darkness was falling, and they could not find a gap in the frontier wire. Thus the two commanders, together with their chiefs of staff, spent the night amid the British and Indian troops in that area – dependent for their safety only on the natural instinct of ordinary soldiers to 'let sleeping generals lie'. For Cruewell's command vehicle was one that had been captured from the British. That also helped them to slip away at dawn unchallenged and get back safely to the headquarters of the 21st Panzer Division.

But on returning there, after twelve hours' 'detention', Rommel found that the 15th Panzer Division had not yet arrived on the frontier, while the Ariete Division had come to a halt at an early stage of its follow-up advance – on sighting the 1st South African Brigade in position across its path. The transport columns bringing up fuel supplies had also failed to arrive. These delays not only hindered but diminished the development of Rommel's counterstroke. He could not carry out his plan of sending a battle-group eastward to Habata, the British railhead, to block both the descents of the escarpment and the main inland route to Egypt along its crest. He also had to drop his idea of sending another battle-group southward to the Jarabub Oasis, along the track past Fort Maddalena, where the Eighth Army's advanced headquarters lay – a move which would have multiplied the confusion and alarm there. Even in the frontier zone, the day slipped away without any more fruitful action than an abortive and costly attack on Sidi Omar by the already weak tank regiment of the 21st Panzer Division. When the stronger 15th Panzer Division belatedly appeared on the scene, its northward sweep along the near side of the frontier merely achieved the destruction of a field workshop where sixteen British tanks were under repair.

Such a slight development of the menace that had loomed so large the day before allowed the British a chance to recover their breath and their balance. Moreover, early on the third day, November 26th, Cunningham was replaced as Commander of the Eighth Army by Auchinleck's Deputy Chief of the General Staff, Neil Ritchie – appointed in this emergency as a way of ensuring that the battle should be continued whatever the risks. It was very fortunate for the British that the enemy's drive had missed the two big supply dumps south of the Trigh el Abd on which they were largely dependent for the possibility of continuing the battle and resuming their advance. The panzer divisions' south-eastward drive from Sidi Rezegh passed well north of the dumps, but the Italians' line of advance, if they had pushed on, would have come closer to the dumps.

But although Rommel's thrust had lost momentum, the British situation remained very precarious on the morning of the 26th. The 30th Corps was so disrupted that it did nothing during the day to relieve the enemy's threat to the rearward parts of the 13th Corps – and these, besides being widely separated, were also isolated by wireless breakdowns. The Germans, however, were also suffering from intercommunication trouble, due to loss of wireless links, and it was far more detrimental in their case. For their prospects depended on quick and coordinated action to develop the threat to the British rear, whereas the best thing that the British troops there could do was to stand firm in their frontier positions while the advanced part of the 13th Corps continued to push on westward and link up with the Tobruk force in a double threat to Rommel's rear. This threat had now begun to produce a succession of signals from Panzer Group HQ, back at El Adem, calling for the return of the panzer divisions to relieve the pressure.

These disturbing calls from the rear combined with wireless breakdowns and fuel shortages in the forward area to upset the continuation of Rommel's counterstroke. He had ordered Cruewell that morning, the 26th, 'to clear the Sollum front quickly' – by a simultaneous attack with the 15th Panzer Division on one side and the 21st on the other. But he was dismayed to find that the 15th had moved back to Bardia early in the morning to replenish its fuel and ammunition, and then, just as it was returning to the battlefield, he found that the 21st had withdrawn from Halfaya, on a misinterpreted order, and was likewise on its way back to replenish at Bardia. So no action developed that day, and in the evening Rommel reluctantly decided to let the 21st Panzer Division continue its return journey to Tobruk. Next day he ordered the 15th to follow suit – after an early morning attack in which it succeeded in overwhelming the headquarters and support elements of the rearmost New Zealand brigade. That was the fade-out finish of a counterstroke that had opened so promisingly.

Retrospective comment on it has naturally been influenced by the knowledge that the thrust failed. Tactically minded critics have taken the view that Rommel should, instead, have concentrated on a more local exploitation of his success at Sidi Rezegh: finishing off what remained of 30th Corps, or crushing the New Zealand Division in its advanced position, or capturing Tobruk – thus clearing his flank and line of supply. But none of these tactical courses offered as great a chance of decisive strategic results against the British, while they carried more risk to him of losing time and being decisively weakened in a fruitless assault. The balance of numbers was so heavily against Rommel from the outset that he was bound to be beaten in a prolonged battle of attrition. If he tried to follow up and wipe out the remaining tanks of the 30th Corps, they could always evade battle – being faster than his own. The other courses meant attacking infantry and artillery in defensive positions. Since he could not afford to fight a battle of attrition, it would have been folly to pursue any of these tactical courses if any better prospect was open. Such a prospect was provided, inherently, by the course he chose – a deep strategic thrust with all his mobile forces. The chances were increased by the fact that he had at last induced Mussolini to put the Italian Mobile Corps under his command.

Rommel's stroke has often been criticized, after the event, as rash. But the history of war shows that a stroke of this kind has many times been successful – especially through its moral effect on the opposing troops and, even more, on their commanders. It was supported, too, by Rommel's own experience. Twice previously, in April and June, he had produced a British retreat – in the first case a collapse – by a similar strategic thrust that was made in lesser strength and did not reach such a threatening position. Two months later – in January 1942 – he produced another collapse by a fourth deep thrust – although it did not go so far as the November one towards cutting the British line of retreat. Moreover, when he launched his November thrust the opposing forces were more scattered and splintered than in any of the three cases when his strategic ripostes were successful.

The causes of his failure on this occasion have already emerged in the account of those crucial days – the delay of the 15th Panzer Division and the inertia of the Italian Mobile Corps in backing up the Rommel-led drive of the 21st Panzer Division; the consequent loss of momentum and spread in the exploiting 'shock-wave'; the fumbling and futile action on the frontier: due in part to lack of accurate information, wireless breakdowns, and misinterpreted orders; the creation by the British of a threat to their opponent's rear; Auchinleck's determination to continue the battle, and press this counter-threat, instead of retreating; the replacement of the Eighth Army's commander at a critical moment. His successor, being appointed in such circumstances, was bound to continue the battle whatever the risks – and this turned out a fortunate decision, although it might have proved fatal. (Two months later, the successor's reaction to a lesser threat was similar to his predecessor's in November.)

There is another factor which deserves attention, and emphasis, in any military analysis of the episode, and its lessons, The decision to continue the battle would have been of no avail, and merely led to worse disaster, if the stampede which Rommel produced had become more widespread. But most of the 'fragments' of the 30th Corps which were not in his path stayed in or near their previous positions, even though isolated, and so did those of the 13th Corps. The very fact of being so split up, and in the 30th Corps so stunned by the battering suffered in the previous days, helped to check the usual tendency of such scattered bodies to fall back towards their base. In this case, the enemy had so clearly outstripped them in his eastward drive that it must have seemed safer to 'stay put', on the edge of the whirlpool, even though the continued arrival of supplies was uncertain.

When Rommel's strategic counter-thrust failed to achieve its purpose, the first question was whether he could recover from the miscarriage, and the next question was whether he could possibly regain the upper hand. Astonishingly, in view of his weakness, he succeeded in his answer to both questions. Yet he was unable to profit by his regained advantage, and had to retreat in the end, through the accumulating effects of attrition. That eventual issue tends to show that he was right in trying his deep, and seemingly rash, strategic counter-thrust of November 24th – as the one move that offered a good chance of tilting the scales decisively in his favour.

When the Afrika Korps turned back westward, with its sixty remaining tanks (of which a third were light tanks), its chances of retrieving the situation at Tobruk by direct action looked dim, while its own situation appeared very precarious. For the New Zealand Division's westward advance, supported by nearly ninety Valentine and Matilda tanks, broke through Rommel's investing curtain on the night of the 26th and linked up with the British force at Tobruk – which comprised more than seventy tanks (including twenty lights). Meanwhile a fresh delivery from the base had brought the tank strength of the 7th Armoured Division up to nearly 130, so that in all the British now had a superiority of 5 to 1 in tanks (and 7 to 1 in gun-armed tanks). If they had been used in a fully concentrated way the Africa Korps would have had a poor prospect of survival, and the 7th Armoured Division alone should have been able to crush it.

The Afrika Korps was in jeopardy during the first stage of its withdrawal, and all the more because the 21st Panzer Division was delayed by a blocking position on its route, and could give no aid to the 15th

Panzer Division when this was intercepted and assailed on the afternoon of November 27th by the two armoured brigades of the 7th Armoured Division – with three times as many tanks as it had. One brigade (the 22nd) barred its path, while the other (the 4th) attacked the marching column from the flank, and caused havoc among the transport. Although the Germans managed to check the attack after some critical hours, their own westward march along the Trigh Capuzzo track was brought to a halt. But as dusk approached the British tanks withdrew southward into the desert to lie up for the night in a protective leaguer, in accordance with their usual practice. That allowed the Germans to push on westward under cover of darkness. On the next day the British armoured brigades renewed their attack, but were kept at bay by the enemy's anti-tank screen – and when night came the Germans were again able to push on unopposed.

Thus by the morning of the 29th the Afrika Korps linked up again with the rest of Rommel's forces, and relieved the pressure on them. Next day Rommel concentrated against the isolated 6th New Zealand Brigade on the Sidi Rezegh ridge, while using the Ariete Division to cover his flank, and his operation, against interference from the British armour lying to the south. His tanks, having got round to the far side of the position, struck from the west while his infantry attacked from the south. By evening the 6th New Zealand Brigade had been driven off the ridge, but a remnant got away and rejoined the main part of the division in the valley below, near Belhamed. The British armour, although brought up to strength again by a fresh delivery of tanks and concentrated under the 4th Armoured Brigade, made no vigorous effort to break through Rommel's 'curtain' and come to the rescue. The commanders had been lured so often into traps, and suffered so much from the enemy's skilful combination of tanks with anti-tank guns, that they had now become excessively cautious.

Early on December 1st Rommel's forces closed in around the New Zealanders at Belhamed, cutting the 'corridor' between them and the Tobruk force. About 4.30 AM the 4th Armoured Brigade was ordered to drive north 'with all speed' at first light and 'at all costs' engage the enemy tanks. It moved off about 7 AM, reached the Sidi Rezegh airfield at 9 AM and, after descending the escarpment, made contact with the New Zealanders. A counterattack was then planned against the enemy tanks – estimated as 'about forty'. But by this time part of the New Zealanders had been overrun, and a general withdrawal was ordered. What was left of the New Zealand Division retreated eastward to Zaafran (and then during the night to the frontier), while the 4th Arm-

oured Brigade made a southward withdrawal of twenty-five miles to Bir
Berraneb.

The outcome of this third round of the battle was an astonishing
achievement on the part of an enemy force that had been outnumbered
7 to 1 in fighting tanks at the start of the round, and when it ended was
still outnumbered 4 to 1 by the total of those on the British side.

Auchinleck now flew up to Eighth Army headquarters again. Correctly gauging the underlying weakness of Rommel's forces, he was
determined to continue the battle, having fresh forces, and reserves of
tanks, which he could bring up for the purpose. The 4th Indian Division was relieved on the frontier by the 2nd South African, and sent
forward to join the 7th Armoured Division in an outflanking move to
cut Rommel's line of supply and retreat.

When Rommel received news of this new and strong threat, he decided to pull back westward, and concentrate his remaining tanks in a
stroke to dislocate the British outflanking move. So on the night of
December 4th the Afrika Korps slipped away to the west, abandoning
the investment of Tobruk.

That morning the leading brigade of the 4th Indian Division had
launched an attack on the Italian position at Bir el Gubi (twenty miles
south of Sidi Rezegh), but the assault broke down under the defenders'
fire. The assault was renewed next morning, but again repelled. During
these operations the British armour had covered the northern flank of
the attack against interference from Rommel, but unfortunately it
moved back to leaguer in the afternoon of the 5th, with the intention of
trying out a new system of leaguering. At 5.30 PM Rommel's panzer
forces suddenly appeared on the scene, at Bir el Gubi, and overran part
of the unshielded Indian brigade – the rest managed to escape as darkness fell.

Following this setback, the commander of the 30th Corps, Norrie,
decided to postpone his intended flank advance to Acroma – a postponement that forfeited the chance of cutting Rommel's line of retreat.
The 4th Armoured Brigade was ordered to seek and destroy the
enemy's armour before a renewed advance was attempted. But the aim
was not achieved, and examination of the records reveals little evidence
of effort to fulfil it, although a fresh delivery of forty tanks had brought
the brigade's total up to 136 – almost three times the remaining
strength of the Afrika Korps. The brigade spent the next two days in
position near Bir el Gubi, with occasional short moves hopefully but
vainly intended to draw the enemy into a direct assault on the gun
positions of the 4th Indian Division.

On December 7th, Rommel decided to withdraw to the Gazala line, having been notified that no reinforcements were likely to arrive before the end of the year; that night the Afrika Korps began to disengage. The British were slow to realize what was happening, and it was not until December 9th that their armour started on a drive for 'Knightsbridge', the road junction south of Acroma. It was checked by an enemy rearguard eight miles short of Knightsbridge – and showed more concern to protect itself than to trap the enemy. By the 11th Rommel's forces had got back safely to Gazala, where a defensive position had earlier been prepared, as a reserve line.

On December 13th, Godwin-Austen's 13th Corps, which had now taken over charge of the pursuit, launched its attack on the Gazala line. The frontal attack was checked, but the Italian Mobile Corps covering Rommel's inland flank gave way rapidly under pressure, and the British left wing reached Sidi Breghisc, fifteen miles behind the Gazala line. But a panzer counterattack then brought the envelopment to a halt.

On the 14th, before renewing the assault, Godwin-Austen sent the 4th Armoured Brigade on a wider flank circuit – to Halegh Eleba, a multiple track junction midway between Gazala and Mechili. This move to get astride Rommel's rear started at 2.30 PM, and the brigade lay up for the night after trekking twenty miles due south. Starting again at 7 AM, with sixty miles to cover in its circuit, it was delayed by bad going and did not reach Halegh Eleba until 3 PM, four hours late by timetable – and too late to aid the main attack by drawing off Rommel's panzer reserve as planned. Moreover, it then sat tight and did nothing to make itself felt, so that the enemy did not become aware of its presence until next morning.

Meanwhile the main attack on the 15th had been a failure. An assault near the coast had gained a foothold in the Gazala position, but an enveloping attack was upset by a panzer counterstroke at midday, which nipped off an advanced part of the attacking force.

The British higher command still hoped that the strong armoured brigade it had placed in the enemy's rear would have decisive results by the next day. But on the morning of the 16th the brigade moved twenty miles south in order to refuel in complete security, and when it returned in the afternoon at a point nearer the front, it was checked by an anti-tank screen – and retired southward again to leaguer for the night. It recorded an interchange of fire, at long range, but no casualties. The impression left on the analyst is that the predominant desire was to see the enemy go – and he went, along the open path that was left for his passage.

For even the small losses incurred in the successful panzer counter-stroke on the 15th had left the Afrika Korps with barely thirty tanks, whereas the British now had nearly 200 on the scene. Weighing the situation, Rommel saw that it was impossible to hold on for long to the Gazala line, and decided to take a long step back, and get well out of reach, while awaiting reinforcements. He would go back to the Mersa Brega bottleneck on the Tripolitanian frontier, a position ideal for defence. It had also been the springboard for his first offensive, and would serve that purpose again. So on the night of December 16th he began his withdrawal – the Afrika Korps and the Italian Mobile Corps travelling by the desert route while the Italian infantry divisions marched back along the coast-road.

The pursuit was slow to get moving. The 4th Armoured Brigade did not start until 1 PM next day, and two hours later halted for the night twelve miles short of its earlier position at Halegh Eleba, while administrative preparations were made for a further advance. On the 18th it advanced along a desert route to a point south of Mechili, but on swinging northwards just missed catching the tail of the enemy's retreating columns.

Meanwhile the 4th Indian Division, mounted in motor transport and accompanied by infantry tanks, pressed on nearer the coast, through the rugged hill-country of the Jebel Akhdar. Derna was taken on the morning of the 19th – but the bulk of the enemy's foot-marching columns had already passed safely through the bottleneck. An attempt to intercept them farther west was hampered by the difficult country and shortage of petrol, and only a few fragments were caught. A large proportion of the pursuing forces were now grounded for lack of petrol.

Motorized infantry were employed to lead the chase across the desert chord of the great Benghazi bend. Reaching Antelat on December 22nd they found the enemy's panzer force (with thirty tanks) posted near Beda Fomm – to cover the coastwise retreat of the Italian foot-marching forces – and were kept at bay until the 26th, when Rommel's rearguard fell back another thirty miles to Agedabia. Meanwhile the re-equipped 22nd Armoured Brigade had come up to reinforce the pursuit force. Following up the enemy rearguard, the Guards Brigade launched a frontal assault on Agedabia – which failed – while the 22nd Armoured Brigade made a turning move thirty miles deeper in the desert, through El Haseiat. This suffered an unexpected reverse. For on the 27th its own flank was suddenly assailed by a German panzer force, and then surrounded in further fighting three days later. Although some thirty of the British tanks managed to escape, sixty-five were lost. In making this riposte Rommel had been helped by the arrival of two fresh tank companies (thirty tanks) which had been landed at Benghazi on the 19th, just before the port was evacuated – the first reinforcement which had reached him since the opening of 'Crusader'.

The British reverse at El Haseiat was a disappointing and frustrating end to the long pursuit – a cold douche to the exhilaration of ultimate success in the battle around Tobruk. But substantial profits were gained through Rommel's enforced retreat, which left the German–Italian garrisons on the frontier isolated and without hope. Bardia surrendered on January 2nd, and the two remaining frontier posts on the 17th. This brought the number of prisoners captured in the frontier positions to 20,000, including those taken earlier at Sidi Omar, and the total Axis casualties to 33,000 – compared with just under 18,000 on the British side. But nearly two-thirds of the Axis loss were Italians, and of the 13,000 Germans a considerable part were administrative personnel, whereas the bulk of the British loss in the six weeks' battle was in the fighting troops, and included many highly trained desert veterans, who were difficult to replace.

The disadvantage of having to rely on inexperienced troops, particularly in the desert, would be shown once again in the next battle. This came in the third week of January – when Rommel, supposedly crippled, delivered another of his unexpected strokes: with startlingly similar results to his opening stroke in 1941.

CHAPTER SIXTEEN

Upsurge in the Far East

From 1931 onward the Japanese were aggressively engaged in expanding their footholds on the Asiatic mainland at the expense of the Chinese, who were weakened by internal conflict, and to the detriment of American and British interests in that sphere. In that year they had invaded Manchuria and converted it into a Japanese satellite state. In 1932 they penetrated China itself, and from 1937 on pursued a consistent effort to establish their control of that vast area, but became enmeshed in the toils of guerrilla warfare, and eventually sought a solution of the problem in further expansionist moves, southward, aimed to shut off the Chinese from outside supplies.

Following Hitler's conquest of France and the Low Countries in 1940, the Japanese took advantage of France's helplessness by getting her to agree, under threat, to their 'protective' occupation of French Indo-China.

In reply President Roosevelt demanded, on July 24th, 1941, the withdrawal of Japanese troops from Indo-China – and to enforce his demand he issued orders on the 26th freezing all Japanese assets in the United States and placing an embargo on oil supply. Mr Churchill took simultaneous action, and two days later the refugee Dutch Government in London was induced to follow suit – which meant, as Churchill had remarked, that 'Japan was deprived at a stroke of her vital oil supplies'.

In earlier discussions, as far back as 1931, it had always been recognized that such a paralysing stroke would force Japan to fight, as the only alternative to collapse or the abandonment of her policy. It is remarkable that she deferred striking for more than four months, while trying to negotiate a lifting of the oil embargo. The United States Government refused to lift it unless Japan withdrew not only from Indo-China but also from China. No Government, least of all the Japanese, could be expected to swallow such humiliating conditions, and such 'loss of face'. So there was every reason to expect war in the Pacific at any moment, from the last week of July onwards. In these circumstances the Americans and British were lucky to be allowed four months' grace before the Japanese struck. But little advantage was taken of this interval for defensive preparation.

On the morning of December 7th, 1941, a Japanese naval force with six aircraft-carriers delivered a shattering air attack on Pearl Harbor, the American naval base in the Hawaiian Islands. The stroke was made ahead of the declaration of war, following the precedent of the attack on Port Arthur in 1904, Japan's opening stroke in her war against Russia.

Until early in 1941 Japan's plan in case of war against the United States was to use her main fleet in the southern Pacific in conjunction with an attack on the Philippine Islands, to meet an American advance across the ocean to the relief of their garrison there. That was the move that the Americans were expecting the Japanese to make, and their expectations had been reinforced by the recent Japanese occupation of Indo-China.

Admiral Yamamoto, however, had in the meantime conceived a new plan – of a surprise attack on Pearl Harbor. The striking force made a very roundabout approach via the Kurile Islands and came down from the north upon the Hawaiian Islands undetected, then launched its attack before sunrise, with 360 aircraft, from a position nearly 300 miles from Pearl Harbor. Four of the eight American battleships were sunk, one was beached, and the others badly damaged. In little over an hour the Japanese had gained control of the Pacific.

By this stroke the way was cleared for an uninterrupted seaborne invasion of American, British and Dutch territories in that ocean. While the main Japanese striking force had been steaming towards the Hawaiian Islands, other naval forces had been escorting troopship convoys into the South-west Pacific. Almost simultaneously with the air attack on Pearl Harbor, landings began in the Malay Peninsula as well as in the Philippines.

The former were aimed at the great British naval base at Singapore, but there was no attempt to attack it from the sea – the kind of attack which the defence had been primarily designed to meet. The approach was very indirect. While a landing was made at Kota Bharu on the north-east coast of the Malay Peninsula, to seize airfields and distract attention, the main forces were disembarked on the Siamese neck of the peninsula, some 500 miles north of Singapore. From these landing-places in the extreme north-east the Japanese forces poured down the *west* coast of the peninsula, successively outflanking the lines on which the British forces attempted to check them.

The Japanese profited not only by their unexpected choice of such a difficult route but by the opportunities for unexpected infiltration which

The Pacific: December 8, 1941

Japanese occupied territory December 1941

the thick vegetation often provided. After almost continuous retreat for six weeks the British forces were forced to withdraw from the mainland into the island of Singapore, at the end of January. On the night of February 8th, the Japanese launched their attack across the mile-wide straits, got ashore at numerous points, and developed fresh infiltrations along a broad front. On February 15th, the defending forces surrendered, and with them was lost the key to the South-west Pacific.

In a smaller, separate operation, the Japanese had launched an attack on the British base at Hong Kong, starting on December 8th, and forced the surrender of the colony, with its garrison, by Christmas Day.

On the main Philippine island of Luzon, the initial landings north of Manila had been quickly followed by a landing in the rear of the capital. Under this dislocating leverage, and the converging threat, the American forces abandoned most of the island and fell back into the small Bataan Peninsula, before the end of December. There, by contrast, they were only open to frontal assault on a narrowly contracted front, and succeeded in holding out until April before they were overwhelmed.

Long before that, and even before the fall of Singapore, the Japanese tide of conquest was spreading through the Malay Archipelago. On January 11th, Japanese forces landed in Borneo and Celebes, and stronger ones followed on the 24th. Five weeks later, on March 1st, the Japanese launched an attack on Java, the core of the Dutch East Indies, after the island had been isolated by flanking moves. Within barely a week, the whole of Java had fallen into their hands like a ripe plum.

But the apparently imminent threat to Australia did not develop. The main Japanese effort was now directed in the opposite direction, westward, towards the conquest of Burma. The direct but wide-fronted advance from Thailand upon Rangoon was an indirect approach to their major object on the Asiatic mainland as a whole, the paralysis of China's power of resistance. For Rangoon was the port of entry for Anglo-American supplies of equipment to China, by way of the Burma Road.

At the same time, this move was shrewdly designed to complete the conquest of the western gateway to the Pacific, and there establish a firm barrier across the main routes by which any overland Anglo-American offensive might subsequently be attempted. On March 8th, Rangoon fell, and within a further two months the British forces were driven out of Burma, over the mountains, back into India.

The Japanese had thus secured a covering position so naturally strong that any attempt at reconquest would be badly handicapped and bound to be a very slow process.

A long time passed before the Allies built up forces sufficient to attempt the recovery of Japan's conquests – beginning at the south-eastern end. Here they benefited from the preservation of Australia, which provided them with a large-scale base close to the chain of Japanese outposts.

Japan was the only country in an advanced industrial state outside Europe and North America – due to the rapid process of modernization which had begun under the Emperor Meiji from 1868 onward. Yet at heart Japanese society remained 'feudal', where the warrior was exalted, not the manufacturer or merchant. The Emperor was divine, and the ruling class all-powerful. Moreover the influence of the military was immense. Fervently patriotic, and often bitterly anti-foreign, they hoped to establish their country's domination over the whole of eastern Asia, particularly China. From the 1930s onward they had, by threats and assassinations, virtually assumed control of Japanese policy.

Japan's approach to political and strategic problems was much influenced by the fact that she had never suffered defeat since her modernization began. Her people's belief in her invincibility became widespread after the war with Russia of 1904–5, when both on land and sea her forces had demonstrated their superiority – and shown that the dominance of Europeans over the rest of the world's peoples could be breached.

In August 1914 Japan, as Britain's ally since 1902, had taken Tsingtao and Shantung, the German concessions in China, together with the Marshall, Caroline, and Mariana groups of islands in the Pacific, all of which were German colonies. The gains were confirmed by the Treaty of Versailles in 1919, at the end of the First World War – thus leaving Japan the predominant power on the west side of the Pacific. Despite this, her people were dissatisfied with her war gains, and left with the feeling that she was a 'have-not' power, like Italy. So the Japanese came to feel that they had something in common with Italy and with Germany.

The sense of frustration probably developed from the failure of Japan's attempt to control China, in 1915, when her '21 Demands' had to be withdrawn under American protest. Significantly, China was always the main goal for the Japanese Army from the Sino-Japanese War of 1895 onward. Although at the end of the First World War the Imperial Defence Policy named the United States as the prime potential enemy, in accord with the naval view, the Army was always more apprehensive about Soviet Russia, whose large land forces in the Far East were regarded as a much greater threat to Japan's continental designs.

Then came a series of humiliations for Japan in the years 1921–4. First, the British politely declined to renew the alliance with Japan. That break was to some extent prompted by various signs of Japanese expansionist plans in the Pacific, but the definite decision was made under strong American pressure. The Japanese took it as an insult, and a sign that the white peoples were lining up against them. Their indignation was increased by successive American legislative steps to restrict Japanese immigration, culminating in the Act of 1924 that excluded Asiatics as immigrants. The double 'loss of face' was bitterly resented.

Meanwhile the British had announced plans for building a Far East naval base at Singapore, adequate for a battle-fleet. That was obviously intended as a check upon Japan, and interpreted by the Japanese as a challenge.

All this reacted to the detriment of the Japanese political leaders, who came under increasing attack for having accepted a 3–5–5 basis in relation to the American and British battle-fleets under the Washington naval limitation treaty of 1921. Other grievances were that they had agreed to return Shantung Province to China, and later had signed the Nine-Power Treaty of 1922 guaranteeing the integrity of China.

Actually, and ironically, the Treaty of Washington assisted Japan's subsequent expansionist moves by weakening checks upon her in the Pacific – the projected American and British naval bases there being either delayed or weakly fortified. She herself found it easier to evade the specifications of gun-power and tonnage during the thirteen-year period before she openly repudiated the treaty.

The more liberal political leaders of Japan also suffered from the world economic crisis that developed in 1929, as she was particularly hard hit by it, with a resulting growth of discontent that the militarists were able to exploit in pressing their argument that expansion was the solution for Japan's economic problem.

In September 1931 the 'Mukden incident' gave the local Japanese Army leaders a pretext, and opportunity, to expand into Manchuria, and turn it into their puppet state of Manchukuo. Their troops guarding the South Manchurian railway, under treaty right, attacked and disarmed the Chinese garrisons in Mukden and neighbouring towns on the excuse of self-defence against a threatened attack. The facts were obscure, and obscured, thus helping the Japanese to overrun the whole of Manchuria within the next few months. Although the occupation was not recognized by the League of Nations, or the United States, protests and widespread criticism gave the Japanese an incentive to withdraw from the League in 1933. Three years later they joined with Nazi Germany and Fascist Italy in the Anti-Comintern Pact.

In July 1937, an alleged clash at the Marco Polo Bridge, another highly suspicious 'incident', led to the Japanese Kwantung Army invading North China proper. The invasion continued and extended during the next two years, but the Japanese became increasingly bogged down in the struggle against the Chinese nationalist forces under Chiang Kai-Shek, while in their attack at Shanghai in the summer of 1937 they suffered a repulse. This, however, turned out to their advantage in the long run, as it spurred them to correct tactical faults and tendencies to overconfidence dating back to the Russo-Japanese War – although not before they had suffered a further lesson, at the hands of the Soviet Army, in a clash over the disputed frontier of West Manchuria. Here, in the Nomonhan region, a Japanese force of some 15,000 men was encircled, and over 11,000 were lost, when the Russians brought up five mechanized brigades with three infantry divisions, in August 1939.

In that same month the unexpected news of the Nazi–Soviet Pact caused a revulsion, and the return of moderate Japanese Governments. But that reaction only continued until Hitler's conquest of Western Europe in 1940, and in July 1940 a pro-Axis Government under Prince Konoye was put into power by the Army. Japanese expansion in China was then accelerated, while at the end of September Japan signed the 'Tripartite Pact' with Germany and Italy, by which these three undertook to oppose any fresh country that joined the Allies – a pact aimed primarily against intervention by America.

In April 1941 the Japanese further reinsured themselves by a neutrality pact with Soviet Russia. That promised to release Japanese forces for southerly expansionist operations – although even then suspicion of Russia and her designs led the Japanese to allot only eleven divisions for such operations, while thirteen were kept in Manchuria, and twenty-two in China.

On July 24th the Japanese, with the reluctant compliance of the Vichy Government, took over French Indo-China. Two days later President Roosevelt 'froze' all Japanese assets, an action that was quickly followed by the British and Dutch Governments. Thus trade with Japan was brought to a stop, particularly in oil.

Japan imported 88 per cent of her peacetime oil consumption. At the time of the embargo she held stocks sufficient for three years of normal use, or half that period at full war consumption. Moreover, a Japanese War Office survey had shown that stocks would be exhausted before the three years that were reckoned as necessary to finish the war in China, so a victory there seemed all the more important. The only available resource left lay in the oilfields of the Dutch East Indies, and it was reckoned that although the Dutch were likely to destroy their installations there before capture these could be repaired and brought into use before home stocks were too badly depleted. Oil from Java and Sumatra would save the situation, and enable China's conquest to be completed.

Conquest of the region, including Malaya, would also bring possession of four-fifths of the world's rubber output, and two-thirds of its tin output. That would not only be a very valuable gain for Japan, but hit her opponents worse than the loss of the oil.

These were the main factors that Japan's leaders had to consider when faced with the trade embargo. Unless America could be induced to lift it, they were faced with a choice between abandoning their ambitions – in which case an Army coup at home might follow – or seizing the oil and fighting the white powers. It was a stark alternative. If they continued the campaign in China, but withdrew from Indo-China and stopped southward expansion, they might obtain some mitigation of the embargo, but Japan herself would be becoming weaker – and less able to withstand any further demands by the United States.

Natural hesitation to make an all-or-nothing choice may explain the puzzle why the Japanese were so tardy in striking, and deferred a decision for four months. There was also the natural instinct of military chiefs to desire ample time for completing preparations, and prolonged arguments over the strategy to be adopted. One school of thought even optimistically hoped, and argued, that America might continue to stand aside if Japan confined herself to seizing Dutch and British territory.

On August 6th Japan besought the United States to lift the embargo. That same month came the American decision to hold the whole of the Philippine Islands in the event of war, and the Japanese request for the cessation of the flow of American reinforcements thither. It met a firm reply, warning the Japanese against further aggression.

After two more months of internal argument, Prince Konoye's Government was replaced by one under General Hideki Tojo – an event that was probably decisive. Even so, there was further prolonged discussion, and the decision for war was not taken until November 25th. One precipitating factor was a report showing oil stocks as having shrunk by a quarter of their total between April and September.

Even then, the Commander-in-Chief of the Japanese Combined Fleet, Admiral Yamamoto, was given orders the same day that the attack on Pearl Harbor was to be cancelled if by any chance the continued negotiations in Washington were successful.

The naval strengths in the Pacific in December 1941 are summarized in the following table: *

	Capital ships	Aircraft Carriers	Heavy Cruisers	Light Cruisers	Destroyers	Submarines
BRITISH EMPIRE	2	—	1	7	13	—
USA	9	3	13	11	80	56
NETHERLANDS	—	—	—	3	7	13
FREE FRENCH	—	—	—	1	—	—
ALLIES TOTAL	11	3	14	22	100	69
JAPAN	10	10	18	18	113	63

The main point to note is that while the two sides were closely balanced in most respects, the Japanese had a great advantage in aircraft-carriers, the crucial arm. Moreover, what such a table cannot show are qualitative differences. The Japanese force was compact and well-trained, especially in night-fighting; it did not suffer command or language difficulties as on the Allied side. There were 6,000 miles of ocean between the two main bases of the Allies, Pearl Harbor and Singapore. Materially, the Japanese Navy was much better. It had many newer ships, while most of them were somewhat better-armed and faster. Of the capital ships, only HMS *Prince of Wales* was a match in these respects for the better Japanese battleships.

In Army strength, the Japanese employed only eleven divisions, out of their overall total of fifty-one, for their operations in the South-west Pacific. That was under a quarter of a million fighting troops, and with administrative troops probably a total of about 400,000. Allied numbers are more uncertain. In deciding to attack, the Japanese estimated the British as having 11,000 in Hong Kong, 88,000 in Malaya, and 35,000 in Burma -- a total of 134,000; the Americans as having 31,000 of their men in the Philippines, with about 110,000 Philippine troops; the Dutch as having 25,000 regulars and 40,000 militia. Superficially, to launch a far-reaching offensive with such small odds might seem a

* Figures from Roskill: *The War at Sea*, vol I, p 560.

daring gamble. In reality, it was a well-calculated gamble, as sea and air control would usually give the Japanese local superiority of numbers, while this would be multiplied by experience and superior quality of training – particularly in amphibious landings, jungle warfare, and night attacks.

In air strength the Japanese employed only 700 out of their total of 1,500 first-line Army aircraft, but these were reinforced by 480 Naval aircraft, of the 11th Air Fleet, based on Formosa – as well as 360 allocated for the Pearl Harbor stroke. Originally, the fleet carriers were allotted, and needed, to provide air cover for the southern operations. But in November, barely four weeks before the war, the range of the Zero fighters – which outclassed the Allied fighters available – was increased, so that they could fly the 450 miles from Formosa to the Philippines, and back. Thus the carriers were freed for the Pearl Harbor stroke.

Opposed to these powerful Japanese air forces were 307 American operational aircraft in the Philippines, including thirty-five long-range B17 bombers, but otherwise inferior in quality; 158 first-line British aircraft in Malaya, mostly of obsolete types; and 144 Dutch in their territories. In Burma, the British then had only thirty-seven fighters. The Japanese superiority in quantity was multiplied by superiority in quality – particularly that of the Zero fighters.

The Japanese also owed much to their development of amphibious warfare, for such an oceanic area of islands and gulfs. Their one serious weakness was the relatively small size of their merchant marine – little more than 6 million tons of shipping – but that did not become a decisive handicap until later in the war.

In sum, the Japanese started the war with a great all-round advantage, especially in quality. In the opening stage, their only real danger lay in the possibility of a prompt intervention by the American Pacific Fleet – but that danger they forestalled by their Pearl Harbor stroke.

Intelligence is a further factor, of which sufficient account is rarely taken in setting out the balance of strength. In general, the Japanese were good in this way, owing to long and careful study of the areas beforehand – but the Allies enjoyed one immense advantage in that the Americans had broken the Japanese diplomatic code in the summer of 1940 (an achievement due to Colonel William F. Friedman). From then on, all Japanese Foreign Office or Command secret messages could be read by the Americans, and during the prewar negotiations they knew the latest Tokyo proposals before they were presented. Only the exact date, and operational points of attack, were not passed to the Japanese ambassador.

Although the Americans were taken by surprise at Pearl Harbor, their knowledge of the Japanese codes was inherently a great basic advantage, and became such as they learnt to use it better.

Japanese strategy was geared to the dual aim, defensive and offensive, of securing the required oil supplies that would enable her to overcome a China that would in the same sweeping process be shut off from the supplies needed to maintain resistance. In taking the risk of challenging America, a power whose potential was vastly greater than their own, the Japanese leaders drew encouragement from the turn of events in Europe, where the Axis now dominated almost the whole Continent, and Soviet Russia was so hard pressed by Hitler's onslaught that she could hardly intervene in the Far East. If the Japanese fulfilled their dream of establishing a concentric defensive ring from the Aleutian Islands in the north round to Burma in the south, they hoped that the United States, after vain efforts to break through the ring, would eventually come to accept Japan's conquests and the establishment of what she called 'The Greater East Asia Co-Prosperity Sphere'.

The plan had a basic likeness to Hitler's concept of establishing offensively a defensive barrier from Archangel to Astrakhan, to shut out and keep out the Asiatic border.

Originally, the Japanese plan had been to seize the Philippines, then await the American recovery-move – which was expected to come through the mandated island territories – while concentrating her own forces to repel it. (Under the three-stage war-plan, the Japanese reckoned to complete the capture of the Philippines in fifty days, that of Malaysia in 100 days, and all the Dutch East Indies after 150 days.) But in August 1939, Admiral Yamamoto, an ardent believer in the value of aircraft-carriers, was appointed to command the Japanese Combined Fleet. He shrewdly saw the necessity of an immediate, and surprise, stroke to paralyse the United States Pacific Fleet – which he termed 'a dagger pointed at the throat of Japan' – and delay its countermoves. The Japanese Naval Staff rather dubiously and reluctantly accepted his argument.

The opening attack-problem was complicated by the timetable – and the zone differences (Sunday, December 7th in Hawaii would be Monday, December 8th in Malaya). But it was arranged that all the main operations would begin between 17.15 hours and 19.00 hours Greenwich Mean Time, and all assaults would take place in the early morning by local time.

On the American side, it had long been considered politically deplorable to abandon the Philippines, but the military argument that it was impossible to defend these islands, 5,000 miles from Pearl Harbor in Hawaii, had prevailed, so that the plan was only to maintain a foothold – on the fortified Bataan peninsula in Luzon, near the capital Manila. In August 1941, however, the plan was changed and the decision taken to hold all the Philippines.

One factor in the change was the pressure of General Douglas MacArthur, who had been military adviser to the Philippine Government since 1935, and then at the end of July 1941 had been recalled to active duty in the United States Army and appointed Commanding General in the Far East; President Roosevelt's high opinion of MacArthur's judgement had earlier been shown by the way he had himself in 1934 extended MacArthur's four-year tenure as Chief of Staff of the United States Army by a year. Another factor was that President Roosevelt had come to feel that since Germany had become entangled in Russia he could venture to take a firmer line with Japan – as he had done in imposing the oil embargo. The third factor was the optimism aroused by the advent of the long-range B17 bombers – which, it was hoped, would effectively hit not only Formosa but Japan herself. She, however, struck before any large number of B17s reinforced the air force in the Philippines. Moreover, what was not seriously considered by the American Chiefs of Staff was a Japanese stroke at Pearl Harbor.

CHAPTER SEVENTEEN

Japan's Tide of Conquest

The execution of the plan of attack on Pearl Harbor owed as much to Admiral Yamamoto's impulsion as had its adoption. For many months a stream of information, particularly about American ship movements, flowed in from the trained naval Intelligence officers who had been posted to the Japanese consulate in Honolulu. In the Japanese fleet itself the crews of ships and aircraft were intensively trained for the operation, and to carry it out in all kinds of weather; at least fifty practice flights were made by the bomber crews.

As already mentioned, the plan was much helped by the recently increased range of the Zero fighter type, which freed the carrier fleet from having to aid the South-west Pacific operations. It profited also from the evidence of the British naval attack on Taranto in November 1940, where the British Fleet Air Arm had succeeded, with only twenty-one torpedo-bombers, in sinking three Italian battleships lying in a strongly fortified harbour. Even then it had not been considered possible to launch aerial torpedoes in water where the depth was less than 75 feet – which was about the average at Taranto – and Pearl Harbor had thus been regarded as immune from that kind of attack, as the depth there was only 30–45 feet. But by 1941 the British, applying their experience at Taranto, had become able to launch aerial torpedoes in barely 40 feet depth of water, by fitting wooden fins that prevented them from 'porpoising' and hitting the shallow sea-bottom.

Learning these details from their embassies in Rome and London, the Japanese were stimulated to press on with similar experiments. Moreover, to make their planned attack more effective, their high-level bombers were equipped with 15-inch and 16-inch armour-piercing shells fitted with fins so that they would fall like bombs. Dropped vertically, no deck-armour could withstand them.

The United States Pacific Fleet could have countered the 'Taranto' danger by fitting its larger ships with anti-torpedo nets – and that possibility worried the Japanese – but Admiral Husband E. Kimmel, its Commander-in-Chief, had taken the view, like the Navy Department,

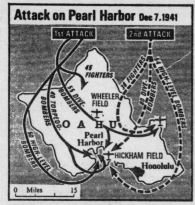

Attack on Pearl Harbor Dec 7, 1941

1st ATTACK   2nd ATTACK

45 FIGHTERS
36 FIGHTERS
51 DIVE BOMBERS
40 TORPEDO BOMBERS
70 DIVE BOMBERS
54 HIGH-LEVEL BOMBERS
50 HIGH-LEVEL BOMBERS

WHEELER FIELD

O A H U

Pearl Harbor

HICKHAM FIELD

Honolulu

0   Miles   15

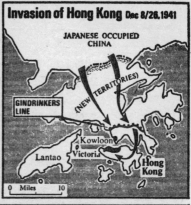

Invasion of Hong Kong Dec 8/26, 1941

JAPANESE OCCUPIED CHINA

GINDRINKERS LINE

(NEW TERRITORIES)

Kowloon
Lantao   Victoria
Hong Kong

0   Miles   10

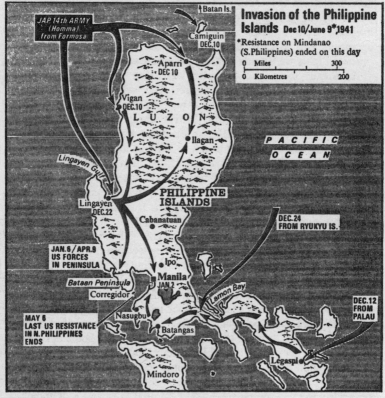

Invasion of the Philippine Islands Dec 10/June 9*, 1941

*Resistance on Mindanao (S. Philippines) ended on this day

0   Miles   300
0   Kilometres   200

Batan Is.

JAP. 14th ARMY
(Homma)
from Formosa

Camiguin
DEC.10

Aparri
DEC.10

Vigan
DEC.10

L U Z O N

Ilagan

P A C I F I C
O C E A N

Lingayen Gulf

Lingayen
DEC.22

Cabanatuan

PHILIPPINE
ISLANDS

DEC.24
FROM RYUKYU IS.

JAN.6/APR.9
US FORCES
IN PENINSULA

Ipo

Manila
JAN.2

Bataan Peninsula
Corregidor

Lamon Bay

DEC.12
FROM PALAU

MAY 6
LAST US RESISTANCE
IN N. PHILIPPINES
ENDS

Nasugbu

Batangas

Legaspi

Mindoro

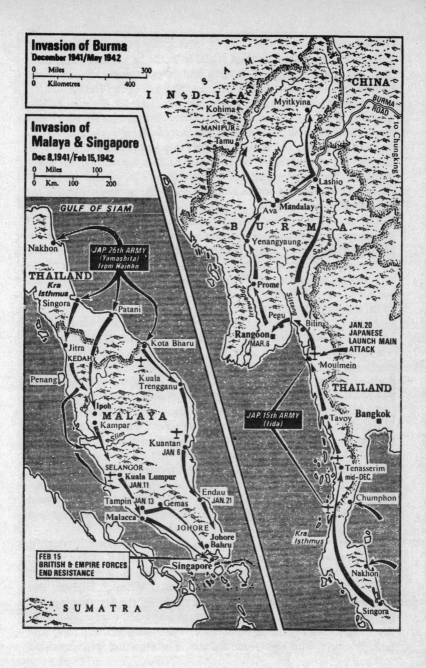

Invasion of Burma
December 1941/May 1942

0 — Miles — 300
0 — Kilometres — 400

Invasion of Malaya & Singapore
Dec 8, 1941/Feb 15, 1942

0 — Miles — 100
0 — Km. 100 — 200

GULF OF SIAM

Nakhon

JAP. 26th ARMY
(Yamashita)
from Hainan

THAILAND
Kra Isthmus
Singora
Patani

Jitra
KEDAH
Kota Bharu

Penang

Kuala Trengganu

Ipoh
MALAYA
Kampar
Slim
Kuantan
JAN 6

SELANGOR
Kuala Lumpur
JAN 11
Tampin JAN 13 — Gemas
Malacca — Endau JAN 21
JOHORE
Johore Bahru
Singapore

FEB 15
BRITISH & EMPIRE FORCES
END RESISTANCE

SUMATRA

I N D I A
Kohima
MANIPUR
Tamu
Chindwin

Myitkyina
CHINA
BURMA ROAD
to Chungking
Lashio

Ava Mandalay
Yenangyaung
BURMA
Irrawaddy
Salween

Prome
Pegu
Biling
Rangoon
MAR. 8

JAN. 20
JAPANESE
LAUNCH MAIN
ATTACK

Moulmein

THAILAND

JAP. 15th ARMY
(Iida)

Tavoy
Bangkok

Tenasserim
mid-DEC.

Chumphon

Kra Isthmus

Nakhon

Singora

that the cumbersome nets then available would be too much of a hindrance to quick movement of ships and to boat traffic. As the event showed, that decision virtually doomed the fleet at Pearl Harbor.

A combination of factors determined the date of the attack. The Japanese knew that Admiral Kimmel always brought his fleet back into Pearl Harbor during the weekend, and that the ships would not be fully manned then, thus increasing the effect of a surprise attack. So a Sunday was the natural choice. After mid-December the weather was likely to be unfavourable for amphibious landings in Malaya and the Philippines, as the monsoon would be at its peak, and unfavourable also for the refuelling at sea of the force to attack Pearl Harbor. On December 8th (Tokyo time), a Sunday at Hawaii, there would be no moonlight, and the consequent cloak of darkness would aid the surprise approach to Hawaii of the carrier force. The tides there would also be favourable for landings, an idea which was originally considered, although eventually rejected for lack of troopships and because the approach of such an invasion force was likely to be detected.

In choosing the approach route of the naval striking force, three alternatives were considered. One was a southerly route via the Marshall Islands, and another was a central route via the Midway Islands. These were the shorter, but they were discarded in favour of a northerly approach from the Kurile Islands – which would mean refuelling – because this avoided the shipping routes and also carried less risk of being spotted by the American reconnaissance aircraft patrols.

The Japanese also benefited from the use of what has been called the 'unequal leg' attack. Approaching in darkness, the carriers launched their planes at first light when at the nearest point to the target, then turned away from the target but not on a directly reversed route, and were rejoined by their aircraft at a point farther from the target than when they had been launched. Thus the Japanese aircraft flew one short, and one long, leg – whereas pursuing American aircraft would have to fly two long legs, one out and one back. That disadvantage had not been considered by the American defence planners.

The targets, in order of importance, were: the American carriers (it was hoped by the Japanese that as many as six, and at least three, would be at Pearl Harbor); the battleships; the oil tanks and other port installations; the aircraft on the main bases at Wheeler, Hickam, and Bellows Field. The force used for this stroke by the Japanese was six carriers, carrying a total of 423 aircraft, of which 360 were employed in the attack – 104 high-level bombers, 135 dive-bombers, and forty torpedo-bombers, with eighty-one fighters. The escorting force consisted of two battleships, three cruisers, nine destroyers, and three submarines, with eight accompanying tankers; it was under Admiral Nagumo. There was also planned to be a simultaneous attack by midget submarines, to take advantage of the expected chaos.

On November 19th the submarine force left Kure naval base in Japan, with five midget sumarines in tow. The main task force assembled on the 22nd at Tankan Bay in the Kurile Islands, and left on the 26th. On December 2nd it received word that the attack orders were confirmed, so ships were darkened; even then there was the proviso that the mission would be abandoned if the fleet was spotted before December 6th – or if a last-minute settlement was reached in Washington. On the 4th the final refuelling took place, and speed was increased from 13 to 25 knots.

Continuous reports were reaching it, via Japan, from the Honolulu consulate, so there was disappointment when on the 6th, the eve of the stroke, no carriers were reported in Pearl Harbor. (Actually one was on the Californian coast, another was taking bombers to Midway, and another had just delivered fighters to Wake, while three were in the Atlantic.) However, eight battleships were reported to be in Pearl Harbor, and without torpedo nets, so Admiral Nagumo decided to go ahead. The aircraft were launched between 06.00 and 07.15 hours (Hawaii time) next morning, about 275 miles due north of Pearl Harbor.

There were two late warnings that might have made a difference to the outcome, but did not. The first was that the approach of the Japanese submarine force was detected, several times from 03.55 hours onward; one of the submarines was sunk at 06.51 by US destroyers and another at 07.00 by naval aircraft. Then the most northerly of the six American radar stations on the island detected a large force of aircraft, evidently over a hundred, approaching soon after 07.00. But this was interpreted by the information centre as being a number of B17s that was expected from California – although it comprised only twelve planes and these were coming from the east, not the north.

The attack started at 07.55 and went on until 08.25; then a second wave, of dive-bombers and high-level bombers, struck at 08.40. But the use of the torpedo-bombers in the first wave had been the decisive factor.

Of the eight American battleships, the *Arizona, Oklahoma, West Virginia* and *California* were sunk, and the *Maryland, Nevada, Pennsylvania,* and *Tennessee* were severely damaged.* Sunk, too, were three destroyers and four smaller vessels, while three light cruisers and a

* The *Nevada* was beached; the *California* was later refloated.

seaplane tender were badly damaged. Of American aircraft, 188 were destroyed, and sixty-three damaged. The Japanese loss was only twenty-nine planes destroyed and seventy damaged – apart from the five midget submarines which were lost in an attack that was a complete failure. Of human casualties, the Americans had 3,435 killed or wounded; while the Japanese figure is more uncertain, the killed were under a hundred.

The returning Japanese aircraft landed on the carriers between 10.30 and 13.30 hours. On December 23rd the main task force itself arrived back in Japan.

The coup brought three great advantages to Japan. The United States Pacific Fleet was virtually put out of action. The operations in the South-West Pacific were made secure against naval interference, while the Pearl Harbor task force could be employed to support those operations. The Japanese now had more time to extend and build up their defensive ring.

The main drawbacks were that the stroke had missed the US carriers – its prime target, and key one for the future. It had also missed the oil tanks and other important installations, whose destruction would have made the American recovery much slower, as Pearl Harbor was the only full fleet base. Coming as a surprise, apparently before any declaration of war, it aroused such indignation in America as to unite public opinion behind President Roosevelt, and in violent anger against Japan.

Ironically, the Japanese had intended to keep within the bounds of legality while profiting from the value of surprise – in other words, going as close to the border as they could without violating it. Their reply to the American demands of November 26th was timed so that it should be sent to the Japanese Ambassador in Washington in the late evening of Saturday, December 6th, and was to be delivered to the United States Goverment at 13.00 hours on the Sunday – which would be 07.30 in the morning by Hawaii time. That would give the United States scant chance – about half an hour – of notifying its commanders in Hawaii and elsewhere that war had come, but could be claimed as legally correct by international law. Owing, however, to the length of the Japanese Note (5,000 words) and delays in decoding it at the Japanese Embassy, it was not ready for delivery by the Ambassador until 14.20 hours Washington time – which was about 35 minutes *after* the start of the Pearl Harbor attack.

The violence of the American denunciation of Pearl Harbor as barbarous behaviour, and the way it came as a surprise, were astonishing in the light of history. For the Japanese attack had a close parallel with their attack on the Russian fleet at Port Arthur, and had been fore-shadowed by it.

In August 1903, negotiations had begun between Japan and Russia for a settlement of their differences in the Far East. But after 5½ months, the Japanese Government came to the conclusion that the Russian attitude offered it no satisfactory arrangement, and on February 4th, 1904, decided to use force. On the 6th, negotiations were broken off – but without any declaration of war. The Japanese fleet, under Admiral Togo, sailed secretly for Port Arthur, the Russian naval base. On the night of the 8th, Togo launched his torpedo-boats against the Russian squadron anchored at Port Arthur. Taking it by surprise, he disabled two of its best battleships, and a cruiser – with the result that Japanese naval supremacy was henceforth established in the Far East. It was only on the 10th that the Japanese declaration of war was issued and the Russian at the same time.

The attitude of the British, who had made an *entente* with Japan two years before, was in ironical contrast to the way they echoed the American denunciation of Japan's behaviour thirty-seven years later. A comment in *The Times* in February 1904 was:

> The Japanese navy, thanks to the masculine decision of the Mikado and his advisers, has taken the initiative, and has opened the war by an act of daring ... Owing to its position in the outer roadstead, the Russian squadron was open to, and invited, attack. The invitation has been accepted with a promptness and a punctuality that do high honour to the navy of our gallant allies ... The moral effect of this exploit promises to be enormous, and may influence and colour the whole conduct of the war ... By these acts of vigour, the Japanese navy have profited by the initiative conferred on them by statesmanship, and have established a moral mastery of the situation.

The article on 'Japan' in the 1911 edition of the *Encyclopaedia Britannica* also praises the action of Japan in choosing war, and for taking up arms 'against a military dictatorship and a policy of selfish restrictions'.

On October 21st, 1904 – the 99th anniversary of Trafalgar – Admiral Sir John Fisher became First Sea Lord in Britain. He promptly began to urge on King Edward VII, and in other influential quarters, a suggestion that the rising danger presented by the growth of the German fleet should be forestalled by 'Copenhagening' it – that a sudden attack should be launched upon it without any declaration of war. He even went so far as to put out propaganda for such a coup. His constant advocacy of such a course naturally came to the ears of the German Government, and as naturally, was taken more seriously than in English political quarters.

It is not clear whether Admiral Fisher's proposals had been mooted prior to the success of the Japanese coup at Port Arthur. In any case, the coup by which Nelson crippled the Danish fleet at Copenhagen without any declaration of war was a famous part of England's naval history, familiar to every sailor. Togo, as a young naval officer, had spent seven years in England studying his profession. Thus the influence of Nelson's Copenhagen coup on Admiral Togo's initiative in 1904 may well have been as great as Admiral Togo's influence on Fisher's scheme.

For Americans, the Pearl Harbor coup of 1941 came as such a surprise, despite the lesson of history, that the shock produced not only widespread criticism of their authorities, headed by President Roosevelt, but a deep suspicion that factors more sinister than blindness and confusion were responsible for the disaster. Such a suspicion became rife, particularly among Roosevelt's critics and political opponents, and has long persisted.

But while it is clear that President Roosevelt had long been hoping and seeking for a way of bringing America's weight into the war against Hitler, the evidence of complacency and miscalculation in army and navy headquarters suffices to outweigh the arguments of American 'revisionist' historians that Roosevelt planned or contrived the Pearl Harbor disaster for that purpose, and the slender evidence on which such arguments have been based.

THE FALL OF HONG KONG

The early loss of this British outpost in the Far East was the clearest of all examples how strategy, and common sense, can be sacrificed vainly for the sake of fanciful prestige.* Even the Japanese never committed

* In March 1935, General Dill, who had become Director of Military Operations and Intelligence, asked me to go to the War Office for a talk with him about current and prospective defence problems. The discussion focused on the Far East, and particularly on the question of trying to hold Hong Kong in the event of war with Japan. According to a note of the discussion made that evening: 'I suggested, and he appeared to agree, that it would be better to risk its loss by holding it too lightly than to strengthen it so much as to make it, morally, a "Verdun" or "Port Arthur" with great danger to our prestige if lost.'

such folly 'for face' as did the British in this case. It was palpably the weak point in Britain's position, and inherently far more difficult to hold than Singapore. This island port, adjoining the coast of China, was barely 400 miles from the Japanese air bases on Formosa whereas it was 1,600 miles from the British naval base at Singapore.

In a review of the situation early in 1937 the British Chiefs of Staff put Japan second to Germany as a possible enemy, and rated Singapore along with Britain herself as the keystones on which the survival of the British Commonwealth would depend, therefore emphasizing that no consideration for the security of British interests in the Mediterranean should be allowed to interfere with the dispatch of a fleet to Singapore. In discussing Hong Kong, they agreed that the period before relief could not be less than ninety days, and went on to say that even if a reinforced garrison could hold the colony the port itself could be neutralized by Japanese air forces operating from Formosa. But, in a more hopeful and less realistic way than the facts of the situation warranted, they rejected the logical conclusion on the ground that evacuation of the garrison would entail a loss of prestige, and of necessary encouragement to China in resisting the Japanese. Their own conclusion was that 'Hong Kong should be regarded as an important though not vital outpost to be defended for as long as possible.'* That conclusion foredoomed the garrison.

Two years later, early in 1939, a new review of the situation produced the same general conclusion, but showed a very significant change in putting the security of the Mediterranean before the Far East in order of priority. That inherently made a defence of Hong Kong more hopeless still, and all the more so because a Japanese expeditionary force was now ensconced on the Chinese mainland north and south of Hong Kong, thus isolating this British possession and exposing it to land attack.

In August 1940, following the fall of France, the situation was reviewed afresh by the new team of Chiefs of Staff – in which Dill represented the Army, as he was now CIGS. This time they faced the fact that Hong Kong was indefensible, and recommended the withdrawal of the garrison – then four battalions. Their view was accepted by the War Cabinet, now led by Mr Churchill. But nothing was done to implement the conclusion. Moreover, a year later they veered round again, and advised Churchill to accept the Canadian Government's offer of two battalions to reinforce the garrison – an offer, and reversal of policy,

* *Official History: The War Against Japan*, vol I, p 17.

that was prompted by the optimistic view of Major-General A. E. Grasett, himself a Canadian, who had recently been commanding in Hong Kong, and on his way back to England had told the Chief of the Canadian General Staff that such an addition would make the place strong enough to withstand attack for a long period. In advising acceptance of the offer, the Chiefs of Staff in Britain expressed the view that even at the worst it would enable the garrison to maintain a 'more worthy' defence of the island – another 'prestige' argument. On October 27th, 1941, the two Canadian battalions sailed for Hong Kong, thus enlarging the vain sacrifice by nearly 50 per cent.

The Japanese attack from the mainland opened early on December 8th, being delivered by a well-armed force more than a division strong (twelve battalions), with ample air cover and artillery support. By next day the British had fallen back to the so-called Gindrinkers Line in the Kowloon peninsula, and early on the 10th a key redoubt here had been seized by a Japanese detachment. This coup precipitated an early abandonment of the Gindrinkers Line and withdrawal to Hong Kong island, while the Japanese were still moving up for their planned attack on the Line.

Initial attempts to cross the straits were repelled, but served to stretch out the defending force. Then on the night of the 18th/19th the main Japanese force landed in the north-east corner, and its concentrated thrust soon drove through to Deep Water Bay in the south, splitting the defending force. One part of it surrendered on the evening of Christmas Day, and the other part followed suit next morning. Despite its reinforcement, Hong Kong had held out for barely eighteen days – a fifth of the time expected. The Japanese casualties were under 3,000, while they had captured the whole of the reinforced garrison, nearly 12,000 men. The loss of the island came in the centenary year of its occupation, and the 99th anniversary of its formal cession, by China, to Britain.

THE FALL OF THE PHILIPPINES

At 02.30 hours on December 8th news of the Japanese attack on Pearl Harbor reached, and alerted, the United States Command in the Philippines. Meanwhile, morning fog on Formosa delayed the planned Japanese airstrike against the islands. But that handicap turned out to the advantage of the Japanese. For on the American side there was a confusion – which has been a continuing cause of controversy – as to whether the B17s were to bomb Formosa in immediate reply. As a result of this they were ordered to fly around the great island of Luzon to avoid being caught on the ground. At 1.30 hours they landed to prepare for their strike – just as the delayed Japanese aircraft arrived overhead. Owing to the defective American warning system, most of the American aircraft were knocked out on that first day, especially the B17 bombers and the modern P40E fighters. The balance of air strength thus swung to the Japanese, who dominated the air from then on with their 190 Army and 300 land-based Naval planes operating from Formosa. On the 17th, the ten remaining B17s were withdrawn to Australia, and from Admiral Hart's pretentiously named Asiatic Fleet its handful of surface ships were also sent away, leaving only his twenty-nine submarines in the area.

As to land forces, despite the new decision – on MacArthur's insistence – that the whole of the Philippines should be held, he had contrarily if shrewdly kept most of the 31,000 regulars (Americans and Filipino Scouts) near Manila, so that the far-stretching coastlines were covered only by low-grade Philippine troops, nominally about 110,000 in total. That decision, however wise strategically, meant that the Japanese would meet little difficulty in getting ashore wherever they chose to land.

The attack was entrusted to the Japanese 14th Army under General Homma. He employed 57,000 men in the landings and initial operations. Relatively, the number was not large, thus making surprise and air superiority the more essential. It was also necessary for the Japanese to capture some outlying islands and weakly-defended coastal regions so that airfields could be quickly built for their short-range Army aircraft.

On the opening day, they seized the main island of the Batan group, 120 miles north of Luzon, and on the 10th made another bound to Camiguin Island, just north of Luzon. That same day two other detachments landed on the north coast itself, at Aparri and Vigau, while on the 12th a fourth one coming from the Palau Islands landed unopposed at Legaspi in the far south-east of Luzon. These paved the way for the main landings, which took place in the Lingayen Gulf, only 120 miles north of Manila, beginning on December 22nd. Eighty-five transports carried General Homma's 43,000 troops. On the 24th another force of 7,000, coming from the Ryukyu Islands, landed in Lamon Bay on the east coast, opposite Manila. None of these forces met any serious opposition, as the raw and poorly equipped Philippine Army crumbled quickly, especially when tanks advanced on them, and the Americans moved to their aid too late. The Japanese casualties hitherto had been less than 2,000.

MacArthur, realizing that he could not fulfil his hope and plan of crushing the invaders before they were properly established ashore, had already on the 23rd reverted to the original plan of withdrawing to the Bataan Peninsula, with all that remained of his forces. His decision was precipitated by reports that overestimated, by almost double, the strength of the Japanese – and discounted most of his own Philippine troops. On the 26th Manila itself was declared an open city. Despite the initial state of confusion, MacArthur's troops managed to carry out a step by step withdrawal, under pressure, and were established in the Bataan Peninsula by January 6th – helped by the fact that the Japanese strength was actually about half their own.

But once back in this peninsula – which was about twenty-five miles long and twenty miles wide – the Americans suffered from having to feed over 100,000 mouths, including civilians, instead of the 43,000 reckoned in the original plan. Moreover the peninsula was extremely malarious, so that very soon barely a quarter of the American forces were fit enough to fight.

The opening Japanese attacks on the peninsular position were repulsed, and so were the amphibious flanking attacks they attempted. On February 8th, after a month's effort, they suspended their attacks as their forces had become so weak – 10,000 being sick with malaria, while their 48th Division had been sent off to help the attack on the Dutch East Indies. By the beginning of March only 3,000 troops were manning the Japanese lines, but the Americans, unaware of this situation, made no attempt to take the offensive. Moreover their own effectives were now down to a fifth of their numbers, and their morale suffered from MacArthur's departure for Australia on March 10th. It was also evident that no effort was being made to come to their relief – a decision made early in January by the authorities in Washington.

By the end of March the Japanese were reinforced with over 22,000 fresh troops, as well as by more aircraft, and many more guns. Their attacks were resumed from April 3rd onward, and the Americans were pushed backward down the peninsula, until on April 9th the remaining commander there, General King, surrendered unconditionally to avoid 'mass slaughter'.

The fight now shifted to the fortified island of Corregidor, which had a garrison of nearly 15,000 men (including those on three smaller islands adjoining it). But only two miles separated it from the Bataan peninsula, which enabled the Japanese to maintain a heavy artillery bombardment over the straits as well as continuous air attacks. This pounding went on week after week, gradually pulverizing the defences and putting most of the American guns out of action, while also hitting the island's water supply. The bombardment rose to an intensity of 16,000 shells on May 4th. Just before midnight on the 5th, 2,000 Japanese troops crossed the straits, and landed. They met fierce resistance and lost more than half their strength before they got ashore, but the landing of tanks turned the scale and caused the defenders to crumble – although only three tanks actually went into action. Next morning, May 6th, General Wainwright, who had been commanding Corregidor since leaving the peninsula, sent out a broadcast message of surrender – to avoid vain loss.

General Homma at first refused to accept such a local surrender while American and Filipino detachments in the southern islands continued to maintain a guerrilla-type struggle, as were others in the more remote parts of Luzon. Wainwright then agreed to order a general surrender, for fear that the now disarmed garrison of Corregidor would be massacred. But some of these detachments still refused to comply – in loyalty to MacArthur's urgings, from Australia, and it was not until June 9th that their resistance ceased.

The Americans had lost some 30,000 troops in the campaign, and their Filipino allies some 110,000. While a large proportion of the latter had melted away by desertion, the total of both who surrendered on the Bataan Peninsula was about 80,000, and a further 15,000 on Corregidor. The Japanese casualties, though more difficult to determine, seem to have been only about 12,000, apart from the sick.

Nevertheless, despite the initial collapse, the defenders of the Philippines eventually held out much longer than anywhere else – four months on Bataan, and six months in all – although they had no effective support or supply from outside the Philippines.

THE FALL OF MALAYA – AND SINGAPORE

In the Japanese plan, the task of conquering Malaya and Singapore was allotted to General Yamashita's 25th Army, comprising three divisions with supporting troops – a combat strength of about 70,000, and a total strength of about 110,000. Moreover the sea-transports available only sufficed to carry a quarter of the force direct across the Gulf of Siam – 17,000 combat troops, and 26,000 in all. This advanced fraction was to seize the northern airfields. The bulk of Yamashita's army was to move overland, from Indo-China through Thailand and down the Kra

Isthmus to reinforce the seaborne force as soon as possible, then pursuing the advance down the west coast of the Malay Peninsula.

Outwardly, it was a remarkably small expedition for such a far-reaching aim – and indeed less in numbers than the British total of 88,000 under General Percival defending Malaya (composed of 19,000 British troops, 15,000 Australian, 37,000 Indian, and 17,000 Malays). But these were a mixed lot, poorly equipped and trained in comparison with Yamashita's three divisions – the Imperial Guards, the 5th, and the 18th – were among the best in the whole Japanese Army. They were supported by 211 tanks – whereas the British in Malaya had none – and 560 aircraft – nearly four times as many as the British aircraft in Malaya, while much superior in quality. Moreover, the Japanese reckoned that the monsoon, prevailing from November to March, would hinder British moves to counter their advance, as during this bad weather only the better roads would be passable. They also reckoned that the mountainous backbone of Malaya, up to 7,000 feet high and covered with dense jungle, would split the defence, and aid their intended switch from the east to the west.

The basic irony of the British dispositions was that the ground forces were widely dispersed to guard airfields that contained no adequate air force, and that these airfields had been built to cover a naval base that contained no fleet. The Japanese were to be the main beneficiaries from both airfields and naval base.

The chief Japanese landings were made at Singora and Patani on the Thai neck of the Malay Peninsula, with four subsidiary landings farther north on the coast of Thailand. The third in importance of the landings was made at Kota Bharu, just inside the frontier of Malaya. This force was intended, after seizing the British airfield there, to carry out a diversionary move down the east coast while the main advance was being made down the west coast. These landings were made in the early hours of December 8th, local time – the landing at Kota Bharu, by a force of 5,500 Japanese, was actually over an hour before the stroke at Pearl Harbor. The airfield there was abandoned to the Japanese after a short fight, while those in Thai territory were taken still more easily. The intended British forestalling advance, 'Operation Matador', started too late because of reluctance to cross the frontier before Thailand's neutrality had been violated by the Japanese. British air reconnaissance had discovered a Japanese fleet in the Gulf of Siam on December 6th, but bad weather obscured its further moves, and aims. The preparatory moves for the 'Matador' offensive merely upset British dispositions for defence. By the morning of December 10th, the Japanese 5th Division had already swung across to the west coast and penetrated the frontier of Malaya, advancing by two roads into Kedah.

That day a decisive disaster befell the British at sea.

After the decision in July to cut off Japan's oil supplies, Winston Churchill had belatedly 'realized the formidable effects of the embargoes' and a month later, on August 25th, proposed the dispatch of what he called a 'deterrent' naval force to the East. The Admiralty were planning to assemble there the *Nelson*, the *Rodney*, and four older battleships, together with a battle-cruiser and two to three aircraft-carriers. Churchill preferred to employ 'the smallest number of the best ships', and proposed to send one of the new *King George V* type battleships, with a battle-cruiser and an aircraft-carrier, telling the Admiralty, on August 29th:

I cannot feel that Japan will face the combination now forming against her of the United States, Great Britain, and Russia ... Nothing would increase her hesitation more than the appearance of the force I mentioned, and above all a *KGV*. This might indeed be a decisive deterrent.*

Accordingly the *Prince of Wales* and the battle-cruiser *Repulse* sailed for Singapore – but without any aircraft-carrier. The one that had been earmarked ran ashore in Jamaica and had to be docked for repairs. There was another actually in the Indian Ocean, and within reach of Singapore, but no orders were given for her to move there. Thus the two big ships had to depend for air cover upon shore-based fighters, and these were scanty – even apart from the early loss of the northern airfields.

The *Prince of Wales* and *Repulse* reached Singapore on December 2nd, and next day Admiral Sir Tom Phillips arrived to take command of the 'Far Eastern Fleet'. On the 6th, as already mentioned, a large Japanese convoy of transports was reported to be sailing from Indo-China in the direction of Malaya. By midday on the 8th Phillips heard that they were disembarking their troops at Singora and Kota Bahru, covered by at least one battleship of the *Kongo* class, five cruisers, and twenty destroyers. In the late afternoon Phillips gallantly sailed north with what was called Force Z – his two big ships and an escort of four destroyers – to strike at the transports, although no shore-based air cover could be provided so far north now that the airfields there were lost.

* Churchill: *The Second World War*, vol III, p 774.

In the evening of the 9th the weather cleared, and with it Phillips' cloak of obscurity. His Force Z was spotted from the air, so he turned south and headed for Singapore. But that night a signal came from there reporting, mistakenly, that a Japanese landing had been made at Kuantan, a midway point. Reckoning that surprise might be possible, and the risk justified, he altered course for Kuantan.

The Japanese were well prepared for any interception move by Force Z, whose arrival at Singapore had been broadcast to the world. Their élite 22nd Air Flotilla, with the best pilots of the Naval Air Arm, was based on the airfields near Saigon, in the south of Indo-China. Moreover, a patrol line of twelve submarines covered the approaches from Singapore to Kota Bharu and Singora. Already, in the early afternoon of the 9th, Force Z's northward move had been sighted and reported by the most easterly submarine of this screen. When the report came, the 22nd Air Flotilla, which had been preparing for a raid on Singapore, hurriedly exchanged its bombs for torpedoes and set off for a night attack on Force Z, but failed to find it because of Phillips' southward turn. However the air flotilla set off again just before dawn, and this time Force Z was found, near Kuantan. The Japanese employed thirty-four high-level bombers and fifty-one torpedo-bombers, the former opening the attack soon after 11.00 hours and the latter following, in successive waves. Both kinds of bombing proved remarkably accurate – despite the fact that it was against ships manoeuvring at high speed, not static and taken by surprise as at Pearl Harbor. Moreover the *Prince of Wales* with 175 anti-aircraft guns could pump out 60,000 shells a minute. Both ships were sunk, the *Repulse* by 12.30 and the *Prince of Wales* by 13.20. The escorting destroyers managed to save over 2,000 men out of 2,800 in the two ships' crews, although Admiral Phillips himself was among those lost. The Japanese abstained from interference with the rescue work. They lost only three aircraft.

Before the war the heads of the Admiralty had scorned the idea that battleships could be sunk by air attack, and Churchill had tended to support their view. The delusion even persisted until the fatal days of December 1941. Moreover, as Churchill wrote: 'The efficiency of the Japanese in air warfare was at this time greatly under-estimated both by ourselves and by the Americans.'*

This stroke settled the fate of Malaya – and Singapore. The Japanese were able to continue their landings unchecked, and establish air bases ashore. The superiority of their air force over the meagre British air strength in Malaya was decisive in crumbling the resistance of the

* Churchill: *The Second World War*, vol III, p 551.

British troops and enabling their own troops to push down the Malay Peninsula and force the backdoor into Singapore. Its fall was the consequence of earlier oversight and misjudgement – mainly in London.

From December 10th onwards, the British retreat down the west coast became almost continuous. Road blocks such as the large one at Jitra were either overcome by Japanese tanks and artillery or by flank threat from Japanese infantry infiltrating through the bordering jungle. The commander in northern Malaya, General Heath, hoped to make a stand on the Perák River, but this line was turned by the Japanese column thrusting obliquely down from Patani. A strong position behind, at Kampar, was turned by flank action from the sea that was carried out by troops using small craft captured in the advance.

On December 27th, Lieutenant-General Sir Henry Pownall took over as C-in-C Far East from Air Chief Marshal Sir Robert Brooke-Popham.

The British fell back at the beginning of January to the Slim River, covering Selangor Province, and the approaches to the southern airfields near Kuala Lumpur. But on the night of the 7th/8th a company of Japanese tanks broke through the ill-organized defence and raced on to seize the road-bridge – which was nearly twenty miles beyond the front line. The British troops north of the river were cut off, losing some 4,000 troops and their equipment – at a cost to the Japanese of only six tanks and a few infantry. The 11th Indian Division was shattered. The disaster entailed the early abandonment of central Malaya and jeopardized the chance of holding northern Johore long enough for adequate reinforcements to reach Singapore by sea from the Middle East.

On the very day of the disaster General Wavell arrived in Singapore on his way to Java to take up the new, emergency post of Supreme Commander, ABDA (American, British, Dutch, Australian) Command. Pownall then became Chief of Staff ABDA, Far East Headquarters being abolished. Wavell decided that the defence was now to be based on Johore, the best troops and the reinforcements being kept there. That meant a quicker withdrawal, instead of the gradual one planned by General Percival. Kuala Lumpur was abandoned on January 11th, and the bottleneck position at Tampin on the 13th (instead of the 24th). It also, by giving the Japanese access to the better road system in Johore, enabled them to employ two divisions simultaneously, instead of in turn – which nullified a tough defence of Gemas by the Australians. Thus the withdrawal through Johore became even quicker than intended.

Meanwhile, a corresponding withdrawal of the British force on the east coast had led to the abandonment of Kuantan and its airfield on January 6th; of Endau on the 21st, following a seaborne threat; and by the 30th both 'Eastforce' and 'Westforce' were back at the extreme southern end of the Malay Peninsula. The rearguards crossed the straits next night, into Singapore Island. The Japanese Army Air Force, less effective than the Naval air arm, had done little to harry the retreat, and only proved effective against airfields.

Thus the Japanese had conquered Malaya in fifty-four days. Their total casualties were only about 4,600 – whereas the British had lost about 25,000 (mainly prisoners), and a large quantity of equipment.

It was on the night of Sunday, February 8th, 1942, that the two leading divisions of the Japanese invading force, which had swept down the 500-mile length of the Malay Peninsula, crossed the narrow channel which separates Singapore Island from the mainland. The crossing was made on an eight-mile stretch of the thirty-mile straits, which here were less than a mile in width. This sector was held by three battalions of the 22nd Australian Brigade.

Armoured landing craft carried the first waves of attackers, but the rest followed in any sort of boats that could be collected, and a number of the Japanese even swam across – with their rifles and ammunition. Some of the craft were sunk, but most of the assault troops landed safely, helped by failures on the defenders' side that have never been satisfactorily explained. The beach searchlights were not employed, means of communication failed or were not used, and the artillery was slow to put down its intended curtain of defensive fire.

By daylight 13,000 Japanese were ashore, and the Australians had fallen back to inland positions. Before midday the invaders' strength had risen to more than 20,000, and they had established a deep lodgement in the north-western part of the island. Later a third Japanese division landed, making the total well over 30,000.

There were two more divisions close behind on the mainland, but General Yamashita did not consider that he could effectively deploy them in the island advance. He did, however, feed in a lot of fresh men as replacements during the days that followed.

Numerically, the defenders had more than sufficient strength in the island to repel the invasion, particularly as it came in the sector where it was most expected. General Percival, even now, had some 85,000 troops under his command – mainly British, Australian, and Indian, with some local Malay and Chinese units. But the majority were ill-trained to match the Japanese attacking force, composed of troops specially selected for the purpose, and had been repeatedly outmanoeuvred in the dense jungle country or rubber plantations. The leadership in general was poor.

The air force had been outnumbered and outclassed from the outset of the campaign, and the little that remained was withdrawn in the final stage. Lack of protection against the enemy's fierce and incessant air attacks was the more demoralizing to troops whose spirits were already depressed by the long retreat down the Malay Peninsula.

The effect of the home Government's failure to provide such essential air cover was not redressed by the appeals that Churchill and his military advisers now sent that 'the battle should be fought to the bitter end at all costs', and that commanders 'should die with their troops' for 'the honour of the British Empire', carry out a 'general scorched-earth scheme' and destroy everything that might be useful to an occupier with 'no thought of saving the troops or sparing the population'. All this showed an extraordinary ignorance of psychology on the part of the authorities at home. The morale of the men in the fighting line was not raised by the sight of black smoke clouds billowing up behind them, from burning oil tanks. Nor did it encourage them to know that they were doomed to death or captivity. A year later, even the tough German veterans in Africa collapsed quickly when, after Hitler's order to hold Tunis at all costs, their front was pierced and behind them lay the sea, with the enemy in command of it. To call on troops to fight with 'backs to the wall' of such a nature is rarely effective in stiffening their spine.

At Singapore the end came on Sunday, February 15th – exactly a week after the Japanese landing. By that time the defenders had been driven back to the suburbs of Singapore city, which lies on the south coast of the island. Food stocks were running low and the water supply was liable to be cut off at any moment. That evening General Percival went out under a white flag to capitulate to the Japanese commander. For a brave man it was a bitter step, but surrender was inevitable, and he chose to go himself in the hope of obtaining better treatment for his troops and the population.

These two black Sundays at Singapore were fatal to the imperial sway of what had been proudly called for many years 'the Empire on which the sun never sets'.

The failure to repel the Japanese Army's attack, however, was not the primary cause. The surrender of Singapore was the sequel to naval defeat – two months before.

It was also the tail end of a long chain of errors and oversights. The development of the new base and its defences had been pitifully slow. Political reluctance to spend money was not the only brake. In the years following the decision to build this base a violent argument raged in Whitehall as to the best means of defending it. The argument was fiercest of all in the Chiefs of Staff Committee – supposedly as united as a trinity. Trenchard, the Chief of the Air Staff, urged the paramount importance of aircraft. Beatty, the First Sea Lord, advocated big guns – while scorning the idea that aircraft could be a grave threat to battleships. Both were famous men, and strong men.

The Government hesitated to decide between their views, and the controversy still continued long after they had retired. On balance, the 'Senior Service' prevailed. The big guns were provided, but not the aircraft. Unfortunately, when the attack eventually came it did not come from the way the guns were pointing, but from behind.

In the 1930s various soldiers who studied the problem began to suggest that the attack might come through the backdoor, by way of the Malay Peninsula. It seemed the more likely because the naval base had been built on the north side of Singapore, in the narrow channel between the island and the mainland. Among the soldiers who took that view was Percival, when Chief General Staff Officer in Malaya 1936–1937. It was endorsed by the then GOC, General Dobbie, who in 1938 began the construction of a defence line in the south of the Malay Peninsula.

Mr Hore-Belisha, who had now become War Minister, was quick to appreciate the necessity for increasing the small garrison – for a main feature of the programme he adopted on taking office was priority for Imperial Defence over Continental action. The danger of war with Germany and Italy combined was becoming so acute that a strengthening of the Mediterranean forces necessarily had first call, but he induced the Government of India to send two brigades to Malaya, for trebling the garrison there. More was hardly possible from the limited prewar resources.

When war came in September 1939, Britain's resources began to multiply. But as the war was then confined to the West it was natural that the bulk of them were devoted to that quarter. Then came the catastrophes of May and June 1940 when France collapsed and Italy entered the war. In that appalling crisis, the first need was to build up the defence of Britain, and the second to provide for the defence of the Mediterranean area. Those two needs were difficult enough to meet simultaneously. Indeed, Churchill's boldest and greatest action was seen in the risks he took to strengthen the defences of

Egypt before Britain itself was secure against invasion.

It would be unjust to find fault with the provision made for Malaya during this period. Taking due account of the circumstances it was remarkable that the garrison was reinforced by six brigades during the winter of 1940–1. Unfortunately, there was no similar increase of air strength – which was more vital.

Early in 1940 the new GOC, General Bond, had expressed the opinion that the defence of Singapore depended on the defence of Malaya as a whole. For that purpose he estimated that three divisions were the minimum required, while suggesting that the RAF should take over the main responsibility for the defence. The authorities at home adopted these views in principle, but with an important modification. Whereas the commanders in Malaya considered that a force of more than 500 modern aircraft was required, the Chiefs of Staff Committee judged that some 300 should suffice, and said that even this total could not be provided until the end of 1941. Moreover, by the time the Japanese invasion came – in December 1941 – the actual first-line air strength in Malaya was only 158, and most of them were out-of-date machines.

During 1941 the bulk of the modern fighter aircraft available, beyond the needs of Britain's air defence, were sent to support the abortive offensive campaigns in the Mediterranean area. In the second half of the year some 600 were sent to Russia. But Malaya received scarcely any. No long-range bombers were sent there, yet hundreds were used nightly in bombing attacks on Germany that were palpably futile at that stage of the war. It is evident that the needs of Malaya's defence received inadequate attention.

The clue to the puzzle is provided by Churchill himself in his war memoirs. Early in May the Chief of the Imperial General Staff, Sir John Dill, submitted a paper to the Prime Minister in which he argued against continuing to build up the striking forces in North Africa at the risk of Britain herself or Singapore.

The loss of Egypt would be a calamity which I do not regard as likely ... A successful invasion alone spells our final defeat. It is the United Kingdom therefore and not Egypt that is vital, and the defence of the United Kingdom must take first place. Egypt is not even second in order of priority, for it has been an accepted principle in our strategy that in the last resort the security of Singapore comes before that of Egypt. Yet the defences of Singapore are still considerably below standard.

Risks must of course be taken in war, but they must be calculated risks. We must not fall into the error of whittling away the security of vital points.*

Churchill was upset by this paper, for it ran contrary to his idea of taking the offensive against Rommel, and to his dream of gaining a decisive victory in North Africa at an early date. 'Compliance with this would have meant a complete reversion to the defensive ... There would be nothing in hand for taking the initiative.' In a sharp reply he said:

I gather you would be prepared to face the loss of Egypt and the Nile Valley, together with the surrender or ruin of the Army of half a million we have concentrated there, rather than lose Singapore. I do not take that view, nor do I think that the alternative is likely to present itself ... should Japan enter the war the United States will in all probability come in on our side; and in any case Japan would not be likely to besiege Singapore at the outset, as this would be an operation far more dangerous to her and less harmful to us than spreading her cruisers and battle-cruisers on the Eastern trade routes.†

It is apparent that Churchill, in his exasperation, distorted the CIGS's argument. It was not a question of weakening the defence of Egypt, but merely of postponing the offensive on which Churchill had set his heart, and about which he had exaggerated expectations. In the event the June offensive in North Africa proved a fiasco, and the renewed offensive in November, with large additional reinforcements, failed to gain any decisive result. Churchill's reply to Field-Marshal Dill also makes it clear how gravely he miscalculated the risk to Singapore. It is astonishing that, in retrospect, he remarked:

Many Governments I have seen would have wilted before so grave a pronouncement by the highest professional authority, but I had no difficulty in convincing my political colleagues, and I was of course supported by the Chiefs of the Navy and the Air. My views therefore prevailed and the flow of reinforcements to the Middle East continued unabated.**

* Churchill: *The Second World War*, vol III, p 375.
† Ibid, p 376.
** Ibid, p 377.

In July President Roosevelt sent his personal adviser, Harry Hopkins, on a mission to London to convey his misgivings about the wisdom of this policy and a warning of the risks involved elsewhere – 'by trying to do too much' in the Middle East. The American military and naval experts endorsed the warning, and expressed the view that Singapore should be given priority over Egypt.

None of these arguments altered Churchill's view. 'I would not tolerate abandoning the struggle for Egypt, and was resigned to pay whatever forfeits were exacted in Malaya.' But he did not really expect danger there. He frankly says: 'I confess that in my mind the whole Japanese menace lay in a sinister twilight, compared with our other needs.' It is clear that the responsibility for the failure to reinforce Malaya's inadequate defences rests principally with Churchill himself – and was due to his insistence on launching a premature offensive in North Africa.

The immediate strategic effects of the loss of Singapore were disastrous, for it was quickly followed by the conquest of Burma and the Dutch East Indies – a two-pronged sweep that brought the Japanese menacingly close to India on the one flank and Australia on the other. Nearly four years of struggle followed, at immense cost, before Singapore was recovered as a result of Japan's own eventual collapse from exhaustion, and atomic bomb-shock.

But the longer and wider effects of Singapore's initial fall were beyond repair. Singapore had been a symbol – the outstanding symbol of Western power in the Far East, because that power had been erected and long maintained on British seapower. So much emphasis had been given since World War I to the creation of a great naval base at Singapore that its symbolical importance had come to surpass even its strategical value. Its easy capture, in February 1942, was shattering to British, and European, prestige in Asia.

No belated re-entry could efface the impression. The white man had lost his ascendancy with the disproof of his magic. The realization of his vulnerability fostered and encouraged the postwar spread of Asiatic revolt against European domination or intrusion.

THE FALL OF BURMA

Britain's loss of Burma was an early sequel to the fall of Malaya, and enabled the Japanese to complete their capture of the western gateways to China, and the Pacific – thus completing the great defensive barrier visualized in their strategic design. Although a sequel, the Burma campaign was an independent operation, and was entrusted to the 15th Army under Lieutenant-General S. Iida.

This 'army' comprised only two divisions, and even with supporting troops totalled only 35,000 men. Its task was to occupy Thailand, including most of the Kra Isthmus, and cover the rear of the 25th Army while this was driving south into Malaya from the landings in the Singora area of the isthmus. The 15th Army was then to set out on its independent task of invading Burma, with Rangoon, the capital, as its immediate goal.

Such a large venture with so small a force was justified by the scantiness, both in quantity and quality, of the forces guarding Burma. Initially, these amounted to little more than a division in numbers, mostly consisting of recently raised Burmese units, with a stiffening of only two British battalions and an Indian brigade – while a second Indian brigade was on its way, to provide a general reserve. When the crisis came, most of the available reinforcements were diverted to Malaya, too late to save Singapore, and not until the end of January did the semi-trained and incomplete 17th Indian Division begin to arrive in Burma as a forerunner of the more substantial reinforcements that were promised. The air situation was even worse, as only thirty-seven aircraft were at first available to meet 100 Japanese – which were doubled by another air brigade after the fall of Manila early in January.

The Japanese invasion of Burma had started as early as mid-December, when a detachment of the 15th Army moved into Tenasserim, on the western or Burmese side of the Kra Isthmus, to seize the three key airfields there and thus block the way for British air reinforcements to Malaya. On December 23rd and 25th heavy Japanese air attacks were delivered on Rangoon, causing the Indian labour force to stream away, blocking the roads and abandoning work on the defences. On January 20th the direct attack opened with an advance from Thailand on Moulmein, which was occupied on the 31st after a stiff but confused struggle – in which the defenders, with the wide Salween River estuary at their backs, had a narrow escape from disaster, and capture.

At the end of December, Wavell had sent his Chief of the General Staff in India, Lieutenant-General T. J. Hutton, to take over the command in Burma, and he in turn had placed the miscellaneous troops defending Moulmein, and the approaches to Rangoon, under Major-General J. G. Smyth, VC, the commander of the newly arriving 17th Indian Division.

After the fall of Moulmein, the Japanese pressed on north-west, and gained crossings of the Salween near there and some twenty-five miles upriver in the first fortnight of February. Smyth had been urging an adequate strategic withdrawal to a position where he could concentrate, but was not permitted to withdraw until too late to organize such a defence on the Bilin River, itself narrow and fordable at many points. That position was soon turned. Then came a race to get the troops back to the mile-wide Sittang River, thirty miles behind (and seventy from Rangoon). Owing to the delayed start, the Japanese were able to forestall the British, despite the handicap of having to pursue their outflanking moves by jungle tracks, and the vital Sittang Bridge was blown up in the early hours of February 23rd, leaving most of Smyth's troops still on the east bank. Barely 3,500 got back, by devious ways, and of these less than half still had their rifles. By March 4th the Japanese, exploiting their advantage, reached and surrounded Pegu, a road and rail junction where the remnants of Smyth's troops and a few reinforcements were assembling.

The next day, General Sir Harold Alexander arrived to take over the command in Burma from General Hutton. That emergency decision by Churchill was quite natural in the circumstances, and the more so in view of the way that the early collapse had been unforeseen in higher quarters. But it was unjust to 'Tom' Hutton who had not only expressed doubt of the possibility of holding Rangoon but shown wise foresight in sending supplies to the Mandalay area 400 miles north of Rangoon, while hastening the construction of a mountain road from the State of Manipur, in India, as an overland link with Mandalay and the Burma Road to Chungking. During this period, and earlier, views at home were much influenced by Wavell's opinion that Japanese skill was overrated – a myth that could be punctured by vigorous counteraction.

On arrival, Alexander at first insisted that Rangoon must be held and ordered an offensive to restore the situation. But when that was attempted, it gained little, despite vigorous action by the newly arrived 7th Armoured Brigade and some infantry reinforcements. So Alexander soon came round to accept Hutton's view, and on the afternoon of March 6th ordered the evacuation of Rangoon, after demolitions carried out the next afternoon. Thus on the 8th the Japanese, to their own surprise, entered a deserted city. Even so, the forces there had luck in escaping, up the road northward through Prome, by finding a gap in the Japanese encirclement.

There was now a temporary pause, during which the Japanese were reinforced by two more divisions, the 18th and 56th, as well as two tank regiments, and their air force was doubled – to over 400 planes.

The British received far fewer troop reinforcements. In the air their three depleted fighter squadrons and the two of the American Volunteer Group (lent by Generalissimo Chiang Kai-Shek), totalling only forty-four Hurricanes and Tomahawks at the start, had effectively beaten off Japanese air raids on Rangoon, while inflicting disproportionately heavy losses on the attackers. But with the abandonment of Rangoon most of the British were withdrawn to India – where an initial reinforcement of some 150 planes, bombers and fighters, was received from the Middle East by the end of March. The loss of Rangoon had disrupted the early warning system, so that the remaining British planes were unable – as in Malaya earlier – to put up any effective resistance to the Japanese.

Early in April the strengthened Japanese 15th Army moved north up the Irrawaddy, towards Mandalay, in fulfilment of its aim of cutting and closing the Burma Road to China. The British, now amounting to some 60,000, were holding an east–west line ˙150 miles south of Mandalay – with the aid of the Chinese forces on their eastern flank. But the Japanese boldly moved round their western flank, enveloping its defenders, and capturing the Yenangyaung oilfields in mid-April. General Joseph Stilwell, the American officer who was Chiang Kai-Shek's right hand, devised a plan to let the Japanese push up the Sittang River and then trap them by a pincer-move, but his plan was forestalled and distracted by a wider Japanese move, round the eastern flank, towards Lashio on the Burma Road. A rapid reflux took place on that flank, and it soon became clear that neither Lashio nor the use of the supply route to China could be preserved.

So Alexander wisely decided not to make a stand at Mandalay – as the Japanese hoped he would – but to withdraw towards the Indian frontier. The long withdrawal, of more than 200 miles, began on April 26th, covered by rearguards, and the Ava bridge over the Irrawaddy was blown up on the 30th – the day before the Japanese flanking advance reached Lashio.

The principal problem now was to reach the Indian frontier, and Assam, before the monsoon began in mid-May and flooded the intervening rivers as well as the roads. The Japanese raced up the Chindwin River to intercept the British retreat, but the British rearguards managed to get through, by a deviation, and reached Tamu a week before the monsoon began. They lost much of their equipment in the final scurry, including all their tanks, but most of the troops were saved. Even so, their casualties in the Burma campaign had amounted to three times those of the Japanese – 13,500 against 4,500. That the forces in Burma got away at all, in their thousand-mile retreat, was largely due to the repeated interventions, by counterattack, from the tanks of the 7th Armoured Brigade – and the cool-headed way in which the retreat was handled after the decision to abandon Rangoon.

CEYLON AND THE INDIAN OCEAN

While the Japanese army in Burma was moving on, in a seemingly irresistible way, from Rangoon to Mandalay, the British were also suffering alarm from the entry of the Japanese Navy into the Indian Ocean. For the great island of Ceylon, off the south-east corner of India, was considered vital by the British – as a potential springboard for the Japanese Navy from which it could threaten Britain's troop and supply route to the Middle East round the Cape of Good Hope, and South Africa, as well as her sea-routes to India and Australia. Rubber from Ceylon, too, had become very important to Britain since the loss of Malaya.

Wavell was told by the British Chiefs of Staff that the preservation of Ceylon was more essential than that of Calcutta. For that reason, no less than six brigades were employed to hold Ceylon at a time when the forces in Burma were palpably inadequate and those in India perilously weak. Moreover a fresh naval force was also built up there in March, under command of Admiral Sir James Somerville – which comprised five battleships (although four of these were old and obsolete), and three carriers, one of which (the *Hermes*) was both old and small.

At the same time the Japanese were preparing an offensive move from Celebes into the Indian Ocean with a more powerful force, comprising five fleet carriers – those used in the Pearl Harbor attack – and four battleships. Thus the prospects of preserving Ceylon looked poor when that news came. But the threat was not so serious, nor so substantial as it appeared. For the Japanese naval offensive was basically defensive in aim. They had not the troops available to carry out an invasion of Ceylon. Their aim was a raid – to disperse the British naval force that was being built up there, and to cover their own troop reinforcements that were on the way to Rangoon by sea.

Expecting attack on April 1st, Somerville's force had been divided into two parts – the faster and more effective part, Force A, being on patrol until it was sent to refuel at Addu Attol, a new secret base in the Maldive Islands some 600 miles south-west of Ceylon. The Japanese stroke actually came on April 5th, when over a hundred planes attacked the harbour at Colombo, inflicting much damage and repelling the air counterattacks. A further attack came in the afternoon, from fifty bombers, which sank two British cruisers. Somerville's two-part force, too late to intervene, then retreated – the older battleships to East Africa, and the faster part to Bombay. But after a successful stroke at Trincomalee on the 9th, the Japanese fleet withdrew, its commerce raiding detachment having meanwhile sunk twenty-three ships (112,000 tons) in the Bay of Bengal during this brief raid.

It was another humiliating defeat for British seapower, but fortunately went no further. Indeed, if the British had not provoked such a stroke by trying to build up a naval force in Ceylon of a palpably obsolescent kind, the Japanese would probably not have attacked – as it was beyond their designed limits.

Another sequel, imposing renewed strain on Britain's relations with the French as well as diversion of force, was the dispatch of a combined army and naval force to seize the harbour of Diego Suarez in the north of French-owned Madagascar – to forestall any possibility of the Japanese occupying it. This rather expensive move in May was followed by a larger expedition in September to take over the whole of the island. As in the case of sinking the French fleet at Mers-el-Kebir, the military port of Oran in Algeria in 1940, fear proved in the long term a bad counsellor.

PART V
THE TURN
1942

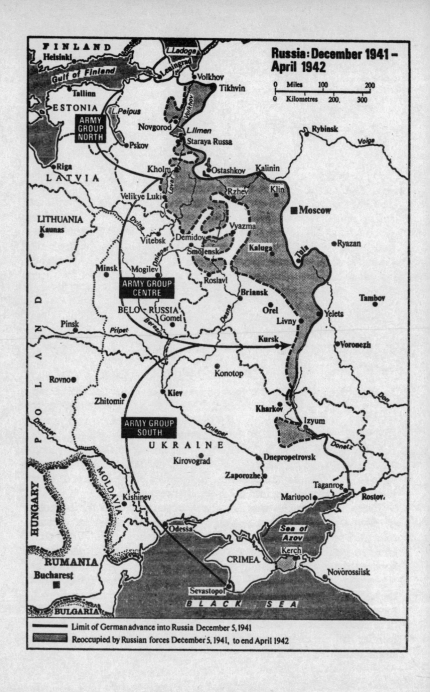

Russia: December 1941 – April 1942

FINLAND
Helsinki
L. Ladoga
Gulf of Finland
Leningrad
Volkhov
Tikhvin
Tallinn
ESTONIA
L. Peipus
ARMY GROUP NORTH
Novgorod
L. Ilmen
Rybinsk
Volga
Pskov
Staraya Russa
Riga
Kholm
Ostashkov
Kalinin
LATVIA
Velikye Luki
Rzhev
Klin
Klin
Moscow
LITHUANIA
Kaunas
Dvina
Vyazma
Vitebsk
Demidov
Ryazan
Dnieper
Smolensk
Kaluga
Tula
Minsk
Mogilev
Roslavl
BELO-RUSSIA
ARMY GROUP CENTRE
Briansk
Tambov
Pinsk
Beresina
Gomel
Desna
Orel
Livny
Yelets
Pripet
POLAND
Kursk
Voronezh
Don
Rovno
Konotop
Zhitomir
Kiev
ARMY GROUP SOUTH
Dnieper
Kharkov
Izyum
Dniester
UKRAINE
Donetz
Kirovograd
Dnepropetrovsk
MOLDAVIA
Zaporozhe
Taganrog
HUNGARY
Kishinev
Mariupol
Rostov
Odessa
Sea of Azov
Kerch
RUMANIA
Bucharest
CRIMEA
Novorossiisk
Sevastopol
BLACK SEA
BULGARIA

0 Miles 100 200
0 Kilometres 200 300

— Limit of German advance into Russia December 5, 1941
▨ Reoccupied by Russian forces December 5, 1941, to end April 1942

CHAPTER EIGHTEEN

The Tide Turns in Russia

In 1940 the Germans had opened their campaign on April 9th with the
spring upon Norway and Denmark. In 1941 they had opened it on
April 6th, with their offensive in the Balkans. But in 1942 there was no
such early opening. That fact showed the exhausting effects on the
Germans of their frustrated attempt in 1941 to gain a quick victory
over Russia, and the extent to which their offensive effort had been
absorbed there. For while weather conditions were unfavourable to an
early spring move on the Russian front, there was no such hindrance to
a move against the eastern or western ends of Britain's precarious position in the Mediterranean. Yet no fresh threat was developed in this
key area of British overseas communications.

In the Russian theatre, the Red Army's winter counteroffensive continued for over three months after its December launching, though with
diminishing progress. By March it had advanced more than 150 miles
in some sectors. But the Germans maintained their hold on the main
bastions of their winter front – such towns as Schlüsselburg, Novgorod,
Rzhev, Vyasma, Briansk, Orel, Kursk, Kharkov, and Taganrog – despite the fact that the Russians were many miles in rear of most of these
places, through pushing into the spaces between them.

These bastion-towns were formidable obstacles from a tactical point
of view; strategically, they tended to dominate the situation, because
they were focal points in the sparse web of communications. While their
German garrisons could not prevent infiltration into the wide spaces
between them, these communication-blocks cramped and curtailed the
exploitation of any penetration so long as they remained intact. Thus
they fulfilled, on a larger scale, the braking function which the French
forts of the Maginot Line had been designed to perform – and might
have succeeded in performing if the chains of forts along the French
frontier had not ended at a halfway point which allowed the Germans
ample room to outflank it.

As the Red Army failed to undercut these bastions sufficiently to cause their collapse, the deep advances it made in the intervening spaces tended to turn out to its own disadvantage later. For the bulges it made were naturally less defensible than bastion-towns, and thus absorbed an excessive quantity of troops in holding them, while they could more easily be cut off by flanking strokes from the German-held bastions, used as offensive springboards.

By the spring of 1942 the battlefront in Russia had become so deeply indented as to appear almost like a reproduction of Norway's coastline, with its fiords penetrating far inland. The way that the Germans had been able to hold on to the 'peninsulas' was remarkable evidence of the power of modern defence when skilfully and tenaciously conducted, and provided with adequate weapons. It was a lesson that went even beyond the Russian defence of 1941 in refuting the superficial deductions drawn from the swift offensive successes earlier in the war against soft opposition – from cases where the attacker had a decisive superiority in weapon-power or encountered an ill-trained and badly bewildered defence. It repeated on a much larger scale the experiences of the St Mihiel salient in the First World War, and proved the possibilities that were foreshadowed by the four-years-long maintenance of that theoretically untenable projection. The experience of the 1941 winter campaign also tended to confirm the longer-view evidence of history that the effect of coincidence is primarily psychological, and that the danger is greatest in the early stages – diminishing if the sudden shock of its realization, by the partially encircled troops, does not produce an immediate collapse.

In retrospect, it is clear that Hitler's veto on any extensive withdrawal worked out in such a way as to restore the confidence of the German troops, and probably saved them from a widespread collapse, while his insistence on the 'hedgehog' system of defence brought the Germans important advantages at the outset of the 1942 campaign.

Nevertheless, they paid a heavy price indirectly for that rigid defence. Its success encouraged the belief that it could be as successfully repeated in the more adverse conditions of the following winters. A more immediate handicap was the strain to which their air force was subjected in the prolonged effort to maintain supplies by air, under winter conditions, to the garrisons of these more or less isolated bastion-towns. Because of the bad weather the accident rate was high, while an excessive number of aircraft had to be used to make up supply shortages in the intervals of good weather – on occasions over 300 transport planes had to be used in the day to provision a single army corps. The effort of providing air transport on such a scale to a whole chain of exposed forward positions damaged the air transport organization of the Luftwaffe, and the withdrawal of experienced air units to other theatres limited the Luftwaffe's combat effectiveness on the Russian front.

The tremendous strain of that winter campaign, on an army that had not been prepared for it, had also a serious delayed effect in other ways. Before the winter ended many divisions were reduced to barely a third of their original strength. They were never fully built up again, and it was well into the summer before they even reached a level sufficient to attempt active operations. Moreover, the additional divisions that were raised at home during the winter created a total figure that was basically fictitious. In 1942 and subsequently, divisions which had been almost destroyed in heavy fighting were maintained in existence, as a camouflage, without the gaps in their ranks being filled up. These nominal divisions sometimes comprised only two or three battalions.

Hitler had been told by his generals that an additional 800,000 men must be provided if the offensive was to be resumed in 1942. Albert Speer, the Minister for Armament Production, said it was not possible to release such a number from the factories for service in the army.

The deficit was eventually met by a radical change in organization. Infantry divisions were reorganized on a basis of seven battalions instead of nine. The battle-strength of the infantry company was fixed at a maximum of 80 men, compared with 180 as formerly. That reduction served a dual purpose, as it was found that with the loss of trained officers the younger officers who replaced them as company commanders were apt to lose control when handling companies of the old bulk, while it was also found that larger losses occurred in the larger-size companies without much difference of effect.

The combined reduction in the number of battalions and number of men gave unreality in subsequent years to the tendency of the Allied Intelligence staffs to continue reckoning the number of German divisions as if they were of similar size to their own. It would have been a better approximation to count two German divisions as equivalent to one British or American division. Even that ratio ceased to be a true guide by the late summer of 1944, when few divisions actually approached their reduced nominal strength.

The 1942 campaign also saw an increase of the German Army's tank strength that was superficial rather than real. Two new armoured divisions were formed during the winter – partly through the conversion of the horsed cavalry division that it had hitherto preserved, only to find it of negligible value. Some additions were made in the tank holdings of the motorized infantry divisions, but barely half of the twenty existing armoured divisions were brought up to strength in tanks.

Thus, in sum, the Germans' balance-sheet represented a precarious foundation for a continuance of the offensive. Even by the most strenuous efforts they could barely regain their former level of numbers, and then only by increased drafts upon their allies' forces, poorer in quality than their own. They could have no margin to meet the losses of another costly campaign. A still greater handicap was their inability to develop their two main offensive assets, their air force and their armoured force, to the scale needed for an assured superiority.*

The unfavourable aspects of the situation were realized by the German General Staff, but its heads had diminished power to influence Hitler's decision. Hitler's pressure was too strong for them to resist, and the pressure of events was too strong for Hitler. He was compelled to go on and on.

The question of resuming the offensive in 1942 was under discussion in November 1941 – even before the final attempt to capture Moscow. Rundstedt claimed to have argued in those November discussions not only for a changeover to the defensive, but the advisability of a withdrawal to the original starting line in Poland. Leeb was said to have agreed. While the other leading generals did not advocate so complete a change of policy, most of them felt an increasing anxiety as to where the Russian campaign was leading them, and showed no keenness for a resumption of the offensive. The failure of the December attack on Moscow and the trials of the winter reinforced their doubts.

But the weight of military opposition was weakened by the changes in the higher commands which followed the miscarriage of the 1941 campaign. Rundstedt had asked, and been allowed, to resign at the end of November, when Hitler overruled his proposal to discontinue the southern drive to the Caucasus and fall back to a winter defence line on the Mius River. He at least was relatively fortunate in the time and manner of his departure. When the failure of the whole campaign was plain to the world, the departure of Brauchitsch on December 19th was

---

* These drawbacks could be deduced even by distant onlookers in the West. In a commentary I wrote in March 1942, my conclusion was that 'it would be reasonable to anticipate this summer not only a repetition of last autumn's German frustration but a definite change in the tide'.

publicly announced in terms which implied that he was the man to blame. That act served the dual purpose of furnishing Hitler with a scapegoat and opening the way for him to take over direct command of the Army. Bock, the too zealous supporter of Hitler's last bid for Moscow, had reported sick in mid-December with a stomach ailment brought on by worry and strain and his resignation was accepted on December 20th. Leeb remained for the moment, and it was less easy to blame him for failure to take Leningrad, since his planned attack on that city had been cancelled by Hitler's own order just as it was about to start – from a fear of the losses that might be incurred in street-fighting. But when Leeb saw that nothing could persuade Hitler to withdraw from the Demyansk salient he asked to be relieved.

The disappearance of Brauchitsch and the three original army group commanders diminished the restraining influence of Halder, the Chief of the General Staff. That effect, and Hitler's advantage, were deepened by the natural tendency of the successors to swallow their doubts and become initially more amenable to the Führer's desires. Hitler well understood the effect of promotion in seducing men's judgement and producing compliance. Professional ambition rarely resists that form of temptation.

Rundstedt was replaced by Reichenau; Bock by Kluge; and Leeb, later, by Küchler. Bock's departure from command of the Central Army Group was due to a temporary illness, and when Reichenau died suddenly from a heart-attack in January, Bock was reinstated as his successor. He was dropped finally in July, however, when the forces in the south were reorganized during the summer offensive. In this reorganization a special 'Army Group A' was created out of Army Group South for the drive to the Caucasus, and command of it was given to Field-Marshal List. The remainder of 'Army Group South' was then redesignated as 'Army Group B' firstly under Bock and then under Weichs.

The plan to launch another great offensive crystallized in the early months of 1942. Hitler's decision was influenced by pressure from his economic experts. They told him that Germany could not continue the war unless she obtained oil supplies from the Caucasus, as well as wheat and ores – a view that was proved mistaken by the fact that Germany failed to secure the Caucasus oil yet managed to continue the war for three more years. But Hitler was the more responsive to such economic arguments because they coincided with his instinctive urge – to do something positive and offensive. The idea of a withdrawal was repugnant to him, whatever the relief and potential advantage it might bring.

Since he recoiled from that step-back he saw nothing else he could do than to push forward again.

That instinct made him insensitive to uncomfortable facts. For example, the German Intelligence Service had information that 600–700 tanks a month were being produced by the Russian factories in the Urals and elsewhere. But when Halder gave him the evidence he slammed the table and declared that any such rate of production was impossible. He would not believe what he did not want to believe.

He was led, however, to recognize the limitation of Germany's resources to the extent of admitting the necessity of limiting the scope of his new offensive. As defined early in the spring, it was to be pursued on both flanks, but not on the whole front.

The main effort was to be made on the southern flank near the Black Sea. It would take the form of a drive down the corridor between the Don and Donetz rivers. After reaching and crossing the lower reach of the Don, between its southerly bend and Black Sea mouth, the drive was to turn south towards the Caucasus oilfields, while also extending eastward to Stalingrad on the Volga.

In formulating that dual aim Hitler originally entertained the idea that the capture of Stalingrad might open the way for a northward wheel to get astride the rear of the Russian armies that were covering Moscow, while some of his entourage even talked of an advance to the Urals. But, after much argument, Halder convinced him that this was an impossibly ambitious project, and the objective actually set was to extend the advance beyond Stalingrad only so far as to provide tactical security for that strategic keypoint. Moreover, the purpose in capturing Stalingrad was now defined as a means of providing strategic flank-cover for the advance into the Caucasus. For Stalingrad lay on the Volga, commanding the land bridge between that river and the Don, and as a focus of communications formed a potential cork for this bottleneck.

Hitler's 1942 plan also comprised a secondary offensive to capture Leningrad during the summer. Apart from the prestige value, this northern move was considered important as a means of securing overland communication with Finland and relieving her isolated situation.

On the rest of the Eastern front, the German armies were to remain on the defensive, merely improving their fortified positions. In brief, the German offensive of 1942 was to be confined to the two wings. That limitation was the measure of the extent to which German reserves were running short. Moreover, the intended drive on the southern wing could only be carried out by drawing more heavily on Ger-

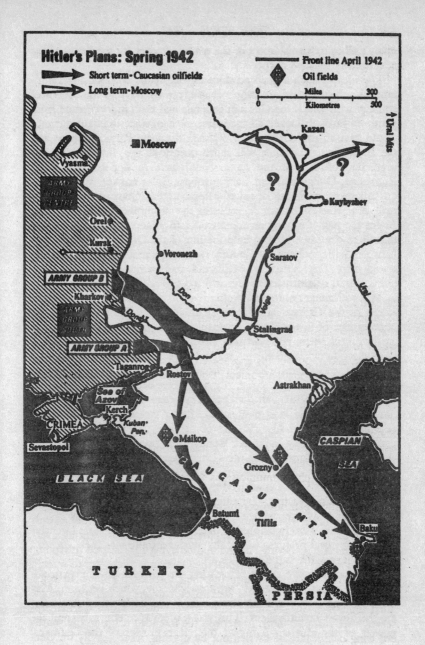

Hitler's Plans: Spring 1942

- ➤ Short term - Caucasian oilfields
- ➤ Long term - Moscow

Front line April 1942

◆ Oil fields

Miles 0 — 300
Kilometres 0 — 500

↑ Ural Mts

Moscow

Vyasma

ARMY GROUP CENTRE

Orel

Kursk

Kazan

Kuybyshev

Voronezh

Saratov

ARMY GROUP B

Kharkov

Donets

ARMY GROUP SOUTH

ARMY GROUP A

Don

Volga

Stalingrad

Taganrog

Rostov

Astrakhan

See of Azov

Kerch

Kuban Pen.

Maikop

CRIMEA

Sevastopol

Grozny

CASPIAN SEA

BLACK SEA

CAUCASUS MTS.

Batumi

Tiflis

Baku

TURKEY

PERSIA

many's allies to furnish most of the rearward cover for the flanks of the advance as it pushed deeper.

The idea of such a deep advance on one flank, without any simultaneous pressure on the enemy's centre, ran contrary to the canons of strategy with which the German generals had been indoctrinated from youth onwards. It looked all the worse to them since the flank advance would have to run the gauntlet between the main Russian armies and the Black Sea. They felt still more uneasy at the thought that the protection of their inland flank would have to depend largely on Rumanian, Hungarian, and Italian troops. Hitler answered their anxious questions with the decisive statement that Germany could only maintain herself in the war by securing the oil supplies of the Caucasus. As for the risk of relying on allied troops to protect their flank, he said that these would be used to hold the line of the Don, and of the Volga between Stalingrad and the Caucasus – where the river lines themselves would help. The capture of Stalingrad, and the holding of that key-point, would be entrusted to German troops.

As a preliminary to the main offensive, on the mainland, the German forces in the Crimea launched a stroke on May 8th to capture the easterly part of it, the Kerch peninsula, where the Russians had managed to check them in the autumn. A well-prepared attack, covered by a concentration of dive-bombers, made a breach in the defences. Pouring through, the Germans wheeled northward and penned a large part of the defenders against the coast, where the dive-bombers soon produced their surrender. With their own path thus cleared, the Germans swept down the fifty-mile long peninsula. After a momentary check at the 'Tartar Ditch' – an historic line of defence twelve miles from the peninsula tip – they captured Kerch itself by May 16th, and thus cleared the Russians out of the Crimea, except for the long-isolated fortress of Sevastopol in the south-western corner.

This coup had been conceived as a means of creating a leverage in aid of the main objective – by a jump across the Kerch Straits onto the Kuban peninsula, which forms the western end of the Caucasus. The German forces were to be used to open the way. But the main offensive made such rapid progress, along the overland route into the Caucasus, that this leverage became unnecessary.

The most effective factor in clearing the path for the German advance was a Russian offensive, towards Kharkov, which began on May 12th, striking at Paulus's 6th Army, which was itself poised to eliminate the Soviet Izyum salient. This was a premature effort, beyond the powers of the Russian Army at this stage in face of the Germans' defensive skill. Ambitious aims, and excessive anticipations, were suggested by Marshal Timoshenko's opening 'Order of the Day' – which started: 'I hereby order the troops to begin the decisive offensive.' The prolongation of this Kharkov offensive played into the Germans' hands, absorbing too large a part of the Russians' reserves, and thus laying them open to a deadly riposte. The Russians penetrated the German defences in the Kharkov area and fanned out north-west and south-west. By Hitler's order the projected offensive against the Izyum salient by Paulus's 6th Army and Kleist's 1st Panzer Army was advanced one day and the Russian offensive was brought to an end by Bock's counter-offensive. Two complete Soviet armies and the elements of two others were cut to pieces, and by the end of May 241,000 Red Army men went into captivity. Few reserves were in hand to meet the Germans when they launched their own main stroke in June.

The German offensive was 'staggered' both in siting and timing. It was planned to take place on the whole German front in South Russia, which ran back obliquely from the coast near Taganrog and along the Donetz towards Kharkov and Kursk. It was a battle-front in echelon. The parts farthest back, on the left, were to move first. The more advanced parts, on the right, were to wait for the left wing to come up before trying to advance, but meanwhile helped to exert a flanking leverage that weakened the resistance facing the left.

On the right was the 17th Army, with the 11th Army in the Crimea. Next to the 17th Army, farther back, was the 1st Panzer Army. After July 9th these two armies comprised List's 'Army Group A', destined to invade the Caucasus. On its left was Bock's 'Army Group B', which included the 4th Panzer Army, the 6th Army, the 2nd Army and the 2nd Hungarian Army. The two panzer armies were to deliver the decisive thrusts, both delivered from the Germans' rear flank against the Russians' most advanced positions – the 1st striking from the Kharkov sector, and the 4th from the Kursk sector. The 'infantry' armies were to follow on and back them up.

As an immediate preliminary to the main offensive, a siege assault was launched against the fortress of Sevastopol on June 7th. This was carried out by Manstein's 11th Army. Although the resistance was tough, the Germans eventually prevailed through superior weight and skill, though it was not until July 4th that the fortress, and with it the whole Crimea, was completely in German hands. The Russians were thus deprived of their chief naval base in the Black Sea. But their fleet was still 'in being', although in fact it was to remain passive.

Meanwhile the opening of this move in the Crimea had been followed by another important diversionary offensive closer to the points where the main operation was being mounted. For on June 10th the Germans exploited their Izyum wedge by forcing the passage of the Donetz, and gaining a foothold on the north bank of the river. After expanding this by degrees into a large bridgehead they delivered a powerful armoured stroke northward from it on the 22nd, and in two days reached the junction of Kupiansk some forty miles north of the river. That created an invaluable flanking leverage to assist the easterly thrust of their main offensive, which was launched on the 28th.

On the left wing of the main offensive there was stiff fighting for several days before the Russian reserves ran short and the 4th Panzer Army broke through in the sector between Kursk and Belgorod. After that the advance swept rapidly across the hundred-mile stretch of plain to the Don near Voronezh. This appeared to foreshadow a direct move across the Upper Don and beyond Voronezh, cutting the lateral rail-link from Moscow to Stalingrad and the Caucasus. Actually, the Germans had no such intention. The orders were to halt on reaching the river and turn it into a defensive flank-cover for the south-easterly continuation of the drive. The 2nd Hungarian Army came up to relieve the 4th Panzer Army, which then wheeled south-eastward down the corridor between the Don and the Donetz, followed by the 6th Army – which had the mission of taking Stalingrad.

The whole of the operations on this left wing tended to cloak the menace that was developing on the right wing. For while attention was focused on the thrust from Kursk towards Voronezh, a more dangerous thrust was being delivered by Kleist's 1st Panzer Army from the Kharkov sector. This profited by the ill-organized position on which the Russian forces stood after the check to their own offensive, as well as by the Kupiansk wedge in the Russians' flank. After achieving a quick breakthrough, Kleist's armoured divisions drove eastward down the Don–Donetz corridor to Chertkovo, on the railway from Moscow to Rostov. Then they made a southerly turn, past Millerovo and Kamensk towards the Lower Don at and above Rostov.

The left wing gained a crossing, with little opposition, on July 22nd – after an advance of some 250 miles from the starting line. Next day the right wing, arriving on the edge of the Rostov defences, drove a wedge into them. Lying on the west bank of the Don, the city was exposed to such thrusts, and in the rapid flux of the retreat its defences had not been properly organized. The German flanking moves accentuated the confusion, and the city quickly fell into their hands. Its capture cut the pipeline from the Caucasus, leaving the Russian armies

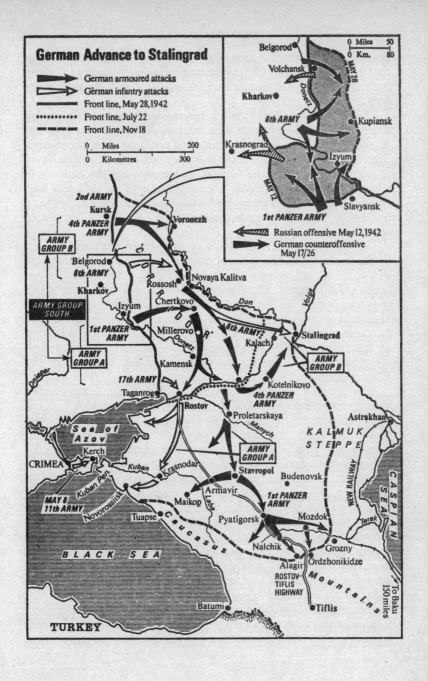

German Advance to Stalingrad

German armoured attacks
Gërman infantry attacks
Front line, May 28, 1942
Front line, July 22
Front line, Nov 18

0 Miles 200
0 Kilometres 300

0 Miles 50
0 Km. 80

Belgorod
Volchansk
MAY 28
Kharkov
6th ARMY
Kupiansk
Krasnograd
Izyum
MAY 12
1st PANZER ARMY
Slavyansk

Russian offensive May 12, 1942
German counteroffensive May 17/26

2nd ARMY
Kursk
4th PANZER ARMY
Voronezh
ARMY GROUP B
Belgorod
6th ARMY
Rossosh
Novaya Kalitva
Kharkov
Chertkovo
Don
Volga
ARMY GROUP SOUTH
Izyum
1st PANZER ARMY
Millerovo
Donetz
4th ARMY?
Stalingrad
ARMY GROUP A
Kamensk
Kalach
17th ARMY
Kotelnikovo
ARMY GROUP B
Taganrog
Rostov
4th PANZER ARMY
Proletarskaya
Astrakhan
Sea of Azov
Menych
KALMUK STEPPE
CRIMEA
Kerch
Kuban
Krasnodar
ARMY GROUP A
Stavropol
Budenovsk
NEW RAILWAY
CASPIAN SEA
MAY 8
11th ARMY
Kuban Pen.
Novorossiisk
Maikop
Armavir
Laba
1st PANZER ARMY
Mozdok
Terek
Tuapse
Caucasus
Pyatigorsk
Nalchik
Grozny
BLACK SEA
Alagir
Ordzhonikidze
ROSTOV-TIFLIS HIGHWAY
Mountains
To Baku 150 miles
Batumi
Tiflis

TURKEY

dependent for their oil supply on what could be brought in tankers up the Caspian Sea and up the new rail route they had hurriedly laid along the steppes west of it. Russia had also lost another huge slice of her bread supply.

The only important offset to this spectacular sweep was that, though large bodies of Russian troops were overrun, the total captured was not nearly so large as in 1941. The pace had not been quite fast enough. That was due, not so much to the resistance met, as to the earlier loss of so many of the best-trained German tank troops, and the tendency to adopt more cautious methods. The panzer 'groups' of 1941 had been reorganized as panzer 'armies', with an increased proportion of infantry and artillery; this increase of support tended to cause a decrease of speed.

Although large numbers of Russian troops were momentarily isolated by the German advance, many of them were able to filter back before they could be rounded up. The south-easterly direction of the German sweep made it natural for them to fall back in a north-easterly direction, thus helping the Russian Command to gather them in or near the Stalingrad area, where they became an inherent threat to the flank of the German advance into the Caucasus. That effect had a vital bearing on the next phase of the campaign, when the German armies forked on divergent courses – part for the Caucasus oilfields, and part for the Volga at Stalingrad.

After crossing the Lower Don, Kleist's 1st Panzer Army wheeled south-eastward into the valley of the Manych River – which is linked by a canal with the Caspian Sea. By blowing up the big dam here, and flooding the valley, the Russians momentarily upset the tanks' onrush. But after two days' delay the German forces succeeded in crossing the river and then continued their drive into the Caucasus, fanning out on a wide front. Encouraged by the lack of opposition and the openness of the country, Kleist's right column drove almost due southward through Armavir to the great oil centre of Maikop, 200 miles south-east of Rostov, which it reached on August 9th. On the same day the van of his centre column swept into Pyatigorsk, 150 miles to the east of Maikop, in the foothills of the Caucasus Mountains. His left column took a still more easterly direction, towards Budenovsk. Mobile detachments had been sent racing ahead, and as a result the pace of this early August onrush beyond the Don was terrific.

But the pace slowed down almost as suddenly as it had developed. The prime causes were a shortage of fuel and an abundance of mountains. That dual brake was subsequently reinforced by the distant effect of the struggle for Stalingrad, which drained off a large part of the forces that might have been used to give a decisive impetus to the Caucasus advance.

It was difficult to keep up the flow of fuel supplies required for such a far-ranging sweep, and the difficulty was increased because it had to come by rail through the Rostov bottleneck, and the track had to be converted from the wide Russian to the central European gauge – the Germans could not venture to send supplies by sea while the Russian fleet remained in being. A limited amount was forwarded by air, but the total that came through by rail and air was insufficient to maintain the momentum of the advance.

The mountains were a natural barrier to the attainment of the German objective, but their effect was increased by the increasingly stubborn resistance that was met on reaching this area. Earlier, there had been little difficulty in swerving round the Russian forces which tried to oppose the advance, and the latter had tended to retreat before they were cut off, instead of fighting on stubbornly as in 1941. The change may have been due to a more elastic defensive strategy, though the German Command was convinced, from the interrogation of prisoners, that there was a growing tendency on the part of troops who were bypassed to look for a way of getting back to their homes, especially among those who came from Asiatic Russia. But when the Caucasus was reached the resistance became stiffer. The defending forces here were largely composed of locally recruited troops, who felt that they were protecting their own homes, and were familiar with the kind of mountainous country in which they were fighting. Those factors multiplied the strength of the defence, whereas the nature of the country cramped the attackers by canalizing the flood-like advance of their armoured forces.

While the 1st Panzer Army had been carrying out its flanking sweep into the Caucasus, the 17th Army had been following up on foot through the bottleneck of Rostov, whence it turned south towards the Black Sea coast.

After the capture of the Maikop oilfields the Caucasus front was divided afresh, and further objectives allotted. The 1st Panzer Army was given responsibility for the main stretch between the River Laba and the Caspian Sea. Its first objective was to capture the mountain stretch of the great highway running from Rostov to Tiflis; its second objective was Baku, on the Caspian. The 17th Army was responsible for the narrower area from the Laba back to the Kerch Straits. Its first task was to advance southward from Maikop and Krasnodar, across the western end of the Caucasus range, to capture the Black Sea ports of Novorossiisk and Tuapse. Its second objective was to force a passage down the coastal road beyond Tuapse, and thus open the way to Batumi.

While the coastal road south from Tuapse was overhung by high mountains, the first task of the 17th Army looked relatively easy, since it had less than fifty miles to go before reaching the coast, and this western end of the mountain chain sloped away into foothills. But the task did not prove easy. The advance had to cross the Kuban River, which had wide marshy borders near its mouth, and the hills farther east were rugged enough to be difficult obstacles. It was nearly the middle of September before the 17th Army captured Novorossiisk. It never reached Tuapse.

The 1st Panzer Army, on the main line of advance, made better progress by comparison, but at a diminishing pace and with increasing pauses. Fuel shortage was the decisive handicap in the advance to the mountains. The panzer divisions were sometimes at a standstill for several days on end, awaiting fresh supplies. This handicap cost the Germans their best chance – of rushing the passes while surprise lasted, and before the defences were strengthened. When it came to a matter of fighting a way into the mountains the 1st Panzer Army was handicapped because most of the expert mountain troops had been allotted to the 17th Army for its attempt to reach Tuapse and open the coast road to Batumi.

The first serious check occurred on reaching the Terek River – which covered the approaches to the mountain road over to Tiflis, as well as the more exposed Grozny oilfields north of the mountains. The Terek has nothing like the awe-inspiring breadth of the Volga, but its swift current made it an awkward obstacle. Kleist then tried a manoeuvre to the east, downstream, and succeeded in forcing a passage near Mozdok, in the first week of September. But his forces were held up again in the densely wooded hills beyond the Terek. Grozny lay only fifty miles beyond the Mozdok crossing, but all the German efforts failed to bring it within their grasp.

An important factor in this frustration was the way that the Russians switched a force of several hundred bombers to the airfields near Grozny. Their sudden appearance proved the more effective, as a brake on Kleist's advance, because most of his anti-aircraft units and much of his air force had been withdrawn from him to help the German forces at Stalingrad. Thus the Russian bombers were able to harass Kleist's army without hindrance, while they also increased its ordeal by setting alight large tracts of the forest through which it was struggling to advance.

The Russians provided a wider distraction by bringing cavalry divisions down the Caspian coast to harass his exposed eastern flank. Operating over the steppes against a widely stretched defensive screen, the Russian cavalry found unusually good scope for their particular qualities. In that vast plain they were able to penetrate his outposts wherever they chose, and cut off supplies. The Russians' growing concentration on this flank was helped by the railway they had built from Astrakhan southward. This was laid across the flat expanse of the steppes without any foundation, and neither cuttings nor embankments were required. The Germans soon found that they gained little by cutting it, since as soon as any section of it was destroyed a fresh set of rails was quickly laid. At the same time the enemy was equally intangible, and his flanking menace continuously increased. Although German mobile detachments penetrated as far as the Caspian shore, the sight of that sea was a 'mirage in the desert'.

Throughout September and October, Kleist went on trying to push south from Mozdok, by surprise attacks at different points. At each attempt he was blocked. Then he decided to switch his weight from his left centre to his right centre, for a pincer-stroke against Ordzhonikidze, the gateway to the Daryal Pass, which carries the mountain highway to Tiflis. This stroke was launched in the last week of October, and for it he was given such air support as could be spared. His right pincer captured Nalchik in a westerly flanking move, and then Alagir – the beginning of the alternative military road over the Mamison Pass. From Alagir it thrust on to Ordzhonikidze in conjunction with a converging thrust up the Terek valley. Rain and snow delayed the final stage, but Kleist's forces were almost within reach of their immediate goal when the Russians launched a well-timed and well-aimed counterattack. This produced the sudden collapse of a Rumanian mountain division, which had done well in the advance but was feeling the strain of the effort. As a result Kleist had to fall back and abandon his plan. The front was then stabilized, with the Germans still facing the mountain barrier which they had vainly tried to pierce.

This final repulse in the central Caucasus coincided with the opening of the great Russian counteroffensive at Stalingrad.

A final effort in the western Caucasus had also been planned, but this never matured. For it Hitler had, very belatedly, decided to play the airborne trump which he had so carefully preserved. The Parachute Division – still called the 7th Air Division as a camouflage – had been assembled in and near the Crimea for a swoop onto the coastal road from Tuapse to Batumi, in conjunction with a renewed push by the 17th Army. But then the Russian counteroffensive at Stalingrad took place, and was followed by a new Russian attack near Rzhev – where Zhukov's armies had nearly broken through in their August attempt to give indirect relief to Stalingrad. Hitler was so alarmed at the dual threat that he cancelled his last bid for Batumi, and ordered the parachute forces to be rushed north by rail to Smolensk, as a reinforcement to the central front.

All these failures and dangers were the fruit of frustration at Stalingrad, where a subsidiary purpose had developed by degrees into a principal effort that drew away the land and air reserves needed to fulfil the primary aim, and ultimately drained Germany's strength to no purpose.

It was ironical that in the first place the Germans should have paid forfeit for fulfilling the canons of orthodox strategy, and subsequently paid forfeit for disregarding them. Out of the original convergence arose a fatal divergence of effort.

The direct advance on Stalingrad was carried out by the 6th Army, under Paulus. It pushed down the north side of the corridor between the Don and the Donetz. Helped by the great armoured drive that was proceeding on the south side, the 6th Army made good progress at first. But as the advance extended its strength dwindled, as more and more divisions had to be detached to cover the ever-extending northern flank along the Don. The shrinkage was increased by the wastage due to long and rapid marches in great heat, as well as to battle-losses. That shrinkage in turn became a handicap in overcoming the successive stands made by the retreating Russians. Harder fighting entailed heavier losses, and thus less power to deal with the next stand.

The effect became pronounced when the 6th Army approached the great eastern bend of the Don. On July 28th one of its mobile spearheads reached the river near Kalach – 350 miles from the starting line and barely forty miles distant from the western bend of the Volga at Stalingrad. But this was a flash in the pan, and the general advance was delayed by stubborn Russian resistance in the Don bend. The narrowed front and the lower proportion of mobile troops in the 6th Army, compared with the panzer armies, handicapped its manoeuvring power. A fortnight passed before the Germans were able to crush the Russian forces in the bend. Even then it was a further ten days before they established bridgeheads across the river.

On August 23rd the Germans were ready to begin the final stage of their advance on Stalingrad. It took the form of a pincer-attack, by the 6th Army from the north-west, and by the 4th Panzer Army from the south-west. That same night German mobile units reached the banks of the Volga thirty miles above Stalingrad and came close to the bend of the Volga fifteen miles south of the city. But the pincers were kept well apart by the defenders. In the next phase the Germans developed an attack from the west, thus completing the semi-circle of pressure, and the tenseness of the situation was manifested in the tone of the call to the Russian troops to hold on at all costs to the last man. They responded to the call with wonderful endurance, for they were fighting under nerve-racking conditions that were also hard for the problem of supply and reinforcement. The two-mile wide river behind their backs was not wholly a disadvantage. With such troops, it helped to stiffen resistance as well as complicating it.

Along the arc of Russian defence, attack followed attack in seemingly endless succession, with frequent changes of site and method, but with only slight progress to compensate the attackers' cost. At times the defence was pierced, but the thrust could never be driven deep enough to cause more than a local withdrawal. More often, the attacks failed to penetrate. As check followed check, the psychological importance of the place increased – as with Verdun in 1916. In this case it was multiplied by the name that the place bore. 'Stalingrad' was an inspiring symbol for the Russians, and a hypnotic symbol for the Germans – especially for their Leader. It hypnotized Hitler into a state in which he lost sight of strategy, and lost all regard for the future. It became more fatal than Moscow – because its name meant more.

The unprofitableness, and risks, of the continued effort were apparent to any analyst of war experience who kept a clear head. Such repetitive attacks rarely pay unless the defending forces are isolated from reinforcement or their country's reserves are running short – whereas in this case it was the Germans who were less able to bear a prolonged process of attrition.

Despite Russia's immense losses, her reserves of manpower remained much greater than those of Germany. Her most serious shortage was in equipment; a shortage due to the 1941 losses which had partly accounted for her renewed defeats in 1942. Artillery was lacking, and was substituted to a large extent by mortars that were brought up on trucks. Tanks and all forms of motor-transport were other serious deficiencies. But towards the end of the summer an increasing flow of fresh equipment came from the new factories in the back areas, as well as from American and British supplies. At the same time the much extended call-up of men that had been applied after the outbreak of war was bearing fruit, and the volume of new divisions from Asia was rising.

The Stalingrad battle-area lay so far east that it was the more accessible to this inflow from the east. That helped the defence of the city, and while the scale of the direct reinforcement was cramped by its awkward situation, the mounting strength of the Russian armies on the northern flank had an indirect effect which was equivalent to an important reinforcement. Their counter-pressure on that flank would have turned the scales long before it did, if it had not been handicapped by material deficiencies in the predominant weapons of modern warfare. But the effect increased as the Germans, through becoming entangled in a localized attrition battle, used up their limited reserves of men and machines. In that kind of battle their expenditure was higher proportionately, being the attackers, and they could afford it less.

The dangers of the process were soon appreciated by the General Staff. On returning from his daily conference with Hitler, Halder would often throw out his hands in a gesture of exasperation and depression that told his assistants of one more vain effort to make Hitler see reason. His arguments against a continuance of the offensive became more urgent as winter came nearer, and the combined effect frayed Hitler's nerves, so that their relations became intolerable to both. In discussing plans Hitler continued his airy habit of waving his hand over the map in big sweeps, although the advances were now so slight that they were hardly discernible. As he became less able to sweep aside the Russians, he became more inclined to sweep obstructive counsellors out of his office. He had always felt that 'the old generals' were half-hearted about his schemes, and the more these failed to progress the more he felt that the General Staff was the brake.

So at the end of September Halder took his departure – following some of his assistants – and was succeeded by Kurt Zeitzler, a much younger man who at the time was Chief of Staff to Rundstedt in the West. In 1940 Zeitzler had been Chief of Staff of Kleist's panzer group, and it was largely due to his bold supply planning that the long-range armoured sweep from the Rhine to the English Channel had proved administratively possible. Apart from that important qualification, Hitler felt that he would have less difficulty in dealing with a younger soldier over the longer-range problem of advancing to the Caspian and the Volga – especially where the latter started with the spur of sudden promotion to the highest post. Zeitzler at first justified his confidence in this respect, for he did not worry Hitler with continual objections as Halder had done. But Zeitzler himself became worried within a short time, and as the prospect of gaining Stalingrad faded he began to argue with Hitler that the idea of maintaining the German front so far forward was impracticable. When events proved the truth of his warning Hitler did not like his advice any the better, and in 1943 took a distant attitude towards him, so that his advice became more and more ineffectual.

The same basic factors that governed the frustration of the Germans' attack on Stalingrad turned it into a fatal reverse, by assisting the eventual Russian counteroffensive.

The more closely the Germans converged on the city, the more their own power of manoeuvre became cramped, whereas the narrowing of the frontage helped the defender in moving his reserves more quickly to a threatened point on the diminished arc. At the same time, the Germans forfeited the advantage which they had formerly enjoyed from their power of distraction. During the opening drive of the summer campaign, as far as the Don, uncertainty as to their aim had helped to paralyse opposition, but now their aim had become obvious – and the Russian Command could commit its reserves with assurance. Thus the attacker's increasing concentration of force on Stalingrad became decreasingly effective as such – concentrated attack meeting concentrated defence.

At the same time, the Germans' concentration at Stalingrad increasingly drained reserves from their flank-cover, which itself was already strained by having to stretch so far – nearly 400 miles from Voronezh along the Don to the Stalingrad 'isthmus', and as far again from there to the Terek, across the Kalmuk Steppes. While these barren wastes restricted the weight of any Russian counterstroke against the second stretch, that limitation did not apply to the Don sector, which, though covered by the river, was liable to become very vulnerable when the river froze or the Russians found unguarded spots for a crossing in strength. Moreover, they had succeeded in retaining a bridgehead over the Don near Serafimovich, 100 miles west of Stalingrad.

The danger to this long-stretched flank was foreshadowed by a number of small exploratory attacks that the Russians delivered from August onwards. These showed them how thinly held it was, and that it was mainly entrusted to Germany's allies – Hungarians from Voronezh southward; Italians around the point where it turned eastwards, near

Novaya Kalitva; Rumanians near the final southward bend west of Stalingrad, as well as beyond Stalingrad. That long flank-front had only a slight German stiffening of odd regiments, or occasionally divisions, interspaced among the allied troops. Divisional sectors were up to forty miles long, and there were no properly fortified positions. The railheads were often a hundred miles or more behind the front, and the country was so bare that little timber was available for constructing defences.

An uncomfortable realization of these handicaps led the German General Staff to tell Hitler as early as August that it would be impossible to hold the line of the Don, as a defensive flank, during the winter. Their warning was not appreciated. All defensive considerations were subordinated to the aim of capturing Stalingrad.

The cramping character of this too direct offensive became more marked after the middle of September, when the Germans penetrated into the straggling suburbs, and then into the factory area. To become entangled in street-fighting is always a handicap on the offensive, and it was specially detrimental to an army whose advantage lay mainly in a superior manoeuvring power. At the same time the defence was able to make use of workers' units, who fought with the ferocity of men whose own homes are the immediate stake. In such circumstances, that local infusion was an important addition to the strength of the defending forces – the 62nd Army under General Chuikov and part of the 64th Army under General Shumilov – during the crucial weeks until the flow of reinforcements began to turn the tide. For the 62nd Army had been badly mauled in the fighting west of the Don, while few immediate resources could be found for it by General Eremenko, who was placed in charge of the sector as a whole.

The Germans' arrival in the built-up area also tended to split up their offensive into a string of localized attacks – which diminished its tidal force. The same limitation fostered a revival of the habit – to which infantry-minded commanders of the old school were prone – of employing tanks in driblets, instead of a flood. Many of the attacks were delivered with a mere twenty of thirty tanks, and although a few of the bigger efforts packed a punch of a hundred tanks, this figure meant only one tank to some 300 men engaged. With so small a proportion it was natural that the anti-tank weapons kept the upper hand. But while these paltry numbers conduced to poor tactics they revealed a growing material deficiency. This became equally marked in the declining scale of air support. The Germans were running short of the two weapons upon which they had mainly depended for their success. As a natural result the burden on the infantry became heavier, and the price of any advance higher.

On the surface, the defenders' position came to appear increasingly perilous, or even desperate, as the circle contracted and the enemy came closer to the heart of the city. The most critical moment was on October 14th, but the German attack was stemmed by General Rodimtsev's 13th Guards Division. Even after this crisis was overcome the situation remained grave, because the defenders now had their backs so close to the Volga that they had little room left in which to practise shock-absorbing tactics. They could no longer afford to sell ground to gain time. But beneath the surface fundamental factors were working in their favour.

The attackers' morale was being sapped by increasing losses, a growing sense of frustration, and the coming of winter, while their reserves were so fully absorbed as to leave the over-stretched flanks without resiliency. They were thus becoming ripe for the counterstroke which the Russian Command were preparing, and for which it had now accumulated sufficient reserves to make it effective against such overstrained opponents.

The counterstroke was launched on November 19th and 20th, and was well-timed. It started in the interval between the strong first frosts, which harden the ground for rapid movement, and the heavy snows, which clog manoeuvre. It was to catch the Germans at the pitch of exhaustion, just as they were feeling most acutely the natural reaction from the failure of their offensive to bring them victory.

The counterstroke was shrewdly aimed strategically and psychologically – exploiting the indirect approach in a double sense. A pair of pincers, each composed of several prongs, was inserted in the flanks of the Stalingrad attack, so as to isolate the 6th Army and 4th Panzer Army from Army Group B. The pincers were driven in at places where the flank-cover was largely provided by Rumanian troops. The plan was devised by a brilliant triumvirate of the Russian General Staff, Generals Zhukov, Vasilevsky, and Voronov. The principal executants were General Vatutin, commander of the South-western front, General Rokossovsky, commanding the Don front, and General Eremenko, commanding the Stalingrad front.

Here it should be mentioned that the Eastern Front as a whole was divided by the Russians into twelve 'fronts' directly under General Headquarters in Moscow. Instead of organizing them permanently in larger groups, it now became the Russian practice to send a senior general and staff from General Headquarters to coordinate the several 'fronts' concerned in any particular series of operations. The 'fronts' comprised an average of about four 'armies' apiece – which were smaller than in the West – and each of these usually controlled the divisions in it direct without the interposition of army corps head-quarters. The armoured and motorized troops were organized in groups of brigades that were called 'corps', but were equivalent to large divi-sions; and these corps were controlled by the 'front' commander.

The corps system was reintroduced by the Russians in the summer of 1943, before the new system had a chance to be tested fully. For by cutting out links in the chain of command, and giving the higher com-manders a larger number of 'sub-units' to handle, operations should be quickened and flexibility of manoeuvre developed. Every additional link in the chain is a *drawback* – in the most literal sense. It tends to cause loss of time both in getting information back to the higher com-mander, and in getting his orders forward to the real executants. More-over, it weakens his power of control, both by making his impression of the situation more remote, and by diminishing the force of his personal influence on the executants. Hence the fewer the intermediate head-quarters, the more dynamic operations tend to become. On the other hand, an increase in the number of sub-units handled by one head-quarters improves the power of manoeuvre by providing more flexi-bility. A more flexible organization can achieve greater striking effect because it has more capacity for adjustment to varying circumstances, and for concentration at the decisive point. If a man had only one or two fingers in addition to his thumb he would find it much more difficult to get a properly adjusted grip on any object, or opponent, than he can with four fingers and a thumb. His hand would have less flexibility and less capacity for concentrated pressure. That cramping limitation was seen in the armies of the Western Powers, where most formations and units were divided into only two or three manoeuvrable parts.

North-west of Stalingrad, Russian spearheads thrust down the banks of the Don to Kalach and the railway running back to the Donetz Basin. South-east of Stalingrad the prongs of the left pincers thrust westward to the railway running south to Tikhoretsk and the Black Sea. After cutting this line they pressed on towards Kalach, and by the 23rd the encirclement was completed. It was welded more firmly in the days that followed, enclosing the 6th Army and a corps of the 4th Panzer Army. In those few days of swift movement the Russians had turned the tables strategically while keeping their defensive tactical advantage – that double score which the indirect approach often achieves. For the Germans were now forced to continue attacking – not to break in, but to break out. Their efforts in reverse were as unsuccessful as their earlier efforts to drive forward.

Meanwhile, another powerful Russian force had burst out of the Serafimovich bridgehead, and spread over the country west of the Don bend, in a multi-pronged drive south into the Don–Donetz corridor, to

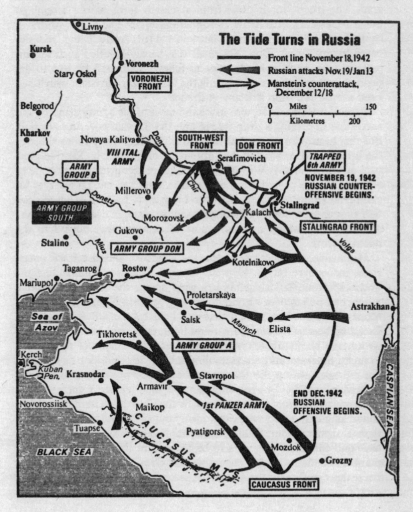

The Tide Turns in Russia

Front line November 18, 1942
Russian attacks Nov. 19/Jan 13
Manstein's counterattack, December 12/18

Miles 0 — 150
Kilometres 0 — 200

Livny
Kursk
Stary Oskol
Voronezh
VORONEZH FRONT
Belgorod
Kharkov
Novaya Kalitva
Don
SOUTH-WEST FRONT
DON FRONT
Serafimovich
TRAPPED 6th ARMY
NOVEMBER 19, 1942 RUSSIAN COUNTER-OFFENSIVE BEGINS.
VIII ITAL. ARMY
ARMY GROUP B
Millerovo
Chir
Stalingrad
Kalach
Donets
Morozovsk
ARMY GROUP SOUTH
Gukovo
STALINGRAD FRONT
Stalino
Mius
ARMY GROUP DON
Kotelnikovo
Volga
Taganrog
Rostov
Mariupol
Proletarskaya
Astrakhan
Sea of Azov
Salsk
Manych
Elista
Tikhoretsk
ARMY GROUP A
CASPIAN SEA
Kerch
Kuban Pen.
Krasnodar
Stavropol
END DEC. 1942 RUSSIAN OFFENSIVE BEGINS.
Novorossiisk
Armavir
Maikop
1st PANZER ARMY
Tuapse
C A U C A S U S   M T S.
Pyatigorsk
BLACK SEA
Mozdok
Grozny
CAUCASUS FRONT

link up on the Chir with the left pincer thrusting on from Kalach. This outer-circle movement was of vital importance to the success of the whole plan, for it upset the enemy's base of operations and dropped an iron curtain across the more direct routes by which relieving forces might have come to the aid of Paulus.

Thus the German reply, in mid-December, was delivered from the south-west, beyond the Don, up the line from Kotelnikovo to Stalingrad. The troops for it came from a scratch force hastily assembled under Manstein's 11th Army Headquarters, which had to be withdrawn from Army Group Centre, Manstein's 11th Army being redesignated 'Army Group Don'. Its small size hardly justified such an impressive title, and for his attempt to relieve Stalingrad he had to depend on meagre reserves, including the 6th Panzer Division, which had been sent by rail from Brittany in France.

By skilful tactics Manstein made the most of his scanty armour, and succeeded in driving a deep wedge into the Russian covering position. But this hastily improvised advance was checked thirty miles short of the beleaguered Army, and then gradually forced back by Russian pressure on its own flank. With the frustration of this attempt any hope of relieving Paulus passed, for the German Command had no reserves for another attempt. Manstein, however, hung on to his own exposed position as long as he could, and longer than was safe, in order to cover the air lifeline by which a meagre flow of supplies was carried to the doomed army.

Meanwhile, on December 16th, the Russians started a fresh outer-circle manoeuvre far to the west. General Golikov, commanding the Voronezh front, launched his left wing across the Middle Don at a number of points on a sixty-mile stretch between Novaya Kalitva and Monastyrshchina – a stretch that was held by the 8th Italian Army. Crossing the hard-frozen Don at first light, tanks and infantry followed up a heavy bombardment which had already put many of the Italians to flight. Snowstorms helped to blind such little opposition as was met, but did not hold up the Russians, who rapidly pushed south towards Millerovo and the Donetz. At the same time Vatutin's forces struck south-westward from the Chir towards the Donetz. Within a week the converging drives had swept the enemy out of almost the whole of the Don–Donetz corridor. While the defence had been too thin and the rout too rapid for many prisoners to be secured in the first bound, larger numbers of the retreating enemy were overrun and rounded up in the next stage, so that by the end of the second week – which was also the end of the year – the bag reached a total of 60,000.

The sweep threatened the rear of all the German armies on the Lower Don and in the Caucasus. But deepening snow and the stubborn resistance of the German troops at Millerovo and several other communication centres north of the Donetz averted the danger for the moment.

Nevertheless the menace was so palpable, and its extension so probable, that Hitler was at last brought to realize the inevitability of a disaster greater even than the Stalingrad encirclement if he persisted in his dream of conquering the Caucasus, and compelled the armies there to cling on while their flank was exposed for 600 miles back. So, in January, the order was sent that they were to retreat. The decision was taken just in time for them to escape being cut off. Their successful extrication prolonged the war, but it preceded the actual surrender of the Stalingrad armies in making clear to the world that the German tide was on the ebb.

The course of the Russian counteroffensive had been marked by the skill with which General Zhukov chose his thrust-points – as much on psychological as on topographical grounds. He hit the moral soft-spots in the enemy's dispositions. Moreover, he had shown his ability to develop an alternative kind of threat once his striking forces lost the immediate local tide, and the chance it carried of producing a general collapse. As a concentrated thrust has a diminishing effect in straining a defender's resisting power, he had renewed the initial effect by developing a widely distributed series of thrusts, aimed to extend the strain. That usually tends to be the more profitable, and less self-exhausting, form of strategy when a counteroffensive grows into an offensive and no longer enjoys its initial recoil-spring impetus.

Beneath all the other factors, material and moral, that governed the course of events lay the basic condition of the ratio between space and force. Space was so *wide* on the Eastern front that an attacker could always find room for outflanking manoeuvre if he did not concentrate upon too obvious an objective – such as Moscow in 1941, and Stalingrad in 1942. Thus the Germans had been able to gain their offensive successes without a superiority in numbers, so long as they kept a qualitative superiority. The fact that space was so *deep* on the Eastern front was, however, a saving factor for the Russians during the time they were unable to match the Germans in mechanized power and manoeuvrability.

But the Germans had lost that technical and tactical advantage, while they had also used up much of their manpower. With that shrinkage of their forces the wide spaces of Russia had turned to their disadvantage, endangering their capacity to hold such an extended front. The question now became whether they could recover their balance by contracting their front, or whether they had expended so much of their strength as to leave them no chance.

CHAPTER NINETEEN

Rommel's High Tide

The campaign of 1942 in Africa saw even more violent and far-reaching reversals of fortune than had taken place in 1941. It started with the rival armies facing one another on the Western border of Cyrenaica – exactly where they had stood nine months before. But when the new year was three weeks old Rommel launched one more of his strategic counterstrokes, which went more than 250 miles deep, and swept the British two-thirds of the way back to the Egyptian frontier before they rallied. There the front crystallized, on the Gazala line.

Near the end of May, Rommel struck again, forestalling a British offensive – just as his own had been forestalled in November. This time, after another whirling battle of breath-catching changes, the British were driven to retreat – so fast and so far that they did not rally until they reached the Alamein line, the final gateway into the Nile Delta. This time Rommel's exploiting thrust had gone more than 300 miles deep in a week. But its momentum, and his strength, were by then nearing exhaustion. His efforts to push on to Alexandria and Cairo were checked, and he was desperately close to defeat before the battle ended in mutual exhaustion.

At the end of August, after being reinforced, he made one more effort for victory. But the British had been more heavily reinforced and – under a new team of commanders, headed by General Sir Harold Alexander and General Sir Bernard Montgomery – his thrust was parried, and he was forced to yield most of his slight initial gains.

Then in late October the British resumed the offensive, in greater strength than ever before – and this time decisively. After a thirteen-day struggle, Rommel's resources were finished, and his tanks almost completely used up. His front then collapsed, and he was fortunate in escaping with the remnants of his army. They were too weak to make any further serious stand, and by the end of the year, eight weeks later, he had been driven back to Buerat in Tripolitania – a thousand miles back from Alamein. Even that was only a halt in a retreat that ended at

Tunis, in the following May, with the complete extinction of the German and Italian forces in Africa.*

At the beginning of January 1942 the British regarded their repulse at Agedabia as no more than a momentary interruption of their advance on Tripoli. They were busy with plans and the build-up for this operation – which was too aptly named 'Acrobat'. Before the month ended they had done a string of somersaults, backwards.

On January 5th a convoy of six ships, which had succeeded in slipping through the British naval and air curtain, reached Tripoli with a fresh batch of tanks that brought Rommel's strength up to just over a hundred. With that aid, and in the light of a report about the weakness of the British advanced forces, he started to plan an immediate counterstroke – keeping his intention secret. He launched it on January 21st. On the 23rd the Italian War Minister arrived at his headquarters to raise objections, but by then Rommel's spearhead had already driven a hundred miles eastward, and the British were moving eastward even faster.

The British advanced force, at the moment when Rommel struck, was formed mainly of a newly arrived armoured division, the 1st, whose armoured brigade (of 150 cruiser tanks) was composed of three converted cavalry regiments – with little experience of armoured operations, and no experience of desert operations. Their handicap was increased because Rommel's new batch of Panzer III tanks were better armoured (with plates of 50 mm thickness) than the older ones, while the German anti-tank gunners had been practising a further development of their offensive tactics in combination with their own tanks. This development is described by Heinz Schmidt:

> With our twelve anti-tank guns we leap-frogged from one vantage point to another, while our Panzers, stationary and hull-down, if possible, provided protective fire. Then we would establish ourselves to give them protective fire while they swept on again. The tactics worked well and, despite the liveliness of his fire, the enemy's tanks were not able to hold up our advance. He steadily sustained losses and had to give ground constantly. We could not help feeling that we were not then up against the tough and experienced opponents who had harried us so hard on the Trigh Capuzzo.†

Worse still, the three British armoured regiments were brought into action separately. They lost nearly half their tanks in the first engage-

* For map, see pp 118–19.
† Schmidt: *With Rommel in the Desert.* pp 125–6.

ments, when the Germans attacked them by surprise near Antelat. Rommel's advance was then temporarily halted by the intervention of the Italian War Minister, General Cavallero, who refused to allow the Italian Mobile Corps to follow up the Afrika Korps. But the British failed to profit from this pause, and the absence of any strong counter-move on their part emboldened Rommel to thrust forward again on the 25th, to Msus, bursting through the line held by the Guards Brigade and the 1st Armoured Division, which fell back northward, away from his line of advance, with its remaining thirty tanks.

Rommel's deep and threatening thrust to Msus produced a hasty order that the 4th Indian Division at Benghazi was to evacuate this port, now crammed with supplies, and withdraw to the Derna–Mechili line. The withdrawal was countermanded that night, and the prepara-tion of a counter-offensive ordered, following the arrival of Auchinleck, who had flown up from Cairo to see Ritchie at Eighth Army head-quarters. But his intervention did not prove so fitting or effective as in November. For it resulted in the British becoming spread out and static in trying to cover the 140 miles stretch between Benghazi and Mechili, while Rommel, from his central position at Msus, was allowed time and freedom to develop his action, as well as a choice of alternative ob-jectives.

This variability of threat on his part produced 'orders, counterorders, and disorders' in the British command during the days that followed. One sequel was that the corps commander, Godwin-Austen, asked to be relieved of his command because of the way that the army commander was issuing orders directly to the subordinate commanders. Worse re-sults followed.

Since Rommel's strength was small, he decided to turn westward against Benghazi as his next move, to quench any threat to his rear from that direction, while making a show of driving eastward to Mechili. The feint hypnotized the British command so that they hur-ried reinforcements to Mechili, while the widely stretched 4th Indian Division was left unsupported. Rommel's rapid switch towards Ben-ghazi came as a shock, and produced a hurried abandonment of the port, with all its accumulated stores. Exploiting the shock effect, he sent two small battle-groups to drive eastward. By their bold blend of thrust and threat they caused the British to abandon a series of possible de-fensive positions, and fall back to the Gazala line – although the bulk of the Afrika Korps, owing to shortage of supplies, had not yet advanced farther east than Msus. It was on February 4th that the British Eighth Army retreated into the shelter of the Gazala defences, but it was not until the beginning of April that Rommel, after overcoming the hesitation of the Italian higher command, was able to move up his forces close to the British position.

By this time the Gazala position was being developed, by constructing field works and laying extensive minefields, from a line into a Line – in the fortified sense of the term. But its preparation for defence was soon overshadowed by the planning for a renewed British offensive, and while it became a suitable springboard for that purpose, it was less suitable for defence – being too linear, and lacking in depth. Except in the coastal sector, the fortified points were too far apart to give one another effective fire-support. They extended fifty miles southward from the coast, with increasing gaps. The left flank position at Bir Hacheim, held by the 1st Free French Brigade under General Koenig, was sixteen miles beyond that at Sidi Muftah. Another complication for the defence was the forward base and railhead established at Belhamed, with a view to the renewed offensive. It was an obvious target for an outflanking thrust by the enemy, and the need to cover the vast amount of supplies piled up there was a constant worry to the British commanders in the battle, cramping their freedom of manoeuvre.

Policy and planning also suffered from a conflict of views on the British side about the practicability and desirability of an early offensive. From February onward, Mr Churchill urged early action, pointing out that the British had 635,000 men standing idle in the Middle East theatre while the Russians were fighting desperately and Malta, closer at hand, was being reduced to an extremity by Kesselring's sustained air attack. But Auchinleck, who had a shrewd sense of the technical and tactical defects of the British forces, wished to wait until Ritchie's strength was raised to a level sufficient to make sure of nullifying Rommel's superiority in quality. Finally Churchill, overruling his arguments, decided to send him definite orders to attack which he 'bust obey or be relieved'. But Rommel struck first, on May 26th – again forestalling the British, whose offensive was intended to start in mid-June.

Reinforcements had brought both sides up to a strength greater than at the start of the November battle, 'Operation Crusader', although the number of divisions remained the same – three German (of which two were armoured) and six Italian (one armoured) against six British (two armoured). Reckoned in terms of divisions, as both statesmen and generals commonly do, Rommel was attacking with nine against six – and such military arithmetic has been used to account for the British defeat.

But the realities in comparative strength were very different, and showed how misleading it can be to reckon in 'divisions'. Four of the five low-strength Italian infantry divisions were unmotorized, so that they could play no active part in a mobile battle of manoeuvre, such as this Battle of Gazala became. The British Eighth Army had not only an abundance of motor transport, but also two independent motor brigade groups and two 'Army' tank brigades additional to its six divisions, while one of its two armoured divisions (the 1st) had two armoured brigades instead of one – as was now the normal pattern. In all, the Eighth Army had fourteen tank units on the scene, and three more on the way, to meet Rommel's seven – of which only the four German were equipped with effective tanks.

In numbers, the British had 850 tanks in the Eighth Army's armoured formations, and 420 more available to send up as reinforcements. Their opponents had 560 tanks altogether, but 230 of these were obsolete and unreliable Italian tanks, and fifty of the 330 German were light tanks. Only the 280 German gun-armed medium tanks would really count in a fight, and there was none available in reserve, apart from about thirty under repair and a new batch of some twenty just landed at Tripoli. Thus on a realistic reckoning the British had a numerical superiority of 3 to 1 for the opening clash of armour, and of more than 4 to 1 if it became a battle of attrition.

In artillery, the British had a numerical superiority of 3 to 2, but that advantage was partly offset because all their guns were distributed among the divisions, whereas Rommel made very effective use of a mobile reserve of fifty-six medium guns which he kept under his own control.

In the air, the two sides were more closely balanced than in any other battle. The British Desert Air Force had a first-line strength of approximately 600 aircraft (380 fighters, 160 bombers, and 60 reconnaissance) against a German–Italian total of 530 (350 fighters, 140 bombers, 40 reconnaissance). But the 120 German Me 109s were qualitatively superior to the British Hurricanes and Kittyhawks.

A greater question is the qualitative balance between the tanks of the two sides. After the Eighth Army's defeat, the British very naturally took the view that their tanks were inferior to the enemy's, and that view was expressed as a fact in Auchinleck's official Despatch. But it is not borne out by analysis of the technical and test data of their respective guns and armour. Most of the German medium tanks were armed with the short 50-mm gun, which had a penetration slightly inferior to the 2-pounder gun, of higher muzzle-velocity, with which all the British-built tanks were armed. In armour, most of the German tanks in 1941 had been more thinly protected than the newer British cruisers (30 mm maximum armour against 40 mm), but were now better protected except on the turret, some of the recent arrivals having thicker hull plates (50 mm), and the rest having additional strips fitted on the most exposed parts of the hull. All the German tanks, however, were more vulnerable than the Matildas (78 mm of armour) and Valentines (65 mm of armour).

A new German medium tank – the Panzer III(J) Special – came into action in this battle, armed with a long 50-mm gun similar to their anti-tank gun. But only nineteen of these tanks had reached the front, while a further batch of the same number had been landed at Tripoli. This reinforcement was far outweighed by the arrival in Egypt of more than 400 of the new American Grant tanks. By the time that the battle opened the two British armoured divisions at Gazala had been equipped with nearly 170 of these Grants – which were armed with a 75-mm gun that had a penetration even better than the long 50-mm gun in the German Panzer III(J) Specials, and also better protection (57 mm thickness of armour compared with 50 mm). Thus there is no basic justification for the oft-repeated assertion that the tanks used by the British were inferior to the German. On the contrary, the British had a qualitative advantage as well as a very large superiority in numbers.*

In anti-tank guns, too, the British had now regained the qualitative advantage through the arrival of their 6-pounder (57-mm), which was 30 per cent superior in penetration to the long 50-mm anti-tank gun of the Germans. Sufficient of the new 6-pounders had arrived to equip both the motorized infantry brigades and the motor battalions of the armoured brigades. Although the German 88-mm gun still remained the most formidable 'tank-killer', Rommel had only forty-eight of these guns, and their high mounting made them much more vulnerable than any of the standard anti-tank guns on either side.

Analysis of the technical factors provides no adequate explanation of the Eighth Army's defeat at Gazala. The evidence clearly shows that it was basically due to the Germans' superior tactics in general, and especially to their tactical combination of tanks with anti-tank guns.

The fortified Gazala Line was held by the 13th Corps, now commanded by Lieutenant-General 'Strafer' Gott, with two infantry divisions forward – the 1st South African on the right, and the 50th on the

* For a fuller examination of this matter, see Liddell Hart: *The Tanks*, vol II, pp 92–8, and 154–6.

left. The 30th Corps, still under Norrie, and comprising most of the armour, was to cover the southern flank and was also to counter any panzer thrust in the centre – which, rather strangely, the British commanders regarded as Rommel's more likely course. This dual task led to the British armour being ill-positioned, the 1st Armoured Division being kept near the Trigh Capuzzo, while the 7th Armoured Division (which had only one armoured brigade) was posted some ten miles southward and stretched widely out to cover and support the French brigade that was holding Bir Hacheim. Auchinleck had written to Ritchie suggesting a closer concentration, but unfortunately his suggestions were not carried out by the men on the spot.

On the moonlit night of May 26th Rommel moved swiftly round the British flank with his three German divisions and the two of the Italian mobile corps – while the four unmotorized Italian divisions 'made faces' at the Gazala Line. Although his outflanking move (with more than ten thousand vehicles) was spotted and reported before dark, and again at dawn as it swept round Bir Hacheim, the opposing commanders still thought that his main attack could come in the centre in accord with their expectation. The British armoured brigades were slow to move, and thus came into action piecemeal, while the two outlying motor brigades on the southern flank were disrupted while separated and unsupported. The headquarters of the 7th Armoured Division was overrun and the commander, Major-General F. W. Messervy, captured – although he later managed to escape. It was his second mishap within a few months, for he had been commanding the 1st Armoured Division when it was surprised and shattered by Rommel at Antelat in January.

But Rommel, despite his opening success, did not succeed in cutting through to the sea – and thus cutting off the divisions in the Gazala Line, as he had hoped. His panzer divisions had a shock on encountering, for the first time, the Grant tanks with their 75-mm guns. They found themselves coming under destructive fire at ranges too long for them to hit back, and only succeeded in making headway when they brought up anti-tank guns, including three batteries of 88s, while their own tanks worked round the flanks of the British armour – whose units as well as brigades were separated, and thus the more susceptible to such flanking leverage. Even so, the panzer divisions had advanced only three miles north of the Trigh Capuzzo by nightfall, at heavy cost – and were still nearly twenty miles short of the sea coast. Rommel himself wrote in his diary: 'Our plan to overrun the British forces behind the Gazala Line had not succeeded ... The advent of the new American tank had torn great holes in our ranks ... far more than a third of the German tanks had been lost in this one day.'*

Rommel's renewed effort to reach the sea on the second day brought little progress and more loss. By nightfall his bid for quick victory had already failed, although the British had done nothing to exploit his loss of balance – their best chance of producing his downfall. But his situation was the more perilous because of the long detour his supply columns had to make round Bir Hacheim, under constant risk of interception by the British armoured and air forces. He himself had a narrow escape from capture when he went forward in his car – and was the more lucky because on his return to his battle headquarters he found that 'during our absence the British had overrun my Staff'. The Afrika Korps had only 150 tanks left fit for action, and the Italians 90, while the British still had 420 in hand.

After another abortive day, he ordered his striking force to take up a defensive position. That was a precarious position. For it lay beyond the fortified Gazala Line, and left him separated from the rest of his forces by the British garrison and their far-stretching belt of minefields. To fight 'with one's back to the wall' is grim, but to fight with one's back to a mined barrier is worse.

During the days that followed, the British air force rained bombs on this position, which was aptly christened 'the Cauldron', while the Eighth Army attacked it on the ground. The newspapers were filled with triumphant reports that Rommel was now trapped, while in the British military headquarters there was a comfortable assurance that he could be dealt with at leisure, and was bound to surrender.

Yet by the night of June 13th the whole outlook had changed. On the 14th Ritchie abandoned the Gazala Line, and started a rapid retreat to the frontier which left the troops in Tobruk isolated. By the 21st Rommel had captured that fortress and 35,000 men in it, together with an immense amount of stores. It was the worst British disaster of the war except for the fall of Singapore. Next day the remainder of the Eighth Army abandoned its position on the frontier near Sollum, and beat a hasty retreat eastward through the desert with Rommel on its heels.

What had caused such a dramatic turnabout? Rarely has there been such a tangled battle, and the threads have never been properly unravelled. The 'mystery of the Cauldron' has continued to baffle those who have tried to write its story from the British side, and been made more puzzling by myths that sprang up.

Besides the myth that Rommel possessed superiority in tanks, an-

* *The Rommel Papers*, pp 207–8.

other myth is that the scales were turned and the bulk of the British
tanks lost in one fatal day, June 13th. In reality that was only the
culmination of a series of disastrous days. The basic clue to the 'mystery of the Cauldron' is to be found in Rommel's notes. On the evening
of May 27th:

> In spite of the precarious situation and the difficult problems I
> looked forward full of hope to what the battle might bring. For
> Ritchie had thrown his armour into the battle piecemeal and had thus
> given us the chance of engaging them on each separate occasion with
> just enough of our own tanks ... They should never have allowed
> themselves to be duped into dividing their forces ...*

He then recorded that he took up what seemed his perilously exposed
defensive position ...

> on the certain assumption ... that the British would not dare to use
> any major part of their armoured formations to attack the Italians in
> the Gazala line [while strong German panzer forces stood in a position to threaten their rear] ... Thus I foresaw that the British
> mechanized brigades would continue to run their heads against our
> well-organized defensive front, and use up their strength in the process.†

Rommel's calculation worked out all too well. The British persisted
in a series of piecemeal assaults on his position, at heavy cost. Such
direct assaults proved the worst form of caution. While beating them
off, he overwhelmed the isolated 'box' at Sidi Muftah held by the 150th
Infantry Brigade, which lay behind his back, and cleared a passage
through the minefield for his supplies.

Four days later, on June 5th, Ritchie launched a larger-scale attack
on Rommel's position. But this again was executed in a piecemeal way,
while the defenders benefited from the long interval they had been
allowed to organize and fortify their position. The complex attack plan
suffered from a series of hitches and became a disjointed succession of
too direct assaults, which were beaten off in turn. By the second evening
the British tank strength had melted, through battle losses and breakdowns, from some 400 down to 170. Moreover, exploiting the attackers'
state of confusion Rommel launched a sudden pincer-like riposte on the

* *The Rommel Papers*, p 208.
† Ibid, p 211.

first evening that scattered one of the brigades of the 5th Indian Division, then closed round the back of another, which was wiped out next day, together with all the artillery supporting the division. The capture of four regiments of artillery, as well as 4,000 prisoners, was a very important 'bag'.

The British armoured brigades were kept at bay while this operation was proceeding. Their relieving efforts were spasmodic and uncoordinated – the breakdown of control being all the worse since the commander of the 7th Armoured Division, Messervy, had been chased off the scene the previous evening when the headquarters of the 5th Indian Division was overrun by the German tanks, his second exit from the stage in this battle.

Meanwhile Rommel was also carrying out the amputation of another important section of the Eighth Army's position. For on the evening of June 1st, immediately after excising the Sidi Muftah 'box', he had sent off a German battle-group and the Trieste Division to attack the still more isolated 'box' at Bir Hacheim on the southern flank held by the 1st Free French Brigade. It proved so tough that Rommel was compelled to go down and take personal command of the assault forces, and he says: 'Nowhere in Africa was I given a stiffer fight.' It was only on the tenth day that he penetrated the defences – and most of the French got away under cover of night.

Rommel was now free to make a fresh and longer pounce. Although the British armoured brigades had been brought up by fresh reinforcements to a total of 330 tanks – more than double the remaining strength of the Afrika Korps – their confidence was badly shaken, and the Germans were smelling the scent of victory. On June 11th Rommel struck eastward, and the next day cornered two of the three British armoured brigades between his panzer divisions – forcing the British to fight in a cramped area where he could batter them with converging fire. They might have made more effort to get out of the trap if they had not been deprived of leadership through Messervy being again cut off from his troops – for the third time in three weeks – by the enemy's advance, when on his way to see the army commander. By mid-afternoon on the 12th the two armoured brigades were trapped, and remnants only escaped, while the third brigade, coming down to the rescue, suffered heavy losses from the well-posted Germans. On the 13th Rommel turned northward, and squeezed the British out of the 'Knightsbridge Box', while continuing to harry what remained of the British armour. By nightfall it had shrunk to barely a hundred tanks. Rommel now for the first time had a superiority in tank strength – and, being in possession of the battlefield, he could recover and repair many of his damaged tanks, unlike the British.

The two divisions holding the Gazala Line were now in imminent danger of being cut off and trapped, for on June 14th Rommel sent the Afrika Korps driving north past Acroma towards the coast road. But it was delayed by the minefield there, which it did not get through until late in the afternoon, and the panzer-troops were by now so tired that they fell asleep where they halted at nightfall – heedless of Rommel's calls to press on and cut the coast road. This was very fortunate for the South Africans, whose motor-convoys were pouring back along the road throughout the night. But part of their rearguard was cut off when the panzer forces raced on to the sea in the morning. The other division in the Gazala Line, the British 50th, only managed to escape by breaking out westward through the Italian front, followed by a long circuit south and then east to the frontier. The 1st South African Division, after slipping out along the coast road, also continued its retreat back to the frontier – over a hundred miles distant and seventy miles beyond Tobruk.

Such a long step back was contrary to Auchinleck's intention, and his instructions to Ritchie were that the Eighth Army should rally and stand on a line west of Tobruk. But Ritchie failed to tell his Commander-in-Chief that the Gazala Line divisions were going back to the frontier, and by the time Auchinleck became aware of this it was too late to stop them. Worse still, the British forces 'fell between two stools'.

For on June 14th, as the British were falling back, Mr Churchill sent an emphatic message saying: 'Presume there is no question in any case of giving up Tobruk.' He repeated this admonition in telegrams on the 15th and 16th. That long-distance advice from London conduced to the crowning blunder. For the hasty step of leaving part of the Eighth Army in Tobruk, while the rest withdrew to the frontier, gave Rommel the chance to overwhelm the isolated force in Tobruk before its defence was properly organized.

Quickly turned eastward again by Rommel, after their thrust to the coast, the panzer forces swept round the Tobruk perimeter, capturing or isolating the 'boxes' that had been established in the Eighth Army's rear, and drove on to capture the airfields at Gambut, east of Tobruk. In this drive, they brushed aside the remnants of the British armoured brigades – which then retreated to the frontier. But Rommel did not pursue them, yet. For as soon as he had secured the Gambut airfields, he turned his forces back westward, and with astonishing quickness mounted an attack on Tobruk. Its reinforced garrison comprised the 2nd South African Division (which included the 11th Indian Brigade) under General Klopper, the Guards Brigade, and the 32nd Army Tank Brigade – with seventy tanks. But, after seeing Rommel's panzer forces drive on eastward, they did not expect an attack, and were not prepared to meet it. At 5.20 AM on June 20th, a hurricane bombardment started against a sector in the south-east of the perimeter, by artillery and dive-bombers, followed by an infantry assault. By 8.30 AM the German tanks were pouring through a breach in the defences, and Rommel himself was on the spot to speed up the exploiting flow. By the afternoon the panzer forces had overcome the resistance of the confused defenders, and drove into Tobruk. By morning the garrison commander, General Klopper, came to the conclusion that continued resistance was hopeless, and retreat impossible, so he took the fateful decision to surrender. Although a few small parties managed to escape, 35,000 troops were taken prisoner.

The consequence of that disaster was the headlong retreat into Egypt of Ritchie's surviving force, with Rommel in hot chase. In maintaining this pursuit Rommel was greatly helped by the huge haul of stores he had made at Tobruk. According to Bayerlein, the Chief of Staff of the Afrika Korps, 80 per cent of Rommel's transport at this time were captured British vehicles. But while this great catch provided him with the transport, fuel, and food to maintain his mobility, it did not restore his fighting strength. When the Afrika Korps moved up to the frontier on June 23rd it had only forty-four tanks left fit for action, and the Italians only fourteen. Nevertheless Rommel determined to follow again the maxim 'press hard on the heels of a rout'.

Field-Marshal Kesselring flew in from Sicily the day after Tobruk's fall to argue against a further advance in Africa – calling for the return of his air force units for an attack on Malta, as earlier agreed. The Italian Supreme Command in Africa were also averse to pushing on, and on the 22nd Bastico actually gave Rommel an order to halt – whereat Rommel replied that he would not 'accept the *advice*', and jocularly invited his official superior to dine with him in Cairo. He could afford to take liberties after such a victory, and all the more because a signal from Hitler's headquarters brought the news of his promotion to field-marshal in reward for the victory. At the same time, Rommel appealed direct to Mussolini and Hitler for permission to drive on. Hitler and his military advisers had become very dubious about the intended assault on Malta, feeling that the Italian Navy would fail to back them up in face of the British Navy, and that the German parachute troops dropped on Malta would be left stranded without supplies and reinforcements. A month earlier, on May 21st, Hitler had decided that, if Rommel succeeded in capturing Tobruk, the attack on Malta, 'Operation Hercules', was to be dropped. Mussolini was also relieved by the possibility of a less formidable alternative to this labour of 'Hercules', and eager to embrace a more glorious prospect. So, early on the 24th, Rommel received a wireless message: 'Duce approves Panzerarmee intention to pursue the enemy into Egypt.' A few days later, Mussolini flew over to Derna, with a white charger following in another aircraft, ready for a triumphant entry into Cairo. Even Kesselring, according to Italian accounts, appears to have agreed that pursuit into Egypt was preferable to an assault on Malta.

The precipitate British retreat from the frontier, even before Rommel had arrived there, provided both a justification and confirmation of his boldness. It was a most striking demonstration of moral effect – and of Napoleon's oft-quoted dictum that 'in war the moral is to the material as three is to one'. For when Ritchie decided to abandon the frontier – 'to gain time with distance' as he telegraphed to Auchinleck – he had three almost intact infantry divisions there, a fourth on the way up that was fresh, and three times as many tanks fit for action as the Afrika Korps.

But the shock of the news from Tobruk had caused Ritchie to abandon any attempt to hold the frontier – a decision which he took on the night of June 20th, six hours before Klopper's decision to surrender.

Ritchie's intention was to make a stand at Mersa Matruh, and fight out the issue there with the divisions brought back from the frontier, reinforced by the 2nd New Zealand Division which was just arriving from Syria. But on the evening of June 25th Auchinleck took over direct command of the Eighth Army from Ritchie. After reviewing the problem with his principal staff officer, Eric Dorman-Smith, he cancelled the order to hold the fortified position at Matruh, and decided to fight a more mobile battle in the Alamein area. It was a hard decision, for not only did it mean many difficulties in getting away troops and stores, but it was bound to cause fresh alarm at home, particularly in Whitehall. In taking this decision, Auchinleck showed a cool head and strong nerve. Although a further withdrawal could not be justified by the balance of material strength, it was probably wise in view of the weaknesses of the Mersa Matruh position, which could be easily bypassed, and of the balance of morale. For although the troops pouring back from the frontier were not demoralized, their confidence was shaken and they were in a state of confusion. Major-General Sir Howard Kippenberger, the New Zealand commander and war historian, watched them arriving in the Matruh area, so 'thoroughly mixed up and disorganized' that he 'did not see a single formed fighting unit, infantry, armour, or artillery'.* Rommel allowed them no time to reorganize, and the speed of his pursuit nullified Ritchie's reason for abandoning the frontier 'to gain time with distance'.

On getting the 'release' from Rome, during the night of June 23rd/24th, Rommel pushed on beyond the frontier and across the desert in the moonlight, and by the evening of the 24th he had covered more than a hundred miles – reaching the coast road well east of Sidi Barrani, close on the heels of the British, although he only caught a small part of the rearguard. By the next evening his forces were close to the positions that the British had taken up at Matruh and to the south of it.

Because of the ease with which Matruh could be by-passed, the mobile forces of the 13th Corps (Gott's) had been posted in the desert to the south, supported by the New Zealand Division, while the Matruh defences were held by the 10th Corps (Holmes) with two infantry divisions. There was a gap of nearly ten miles between the two corps, covered by a minefield belt.

There was no pause to mount a carefully prepared attack. For lack of strength, Rommel had to depend on speed and surprise. While the British armour had been brought up to a total of 160 tanks (of which nearly half were Grants), he had barely 60 German tanks (of which a quarter were light Panzer IIs) and a handful of Italian tanks. The total infantry strength of his three German divisions was a mere 2,500, and that of the six Italian divisions only some 6,000. It was sheer audacity to launch any attack with such a weak force – but audacity triumphed, with the aid of moral effect plus speed.

The three very diminished German divisions, leading the advance, started their attack on the afternoon of the 26th. Two of them had arrived opposite the gap already mentioned. The 90th Light was fortunate in arriving on the shallowest part of the mined belt, and by midnight was twelve miles beyond (it reached the coast road, again, on the next evening and thus blocked the direct line of retreat from Matruh). The 21st Panzer took longer in getting through the doubled belt of mines that it met, but at daylight drove on twenty miles deep and then swung round on to the rear of the New Zealand Division at Minqar Qaim, scattering part of its transport before being checked.

* Kippenberger: *Infantry Brigadier*, p 127.

The 15th Panzer, farther south, ran into the British armour and was held in check most of the day. But the swift and deep thrust of the 21st Panzer, and its threat to the British line of retreat, had produced such an effect that in the afternoon Gott ordered a retreat – which soon developed into a very disorderly retreat. The New Zealand Division was left isolated, but succeeded in breaking through the enemy's thin ring after dark. The 10th Corps in Matruh received no word of the retreat of the 13th Corps until almost dawn on the next day – nine hours after its line of retreat had been blocked. Nearly two-thirds of the Matruh force managed to escape on the following night, however, by breaking out southward in small groups under cover of darkness. But 6,000 were taken prisoner – a number larger than Rommel's whole striking force – and a vast quantity of supplies and equipment was left behind, to Rommel's benefit.

Meanwhile his panzer spearheads were pushing on, so fast that they forestalled the British hope of making a temporary stand at Fuka. By their quick arrival on the coast road there, in the evening of the 28th, they caught and overwhelmed the remnants of an Indian brigade which had been scattered in the opening attack, and next morning they trapped some of the columns that had escaped from Matruh. The 90th Light, which had been mopping up at Matruh, resumed its eastward drive along the coast road that afternoon; by midnight it had travelled ninety miles, and overtaken the panzer spearheads. Next morning, June 30th, Rommel wrote to his wife exultantly: 'Only 100 more miles to Alexandria!' By evening he was barely sixty miles distant from his goal, and the keys of Egypt seemed within his grasp.

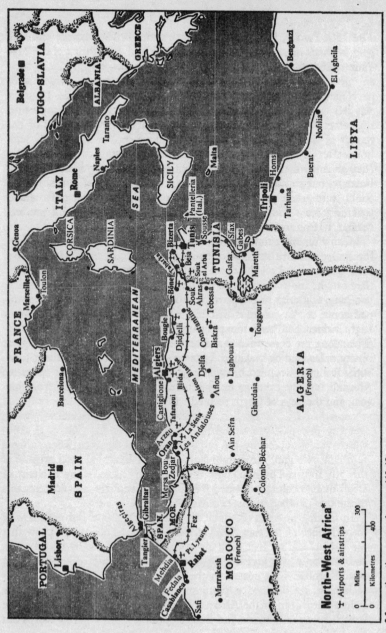

North–West Africa*

✈ Airports & airstrips

| 0 | | Miles | 300 |
| 0 | | Kilometres | 400 |

* for continuation eastward see pp. 118–19

CHAPTER TWENTY

The Tide Turns in Africa

On June 30th the Germans moved up close to the Alamein line, a relatively short advance, while waiting for the Italians to arrive. This brief pause to gather strength turned out to the detriment of Rommel's chances. For that morning what remained of the British armoured brigades were still lying in the desert south of the coast route, unaware that they had been outstripped in their retreat by Rommel's armour. Only the thinness of the pursuing force saved them from being trapped and 'put in the bag' before they got back into the shelter of the Alamein line.

Rommel's momentary pause may have been caused by mistaken Intelligence reports about the strength of that defensive position. Actually, it comprised four 'boxes', which had been laid out in the thirty-five-mile stretch between the coast and the steep drop into the great Qattara Depression – which, because of the salt marsh and soft sand, limited an outflanking move. The largest and strongest 'box' lay on the coast at Alamein, and was occupied by the 1st South African Division. The next, similar, to the south, was a newly made one at Deir el Shein, occupied by the 18th Indian Brigade. The third, seven miles beyond, was the Bab el Qattara Box (called by the Germans Qaret el Abd) which was occupied by the 6th New Zealand Brigade. Then, after a fourteen mile gap, came the Naqb el Dweis Box held by a brigade of the 5th Indian Division. The intervals were covered by a chain of small mobile columns formed from these three divisions and remnants of the two that had garrisoned Mersa Matruh.

In making his plan of attack, for July 1st, Rommel did not know of the existence of the new 'box' at Deir el Shein. Nor did he know that the British armour had been outstripped in its retreat by his advance, and was only just arriving back at Alamein. So he reckoned that it would probably be posted in the south to cover that flank. On this reckoning, he planned a pinning attack there, followed by a quick switch northward of the Afrika Korps for a breakthrough thrust in the stretch between Alamein and Bab el Qattara. But the Afrika Korps ran into the 'unknown' Deir el Shein Box, and was held up until the evening before it succeeded in capturing the 'box', with most of its defenders. But they had held out long enough to annul Rommel's hope of a quick breakthrough and its swift exploitation. The British armour arrived on the scene too late to save the 'box', but its belated appearance helped to check the Afrika Korps from continuing the advance. Rommel ordered it to push on by moonlight, but that intention was frustrated by the British aircraft which utilized the moonlight to bomb and disperse the German supply columns.

This day – Wednesday, July 1st – was the most dangerous moment of the struggle in Africa. It was more truly the turning point than the repulse of Rommel's renewed attack at the end of August or the Octo-

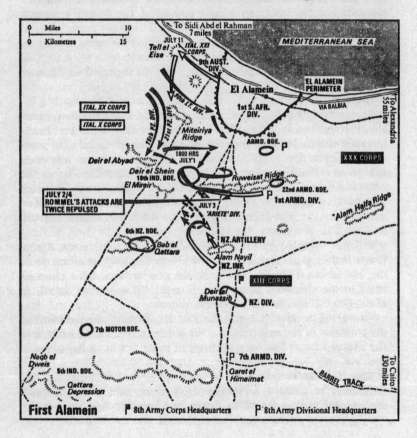

First Alamein

ber battle that ended in Rommel's retreat – the battle which, because of its more obviously dramatic outcome, has come to monopolize the name of 'Alamein'. Actually, there was a series of 'Battles of Alamein', and the 'First Alamein' was the most crucial.

The news that Rommel had reached Alamein had led the British fleet to leave Alexandria, and withdraw through the Suez Canal into the Red Sea. Clouds of smoke rose from the chimneys of the military head-quarters in Cairo as their files were hastily burned. In grim humour, soldiers called it 'Ash Wednesday'. Veterans of World War I re-membered that it was the anniversary of the opening day of the Somme offensive in 1916, when the British Army lost 60,000 men – the worst day's loss in all its history. Seeing the black snowstorm of charred paper, the people of Cairo naturally took it as a sign that the British were fleeing from Egypt, and crowds besieged the railway station in a rush to get away. The world outside, on hearing the news, took it to mean that Britain had lost the war in the Middle East.

But by nightfall the situation at the front had become hopeful, and the defenders more confident – in contrast to the state of panic at the back of the front.

Rommel continued his attack on July 2nd, but the Afrika Korps had less than forty tanks left fit for action and the troops were dead tired. Its renewed attack did not get going until the afternoon, and soon came to a halt on sighting two larger bodies of British tanks – one in its path and the other moving round its flank. Auchinleck had coolly gauged the situation, realized the weakness of Rommel's attacking forces, and planned what he hoped would prove a decisive counterstroke. His plan was not carried out as intended, and the hitches in execution frustrated his hopes, but it served to foil Rommel's aim.

Rommel made a further effort on July 3rd, but by then the Afrika Korps had only twenty-six tanks fit for action, and its eastward push that morning was checked by the British armour, although a renewed effort in the afternoon advanced nine miles before it was halted. A converging advance by the Ariete Division was also repelled, and dur-ing the action a New Zealand battalion, the 19th, captured almost the whole of the Ariete's artillery in a sudden counterattack on its flank – and 'the remainder took to their heels in panic'.* That collapse was a clear sign of overstrain.

Next day, July 4th, Rommel ruefully wrote home: 'Things are, un-fortunately, not going as we should like. The resistance is too great, and our strength is exhausted.' His thrusts had not only been parried but

* *The Rommel Papers*, p 249.

answered by upsetting ripostes. His troops were too tired as well as too few to be capable of making a fresh effort for the moment. He was forced to break off the attack and give them a breather, even though it meant giving Auchinleck time to bring up reinforcements.

Moreover Auchinleck had regained the initiative, and he came close to turning the tables decisively even before reinforcements arrived. His plan that day was broadly the same as on the previous day – to hold the Panzerarmee's attack in check with Norrie's 30th Corps, while Gott's 13th Corps in the south struck upward across the enemy's rear. But this time the bulk of the armour was kept in the north under the 30th Corps, although the 13th Corps included the recently reorganized 7th Armoured Division, now called a 'light armoured division' and composed of a motor brigade, armoured-cars, and Stuart tanks. It lacked punch, but had the mobility for a quick and wide drive round the enemy's rear while the strong New Zealand Division attacked his flank.

Unfortunately, a lack of wireless security allowed the German 'intercept' services to hear, and warn Rommel, of Auchinleck's design. The 21st Panzer Division was moved back to meet the enveloping attack, and that countermove may have increased the hesitation which the executive commanders showed in fulfilling Auchinleck's decisive intention. Similar hesitation was shown in the northern sector. When the 21st Panzer Division moved back, some of the 1st Armoured Division's Stuart tanks started to push forward, and this insignificant advance produced a very significant effect – a sudden panic among the scanty troops of the 15th Panzer Division (whose fighting strength now was only fifteen tanks and some 200 riflemen). Such a panic in such tough German troops revealed how badly overstrained they were. But nothing was done to seize the opportunity for a general attack – by the armoured division, and the corps – which might well have proved decisive.

That night Auchinleck, even more emphatically than before, ordered his forces to drive home their attack, saying in his orders: 'Our task remains to destroy the enemy as far east as possible and not to let him get away as a force in being ... the enemy should be given no rest ... Eighth Army will attack and destroy the enemy in his present position.' But he did not succeed in passing his own vigorous spirit down the 'chain of command'. He had moved his tactical headquarters up close to 30th Corps HQ, but that had been established nearly twenty miles behind the front, while it was equally far from 13th Corps HQ in the south. Panzerarmee HQ was only six miles behind the front, and Rommel himself was often up with the forward troops, applying a personal impulse on the spot. Rommel has been much criticized by more orthodox soldiers, German as well as British, for the frequency with which he was away from his headquarters and his fondness for taking direct control of the fight. But that direct control, although it caused some of his troubles, was a prime cause of his great successes. It revived in modern war the practice of, and influence exerted by, the Great Captains of the past.

On July 5th the 13th Corps did little, and the 30th Corps even less, to carry out Auchinleck's aim and orders. The brigades of the New Zealand Division, which were cast for the leading role in the attack on Rommel's rear, were not informed of their Commander-in-Chief's intentions, and the decisive action expected of them. Auchinleck may reasonably be criticized for leaving the bulk of the armour with the 30th Corps instead of sending it to reinforce the intended rear thrust by the 13th Corps, but there is little reason to think that it would have been more vigorously employed there than it was in the centre – where a vigorous thrust might easily have succeeded in view of the enemy's weakness. The 1st Armoured Division had now been brought up to a strength of ninety-nine tanks, while the 15th Panzer Division facing it had only fifteen left, and the whole Afrika Korps barely thirty.

The best excuse, and basically the truest explanation, was sheer tiredness – resulting from prolonged strain. That was the factor which in this first crucial phase finally settled the issue – as a stalemate settlement.

On balance, this was probably to the immediate advantage of the Germans and Italians, although to their ultimate disadvantage. The British situation was never so desperate as it outwardly appeared, whereas by July 5th Rommel's forces were nearer to complete collapse than they had ever been to complete victory.

During the short lull which followed, the remainder of the Italian infantry divisions came up, and these took over the now static front in the northern sector, thus setting free the Germans for the new thrust in the southern sector that Rommel was planning. But on July 8th, when he was about to try this thrust, the fighting strength of his three German 'divisions' had risen to no more than fifty tanks and about 2,000 infantry, while that of the seven Italian 'divisions' (including the recently arrived Littorio armoured division) was only fifty-four tanks and about 4,000 infantry. The British were reinforced by the arrival of the 9th Australian Division, which had so vigorously defended Tobruk in 1941, and by two fresh regiments, which brought them up to a strength of more than 200 tanks. The Australian division was sent to join the 30th Corps, which was now given a new commander, Lieutenant-

General W. H. Ramsden – previously commanding the 50th Division.

Rommel's intention to switch his effort southward fitted in well with Auchinleck's desires, and new plan – which was to use the Australians for an attack westwards along the coast road. When the Germans moved south, the New Zealanders withdrew eastward, evacuating the Bab el Qattara Box, so that all the Germans gained by this thrust on July 9th was 'vacant possession' of this 'box'.

Early next morning, the Australians launched their attack near the coast, and speedily overran the Italian division holding that sector. Although they were checked, and some of the lost ground regained, by German troops who were rushed to the spot, this strong threat to Rommel's coast-road line of supply forced him to abandon his thrust in the south. Auchinleck promptly sought to exploit the effect by a thrust aimed at the now weakened centre of Rommel's line, on the Ruweisat Ridge. But, again, a well-conceived plan miscarried through mismanagement by the subordinate commanders, and lack of skilful combination between armour and infantry – to which the Germans owed so many of their successes.

The faulty tactical combination between the arms was made all the worse by the distrust that had long been growing among the infantry of the support they were likely to get from their own armour if, by pushing forward, they exposed themselves to counterattack from the panzer troops :

At this time there was throughout the Eighth Army, not only in the New Zealand Division, a most intense distrust, almost hatred, of our armour. Everywhere one heard tales of the other arms being let down; it was regarded as axiomatic that the tanks would not be where they were wanted in time.*

Even so, the thrust and threat strained Rommel's meagre resources, while a counterattack he attempted in the north had little success. Although the British tanks were slow in meeting German tank counterstrokes against their own infantry, they helped to frighten the Italian infantry into large surrenders. Writing home on July 17th Rommel said :

Things are going downright badly for me at the moment, at any rate, in the military sense. The enemy is using his superiority, especially in infantry, to destroy the Italian formations one by one, and the

* Kippenberger: *Infantry Brigadier*, p 180.

German formations are much too weak to stand alone. It's enough to make one weep.*

Next day the 7th Armoured Division developed a threat to Rommel's southern flank, to extend the strain while Auchinleck prepared a new and heavier attack with further reinforcements which had now arrived. It was again aimed to achieve a breakthrough in the centre, but this time on the southern side of the Ruweisat Ridge, towards El Mireir. A fresh armoured brigade, the 23rd, which had just arrived (with 150 Valentines), was to be used in this attack – but one of its three regiments was sent to help the Australians in a subsidiary attack on the Miteiriya Ridge in the north.

The prospects looked all the better since the Eighth Army, with this additional brigade and fresh deliveries to the others, now had nearly 400 tanks on the scene. Rommel's tank strength was even lower than his opponents realized – the Afrika Korps had less than thirty tanks left. But, by a combination of luck and judgement, they were posted just at the point where the main British thrust was looming – and, in the event, only a small proportion of the British tanks were actually brought into action there.

Auchinleck's plan this time was to burst through the enemy's centre by a wide-fronted night attack with infantry – the 5th Indian Division – advancing straight along the Ruweisat Ridge, and the valley south of it, after the resistance had been lowered by a northward sweeping flank attack of the New Zealand Division. Then, at daylight, the new 23rd Armoured Brigade was to drive through to the El Mireir end of the valley, and the 2nd Armoured Brigade would then pass to carry on the exploiting drive. It was a finely conceived plan, but required thorough working out of the detailed process by the executives, which it did not get. The successive steps were not adequately coordinated at a corps conference, and Gott's subordinates remained hazy about each other's part.

The attack was launched on the night of July 21st, and the New Zealanders arrived on their objective. But then German tanks came up and counterattacked them in the dark, causing confusion. At daylight they smashed the most advanced New Zealand brigade – while the 22nd Armoured Brigade, which was to have protected the flank of the New Zealand advance, had not appeared on the scene. For its commander, in contrast to the Germans, had declared that tanks could not move in the dark.

* *The Rommel Papers*, p 257.

Meanwhile the 5th Indian Division's night attack had failed to reach its objectives. Worse still, it failed to clear a gap in the minefields for the follow-up advance of the 23rd Armoured Brigade. When its 40th and 46th Royal Tank Regiments were launched to the attack in the morning, they met the Indians falling back, but could get no clear information as to whether the mines in their path had been cleared. So they most gallantly drove on, and carried out what the New Zealanders, admiringly but too aptly, called 'a real Balaclava Charge'. They soon found that the minefield had not been gapped, and that they had charged into a triple trap – coming under intense fire from the German tanks and anti-tank guns when they ran onto the minefield and became stranded there. Only eleven tanks returned. The one redeeming aspect of this ill-fated attack was that these two fresh regiments of the RTR helped to restore the confidence of the infantry, and of the New Zealanders particularly, that they would not be left in the lurch by the excessive caution of their own armour. The other regiment of the brigade had shown a similar thrustfulness in the northern attack. But the price was heavy – altogether, 118 tanks were lost this day, compared with the Germans' loss of three. Even so, the British tank strength was still ten times as large as Rommel's. But the miscarriage of the initial attack had such a damping effect that little further effort was made to resume the attack and use the potentially overwhelming weight of the forces on the British side.

After four days' interval, for reorganization and regrouping, one further attempt was made to break through Rommel's front – by a thrust in the north. It opened well with the Australians' capture of the Miteiriya Ridge by moonlight, and the 50th Division to the south of them also made a good start. But the commander of the 1st Armoured Division, which was to follow up and pass through, was not satisfied that a sufficiently wide gap had been cleared in the minefield. His delay spoilt the prospects of the attack as a whole. It was mid-morning before the leading tanks started to move through the minefield, and they were then pinned down by German tanks which had been rushed north. The infantry on the far side of the minefield were cut off, and then cut up by a counterattack. Meanwhile, the Australians had also been driven off the ridge, and a part of them similarly trapped.

Auchinleck now reluctantly decided to suspend the attack. Many of the troops were showing signs of exhaustion after the prolonged struggle, and an increasing tendency to surrender if isolated. It was also clear that the defence had the advantage on such a restricted front, and that the advantage would grow with the reinforcements that were now at last reaching Rommel – by the start of August his tank strength increased to more than five times what it had been on July 22nd.

While the battle ended in disappointment for the British, their situation was far better than when it opened. The final sentence of Rommel's account of the battle utters the final verdict: 'Although the British losses in this Alamein fighting had been higher than ours, yet the price to Auchinleck had not been excessive, for the one thing that had mattered to him was to halt our advance, and that, unfortunately, he had done.'*

Although the Eighth Army had suffered over 13,000 casualties during the July battle at Alamein, it had taken over 7,000 prisoners, including more than a thousand Germans. The price would have been lower, and the gains much greater, if the execution of the plans had been more vigorous and efficient. But, even as it was, the difference in the total loss on either side was not large, and Rommel was much less able to afford the loss. His frustration was almost certainly bound to prove fatal in view of the flood of British reinforcements that was now pouring into Egypt.

His own account makes it clear how perilously close to defeat he came by mid-July. Even clearer in his own confession at the time, in a letter to his wife on the 18th: 'Yesterday was a particularly hard and critical day. We pulled through again. But it can't go on like it for long, otherwise the front will crack. Militarily, this is the most difficult period I've ever been through. There's help in sight, of course, but whether we will live to see it is a question.'† Four days later, with reserves still fewer, his troops had to meet an even weightier blow, and were fortunate in surviving it.

Rommel's subsequent account of the battle pays a high tribute to the British Commander-in-Chief: 'General Auchinleck who had ... taken over command himself at El Alamein, was handling his forces with very considerable skill ... He seemed to view the situation with decided coolness, for he was not allowing himself to be rushed into accepting a "second-class" solution by any moves we made. This was to be particularly evident in what followed.'**

But each of the successive 'first-class' solutions which Auchinleck devised (with the aid of his fertile-minded chief staff officer, Dorman-Smith) went wrong in the third-class compartments of the executants' train. Its corridors also became blocked. One important cause of block-

* *The Rommel Papers*, p 260.
† Ibid, p 257.
** Ibid, p 248.

age was the presence of such a mixture of contingents from the different countries of the British Commonwealth, under such conditions of strain, and the way that the commanders were distracted by anxious questions and cautions from their respective Governments. While such anxiety was very natural after the unhappy experience of recent months, it multiplied the usual friction of war.

It was also natural that the prevailing disappointment at the end of the battle in July should have renewed the impression of bad leadership left by the disaster in June, and developed an impulsive feeling that drastic changes were needed in the higher command. As usual, criticism was focused on the top of the ladder, rather than where the slips and bungles had occurred, lower down. There was better justification in the need to restore the confidence of the troops, which had been shaken afresh by the failure of Auchinleck's counteroffensive. In such conditions, a change of command is the easiest way to provide a tonic and may be essential as a stimulant – however unjust to the commander who is replaced.

Churchill decided to fly out to Egypt, to size up the situation, and arrived in Cairo on August 4th – the fateful anniversary of Britain's entry into World War I. Although Auchinleck had 'stemmed the adverse tide', as Churchill recognized and said, it was not so apparent that the tide had actually turned, as can be seen in retrospect. Rommel still stood barely sixty miles from Alexandria and the Nile Delta – disturbingly close. Churchill was already thinking of making a change in the command, and his inclination turned into decision after finding that Auchinleck strongly resisted his pressure for an early renewal of the offensive, and insisted that it must be deferred until September in order to give the new reinforcements time to become acclimatized and have some training in desert conditions.

His decision was also influenced and fortified by discussion with Field-Marshal Smuts, the South African Prime Minister, who had flown to Egypt at his request. Churchill's first idea was to offer the command to the very able Chief of the Imperial General Staff, General Sir Alan Brooke – but Brooke, from motives of delicacy as well as of policy, did not wish to leave the War Office and take Auchinleck's place. So after further discussion, Churchill telegraphed to the other members of the War Cabinet in London that he proposed to appoint Alexander as Commander-in-Chief, and to give the command of the Eighth Army to Gott – a surprising choice in the light of this gallant soldier's fumbling performance as a corps commander in the recent battles. But Gott was killed in an air crash next day, on his way to

Cairo. Montgomery was then, fortunately, brought out from England to fill the vacancy. Two fresh corps commanders were also flown out – Lieutenant-General Sir Oliver Leese to take over the 30th Corps and Lieutenant-General Brian Horrocks to fill the vacancy in the 13th.

But an ironical result of these changes was that the resumption of the British offensive was put off to a much later date than Auchinleck had proposed. For the impatient Prime Minister had to give way to Montgomery's firm determination to wait until preparations and training were completed. This entailed leaving the initiative to Rommel, and allowing him another chance to bid for victory in what was to be called the 'Battle of Alam Halfa' – but in effect only gave him 'enough rope to hang himself'.

During August only two fresh formations arrived to reinforce Rommel – a German parachute brigade and an Italian parachute division. Both came 'dismounted', for employment as infantry. But the losses in the divisions already engaged were made up to a considerable extent by drafts and fresh supplies of equipment – although much more arrived for the Italian divisions than for the German. By the eve of the attack, which Rommel was planning to deliver at the end of August, he had about 200 gun-armed tanks in the two panzer divisions, and 240 in the two Italian armoured divisions. While the Italian tanks were still of the old model, now more obsolete than ever, the German Panzer IIIs included seventy-four with the long 50-mm gun, and twenty-seven of the Panzer IVs mounted the new long 75-mm gun. That was an important qualitative gain.

But the British tank strength at the front had been brought up to a total of over 700 (of which some 160 were Grants). In the event, only some five hundred were used in the armoured battle – which this time was brief.

The fortified front was still held by the same four infantry divisions as in July, with strength rebuilt, and the 7th (Light) Armoured Division remained, while the 1st Armoured Division went back to refit and was replaced by the 10th (commanded by Major-General A. H. Gatehouse) – which comprised two armoured brigades, the 22nd and the newly arrived 8th, while the re-equipped 23rd was also put under its command after the battle started. A newly arrived infantry division was also brought to the front to hold the rearward position on the Alam Halfa Ridge.

No radical change was made in the defence that had been designed by Dorman-Smith and approved by Auchinleck while he was still in command. After the battle was won, it was widely reported that the plan was completely recast following the change of command. So it should be emphasized that Alexander, in his Despatch, stated the facts with an honesty shattering to such stories and claims. He said that when he took over the command from Auchinleck:

> The plan was to hold as strongly as possible the area between the sea and Ruweisat ridge and to threaten from the flank any enemy advance south of the ridge from a strongly defended prepared position on the Alam el Halfa ridge. General Montgomery, now in command of Eighth Army, acepted this plan in principle, to which I agreed, and hoped that if the enemy should give us enough time he would be able to improve our positions by strengthening the left or southern flank.*

The Alam Halfa position was reinforced before Rommel attacked, but its defence was not seriously tested – for the issue of the battle was decided by the well-judged positioning of the armour, and its very effective defensive action.

The northern and central sectors of the front were so strongly fortified that the southern stretch of fifteen miles, between the New Zealanders' 'box' on the Alam Nayil Ridge and the Qattara Depression, was the only part of the front where a quick penetration could possibly succeed. Thus in trying to achieve a breakthrough Rommel was bound to take that line of advance. That was obvious – and was what the defence plan evolved under Auchinleck had been designed to produce.

Surprise in aim-point was thus impossible, so Rommel had to depend on achieving surprise in time and speed. He hoped that if he broke through the southern sector quickly, and got astride the Eighth Army's communications, it would be thrown off balance and its defence disjointed. His plan was to capture the mined belt by a night attack, after which the Afrika Korps with part of the Italian Mobile Corps would drive on eastward for about thirty miles before daylight, and then wheel north-east to the coast towards the Eighth Army's supply area. This threat, he hoped, would lure the British armour into a chase, giving him the chance to trap and destroy it. Meanwhile the 90th Light Division and the rest of the Italian Mobile Corps were to form a protective corridor strong enough to resist counterattacks from the north until he had won the armoured battle, in the British rear. In his own account, he says that he 'placed particular reliance on the slow reaction of the

* Alexander: *Despatch*, p 841.

British command, for experience had shown us that it always took them some time to reach decisions and put them into effect'.

But when the attack was launched, on the night of August 30th, it was found that the mined belt was much deeper than expected. At daylight, Rommel's spearheads were only eight miles beyond it, and the bulk of the Afrika Korps was not able to start on its eastward drive until nearly 10 AM. By that time its mass of vehicles was being heavily bombed by the British air force. The corps commander, General Walter Nehring, was wounded at an early stage, and during the rest of the

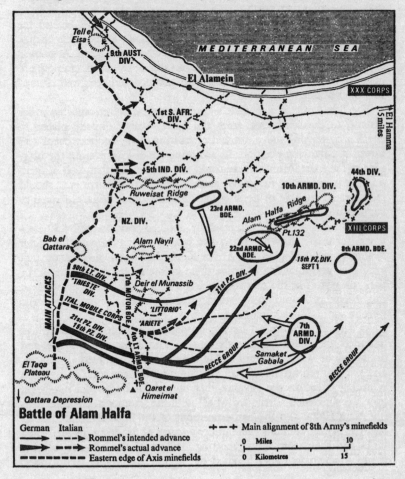

Battle of Alam Halfa

German Italian

⟶ ⤏ Rommel's intended advance
➤ ➤ Rommel's actual advance
▬ ▬ ▬ Eastern edge of Axis minefields

+—+ Main alignment of 8th Army's minefields

0 Miles 10
0 Kilometres 15

battle, the Afrika Korps was commanded by its Chief of Staff, Lieutenant-General Fritz Bayerlein.

When it was clear that any surprise-effect had vanished, and that the rate of advance was badly behind time, Rommel thought of breaking off the attack. But after discussion with Bayerlein, and following his own natural inclination, he decided to continue it – although with modified aims and more limited objectives. As it was obvious that the British armour had been allowed time to take up its battle positions, and could thus threaten the flank of a deeply extended drive, he felt bound to make 'an earlier turn north than we had intended'. He therefore ordered the Afrika Korps to make an immediate wheel, so that it headed for Point 132, the dominant feature of the Alam Halfa Ridge. This change of direction brought it towards the area where the 22nd Armoured Brigade was posted – and also towards an area of soft sand, cramping to manoeuvre. The line of thrust originally planned had been well clear of this 'sticky' area.

The 8th Armoured Brigade's battle positions were some ten miles distant, to the south-east, from the 22nd – more directly placed to check a by-passing move, instead of trusting to the indirect check and threat of a flanking position. In accepting the risk of posting the brigades so far apart, Montgomery could rely on the fact that each of them was almost as strong in armour as the whole Afrika Korps, and should therefore be capable of holding out until the other brigade arrived to support it.

The 8th, however, did not reach its assigned position until 4.30 AM – it was fortunate that the enemy had been so much delayed, for under Rommel's original plan the Afrika Korps had been directed on that same area and intended to arrive there before dawn. A collision in the dark, or assault in the morning, before the 8th was firmly in position, might have produced an awkward situation, especially for troops who were in action for the first time.

As a result of Rommel having to wheel north earlier than he had intended, the attack fell directly on the 22nd Armoured Brigade, and on that alone – but not until late in the day. For continued air attacks, and the delayed arrival of fuel and ammunition convoys, had such a retarding effect on the advance that the Afrika Korps did not begin even the shortened northward wheel until the afternoon. On approaching Alam Halfa, and the battle positions of the 22nd Armoured Brigade, the panzer columns came under a storm of fire from the well-sited tanks and then from the supporting artillery of this all-arms brigade group – which was ably handled by its new and young commander,

'Pip' Roberts. Repeated advances and attempted local flank moves were checked – until nightfall closed down the fight, bringing well-earned respite to the defenders and spreading depression among the attackers.

The abortiveness of the attack was due, however, not only to these actual repulses. For fuel was so short in the Afrika Korps that in mid-afternoon Rommel had cancelled his orders for an all-out effort to capture Point 132.

Even when morning came on September 1st, there was still such a shortage of fuel that Rommel was forced to give up the idea of carrying out any large operation that day. The most that he could attempt was a local and limited attack with one division, the 15th Panzer, to seize the Alam Halfa Ridge. The Afrika Korps was now in a very awkward predicament, and it suffered growing loss as the battering it had endured during the night from British bombers and the artillery of Horrocks's 13th Corps continued throughout the day. The diminished attacks of the German armour were successively checked, by a reinforced defence – for early that same morning Montgomery, now sure that the enemy was not driving on east towards his rear, had ordered the two other armoured brigades to concentrate alongside Roberts'.

By the afternoon Montgomery 'ordered planning to begin for a counterstroke which would give us the initiative'. The idea was, by a wheeling attack southward from the New Zealanders' position, to cork the neck of the bottle into which the Germans had pushed. He also made arrangements to bring up the headquarters of the 10th Corps 'to command a pursuit force', that was 'to be prepared to push through to Daba with all reserves available'.

The Panzerarmee now had only one day's fuel issue left in hand – a quantity sufficient only for about sixty miles movement for its units. So, after a second night of almost continuous bombing, Rommel had decided to break off the offensive, and make a gradual withdrawal.

During the day, the Germans facing Alam Halfa were seen to be thinning out, and starting to move westward. But requests for permission to follow them up were refused – for it was Montgomery's policy to avoid the risk of his armour being lured into Rommel's traps, as had happened so often before. At the same time Montgomery gave orders that the southward attack by New Zealanders, reinforced by other troops, was to start on the next night but one, September 3rd/4th.

But on September 3rd Rommel's forces began a general withdrawal, and were only followed up by patrols. The 'bottling' attack was launched that night, against the enemy's rear flank, which was being guarded by the 90th Light and Trieste Divisions. The attack became badly mixed up, suffering heavy loss, and was broken off.

On the next two days, September 4th and 5th, the Afrika Korps continued its gradual withdrawal, and no further effort was made to cut it off, while it was only followed up in a very cautious way, by small advanced parties. On the 6th the Germans halted on a line of high ground six miles east of their original front, and were obviously intending to make a strong stand there. Next day, Montgomery decided, with Alexander's approval, to break off the battle. So Rommel was left in possession of this limited gain of ground in the south. It was small consolation for his losses, and the decisive frustration of his original aims.

For the troops of the Eighth Army, the fact of seeing the enemy in retreat, even though only a few short steps back, far outweighed the disappointment of failing to cut him off. It was a clear sign that the tide had turned. Montgomery had already created a new spirit of confidence in the troops, and their confidence in him was confirmed.

The question remains, however, whether a great opportunity was missed of destroying the enemy's capacity for further resistance while the Afrika Korps was 'bottled'. That would have saved all the later trouble and heavy cost of assaulting him in his prepared positions. But so far as it went the Battle of Alam Halfa was a great success for the British. When it ended, Rommel had definitely lost the initiative – and, in view of the swelling stream of reinforcements to the British, the next battle was bound to be for Rommel a 'Battle Without Hope' – as he himself aptly called it.

In the clearer light of postwar knowledge of the respective forces and resources, it can be seen that Rommel's eventual defeat became probable from the moment his dash into Egypt was originally checked, in the July battle of First Alamein, and this accordingly may be considered the effective turning point. Nevertheless, he still looked a great menace when he launched his renewed and reinforced attack at the end of August, and as the strength of the two sides was nearer to an even balance than it was either before or later, he still had a possibility of victory – and might have achieved it if his opponents had faltered or fumbled as they had done on several previous occasions when their advantage had seemed more sure. But in the event the possibility vanished beyond possibility of recovery. The crucial significance of 'Alam Halfa' is symbolized in the fact that although it was fought out in the same area as the other battles of Alamein, it has been given a separate and distinctive name.

Tactically, too, this battle has a special interest. For it was not only won by the defending side, but decided by pure defence, without any counteroffensive – or even any serious attempt to develop a counteroffensive. It thus provides a contrast to most of the 'turning point' battles of the Second World War, and earlier wars. While Montgomery's decision to abstain from following up his defensive success in an offensive way forfeited the chance of trapping and destroying Rommel's forces – momentarily a very good chance – it did not impair the underlying decisiveness of the battle as a turning point in the campaign. From that time onwards, the British troops had an assurance of ultimate success which heightened their morale, while the opposing forces laboured under a sense of hopelessness, feeling that whatever their efforts and sacrifices they could achieve no more than a temporary postponement of the end.

There is also much to be learned from its tactical technique. The positioning of the British forces, and the choice of ground, had a great influence upon the issue. So did the flexibility of the dispositions. Most important of all was the well-gauged combination of airpower with the ground forces' plan. Its effectiveness was facilitated by the defensive pattern of the battle, with the ground forces holding the ring while the air forces constantly bombed the arena, now a trap, into which Rommel's troops had pushed. In the pattern of this battle, the air forces could operate the more freely and effectively because of being able to count on all troops within the ring as being 'enemy', and thus targets – in contrast to the way that air action is handicapped in a more fluid kind of battle.

Seven weeks passed before the British launched their offensive. An impatient Prime Minister chafed at the delay, but Montgomery was determined to wait until his preparations were complete and he could be reasonably sure of success, and Alexander supported him. So Churchill, whose political position was at this time very shaky after the series of British disasters since the start of the year, had to bow to their arguments for putting off the attack until late in October.

The exact date of D-day was determined by the phases of the moon, for the offensive was planned to start with a night assault – to hamper the enemy's defensive fire – while adequate moonlight was needed for the process of clearing gaps in his minefields. So the delivery of the assault was fixed for the night of October 23rd – full moon being on the 24th.

One key factor in Churchill's desire for an earlier attack was that the great project of a combined American and British landing in French North Africa, named 'Operation Torch', was now planned for launching early in November. A decisive victory over Rommel at Alamein would encourage the French to welcome the torch-bearers of liberation from Axis domination, and would also help to make General Franco more disinclined to welcome the entry of German forces into Spain and Spanish Morocco – a countermove that could upset and endanger the Allied landings.

But Alexander considered that if his attack, 'Operation Lightfoot', was launched a fortnight in advance of 'Torch', that interval 'would be long enough to destroy the greater part of the Axis army facing us, but on the other hand it would be too short for the enemy to start reinforcing Africa on any significant scale'. In any case, he felt, it was essential to make sure of success at his end of North Africa if there was a good result from the new landings at the other end. 'The decisive factor was that I was certain that to attack before I was ready would be to risk failure if not to court disaster.' These arguments prevailed, and although the date he now proposed was nearly a month later than Churchill had earlier suggested to Auchinleck, the postponement to October 23rd was accepted by him.

By that time, the British superiority in strength – both in numbers and quality – was greater than ever before. On the customary reckoning by 'divisions', the two sides had the appearance of being evenly matched – as each had twelve 'divisions', of which four were of armoured type. But in actual number of troops the balance was very different, the Eighth Army's fighting strength being 230,000, while Rommel had less than 80,000, of which only 27,000 were German. Moreover the Eighth Army had seven armoured brigades, and a total of twenty-three armoured regiments, compared with Rommel's total of four German and seven Italian tank battalions. More striking still is the comparison in actual tank strength. When the battle opened the Eighth Army had a total of 1,440 gun-armed tanks, of which 1,229 were ready for action – while in a prolonged battle it could draw on some of the further thousand that were now in the base depots and workshops in Egypt. Rommel had only 260 German tanks (of which twenty were under repair, and thirty were light Panzer IIs), and 280 Italian tanks (all of obsolete types). Only the 210 gun-armed German medium tanks could be counted upon in the armoured battle – so that, in terms of reality, the British started with a 6 to 1 superiority in numbers fit for action, backed by a much greater capacity to make good their losses.

In fighting power, for tank *versus* tank action, the British advantage was even greater, since the Grant tanks were now reinforced by the still newer, and superior, Sherman tanks that were arriving from America in large numbers. By the start of the battle the Eighth Army had more than 500 Shermans and Grants, with more on the way, while Rommel had only thirty – four more than at Alam Halfa – of the new Panzer IVs (with the high velocity 75-mm guns) that could match these new American tanks. Moreover, Rommel had lost his earlier advantage in anti-tank guns. His strength in anti-tank '88s' had been brought up to eighty-six and although these had been supplemented by the arrival of sixty-eight captured Russian '76s', his standard German 50-mm anti-tank guns could not penetrate the armour of the Shermans and Grants, or the Valentines, except at close range. That was all the worse handicap since the new American tanks were provided with high explosive shells that enabled them to knock out opposing anti-tank guns at long ranges.

In the air, the British also enjoyed a greater superiority than ever before. Sir Arthur Tedder, the Air Commander-in-Chief in the Middle East, now had ninety-six operational squadrons at his disposal – including thirteen American, thirteen South African and one Rhodesian, five Australian, two Greek, one French and one Yugo-Slav. They amounted to more than 1,500 first-line aircraft. Of this total, 1,200 serviceable aircraft based in Egypt and Palestine were ready to aid the Eighth Army's attack, whereas the Germans and Italians together had only some 350 serviceable in Africa to support the Panzerarmee. This air superiority was of great value in harassing the Panzerarmee's movements and the immediate supply of its divisions, as well as in protecting the Eighth Army's flow of supplies from similar interruption. But much more important for the issue of the battle was the indirect and strategic action of the air force, together with the British Navy's submarines, in strangling the Panzerarmee's sea-arteries of supply. During September, nearly a third of the supplies shipped to it were sunk in crossing the Mediterranean, while many vessels were forced to turn back. In October, the interruption of supplies became still greater, and less than half of what was sent arrived in Africa. Artillery ammunition became so short that little was available for countering the British bombardment. The heaviest loss of all was the sinking of oil tankers, and none reached Africa during the weeks immediately preceding the British offensive – so that the Panzerarmee was left with only three issues of fuel in hand when the battle opened, instead of the thirty issues which were considered the minimum reserve required. That severe shortage cramped counter-manoeuvre in every way. It compelled piecemeal distribution of the mobile forces, prevented their quick concentration at the points of attack, and increasingly immobilized them as the struggle continued.

The loss of food supplies was also an important factor in the spread of sickness among the troops. It was multiplied by the bad sanitary condition of the trenches, particularly those held by the Italians. Even in the July battle, the British had often been driven by the filth and smell to evacuate Italian trenches which they captured, and had thereby been caught in the open on several occasions by German armour before they could dig fresh trenches. But the disregard of sanitation eventually became a boomerang, spreading dysentery and infectious jaundice not only among the Italian troops but also among their German allies – and the victims included some of the key officers of the Panzerarmee.

The most important 'sick casualty' of all was Rommel himself. He had been laid up in August, before the Alam Halfa attack. He recovered sufficiently to exercise command during that battle but medical pressure subsequently prevailed, and in September he went back to Europe for treatment and rest. He was temporarily replaced by General Stumme, while the vacant command of the Afrika Korps was filled by General von Thoma – both of these commanders coming from the Russian front. Rommel's absence, and their inexperience of desert conditions, was an additional handicap in the planning and preparation of the measures to meet the impending British offensive. On the day after this opened, Stumme drove up to the front, ran into a heavy burst of fire, fell off his car, and died from a heart attack. That evening, Rommel's convalescence in Austria was cut short by a telephone call from Hitler to ask if he could return to Africa. He flew back there next day, October 25th, arriving near Alamein in the evening – to take charge of a defence which had by then been deeply dented and had lost nearly half its effective tanks that day in fruitless counterattacks.

Originally, Montgomery's plan had been to deliver simultaneous right and left hand punches – by Oliver Leese's 30th Corps in the north and Brian Horrocks's 13th Corps in the South – and then push through the mass of his armour (concentrated under Herbert Lumsden in the 10th Corps) to get astride the enemy's supply routes. But early in October he came to the conclusion that it was too ambitious, 'because of shortcomings in the standard of training in the Army', and changed to a more limited plan. In this new plan, 'Operation Lightfoot', the thrust was concentrated in the north, near the coast, in the four mile stretch between the Tell el Eisa and Miteiriya ridges – while the 13th Corps was to make a secondary attack in the south, to distract the enemy, but

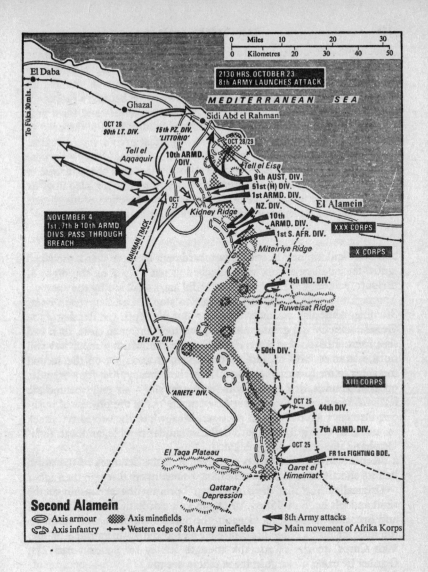

Second Alamein

not to press it unless the defence crumbled. This cautiously limited plan led to a protracted and costly struggle, which might have been avoided by the bolder original plan – taking account of the Eighth Army's immense superiority in strength. The battle became a process of attrition – of hard slogging rather than of manoeuvre – and for a time the effort appeared to hover on the brink of failure. But the disparity of strength between the two sides was so large that even a very disparate ratio of attrition was bound to work in favour of Montgomery's purpose – pressed with the unflinching determination that was characteristic of him in all he undertook. Within the chosen limits of his planning, he also showed consummate ability in varying the direction of his thrusts and developing a tactical leverage to work the opponent off balance.

After fifteen minutes' hurricane bombardment by more than a thousand guns, the infantry assault was launched at ten o'clock on the night of Friday, October 23rd. It had a successful start – helped by the enemy's shortage of shells, which led Stumme to stop his artillery from bombarding the British assembly positions. But the depth and density of the minefields proved a greater obstacle, and took longer to clear, than had been reckoned, so that when daylight came the British armour was still in the lanes or held up just beyond them. It was only on the second morning, after further night attacks by the infantry, that four brigades of armour succeeded in deploying on the far side – six miles behind the original front – and they had suffered much loss in the process of pushing through such constricted passages. Meanwhile, the subsidiary attack of the 13th Corps in the south had met similar trouble, and was abandoned on the second day, the 25th.

But the wedge that had been driven into the defences in the north looked so menacing that the defending commanders threw in their tanks piecemeal during that day in efforts to prevent the expansion of the wedge. This action fulfilled Montgomery's calculation and enabled his armour, now established in good positions, to inflict heavy losses on these spasmodic counterattacks. By evening the 15th Panzer Division had only a quarter of its tank strength left fit for action – the 21st Panzer Division was still in the southern sector.

Next day, October 26th, the British resumed the attack, but their attempt to push forward was checked, and their armour paid a heavy price for the abortive effort. The chance of developing the break-in to a breakthrough had faded, and the massive British armoured wedge was embedded in a strong ring of German anti-tank guns. Lumsden and his divisional commanders had already raised objections on the second night to the way that the armour was being used, to ram a passage through such narrow lanes, and the feeling that it was being misused became increasingly widespread among officers and men as losses multiplied in the still narrow-fronted pushes.

While maintaining an air of supreme confidence, Montgomery shrewdly realized that his initial thrust had failed, that the breach was blocked, that he must devise a fresh plan, and meanwhile give his main striking forces a rest. His readiness to vary his aim according to circumstances, on this and later occasions, was a better tonic to the troops and a greater tribute to his generalship than his habit of talking in retrospect as if everything had gone 'according to plan'. Ironically, that habit has tended to obscure and diminish the credit due to him for his adaptability and versatility.

The new plan was christened 'Operation Supercharge' – a good name to impress the executants that it was decisively different and carried a better promise of success. The 7th Armoured Division was brought north as a reinforcement. But Rommel also took the opportunity of regrouping his forces during the lull, and the 21st Panzer Division was already on its way north, followed by the Ariete. The secondary attack in the south by the British 13th Corps had not fulfilled its purpose of distracting the enemy's attention and making him keep part of his armour in the south. The switch northward, and the consequent closer concentration of both armies there, was tactically an advantage to Rommel. It left the British more dependent on sheer slogging power, and attrition. Fortunately for them, their numerical advantage was so large that attrition, even at a very adverse ratio, was bound to decide the issue in their favour if the 'killing' process was pursued with unflinching determination.

Montgomery's new offensive opened on the night of October 28th – with a northward thrust towards the coast, from the big wedge that had been driven into the enemy's front. Montgomery's intention was to pinch off the enemy's coastal 'pocket', and then start an exploiting drive westward along the coast road, towards Daba and Fuka. But the new thrust became hung up in the minefield, and its prospects waned with Rommel's quick countermove in switching the 90th Light Division to this flank. Even so, Rommel counted himself lucky when this attack came to a halt, for by now his resources were running low. The Afrika Korps had only ninety tanks left, while the Eighth Army still had more than eight hundred serviceable tanks on the spot – so that although it had paid a price of nearly four British tanks for one German, its ratio of superiority had risen, and was now 11 to 1.

Writing to his wife on the 29th, Rommel said: 'I haven't much hope left. At night I lie with my eyes wide open, unable to sleep, for the load that is on my shoulders. In the day I'm dead tired. What will happen if things go wrong here? That is the thought that torments me day and night. I can see no way out if that happens.'* It is very evident from this letter that the strain was wearing down not only the troops but also their commander, who was still a sick man. Early that morning he had thought of ordering a withdrawal to the Fuka position, sixty miles to the westward, but had been reluctant to take such a step back because it meant sacrificing a large part of his immobile infantry, and therefore deferred such a fateful decision in the hope that one more check would lead Montgomery to break off his offensive. In the sequel, the check to the coastward attack turned out to the British advantage. For if Rommel had slipped away at this moment, all the British planning would have been thrown out of gear.

As soon as Montgomery saw that his coastward thrust had miscarried, he decided to revert to his original line of thrust – hoping to profit by the northward shift of the enemy's scanty reserves. It was a well-judged decision, and another example of his own flexibility. But his forces were not as flexible, and time consumed in regrouping prevented the fresh thrust being launched until November 2nd.

This further pause, following the repeated checks, deepened the depression and anxiety in London. Churchill was feeling bitter disappointment about the slow progress of the offensive, and was with difficulty restrained from sending off an acid telegram to Alexander. The brunt fell on the CIGS, General Sir Alan Brooke – who strove to reassure the Cabinet, but inwardly had growing doubts, and anxiously wondered whether 'I was wrong and Monty was beat'. Even Montgomery himself was no longer so confident as he outwardly appeared, and privately confessed his anxiety.

The start of the new attack, in the early hours of November 2nd, was again damping – and increased the feeling that the offensive might have to be broken off. For, once again, the minefields caused more delay, and the resistance proved tougher, than expected. When daylight came, the leading armoured brigade 'found itself on the muzzles of the powerful screen of anti-tank guns on the Rahman track, instead of beyond it as had been planned'.† In that cramped position it was counterattacked by what remained of Rommel's armour, and in the day's fighting lost

---

* *The Rommel Papers*, p 312.
† Alexander: *Despatch*, p 856.

three-quarters of its tank strength. The remainder gallantly held on, and thus enabled the follow-up brigades to push through the gap, but they in turn were held up just beyond the Rahman track. When nightfall put an end to the fight, the British had lost nearly two hundred more tanks in combat and mechanical casualties.

Gloomy as the situation looked after this further check – particularly when viewed from afar – the cloud was about to lift. For by the end of the day Rommel was at the end of his resources. It is amazing that the defence had held out so long. The hard core of it was the two panzer divisions of the Afrika Korps, but even at the start of the battle, their fighting strength had been only 9,000, and had withered in the fire to little more than 2,000. Worse still, the Afrika Korps was left with barely thirty tanks fit for action, whereas the British still had more than 600 – so that their superiority over the Germans was now 20 to 1. As for the thin-skinned Italian tanks, they had been pulverized by the British fire, and many of the survivors had vanished from the battlefield in westward flight.

That night Rommel took the decision to fall back to the Fuka position in a two-step withdrawal. This was well in progress when, soon after midday on the 3rd, an overriding order came from Hitler – insisting that the Alamein position must be held at all costs. So Rommel, who had not previously suffered from Hitler's interference, nor learned the necessity of disobedience, stopped the withdrawal and recalled the columns that were already on the way back.

The turnabout was fatal to the chance of making an effective stand farther back, while the attempt to resume a stand at Alamein was futile. The westward withdrawal had been spotted and reported from the air early on the 3rd, and naturally stimulated Montgomery to continue and intensify his efforts. Although two attempts to get round the enemy's screen were checked during the day, a fresh infantry attack that night (by the 51st Highland and 4th Indian Divisions), made with a south-westerly slant, succeeded in piercing the joint between the Afrika Korps and the Italians. Soon after dawn on the 4th, the three armoured divisions passed through the breach and deployed – with orders to swing northward and bar the enemy's line of retreat along the coast road. Their exploiting drive was reinforced by the motorized New Zealand Division, and a fourth armoured brigade, under its command.

There was now a magnificent opportunity of cutting off and destroying Rommel's entire army. The chance was all the greater because the commander of the Afrika Korps, Thoma, was captured in the confusion of the morning, and the order for retreat was not given until the afternoon – while Hitler's belated permission was not received until next day. But as soon as the retreat order was given by Rommel, the German troops moved very fast, packed into such motor transport as remained to them, while the British exploitation suffered from its old faults of caution, hesitation, slow motion, and narrow manoeuvre.

After passing through the gap and deploying, the three armoured divisions were directed northward to the coast road at Ghazal, only ten miles behind the broken front. That narrow wheel gave the remnant of the Afrika Korps a chance to block them, by a quick and short side-step. After advancing a few miles they were checked by this thin screen, and kept in check until the afternoon, when the Panzerarmee began to withdraw as ordered. Then when darkness came the British cautiously halted for the night. That was the more unfortunate because they were well beyond, and behind, the bulk of what remained of the Panzer-armee.

Next day, November 5th, the cutting-off moves were again too nar-row and too slow. The 1st and 7th Armoured Divisions were at first directed on Daba, only ten miles beyond Ghazal, and the leading troops did not arrive at Daba until midday – to find that the retreating enemy had slipped past them. The 10th had been directed on Galal, fifteen miles farther west, and there caught the enemy's tail, capturing some forty tanks – most of these being Italian tanks that had run out of fuel. No effort was made to chase the main retreating columns until the evening, and the British armour then halted for the night as usual, after a short advance of eleven miles – when six miles short of its new objective, the escarpment at Fuka.

The New Zealand Division and its attached armour had been told to go for Fuka when the breakthrough was achieved, but it was delayed in following the armoured divisions through the gap – partly owing to bad traffic control – and then lost more time in mopping up Italians in its path. So it was less than halfway to Fuka when it halted at nightfall on the 4th. It arrived near its objective at midday on the 5th, but then halted in face of a suspected minefield – which was, in fact, a dummy that the British had laid to cover their own retreat to Alamein. Dark-ness was approaching before the New Zealanders pushed through it.

Meanwhile the 7th Armoured Division, after its too early wheel in-wards at Daba, had been sent back into the desert to drive for Baqqush, fifteen miles beyond Fuka. But it was delayed in crossing the New Zealanders' tail, as well as by the suspected minefield – and then halted for the night.

Next morning these three pursuing divisions closed in around Fuka and Baqqush – but the retreating enemy had already slipped away westward. All they caught were a few hundred stragglers and a few tanks that had run out of fuel.

The main hope now of catching Rommel's columns depended on the 1st Armoured Division – which, after missing them at Daba, had been ordered to make a longer circuit through the desert and cut the coast road west of Mersa Matruh. But its drive was twice halted by fuel shortage – the second time when only a few miles from the coast road. That was all the more exasperating to its commander, because he and others had urged that at least one of the armoured divisions should be prepared for a long pursuit, to Sollum, by replacing some of the ammunition in the transport with extra fuel.

In the afternoon of November 6th, rain started to fall in the coastal belt, and became very heavy during the night. That put a brake on all the pursuit moves, and ensured Rommel's get-away. After the event, it formed the main excuse for the failure to cut off his retreat. But, in analysis, it becomes clear that the best opportunities had already been forfeited before the rain intervened – by too narrow moves, by too much caution, by too little sense of the time-factor, by unwillingness to push on in the dark, and by concentrating too closely on the battle to keep in mind the essential requirements of its decisive exploitation. If the pursuit had driven deeper through the desert, to reach a more distant blocking point such as the steep escarpment at Sollum, it would have avoided the risk of interception either by resistance or weather – for while rain is a likely risk in the coastal belt it is rare in the desert interior.

During the night of the 7th Rommel withdrew from Mersa Matruh to Sidi Barrani, and there made another brief stand while his transport columns were filtering through the frontier bottleneck by the passes up the escarpment at Sollum and Halfaya, which were being heavily bombed by the British air force. For a time there was a huge traffic jam on the coast road, a queue twenty-five miles long, but with well-organized traffic control most of it got through on the following night, despite the British bombing. So on the 9th, although about a thousand vehicles still had to pass through the bottleneck, Rommel ordered his rearguards to withdraw to the frontier.

Meanwhile Montgomery had organized a special pursuit force, consisting of the 7th Armoured and New Zealand Divisions, and grounded the other two armoured divisions as a safeguard against running out of fuel and giving Rommel a chance for one of his ripostes, against a stranded force. This longer pursuit started on the 8th, but the New

Zealanders did not reach the frontier until the 11th, and although the two armoured brigades of the 7th Armoured Division, advancing through the desert south of the coast road crossed it the afternoon before, they just missed catching the enemy's tail when it passed through Capuzzo on the 11th.

While Rommel had slipped out of Montgomery's clutches, successfully evading each successive attempt to cut off his retreat, he was too weak to re-establish a new defence line on the frontier, or farther back in Cyrenaica. His fighting strength at the moment was about 5,000 Germans and 2,500 Italians, with eleven German and ten Italian tanks, thirty-five German anti-tank guns, sixty-five German field-guns, and a few Italian guns. For although some 15,000 German fighting troops had got away, safely, two-thirds of them had lost all their fighting equipment, and a still larger proportion of the Italians who had escaped had left theirs behind. The Eighth Army, besides killing several thousand, had captured some 10,000 Germans and over 20,000 Italians – including administrative personnel – together with some 450 tanks and over 1,000 guns. That was a very big compensation for its own 13,500 casualties, as well as for the disappointment of seeing Rommel slip away 'to fight again another day'.

After a short pause to bring up supplies, the British advance was resumed. But it was a follow-up rather than a pursuit, and Rommel's past counterstrokes had left so deep an impression that the advance proceeded cautiously along the coastal circuit instead of driving across the desert chord of the Benghazi arc. The leading armour did not reach Mersa Brega until November 26th, more than two weeks after crossing the eastern frontier of Cyrenaica – and long after Rommel had regained the shelter of that bottleneck position. The only serious trouble and danger to his forces during the retreat through Cyrenaica had come from shortage of fuel. At Mersa Brega he was reinforced by a fresh Italian armoured division, the Centauro, and elements of three Italian infantry divisions – although these, being unmotorized, were more of a complication than an asset.

There was now a further fortnight's pause while the British brought up reinforcements and supplies for an assault on the Mersa Brega position. Montgomery again prepared a plan 'to annihilate the enemy in his defences' – by pinning Rommel with a strong frontal assault, while sending another strong force on a wide outflanking manoeuvre to block his line of retreat. The frontal assault was to be launched on December 14th, preceded by large-scale raids on the night of the 11th/12th to distract attention from the outflanking manoeuvre, which then started on its desert circuit. But Rommel slipped away during the night of the 12th – thus stultifying the British plan. He went back in a rapid bound to a position near Buerat, 250 miles west of Mersa Brega – and double that distance beyond the Eighth Army's new advanced base at Benghazi.

Rommel was still holding the Buerat position when the year ended, for this time there was a month's pause, for a move-up and build-up, before Montgomery was ready to resume his drive. But it was nonetheless clear that the tide of war in Africa had definitely turned. For there was little chance that Rommel's army could be brought up again to a strength capable of matching the Eighth Army's build-up capacity, while his rear areas, and possible rearward positions, were now imperilled by the Anglo-American First Army's advance eastward from Algeria into Tunisia.

Yet Hitler's illusions soon revived, while Mussolini desperately clung to his because he could not bear to see Italy's African empire crumbling away. Indeed, their illusions had become uppermost again even while it was still uncertain whether Rommel would succeed in evading his pursuers and extricating the remnants of his battered army. On reaching Mersa Brega safely he had received orders to hold that line 'at all costs', and prevent the British from penetrating into Tripolitania. As a reinforcement to that dreamland demand he was also put under Marshal Bastico's command again, as he had been before the advance into Egypt. When he saw Bastico on November 22nd he had told him bluntly that the order 'resist to the end' on that desert frontier spelt the certain destruction of the remaining troops – 'we either lose the position four days earlier and save the army, or lose both position and army four days later'.

Then Cavallero and Kesselring came to see Rommel on the 24th and he told them that, as barely 5,000 of his German troops had weapons, to hold the Mersa Brega position he would need the speedy delivery, before Montgomery attacked, of fifty Panzer IV tanks armed with the new long-barrelled 75-mm guns, and fifty anti-tank guns of the same kind, besides an adequate supply of fuel and ammunition. It was a modest estimate of his need, but it was all too evident that there was no likelihood of its being met, as most of the available equipment and reinforcements was being diverted to Tunisia. Yet they still pressed the order to stand at Mersa Brega.

So, in the hope of getting Hitler to face the realities of the situation, Rommel flew to the Führer's headquarters near Rastenburg, in the East Prussian forests. He had a chilly reception, and when he suggested that the wisest course would be to evacuate North Africa, Hitler 'flew into a fury', and would not listen to any further argument. This explosion did more than anything before to shake Rommel's faith in his Führer. As he wrote in his journal: 'I began to realize that Adolf Hitler simply did not want to see the situation as it was, and that he reacted emotionally against what his intelligence must have told him was right.' Hitler insisted that 'it was a political necessity to continue to hold a major bridgehead in Africa and there would, therefore, be no withdrawal from the Mersa el Brega line'.*

But when Rommel went to Rome on the way back he found Mussolini more open to reason, while more aware of the difficulties of shipping sufficient supplies to Tripoli and getting them forward to Mersa Brega. So he had managed to obtain Mussolini's permission to prepare an intermediate position at Buerat, to move the non-motorized Italian infantry back there in good time and to withdraw the rest of his slender force if and when the British attacked. Rommel had been prompt to act on this permission and slip away in the darkness immediately the British showed signs of launching their attack. Moreover, he had made up his own mind that he was not going to stop at Buerat or in front of Tripoli, and provide Montgomery with a chance of trapping him. His plan, already formed, was to withdraw right back to the Tunisian frontier and the Gabes bottleneck, where he could not easily be out-flanked and could deliver an effective counterstroke with the reinforcements that would be more closely at hand there.

* *The Rommel Papers*, p 366.

CHAPTER TWENTY-ONE

'Torch' – The New Tide from the Atlantic

The Allied landings in French North Africa took place on November 8th, 1942.* This entry into north-west Africa came a fortnight after the launching of the British offensive on Rommel's position at Alamein, in the extreme north-east of Africa, and four days after the collapse of that position.

At the 'Arcadia Conference' in Washington at Christmas 1941 – the first Allied conference following the Japanese stroke at Pearl Harbor which brought the United States into the war – Mr Churchill put forward the 'North-west Africa Project' as a step towards 'closing and tightening the ring around Germany'. He told the Americans that there was already a plan, 'Gymnast', for a landing in Algeria if the Eighth Army gained a sufficiently decisive success in Cyrenaica for it to push westward to the Tunisian border. He went on to propose that 'at the same time United States forces, assuming French agreement, should proceed to land on the Moroccan coast by invitation'. President Roosevelt favoured the project, being quick to see its political advantages in grand strategy, but his Service advisers were dubious about its practicability while anxious lest it should interfere with the prospects of an early and more direct attack against Hitler's hold on Europe. The most they were willing to agree was that study of the operation, now re-christened 'Super-Gymnast', should continue.

During the next few months discussion concentrated on the project of a cross-Channel attack, to be launched in August or September, to meet Stalin's demand for the opening of a 'Second Front'. The Cotentin (Cherbourg) peninsula came to be the most favoured site, as urged by General Marshall, the Chief of Staff of the United States Army, and by Major-General Eisenhower, whom he had chosen and sent to London as Commander of the American forces in the European theatre. The British emphasized the drawbacks of a premature landing in Europe with inadequate strength, pointing out the risks of such a bridgehead being bottled up, or overwhelmed, without bringing appreciable relief

* For map, see p 292.

to the Russians. But President Roosevelt swung his weight in support of the project, and committed himself, when Molotov visited Washington at the end of May, to an assurance that he 'hoped' and 'expected' to create 'a Second Front in Europe in 1942'.

A reversion to the project of a landing in north-west Africa was spurred on by the unexpected British collapse in north-east Africa which occurred in June, following Rommel's forestalling attack on the Gazala Line.

The battle of Gazala had already taken a bad turn when Churchill flew to Washington on June 17th, with his Chiefs of Staff, for a fresh conference. On arrival Churchill went on by air to Hyde Park, Roosevelt's family home on the Hudson, for a private talk. Here he re-emphasized the drawbacks and dangers of a premature landing in France, while suggesting the revival of 'Gymnast' as a better alternative. The British and American Chiefs of Staff, meeting in Washington on June 21st, had disagreed over the Cherbourg project but found themselves in complete agreement that the North Africa project was unsound.

Their combined negative conclusion about this project was soon reversed by the pressure of events, combined with Roosevelt's pressing desire for some positive action in 1942 that would fulfil, even if not so directly as intended, his promise to the Russians. On June 21st, news came that the fortress of Tobruk had fallen to Rommel's assault and that the remains of the British Eighth Army were in retreat to Egypt.

During the weeks that followed, the British situation worsened, and the argument for direct or indirect American intervention in Africa was correspondingly strengthened. By the end of June, Rommel reached and started to attack the Alamein Line, following on the heels of the British retreat. On July 8th Churchill cabled to Roosevelt that 'Sledgehammer', the plan for a landing in France that year, must be discarded, and went on to urge, once again, the case for 'Gymnast'. He followed it up with a message through Field-Marshal Sir John Dill, who was now head of the British Joint Staff Mission in Washington: 'Gymnast affords the sole means by which the US can strike at Hitler in 1942,' and that otherwise both the Western allies would have to remain 'motionless in 1942'.

The American Chiefs of Staff reacted to this contention with renewed objections to 'Gymnast' – Marshall's condemnation of it as 'expensive and ineffectual' was supported by Admiral King's declaration that it was 'impossible to fulfil naval commitments in other theatres and at the same time to provide the shipping and escorts which would be essential should that operation be undertaken'. They also agreed in viewing the British refusal to attempt a landing in France in 1942 as clear evidence that the British did not really want to risk it even in 1943. So Marshall, readily supported by King, proposed a radical change of strategy – that unless the British accepted the American plan for an early cross-Channel attack 'we should turn to the Pacific and strike decisively against Japan; in other words assume a defensive attitude against Germany, except for air operations; and use all available means in the Pacific'.

But the President objected to the idea of delivering such an ultimatum to his British allies, expressed his disapproval of the proposed strategic switch, and told his Chiefs of Staff that unless they could persuade the British to undertake a cross-Channel operation in 1942 they must either launch one into French North Africa or send a strong reinforcement to the Middle East. He emphasized that it was politically imperative to take some striking action before the year ended.

Faced with the President's decision, the Chiefs of Staff might have been expected to choose the course of temporarily reinforcing the British in the Middle East, rather than embarking on the 'Gymnast' plan which they had so strongly and persistently opposed. Moreover, after reviewing the two courses, Marshall's planning staff reached the conclusion that the former was the lesser of two evils. But contrary to expectation, he and King swung round in favour of 'Gymnast'. This became their preferred alternative when they flew to London in mid-July along with Harry Hopkins, as the President's representatives, and found that the British Chiefs of Staff were firmly opposed to Eisenhower's plan for an early landing near Cherbourg.

In choosing north-west Africa as the alternative, rather than a reinforcement to the Middle East, Marshall's prime reason, according to Harry Hopkins, was 'the difficulty of mixing our troops with the British in Egypt'. While a mixture would also occur in the case of a combined operation in north-west Africa, it was obvious that American reinforcements to the Middle East would have come under a British Commander-in-Chief.

The adoption of 'Super-Gymnast' was formulated at two further meetings of the Combined Chiefs of Staff, American and British, in London on July 24th and 25th – and promptly endorsed by Roosevelt. Moreover, he emphasized in his cable that the landing should be planned to take place 'not later than October 30th' – a directive that Hopkins had suggested, in a personal message, as a means 'to avoid procrastination and delays'. On Churchill's initiative the operation was rechristened 'Torch', as a more inspiring name. It was also agreed that the supreme command should be given to an American – an ointment to the sore feelings of the American Service chiefs that Churchill was very ready to provide – and on the 26th Eisenhower was told, by Marshall, that he was to have the post.

While the decision for 'Torch' was now definite, it had been made before the questions of time and site were settled, or even fully examined. Thus fresh conflicts of view arose over both these problems.

On the question of time the British Chiefs of Staff, spurred by Churchill, proposed October 7th as the target date. But the American Chiefs of Staff recommended November 7th, as being 'the earliest reasonable date for landing of the forces based on availability of combat loaders'.

On the question of site, the respective views were even wider apart. The British urged that the landings should be made on the north coast of Africa, inside the Mediterranean, so that a quick advance to Tunisia would be possible. But the American Chiefs of Staff stuck to the limited objective of the 'Gymnast' plan, as modified in June, when it was envisaged as a purely American operation, and were anxious to confine the landings to the Casablanca area on the west coast – the Atlantic coast – of Morocco. They feared not only the dangers of French opposition but of hostile Spanish reaction and a German counterstroke to block the gateway into the Mediterranean by seizing Gibraltar. The British on this issue were dismayed by such a cautious approach to the strategic problem. They argued that it would allow the Germans time to seize Tunisia, stiffen or replace French opposition in Algeria and Morocco, and thus frustrate the aim of the Allied operation.*

Eisenhower and his staff were inclined to agree with the British view. His first outline plan, formulated on August 9th, was devised as a compromise. It proposed simultaneous landings inside and outside the

* I was asked for my views on the question of the North-west Africa Project on June 28th, immediately after the Washington Conference when its revival was mooted. On being told that the main landing was then intended to be at Casablanca, on the Atlantic coast, I pointed out that this site was 1,100 miles distant from Bizerta and Tunis, the strategic keys, and that the best chance of early success lay in capturing them as quickly as possible, which meant that the landings should be made as near them as possible. I also emphasized the importance of landing on the north coast, in Algeria, 'on the backs of the French' as a means to diminish the opposition that was likely to develop in face of a frontal attack at, and slow advance from, Casablanca.

Mediterranean, but not farther eastward than Algiers – because of the risk of enemy air attacks from Sicily and Sardinia – except for a minor one at Bône to seize the airfield there (Bône is 270 miles east of Algiers but 130 miles short of Bizerta). This compromise did not satisfy the British planners, as it did not seem likely to fulfil the principal condition of success, which they defined as being: 'We must have occupied the key points of Tunisia within 26 days of passing Gibraltar and preferably within 14 days.' In their view, a major landing at Bône, or even farther east, was essential to achieve a quick enough advance to Tunisia.

These arguments impressed the President, who directed Marshall and King to restudy the project. They had also impressed Eisenhower, who reported to Washington that the American members of his staff were now convinced of the soundness of the British reasoning, and that he was now drawing up a new plan that would eliminate the Casablanca landings, and advance the date of the others.

His staff produced (on August 21st) a second outline plan which largely followed the British idea. Discarding the Casablanca landing, it provided for an American landing at Oran (250 miles east of Gibraltar) as well as for British landings at Algiers and Bône. But Eisenhower's own endorsement of it was tepid, and emphasized that such an expedition, wholly inside the Mediterranean, would be badly exposed on its flank. That conclusion tuned in with Marshall's opinion.

The second outline plan was as unpalatable to the American Chiefs of Staff as the first had been to the British. Marshall told the President that 'a single line of communication through the Straits is far too hazardous' and he was against any landing being made inside the Mediterranean farther east that Oran (600 miles short of Bizerta).

Churchill received the news of this cautious turn after returning from his visit with General Brooke to Egypt and Moscow – where Stalin had taunted them about the failure of the Western Powers to open a 'Second Front', with such scornful questions as 'Are you going to let us do all the work while you look on? Are you never going to start fighting? You will find it is not too bad when once you start!' That had, naturally, stung Churchill, but he had managed to arouse Stalin's interest in the potentialities of 'Torch', and had vividly depicted how it could indirectly relieve the pressure on Russia. So he was shocked to find that the Americans were proposing to whittle down the plan.

On August 27th he sent off a long cable to Roosevelt protesting that the changes which the American Chiefs of Staff suggested might be 'fatal to the whole plan', and that 'the whole pith of the operation will be lost if we do not take Algiers as well as Oran on the first day'. He emphasized the bad impression that a narrowing of the aim would have on Stalin.

Roosevelt's reply, on the 30th, insisted that 'under any circumstances one of our landings must be done on the Atlantic'. So he proposed that the Americans should carry out the Casablanca and Oran landings, leaving the British to make the eastward ones. Moreover, mindful of British military action against Vichy French forces in North Africa, Syria and elsewhere, he raised a fresh issue:

> I feel very strongly that the initial attacks must be made by an exclusively American ground force ... I would even go so far as to say I am reasonably sure a simultaneous landing by British and Americans would result in full resistance by all French in Africa, whereas an initial American landing without British ground forces offers a real chance that there would be no French resistance, or only a token resistance ... It is our belief that German air or parachute troops cannot get to Algiers or Tunis in any large force for at least two weeks after the initial attack.*

The British were appalled at the idea of a week's pause before making eastward landings, more important and urgent for the strategic goal than the westerly ones, and were far from happy about the Americans' optimistic estimate that the Germans could not intervene effectively in less than two weeks.

Churchill was very willing to profit from the persuasive influence of the American Ambassador to the Vichy Government, Admiral Leahy, towards easing the way politically and psychologically. While he was 'anxious to preserve the American character of the expedition', and therefore willing to keep the British forces 'as much in the background as was physically possible', he did not believe it possible to conceal the fact that the larger part of the shipping, the air support, and the naval forces would be British – and these elements would become visible first, before the ground forces. He touched on these points in a tactful reply to Roosevelt on September 1st, and emphasized that if 'the political bloodless victory, for which I agree with you there is a good chance, should go amiss, a military disaster of very great consequences would ensue'. He continued:

> Finally, in spite of the difficulties it seems to us vital that Algiers should be occupied simultaneously with Casablanca and Oran. Here

* Churchill: *The Second World War*, vol IV, p 477.

is the most friendly and hopeful spot where the political reaction would be most decisive throughout North Africa. To give up Algiers for the sake of the doubtfully practicable landing at Casablanca seems to us a very serious decision. If it led to the Germans forestalling us not only in Tunis but in Algeria, the results on balance would be lamentable throughout the Mediterranean.*

This good argument for maintaining the landing at Algiers as part of the plan did not mention the importance of landings farther east, and nearer Bizerta – an omission, and concession, which was of fateful consequence to the chances of early strategic success.

Replying to Churchill's cable, on September 3rd, Roosevelt agreed that a landing at Algiers should be included in the plan, while suggesting that American troops should land first 'followed within an hour by British troops'. Churchill immediately accepted this solution, provided that there was such a reduction in the force earmarked for Casablanca as to make the Algiers landing effective. To this Roosevelt agreed, in a modified form, suggesting a reduction of 'one regimental combat team' at Casablanca, and another at Oran, to provide '10,000 men for use at Algiers'. Churchill cabled back on September 5th: 'We agree to the military lay-out you propose. We have plenty of troops highly trained for landing. If convenient they can wear your uniform. They will be proud to do so. Shipping will be all right.' That same day, Roosevelt replied in a one word cable 'Hurrah!'

Thus the matter was finally settled in this exchange of cables between Roosevelt and Churchill. Three days later Eisenhower specified November 8th as the date of the landings, while declining Churchill's offer to put the British Commandos in American uniform, as he was anxious to preserve an all-American look to the initial landings. Churchill reconciled himself to the delay, and to the modification of the plan. Indeed, in a subsequent cable to Roosevelt on September 15th, he submissively said: 'In the whole of "Torch", military and political, I consider myself your lieutenant, asking only to put my view-point plainly before you.'†

Roosevelt's 'Hurrah!' cable on September 5th settled what was aptly called 'the transatlantic essay competition' – although Marshall continued to express doubts, while his immediate political chief, Henry Stimson, the Secretary for War (ie for the Army) made a bitter complaint to the President about the decision to land in North Africa. But

* Churchill: *The Second World War*, vol IV, pp 479–80.
† ibid, p 488.

the President's decision enabled detailed planning to be pushed on in a hurried effort to remedy the effects of procrastination. The plan, however, carried the two-edged effects of a compromise. By diminishing the chances of a quickly decisive success in North Africa it made more certain the prolonged diversion of Allied effort in the Mediterranean – as American official historians have recognized and emphasized.*

In the final plan, the Atlantic coast landing to capture Casablanca was to be made by the all-American force under Major-General George S. Patton, with 24,500 troops, carried by the Western Naval Task Force under Rear-Admiral H. Kent Hewitt. It sailed direct from America – the main part from Hampton Roads in Virginia – and consisted of 102 ships, of which twenty-nine were transports.

The capture of Oran was entrusted to the Centre Task Force, which comprised 18,500 American troops under Major-General Lloyd R. Fredendall, but was escorted by a British naval force under Commodore Thomas Troubridge. It sailed from the Clyde, as it was composed of American troops who had been brought over to Scotland and Northern Ireland early in August.

For the operation against Algiers, the Eastern Naval Task Force was also entirely British, commanded by Rear-Admiral Sir Harold Burroughs, but the Assault Force consisted of 9,000 British and 9,000 American troops, and its commander, Major-General Charles Ryder, was American. Moreover, American troops were incorporated in the 2,000-strong British Commando units. This curiously mixed composition was inspired by the hope that putting Americans in the front of the shop window would lead the French to assume that the assault force was all-American. On November 9th, the day after the landings, overall command of all the Allied troops in Algeria was taken over by the commander of the newly created British First Army, Lieutenant-General Kenneth Anderson.

The assault forces for both Oran and Algiers sailed together from Britain in two large convoys, a slow one starting on October 22nd and a fast one four days later. This timing was arranged so that they could pass through the Straits of Gibraltar simultaneously during the night of November 5th, and from there they were covered by part of the British Mediterranean Fleet under Admiral Sir Andrew Cunningham. Its presence sufficed to deter the Italian fleet from interfering, even after the

---

* See, in particular, the very able and penetrating analysis in *Strategic Planning for Coalition Warfare* 1941–1942, by Maurice Matloff and Edwin M. Snell.

landings – so that, as Cunningham regretfully remarked, his powerful force had 'to be kept cruising idly'. But he had plenty of work on his hands, as he was Allied Naval Commander, under Eisenhower, and thus responsible for the whole of the maritime side of 'Torch'. Including storeships that had come in advance convoys early in October, over 250 merchantmen sailed from Britain, of which some forty were transports (including three American), while the British naval force employed in the operation, as escort and cover, amounted to 160 warships of various types.

The diplomatic prelude to the landings was akin to a mixture of a spy story and a 'Western', with comic interludes, carried into the field of history. Robert Murphy, the chief American diplomatic representative in North Africa, had been active in preparing the way for the landings by discreet sounding among French officers whom he felt were likely to be in sympathy with, and to give aid to, the project. He relied particularly on General Mast, commander of the troops in the Algiers sector (and previously Chief of Staff to General Juin, the Commander-in-Chief) and General Béthouart who commanded the troops in the Casablanca sector – although that sector as a whole was under the command of Admiral Michelier, a fact that the Americans failed to realize.

Mast had urged that a senior Allied military representative should come secretly to Algiers for backstage talks, and discussion of plans, with Juin and others. Accordingly General Mark Clark (who had just been appointed Deputy Commander-in-Chief for 'Torch'), flew to Gibraltar with four key staff officers, and the party were carried on by a British submarine, HMS *Seraph* (Lieutenant N. A. A. Jewell), to a rendezvous at a villa on the coast some sixty miles west of Algiers. The submarine arrived off the coast early on October 21st but too late to land Mark Clark's party before daylight, so had to stay submerged all day, while the puzzled and disappointed French party went home. A message from the submarine to Gibraltar, relayed to Algiers over a secret radio chain, brought Murphy and some of the French back to the villa the next night, when Clark's party came ashore in four canvas canoes – one of which upset when they embarked. They had been guided to the meeting place by a lamp, with a white blanket behind, shining through a window.

Mark Clark told Mast, in a broad way, that a large American force was being prepared for dispatch to North Africa, and would be supported by British air and sea forces – a statement which was lacking in frankness. Moreover he abstained, in the interests of security, from giving Mast a clear idea of the time and places of the Allied landings. This excess of secrecy in dealing with a man whose help was of key importance was unwise, since it deprived him and his associates of the information and time necessary to plan, and take, cooperative steps. Clark authorized Murphy to inform Mast immediately before the landings of the date, but even then not of the places. That was too late for Mast to notify his associates in Morocco.

The conference was temporarily, and dramatically, interrupted by the appearance on the scene of suspicious French police. Mark Clark and his companions were hurriedly hidden in an empty wine cellar while the police searched the villa. Danger became more acute when one of the British Commando officers who had piloted the party began coughing. Mark Clark passed him a bit of chewing gum as a remedy, but he soon asked for more, saying that it had not got much taste – to which Clark replied: 'That is not surprising, as I have been chewing it for two hours!' After the police at last went away, still suspicious and likely to return, Clark and his party ran into fresh trouble when they tried to re-embark at dusk, for the surf had become heavy, and he had a narrow escape from drowning when his canoe overturned. At a further attempt shortly before dawn, the others capsized, but all of the party got through the breakers in the end and reached the submarine, safe though soaked. The next day they were transferred to a flying-boat, which carried them back to Gibraltar.

An important issue which came into further discussion at this conference was the choice of the most suitable French leader to rally the French forces in North Africa to the Allied side. While Juin, their Commander-in-Chief, had privately expressed a favourable inclination, he showed a tendency to 'sit on the fence' as long as possible, and a reluctance to take the initiative. His chief subordinate commanders lacked sufficient prestige, and were no less reluctant to take any definite step in disregard or defiance of orders from the Vichy Government. Admiral Darlan, the Commander-in-Chief of its forces as a whole, and potential head of State if the aged Marshal Pétain were to die, had hinted to Leahy in 1941 and more recently to Murphy that he might be willing to break away from the policy of collaboration with Germany and bring the French over to the Allied side if assured of American military aid on a sufficiently large scale. But he had played in with Hitler so long that his hints did not inspire confidence. Moreover he had an anti-British bias, which had naturally been increased by the British action against the French fleet at Oran and elsewhere, after the collapse of France in 1940. This made his attitude all the more doubtful in view of the difficulty of disguising the fact that the British were playing a large part in 'Torch'.

General de Gaulle was ruled out for the opposite reason – that his defiance of Pétain in 1940 and subsequent part in Churchill's moves against Dakar, Syria, and Madagascar would make all French officers who had remained loyal to the Vichy Government unwilling to accept his leadership – even those who were most eager to throw off the German yoke. That was emphasized by Murphy and readily assumed by Roosevelt, who had developed a deep distrust of de Gaulle's judgement and dislike of his arrogance.

Churchill, who had recently dubbed himself 'your lieutenant', bowed to his master's voice, and de Gaulle was given no information of the project until the landings had taken place.

In these circumstances the Americans, from the President downward, readily accepted the view of General Mast and his associates that General Giraud was the most desirable and acceptable candidate for the leadership of the French in North Africa – as Murphy had already conveyed before the conference took place. Giraud, an army commander in May 1940, had been taken prisoner by the Germans, but had managed to escape in April 1942, and reached the unoccupied part of France, where he was allowed to stay, on promising to support Pétain's authority. He took up residence near Lyons. From there, although under surveillance, he got into communication with many officers, both in France itself and in North Africa, who shared his desire to organize a revolt against German domination with American help. Giraud's viewpoint was expressed in a letter to one of his supporters, General Odic: 'We don't want the Americans to free us; we want them to help us free ourselves, which is not quite the same.' Moreover, in his private negotiations with them he made it one of his conditions that he should be commander-in-chief of Allied troops in French territory wherever French troops were fighting. From a message he received he understood that his conditions were accepted by Roosevelt, but they came as a complete surprise to Eisenhower when Giraud arrived at Gibraltar to meet him on November 7th – the eve of the landings.

Giraud had been picked up, at a rendezvous on the south coast of France, by the same British submarine, HMS *Seraph*,* that had car-

---

* Giraud had stipulated that an American ship must be sent to convey him, for political reasons, so his demand was met by putting HMS *Seraph* under nominal command of an American naval officer, Captain Jerauld Wright, and carrying an American flag that could be displayed if necessary. Giraud was accompanied by his son and two young staff officers – one of whom, Cap-

ried Mark Clark on the secret mission to the Algerian coast. He was then transferred to a flying-boat, though nearly drowned in doing so, and carried on to Gibraltar. On reaching there, he was staggered at the news that the Allied landings in North Africa were taking place early next morning – as he had been told that they were planned for the following month – and also by the discovery that the command of them was in the hands of Eisenhower, instead of his own. This led to a heated argument, in which he based himself on his higher rank as well as on the assurances he had received, and constantly reiterated that to take anything less than supreme command would be a surrender of his country's prestige and his own. But when talks were resumed in the morning (of the 8th) he reconciled himself to the situation, after explicit assurance that he would be head of the French forces and administration in North Africa – a promise that was soon to be set aside on grounds of expediency and the superior assets of Admiral Darlan.

In bringing the 'Torch' of liberty to French North Africa, the Americans had achieved surprise too fully, throwing their friends and helpers into confusion – more confusion than was caused on the enemy's side. Their French collaborators were caught unready to aid effectively in clearing the way, and under the shock of the sudden invasion most of the French commanders reacted in the way that was natural in such circumstances, and in conformity with their loyalty to legitimate authority, embodied in Marshal Pétain at Vichy. Thus the landings met resistance initially – although less at Algiers than at Oran and Casablanca.

At Casablanca, General Béthouart, the French divisional commander, received a message late in the evening of the 7th that the landing would take place at 2 AM on the 8th. He sent off parties of his troops to arrest the German Armistice Commissions, and posted some of his officers to welcome the Americans on the beach at Rabat, fifty miles to the north, as he assumed that they would land there, since it had no coast defence batteries and was the seat of French Government in Morocco.

After these preliminary steps, Béthouart himself went with a battalion to occupy Army headquarters at Rabat, and sent the Army Commander off under escort. Béthouart had also dispatched letters to General Noguès, the Resident-General (and overall Commander-in-Chief)

---

tain André Beaufre, had played an influential part in the planning of this dramatic move to swing the French Army into action against the Germans. Both Wright and Beaufre in later years rose to high places in their respective Services, and in the NATO command structure.

in Morocco, and to Admiral Michelier, informing them that the Americans were about to land, that Giraud was coming to take over command of French North Africa as a whole, and that he himself had been appointed by Giraud to take over command of the Army in Morocco. His letter to Noguès and Michelier asked them to back the order he had issued for allowing the Americans to land unopposed, or else keep out of the way until it was more convenient for them to accept the *fait accompli*.

On receiving the letter, Noguès tried to 'sit on the fence' until the situation was clearer. While Noguès hesitated, Michelier took prompt action. His air and submarine patrols had not spotted the approaching armada before nightfall, so he jumped to the conclusion that Béthouart was deluded or hoaxed. Michelier's assurance that no strong force had been sighted off the coast so impressed Noguès that even when the first reports of the landing reached him, shortly after 5 AM, he believed that they were no more than Commando raids. He therefore jumped down off the fence, on the anti-American side, and ordered the French forces to resist the landings, while putting Béthouart under arrest on a charge of treason.

Patton's main landing was made at Fedala, fifteen miles north of Casablanca, with subsidiary ones at Mehdia, fifty-five miles farther north, and Safi, 140 miles south of Casablanca. Fedala offered the nearest suitable landing beaches to that city and its strongly defended harbour – the only large and well-equipped one on the Atlantic coast of Morocco. Mehdia was chosen because it was the nearest landing place to the Port Lyautey airfield, the only one in Morocco with a concrete runway. Safi was chosen because a right-wing force operating there might ward off the strong French garrison of the inland city of Marrakesh from intervening at Casablanca, and also because it had a harbour where medium tanks could be disembarked – for the new LSTs (Landing Ships Tank) then being produced were not ready in time for 'Torch'.

As the American armada approached the coast of Morocco on November 6th, after a smooth ocean passage, 'heavy seas' were reported there and the forecast for the 8th was that the surf would be so high as to make landings impossible. But Admiral Hewitt's own weather expert predicted that the storm would pass away, and he decided to take the risk of pursuing the plan of landing on the Atlantic coast. On the 7th the sea began to subside, and on the 8th it was calm, with only a moderate ground swell. The surf was slighter than on any morning in the month. Even so, many mishaps and delays arose from inexperience.

But things at least went better than Patton had forecast in a characteristically bombastic 'blood and guts' speech at the final conference before embarkation, when he had caustically told the naval members that their elaborate landing plans would break down 'in the first five minutes' and gone on to declare: 'Never in history has the Navy landed an army at the planned time and place. But if you land us anywhere within fifty miles of Fedala and within one week of D-day, I'll go ahead and win.'

It was fortunate that the confusion and hesitation among the French were such that the landing attack waves were safely ashore before the defenders' fire became serious, and by then the light was good enough to help the American naval gunners in subduing the coastal batteries. But fresh trouble developed in the beachhead, and in extending it, from the inexperience and muddles of the Army's shore parties, so that Patton switched his explosive criticism to the faults of his own force and Service. Both the troops and the boats had been overloaded. Although the advance on Casablanca got going on the second day, and met no serious opposition, it was abruptly halted by the pull on its tail that was caused by lack of equipment – which was piling up on the beaches but failed to come forward to the combat troops. Little progress was made on the third day, and there was an increase of opposition, so that the outlook became gloomy.

The situation would have been more serious if the French naval threat had not been quelled on the first day. This was achieved in a battle off Casablanca that had an old-style flavour. It started just before 7 AM, when the coast defence battery on Cap El Hank and *Jean Bart* in the harbour – this was the newest French battleship but still uncompleted, and unable to move from her berth – opened fire on Rear-Admiral R. L. Giffen's Covering Group, which comprised the battleship *Massachusetts*, two heavy cruisers and four destroyers. These suffered no hits, although there were several near misses, and their reply was sufficiently effective to silence temporarily both the El Hank battery and *Jean Bart*. But they became so absorbed in this lively action that they neglected their task of keeping the other French ships penned there. By 9 AM one light cruiser, seven destroyers and eight submarines had slipped out. The destroyers headed for Fedala, where the American transports were 'sitting ducks'. Fortunately they were headed off and driven to withdraw by a heavy cruiser, a light cruiser and two destroyers which Admiral Hewitt had ordered to intercept them. Then, on his summons, the Covering Group came up to cut off their retreat. Thanks to able seamanship, the skilful use of smokescreens, and the disturbing effect of a relief attack by their submarines, the French managed to survive this overwhelming concentration of heavyweight fire with the loss of only one destroyer, and then made another gallant effort to reach the transport area. In this second engagement, however, another was sunk, and only one of the eight French ships returned to harbour undamaged. There two more sank and others were further crippled by bombing.

But the result was not decisive, as the El Hank batteries and *Jean Bart*'s 15-inch guns had come to life again, while the American ships had used up so much of their ammunition that they might not have been able to drive off the French warships based on Dakar if these had come up, as it was feared they might.

Fortunately, the situation at Casablanca, and on the Atlantic coast as a whole, was decisively changed by favourable political developments in Algiers. In the late afternoon General Noguès heard indirectly that the French authorities there, headed by Admiral Darlan, had on the 10th issued an order to stop fighting. Noguès was prompt to act on this unconfirmed report, and ordered his own subordinate commanders to cease active resistance pending an armistice.

Meanwhile, the American landings at Oran had met somewhat stiffer opposition than those of the Western Naval Task Force in the Casablanca area. Yet there was remarkably good joint planning and cooperation between the American military task force and the British naval force which brought it to the scene and delivered it ashore. Moreover its spearhead, the US 1st Infantry Division, commanded by Major-General Terry Allen, was a highly trained formation, and it was backed up by half the 1st Armored Division.

The plan was to capture the port and city of Oran by a double envelopment – two of Terry Allen's regimental combat teams landing on beaches in the Gulf of Arzeu, twenty-four miles to the east, while the third (under Brigadier-General Theodore Roosevelt) landed on beaches at Les Andalouses, fourteen miles to the west of the city. Then a light armoured column was to drive inland from the beachhead at Arzeu, and a smaller one from a further landing point at Mersa Bou Zedjar, thirty miles west of Oran, to capture the airfields south of Oran and close on the city to the rear. To shut it off quickly was the more important because, as estimated, its garrison of 10,000 troops could be almost doubled within twenty-four hours by reinforcement from inland stations.

The operation started well. At nightfall on November 7th the convoy had deceptively passed Oran, heading east, but then doubled back in the dark. The landings began promptly to time (1 AM) at Arzeu and only half an hour late at Les Andalouses and Mersa Bou Zedjar. Surprise was complete and no opposition was met on the beaches. Although thirteen coast defence batteries covered this stretch, there was no harrassing fire until after daylight, and even then it caused very little damage, thanks to effective naval support and the cloak it provided with smoke-screens. Disembarkation and unloading went smoothly on the whole, although slowed down by the overloading of the troops, who were carrying nearly ninety pounds of equipment apiece. The medium tanks were carried in transports and unloaded on the quay after the harbour at Arzeu was captured.

The only serious reverse was suffered in an attempt to take Oran harbour by direct assault, to forestall sabotage of its apparatus and the ships lying there. Two small British cutters, HMS *Walney* and *Hartland*, carrying 400 American troops, and accompanied by two motor launches, were employed to carry out this daring plan – which the American naval authorities had deprecated as rash. The outcome confirmed their view that it was a 'suicide mission'. Unwisely, it was timed to start two hours after H-hour, just when the French had been aroused by the landings elsewhere. The precaution of displaying a large American flag failed to deter the French from replying with sustained blasts of fire which crippled both cutters, killed half of their crews and troops, while the remainder, mostly wounded, were taken prisoner.

The advance from the beachheads got going by 9 AM or earlier, and soon after 11 AM Colonel Waters' light armoured column from Arzeu reached Tafaraoui airfield, which was reported an hour later as ready to receive aircraft from Gibraltar. But when the column turned north it was checked short of La Sénia airfield, and so was Colonel Robinett's column from Mersa Bou Zedjar. The converging infantry advances from Arzeu and Les Andalouses also became hung up when they met resistance as they approached Oran.

On the second day little progress was made, as French resistance stiffened and a counterattack on the flank of the Arzeu beachhead dislocated the whole plan of operations through the threat being magnified by lurid reports – which led General Fredenhall to divert forces from other missions. While La Sénia airfield was captured in the afternoon, most of the French aircraft had already flown off, and it could not be used because of persistent shellfire. A concentric attack towards Oran was mounted on the third morning, after some of the islands of resistance on the approach roads had been by-passed during the night. The infantry attacks from east and west again met checks, but helped to fix the attention of the defenders, while advance parties of the two light armoured columns drove into the city from the south without being opposed, apart from occasional sniping, and reached the French military headquarters before midday. The French commanders then agreed to surrender. The American casualties in the three days' fighting on land were under four hundred, and the French even less. These light losses, and particularly the diminishing resistance on the final day, were influenced by the French commanders' awareness that negotiations were proceeding at Algiers.

The landings at Algiers had run a smoother and shorter course, thanks largely to the local commander, General Mast, and his collaborating associates. No serious resistance was met anywhere, except in trying to force an early entry into the harbour, as at Oran.

One transport, USS *Thomas Stone*, was temporarily disabled at daybreak on the 7th by a torpedo fired by a U-boat when 150 miles short of Algiers, but after that the seaborne approach deeper into the Mediterranean met no further trouble. Although sighted by a few enemy observation planes, no air attack came before the convoy made its southward turn after dark to the landing beaches. One group landed near Cap Matifou, some fifteen miles east of Algiers, another near Cap Sidi Ferruch, ten miles west of the city, and the third group ten miles further west near Castiglione. For political camouflage the landings nearest Algiers were made by the Americans, with an admixture of British Commandos, and the main British one was on the more westerly beaches near Castiglione.

Here the landings began promptly at 1 AM, and proceeded without mishap despite rough and dangerous beaches. French troops met a short way inland said that they had been instructed to offer no resistance. Blida airfield was reached about 9 AM. On the eastern side of Algiers the landings were a little late and suffered some confusion, but in the absence of resistance it was possible to straighten out the situation quickly.

The important Maison Blanche airfield was reached soon after 6 AM and occupied after a few shots had been fired as token resistance. The advance on Algiers itself, however, met a village strong-point that refused passage and was then brought to a stop by a threat of attack from three French tanks. The coast battery on Cap Matifou also rejected calls to surrender, and only yielded after being twice bombarded by warships and dive-bombed in the afternoon.

The attempt to rush the port of Algiers fared worse. The British destroyers, *Broke* and *Malcolm*, flying large American flags and carrying an American infantry battalion, were used for this venture – which was planned to enter the harbour three hours after the landings, in the hope that the defenders would have been drawn off, even if their acquiescence had not been secured. Instead, the destroyers came under heavy fire as soon as they approached the entrance. *Malcolm* was badly hit and withdrew. *Broke*, at the fourth try, succeeded in running the gauntlet, and berthed alongside a quay, where her troops disembarked. At first they were allowed to occupy installations unopposed, but about 8 AM guns started to shell *Broke*, forcing her to cast off and withdraw. The landing party was hemmed in by French African troops, and surrendered soon after midday, as its ammunition was running low and there were no signs of relief by the main force. The French fire, however, had been directed to keep the landing party in check rather than to destroy it.

In the landings west of Algiers near Cap Sidi Ferruch there was much more delay and confusion, while a number of the landing craft went astray and arrived on the British beaches further west. Components of each battalion were scattered over fifteen miles of coast, while many of the landing craft were wrecked in the surf or delayed by engine trouble. Fortunately, the troops had a friendly or passive reception at first, Mast and some of his officers coming to meet them and clear the way – otherwise these landings would have turned into a costly fiasco. But when, after hasty reorganization, columns pushed on towards Algiers they encountered resistance in several places. For Mast had by now been relieved of command, his orders for cooperation cancelled, and his troops bidden to oppose the Allied advance.

The Allies' collaborators in Algiers had played their part remarkably well under the difficulties caused by the very short notice they had been given of the landing, and the little they had been told about its objectives. Their own plans to aid such a landing were promptly put into action. Officers were posted along the coast to welcome and guide the Americans, control points seized by organized parties, the telephone service largely blocked, police headquarters and outlying stations occupied, unsympathetic higher officials locked up, and the radio station taken over in readiness for a broadcast by Giraud or on his behalf which it was hoped would be of decisive effect. In sum, the collaborators achieved enough to paralyse opposition by the time that the landings took place, and they kept control of the city until about 7 AM – longer than they had reckoned on doing or had regarded as necessary. But the advance from the landing beaches was too slow to match the need.

When the Americans failed to appear by 7 AM, the limitations of the collaborators' influence on their countrymen became manifest. Moreover, when they broadcast an appeal in the name of Giraud, who had also failed to arrive as expected, this fell so flat as to show that the weight of his name had been overestimated by them. They soon began to lose control of the situation, and were brushed aside or put under arrest.

Meanwhile fateful discussions were proceeding on a higher level. Half an hour after midnight Robery Murphy had gone to see General Juin, broken the news to him that overwhelmingly strong forces were about to land, and urged him to cooperate by prompt instructions that they were not to be resisted. Murphy said that they had come on the invitation of Giraud, to help France in liberating herself. Juin showed no readiness to accept Giraud's leadership or regard his authority as sufficient, and said that the appeal must be submitted to Admiral Darlan – who was, by chance, in Algiers at that moment, having flown there to see his son, who had fallen dangerously ill. Darlan was awakened by a telephone call and asked to come to Juin's villa to receive an urgent message from Murphy. On arrival, when told of the impending stroke, his first reaction was to exclaim angrily: 'I have known for a long time that the British were stupid, but I always believed that the Americans were more intelligent. I begin to believe that you make as many mistakes as they do.'

After some discussion he eventually agreed to send a radio message to Marshal Pétain reporting the situation and asking for authorization to deal with it freely on the Marshal's behalf. Meanwhile the villa had been surrounded by an armed band of anti-Vichy French, so that Darlan was virtually under guard. But a little later they were driven off by a detachment of *gardes mobiles*, who put Murphy under arrest. Then Darlan and Juin, eyeing one another like suspicious cats, went off to the headquarters in Algiers. From here Juin took steps to regain control, releasing General Koeltz and other officers who had been arrested by Mast and his associates, while putting the latter under arrest in their turn. Darlan, however, sent a further telegram to Marshal Pétain, just before 8 AM, in which he emphasized that: 'The situation is getting worse and the defences will soon be overwhelmed' – a palpable hint that it would be wise to bow to *force majeure*. Pétain's reply gave the authorization requested.

Just after 9 AM the American chargé d'affaires in Vichy, Pinkney Tuck, had gone to see Pétain and deliver Roosevelt's letter requesting his cooperation. Pétain handed him a reply, already prepared by then, expressing 'bewilderment and sadness' at American 'aggression', and declaring that France would resist attack on her empire even by old friends – 'This is the order I give.' But his attitude to Tuck was very pleasant, and he seemed to be far from sad. Indeed, his behaviour conveyed the impression that his formal reply was really meant to allay German suspicions and intervention. But a few hours later Pierre Laval, the Prime Minister, accepted under Hitler's pressure an offer of German air support – and by evening the Axis powers were preparing forces for dispatch to Tunisia.

Meanwhile Darlan, on his own responsibility, had issued orders to the French troops and ships in the Algiers area to cease firing. Although this order did not apply to the Oran and Casablanca areas, Darlan authorized Juin to arrange a settlement for the whole of North Africa. Moreover it was agreed early in the evening that control of Algiers should be transferred to the Americans at 8 PM and that the Allies should have the use of the harbour from first light the next morning, the 9th.

The afternoon of the 9th saw the arrival of Mark Clark to conduct the fuller negotiations necessary, and of Kenneth Anderson to assume command of the Allied troops for the advance to Tunisia. Giraud also arrived, a little earlier, but found that he was far from welcome among his chief compatriots there, and took refuge with a family who lived in an out of the way place. Mark Clark remarks 'he practically went underground' – although he emerged next morning for Clark's first conference with Darlan, Juin, and their chief subordinates.

Here Clark pressed Darlan to order an immediate cease-fire everywhere in French North Africa, and when he hesitated, arguing that he had sent a summary of the terms to Vichy and must await word from there, Clark began pounding the table and said that he would get Giraud to issue the order in his place. At that, Darlan pointed out Giraud's lack of legal authority or sufficient personal weight. He also declared that such an order 'would result in the immediate occupation of southern France by the Germans' – a forecast that was soon borne out. After some more argument, with an accompaniment of table-pounding, Clark pungently told Darlan that unless he issued the order immediately he would be taken into custody – Clark having taken the precaution of posting an armed guard around the building. Darlan then, after a brief discussion with his staff, accepted this ultimatum – and his order was sent out at 11.20 AM.

When it was reported to Vichy, Pétain's own reaction was to approve it, but when Laval heard of it en route to Munich, in response to a brusque summons from Hitler, he got on the telephone to Pétain and induced him to disavow it. Early in the afternoon, Clark received the news that Vichy had rejected the armistice. When Darlan was told of this by Clark, he dejectedly said: 'There is nothing I can do but revoke the order I signed this morning.' Thereupon Clark retorted: 'You will do nothing of the kind. There will be no revocation of these orders; and, to make it certain, I shall hold you in custody.' Darlan, who had already hinted at this solution, showed himself very ready to accept it – and sent the reply to Pétain: 'I annul my orders and constitute myself a prisoner' – the annulment being only for Vichy and German ears. Next day, under pressure from Hitler via Laval, Pétain announced that all authority in North Africa had been transferred from Darlan to Noguès, but had already sent Darlan a secret message that the disavowal had been made under German pressure and was contrary to his own wishes. Such double-talk was a subterfuge compelled by the perilous situation in France, but left the situation and French commanders in North Africa, outside Algiers, still confused.

Fortunately, Hitler helped to clarify it and resolve their doubts by ordering his forces to invade the unoccupied part of France that, by the 1940 armistice agreement, had been left under the control of the Vichy Government. On November 8th and 9th Vichy had stalled on the offers of armed support which Hitler pressed on them, making reservations which inflamed his suspicions. On the 10th Laval arrived in Munich to face Hitler and Mussolini, and that afternoon Hitler insisted that the ports and air bases in Tunisia must be made available to the Axis forces. Laval still tried to hedge, saying that France could not agree to the Italians moving in, and that in any case only Pétain could decide. Hitler then lost all patience, and soon after the talk ended gave orders for his forces to drive into the unoccupied part of France at midnight – a move already mounted in readiness – as well as to seize the Tunisian air and sea bases, along with the Italians.

Southern France was speedily overrun by the German mechanized forces while six Italian divisions marched in from the east. German planes had started to arrive on an airfield near Tunis in the afternoon of the 9th, together with an escort of troops to protect them on the ground, but had been confined to the airfield by a ring of French troops. Now, from the 11th onward, the airlift was multiplied, the adjacent French troops disarmed, while tanks, guns, transport vehicles and stores were brought over by sea to Bizerta. By the end of the month 15,000 German troops had arrived, with about 100 tanks, although a large proportion were administrative personnel to organize the base. Some 9,000 Italians had also arrived, largely by road from Tripoli, and were primarily used to cover the southern flank. For a hastily improvised move, at a time when the Axis forces were hard pressed everywhere, that was a fine achievement. But such a scale of force was very small compared with what the Allies had brought to French North Africa, and would have had slight chance of resisting them if the 'Torch' plan had provided for a larger proportion of the Allied expeditionary force to be used for the advance to Tunisia, or if the Allied Command had developed the advance more rapidly than it did.

The German invasion of southern France did more than anything else to help the Allied situation in Africa by the shock it gave to the French commanders there. On the morning of the 11th, before the news came, there had been another see-saw in Algiers. The first sign was when Clark went to see Darlan, and pressed him to take two urgent steps – to order the French fleet at Toulon to come to a North African port, and to order the Governor of Tunisia, Admiral Esteva, to resist the Germans' entry. Darlan was at first evasive, arguing that his orders might not be obeyed in view of the broadcast announcement that he had been dismissed from command of the French forces – and, when further pressed, he refused to comply with Clark's demands. Clark marched out of the house, slamming the door to relieve his feelings. But in the afternoon he had a telephone message asking him to see Darlan again, and Darlan now agreed to comply with Clark's wishes, in view of developments in France – although his message to the commander of the fleet at Toulon was worded as urgent advice rather than as an order. Another favourable turn was that General Noguès, Darlan's Vichy-nominated successor, agreed to come to Algiers for a conference next day.

But in the early hours of the 12th Clark had a fresh jolt on hearing that Darlan's order for resistance in Tunisia had been revoked. Summoning Darlan and Juin to his hotel, it soon became apparent that the change was due to Juin, who argued that it was not a revocation but only a suspension of the previous order pending the arrival of Noguès, who was now his legitimate superior. Such scruples about legality, while characteristic of the French military code, appeared to Clark as merely legalistic quibbles. Although they bowed to his insistence that the order to Tunisia must be reissued immediately, without waiting for the arrival of Noguès, his suspicion was renewed by their reluctance to accept Giraud's participation in the conference. Clark was so exasperated at their procrastination that he spoke of putting all the French leaders under arrest, and locking them up aboard a ship in the harbour, unless they came to a satisfactory decision within twenty-four hours.

Meanwhile, Darlan's position in relation to the other French leaders in Africa had been strengthened by the receipt of a second clandestine message from Pétain reaffirming his confidence in Darlan and emphasizing that he himself was in *accord intime* with President Roosevelt, although he could not speak his mind openly because of the Germans' presence. This helped Darlan, who had a shrewder sense of realities than many of his compatriots, to secure the agreement of Noguès and the others for a working agreement with the Allies, including the recognition of Giraud. Their discussions at a further conference on the 13th were expedited by a fresh threat by Clark that he would lock up the lot. That afternoon it was settled, and promptly endorsed by Eisenhower who had just flown over from Gibraltar. Under its terms, Darlan was to be High Commissioner and Commander-in-Chief of Naval Forces; Giraud to be Commander-in-Chief of Ground and Air Forces; Juin, Commander of the Eastern Sector; Noguès, Commander of the Western Sector, as well as Resident-General of French Morocco. Active cooperation with the Allies in liberating Tunisia was to begin immediately.

Eisenhower endorsed the agreement all the more readily because he had come to realize, like Clark, that Darlan was the only man who could bring the French round to the Allied side, and also because he remembered Churchill's remark to him just before he left London: 'If I could meet Darlan, much as I hate him, I would cheerfully crawl on my hands and knees for a mile if by doing so I could get him to bring that fleet of his into the circle of the Allied forces.' Eisenhower's decision was no less promptly endorsed by Roosevelt and Churchill.

But such a 'deal with Darlan', who had so long been presented in the press as a sinister pro-Nazi figure, aroused a storm of protest in Britain and America – a worse storm than either Churchill or Roosevelt had foreseen. In Britain it was the greater, since de Gaulle was there, and his supporters did their utmost to increase the outburst of popular indignation. Roosevelt sought to calm the tumult by a public statement of explanation in which he adopted a phrase from Churchill's private cable to him, saying that the arrangement with Darlan 'is only a temporary expedient, justified solely by the stress of battle'. Moreover, in an off-the-record press conference, he described it as an application of an old proverb of the Orthodox Church: 'My children, it is permitted you in time of grave danger to walk with the devil until you have crossed the bridge.'

Roosevelt's way of explaining away the arrangement as 'only a temporary expedient' naturally came as a shock to Darlan, who felt that he had been tricked. In a letter of protest to Mark Clark he bitterly remarked that both public statement and private word appeared to show that he was regarded as 'only a lemon which the Americans will drop after they have squeezed it dry'. Roosevelt's statement was still more hotly resented by the French commanders who had supported Darlan in reaching an agreement with the Allies. Eisenhower, very perturbed, cabled to Washington emphasizing that 'existing French sentiment does not even remotely resemble prior calculations, and it is of utmost importance that no precipitate action be taken which will upset such equilibrium as we have been able to establish'. General Smuts, who flew to Algiers on his way back from London to South Africa, cabled Churchill: 'As regards Darlan, statements published have had unsettling effect on local French leaders, and it would be dangerous to go further on these lines. Noguès has threatened to resign, and as he controls the Moroccan population the results of such a step may be far-reaching.'

Meanwhile, Darlan had made a definite and detailed agreement with Clark for cooperative action. He also induced the French leaders in West Africa to follow his lead, and make the key port of Dakar, together with the air bases, available to the Allies. But, on Christmas Eve, he was assassinated by a fanatical young man, Bonnier de la Chapelle, who belonged to the Royalist and Gaullist circle, which had been pressing for Darlan's removal from power. That accelerated removal helped to solve the Allies' awkward political problem, and to clear the way for de Gaulle's advent, while the Allies had already reaped the benefit of their 'deal with Darlan'. Churchill's comments in his memoirs: 'Darlan's murder, however criminal, relieved the Allies of their embarrassment in working with him, and at the same time left them with all the advantages he had been able to bestow during the vital hours of the Allied landings.' His assassin was promptly tried by court-martial on Giraud's orders, and quickly executed. On the following day the French leaders agreed to choose Giraud as High Commissioner in succession to Darlan. He 'filled the gap' – for a short time.

If the Allies had not succeeded in enlisting Darlan's help their problem would have been much tougher than it turned out. For there were nearly 120,000 French troops in North Africa – about 55,000 in Morocco, 50,000 in Algeria, and 15,000 in Tunisia. Although widely spread, they could have provided formidable opposition if they had continued to resist the Allies.

The only important respect in which Darlan's aid and authority failed to achieve the desired effect was over bringing the main French fleet across from Toulon to North Africa. Its commander, Admiral de Laborde, hesitated to respond to Darlan's summons without confirming word from Pétain, and a special emissary sent by Darlan to convince him was picked up by the Germans. Laborde's hesitation was prolonged, and his anxiety lulled, by the Germans' shrewdness in halting on the outskirts of the naval base and allowing it to remain an unoccupied zone garrisoned by French troops. Meanwhile they prepared a plan for a coup to seize the fleet intact, and launched it on November 27th, after blocking the harbour exits with a minefield. But although delay had forfeited the chance of breaking out, the French managed to carry out their prepared plan for scuttling the fleet quickly enough to frustrate the German attempt to capture it – thus fulfilling the assurance that Darlan had given in his initial conference with Clark at Algiers on November 10th: 'In no circumstances will our fleet fall into German hands.' The Allies' disappointment that it had not come to North Africa was outweighed by their relief that the danger of it being used against them had vanished with its sinking.

Another cause of relief during this critical period, and especially the first few days, was that the Spanish had abstained from any intervention and that Hitler had not attempted to strike back through Spain against the western gateway into the Mediterranean. The Spanish Army could have made the harbour and airfield at Gibraltar unusable by artillery fire from Algeçiras, and could also have cut communications between Patton's force and the Allied forces in Algeria, as the railway from Casablanca to Oran ran close to the border of Spanish Morocco – as close as twenty miles. When 'Torch' was being planned, the British had said that if Franco were to intervene it would be impossible to preserve the use of Gibraltar,* while Eisenhower's planning staff reckoned that a force of five divisions would be necessary to occupy Spanish Morocco and that the task would take three and a half months. Fortunately Franco was content to stay quiet, as a 'non-belligerent' ally of the Axis – and the more contentedly because the Americans were both buying Spanish products and allowing him to obtain oil from the Caribbean. Moreover, the Axis archives show that Hitler,

---

* It was no new conclusion. I had emphasized this point in numerous articles, lectures, and private discussions after the Spanish Civil War broke out in 1936, when discussing the danger that might develop if Spain came to be dominated by a Fascist régime, and if this should decide to cooperate actively with the Axis powers.

after his earlier experience of Franco's skill in evading his desires for a move through Spain against Gibraltar, did not really consider attempting such a counterstroke in November 1942. The idea was only revived, and then by Mussolini, the following April – when the Axis forces in Tunisia were hard pressed and an early Allied invasion of Italy was feared. Even then Hitler turned down Mussolini's plea, both because he feared that a move through Spain would be fiercely and stubbornly resisted by his 'non-belligerent' ally, and because he remained confident that the Axis forces could maintain their hold on Tunisia. That confidence of his was bolstered by the remarkable success of the very slender Axis forces sent to Tunisia by the end of November in holding up the Allied advance at that time.

CHAPTER TWENTY-TWO

*The Race for Tunis**

The advance on Tunis and Bizerta started with a seaborne move, but one of very short extent – to the port of Bougie, about a hundred miles east of Algiers and only a quarter of the distance to Bizerta. This was a diminution of the original plan which, assuming full and prompt French cooperation, was to use parachute troops and seaborne Commandos to seize the airfields at Bône, Bizerta, and Tunis on successive days – November 11th, 12th, and 13th – while a floating reserve of the force landed at Algiers was to sail for, and seize, the port of Bougie and the Djidjelli airfield forty miles beyond the forward base. But in the state of uncertainty after the landing at Algiers, this plan was considered too hazardous, and the more distant moves were dropped. Instead, it was decided on the 9th to occupy Bougie and the airfield, and then rush a force to a railhead at Souk Ahras close to the Tunisian border, while a second seaborne and airborne force occupied Bône.

On the early evening of the 10th two well-protected convoys sailed from Algiers, carrying the leading brigade group (the 36th) of the British 78th Division (Major-General Vyvyan Evelegh) and the stores for the expedition. It arrived off Bougie early next morning, but lost time by landing on nearby beaches, in heavy surf, from fear of a hostile reception – although in the event it proved a friendly one. Because of heavy surf an intended landing close to Djidjelli was not attempted, and the airfield was not occupied in time to provide effective fighter protection until two days later, so that several ships were destroyed in air raids. Early on the 12th, however, a Commando force slipped into the port of Bône and a parachute detachment dropped on the airfield, both being well received by the French there.

By the 13th the brigade group at Bougie was moving forward, while other elements of the division were advancing overland from Algiers, quickly followed by Blade Force, an armoured column just landed, which was composed of the 17th/21st Lancers and attached troops, under Colonel R. A. Hull – it was the leading contingent of the 6th

* For maps, see pp 292, 423, 432.

Armoured Division.* To pave the way it was planned that on the 15th
a British parachute battalion would be dropped ahead at Souk el Arba
eighty miles from Tunis inside the Tunisian border, and an American
parachute battalion near Tebessa to cover the southern flank and secure
a forward airfield there. The American drop was carried out as planned
– and two days later this battalion, under Colonel E. D. Raff, made an
eighty miles bound south-eastward to secure the airfield at Gafsa,
barely seventy miles from the Gulf of Gabes and the bottleneck approach from Tripoli. The British drop was delayed a day because of
weather conditions, and the leading ground troops came up so fast that
they also reached Souk el Arba on the 16th. By then, too, the small
Tunisian port of Tabarka, on the road to Bizerta, was reached by another column advancing along the coast road.

Next day, the 17th, General Anderson gave orders for the 78th
Division 'to advance on Tunis and destroy the Axis forces' after completing its forward concentration. That pause to concentrate, however
desirable it seemed, was unfortunate in view of the slenderness of the
Axis forces that had so far arrived – an under-strength parachute regiment of two battalions at Tunis, which had been flown over from Italy
on the 11th, and two battalions at Bizerta (one of parachute engineers,
and one of infantry). On the 16th General Nehring – the former Commander of the Afrika Korps, who had been badly wounded in the Alam
Halfa battle and just recovered – arrived with a solitary staff officer to
command this nucleus, some 3,000 troops of what was entitled the
'90th Corps'. Even at the end of the month it had only the strength of a
division.

The Germans, without waiting to concentrate, quickly thrust to the
westward, and by that boldness disguised their weakness. The French
troops in Tunisia, although much more numerous, fell back before them
to avoid a premature clash before Allied reinforcements arrived. On the
17th a German parachute battalion (of some 300 men only) under Captain Knoche pushed out along the Tunis–Algiers road, and the French
group posted there withdrew to the road-centre of Medjez el Bab
(thirty-five miles west of Tunis), with its important bridge across the
Medjerda River. Here the French were reinforced on the night of the
18th by elements of Blade Force, including a British parachute bat-

---

* In the 17th/21st Lancers, and other armoured regiments of this division,
two troops of each squadron had the new, and fast, Crusader III tank armed
with the powerful 6-pounder gun, while the other two troops were equipped
with the 2-pounder armed Valentine which, although slower, was far more
reliable and also better armoured.

talion and an American field artillery battallion. (The 17th/21st Lancers and their tanks had not yet arrived; the leading squadron reached Souk el Arba on the 18th, but was not sent forward.)

At 4 AM the French commander in Tunisia, General Barré, was called there to meet a German envoy who presented an ultimatum from Nehring that French troops must withdraw to a line near the border of Tunisia. Barré tried to parley, but the Germans realized that it was merely an attempt to gain time, and early morning reconnaissance spotted the presence of Allied troops. So at 9 AM they broke off parleys, and a quarter of an hour later opened fire. An hour and a half later German dive-bombers came on the scene to add punch to the bluff. Following up the bombing attacks, which shook the defenders badly, the paratroopers made two small ground attacks, and that air of vigorous effect created an exaggerated impression of their strength. The opposing commanders felt that they could not hold out unless further reinforcements came to the rescue – and General Anderson's instructions curbed such aid pending the completion of the Allied concentration for the planned advance on Tunis.

After dark Captain Knoche sent small parties to swim across the river, and these very effectively simulated an attack with growing strength. The Allied troops fell back from the bridge, leaving it intact. Just before midnight the local British commander called the French commander to his command post and insisted that an immediate withdrawal should be made to a more secure position on the high ground eight miles back. This was done, and the Germans occupied Medjez el Bab. It was a striking example of bluff achieved by boldness by a small detachment less than a tenth of the size of the force in possession.

Farther north, Major Witzig's parachute engineer battalion from Bizerta, with some tanks, had pushed west along the coast road, and met the leading battalion of the 36th Infantry Brigade Group, the 6th Royal West Kents, at Jebel Abiod. But although the Germans overran part of the battalion it held on until the rest of the brigade came up to its relief.

Meantime smaller German parties, sent south, had secured the key towns on the approach from Tripoli – Sousse, Sfax, and Gabes. Some fifty paratroopers, carried by air, bluffed the French garrison into evacuating Gabes. They were reinforced on the 20th by two Italian battalions marching from Tripoli, which arrived just in time to foil an American move on Gabes by Colonel Raff's paratroopers. On the 22nd a small German armoured column drove the French out of the central road junction at Sbeitla, and installed an Italian detachment there before returning to Tunis – but this was promptly expelled by another detachment of Raff's battalion.

Nevertheless, Nehring's skeleton force had not only preserved their bridgeheads at Tunis and Bizerta, but extended these into a very large bridgehead embracing most of the northern half of Tunisia.

Anderson's planned offensive to capture Tunis did not start until the 25th. During the interval the slender German strength had been trebled, although its close combat component comprised only two small parachute regiments (of two battalions apiece), a battalion of parachute engineers, three infantry draft-holding battalions, and two companies of a panzer battalion (the 190th) with thirty tanks. These included a number of the new model Panzer IV with the long 75-mm gun, an important asset. Thus the extreme disparity between the Axis and Allied forces had diminished through Anderson's lengthy pause near the border of Tunisia to complete the process of concentration.

He himself on the 21st expressed doubt whether his strength was sufficient to gain that objective. So he was hurriedly reinforced with more American units on Eisenhower's orders, particularly Combat Command B of the 1st Armored Division, which came all the way from Oran, 700 miles back – the wheeled and half-track vehicles by road, and the tanks by rail.* Only part of this, however, arrived in time for the start of the operation.

It was a three-pronged offensive, the 36th Infantry Brigade Group on the left near the coast, the much larger Blade Force in the centre, and the 11th Infantry Brigade Group on the right along the main highway – each reinforced with American armoured and artillery units.

The left prong, on the hilly coastal road, started a day late and advanced only six miles on each of the first two days, in a cautious way – Witzig's small battalion of parachute engineers falling back before it. Then on the 28th it pushed on twice as far, but ran into an ambush that Witzig had laid in a pass near Djefna station, and the leading battalion was badly mauled. A larger attack on the 30th failed against a strengthened defence, and the attack was then abandoned. That repulse, in turn, led to the failure of an amphibious move by a mixed Anglo-American Commando which landed on the coast north of Djefna early next morn-

---

* American armoured divisions at this period of the war included two armoured regiments, each comprising one light and four medium battalions, an armoured infantry regiment of three battalions, and three armoured field artillery battalions. It had an establishment of 390 tanks – 158 light and 232 medium tanks. Operationally, it was distributed in two Combat Commands, A and B, and a third was later added.

ing, and blocked the road behind, east of Mateur, but was driven to withdraw three days later as no sign of relief had come and its supplies were running low.

The centre prong was formed by Blade Force, which had been further strengthened by the inclusion of an American light tank battalion (the 1st Battalion, 1st Armored Regiment, equipped with Stuarts), so that it now had well over a hundred tanks. It thrust forward thirty miles on the 25th to the Chouigui pass, after breaking through an outpost line held by a small Axis detachment. Next morning, however, a check came from a German detachment, a panzer company of ten tanks followed by two foot-fighting companies, which stuck southward from Mateur. Eight of these tanks were knocked out, most by the American 37-mm anti-tank guns, but their sacrifice in creating this flank threat led the British higher command to break off Blade Force's thrust, and distribute this force to cover the flank of the right prong.

Both sides were groping in 'the fog of war' but such caution at a crucial moment was in unwise contrast to the Germans' boldness – and all the more because on the previous afternoon a small detachment of Blade Force had by chance given the German higher command a bad fright. Hull had ordered Lieutenant-Colonel John K. Waters, commanding the American light tank battalion, to reconnoitre the bridges across the Medjerda River near Tebourba and Djedeida. Company C, under Major Rudolph Barlow, was sent on this mission and thus happened to arrive on the edge of the Djedeida airfield, newly brought into use. Seeing and seizing the opportunity, Barlow swept over the airfield with his seventeen tanks and destroyed some twenty aircraft – in reports it was magnified to forty. This deep penetration, also magnified in the reports that reached Nehring, came as such a shock that he pulled back his forces for a close-in defence of Tunis.

The Allied right prong, on the main highway, had met an early check in attacking Medjez el Bab,* and small counterattacks produced a disorganized retirement. But after nightfall on the 25th Nehring – shaken by the Djedeida raid – ordered the defenders to withdraw, fearing that they might be overwhelmed by a renewed attack. Following them up, the Allied column occupied Tebourba, twenty miles farther on, in the early hours of the 27th. But after a short advance next day it was abruptly checked at Djedeida, twelve miles from Tunis, by a mixed battalion group. A renewed assault on the 29th was also repulsed.

* Medjez el Bab was held by a German parachute battalion, an Italian anti-tank company, and two 88-mm guns, supported by a company of the 190th Panzer Battalion, with 17 tanks.

General Evelegh then advised a pause until further reinforcements came up and closer fighter protection had been provided against the German dive-bombers, which had harrassed Allied troops increasingly and frayed their nerves.

This recommendation was accepted by Anderson, and by Eisenhower. He visited the forward area on those two days, and was greeted by American officers with 'the constant plaint, "Where is this bloody Air Force of ours? Why do we see nothing but Heinies?".' In his memoirs he remarks: 'Every conversation along the roadside brought out astounding exaggerations' about the damage, but it was nonetheless ominous to hear such comments as: 'Our troops will surely have to retreat; humans cannot exist in these conditions.'*

Meanwhile Field-Marshal Kesselring, who visited Tunis at the same time, was reproaching Nehring for being too cautious and defensive. He brushed aside arguments about the much larger strength of the Allied forces, and the fact that the inflow of Axis reinforcements was badly hindered by Allied bombing of the airfields. Criticizing the decision to withdraw from Medjez el Bab, he ordered him to regain the lost ground, as far as Tebourba at least. So, on December 1st, a counter-thrust was delivered by three panzer companies† with some forty tanks and a few supporting elements, including a field battery of three guns and two companies of anti-tank guns. The counter-thrust was aimed, not direct at the force which had attacked Djedeida, but from the north towards the Chouigui pass, on the flank, with the intention of swinging round onto its rear near Tebourba. The Germans, in two converging columns, first hit Blade Force, which suffered from being widely distributed in its flank protective role, part of it being overrun and destroyed. Then, in the afternoon, the Germans pushed towards Tebourba but were checked by artillery fire and bombing before they reached their objective and got astride the main road.

But their continued pressure produced such a close threat to this artery that the Allies' spearhead at Djedeida was pulled back to a position nearer Tebourba. On the 3rd the pressure was increased to strangling pitch, and became concentric as Nehring threw in all the other German detachments that were within reach, leaving only a tiny hand-

---

* Eisenhower: *Crusade in Europe*, p 120.

† The leading elements of the 10th Panzer Division had just arrived in Tunisia, and included two companies of a fresh panzer battalion – with 32 Panzer IIIs and two of the new model Panzer IVs. These two companies were immediately used for the counterthrust along with one company of the panzer battalion that had arrived earlier.

ful on guard in the city of Tunis. That night the Allies' spearhead force was squeezed out of Tebourba, and barely managed to escape – by using a dirt track along the river bank, which entailed the abandonment of much equipment and transport. The Germans in their counterstroke took more than a thousand prisoners, and their 'bag' also included more than fifty tanks.

It deserves mention that the recent German reinforcements included five of the new fifty-six ton Tiger tanks, mounting a long 88-mm gun. These monsters were a 'secret weapon', but Hitler had decided to send a few to Tunis for test in combat, and two of them were attached to the Djedeida combat group in this fight for Tebourba.

In the days that followed, the Allied commanders planned an early renewal of their offensive, with increased strength. But the prospect was soon diminished by Nehring's early action to extend his gains. He now planned to use his small armoured force to recapture Medjez el Bab by a wide outflanking move south of the Medjerda River. Here Combat Command B of the US 1st Armored Division had just been deployed, with a view both to the renewed advance and to keeping it separate from the British, so that it could fight as an integrated team. An advanced detachment was posted at Jebel el Guessa, a piece of high ground south-west of Tebourba which overlooked the flat country farther south. As a preliminary to their own outflanking move, the Germans attacked this observation point early on December 6th, and overran its defenders, who had become disorganized in a hasty attempt to withdraw. Reinforcements had been sent, but were slow in starting, and when they arrived on the scene suffered a costly repulse.

This fresh German stroke, and threat, caused the newly arrived commander of the British 5th Corps, Lieutenant-General Allfrey, to order a withdrawal of his troops north of the river, from their position near Tebourba to one near Hill 290 (which the British had named 'Longstop Hill') closer to Medjez el Bab. Moreover, he advised a longer withdrawal, to a line west of Medjez el Bab. This proposal was endorsed by Anderson but turned down by Eisenhower. Longstop Hill, however, was evacuated.

Writing on the 7th to a friend, General Handy, Eisenhower remarked: 'I think the best way to describe our operations to date is that they have violated every recognized principle of war, are in conflict with all operational and logistic methods laid down in textbooks, and will be condemned in their entirety by all Leavenworth and War College classes for the next twenty-five years.'

Resuming their flank thrust on December 10th, with a force including about thirty medium and two Tiger tanks, the Germans were checked two miles short of Medjez el Bab by a well-posted French battery, became temporarily bogged when they tried to move off the road to outflank it, and were then led to withdraw by an American threat to their own rear from a detachment of Combat Command B. But they scored an indirect and unforeseen success when Combat Command B started to withdraw after dark from its exposed position, became confused, reversed course on a false rumour of German threat, and turned off along a muddy track near the river, where many of its remaining tanks and other vehicles became stuck, and were abandoned. This disaster was temporarily crippling, while very damaging to the prospect of an early resumption of the Allied push for Tunis. For the moment, Combat Command B had only forty-four tanks left fit for action – barely a quarter of its full strength. The two German counter-strokes had all too effectively upset the Allies' plan and prospects.

Meanwhile Colonel-General Jurgen von Arnim had been sent by Hitler to take supreme command of the Axis forces, which were re-christened the 5th Panzer Army. He took over from Nehring on the 9th and, with the arrival of further reinforcements, proceeded to expand the two perimeters covering Tunis and Bizerta into a general bridgehead, formed by a hundred-mile chain of defence posts, and stretching from the coast some twenty miles west of Bizerta to Enfidaville on the east coast. It was divided into three sectors, the northern one held by the improvised Division von Broich (named after its commander), the central one (from west of Chouigui to just beyond Pont-du-Fahs) by the 10th Panzer Division, which had been arriving in driblets, and the southern sector by the Italian Superga Division. The Allied Intelligence estimated the Axis forces in mid-December as about 25,000 fighting troops and 10,000 administrative personnel, with eighty tanks – an estimate which was in excess of the mark. The Allies' effective fighting troops numbered close on 40,000 – some 20,000 British, 12,000 American, and 7,000 French – and their total strength was much larger, as their administrative organization was more lavish.

Delays in the build-up, partly due to bad weather, led Anderson to postpone the renewal of the offensive. But on the 16th he decided that it should start on the 24th, so as to utilize a full moon for an infantry night assault. It was to be delivered by the British 78th Division and 6th Armoured Divisions, together with part of the US 1st Infantry Division.

To gain room for deployment, preliminary attacks were made to regain Longstop Hill and also Hill 466 on the more northerly line of approach to Tebourba. Both suffered from confusion in bad weather and developed into protracted see-saw battles, so that the main attack had to be postponed. By the 25th the Germans had completely regained their original positions – and, very naturally, now gave 'Longstop Hill' the name 'Christmas Hill'.

Already, on Christmas Eve, Eisenhower and Anderson had reluctantly decided to abandon the intended offensive in view of these setbacks and the torrential rain, which was turning the battleground into a morass. The Allies had lost 'the race for Tunis'.

Yet, by the irony of luck, this failure turned out one of the biggest blessings in disguise that could have happened. For without such a failure Hitler and Mussolini would not have had the time or encouragement to pour very large reinforcements into Tunisia and build up the defence of that bridgehead to a strength of over a quarter of a million men – who had to fight with an enemy-dominated sea at their back, and if defeated would be trapped. When the Axis forces were eventually overwhelmed, in May, the south of Europe was left almost bare, so that the follow-up Allied invasion of Sicily in July had an easy run. But for the Allied failure in December which led to that huge 'bag' in May, it is all too probable that the Allied re-entry into Europe would have been repelled. What Churchill was fond of calling the 'soft under-belly' was so mountainous as to be very hard country for an invading force, and only became soft when there was a lack of defenders.

CHAPTER TWENTY-THREE

The Tide Turns in the Pacific

Japan's offensive aims in the Pacific, to establish what she called 'The Greater East Asia Co-Prosperity Sphere', had been virtually achieved within four months.* By that time Malaya and the Dutch East Indies had been completely conquered, as well as Hong Kong; so had almost the entire Philippines and the southern part of Burma. Within another month the surrender of the island-fortress of Corregidor brought the fall of America's last foothold in the Philippines. A week later the British had been driven out of Burma, back into India, and China was thus cut off from her allies. This vast run of conquest had cost the Japanese only about 15,000 men, 380 aircraft, and four destroyers.

After such a series of easy triumphs the Japanese were, naturally, reluctant to change over to the defensive – as their strategic plan ordained. They feared that such a change might bring a gradual decline of fighting spirit, while giving their Western opponents, economically much stronger, a breathing space for recovery. The Japanese Navy, in particular, was anxious to eliminate the two possible bases for an American comeback in the Pacific – Hawaii and Australia. As they pointed out, the US Navy's carrier force could still operate from Hawaii, while Australia was obviously being turned into a springboard, as well as a stronghold.

The Japanese Army, with its mind still focused on China and Manchuria, was unwilling to release the troops required for such expeditions, which in the case of an expedition to invade Australia would have to be large. It had already declined to cooperate in a plan of the Combined Fleet Staff to take Ceylon.

The Navy, however, hoped that by a further successful stroke in either direction it might overcome the Army chiefs' objection and induce them to provide the troops required for one or other of these expeditions, but was itself divided in mind about the best direction. Admiral Yamamoto and the Combined Fleet Staff favoured a plan to take Midway Island (1,100 miles west of Pearl Harbor) – as a bait to

* For map, see pp 210–11.

draw the US Pacific Fleet into action, and crush it. The Naval Staff, however, preferred a thrust through the Solomon Islands to take New Caledonia, Fiji, and Samoa – and, by capturing this island chain, block the sea-routes between America and Australia. A weighty argument for the latter plan, of isolating Australia, was that the Japanese had already gone a long way towards completing the ring. For by the end of March they had advanced from Rabaul into the Solomon Islands as well as into the northern coast of New Guinea.

The debate between the alternative naval plans was interrupted, and diverted, by the American air raid on Tokyo, of April 18th, 1942.

THE TOKYO RAID

This air strike at the Japanese capital, the heart of Japan's homeland, was inspired by the idea of retaliation for Pearl Harbor, and planning for it had begun in January. As the distance from any surviving American base was too far, the raid must necessarily be made from naval carriers. But as the Japanese were known to have a picket boat patrol operating 500 miles out from the mainland, the strike aircraft would have to be launched from a distance of about 550 miles, involving an out and back flight of at least 1,100 miles – which was too far for naval carrier planes. Moreover the US Navy's few, and precious, carriers would be endangered if they had to wait in the area until the raiding planes returned. So it was decided to use US Army Air Force bombers, of longer range, and also that they should fly westward after bombing Tokyo to land on Chinese airfields.

That entailed a flight of more than 2,000 miles, and the ability to take off from carriers. So the B25 Mitchell was selected. These bombers, with extra fuel tanks fitted, could carry a 2,000 lb bomb load for 2,400 miles. The pilots, led by Lieutenant-Colonel James H. Doolittle, practised short take-offs and long overwater flights. Only sixteen planes were employed, as they were too large to be stowed below deck, while they had to be allowed sufficient space for the take-off.

On April 2nd the carrier selected for the task, *Hornet*, sailed fom San Francisco with its escort of cruisers and destroyers. On the 13th it was joined by Task Force 16, organized round the carrier *Enterprise*, which was to give air support – as the *Hornet*'s own planes were stowed below deck. Early on the 18th the carrier force was sighted by a Japanese patrol boat while still more than 650 miles from Tokyo. The naval commander, Vice-Admiral William F. Halsey, conferred with Doolittle, and they agreed that it would be better to launch the bombers immediately despite the extra distance involved. It proved a wise and fortunate decision.

Taking off in a heavy sea between 08.15 and 09.24, the bombers reached Japan within four hours, catching the defences by surprise, and dropped their bombs (including incendiaries), on Tokyo, Nagoya, and Kobe. They then flew on to China, aided by a tail wind. Unfortunately, by a misunderstanding, Chuchow airfield was not ready to receive them, so that the crews had to make a crash-landing or drop by parachute. Out of the eighty-two man total, seventy returned – three who did not were executed by the Japanese for bombing civilian targets. The two carriers escaped unhurt, and reached Pearl Harbor on the 25th.

Another piece of good fortune was that, despite the patrol boat's warning, the Japanese had expected the raid to come a day later than it did, on the 19th – when, as they reckoned, the carriers would be close enough to launch their naval bombers. By then the air forces would have been ready and Admiral Nagumo's carriers would have reached their planned position for a counterstroke.

The prime result of the raid was the fillip it gave to American morale, which had been badly shaken by Pearl Harbor. But it also forced the Japanese to keep four Army fighter groups at home for the defence of Tokyo and other cities, while another resultant diversion was the dispatch of a punitive expedition of fifty-three battalions to drive through Chekiang Province, where the American bombers had landed. A still more important effect, inherently causing a diversion of strength, was the decision to forestall further raids by undertaking the Midway operation as well as the thrust to cut Australia off from America. The dual effort was detrimental to concentration of effort and strength.

Under the revised Japanese plan the first move, itself dual, was to be an advance deeper into the Solomon Islands to seize Tulagi as a seaplane base to cover a further leap south-eastward, coupled with the capture of Port Moresby on the south coast of New Guinea, which would bring Queensland within range of Japanese bombers. Then the Combined Fleet under Yamamoto was to carry out the occupation of Midway Island and key points in the Western Aleutians. After the desired destruction of the US Pacific Fleet, the third move would be a resumption of the advance in the south-east to block the sea-routes from America to Australia.

The first of these moves led to the Battle of the Coral Sea, the second to the Battle of Midway, and the third to the prolonged and intense struggle for Guadalcanal, the large island close to Tulagi.

An ironical, and indirect, effect of this diverse Japanese plan was that it helped to cement a split in American planning and command arrangements.

At the beginning of April the United States had assumed responsibility for the whole Pacific area, except Sumatra, while the British would remain responsible for Sumatra and the Indian Ocean area. China was a separate theatre of war, under American tutelage. The American sphere was divided in two – the South-west Pacific area under General MacArthur, whose headquarters were now established in Australia, and the Pacific Ocean area under Admiral Chester W. Nimitz. Both were strong and forceful men, likely to clash. The Japanese plan provided ample call on, and scope for, the activity of each. Moreover the borderline between their respective spheres came in the Solomon Islands, where the Japanese amphibious threat required the conjoint use of MacArthur's ground forces and Nimitz's naval forces. Thus they had to develop a working arrangement.

THE BATTLE OF THE CORAL SEA

The Japanese ground and air forces for the first move assembled at Rabaul in New Britain, and the naval forces at Truk in the Caroline Islands, a thousand miles to the north. Behind the amphibious groups destined for the two invasions lay a carrier striking force ready to beat off any American intervention. It comprised the carriers *Zuikaku* and *Shokaku*, with an escort of cruisers and destroyers, and carried 125 naval aircraft (42 fighters and 83 bombers). A further 150 aircraft at Rabaul could aid it.

American Intelligence, the Allies' chief advantage, had discovered the main threads of the Japanese plan, and Admiral Nimitz sent all his available forces southward – the carriers *Yorktown* and *Lexington* from Pearl Harbor, with 141 aircraft (42 fighters, 99 bombers), and two groups of cruisers to escort them. (The two other American carriers, *Enterprise* and *Hornet*, returning from their part in the Tokyo raid, were also ordered to hurry down to the Coral Sea, but arrived too late for the battle.)

On May 3rd the Japanese landed on Tulagi and took that island unopposed – as the small Australian garrison, forewarned, had been withdrawn. At that moment the *Lexington* was refuelling at sea while the *Yorktown* under Rear-Admiral Fletcher was farther away from the scene. But the next day it launched a number of strikes when about 100 miles distant from Tulagi. These had little effect beyond sinking a

Japanese destroyer. The *Yorktown* was fortunate in escaping retaliation. For the two Japanese carriers had been sent to deliver a handful of
fighter planes to Rabaul – sent off the scene merely to save an extra
ferrying mission. It was the start of a series of mistakes or misunder-
standings on both sides from which the Americans eventually profited
on balance.

Admiral Takagi's carrier group now came south, passing to the east
of the Solomons and round into the Coral Sea, hoping to take in rear
the American carrier force. Meanwhile the *Lexington* had joined the
Yorktown and the two were steering north to intercept the Japanese
invasion force that was on the way to Port Moresby. On May 6th – the
black day of Corregidor's surrender – the opposing carrier groups
searched for one another without making contact, although at one time
they were only seventy miles apart.

Early on the 7th the Japanese searching planes reported that they had
spotted a carrier and a cruiser, whereupon Takagi promptly ordered an
all-out bombing attack on the ships, and speedily sank both. But, actually, they were only a tanker and escorting destroyer, so that time and
effort were wasted. That evening Takagi tried another and lesser strike,
but the result was that twenty of the twenty-seven planes he employed
were lost. Meanwhile Fletcher's carrier aircraft, likewise led astray by a
false report, expended their effort in an attack upon the close-covering
force of the Port Moresby invasion. In this stroke they sank the light
carrier *Shoho*, and did so in ten minutes – one of the quickest sinkings
on record in the entire war. A more important effect was that the Japanese were led to postpone the invasion and order their force to turn
back. It was an ironical benefit from the mistake of attacking the wrong
ship. It was, also, one of several blind shots that day.

On the morning of May 8th the two opposing carrier forces at last
came to grips. The two sides were closely matched, the Japanese having
121 aircraft and the Americans 122, while their escorts were almost
equal in strength – four heavy cruisers and six destroyers on the Japanese side, five heavy cruisers and seven destroyers on the American
side. The Japanese, however, were moving in a belt of cloud while the
Americans had to operate under a clear sky. The primary consequence
of this was that the carrier *Zuikaku* escaped attention. The *Shokaku*,
however, suffered three bomb-hits and had to be withdrawn from the
battle. On the other side, the *Lexington* suffered two torpedo-hits and
two bomb-hits, and subsequent internal explosions compelled the abandonment of this much cherished ship – which sailors called the 'Lady
Lex'. The nimbler *Yorktown* escaped with only one bomb hit.

In the afternoon, Nimitz ordered the carrier force to withdraw from the Coral Sea – and the more readily as the threat to Port Moresby had vanished for the time being. The Japanese also retired from the scene, in the mistaken belief that both the American carriers had been sunk.

In absolute losses the Americans came off slightly better in aircraft, seventy-four compared with over eighty, while their loss in men was only 543 compared with over a thousand, but they had lost a fleet carrier whereas the Japanese had lost only a light carrier. More important, the Americans had thwarted their enemy's strategic object, the capture of Port Moresby in New Guinea. And now by a superiority in technical achievement they managed to repair the *Yorktown* in time for the next stage of the Pacific conflict, whereas neither of the two Japanese carriers in the Coral Sea fight could be got ready for use in the second and more decisive fight.

The Battle of the Coral Sea was the first in history fought out between fleets that never came in sight of one another, and at ranges that had been extended, from the battleship's extreme limit of about twenty miles, to a hundred miles and more. A greater repetition was soon to follow.

THE BATTLE OF MIDWAY

Imperial General Headquarters in Japan had already set this next stage going by its order of May 5th. The plan produced by the Combined Fleet staff was extraordinarily comprehensive and elaborate, but lacking in flexibility. Almost the entire Navy was to be used in the operation. The total of some 200 ships included 8 carriers, 11 battleships, 22 cruisers, 65 destroyers, 21 submarines. They were assisted by more than 600 aircraft. Admiral Nimitz could scrape together only 76 ships, and of these a third, belonging to the North Pacific Force, never came into the battle.

For the main, the Midway operation, the Japanese employed (1) an advanced submarine force, patrolling in three cordons, and intended to cripple American naval countermoves; (2) an invasion force under Admiral Kondo of twelve escorted transports, carrying 5,000 troops, with close support by four heavy cruisers, and more distant cover from a force comprising two battleships, one light carrier and a further four heavy cruisers; (3) Nagumo's First Carrier Force of four fleet carriers – carrying over 250 planes – escorted by two battleships, two heavy cruisers and a destroyer screen; (4) the main battle fleet under Yamamoto, comprising three battleships, with a destroyer screen, and one

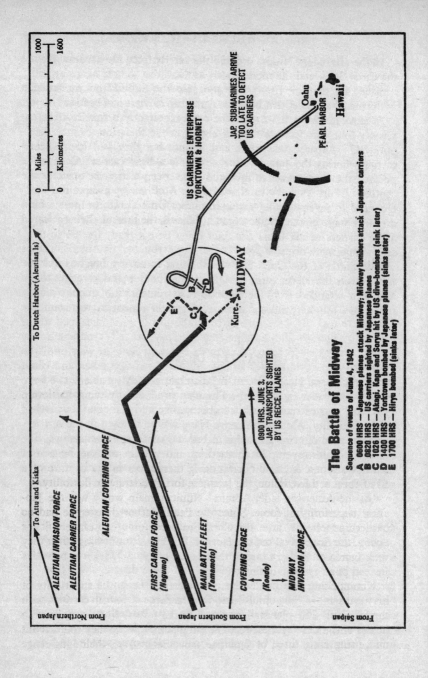

The Battle of Midway

Sequence of events of June 4, 1942

A 0600 HRS — Japanese planes attack Midway; Midway bombers attack Japanese carriers
B 0820 HRS — US carriers sighted by Japanese planes
C 1026 HRS — Akagi, Kaga and Soryu hit by US dive-bombers (sink later)
D 1400 HRS — Yorktown bombed by Japanese planes (sinks later)
E 1700 HRS — Hiryu bombed (sinks later)

ALEUTIAN INVASION FORCE

ALEUTIAN CARRIER FORCE

ALEUTIAN COVERING FORCE

To Attu and Kiska

To Dutch Harbor (Aleutian Is)

From Northern Japan

FIRST CARRIER FORCE
(Nagumo)

MAIN BATTLE FLEET
(Yamamoto)

COVERING FORCE
(Kondo)

MIDWAY INVASION FORCE

From Southern Japan

From Saipan

0900 HRS, JUNE 3,
JAP. TRANSPORTS SIGHTED
BY US RECCE. PLANES

MIDWAY

Kure.

US CARRIERS: ENTERPRISE
YORKTOWN & HORNET

JAP. SUBMARINES ARRIVE
TOO LATE TO DETECT
US CARRIERS

Oahu

PEARL HARBOR

Hawaii

Miles

Kilometres

0   1000

0   1600

light carrier. One of the battleships was the recently built giant, the *Yamato*, of 70,000 tons and mounting nine 18-inch guns.

For the Aleutians operation the Japanese allotted (1) an invasion force of three escorted transports, carrying 2,400 troops, with a support group of two heavy cruisers; (2) a carrier force of two light carriers; (3) a covering force of four older battleships.

The battle was to open in the Aleutians, with air strikes against Dutch Harbor on June 3rd, followed by landings at three points on the 6th. Meanwhile, on the 4th, Nagumo's carrier planes were to attack the airfield on Midway, and next day Kure Atoll (sixty miles to the west) was to be occupied for a seaplane base. On the 6th, cruisers would bombard Midway, and the troops be landed, the invasion being covered by Kondo's battleships.

The Japanese expectation was that there would be no American ships in the Midway area until after the landing, and their hope was that the US Pacific Fleet would hurry northward as soon as news came of the opening air strike in the Aleutians. That would enable them to trap it between their two carrier forces. But in pursuing this strategic aim, the destruction of the American carriers, the Japanese handicapped themselves by their tactical arrangements. Because of the favourable moon conditions of early June, Yamamoto was unwilling to wait until the *Zuikaku* had replaced her aircraft losses in the Coral Sea and could reinforce the other carriers. As for the eight available carriers, two were sent to the Aleutians and two more were accompanying battleship groups. At the same time, fleet movements were tied to the speed of slow troop transports. Moreover, it is hard to see the point of a diversionary move to the Aleutians if the Japanese main object was the destruction of the American carriers, and not merely the capture of Midway. Worst of all, by committing themselves to the capture of a fixed point at a fixed time, the Japanese forfeited strategic flexibility.

On the American side, Admiral Nimitz's main worry was the Japanese superiority of force. Since the Pearl Harbor disaster he had no battleships left, and after the Coral Sea battle only two carriers fit for action, the *Enterprise* and the *Hornet*. But by an astonishing effort they were increased to three through the repair of the *Yorktown* in two days instead of an estimated ninety.

Nimitz's one great, and offsetting, advantage was the superiority of his means and supply of information. The three American carriers, with their 233 planes, were stationed well to the north of Midway, so as to be out of sight of Japanese reconnoitring planes, while they could count on getting early word of Japanese movements from their long-range

Catalinas based in Midway. Thus they hoped to make a flank attack on the Japanese forces. On June 3rd, the day after the carriers were in position, air reconnaissance sighted the slow-moving Japanese transports 600 miles west of Midway. Gaps in the search patterns flown by Japanese aircraft allowed the American carriers to approach unseen, from the north-east. They were also helped by the belief of Yamamoto and Nagumo that the US Pacific Fleet would not be at sea.

Early on June 4th, Nagumo launched a strike by 108 of his aircraft against Midway, while a further wave of similar size was being prepared to attack any warships sighted. The first wave did much damage to installations on Midway, with little loss to itself, but reported to Nagumo that there was need for a second attack. Since his own carriers were being bombed by planes from Midway, he felt that there was still need to neutralize the island's airfields, so ordered his second wave to change from torpedoes to bombs for this purpose, as there was still no sign of the American carriers.

Shortly afterwards, a group of American ships was reported about 200 miles away, although it was at first thought to consist only of cruisers and destroyers. But at 08.20 came a rather more precise report saying that the group included a carrier. This was an awkward moment for Nagumo, as most of his torpedo-bombers were now equipped with bombs, and most of his fighters were on patrol. He had, also, to recover the aircraft returning from the first strike at Midway.

Nevertheless, the change of course north-eastward which Nagumo made on receiving the news helped him to avoid the first wave of dive-bombers dispatched against him from the American carriers. And when three successive waves of torpedo-bombers – relatively slow machines – attacked the Japanese carriers between 09.30 and 10.24, thirty-five of the forty-one used were shot down by the Japanese fighters or anti-aircraft guns. At that moment the Japanese felt that they had won the battle.

But two minutes later thirty-seven American dive-bombers from the *Enterprise* (under Lieutenant-Commander Clarence W. McClusky) swooped down from 19,000 feet, so unexpectedly that they met no opposition. The Japanese fighters that had just shot down the third wave of torpedo-bombers had no chance to climb and counterattack. The carrier *Akagi*, Nagumo's flagship, was hit by bombs which caught its planes changing their own projectiles and exploded many of the torpedoes, compelling the crew to abandon ship. The carrier *Kaga* suffered bomb-hits that destroyed her bridge and set her on fire from stem to stern; she eventually sank in the evening. The carrier *Soryu* suffered three hits with half-ton bombs from the *Yorktown*'s dive-bombers, which now arrived on the scene, and was abandoned within twenty minutes.

The only still intact fleet carrier, the *Hiryu*, struck back at the *Yorktown* and hit her so badly in the afternoon as to cause her abandonment – she was weakened by the damage, hastily repaired, that she had suffered in the Coral Sea battles. But twenty-four American dive-bombers, including ten from the *Yorktown*, caught the *Hiryu* in the late afternoon and hit her so severely that she had to be abandoned in the early hours of the 5th, and sank at 09.00 hours.

This battle of the Fourth of June saw the most extraordinarily quick change of fortune known in naval history, and also showed the 'chanciness' of battles fought out in the new style by long-range sea-air action.

Admiral Yamamoto's first reaction to the news of the disaster to his carrier force was to bring up his battleships, while bringing back his two light carriers from the Aleutians – still in the hope of fighting a sea-battle more in the old style to restore the prospect. But the subsequent news of the loss of the *Hiryu*, and Nagumo's gloomy reports, led to a change of mind, and early on the 5th Yamamoto decided to suspend the attack on Midway. He still hoped to draw the Americans into a trap, by withdrawing westward, but was foiled by the fine combination of boldness with caution shown by Admiral Raymond A. Spruance, who commanded the two American carriers *Enterprise* and *Hornet* in this crucial battle.

Meantime, the Japanese attack on the Aleutian Islands in the North Pacific had been delivered as planned early on June 3rd, when two light carriers allotted for the operation launched twenty-three bombers, with twelve fighters, against Dutch Harbor. It was too small a force for serious effect except by luck, and did little damage, as cloud obscured the ground. A repetition next day, in clearer weather, achieved some hits but nothing drastic. Then on June 5th the carriers were called southward to help in the main operation. On the 7th, however, the small seaborne force of Japanese troops landed on, and captured unopposed, two of the three islands – Kiska and Attu – which had been assigned as objectives. Japanese propaganda made the most of this minor achievement, to offset the crucial failure at Midway. Superficially, the capture of these points looked an important gain, as the Aleutian chain of islands stretching across the North Pacific lay close to the shortest route between San Francisco and Tokyo. But in reality these bleak and rocky islands, often covered in fog or battered by storms, were quite unsuitable as air or naval bases for a trans-Pacific advance either way.

In sum, the operations of June 1942 were a crushing defeat for the Japanese. They had lost in the Midway battle itself four fleet carriers and some 330 aircraft, most of which went down with the carriers, as well as a heavy cruiser – whereas the Americans lost only one carrier and about 150 aircraft. The dive-bombers had been the key weapon on the American side – in contrast, over 90 per cent of the torpedo-bombers had been shot down, while the large B17 bombers of the Army had proved quite ineffective against ships.

Beside the strategic errors earlier mentioned, the Japanese also suffered from other handicapping faults of various kinds. Among 'command' faults was Yamamoto's virtual isolation, on the bridge of the battleship *Yamato*, Nagumo's loss of nerve, and the naval tradition that led Yamaguchi and other leaders to go down with their ships instead of seeking to recover the initiative. Nimitz, by remaining on shore, was able to keep an overall grip on the strategic situation, in contrast to Yamamoto.

Japanese troubles were multiplied by a string of tactical errors – the failure to fly sufficient search planes to spot the American carriers; lack of fighter cover at high altitude; poor fire precautions; striking with the planes of all four carriers, which meant that they had to recover and rearm their aircraft at the same time, so that there was a period when their carrier force had no striking power; steering towards the enemy when the changes were taking place, which gave the American planes the chance to locate Nagumo's force more easily and to hit it before it could hit back or even defend itself with its fighters. Most of these faults could be traced to complacent overconfidence.

Once the Japanese had lost these four fleet-carriers, and their well-trained aircrews, their continued preponderance in battleships and cruisers counted for little. These ships could only venture out in areas that could be covered by their own land-based aircraft – and the Japanese defeat in the long struggle for Guadalcanal was principally due to lack of air control. The Battle of Midway gave the Americans an invaluable breathing space until, at the end of the year, their new '*Essex*' class fleet carriers began to become available. Thus it can reasonably be said that Midway was the turning point that spelt the ultimate doom of Japan.

THE SOUTH-WEST PACIFIC AFTER MIDWAY

Even so, although the outcome of the Midway battle severely handicapped – and, indeed, curbed – the Japanese advance in the South-west

Pacific, it did not halt it. While the Japanese could no longer use their fleet to press their advance, they still chose to continue it, and in a two-pronged way – in New Guinea, by overland attack across the Papuan Peninsula in the east of that vast island; and in the Solomons by a process of hopping from island to island, establishing airfields along the chain to cover successive short hops.

NEW GUINEA AND PAPUA

When the Japanese entered the war in December 1941, most of Australia's operational forces were fighting with the British Eighth Army in North Africa – although they were to be recalled when the emergency developed. In New Guinea, so menacingly close to Australia itself, the only considerable force was one of brigade size posted at Port Moresby, the capital of Papua, on the south coast. The very small Australian garrisons on the north coast, as well as in the Bismarck Archipelago and the Solomons, were withdrawn as soon as the Japanese approached. But it was considered essential to hold on to Port Moresby, because Japanese air attacks from there could have reached Queensland itself, on the Australian mainland. The Australian people were, naturally, sensitive to such a threat.

Early in March 1942, the Japanese, from Rabaul, had landed at Lae on the north coast of New Guinea, close to the Papuan Peninsula. But, as already related, their seaborne expeditionary force to capture Port Moresby was turned back in consequence of the otherwise indecisive Battle of the Coral Sea in May. Meanwhile General Douglas Mac-Arthur had been appointed Allied Commander-in-Chief of the South-west Pacific area. And after the Battle of Midway early in June, the Allied position became much more secure, directly as well as indirectly, since most of the Australian troops had by now returned home, and new divisions were being formed, while the United States had placed two divisions and eight air groups in Australia. In Papua, too, Australia's strength was increased to more than the size of a division – two brigades at Port Moresby, and a third at Milne Bay on the eastern tip of the peninsula, while two battalions were pushing forward over the Kokoda trail to Buna, on the north coast, with the aim of establishing an airbase there to provide cover for the planned amphibious advance by the Allies westward along the coast of New Guinea.

But on July 21st this move was forestalled, and the apparently fading Japanese threat revived, when the Japanese landed near Buna – with some 2,000 men – as part of their renewed attempt to capture Port

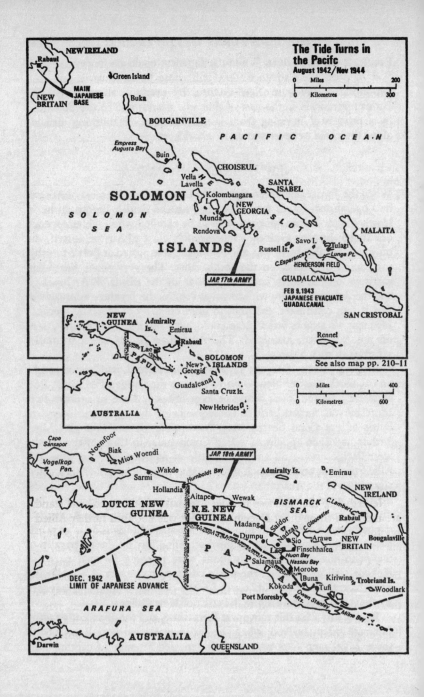

The Tide Turns in the Pacifc
August 1942/Nov 1944

Moresby, this time by overland attack. The Allies had a further shock when, on the 29th, the Japanese took Kokoda, nearly halfway across the peninsula – and by mid-August, with a force built up to a strength of over 13,000 men, they were pressing the Australians back along the jungle track. But although the peninsula here was little more than a hundred miles wide, the trail had to cross the Owen Stanley Mountains, at a point 8,500 feet high, and the growing difficulties of supply across such difficult terrain – naturally worse for the attacking side – were multiplied by Allied air attacks. Within a month the Japanese advance was brought to a halt some thirty miles short of its objective. Meantime, a smaller Japanese force (of 1,200 men, reinforced to 2,000) had landed in Milne Bay on August 25th, and succeeded in reaching the edge of the airstrip there after five days' fierce fighting, but was then counterattacked by the Australians and driven to reembark.

My mid-September MacArthur had concentrated in Papua the bulk of the 6th and 7th Australian Divisions, and an American regiment, ready to take the offensive. On the 23rd General Sir Thomas Blamey, the Australian Commander-in-Chief of the Allied Land Forces, Southwest Pacific, arrived at Port Moresby to take control of the operations. His forces in their turn met fierce resistance as they strove to fight their way back to Kokoda, and on to Buna, but their difficulties of supply were eased by increasing use of air transport. By the end of October the Japanese were dislodged from the last of the three successive positions they had constructed near Templeton's Crossing, at the top of the range, and on November 2nd the Australians reoccupied Kokoda, reopening the airfield there. The Japanese tried to make a fresh stand on the Kumusi River, but their defence was overcome with the aid of bridging material dropped by air, and the flank threat of fresh Australian and American troops who were brought forward by air to the north coast.

Nevertheless the Japanese managed to make a prolonged final stand around Buna throughout December, and it was not until further Allied reinforcements had arrived, by sea and air, that the last pocket of Japanese resistance on the coast was liquidated, on January 21st, 1943. In the six months' campaign they had lost over 12,000 men. The Australian battle-casualties were 5,700 and the American 2,800 – a total of 8,500 – while they had suffered three times as many from sickness in the tropical damp-heat and malarial jungles. They had proved, however, that they could successfully fight the Japanese even in such appalling jungle conditions, and that airpower in all its varied forms provided a decisive advantage.

GUADALCANAL

The Guadalcanal campaign developed from the mutual, and natural, desire of General MacArthur and Admiral Nimitz to exploit the Midway victory by a speedy change-over from the defensive to the counter-offensive in the Pacific. Their desire was backed by their respective chiefs in Washington, General Marshall and Admiral King, in so far as such an offensive could be reconciled with the grand strategy, agreed with the British, of 'beat Germany first'. For any early counteroffensive the only feasible area was the South-west Pacific, and on that all were agreed. But a conflict of opinion arose, also quite naturally, as to who should direct and command the counteroffensive. Now that enemy pressure on the Hawaiian Islands, in the Central Pacific, had been not only relieved but removed, the Navy became all the more eager to play its full part in what basically had to be an amphibious operation. It was only with reluctance that Admiral King had accepted the policy of tackling Germany first and building up American strength in Britain for that purpose. British arguments against an early cross-Channel attack, in 1942, had caused Marshall to veer round towards the idea of giving the Pacific priority, and King was delighted to welcome such a change of view, even if it were no more than temporary – and unlikely to be endorsed by President Roosevelt as a definite change of policy.

But agreement about a changeover to the offensive in the South-west Pacific immediately sharpened the argument as to who should be in charge of it, and in the last part of June the debate became passionate. The outcome was a compromise, expressed in the Joint Chiefs of Staff directive of July 2nd, inspired by Marshall. The offensive was to be carried out in three stages, the first being the occupation of the Santa Cruz islands and the eastern Solomons, especially Tulagi and Guadalcanal. For this purpose the boundary between the zones was shifted, so that this area came under Nimitz, who would therefore conduct the first stage of the offensive. The second stage would be the capture of the rest of the Solomons, and of the New Guinea coast as far as the Huon Peninsula, just beyond Lae, while the third stage would be the capture of Rabaul, the main Japanese base in the South-west Pacific, and the rest of the Bismarck Archipelago – these two stages falling to MacArthur's direction under the redistribution of zones.

The plan under this compromise did not please MacArthur who, immediately after the Midway victory, advocated a speedy and large-scale attack on Rabaul, confidently predicting that he could quickly capture it, with the rest of the Bismarcks, and drive the Japanese back to Truk (in the 700-miles-distant Caroline Islands). But he was brought to recognize that he could not hope to obtain the force he considered necessary – a marine division and two carriers, in addition to the three infantry divisions he already had. So the compromise three-stage plan was adopted – and took much longer to complete than any of the leaders had expected.

The Allies' plan, for capturing the eastern Solomons, was forestalled – as it had been in Papua. On July 5th reconnaissance planes reported that the Japanese had moved some forces from Tulagi to the larger nearby island of Guadalcanal (ninety miles long and twenty-five miles wide), and were building an airstrip at Lunga Point (this later came to be called 'Henderson Field'). The obvious danger of Japanese bombers operating from there caused an immediate reconsideration of American strategy, and Guadalcanal itself became the primary objective. With its backbone of wooded mountains, heavy rainfall, and unhealthy climate it was not a favourable objective for any campaign.

The overall strategic direction of the operation, under Nimitz, was entrusted to Vice-Admiral Robert L. Ghormley, the area C-in-C, while Rear-Admiral Fletcher was in tactical command of it – he also controlled the three covering carrier groups built around the *Enterprise*, *Saratoga*, and *Wasp* respectively. Land-based air support came from Port Moresby, Queensland, and various island airstrips. The landing force, commanded by Major-General Alexander A. Vandegrift, comprised the 1st Marine Division and a regiment of the 2nd, totalling 19,000 Marines carried in nineteen transports, with escorts. No sign of the enemy was seen as the armada approached, and early on August 7th the air and naval bombardment opened, while the landings began at 09.00 hours. By evening 11,000 Marines were ashore, and the airfield was occupied next morning; it was found to be nearly completed. The 2,200 Japanese on Guadalcanal, who were largely construction workers, had mostly fled into the jungle. On Tulagi, the Japanese garrison of 1,500 troops had put up a tougher resistance, and it was not until the second evening that they were overcome and wiped out, by the 6,000 Marines who had landed there.

Japanese reaction was prompt – and, ironically, all the quicker because reports had led the Japanese to believe that the American landing force was only a fraction of its actual numbers. Thus they did not pause to prepare an adequate response, but sent off a series of reinforcing driblets, repeatedly increased, so that what the two sides had conceived as a swift stroke and counterstroke developed into a protracted campaign.

The Japanese naval escorts were stronger, however, and their successive advances produced a series of momentous naval clashes. The first of these, and the worst for the Americans, was the Battle of Savo Island, off the north-west coast of Guadalcanal. On the evening of August 7th, Vice-Admiral Mikawa, the Japanese Commander-in-Chief at Rabaul, assembled a force of five heavy cruisers, with two light cruisers, and set off for Guadalcanal. Slipping undetected next day through what was called 'the Slot', the narrow waters between the two chains of the Solomons, he approached Savo Island in the evening – just after Fletcher had withdrawn the American carriers because their fuel and fighter strength were running short. Although the Allied cruiser and destroyer force had taken up precautionary dispositions for the night, cooperation and watch-keeping were poor. In the early hours of the morning Mikawa took by surprise in turn its southerly and northerly groups, and within an hour was steaming back through the Slot, leaving behind four Allied heavy cruisers sunk or sinking, and one badly damaged – five out of five – while his own were almost undamaged.

The Japanese profited greatly from their superior skill at night-fighting, helped by their superior optical instruments, and especially their 24-inch 'long lance' torpedoes. It was one of the worst defeats that the US Navy suffered at sea in the war. Fortunately for the Allies, Mikawa did not complete his mission by destroying the mass of transport and supply ships lying defenceless in Lunga Roads – being unaware that the Allied carriers had been withdrawn, and thus expecting early counterattack from the air if he did not quickly regain the relative shelter of the Slot. Moreover, he did not know that the American landing on Guadalcanal was on any such large scale as it actually was. A commander should be judged in the light of the information he has at the moment he makes his decisions.

But all that remained of the Allied naval forces withdrew southward that afternoon to avoid further attack, although less than half the Marines' supplies of food and ammunition had been unloaded by then. Troop rations were reduced to two meals a day, and for the next two weeks the Marines were isolated – without naval support and also without air cover until Henderson Field was brought into use on the 20th with the arrival of the first squadrons of Marine aircraft. Even then, such air cover was narrowly limited.

The Japanese forfeited the opportunity largely because they still greatly underestimated the strength of the Marine force landed on

Guadalcanal – estimating it at 2,000 men, and assuming that a force of 6,000 would be sufficient to overcome them and regain the island. They sent off two advanced detachments, totalling 1,500 men, carried in destroyers, which landed east and west of Lunga Point on August 18th; these attacked without waiting for the follow-up convoy, and were promptly wiped out by the Marines. The follow-up convoy – of only 2,000 men – sailed from Rabaul on the 19th. While small in itself, it was given strong naval aid – being intended as a bait to draw the US fleet into a trap, as had been the idea at Midway. The advance was led by the light carrier *Ryujo*, itself part of the bait, while behind came two battleships and three cruisers under Admiral Kondo, and behind them the fleet carriers *Zuikaku* and *Shokaku* under Admiral Nagumo.

This baited plan led to what was called the Battle of the Eastern Solomons, but not to the achievement of the trap that the Japanese intended. For Admiral Ghormley received timely warning of their approach from 'Coast-watchers' – an organization composed mostly of Royal Australian Navy Intelligence officers and local planters. He concentrated three naval task forces south-east of Guadalcanal, built round the carriers *Enterprise*, *Saratoga*, and *Wasp*. The *Ryujo* was sighted on the morning of the 24th, and sunk in the afternoon by aircraft from the American carriers. Meanwhile the two Japanese fleet carriers had also been sighted, so that when the expected attacks came from them the American carriers had their full fighter strength in the air to meet them, and took heavy toll, knocking out over seventy of eighty enemy planes employed, and losing only seventeen of their own. The *Enterprise* was the only ship that suffered any serious damage. After this indecisive battle the Japanese fleet retired during the night, and so did the American.

After this ineffectual naval effort there was a lull, except on land, where the weak Japanese forces made unsuccessful efforts to reach Henderson Field, being beaten off by the Marines, although they so 'fought to the death' that almost all of them were killed. But they were replaced by a series of small detachments brought along by destroyers – in such regular succession that the process came to be called by the Marines the 'Tokyo Express'. Thereby the Japanese ground strength on Guadalcanal was steadily increased, a further 6,000 men being shuttled there by early September. On the night of September 13th/14th this force fiercely attacked the Marines' position – which came to be called 'Bloody Ridge' – but all its attacks were repelled, and its loss was over 1,200 men.

Meanwhile, however, the US Navy in that area was badly depleted by the loss of the carriers *Saratoga* and *Wasp* to Japanese submarine attacks – the former badly damaged and the latter sunk. As the *Enterprise* was still under repair, this left only the *Hornet* to provide air cover.

After the failure of the earlier Japanese attempts to retake Guadalcanal, Imperial General Headquarters issued a new directive on September 18th that gave this campaign priority to the one in New Guinea. But the Japanese still greatly underestimated the size of the Marine force there, putting it as no more than 7,500, and on this calculation reckoned that the dispatch of a division would suffice, in cooperation with the temporary use of their Combined Fleet. The preliminary sea-borne move of the first reinforcing contingent led to another naval battle off the coast of Guadalcanal, on October 11th/12th. In this fight, called the Battle of Cape Esperance, the respective losses were not heavy but on balance favourable to the Americans – which came as a moral tonic. During the battle, however, the Japanese managed to land reinforcements that brought their total of troops up to 22,000. At the same time the Americans brought their strength up to 23,000 – with 4,500 more on Tulagi.

Even so, mid-October was the most critical period of the campaign for them, particularly when a bombardment from two Japanese battleships ploughed up Henderson Field, set fuel stocks on fire, and reduced the number of their planes there from ninety to forty-two – while they also forced the US Army's heavy bombers to fly back to the New Hebrides. Repeated Japanese bombing attacks were another strain, while the humid heat and inadequate diet were taking a heavy toll.

On October 24th the Japanese land offensive developed, having been delayed by torrential rain and the dense jungle. The main attack came up from the south, but the Marines were well-posted in their defensive position and their artillery was well handled. The Japanese were beaten off, their losses running into thousands compared with a few hundred on the American side, and by the 26th they were driven to retreat, leaving behind about 2,000 dead.

Meanwhile the Combined Fleet under Yamamoto had advanced with two fleet carriers, two light carriers, four battleships, fourteen cruisers, and forty-four destroyers, and cruised to the north-east of the Solomons, awaiting the expected news that Henderson Field had been captured by the Army. On the American side, the naval strength was barely half, despite the arrival of the new battleship *South Dakota* and several cruisers. In battleships, there was only one against four. But the carrier *Hornet* had now been reinforced by the repaired *Enterprise*, and that was more important in modern naval terms. Fresh vigour also came with the appointment of Admiral Halsey to replace the overtired Ghormley. The two fleets clashed on October 26th in what was called the Battle of the Santa Cruz Islands, a battle once again dominated by air action on either side. The *Hornet* was sunk and the *Enterprise* damaged, while on the other side the *Shokaku* was badly damaged and also the light carrier *Zuiho*, before the two fleets retired from the scene on the 27th. But in planes lost the Japanese suffered much the worse – seventy of them failed to return, and in the ten-day period culminating in this battle they lost 200 – to add to the 300 they had lost since the last week of August. Moreover the Americans soon received a reinforcement of over 200 planes, as well as the rest of the 2nd Marine Division and part of the American Division.

Nevertheless the Japanese were also reinforced sufficiently to resume their efforts – impelled by pride, and also gulled by absurdly optimistic reports of the damage they had inflicted. These efforts led to the two clashes known as the 'Naval Battle of Guadalcanal'. The first took place in the early hours of Friday November 13th, and although it lasted barely half an hour, the Americans had two cruisers sunk while the Japanese battleship *Hiei* was so badly crippled that it had to be scuttled next day – the first Japanese battleship lost in the war.

The second part of this naval battle came on the night of the 14th/15th, and with roles reversed, when the Japanese tried to bring down a reinforcement of 11,000 troops in a convoy with a large destroyer escort under the indomitable Rear-Admiral Tanaka, covered by Admiral Kondo's heavier ships. Seven of the transports were sunk in the approach, and although the other four reached Guadalcanal they were smashed by air attack in the morning, so that only 4,000 of the troops were landed, and very few of the urgently needed supplies.

In the accompanying naval battle, the American destroyers suffered badly, but then Kondo's remaining battleship, the *Kirishima*, was crippled when, at midnight, the radar-controlled guns of the US battleship *Washington* opened fire on it at a range of 8,400 yards, and hit it so devastatingly that it was put out of action within seven minutes, and soon had to be scuttled.

Meanwhile on land the Marines and the other American troops, having now the advantage in supplies, had gone over to the offensive, and were expanding their perimeter. By the end of the month the American air strength on the island had risen to 188, and the Japanese no longer dared to ship either reinforcements or supplies by slow convoy. In December they were reduced to sending driblets of both in submarines.

The Japanese Navy had suffered so heavily that its chiefs urged the abandonment of Guadalcanal, but the Army chiefs, who had now assembled 50,000 troops at Rabaul, were still hoping to send them to reinforce the 25,000 now on the island. Meanwhile, however, the Americans had built up their strength on Guadalcanal to over 50,000 by January 7th, 1943, which were now well-supplied, while the Japanese, who had been reduced to one-third of normal rations, were so weakened by hunger and malaria that they could not hope to take the offensive – tenaciously as they still fought on the defensive.

So on January 4th Imperial GHQ reluctantly faced realities, and gave the order for them to be gradually evacuated. Unaware of this decision, the Americans pushed forward cautiously, so that the Japanese were able to take away all their troops in three moves, starting on the night of February 1st and completed on the night of February 7th, losing only one destroyer in the process.

On balance, however, the prolonged struggle for Guadalcanal was a very serious defeat for Japan. She had lost some 25,000 men, including 9,000 from hunger and disease, while American losses were much smaller. Worse still she had lost at least 600 planes, with their trained crews. At the same time America's strength in all spheres was continually increasing, as her mobilization of manpower and industry got into its stride.

BURMA MAY 1942–MAY 1943 – THE RIPOSTE MISCARRIES

By May 1942, with the British withdrawal from Burma into India, the Japanese had achieved the planned limit of their expansion in Southeast Asia, so they changed over to the defensive and sought to consolidate their conquests. Meanwhile the British made plans for a comeback when the next dry season came, in November 1942. None of them proved feasible – because of logistical difficulties. And the only one even attempted, the very limited Arakan offensive, resulted in a disastrous failure.*

The crucial area logistically, Assam and Bengal, had never been regarded or planned as a military base area. Airfields, depots, roads, railways, and pipelines all had to be built, ports enlarged, and the whole region reorganized.

First of the major difficulties facing the India Command was shipping, as most of its needs had to come from overseas. But all other

* For map, see p 538.

theatres of war had priority, and little shipping was left for India, even when threatened with invasion, after providing for the Atlantic and Arctic convoys, the Mediterranean and Pacific theatres. The amount allotted for India was only about one-third of what was necessary for the build-up of the area as the springboard for an offensive.

Internal transport was also a major difficulty. The road and rail systems of north-east India were old and haphazard. They required great improvement before the supplies coming from Calcutta and the other ports could be carried to the front line. Shortages of all kinds hampered the progress of the work. So did the monsoons, which caused landslides and carried away bridges. Japanese air raids also contributed, while labour troubles and political unrest were worse hindrances – particularly the widespread disorder and risks that followed the failure of the Cripps mission in the late summer of 1942, when the Indian Congress called for a civil disobedience campaign. This was fomented by pro-Japanese elements as well as by the worsening economic situation in India. The worst handicap of all was the lack of locomotives – Wavell had begged for at least 185, but was given four!

Yet the logistical problem had been vastly multiplied by the decision that India was to be built up as a base, to hold thirty-four divisions and 100 air squadrons. Over a million men were employed in building the 220 new airfields, thus greatly reducing the labour force available for other projects – of which road-building was the primary need. Moreover the supply problem was increased by the need to feed 400,000 civilian refugees from Burma.

Although the Indian Command now comprised a large number of divisions, most of them were newly formed ones produced by the wartime expansion of the Indian Army; they lacked equipment and training, as well as experienced officers and NCOs. The few that had some battle experience were exhausted and depleted not only by the Burma campaign but by the ravages of malaria, while they had lost most of their equipment in the retreat. Only three of some fifteen divisions nominally available were in any respect fit for operations in the near future.

Administrative problems were accentuated by Command problems, especially with the Chinese forces which had withdrawn into India, with the 10th US Army Air Force, and with the prickly General Stilwell.

Another crucial factor was the need for air superiority – to protect India itself, to ensure continual supplies to China, and to provide the air cover essential for the success of any attempt to reconquer Burma.

Fortunately, as soon as the monsoon had come, in May 1942, the Japanese had sent a large number of their aircraft to help the South-west Pacific campaigns, and had given the remainder a period of rest. That enabled the Allies to build up their own air strength in comparative peace. By September, 1942 there were thirty-one British and Indian squadrons in India. Of these, however, six were unfit for operations, nine were kept for the defence of Ceylon, and five were employed for transport and reconnaissance duties – leaving only seven fighter and four bomber squadrons for operations in north-east India. But the flow of aircraft, from both Britain and the USA, was increasing monthly, and by February 1943 there would be fifty-two squadrons. Moreover the aircraft themselves were being replaced by newer types – Mitchells, Hurricanes, Liberators, Beaufighters. Most of them could go straight to the new airfields in Assam and Bengal, as the possibility of a seaborne invasion of India had become slight after the naval battles of the Coral Sea and Midway.

In April 1942 Wavell had reorganized the India Command. The Central Command HQ now at Agra, was responsible for training and supply, while there were three regional Army Commands: the Northwestern, the Southern, and the Eastern, which was the operational one.

Planning for the reconquest of Burma entailed cooperation with the Chinese armies, both those now in Assam and those in the Yunnan province of China. The Chinese plan, of October 1942, was for a converging advance on Burma by fifteen Chinese divisions, so called, from Yunnan and three from Assam, together with some ten British or Indian divisions. The role of the latter, in the Chinese plan, was not only to invade northern Burma but to launch a seaborne attack on Rangoon. Wavell agreed to the plan in principle, although dubious whether what he considered the two essential requirements were obtainable – sufficiently powerful air forces to dominate the sky over Burma; and a strong British fleet, with four or five carriers, to dominate the Indian Ocean and cover the Rangoon attack. The second requirement was, in fact, impossible – in view of naval commitments elsewhere. Chiang Kai-Shek – regarding these essential conditions as Wavell's quibbles and as a sign that the British were not going to make a serious effort, angrily abandoned his part in the operation, at the end of 1942.

THE ARAKAN OFFENSIVE, DECEMBER 1942–MAY 1943

Wavell nevertheless decided to carry out a limited offensive to recover the Arakan coastal region by a hundred-mile advance down the Mayu

Peninsula, combined with a seaborne invasion of Akyab island, at the tip of the next peninsula, to recapture the airfields there – from which Japanese squadrons could attack most of north-east India. If the Allied squadrons could be re-established there they could cover all of north and central Burma. This important part of the plan, however, was dropped because of the lack of landing craft.

Even so, Wavell persisted with the overland advance into Arakan rather than do nothing. The 14th Indian Division started to advance in December 1942, but moved so slowly that the commander of the Japanese 15th Army, General Iida, was able to send reinforcements thither and halt the British advance by the end of January – while he sent still more in February. Yet Wavell insisted that the advance must be continued, despite the arguments and protests of General Noel Irwin, the Commander of the Eastern Army, who warned him that the troops were badly depleted, and their morale affected, by malaria. Thus the Japanese were able to strike against the 14th Division's rear, and reached Htizwe on the Mayu River by March 18th, thereby uncovering its flank and causing it to retreat. The 14th Indian Division was now replaced by the 26th, but the Japanese counterstroke continued, over the Mayu, reaching the coast at Indin early in April. The Japanese then pushed on northward, with the aim of capturing the line Maungdaw–Buthidaung by May, when the monsoon season was due, and thus dislocate any British plans for a renewed advance into Burma during the next dry season – from November 1943 to May 1944.

On April 14th Lieutenant-General W. J. Slim, 15th Indian Corps, took over command of the forces in Arakan, and was appalled to find how badly their physical and moral state had suffered from the ravages of malaria and the battle-losses due to frontal attacks on Japanese positions. While hoping to hold the Maungdaw–Buthidaung line, between the sea and the Mayu River, he planned to withdraw farther if necessary to a line running inland from Cox's Bazar, a further fifty miles northward and just over the frontier. Here the country was comparatively open, and thus more suited to the British advantage in artillery and tanks than the jungles and swamps of the Mayu Peninsula, while the Japanese communications up the coast would be more stretched and thus more vulnerable.

But neither plan came into effect. For the Japanese drove the British to abandon Buthidaung after dark on May 6th, and that flanking threat led to the abandonment of Maungdaw, on the coast. And the Japanese then decided to stop on the newly captured line, as the monsoon was due. In sum, the British attempt to recapture Akyab and its airfields –

by an overland advance and without seaborne aid – had proved a complete, and dismal, failure. The Japanese had shown their skill in flanking moves and infiltrations through the jungle, while the British had damped the spirit of their troops by costly frontal attacks and blundering disregard for the indirect approach. By May 1943 they were back on the line they had held the previous autumn.

THE CHINDITS

The only glimmer of light in this darkly clouded phase of the war came, at the northern end of the Burmese theatre, from the first 'Chindit' operation – a name taken by its initiator, Orde Wingate, from a mythical beast, the Chinthe, half lion and half eagle, of which statues are numerous in Burmese pagodas. His imagination was caught by the way this griffin-like beast symbolized the close ground-and-air cooperation needed in such operations and by such forces. The fact that the first operations were carried out across and beyond the Chindwin River, in northern Burma, may have helped to engrave the name on the minds of the public.

In the autumn of 1938 Orde Wingate, then a captain on leave from Palestine, had met, and made a strong impression on, a number of influential people – as he had earlier that year on General Wavell, then the Commander in Palestine, and Brigadier John Evetts, who was in charge of the northern area.* But on returning to Palestine in December he found that his political activities in Zionist circles had made him such an object of suspicion in British official quarters that Wavell's successor, General Haining – who had originally approved the 'SNS' organization – had decided to remove him from control of it and appoint him to an innocuous job at his own headquarters. Then, in May 1938, he was sent home at Haining's request, and given a minor staff post in Anti-Aircraft Command.

But in the autumn of 1940 he was rescued from this backwater and

---

* He came to see me several times to discuss the training of the 'SNS' – 'Special Night Squads' – that he had been allowed to organize in the spring, from young and picked members of the 'underground' Jewish defence force, the Hagana, to tackle the Arab armed bands which had been causing much trouble in Palestine. He told me how he had been applying my tactical ideas in such guerrilla-type operations, and gave me a set of his papers on the subject. He also emphasized with evident pride, at that time, that he was a distant cousin of T. E. Lawrence – although he later tended to disparage Lawrence when he himself became famous. At Wingate's request I wrote to Winston Churchill about him, to effect an introduction.

sent to organize a guerrilla campaign in Ethiopia against the Italian control of East Africa. The appointment, suggested by Leo Amery, who had joined the Cabinet, was clinched by Wavell's prompt acceptance of the proposal. The successful conclusion of this East African Campaign in May 1941 was followed by another slump in Wingate's personal fortunes, and to a state of depression that caused him to attempt suicide during a bout of malaria. But when convalescing at home he was rescued by a call to fresh opportunity, this time arising from the British disasters in the Far East. The opportunity was once again provided by Wavell, who had himself been removed from the Middle East Command in June, after the failure of the summer offensive there, and sent to India. At the end of the year Wavell found himself caught up in a greater crisis when the Japanese invaded Malaya and Burma successively. In February 1942, when the situation even in Burma was looking bleak, Wavell asked for Wingate to be sent to him with a view to developing guerrilla operations there.

After his arrival Wingate urged the creation of what were called 'Long Range Penetration Groups' trained to operate in the Burmese jungle and strike at the Japanese communications as well as against the Japanese outposts. He argued that the force must be sufficiently large to strike with strong effect, while small enough to evade the enemy. Brigade size was considered suitable, and the 77th Indian Brigade was reorganized for the purpose. These 'Chindits' must be better jungle fighters than the Japanese, and they needed to comprise experts in such kinds of fighting, particularly experts in demolition and radio communication. They must also develop ground-and-air cooperation, as they would be dependent on supply by air; for that reason a small RAF section was attached to each column. Within the column, pack-animals would provide the transport.

Wingate pressed for an early operation, both to restore British morale by demonstrating their power to upset the enemy's morale, and as a test of the working of such Long-Range Penetration Groups. Wavell preferred that they should be used immediately before, and during, a British general offensive, but decided in response to Wingate's desire that an earlier experiment was worth risking because of the experience and the information that could be gained.

The Brigade comprised seven columns, and for the planned operation was divided into two groups – a Northern Group of five columns, totalling 2,200 men with 850 mules, and a Southern Group of two columns, totalling 1,000 men with 250 mules. The two groups crossed the Chindwin River on the night of February 14th, 1943, assisted by diverting actions on the part of the regular forces. Moving on eastward, the groups split up into their prearranged columns, and then carried out a series of attacks on Japanese outposts, as well as to cut railway lines, blow up bridges and create ambushes on the roads. In mid-March the columns crossed the Irrawaddy, a hundred miles east of the Chindwin. By then, however, the Japanese had awoken to the threat and deployed a large part of two divisions, of their five in Burma, to counter it. Under the counterpressure and other difficulties the columns were forced to withdraw, and by mid-April were back in India, having lost one-third of their strength and left behind most of their equipment.

The operation had little strategic effect, and Japanese casualties had been slight, but it did show that British and Indian troops could operate in the jungle, and it had provided useful experience in air supply, as well as the need for air superiority.

It also led General Mutagachi, Commander of the Japanese 15th Army, to recognize that he could not regard the Chindwin as a secure barrier, and that to forestall a British counteroffensive he would have to continue his own advance. Thereby it led to the Japanese advance across the Indian frontier in 1944, and the crucial battle of Imphal.

FUTURE PLANNING

A serious British offensive in the dry season of 1942-3 had been annulled by the combination of administrative difficulties and lack of resources. The main plan for the next dry season, of 1943-4, as decided at the Casablanca conference of January 1943, was intended to be a seaborne assault on Rangoon, called 'Operation Anakim', following British and Chinese offensives in the north of Burma and the capture of key-points on the coast. Those aims meant that air superiority had to be gained, and a strong naval force assembled, with ample landing craft – as well as the solution of the administrative and overland transport problems.

The difficulties of meeting all these requirements were, clearly, so great that in the spring of 1943 Wavell was inclined to turn away from Burma, and to favour a move against Sumatra as an indirect way of approach to the defeat of the Japanese. His talks with Churchill and the Chiefs of Staff on a visit to London in April convinced them that 'Operation Anakim' must be deferred or discarded, and in its place the Sumatra move was chosen – a move code-named 'Culverin'. This indirect move became attractive to Churchill, but it had to be abandoned in its turn for the same reasons that 'Anakim' had been given up, and also because of American insistence on the importance of reopening the land route of supply to China as soon as possible. Hence southern operations were shelved, although planning for them continued. If anything at all was to be done in this theatre of war, it would have to be in the north of Burma.

CHAPTER TWENTY-FOUR

The Battle of the Atlantic

The most critical period in the Battle of the Atlantic was during the second half of 1942 and the first half of 1943, but its long and fluctuating course was co-existent with the whole six years' course of the war. Indeed, it can be said to have started before the war itself, as the first ocean-going U-boats sailed from Germany to their war stations in the Atlantic on August 19th, 1939. By the end of that month, on the eve of the German invasion of Poland, seventeen were out in the Atlantic, while some fourteen coastal-type U-boats were out in the North Sea.

Despite their late start in rearming themselves with submarines, the Germans had a total strength of fifty-six (although ten were not fully operational) on the outbreak of war, which was only one less than that of the British Navy. Of these, thirty were 'North Sea Ducks', unsuitable for the Atlantic.

The first score achieved was the sinking of the outward-bound liner *Athenia* on the evening of September 3rd, the same day that Britain declared war, two days after the German invasion of Poland. It was actually torpedoed without warning, contrary to Hitler's specific order that submarine warfare was to be conducted only in accordance with The Hague Conventions; the U-boat commander justified his action by asserting his belief that the liner was an armed merchant cruiser. During the next few days several more ships were sunk.

Then on the 17th a more important success was gained when the aircraft-carrier *Courageous* was sunk by *U29* off the Western Approaches to the British Isles. Three days earlier the aircraft-carrier *Ark Royal* had had a narrow escape from *U39* – which, however, was promptly counterattacked and sunk by the escorting destroyers. The manifest risks led to the fleet aircraft-carriers being withdrawn from submarine-hunting.

U-boat attacks against merchant-shipping also had considerable success. A total of forty-one Allied and neutral ships, amounting to 154,000 tons, were sunk in the opening month, September, and by the end of the year the losses reached 114 ships, and over 420,000 tons.

Moreover in mid-October the *U47* under Lieutenant Prien had penetrated the fleet anchorage at Scapa Flow and sunk the battleship *Royal Oak*, causing the temporary abandonment of this main base until the defences were improved.

It is significant, however, that in November and December, merchant shipping losses were less than half what they had been the first two months, and more shipping had been lost to mines than to U-boats. Moreover, nine U-boats had been sunk – a sixth of the total strength. Air attacks on shipping had been a nuisance, but no worse.

During this early part of the war, the German Navy placed great hopes in its surface warships, and not only in its U-boats, but such hopes were not borne out by experience. On the outbreak of war the pocket-battleship *Admiral Graf Spee* was in position in mid-Atlantic, and her sister-ship *Deutschland* (later renamed *Lützow*) in the North Atlantic – although Hitler did not allow them to start attacks on British shipping until September 26th. Neither of them achieved much – and the *Graf Spee*, cornered in the mouth of the River Plate, was driven to scuttle herself in December. The new battle-cruisers *Gneisenau* and *Scharnhorst* made a brief sortie in November, but after sinking an armed merchant cruiser in the Iceland–Faeroes channel bolted for home. Allied ships were already sailing in convoy, after their experience in 1917–18, and although escorts were inadequate – and all too many ships still had none – they proved a remarkably effective deterrent.

After the fall of France in June 1940 the danger to Britain's shipping routes became much more severe. All ships passing south of Ireland were now exposed to German submarine, surface, and air attack. Except at great hazard, the only remaining route in and out was round the north of Ireland – the North-Western Approaches. Even that route could be reached, reported on, and bombed by the first of the German long-range aircraft, the four-engined Focke-Wulf 'Kondor' (the FW 200), operating from Stavanger in Norway and Merignac near Bordeaux. In November 1940 these long-range bombers sank eighteen ships, of 66,000 tons. Moreover the U-boats' toll had risen greatly – to a total sixty-three ships, amounting to over 350,000 tons, in the month of October.

The threat had become so serious that a large number of British warships were pulled back from anti-invasion duties and sent to the North-Western Approaches. Even so, surface and air escorts were perilously weak.

In June, the first month of the changed strategic situation, U-boat

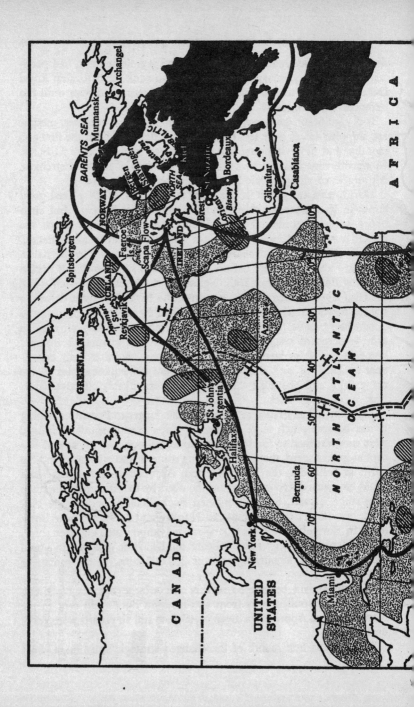

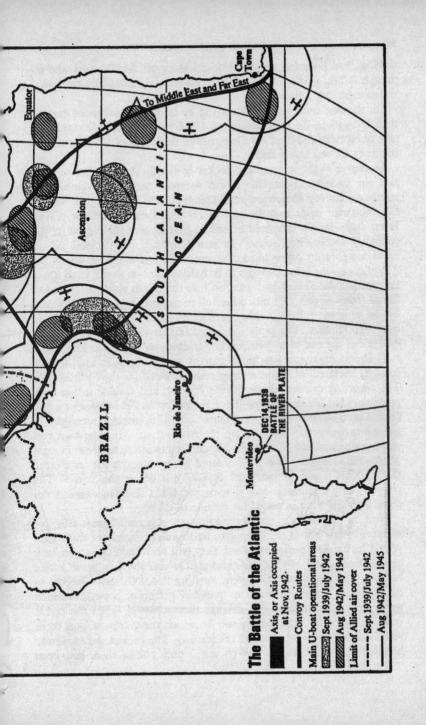

The Battle of the Atlantic

Axis, or Axis occupied at Nov. 1942.

Convoy Routes

Main U-boat operational areas

Sept 1939/July 1942

Aug 1942/May 1945

Limit of Allied air cover

Sept 1939/July 1942

Aug 1942/May 1945

Equator

To Middle East and Far East

Cape Town

SOUTH ATLANTIC OCEAN

Ascension

BRAZIL

Rio de Janeiro

Montevideo

DEC 14, 1939
BATTLE OF
THE RIVER PLATE

sinkings had bounded up to fifty-eight ships of 284,000 tons, and although falling a little in July, they averaged over 250,000 tons during the months that followed.

On the east coast route, minelaying by air had caused more damage than U-boats in the later months of 1939, and after the German invasion of Norway and the Low Countries in the spring of 1940 its menacing pressure was intensified.

Moreover in the autumn the pocket-battleship *Admiral Scheer* slipped out undetected into the North Atlantic, and on November 5th attacked a convoy homeward-bound from Halifax, Nova Scotia, sinking five merchant ships and the sole escort, the armed merchant cruiser *Jervis Bay* – which sacrificed herself in gaining time for the rest of the convoy to escape. The *Scheer*'s sudden appearance on this vital convoy route temporarily disorganized the entire flow of shipping across the Atlantic, causing other convoys to be held up for two weeks, until it was known that the *Scheer* had gone on into the South Atlantic. Here she found fewer targets, but raised her toll to sixteen ships, of 99,000 tons, by the time she returned safely to Kiel on April 1st after a 'cruise' of over 46,000 miles. The cruiser *Admiral Hipper* also broke out into the Atlantic at the end of November, but at dawn on Christmas Day had a rude shock when she attacked a convoy which she soon found to be strongly escorted, as it was a troop convoy bound for the Middle East. The escorting cruisers drove off the *Hipper*, and trouble in her own machinery led her to make for Brest. From here in February she made a second sortie, and was somewhat more successful, sinking seven ships in an unescorted group steaming up the African coast, but her own fuel was running low and her captain thus decided to return to Brest. In mid-March the German Naval Staff ordered her to return home for a more thorough refit, and she got back to Kiel just before the *Scheer*. The *Hipper*'s low endurance had shown that, apart from mechanical defects, her type was not suited for commerce raiding.

Next to the U-boats and minelaying, the Germans' most effective weapon in the war at sea proved to be disguised merchant ships converted for raiding purposes, which they had been sending out on long cruises since April 1940. By the end of that year the first 'wave' of six had sunk fifty-four merchantmen, totalling 366,000 tons – largely in distant seas. Their presence, or possible presence, caused as much worry and dislocation as the sinkings they achieved, while the threat was multiplied by the masterly way in which the Germans kept them refuelled and supplied at secret rendezvous. The raiders were skilfully handled and their targets well-chosen – only one of them had been brought to action, and that had escaped serious damage. Yet their captains, with one exception, had behaved humanely, allowing the crews of the ships attacked time to take to the boats, and treating their prisoners decently.

In the face of the manifold threat, above all that of U-boats in the Atlantic approaches to Britain, the Royal Navy's escort resources were heavily strained, and overstrained. From the French Atlantic ports – Brest, Lorient, and La Pallice near La Rochelle – U-boats were able to cruise as far as 25° West, whereas during the summer of 1940 the British could only provide escorts up to about 15° West, some 200 miles west of Ireland, and outward bound convoys then had to disperse, or steam on unescorted. Even in October, close escort was only extended to about 19° West – about 400 miles west of Ireland. Moreover, the usual escort was merely one armed merchant cruiser, and it was not until the end of the year that the average could be increased to two vessels. Only convoys to the Middle East were given more powerful protection.

Here it should be mentioned that Halifax in Nova Scotia was the main Western terminal for the Atlantic convoys, and that homeward-bound convoys – carrying supplies of food, oil, and munitions – were escorted by Canadian destroyers for the first 300–400 miles, after which the ocean escort took over, until the convoy reached the better-protected area of the Western Approaches.

Valuable aid towards meeting the escort problem came from the advent of the corvettes in the spring of 1940. These small vessels, of a mere 925 tons, were exhausting for the crews in rough weather, and suffered the handicap of not being fast enough to overtake, or even to keep up with, a U-boat on the surface, but they did most gallant work in escorting convoys in all weathers.

A larger aid came from the agreement which Churchill negotiated with President Roosevelt, in September, after two months' persuasive efforts, whereby fifty of the US Navy's old and surplus destroyers from World War I were obtained in exchange for a ninety-nine year lease of eight British bases on the far side of the Atlantic. Although these destroyers were obsolescent, and had to be fitted with the Asdic submarine-detecting device before they could be brought into use, they were soon able to make an important contribution to the escort problem and the anti-submarine campaign. Moreover the double transfer enabled the United States to prepare bases for the protection of its own seabound and coastal shipping, while taking the first of the steps which involved that great neutral country in the Battle of the Atlantic.

The coming of winter, and bad weather, naturally brought an increase of the difficulties of convoy, and convoy escorts, but also a diminution of German submarine activity. By July 1940 German figures show that U-boat strength had been increased 50 per cent since the start of the war, that twenty-seven had been destroyed, and fifty-one remained. By the following February the effective total fell to twenty-one. But with the French bases the Germans could keep more U-boats at sea out of a reduced smaller total strength, and could also use their smaller coastal-type U-boats on the ocean routes.

On the other hand, the Italian Navy's contribution to the struggle proved negligible. Although their submarines had begun to operate in the Atlantic from August on, and by November no less than twenty-six were out on the ocean, they achieved virtually nothing.

Although the pressure of the U-boat campaign diminished during the winter, mainly due to bad weather, it was renewed early in 1941, and at the same time multiplied by Admiral Dönitz's introduction of 'wolf-pack' tactics – by several U-boats working together, instead of individually. These new tactics had been introduced in October 1940, and were developed in the months that followed.

The way they operated was that, when the existence of a convoy had been approximately established, U-boat Command HQ ashore would warn the nearest U-boat group, which would send a submarine to find and shadow the convoy and 'home' the others onto it by wireless. When they were assembled on the scene, they would launch night attacks on the surface, preferably up-wind of the convoy, and continue these for several nights. During daylight the U-boats would withdraw well clear of the convoy and its escort. Attacking on the surface, they had an advantage in speed over most of the escorts. Night surface attacks had been made in World War I, and Dönitz himself had described in a book before the second war how he would do them.

These new tactics took the British unawares, as they had been thinking mainly of submerged attack, and pinned their faith to the Asdic device, the underwater detecting device, which had a range of about 1,500 yards. The Asdic could not detect U-boats that were operating on the surface like torpedo-boats near the convoy, and when these submarines were employed at night, escorts were virtually blindfolded. This German exploitation of the value of night attacks by surfaced U-boats thus nullified the British preparation for submarine warfare, and threw it off balance.

The best chance of countering the new tactics lay in early location of the shadowing U-boat, the 'contact-keeper', and driving it away. If the escort could make the U-boats dive, these would be handicapped, their periscopes being useless at night. A very important countermeasure to night attacks was the illumination of the sea. At first this was dependent on star-shell and rocket flares, but these were superseded by a more efficient illuminant known as 'snowflake', which went far towards turning darkness into daylight, while a powerful searchlight, called the Leigh Light after its inventor, was fitted in aircraft that were employed in convoy escorts and anti-submarine patrols. Still more important was the development of radar to supplement visual sighting. Along with new instrumental devices came more thorough training for escort vessels and escort groups and a marked improvement in the intelligence organization.

But all the improvements took time, and it was fortunate that the small number of U-boats at this period restricted the activity of the new 'wolf-packs'. Before the war Admiral Dönitz had estimated that if the British adopted a world-wide convoy system Germany would need 300 U-boats for decisive results, whereas in the spring of 1941 she had an operational strength of only a tenth of that scale.

That was the more fortunate because the commerce raids by other warships, and by aircraft, reached a new peak in March. The pocket-battleship *Scheer* and the battle-cruisers *Scharnhorst* and *Gneisenau* sank or captured seventeen ships, the long-range bombers sank forty-one, and the U-boats the same number – from all causes a total of 139 ships, and over half a million tons of shipping, destroyed.

After reaching Brest on March 22nd, however, the battle-cruisers were immobilized there, by damaging British air attacks on the port during April.

Just after the middle of May the new German battleship *Bismarck*, accompanied by the new cruiser *Prinz Eugen*, sailed out into the Atlantic to multiply the threat. British Intelligence worked well and warning of their presence in the Kattegat was received in London early on May 21st, while later the same day they were spotted by Coastal Command aircraft near Bergen. The battle-cruiser *Hood* and the battleship *Prince of Wales*, under Vice-Admiral L. Holland, at once sailed from Scapa Flow to intercept their expected passage round the north of Iceland, and next evening, after air reconnaissance had shown they were no longer in the Bergen area, the main fleet (under Admiral Tovey), also sailed from Scapa in the same direction. On the evening of the 23rd the two German ships were sighted, by the cruisers *Norfolk* and *Suffolk*, in the Denmark Strait – between the west of Iceland and the edge of the icefields east of Greenland. By that time Admiral Holland's force was close to the southerly end of the Strait.

On paper, this force had a big advantage, as the 42,000-ton *Hood* was nominally the largest ship in either Navy, and mounted eight 15-inch guns, while it was accompanied by the new battleship *Prince of Wales* (35,000 tons and ten 14-inch guns). But the *Hood*, built in 1920, before the Washington Treaty, had never been thoroughly modernized – the coming of war in 1939 had forestalled the Board of Admiralty's decision in March that year to give her better armour-protection, horizontal and vertical – and the *Prince of Wales* was so new that her armament had not been fully tested.* The German ships, although supposed to conform to the treaty limitations – 35,000 tons for battle-ships and 10,000 for heavy cruisers – actually displaced about 42,000 tons and 15,000 tons respectively, which enabled them to be given heavier armour-protection than appeared. Moreover their disadvantage in main armament – eight 15-inch guns in the *Bismarck* and eight 8-inch guns in the *Prinz Eugen* – was offset not only by defects in the guns of the *Prince of Wales* and superior range-finding equipment on the German side, but by the way the British ships came into action.

The Germans were sighted (in the twilight) at 5.35 AM, an hour before sunrise, and at 5.52 all four ships opened fire – at a range of about 25,000 yards (fourteen miles). On the British side the *Hood* was leading, and both the German ships concentrated their fire on her. Besides being the flagship, she was the most vulnerable, and particularly vulnerable to plunging fire – a reason for seeking to close the range as soon as possible. The approach was nearly end-on, so the British could not bring their after turrets to bear, whereas the Germans could use their entire broadsides. Their second or third salvo took effect, and such effect that at 6 AM the *Hood* blew up, and sank within a few minutes – only three of her crew of over 1,400 surviving. That was all too grimly reminiscent of the fate of the British battle-cruisers at Jutland a quarter of a century earlier.

The *Prince of Wales*, on which both German ships were now able to concentrate, also suffered from damaging hits from the *Bismarck*, as well as three from the *Prinz Eugen*, within a few minutes. So, at 6.13 AM the captain of the *Prince of Wales* wisely decided to break off the fight, and turned away under cover of a smokescreen. The range was now down to 14,600 yards. Rear-Admiral Wake-Walker, commanding the two cruisers – and now the whole force since Holland's death –

---

* There were, in fact, still some Clydeside workers on board.

confirmed the decision, and decided merely to keep touch with the enemy until the main fleet under Tovey arrived on the scene. This was now about 300 miles away, and the prospects of catching the Germans were not good, since the visibility became worse during the morning. It was thus a relief to Tovey when he heard in the early afternoon that the *Bismarck* had altered course and dropped its speed to about 24 knots.

For in the brief morning action the *Prince of Wales* had made two hits on the *Bismarck*, and one of these had caused an oil leak which reduced its fuel endurance, and led the German admiral, Lütjens, to make for a western French port, abandoning his raid into the Atlantic – and the alternative of turning back to Germany before the several British forces now converging towards the scene could intercept him.

That afternoon Tovey detached the 2nd Cruiser Squadron under Admiral Curteis and the aircraft-carrier *Victorious* – which had been about to start for the Mediterranean with a cargo of fighters – to proceed to a position within 100 miles of the *Bismarck* and near enough to launch the *Victorious*'s nine torpedo-bombers. These took off soon after 10 PM, in very bad weather, and had difficulty in finding the *Bismarck*, but eventually delivered successive attacks on her soon after midnight. One hit was achieved, but did no serious damage to the heavily armoured battleship. Moreover she managed to give her pursuers the slip early on the 25th, and the rest of that day was spent in fruitless efforts to find her again.

Not until 10.30 AM on the 26th was she spotted and reported, by a patrolling Catalina aircraft of Coastal Command, about 700 miles distant from Brest. Tovey's widely spread fleet was by then badly placed to catch her before she reached shelter, and was also running short of fuel. But Admiral Somerville's Force H, coming up from Gibraltar, was now close enough to intercept the *Bismarck*. Moreover this force included the large carrier *Ark Royal*. The first strike miscarried, but a second one, around 9 PM, was more successful. Two of the thirteen torpedoes released reached their mark. Although one hit was on the *Bismarck*'s armour belt and had little effect, the other, right aft, damaged her propeller, wrecked her steering gear, and jammed the rudders. That proved decisive.

While Captain Vian's destroyers held the ring, as well as making further torpedo attacks during the night, the battleships *King George V* and *Rodney* arrived on the scene, and pounded the crippled *Bismarck* with armour-piercing shell from their heavy guns for 1½ hours. By 10.15 she was a flaming shambles. On Tovey's order the British battleships then withdrew, before U-boats or the Luftwaffe's heavy bombers arrived to endanger them, leaving the cruisers to finish off the sinking ship. The *Dorsetshire* did this, with three torpedoes, and the *Bismarck* disappeared under the waves at 10.36.

Before the end came she had suffered, and survived, at least eight, and possibly twelve, torpedo hits, and many more heavy shell hits. That was a remarkable tribute to her designers.

The *Prinz Eugen* had left the *Bismarck* on the 24th, to refuel in mid-Atlantic, but after doing so she had developed engine defects, so her Captain had decided to abandon his excursion and make for Brest. Although her approach to that port was detected, she reached it safely on June 1st.

However, in the end these dramatic events of May 1941 marked the climax, and final defeat, of the German plans and efforts to win the Battle of the Atlantic with surface ships.

The U-boat campaign continued for a much longer time, and became a grave menace, although it ran a fluctuating course.

In May U-boat sinkings rose sharply and in June again reached the high figure of over 300,000 tons – to be exact, sixty-one ships of 310,000 tons. That was as many ships as there were in a single large convoy. It was remarkable that sailors were not deterred from manning them, and there was never a shortage of crews.

A number of important counteracting factors came into play, however, that spring. On March 11th the United States Lend-Lease Bill became law, and in that same month the American 'Atlantic Fleet Support Group', of destroyers and flying-boats, was formed. In April, the American 'Security Zone', patrolled by US Navy forces, was extended eastward from 60° to 26° West.

Also in March, American air bases were opened on the east coast of Greenland, and installations in Bermuda, while in May the US Navy took over the leased base at Argentia in the south-east of Newfoundland. Early in July US Marines relieved the British garrison at Reykjavik in Iceland, and from then on US naval forces protected American shipping to and from Iceland. American 'neutrality' in the Atlantic was becoming markedly less neutral. The refitting of British ships in American yards had already been approved in April, while the building of warships and merchant-ships on Lend-Lease account had started.

Meanwhile Canada was becoming more strongly a relief to Britain in the Atlantic struggle. A Canadian Escort Force was created in June, and based on St John's, Newfoundland. The Royal Canadian Navy now took the responsibility for ocean anti-submarine escort eastwards to a rendezvous south of Iceland. Thus the British Admiralty's plans for continuous escort became possible.

In the summer of 1941, Canadian and British escorts met and handed over their convoys to one another at the Mid-Ocean Meeting Point in about 35° West. The Iceland escorts and the Western Approaches escorts met, and handed over at the Eastern Ocean Meeting Point in about 18° West.

From July onwards, too, a close escort group accompanied Gibraltar convoys the whole way there, and continuous escort, down the West African coast, was also given to the Sierra Leone convoys.

Convoys now could be provided with an average of five escort vessels. A convoy of forty-five ships had a perimeter of over thirty miles to protect. Even so, each escort vessel's Asdic would only sweep an arc of a mile – so there were still wide gaps through which a U-boat could penetrate without being detected.

As to air cover, the addition of Lend-Lease Catalina flying-boats from the spring onward extended such cover to some 700 miles from the British Isles (forcing the U-boats away from Western Approaches) 600 miles from Canada, and 400 miles to the south of Iceland. But a gap about 300 miles wide remained in mid-Atlantic, and the very long-range American Liberators, which could have covered it, were not regularly available until the end of March 1943, and by mid-April only forty-one were in service.

Meanwhile, the number of U-boats was increasing. By July 1941, sixty-five were operational and in October eighty. The total U-boat strength on September 1st was 198 – while forty-seven had been lost so far. In sum, new U-boats were entering service much faster than they were being sunk. Moreover U-boats were being made stronger. Their welded pressure hulls were proving more difficult to break than the British plated and riveted hulls and a depth-charge had to explode much closer than before for a kill.

During September four convoys suffered heavy losses – all of these lacking adequate air cover.

That month, however, following an August meeting between Roosevelt and Churchill, cooperation between the two navies was increased still more by the President's approval of the well-planned American 'Western Hemisphere Defence Plan Number 4'. Under this the US Navy was permitted to escort convoys of non-American ships, and started to provide escorts for certain Atlantic convoys eastwards as far as the Mid-Ocean Meeting Point, while this Meeting Point was moved eastwards to about 22° West.

This helped to ease the British problem of providing adequate escorts between the British Isles and the Mid-Ocean Meeting Point. By the end of the year they had been increased to eight groups, each of three destroyers and about six corvettes. A further eleven groups, each of five destroyers, were nominally in reserve to reinforce the escort of any convoy that might be in trouble, or to deal with the U-boat concentrations, but were largely occupied with routine tasks.

In October U-boat sinkings fell to thirty-two ships of 156,000 tons. Significantly no ships were sunk within 400 miles of a Coastal Command base. That showed the reluctance of U-boats to enter zones covered by long-range reconnaissance and bomber aircraft, although the drop was also due in part to the dispatch of U-boats to the Mediterranean to support Rommel's operations in North Africa.

In November, U-boat sinkings fell again – to little more than a third of the October total – and in December they were smaller still in the North Atlantic. But the heavy losses in the Far East that followed Japan's entry into the war raised the total sinkings from all causes to 282 ships of nearly 600,000 tons.

In the West, the German long-range bombers had become a greater menace than U-boats during the second half of 1941, especially to the Gibraltar convoys. This led to a realization of the need for fighters in close support of any convoy, and thus to the introduction of the first escort carrier, HMS *Audacity*, in June. She played a key part in the successful defence of a homeward-bound Gibraltar convoy in December, although herself sunk in the nine-day fight.

At the end of that year the total of operational U-boats was eighty-six, and about 150 more were in training or running trials. But as fifty were now in the Mediterranean or its approaches, only thirty-six were left for use in the North Atlantic. A sweep for supply ships there in June had resulted in nine being intercepted, and to the withdrawal of U-boats from the South Atlantic. During the nine months April to December 1941 the total German and Italian submarine sinkings had been 328 ships of 1,576,000 tons, but only one-third of these had been sailing in convoy. Moreover twenty of the thirty submarines lost had been destroyed by convoy escorts. It was clear that stronger escorting, and evasive routing, had temporarily gained the upper hand over the U-boats.

It may be useful to give here a summary of the escort situation at the beginning of 1942. The three great operational bases of the Western

Approaches Command under Admiral Sir Percy Noble were Liverpool, Greenock and Londonderry, and controlled twenty-five escort groups – totalling about seventy destroyers and ninety-five smaller craft.

They were in four categories: (i) short-endurance destroyers for Middle East and Arctic convoys on the first part of their passage, and for the liners when they started bringing American troops across; (ii) long-distance destroyers and corvettes for the North Atlantic convoys, from the Western Ocean Meeting Point to Britain, and for the Gibraltar convoys; (iii) long-range sloops, destroyers, and cutters for the Sierra Leone convoys on the main part of their journey; (iv) anti-aircraft groups to back up escort of convoys within reach of German bombers, and for the Arctic and Gibraltar convoys.

There were also the equivalent of two groups at Gibraltar for local escort, and the Freetown Escort Force of one destroyer flotilla and about two dozen corvettes. The Newfoundland Escort Force, provided mainly by the Canadian Navy, had fourteen destroyers and about forty corvettes, as well as a score of other vessels for local escort.

But the improving prospect in the Battle of the Atlantic suffered bad handicaps in the early part of 1942. One was a lack of aircraft. On taking over Coastal Command in the previous summer, Sir Philip Joubert de la Ferté had assessed its needs as approximately 800 aircraft of all types, and particularly emphasized the importance of long-range bombers. But in the New Year, Coastal Command's bombers were transferred to Bomber Command, and all the new ones allotted to it, for the air offensive against Germany. The clash of priorities became intense. Moreover the Fleet Air Arm was having difficulties in obtaining fighters for the thirty-one new escort carriers that had been ordered.

Another handicap was that the new frigates that were being built in America for the British were not entering service as fast as was hoped – largely because priority was being given to the landing-craft needed for a cross-Channel operation, which the Americans still hoped to launch in 1943, if not in 1942. This priority contributed greatly to the continuing weakness of British Atlantic efforts, and to the further heavy shipping losses.

A third handicap came in the early months of 1942 from America's own maritime troubles – troubles which came not only in the Pacific, from the Pearl Harbor disaster, but also in the Atlantic, from the extension of U-boat activities and America's own consequent shipping losses.

Admiral Dönitz and his staff estimated in May 1942 that to defeat Britain their sinkings must average 700,000 tons a month. They knew that in 1941 these had not reached such an average – although they did not know that the monthly average had actually been no more than 180,000 tons. But they had thought that America's entry into the war would give them increased freedom of action in the Western Atlantic, and more opportunity of finding unescorted targets.

Only a small number of U-boats could be sent to operate off the American coast, but these achieved disproportionately large results. For the American admirals were slow, and reluctant, to start convoys – as the British admirals had been in the First World War. The Americans were also slow to take other precautions. Lighted channel markers and the unrestricted use of ship's radio gave the U-boats all the help they wanted. Coastal resorts, such as Miami, continued to illuminate their sea-fronts at night with miles of neon-lighted beaches – against which the shipping was clearly silhouetted. The U-boats lay submerged off-shore during the day, and moved in to attack, with guns or torpedoes, on the surface at night time.

Although there were never more than about a dozen U-boats operating off the American coast, they sank nearly half a million tons of shipping by the beginning of April – and 57 per cent consisted of tankers.

The reaction on Britain's situation was serious. The United States Navy was having to withdraw its escort vessels and aircraft to its own coastal waters, and British merchant ships, after surviving the crossing of the Atlantic, became an easy prey in American waters.

Admiral Dönitz was so encouraged by the results that he wanted to send every U-boat he could to the American seaboard. Fortunately for the Allies, Hitler's 'intuition' came to their aid at this critical moment. At his conference on January 22nd he announced his conviction that Norway was 'the zone of destiny' and insisted that every surface war-ship and U-boat available should be sent thither to ward off an Allied invasion. Three days later Dönitz received a completely unexpected order to dispatch an initial batch of eight U-boats to cover the sea approaches to that country. The new battleship *Tirpitz* was also moved to Norway in January, and was followed by the *Scheer*, *Prinz Eugen*, *Hipper*, and *Lützow*.

There was something in his foresight, as in April Churchill did tell the British Chiefs of Staff to examine the feasibility of a landing in Norway, with the aim of relieving German pressure on the Arctic con-voys – but their doubts were reinforced by the Americans, and the project never matured.

Another piece of good fortune for the Allies was that the severe winter of 1941–2 delayed U-boat training in the Baltic, with the effect that only sixty-nine submarines in all were made ready for operations in the first half of 1942. Of these, twenty-six were eventually sent to northern Norway, two to the Mediterranean, and twelve replaced losses, so that the net gain in the Atlantic was only twenty-nine.

Even as it was, Axis submarine sinkings increased monthly – in February to nearly 500,000 tons, in March to over 500,000 tons; in April there was a drop to 430,000 tons, but in May 600,000 tons and in June sinkings reached the ominous figure of 700,000 tons. By the end of June the toll for the half-year was over 3 million tons out of 4,147,406 tons sunk from all causes – of which nearly 90 per cent was in the Atlantic and Arctic. It was not until July that the monthly loss from submarines fell to just under 500,000 tons, thanks to an all-round improvement in anti-submarine methods, and the American adoption of convoy.

The improvement in the summer of 1942 proved illusory. By August the advent of freshly built U-boats had raised the total strength to over 300, and of the total about half was operational. It comprised groups off Greenland, off the Canadian coast, off the Azores, off North-west Africa, in or near the Caribbean, and off Brazil. Sinkings by U-boats in August went above the 500,000 tons mark again. In the next few months they made a particularly large bag near Trinidad, where many ships were still travelling independently. A more dubious action, politically and in terms of grand strategy, was the sinking of five Brazilian ships in mid-August, which led to a prompt declaration of war by Brazil. The use of Brazilian bases enabled the Allies to exercise much stronger control of the whole South Atlantic, and drive out surface raiders from then on.

That, however, mattered less than it would have earlier, as the place of the German armed merchant ship for commerce raiding in the far oceans was being taken over by new and larger U-boats – the so-called 'U-cruisers' of 1,600 tons, whose radius of action was 30,000 miles.

U-boats were now able to dive much deeper, to depths of 600 feet, or even more in emergency – an advantage that was soon offset, however, by the fact that depth-charges were being set to explode at greater depths – as well as being produced in greater quantity. The U-boats were also benefiting from the way that the new U-tankers could refuel them on the oceans, and from increasingly efficient wireless Intelligence. Moreover the Germans were now able to read many of the British ciphered convoy control signals again, as they had done up to August 1940.

On the other side, the new 10-centimetre radar set – which the U-boats could not intercept – was paramount among all the achievements of British scientists. When it came into full use in aircraft early in 1943, in conjunction with the Leigh Light, it restored the Allied initiative by night or in low visibility, and defeated the U-boats' radar search receivers working on $1\frac{1}{2}$ metres.

Dönitz's war diary for this period shows how worried he was about the effect of this new British location device, as well as about the increased number of British aircraft in the Eastern Atlantic.

Throughout the campaign Dönitz had shown himself a very able strategist, always probing for the soft spots and concentrating to strike when the defence was weak. He had held the initiative from the outset, and the Allied anti-submarine forces were always a stage behind.

In the second half of 1942 his plan focused on the air escort gap south of Greenland, aiming to locate Allied convoys before they reached it, to concentrate against them while they traversed it, and to withdraw when air cover was resumed.

Moreover by the autumn Dönitz had sufficient U-boats to allow a 'pack' to strike on its own initiative whenever opportunity offered.

Thus U-boat pressure increased from July on, and in November sinkings rose to 119 ships of 729,000 tons. A large proportion, however, were caught by U-boats when sailing independently, out of convoy, off South Africa or South America.

The call for escorts was increased by the naval requirements of 'Operation Torch', the American–British landings in North-west Africa, which was carried out that autumn. The Gibraltar, Sierra Leone, and Arctic convoys had to be temporarily suspended. There was also fresh demand for escorts to the troopship convoys carrying American troops from Iceland to Britain. These fast convoys had at least four destroyers to escort three troopships.

An exception to the demand for escort was provided by the conversion of the two giant 80,000-ton liners *Queen Mary* and *Queen Elizabeth* into troopships, with a carrying capacity of 15,000 men and more – the major part of a division. Their speed, over 28 knots, was too high for any destroyers to accompany them except at the start and finish of their voyages, so it was on speed alone, combined with zigzagging and ever-changing routes, that such giant liners depended for their safety. The hazardous policy succeeded so well that no submarine ever managed to intercept them on their many transatlantic journeys from August onward.

In general, the provision of naval escorts and air cover did not, and could not, keep up with the increasing menace from the output of U-boats. Of these an average of about seventeen had entered the service each month, and at the end of 1942 there were 212 operational, out of a total of 393 – compared with ninety-one operational, out of 249, at the start of the year. The number destroyed was eighty-seven German, and twenty-two Italian – a total quite insufficient to offset the construction rate.

During the year Axis submarines had sunk, in all waters, 1,160 ships totalling 6,266,000 tons – while the enemy's other weapons had raised the total loss to 1,664 ships and over 7,790,000 tons.

Although about 7 million tons of new Allied shipping was put into service, even that left a further deficit of nearly a million tons to the adverse balance shown in each year's accounts since the outbreak of war. British imports during the year fell below 34 million tons – one-third less than the figure in 1939. In particular, stocks of commercial bunker fuel in Britain had fallen precariously low – only 300,000 tons, compared with a monthly consumption of 130,000 tons. Although it could be eked out from the Navy's reserve stocks, that was a course to be avoided save in grave emergency.

Thus when the Allied Conference assembled at Casablanca, on the Moroccan coast, in January 1943, to settle the next steps in Allied strategy, it was faced with a very disturbing balance-sheet of mercantile tonnage. Until the U-boat menace was overcome, and the Battle of the Atlantic won, an effective invasion of Europe was not practicable. That battle had become as crucial as the Battle of Britain in 1940. The issue depended, basically, on which side could endure the longer, materially and psychologically.

The course of the struggle was affected by changes of command. In November, Admiral Sir Percy Noble was appointed head of the British Naval Mission in Washington, and thus became the First Sea Lord's representative on the American side of the Combined Chiefs of Staff organization. During his twenty months' tenure as C-in-C of the Western Approaches he had done much to improve the anti-submarine measures, and to keep up morale among the escort and aircraft crews by the understanding he showed of their problems and the close personal touch he established. His successor, fortunately, was well chosen. This was Admiral Sir Max Horton, who had been an outstanding submarine commander in World War I, and in command of Britain's home-based submarines since early 1940. He brought an expert knowledge of submarines, and submariners, to the anti-submarine campaign, coupled with driving energy and imagination. This combination of qualities made him a fit man to match Dönitz.

Horton's plan was to develop a more powerful and concentrated counterattack on the U-boats. The corvettes and other small craft had not got the speed sufficient to follow through in their fights with U-boats, for if they pursued them far they could not catch up with the convoys they were escorting. More destroyers and frigates were needed, working separately, to come to the aid of convoy escorts and, after making contact with the U-boats, hunt them to the death. Support groups for this purpose had already begun to be formed in September, but Horton at once developed them intensively, and even reduced the strength of the close-escort groups in order to do so. He aimed to surprise the enemy in mid-Atlantic with a coordinated counterattack by several of the new support groups and carrier-borne aircraft, working in cooperation with the escorts and with very long-range aircraft. He emphasized that the support groups should not waste time searching widely for the U-boats – the mistake in the past. The place to find them was near the convoys, and the support groups should work closely with the convoy escort groups. Each of these while in the Greenland air gap was to be reinforced by a support group, and whenever possible by aircraft. He reckoned that the U-boats, accustomed to being attacked from the direction of the convoy, would be thrown off balance when the support groups came in attacking from all quarters.

On the German side Hitler was enraged by the ineffective result of a New Year's Eve attack on an Arctic convoy by the *Hipper, Lützow* and six destroyers, emerging from Altenfiord, and this had important effects. In his disgust he expressed his 'firm and unalterable resolve' to pay off his big ships. This brought about the resignation of Grand Admiral Raeder a month later, and his replacement, as Naval Commander-in-Chief, by Dönitz – who at the same time retained his title and office as Commander, U-boats. Dönitz had a better knack of handling Hitler, and in the end obtained Hitler's agreement to the retention of the *Tirpitz, Lützow,* and *Scharnhorst* in Norway as 'a fairly powerful task force'.

There was a lull in the Atlantic during December and January, when U-boat sinkings fell to barely 200,000 tons. That was largely due to stormy weather. But the respite was offset by the dispersing effect and havoc caused to the merchant ships in convoy, especially the more weakly powered ones.

In February the U-boat sinkings were almost doubled, while in March they amounted to 108 ships of 627,000 tons – thus approaching once again the peak figures of June and November 1942. Most worryingly, nearly two-thirds were sunk in convoy. In the middle of March thirty-eight U-boats were concentrated on two homeward-bound convoys, which happened to be close together, and sank twenty-one ships of 141,000 tons, for a loss of only one U-boat, before air cover was resumed on the 20th. This was one of the biggest convoy battles of the whole war.

In retrospect, the Admiralty recorded that 'the Germans never came so near to disrupting communication between the New World and the Old as in the first twenty days of March, 1943'. Moreover, the Naval Staff was brought to the point of wondering whether convoy could continue to be regarded, and used, as an effective system of defence.

But in the last eleven days of March – the last third of that fateful month – a great change came over the scene. Only fifteen ships were sunk in the North Atlantic compared with 107 in the first two-thirds. In April the month's toll was halved, and in May it was much less still. Max Horton's coordinated counteroffensive had come into effect – and fulfilled its desired effect in a remarkably short time.

The Americans, at the most critical time in March, had asked to withdraw from the North Atlantic escort system, taking responsibility for the South Atlantic routes, particularly to the Mediterranean. They also had the Pacific much in mind. However, the practical effect was not great. The US Government put the first support group carrier under British Command and provided the vital VLR (very long range) Liberators. So from April 1st, Britain and Canada had taken complete charge of all convoys between the American continent and Britain.

During the spring of 1943, the U-boats met defeat in a series of convoy battles, and suffered heavy losses in them. In mid-May Dönitz perceptively reported to Hitler: 'We are facing the greatest crisis in submarine warfare, since the enemy, by means of new location devices ... makes fighting impossible, and is causing us heavy losses.' For U-boat losses in May had more than doubled, rising to 30 per cent of those at sea – a rate of loss that could not be borne for long. Hence on May 23rd Dönitz withdrew his U-boats from the North Atlantic until he had new weapons to use.

By July, more Allied merchant ships were being built than were being sunk. That was the crux of the matter and the proof that the U-boat offensive had been defeated.

Yet, looking back, it is evident that Britain had herself narrowly escaped defeat in March. It is also evident that the primary cause of her danger was the lack of long-range aircraft for the protection of convoys. From January to May, only two ships were sunk in convoy, in the Atlantic, while an air escort was present. Once adequate air cover of this kind was provided for convoys, particularly by the long-range Liberators, it became increasingly difficult for U-boats to operate in 'wolf-packs'. They might now at any moment suddenly find an aircraft over them, directing a support group to their position.

But radar, on the new 10-cm wavelength that the U-boats could not intercept, was certainly a very important factor, as Dönitz realized and emphasized. New weapons such as the 'Hedgehog', an anti-submarine rocket device, and heavier depth-charges, also contributed. So did the analytical work of the Western Approaches Tactical Unit set up early in 1942 to evolve the best tactical system for dealing with U-boats, and Professor P. M. S. Blackett's operational analysis of convoy deployment. Moreover a new cipher, for shipping control, introduced at the end of May 1943, deprived the Germans of their most valuable source of Intelligence.

Probably the most important factors in the victory, however, were the improvement in training standards of the escorts and aircraft, and the increased cooperation between sailors and airmen.

Among individuals, the outstanding part in the defeat of the U-boats was played by Admiral Sir Max Horton, as already emphasized. Much was also due to Air Marshal Sir John Slessor, who became Commander-in-Chief of Coastal Command in February 1943, the crucial period of the battle. Among the fine band of escort group commanders, two deserve special mention for their exploits – Captain F. J. Walker, from 1941 on, and Commander P. W. (later Vice Admiral Sir Peter) Gretton in 1942–3.

No convoys were attacked in the North Atlantic during the month of June 1943, while July was very costly for the U-boats, particularly in the Bay of Biscay, where Coastal Command's air patrols had a rich harvest. Of eighty-six U-boats which tried to cross the Bay that month, fifty-five were sighted, seventeen were sunk (all save one by aircraft), and six forced to turn back. Their only outward route had become a narrow line in the Bay of Biscay, hugging the Spanish coast, as Dönitz gloomily reported to Hitler. The anti-submarine patrols, however, paid a considerable price for their successes, fourteen planes being lost.

During the three months June to August 1943, the German U-boats sank no more than fifty-eight Allied merchant ships in all waters excluding the Mediterranean, and nearly half of them were off South Africa and in the Indian Ocean. They gained that very moderate result at a cost of seventy-nine U-boats – of which no less than fifty-eight were sunk by aircraft.

In the hope of regaining the upper hand, Dönitz pressed Hitler for more long-range air reconnaissance in the Atlantic and stronger air cover on the transit routes – and did get a more sympathetic hearing than Raeder had for his arguments towards overcoming Göring's unwillingness to provide air cooperation. Dönitz also obtained approval to increase U-boat production from thirty to forty a month, and to give priority to new types of submarine which would be capable of higher speed when submerged. But the very promising 'Walter' type submarine, driven by a combination of diesel fuel and hydrogen peroxide, suffered so many 'teething' troubles that none was ready for service before the war ended in 1945. A new and important development, however, came with the fitting of the 'Schnorkel' air intake and diesel exhaust mast, a device of pre-1940 Dutch origin, that enabled submarines to charge their batteries while remaining at periscope depth. Thirty of them were fitted with it by the middle of 1944.

Two other new German devices of the mid-1943 period were the 'homing' torpedo, acoustically guided to ships' propellers, and the glider bomb. But during September and October, the first two months of the renewed U-boat campaign, the Allies lost only nine merchant ships – out of the 2,468 which sailed in sixty-four North Atlantic convoys – whereas twenty-five U-boats were sunk. After that further heavy defeat Dönitz gave up working the U-boats in large mobile groups.

On October 8th Britain took over two air bases in the Azores, by agreement with Portugal, and from then onward air cover could be provided over the whole North Atlantic.

In the first three months of 1944 the U-boats suffered still worse losses. Only three merchant ships were sunk – out of 3,360 which crossed the North Atlantic, in 105 convoys – whereas thirty-six U-boats were lost. Dönitz now cancelled all further operations against convoys, telling Hitler that they could not be renewed until the new types of U-boat and new defensive devices were available, and better air reconnaissance provided.

At the end of March, 1944, Dönitz was ordered to form a group of forty U-boats for inshore operations in the event of an Allied invasion of Western Europe. By the end of May he had concentrated seventy in Biscay ports, and only three remained in the North Atlantic, while these were merely kept on the task of weather reporting.

The German abandonment of the U-boat campaign in the North Atlantic was a relief to Coastal Command, whose aircraft, of No. 19 Group, had sunk fifty U-boats and damaged fifty-six (out of 2,425 passages in and out from the Biscay bases) by May 1944, during forty-one months of anti-submarine operations. No. 19 Group had lost 350 aircraft in the Bay during that period. Its losses would probably have been less, and its effect even greater, if Coastal Command had been allotted a larger scale of aircraft, more appropriate to the key importance of its task.

Among other events of the period were two damaging attacks on the *Tirpitz* at her moorings in northern Norway – by three midget-submarines in September, 1943, and by the Fleet Air Arm in March 1944 – which preceded her eventual sinking by RAF heavy bombers in November that year. She had only once fired her main armament in earnest (in a raid on Spitzbergen), but the amount of damage she survived was testimony to the design and strength of German naval construction. Moreover, her mere existence as a 'ship in being', and threat in the offing, had a great influence on Britain's maritime strategy, while absorbing a remarkably large amount of her naval strength.

The threat of the *Scharnhorst* had been brought to an end in the previous December, when she was intercepted and sunk by a strong force from the British Home Fleet, when herself attempting to intercept an Arctic convoy.

During the first half of 1944, Britain's chief trouble in home waters came from the small motor torpedo-boats, called 'E-boats', which the Germans had developed. Although their number was never more than about three dozen, they could be switched rapidly from one convoy route to another and, by choosing suitable opportunities, became a harassing nuisance.

The U-boats that had been concentrated in the western ports of France to oppose an Allied cross-Channel move proved of little effect, although they benefited from having been fitted with the Schnorkel device by the time the Normandy invasion came in June, and were thus less vulnerable to air attack.

When the American Third Army, breaking out from Normandy, arrived close to these western ports – Brest, Lorient, and St Nazaire – in mid-August, most of the U-boats were moved to Norway. And from then shipping to and from Britain could again use the old, and normal, route round the south of Ireland, as well as the route round the north coast.

From the later part of August onward, a stream of U-boats started to come out from Norway, and Germany, by passing round the north of Scotland and Ireland, and positioned themselves close inshore, at busy corners – as far south as Portland Bill on the south coast of England. But they achieved little by this inshore campaign – although, thanks to constant submergence and use of their Schnorkels they suffered fewer losses than before. During the four months September–December 1944, they sank only fourteen ships in British coastal waters.

THE ARCTIC CONVOYS

British convoys to North Russia were started at the end of September, 1941. Ice blocked Archangel in the winter, so Murmansk was used, Russia's only important ice-free port. The Germans' failure to capture that port by a strong overland move was a strange strategic omission as it lost them the chance to strangle this northern supply-route when it was most vulnerable.

As the Germans came to realize the large scale on which British, and then also American, ships were carrying aid to Russia by this route, they hastened to reinforce their naval and air strength in Norway, and developed a series of powerful attacks on the Allies' Arctic convoys in March, April, and May, 1942. The worst hit was eastbound convoy PQ 17, sailing at the end of June. The Admiralty, believing that the convoy and its escort were about to be overwhelmed by German warships, ordered the convoy to scatter in the Barents Sea on July 4th. The helpless merchant ships were attacked by aircraft and U-boats, only thirteen out of thirty-six surviving. Of the aircraft which this convoy was carrying eighty-seven were delivered, but 210 lost; of the tanks 164 were delivered, but 430 lost: of non-fighting vehicles 896 were delivered, but 3,350 lost – along with two-thirds of the other cargo, some 99,316 tons.

After that disaster, the next convoy to Russia was not dispatched until September. It was given a much stronger escort and Admiral Raeder, warned by radio intelligence, cautiously held back his larger warships – which might have overwhelmed the escorts. As it was, twenty-seven of PQ 18's forty merchant ships got safely through to Archangel, while the German aircraft and U-boats suffered badly. Never again did the Germans deploy such great air strength in the far north.

After another interval, a few smaller convoys were sent in the winter. But the Russians, while repeatedly pressing for more convoys to be run, gave no help in protecting them on the long ocean passage and only a little at the receiving end. From March 1943 onward the C-in-C, Home Fleet, Admiral Tovey, was unwilling to risk further convoys as the daylight lengthened. The critical situation in the Atlantic decided the argument, and the Arctic escorts were diverted to the Atlantic, where they played a great part in the decisive defeat of the U-boats that spring.

By November, when the Arctic convoys were resumed, much stronger escorts were available, and included the new escort carriers. These inflicted heavy loss on the weakening Luftwaffe as well as on the U-boats, while bringing huge cargoes safely through to Russia.

In the forty outward Arctic convoys from 1941 on, 811 ships sailed, of which fifty-eight were sunk and thirty-three turned back for one reason or another, while 720 came safely through – and delivered about four million tons of cargo to Russia. The deliveries included 5,000 tanks and over 7,000 aircraft. In delivering that large-scale aid the Allies had lost eighteen warships and ninety-eight merchant ships, including those on the homeward convoys, while the Germans had lost the battle-cruiser *Scharnhorst*, three destroyers, and thirty-eight U-boats in trying to stop it.

THE LAST PHASE

During the early months of 1945 the size of the U-boat fleet was still increasing – through new production and reduced losses, thanks to the Schnorkel device as well as to the suspension of long-range operations in the Atlantic. In January, thirty new boats were put into service, compared with the recent monthly average of eighteen. Some of them were of the new and improved models with longer cruising range and higher speed when submerged – the ocean-going Type XXI of 1,600 tons, and the coastal Type XXIII of 230 tons (of which about two-thirds were of the larger type). In March, the U-boat fleet reached its peak strength, a total of 463.

It was not until March that the bombing campaign began to have a serious effect on production. Fortunately for the Allies the air minelaying in the Baltic, although it did little material damage compared with the effort, had an important effect – more than was realized by their naval chiefs – in hindering U-boat trials and training, and thus the operational advent of the new submarine types in large numbers. If the new types had ever got to sea in strength they might have revived the U-boat menace as dangerously as in 1943.

But once the Allied armies crossed the Rhine in March, closing on

Berlin in conjunction with the Russian advance from the east, all forms of pressure could be, and were, intensified – with crippling effect.

During the last few weeks of the war, the U-boats' activity was mainly off the east and north-east coasts of Britain. Although they achieved little, it is significant that none of the new types was ever sunk in these waters.

After Germany's capitulation in May, 159 U-boats surrendered, but a further 203 were scuttled by their crews. That was characteristic of the U-boat crews' stubborn pride and unshaken morale.

During the 5½ years of war, the Germans had built and commissioned 1,157 U-boats and fifteen ex-foreign submarines were taken over by them: 789 (including 3 ex-foreign) had been lost. They had also commissioned some 700 midget submarines. By far the largest proportion of those sunk *at sea* – 500 out of 632 – were destroyed by British or British-controlled forces. On the other side, submarines – German, Italian, and Japanese – sank 2,828 ships, totalling nearly 15 million tons. Much the greatest proportion of that huge total was sunk by the Germans – whose U-boats also sank 175 Allied warships, most of them British. Of the Allied losses to U-boats, 61 per cent of the total was made up of ships sailing independently of convoys, 9 per cent was of stragglers from convoys, and only 30 per cent came from ships in convoy – and very few were lost in convoy when air cover was available.

The Germans' possession of the French naval bases on the Bay of Biscay, for four years, and Eire's refusal to allow the Allies use of her western and southern coastlines, even though she herself depended largely upon the supplies the convoys brought her, contributed immensely to the Allied losses in the Atlantic. And it was largely the Allies' hold on Northern Ireland and Iceland that kept open the one remaining route to Britain.

PART VI

THE EBB
1943

CHAPTER TWENTY-FIVE

The Clearance of Africa

The first consequence of the Allied failure to capture Tunis in December 1942 was the abandonment of the original idea of trapping Rommel between the pursuing British Eighth Army and the new First Army in Tunisia pushing eastward to meet it.* The two armies would now for a time have to deal separately with the respective forces of Rommel in Tripolitania and Arnim in Tunisia, while these, as Rommel's drew nearer to Arnim's, would enjoy the strategic advantage of a central position – enabling them to switch their combined weight against one or other of their assailants.

When checked before Tunis at Christmas, and faced with the prospect of continued mud there until the rainy season ended, Eisenhower sought to develop a more southerly thrust to reach the coast near Sfax, thus blocking Rommel's line of supply and retreat. For this 'Operation Satin' he planned to use mainly American troops, concentrating them around Tebessa to form what was entitled the US 2nd Corps (Major-General Fredendall). But when he reported his intention to the Combined Chiefs of Staff – who came along with Roosevelt and Churchill to Africa in mid-January for a fresh Allied Conference at Casablanca, to settle future aims – the riskiness of such a thrust by raw troops into an area where Rommel's veterans might soon be arriving was emphasized in discussion of Eisenhower's new plan – particularly by General Alan Brooke – and he was moved to cancel it.

That decision left the next move to Montgomery, who had paused near Nofilia in mid-December to build up his strength before attacking the Buerat position, 140 miles west, to which Rommel had withdrawn the remnant of his army in the previous stage of his long retreat from Egypt.

Montgomery launched his fresh offensive in mid-January. It was planned on the same pattern as before – a pinning attack on the enemy's front combined with an outflanking manoeuvre through the desert interior to close the way of retreat. This time, however, he eschewed any

* For map, see p 292.

preliminary probing that would show his intention and 'scare the enemy off his present line'. Moreover, only an armoured-car screen was used to watch the enemy's position, and the main bodies of Montgomery's force were held far back until the day before the attack, and then started on a long approach march from which they went straight into action, on the morning of the 15th. The 51st Division with armoured support attacked along the coast road, while the 7th Armoured and the New Zealand Divisions carried out the planned manoeuvre. But no opposition was encountered at first, and when it was met west of Buerat it came only from rearguards. Rommel had slipped away from the Buerat position and, once again, out of the intended trap. That proved the easier because, as Alexander's Despatch remarked in gentle rebuke, 'the New Zealanders and the 7th Armoured Division felt with some caution round the southern end of the enemy's anti-tank screen'.

Rommel's main battle had also, once more, been with the Axis Supreme Command. Back in safely remote Rome, Mussolini had again lost touch with realities, and the week before Christmas had sent an order to 'resist to the utmost' on the Buerat position. Thereupon Rommel inquired by radio of Marshal Cavallero, the Chief of the Comando Supremo, what he was to do if the British were to ignore that position, which was easy to by-pass, and drive on westward. Cavallero did not answer the question, but emphasized that the Italian troops must not be left in the bag again as at Alamein.

Rommel pointed out to Bastico the obvious contradiction between Mussolini's order and Cavallero's stipulation. Like most servants of an authoritarian régime, Bastico sought to avoid making a choice and taking responsibility for a course that would not correspond to the hopes and dreams of his leader. But by persistence Rommel had got him to agree to, and give an order for, the withdrawal of the non-motorized Italian troops to the Tarhuna–Homs line, 130 miles farther back nearer Tripoli. Then, in the second week of January, Cavallero asked that a German division should be sent back to the Gabes defile to guard against the threatened American thrust there – which, as already related, did not mature. Rommel, naturally, was not unwilling to respond to a request that fitted in well with the plan he had conceived, and sent the 21st Panzer Division. That left him with only the thirty-six tanks of the 15th Panzer Division, and the fifty-seven obsolete Italian tanks of the Centauro Division, to meet the 450 that Montgomery had brought up for his fresh thrust. Rommel had no intention of fighting a hopeless battle against such overwhelming strength, so withdrew from the Buerat position as soon as he heard – through his wireless interception service – that the British would be ready to strike on January 15th.

After imposing checks on them in the first two days – during which they were made cautious not only by widely strewn mines but by losing some fifty tanks in efforts to pierce his screen – Rommel withdrew his motorized forces to the Tarhuna–Homs line on the 17th, and immediately told the Italian infantry already there to go back to Tripoli. The Tarhuna–Homs line was more defensible than the Buerat position, but the weight of armour that Montgomery brought against its inland flank convinced Rommel by the 19th that a prolonged stand there would be hopeless, and imperil his line of retreat. So he began to withdraw his remaining forces during the night, while the port installations at Tripoli were blown up.

Early in the morning a signal came from Cavallero conveying Mussolini's sharp disapproval of the withdrawal and insistent demand that the line must be held for at least three weeks. That afternoon Cavallero arrived on the scene to reinforce the message. Rommel caustically pointed out that any such time-limit was dependent on the enemy's action in the absence of adequate reinforcements to counter it. He ended by putting the crux of the matter to Cavallero in the same way as he had done to Bastico in November over the demand to hold on to the Mersa Brega line: 'You can either hold on to Tripoli a few more days and lose the army, or lose Tripoli a few days earlier and save the army for Tunis. Make up your mind.' Cavallero avoided giving a definite decision, but provided it indirectly by telling Rommel that the army must be preserved although Tripoli must be held as long as possible. Rommel promptly started to withdraw the non-motorized Italian troops, and also most of the movable stores. Then on the night of the 22nd he withdrew the rest of the troops from the Tarhuna–Homs line, going right back to the Tunisian frontier, a hundred miles west of Tripoli, and then to the Mareth Line, eighty miles beyond.

The British follow-up from beyond the Buerat line had been 'sticky', as Montgomery himself described it. That was due not only to mines and road-demolitions but also to extreme caution in tackling the enemy's rearguard screens. Montgomery, in his memoirs, emphasizes that the advance on the coast road 'generally displayed a lack of initiative and ginger', reinforcing this comment by quoting a note in his diary on the 20th: 'Sent for the GOC 51st (Highland) Division, and gave him an imperial "rocket"; this had an immediate effect'. But, in fact, Rommel had already pulled back to the Tarhuna–Homs line, and it was not the stronger push on the coast road but the weight of armour building up against his inland flank which had expedited his order, on the 22nd, to give up that line and withdraw to the Tunisian frontier. When the 51st Division advanced by moonlight, with the leading infantry riding on the tops of the tanks, they found that the enemy had vanished. By daybreak on January 23rd the speartips of the converging British columns had driven into Tripoli unopposed.

The attainment of that objective, which had been the goal of successive British offensives since 1941, crowned the 1,400-mile advance from Alamein in pursuit of Rommel. It was reached exactly three months, to the day, after the launching of the offensive. For Montgomery and his troops it was an exhilarating achievement, but in him it also produced a sigh of relief – for, as he wrote: 'I was experiencing the first real anxiety I had suffered since assuming the command of the Eighth Army.' A gale in the first week of January had played havoc in the harbour at Benghazi, reducing the intake of stores from three thousand tons a day to less than a thousand, and compelling him to fall back on the use of Tobruk, nearly eight hundred miles from Tripoli, which meant considerably lengthening the already very long line of supply by road. To provide the extra lift he had 'grounded' the 10th Corps and used its transport, but feared that he would have to suspend the advance unless he could reach Tripoli within ten days of the start of his new push.

The enemy, fortunately for him, were not aware of his time and supply problem, whereas it was clear to them that he was advancing on them with an overwhelming superiority in tanks – 14 to 1 against those of the 15th Panzer Division, the only really effective tanks they had. If the 21st Panzer Division had not been called away to meet the threatened American thrust towards the Gabes bottleneck – a thrust that was cancelled two days after the dispatch of this division, on the 13th – a stand on the Tarhuna–Homs line would have been more possible. In that case Montgomery, on his own evidence, might have had to break off the advance and withdraw to Buerat, for when he entered Tripoli he was within two days of the expiry of his ten-day time limit.

At Tripoli he paused for several weeks to build up and clear the demolition-blocked harbour. It was not until February 3rd that the first ship was able to enter, and it was the 9th before the first convoy came in. Only light troops had followed up the enemy's withdrawal, and Montgomery's leading division did not advance across the Tunisian frontier until the 16th – Rommel's rearguard having withdrawn on the previous night into the forefield of the Mareth Line, which the French had originally built to check an Italian invasion of Tunisia from Tripolitania. It consisted merely of a chain of antiquated block-houses, and Rommel thought it better to rely on field entrenchments newly dug in the spaces between them. Indeed, after inspecting the Mareth Line, he urged that it would be wiser to base the defence of this approach route to Tunis on the line of the Wadi Akarit – forty miles back, and fifteen miles west of Gabes – which could not be outflanked, as its inland flank rested on the saltmarsh area of the Chott el Jerid. But his proposal was not acceptable to distant dictators who were still hopefully erecting 'castles in the air', and his own stock was at its lowest point.

Mussolini vented his spleen at the loss of Tripoli by recalling Bastico and dismissing Cavallero – who was replaced by General Ambrosio. Meanwhile Rommel had received a telegram, on January 26th, notifying him that in view of the bad state of his health he would be relieved of command after consolidating his new position in the Mareth Line, and that his army was to be renamed the First Italian Army, with General Giovanni Messe as its commander. He was, however, left to choose the date of hand-over and departure – a concession of which he took advantage, to the Allies' detriment.

Rommel was a sick man and the strain of the last three months had not improved his condition. But he was to show, in February, that he still had a strong kick in him.

Instead of being dismayed by the Americans' close approach to his line of retreat through southern Tunisia, he scented a fine opportunity of striking there before Montgomery could again catch up with him. Although the Mareth defences were poor, they did provide an obstacle to tank attack and should at least delay Montgomery. Moreover, Rommel's own strength was reviving. In retreating westward, he had come nearer to his supply ports and had gained more than he had lost during the long retreat, while in number of troops he had now as many as when the autumn Battle of Alamein opened. At the time he arrived in Tunisia his army totalled close on 30,000 Germans,* and about 48,000 Italians – although this roll included the 21st Panzer Division, which had been sent back to the Gabes-Sfax area, and also the Centauro Armoured Division, which was being sent to guard the El Guettar defile, facing the American position at Gafsa. In armament, however, the situation was not nearly so good – the German units were about one-third of full strength in tanks, one-fourth in anti-tank guns, and one-sixth in artillery. Moreover, out of approximately 130 tanks, less than half were fit for action. Nevertheless the overall situation was relatively

* This was about half their full strength, on establishment scale – the same as it had been when the Alamein battle began.

better than it was likely to become once Montgomery had time to make full use of the port of Tripoli, and mass his superior strength on the Tunisian frontier. Rommel was eager to profit by the interval.

So he now planned a double stroke in Napoleonic style to exploit what strategists term the 'interior lines' theory – taking advantage of a central position, between two converging enemy forces, to strike at one of them before the other can aid it. If he could crumple up the Americans poised behind him, he would have both hands free to tackle Montgomery's Eighth Army which was now thinned out by the way its lines of supply had been stretched.

It was a brilliant plan, but Rommel's biggest handicap in putting it into effect was that it had to depend largely on forces which were not under his own control. He could spare only enough from the Mareth Line to form one large combat-group, less than half the size of a division, under Colonel von Liebenstein. His famous and trusty 21st Panzer Division, sent back to Tunisia earlier, was right on the spot where he wanted to strike, but it had passed under the command of General von Arnim's army. It was thus left to Arnim, at the outset, to decide the aims of the main thrust and the strength that should be employed, while Rommel was limited to helping it on so far as he could.

The American 2nd Corps (which included a French division) was the target of this counterstroke. Its front covered ninety miles, but was really focused on the three routes through the mountains to the sea, with spearheads at the passes near Gafsa, Faid, and Fondouk – where it linked up with the French 19th Corps under General Koeltz. These passageways were so narrow that the occupiers felt secure, and the attention of the Allied higher command had been largely absorbed in checking a series of Axis probing attacks in the sector north of Fondouk.

But at the end of January, the veteran 21st Panzer made a sudden spring at the Faid Pass, overwhelmed the poorly armed French garrison there before American aid belatedly arrived, and thus gained a sally-port for the bigger attack to follow. This coup made the Allied higher commanders suspect that such an offensive was being planned by the enemy, but they did not expect it where it came. Regarding the preliminary Faid stroke as a diversion, they believed that the attack would be delivered near Fondouk. As General Omar Bradley remarked in his memoirs: 'This belief came to be a near-fatal assumption.' It prevailed both at Eisenhower's headquarters and at those of the British First Army, under Anderson, who had now been placed in charge of the whole Allied front in Tunisia pending the arrival of Alexander. The latter had been appointed at the Casablanca Conference to command, under Eisenhower, the new 18th Army Group made up of the First and Eighth Armies, which was to be constituted when the latter entered Tunisia. To guard the expected line of attack, Anderson was led to keep Combat Command B, with half the American armour, back in reserve behind Fondouk. That miscalculation helped to ease the way for the enemy's advance.

By the beginning of February the Axis forces in Tunisia had risen to a total of 100,000 – 74,000 Germans and 26,000 Italians – which was a much better ratio to the Allied strength than it had been in December, or was likely to be when the Allied concentration was completed. About 30 per cent were administrative personnel. The available strength in armour, which was almost entirely dependent on the German contribution, was just over 280 tanks – 110 with the 10th Panzer Division, 91 with the 21st Panzer Division (exactly half the full complement on the existing establishment scale), a dozen Tigers in a special unit, while Rommel was bringing a battalion of twenty-six tanks in Liebenstein's combat-group to reinforce twenty-three surviving Italian tanks of the Centauro Division on the Gafsa road. This total fell a long way short of the Allied strength, and even if the whole of it was employed would not provide a numerical superiority on the intended front of attack in the southerly part of Tunisia. For the US 1st Armored Division supporting that sector, although still short of full strength, had about 300 tanks in operation – although ninety were Stuarts – and thirty-six tank destroyers, and was much stronger in artillery than a panzer division.* But

* These figures, from the records, significantly show how fallacious it can be to compare Allied and Axis strength in terms of the number of 'divisions' engaged on either side – as the Allied commanders, and many of the official historians, have done in their accounts. At this period the tank establishment of an American armoured division (390 tanks) was more than twice as large as that of a normal German panzer division (180). But the actual ratio was usually greater, as the Germans had more difficulty in making up shortages. As can be seen, even the depleted 1st Armored Division had approximately three times as many tanks as the average of the panzer divisions opposed to it.

The establishment of a British armoured division had recently been reduced to approximately 270 tanks, exclusive of specialized ones, and American divisions, with certain exceptions, were reorganized on a similar scale later in the year. But in 1944 the British armoured divisions were raised to a scale of 310, by equipping their reconnaissance unit with tanks instead of armoured-cars – and the actual strength of the Allied armoured divisions, in number of tanks available for action, was usually two to three times as large as the German. To maintain a balance the Germans had to depend on a qualitative advantage.

to Rommel's disappointment only part of the 10th Panzer Division (with one medium tank battalion and a company of four Tigers) was sent down to reinforce the 21st, and merely for the opening phase, as Arnim was planning to use the 10th for a thrust he planned to deliver farther north.

On February 14th the real offensive opened, when the 21st Panzer Division pounced again, from Faid, together with the contingent from the 10th. Arnim's deputy, General Ziegler, was in immediate charge of the attack. While the two small combat-groups from the 10th Panzer Division swept forward from the Faid Pass, opening out like pincer arms to grip the advanced part of the US 1st Armored Division – Combat Command A – two more from the 21st Panzer Division (each with a tank battalion as its core) made a wider circuit southward, during the night, to outflank and trap the Americans. Although fragments managed to escape before the ring was closed, around Sidi Bou Zid, loss of equipment was very heavy. The battlefield was strewn with blazing American tanks, forty being lost in this action. Next morning Combat Command C was hastily sent forward to deliver a counter-attack, and was promptly trapped by encircling German moves, only four of its tanks getting away. Thus two fine battalions of medium tanks had been wiped out successively in these piecemeal fights against the enemy's skilful concentration of superior force from inferior resources. Fortunately for the Allies, the Germans were slow in their follow up.

Rommel had urged Ziegler, on the 14th, to drive on during the night and exploit the opening success to the full – 'The Americans had no practical battle experience, and it was for us to instil them with a deep inferiority complex from the outset.' But Ziegler felt bound to wait until he had obtained Arnim's authorization, and it was only on the 17th that he pushed forward twenty-five miles to Sbeitla, where the Americans had rallied. There, in consequence, the Germans met stiffer opposition, as Combat Command B (now led by Brigadier-General Paul Robinett) had been rushed south. It kept the Germans at bay until late in the afternoon, and helped to cover the retreat of the battered remnants of the other two Combat Commands before withdrawing itself – as part of a general wheel back of the Allies' southern wing, ordered by Anderson, to the line of the Western Dorsal mountain ridges. Although the Germans' entry into Sbeitla had been delayed, their total bag had risen to more than a hundred tanks and nearly three thousand prisoners.

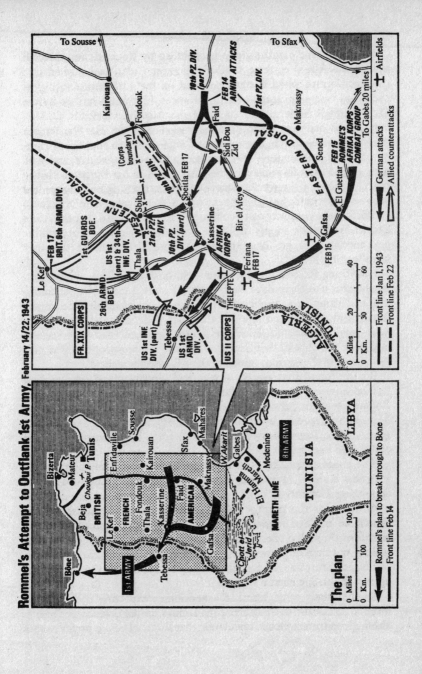

Rommel's Attempt to Outflank 1st Army, February 14/22, 1943

To Sousse   To Sfax

Kairouan

FEB 14
ARNIM ATTACKS

10th PZ. DIV. (part)

21st PZ. DIV.

Fondouk

Faid

Maknassy

Sidi Bou Zid

FEB 14
ARNIM ATTACKS

(Corps boundary)

Sbeitla FEB 17

10th PZ. DIV.

Sened

El Guettar

FEB 15
ROMMEL'S
AFRIKA KORPS
COMBAT GROUP

To Gabes 20 miles

EASTERN DORSAL

Le Kef

FEB 17
BRIT. 6th ARMD. DIV.

1st GUARDS BDE.

Sbiba

WESTERN DORSAL

21st PZ. DIV.

Kasserine

Bir el Afley

Gafsa

FEB 15

1st GUARDS
BDE.

US 1st
DIV. & 34th
INF. DIV.

Thala

10th PZ.
DIV. (part)

AFRIKA
KORPS

Feriana
FEB 17

Airfields

German attacks

Allied counterattacks

26th ARMD.
BDE.

FR. XIX CORPS

TELEPTE

Front line Jan 1, 1943

Front line Feb 22

1st INF.
DIV. (part)

Tebessa

US 1st INF.
DIV. (part)

US 1st
ARMD. DIV.

US II CORPS

ALGERIA
TUNISIA

Miles   0   20   40
Km.   0   30   60

The plan

Bône

Bizerta

Mateur

Chouigui P.

Tunis

Enfidaville

Sousse

BRITISH

Beja

Le Kef

FRENCH

Fondouk

Kairouan

Sfax

Mahares

Thala

Kasserine

Faid

Maknassy

AMERICAN

Tebessa

Gafsa

Chott el Jerid

MARETH LINE

El Hamma

Medenine

Mareth

Gabes

N. Akarit

8th ARMY

LIBYA

TUNISIA

1st ARMY

Miles   0   100
Km.   0   100

Rommel's plan to break through to Bône

Front line Feb 14

Meanwhile the combat-group brought up by Rommel, and directed against the Allies' extreme southern flank at Gafsa, had pushed into that road-centre when it was evacuated on the 15th. Accelerating its pace, and swinging north-west, it advanced fifty miles farther by the 17th, through Feriana, and captured the American airfields at Thelepte. So it had now come up almost level with the 21st Panzer but thirty-five miles to the west of it, and thus closer to the Allies' communications. Alexander – who arrived on the scene that day, and took over charge of both armies on the 19th – said in his Despatch that in the 'confusion of the retreat American, French, and British troops had become inextricably mingled, there was no coordinated plan of defence and definite uncertainty as to command.' Rommel heard that the Allies had set fire to their supply depots at Tebessa, forty miles on beyond the next mountain range. That appeared to him clear evidence that they were 'getting jittery'.

Now came the real turning point – although the Allied commanders imagined it was three days later. Rommel wanted to exploit the confusion and panic by a combined drive with all the available mechanized forces through Tebessa. He felt that such a deep thrust towards the Allies' main communications 'would force the British and Americans to pull back the bulk of their forces to Algeria – a prospect that was now prominent in the anxious minds of the Allied commanders'.

But he found that Arnim – who had already called off the 10th Panzer Division – was unwilling to embark on such a venture. So Rommel sent his proposals to the Comando Supremo – counting on Mussolini's desire for a 'victory to bolster up his internal political position' – while Bayerlein won over the air force commander in Tunisia and gained his support for the plan.

The hours slipped by, and it was not until almost midnight on the 18th that a signal came from Rome authorizing the continued attack, appointing Rommel to conduct it, and placing both panzer divisions under him for the purpose. But the order conveyed that the thrust should be made *northward* to Thala and Le Kef, instead of *north-westward* through Tebessa. In Rommel's view that change was 'an appalling and incredible piece of shortsightedness' – for it meant that the combined thrust was 'far too close to the front and bound to bring us up against the strong enemy reserves'.

So the attack came where Alexander was expecting it, as he had ordered Anderson 'to concentrate his armour for the defence of Thala' – although on the erroneous calculation that Rommel would prefer to seek a 'tactical victory' than to pursue a less direct strategic aim. This mistaken assumption turned out fortunately for the Allies as things went, thanks to the Comando Supremo – but the Allied forces would have been caught badly off balance had Rommel been allowed to drive the way he wished. For the bulk of the reinforcements, American and British, that had been rushed south were sent to Thala and the Sbiba sector east of it, while Tebessa was meagrely covered by what remained of the US 1st Armored Division.

The main British reinforcement was the 6th Armoured Division. Its armoured component, the 26th Armoured Brigade, was posted at Thala while additional infantry and also the artillery of the now arriving US 9th Infantry Division were brought there to support it. The 1st Guards Brigade, the lorried infantry component of the 6th Armoured Division, was posted to guard the Sbiba gap, due north of Sbeitla, along with three Regimental Combat Teams from the US 1st and 34th Infantry Divisions.

Rommel's thrust was launched early on February 19th, within a few hours of receiving the Comando Supremo's sanction. But the prospects were diminished both by the earlier delays and by Arnim's action in calling the 10th Panzer Division northward, so that it had to be recalled and could not arrive in time to play a part in the first phase of the new attack. Thus handicapped, Rommel decided to swing his Afrika Korps combat-group round to lead the advance on Le Kef through Thala, while using the 21st Panzer Division for an effort to reach Le Kef by the converging road through Sbiba, so that the two lines of thrust might develop a mutual leverage helpful to both.

The approach to Thala was through the Kasserine Pass, midway between Sbeitla and Feriana, and the position here was held by an American composite force under Colonel Stark. An initial attempt to rush the pass by surprise was checked, and in the afternoon various reinforcements arrived that brought Stark's force up to a strength considerably exceeding that of the Africa Korps group (three small battalions – one of tanks and two of infantry) which was carrying out the attack. But the defence was not well coordinated, so that the Germans managed to infiltrate at some points in the evening, and still farther after dark. Meanwhile the 21st Panzer Division's push for Sbiba had been blocked by a minefield and the strong Allied force deployed behind it – eleven infantry battalions against the attacker's two, as well as a superior number of guns and tanks (for the 21st Panzer Division now had less than forty in operation). So during the night Rommel decided to concentrate on forcing the Kasserine Pass, where the defence seemed more shaky, and to employ there the belatedly arriving 10th Panzer Division. The now shrinking prospect was diminished, however, as it included only one tank battalion, two infantry battalions, and a motor-cycle battalion. Arnim had kept back almost half the division, and its attached battalion of Tiger tanks, on which Rommel had been counting as a trump card in playing his hand.

His concentrated attack on the Kasserine Pass could not be delivered until the afternoon of the 20th, as the elements of the 10th Panzer Division did not arrive until then – a delay which made him 'extremely angry'. A morning attack had been checked by the defenders' fire, but at 4.30 PM, having come close up to the front himself, he threw all the available infantry – five battalions (including one, the 5th Bersaglieri Battalion, of Italians) – into a simultaneous assault, and this quickly broke through. But the attackers then met stubborn resistance from a very small British detachment (an armoured squadron, an infantry company, and a field battery) under Lieutenant-Colonel A. C. Gore which had been sent to support the defence of the pass, and this was only overcome after a panzer battalion had been brought up, and its eleven tanks had been knocked out. The American official history, with an honesty rare in the official histories of any country, not only empha-sizes the exceptionally tough resistance put up by this detachment, but significantly remarks with reference to the easy breakthrough else-where: 'The enemy was amazed at the quantity and quality of the American equipment captured more or less intact.'*

After capturing the pass, Rommel sent reconnoitring detachments up the road towards Thala and also up the fork road to Tebessa, in order to put the Allies on the horns of a dilemma in moving their reserves, and also to explore the possibility of pursuing his own original aim of capturing the vast American supply dumps at Tebessa. The first aim, and effect, had already been produced by the news of Rommel's pro-gress. For Fredendall, after ordering Robinett's Combat Command B in the morning to switch from the extreme right flank to Thala, had later diverted it to cover the fork road from Kasserine to Tebessa. Meanwhile, the British 26th Armoured Brigade Group (under Briga-dier Charles Dunphie) – with two armoured regiments and two in-fantry battalions – had moved south from Thala, and taken up a position about ten miles from the Kasserine Pass, in expectation of Combat Command B's arrival to support it. Fortunately for the

* Howe: *U.S. Army in World War II. Northwest Africa: Seizing the Initiative in the West*, p 456.

Allies, the attacker's strength was much weaker than they imagined.

Next morning, February 21st, Rommel at first stood fast in expectation of an Allied counterattack, to recapture the Kasserine Pass. That pause seemed surprising to his opponents, who did not realize how slender was his strength compared with what they had now gathered. When he found that they remained static, he pushed on up the road to Thala with such part of the 10th Panzer Division as he had under command – it amounted only to a combat group, comprising thirty tanks, twenty self-propelled guns and two panzer-grenadier (motorized infantry) battalions. Dunphie's brigade group fell back gradually before the Germans, making a stand on successive ridges until outflanked and enfiladed. But when its tanks withdrew at dusk into the Thala position already prepared, a string of German tanks followed close on their tail – cunningly headed by a captured Valentine, so that they were assumed to be British stragglers. Thus the Germans burst into the position, overrunning part of the infantry, shooting up many vehicles, and spreading confusion. Although checked after a three-hour mêlée, they carried away 700 prisoners on withdrawing. In this series of fights up the road from Kasserine they had lost a dozen tanks, but had knocked out nearly forty of the opposing tanks, including those of a squadron which lost direction and ran into the midst of their tank leaguer in a dawn counterattack next morning.

Expecting a larger counterattack to follow, Rommel decided to await it, with the idea of following up its repulse. But, during the morning, air reconnaissance showed that large Allied reinforcements had arrived on the scene and that more were approaching. So it became evident that the prospect of further exploitation through Thala had waned, while the Axis left flank was now in growing danger. On the previous afternoon the Afrika Korps combat group had pushed up the Tebessa fork road with the aim of securing the passes there, to cover the flank of the thrust for Thala, but had been checked by a heavy concentration of fire from the American artillery positions on the high ground. A renewal of the effort on the morning of the 22nd brought only slight gain and more serious losses than the attackers could afford – for in this sector they were now greatly outnumbered by the American forces assembled there, Robinett's Combat Command B and part of Terry Allen's 1st Infantry Division.

That afternoon Rommel and Kesselring, who had flown to see him, came to the conclusion that no further advantages could be achieved by pursuing the westward counterstroke, and that it should be broken off in order to switch the striking force back for the eastward counterstroke against the British Eighth Army. Following this decision, the Axis troops were ordered to begin withdrawing that evening – to the Kasserine Pass in the first place.

Meanwhile Allen had been trying since early in the morning to organize a counterattack against the Axis flank, but it was delayed by the difficulty of getting into communication with Robinett, and did not develop until late in the afternoon. It then hastened and hustled the Afrika Korps group's withdrawal to the Kasserine Pass, the Italian elements retreating in disorder. Rommel was impressed by the growing tactical skill here shown by the American troops and the accuracy of their artillery fire, as well as by the abundance of their armament. His relatively weak forces would have been in grave danger if a larger and wider counterattack had developed.

But his weakness and the way that the situation had changed were not realized on the higher level of the Allied Command. As the US official history remarks, Fredendall's direction of 'ground operations against the retreating enemy became extraordinarily hesitant at just the time that the enemy was most vulnerable'. Anderson, too, was still thinking defensively. Indeed, the large Allied force at Sbiba was that night withdrawn some ten miles northward in fear that Rommel might break through at Thala and threaten its rear. Under a similar fear the evacuation of Tebessa on the other flank was being contemplated. Even when the enemy's withdrawal from Thala was discovered, on the morning of the 23rd, nothing was done to press upon it, and not until late that night were orders given for a general counterattack to be mounted – for launching on the 25th. By that time the enemy had safely withdrawn through the Kasserine bottleneck, and the Allied effort to 'destroy' the enemy and 'recapture' the pass became merely a processional march, meeting only the road demolitions and mines which the vanished enemy had strewn in his wake.

When due account is taken of the balance of the forces, and the hardening resistance, it becomes clear that the termination of the Axis offensive was very well judged. To press it any further would have been folly in face of the vastly superior strength by now assembled on the Allied side. Materially, the profits of the offensive were large in comparison with its cost – over 4,000 prisoners had been taken at the price of little more than a thousand casualties, and some 200 tanks destroyed or disabled at an even smaller ratio of loss. Thus as a 'limited objective' stroke it had been a brilliant success. But it had fallen short of, although coming dangerously near to, the strategic object of producing an Allied retreat from Tunisia. Such a result would have been probable if the whole of the 10th Panzer Division had been allotted for the counter-stroke and Rommel had been in charge of the operation from the outset with freedom to direct it against Tebessa. A swift seizure of that American main base and airfield centre, with its huge accumulation of supplies, would have made it impossible for the Allied forces to main-tain their position in Tunisia.

The irony of fortune was demonstrated by the arrival of an order from Rome, on February 23rd, placing all the Axis forces in Tunisia under Rommel's command. While this appointment to command the newly constituted 'Army Group Afrika' showed how the dramatic effect of the counterstroke had revived his stock in the minds of Mussolini and Hitler, its timing had a bitter flavour for Rommel, since it came the morning after the withdrawal had begun – and far too late to redeem the lost opportunity.

It also came too late to cancel Arnim's intended thrust in the north, for which Arnim had kept back reserves that could have been much better employed in Rommel's. As planned, the capture of Medjez el Bab was to be the limited objective, and the attack was to be launched on the 26th, with two panzer battalions and six others. But at dawn on the 24th Arnim, after sending one of his staff to inform Rommel about this limited plan, flew to see Kesselring in Rome and from their discus-sion a far more ambitious plan emerged later that day. Under it, attacks were to be launched at eight different points along the seventy-mile stretch of front between the north coast and Pont-du-Fahs, against the British 5th Corps (46th, 78th, and Y Divisions, with a French Regi-mental Group near the coast). The main thrust, by an armoured group, was to be aimed at the road-centre of Beja (sixty miles west of Tunis), and combined with a shorter-range pincer attack to capture Medjez el Bab. Though all available forces were employed, the increase of strength was nowhere near equal to the extension of the assault. For the Beja thrust the armoured group, of two panzer battalions, was raised to a total strength of seventy-seven tanks (including fourteen Tigers), but even this slender scale was only attained by purloining fifteen that had just arrived at Tunis on their way to the 21st Panzer Division in the south. Rommel was taken aback when informed of the new plan, and described it as 'completely unrealistic' – although ascribing it mis-takenly to the Italian Comando Supremo, which had been as staggered as he was when informed of it.

Arnim's operation order was issued on the 25th, and the offensive was launched next day – thus keeping to the intended date of the smaller plan. That was remarkable testimony to the speed and elasticity of German planning, if too hurried for such extensive changes. Even so, the best performance was achieved by the newly added attacks carried out by Manteuffel's division, on the northernmost sector, which almost reached the Allies' main lateral road at Djebel Abiod, and took 1,600 prisoners from the French and British troops holding this sector. But the main attack by the German armoured group, after overrunning the British forward position near Sidi Nsir, became trapped in a narrow and marshy defile ten miles short of Beja, where the British field and anti-tank guns took heavy toll. All save six of the German tanks were put out of action, and the push petered out. The secondary attack to pinch off Medjez el Bab ended in failure, after some initial success, and so did the other attacks further south. Altogether Arnim's offensive took 2,500 prisoners at a cost of just over 1,000 casualties, but that was outweighed by the fact that seventy-one of his tanks were destroyed or disabled, while the British lost less than a score. For the Germans were already suffering from a shortage of tanks and theirs could not be so easily replaced.

Worse still, this abortive offensive caused delay in releasing the divisions needed for Rommel's intended second stroke – against Montgomery's position at Medenine, facing the Mareth Line. For Kesselring had asked that the 10th and 21st Panzer Divisions should stay near enough to the Americans' flank for long enough to deter them from sending reserves northward to help in meeting Arnim's offensive. This delay made a vital difference to the prospects of Rommel's eastward counterstroke. Until February 26th Montgomery had only one division up forward at Medenine. He admitted that for once he was worried, and his staff worked feverishly to redress the balance before Rommel could strike. By March 6th, when the blow came, Montgomery's strength was quadrupled – the equivalent of four divisions with nearly 400 tanks, 350 guns, and 470 anti-tank guns.

Thus, in the interval, Rommel's chance of striking with superior force had vanished. His three panzer divisions (the 10th, 15th, and 21st) mustered only 160 tanks – less than one would have had at full strength – and were supported in the attack by no more than 200 guns and 10,000 infantry, apart from the string of weak Italian divisions stationed in the Mareth Line. Moreover, Montgomery now had three fighter wings operating from forward airfields, so was assured of air superiority, while Rommel's chance of achieving surprise was annulled when the panzer divisions' approach was spotted and reported on March 4th, two days in advance of their attack.

In such a situation, Montgomery was able to make the most of his ability for planning a well-woven defence, and the attack was shattered even more effectively than at Alam Halfa six months earlier. The advancing Germans were soon pinned down and whittled away by the British concentration of fire. Realizing the futility of continuing, Rommel broke off his attack in the evening. But by that time he had lost more than forty tanks, although in men the casualties were only 645. The defenders' losses were much slighter.

This repulse dispelled any reasonable hopes that the outnumbered and outweaponed Axis forces might be able to cripple one of the two Allied armies before they linked up and developed a combined pressure. Already the week before, Rommel had sent Kesselring a sober and sombre appreciation of the situation which embodied the view of his two army commanders, Arnim and Messe, as well as his own. In it he had emphasized that the Axis forces were holding a front of nearly 400 miles against much superior forces – twice as strong in men while six times as strong in tanks* – and were strung out perilously thin. He had urged that the front should be shortened to a ninety-mile arc covering Tunis and Bizerta, but said that this could only be held if supplies were increased to 140,000 tons a month, and had pointedly asked for enlightenment as to the higher command's long-term plans for the Tunisian campaign. The reply he received, after several urgent reminders, simply said that the Führer did not agree with his judgement of the situation. Attached to it was a table setting forth the number of formations on either side, irrespective of actual strength and equipment – the same false basis of comparison which the Allied commanders used, then and later, in rendering account of their successes.

After the failure at Medenine, Rommel came to the conclusion that it would be 'plain suicide' for the German–Italian forces to stay in Africa. So on March 9th, taking his long deferred sick leave, he handed over command of the Army Group to Arnim, and flew to Europe in an effort to make his masters understand the situation. As it turned out, the result was merely to terminate his connexion with the campaign in Africa.

---

* He estimated the Allies' strength as 210,000 men, with 1,600 tanks, 850 guns and 1,100 anti-tank guns – an estimate which was under the mark. The Allies' actual strength early in March was over 500,000 men, although barely half of them were fighting troops. The total of tanks was nearly 1,800, with over 1,200 guns and over 1,500 anti-tank guns. The Axis fighting troops numbered 120,000, with barely 200 effective tanks.

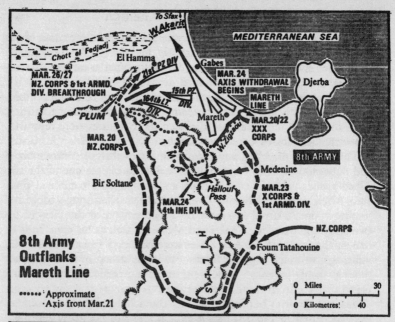

MEDITERRANEAN SEA

To Sfax
W.Akarit

El Hamma

21st PZ DIV.

Gabes

MAR.24
AXIS WITHDRAWAL
BEGINS

Djerba

MAR.26/27
NZ. CORPS & 1st ARMD.
DIV. BREAKTHROUGH

15th PZ
DIV.

164th L.T.
DIV.

MARETH
LINE

'PLUM'

Mareth

MAR.20/22
XXX
CORPS

W.Zigzaou

MAR.20
NZ.CORPS

8th ARMY

Bir Soltane

Medenine

MAR.24
4th INF. DIV.

Hallouf
Pass

MAR.23
X CORPS &
1st ARMD. DIV.

NZ. CORPS

Foum Tatahouine

**8th Army
Outflanks
Mareth Line**

•••••• Approximate
Axis front Mar.21

0   Miles   30

0   Kilometres   40

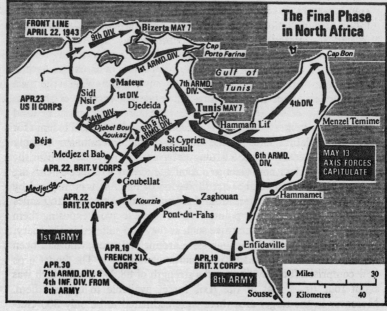

**FRONT LINE
APRIL 22, 1943**

9th DIV.

Bizerta MAY 7

**The Final Phase
in North Africa**

Cap
Porto Farina

1st ARMD. DIV.

Cap Bon

Mateur

1st DIV.

7th ARMD.
DIV.

**Gulf of
Tunis**

APR.23
US II CORPS

Sidi
Nsir

34th DIV.

Djedeida

Tunis MAY 7

4th DIV.

Menzel Temime

Béja

Djebel Bou
Aoukaz

6th & 7th
ARMD. DIV.

St Cyprien
Massicault

Hammam Lif

MAY 13
AXIS FORCES
CAPITULATE

Medjez el Bab

Goubellat

6th ARMD.
DIV.

APR.22, BRIT. V CORPS

Medjerda

Zaghouan

Hammamet

APR.22
BRIT. IX CORPS

Kourzia

Pont-du-Fahs

1st ARMY

APR.19
FRENCH XIX
CORPS

Enfidaville

APR.19
BRIT. X CORPS

APR.30
7th ARMD. DIV. &
4th INF. DIV. FROM
8th ARMY

8th ARMY

Sousse

0   Miles   30

0   Kilometres   40

On landing in Rome he saw Mussolini, who 'seemed to lack any sense of reality in adversity, and spent the whole time searching for arguments to justify his views'. Then Rommel went on to see Hitler, who was impervious to Rommel's arguments and made it plain that in his view 'I had become a pessimist'. He barred Rommel from returning to Africa for the moment, and told him that he might thus get fit in time 'to take command of operations against Casablanca'. In view of Casablanca's remoteness on the Atlantic coast, it is evident that Hitler was still imagining that he could throw the Allies completely out of Africa – which showed his extreme state of delusion.

Meanwhile a converging Allied offensive was being mounted with greatly superior strength to capture the southern gateway into Tunisia, enable the Eighth Army to join up with the First, and pinch out Messe's 'First Italian Army' – formerly Rommel's 'Panzerarmee Afrika'. (Bayerlein, although nominally no more than Messe's German Chief of Staff, held direct and complete control of all the German components.)

Following the heavy repulse of the German counterstroke at Medenine, Montgomery did not try to exploit this defensive success and the enemy's shaken state by an immediate follow-up, but proceeded methodically to continue building up his forces and supplies for a deliberate attack on the Mareth Line. This was planned for delivery on March 20th, two weeks after the Medenine battle.

To aid it, by leverage on the enemy's back, an attack by the American 2nd Corps in southern Tunisia was launched three days earlier, on March 17th. Its aims, prescribed by Anderson and endorsed by Alexander, were threefold – to draw off enemy resources that might be used to block Montgomery; to regain the forward airfields near Thelepte for use in aiding Montgomery's advance; and to establish a forward supply centre near Gafsa, to help in provisioning him as he advanced. But the attacking force was not asked to cut off the enemy's retreat by driving through to the coast road. That limitation of its aims was inspired by doubts of the Americans' capability for such a deep thrust – 160 miles to the sea from its starting points – and a desire to avoid exposing them to another German counterstroke such as they had suffered in February. But the restraint galled the aggressive ardour of Patton, who had been appointed to replace Fredendall as corps commander. The 2nd Corps now comprised four divisions and a strength of 88,000 men, which was about four times that of the Axis forces available to oppose them. Moreover in the target area there were estimated to be only 800 Germans and 7,850 Italians, the latter mainly with the Centauro Division near Gafsa.*

The American attack started promisingly. On the 17th Allen's 1st Infantry Division occupied Gafsa without a fight, the Italians withdrawing nearly twenty miles to a defile position east of El Guettar, astride the forking roads to the coastal towns of Gabes and Mahares. On the 20th Ward's 1st Armored Division drove down from the Kasserine area on to the flank of the third route from Gafsa to the coast, and the next morning occupied Station de Sened, prior to advancing eastward through Maknassy to the pass beyond.

That day Alexander loosened the rein on Patton by telling him to prepare a strong armoured thrust to cut the coast road, as a greater aid to Montgomery's offensive against the Mareth Line, which had just been launched. But it was stultified by the stubborn defence of the pass and surrounding heights by the very small German detachment posted there, under Colonel Rudolf Lang. Successive attacks on the 23rd to capture the dominating Hill 322 were checked, although it was defended by only some eighty men composed of what had formerly been Rommel's bodyguard. A renewed attack next day - by three battalions of infantry supported by four battalions of artillery and two companies of tanks - was again repulsed, although the defending force had only risen to 350 men. A fresh attempt was made on the 25th, led personally by Ward - on a peremptory telephone order from Patton, who insisted that the attack had to succeed. But it did not succeed and had to be abandoned in face of the enemy's increased reinforcements. Patton had already complained that the division had 'dawdled', and Ward was subsequently relieved of command. But Patton was so attack-minded that he did not realize the inherent advantages of defence, even against much superior numbers - especially when conducted by highly skilled troops against inexperienced attackers.

Those advantages meanwhile had another demonstration in the El Guettar sector, and by troops who were comparatively inexperienced but particularly well trained - the US 1st Infantry Division. Here Allen's troops had broken into the Italian position on the 21st, and made some further progress next day, but on the 23rd were hit by a German counterstroke. This was delivered by the depleted 10th Panzer Division, the Army Group Afrika's main reserve, which had been rushed up from the coast. (It comprised two tank and two infantry battalions with one motorcycle and one artillery battalion.) The at-

* Even this was an overestimate - the Centauro Division was only 5,000 strong before the February battles, and further depleted then.

tackers overran the American forward positions but were then checked by a minefield, and then heavily hammered by Allen's artillery and tank destroyers. That blunted the edge of the attack, and a renewal of it in the evening had no better success – as an American infantry report exultantly put it: 'Our artillery crucified them with high explosive shells and they were falling like flies.' Although the German loss in their second attack was not so heavy as here picturesquely reported, some forty tanks were knocked out by fire or disabled by mines during the day.

By drawing the enemy's main armoured reserve into this costly counterstroke, the Americans' limited thrust had brought compensation for its own failure at Maknassy. It had not only drawn off an important counterweight to Montgomery's prospects, but drained away more of the enemy's scanty tank strength. For their ultimate victory the Allies owed more to the enemy's three unsuccessful counterstrokes, which followed the advantageous mid-February one at Faid, than they did to their own assaults. The possibility of gaining the ascendency came only after the enemy had overstrained and drained his own strength. Later the enemy might still have protracted the struggle but for the way he continued to use up his remaining strength in abortive retorts.

Montgomery's attack on the Mareth Line was launched on the night of March 20th. For it he had brought up both the 10th and the 30th Corps, with about 160,000 men, 610 tanks, and 1,410 guns. While Messe's army comprised a nominal nine divisions compared with Montgomery's six, it mustered less than 80,000 men, with 150 tanks (including those with the 10th Panzer division near Gafsa) and 680 guns. Thus the attacker had a superiority of more than 2 to 1 in men and guns – as well as in aircraft – and 4 to 1 in tanks.

Moreover, the Mareth Line stretched for twenty-two miles, from the sea to the Matmata Hills, and beyond this range had an open desert flank. In the circumstances it would have been wiser for the relatively weak Axis forces to attempt merely a delaying defence of the Mareth Line, with mobile forces, and to make their stand on the Wadi Akarit position north of Gabes – a bottleneck barely fourteen miles wide between the sea and the saltmarshes, the 'Chotts'. That was the course Rommel had advocated, and the position he had proposed, ever since the retreat from Alamein in November. When he saw Hitler on March 10th, he had succeeded in getting Hitler to agree, and to instruct Kesselring that the non-mobile Italian divisions in the Mareth Line should be moved back to the Wadi Akarit to build a position there. But the Italian leaders preferred to hold on to the Mareth Line, and Kesselring, who shared their views, induced Hitler to cancel the new orders.

Montgomery's original plan was code-named 'Pugilist Gallop'. Under it the main blow was a frontal one, by the three infantry divisions of Oliver Leese's 30th Corps, intended to break through the defence near the sea and make a gap through which the armoured force of Brian Horrocks's 10th Corps would drive to exploit success. At the same time, the provisionally formed New Zealand Corps under Bernard Freyberg made a wide outflanking march towards El Hamma (twenty-five miles inland from Gabes) to menace the enemy's rear and pin down his reserves.

The frontal attack was a failure. Launched on a narrow sector near the coast, by one infantry brigade and a regiment of fifty infantry tanks, it made only a shallow dent in the enemy position – which was covered by the Wadi Zigzaou, 200 feet wide and 20 feet deep, and an anti-tank ditch beyond this. The soft bed of the wadi, and the mines laid there, hindered the advance of the tanks and supporting guns, while the infantry foothold in the enemy's position beyond it became a concentrated target for the enfilading fire. A reinforced renewal of the assault on the following night achieved some expansion of the bridgehead, and many of the Italian troops took the opportunity of surrendering when the British got in among them. But the arrival of the anti-tank guns was still delayed by the marshy ground they had to cross, and in the afternoon the forward infantry were overrun by a German counterattack* while still inadequately supported, and under cover of darkness the British fell back across the wadi. Thus by the night of the 22nd the frontal attack had not only failed to make an adequate breach, but abandoned its lodgement in the enemy defences.

Meanwhile the outflanking move had started well but then been held up. After a long approach march from the Eighth Army's rear area, across a difficult stretch of desert, the New Zealand Corps had brought its 27,000 men and 200 tanks close to the hill-gap called 'Plum' – thirty miles west of Gabes and fifteen miles south-west of El Hamma – by the night of the 20th when the coastal assault opened. But after clearing the approaches it met a prolonged check at this hill-gap, where the Italian defenders were reinforced successively by the 21st Panzer Division from the reserve, and then by the four battalions of the 164th Light Afrika Division, which was brought back from the right of the Mareth Line.

In the early hours of March 23rd, when there was clearly no chance

---

* It was delivered by just under thirty tanks and two infantry battalions of the 15th Panzer Division.

of reviving the coastal attack, Montgomery decided to recast his plan, and concentrate all his resources on the inland flank, as there was better ground for hope there that a renewed attack in greater strength might break through to El Hamma. He ordered Horrocks with the headquarters of his 10th Corps and the 1st Armoured Division, commanded by Major-General Raymond Briggs (160 tanks), to start moving inland that night and make a long circuit through the desert to reinforce the New Zealanders. At the same time the 4th Indian Division (Major-General Francis Tuker) was to side-step inland from Medenine and clear the Hallouf Pass, through the Matmata Hills, the use of which would shorten by more than a hundred miles the supply route to the mass of manoeuvre advancing on the desert flank. After clearing the pass, Tuker was to push northward along the hill-tops, past the immediate flank of the Mareth Line, thus producing an additional threat to the enemy's flank and opening an alternative line of thrust for exploitation if the wider manoeuvre through the 'Plum' gap was blocked.

The new plan was a fine conception and masterly switch. It showed Montgomery's capacity for flexibility in varying his thrust-point, and creating fresh leverage when checked, even better than at Alamein – although, as was his habit, he subsequently tended to obscure the credit due to him for such flexibility, the hallmark of generalship, by talking as if everything had gone 'according to plan' from the outset. In many respects Mareth was his finest battle performance in the war, despite the troubles ensuing from his initial plan in trying to force a breakthrough on a narrow and marshy sector near the coast, and disclosing the potentialities of the desert manoeuvre without using sufficient strength to ensure its speedy fulfilment.

This premature disclosure became the chief handicap to the new plan of attack, called 'Supercharge II' – a name prompted by memories of the finally successful plan at Alamein. For having been alerted by the New Zealanders' arrival near 'Plum' on the 20th, the Axis command was quick to deduce that the further movements in that direction which were spotted on the evening of the 23rd and again on the 24th, by observers on the hills, portended a change in Montgomery's plan and the switching of his weight to the desert flank. Accordingly, the 15th Panzer Division was brought back near to El Hamma, in readiness to support the 21st Panzer and 164th Light, two days before the British reinforcements reached that area – only just in time for the planned launch of the attack on the afternoon of March 26th.

The prospects of 'Supercharge II' diminished when surprise vanished, but that loss was compensated by the combination of four other factors. The primary one was that Arnim had decided, on the 24th, to withdraw Messe's army to the Wadi Akarit position rather than risk it being trapped, and overruled Messe's desire to cling on to the Mareth Line – so that the defenders of the hill-gap were only required to hold up the assault long enough to extricate the non-mobile divisions in the Mareth Line. The second factor was the way that the path of the assault was swept by an air 'barrage' – produced by successive low-level attacks, with bombs and cannon-fire, by sixteen squadrons of fighter-bombers, operating in fifteen-minute relays of two squadrons at a time. This defence-stunning adaptation of the German 'blitz' method was organized by Air Vice-Marshal Harry Broadhurst, commanding the Desert Air Force, and worked very effectively – although frowned on by his distant RAF superiors as a breach of Air Staff doctrine. The third factor was the bold decision to press on the armoured advance during the night – a course which the Germans had often pursued with profit, but which the British had been reluctant to try. The fourth factor was a stroke of good luck – that a sandstorm blew up which cloaked the assembly of the British armour and the first stage of its advance through a hill-gap bristling with the enemy anti-tank guns on both flanks.

The attack was launched at 4 PM on the 26th, with the sun low behind it to help in blinding the defenders. The 8th Armoured Brigade and the New Zealand infantry led the way. Then Raymond Briggs' 1st Armoured Division passed through them about 6 PM, penetrated five miles under cover of dust and dusk, paused at 7.30 PM when darkness fell, and drove forward again 'in a solid phalanx' just before midnight when the moon rose. By daybreak, on March 27th, it was safely through the bottleneck and had arrived on the edge of El Hamma.

But here the British were checked for two days by the Germans' anti-tank screen, and a counterattack against their flank by some thirty tanks of the 15th Panzer Division. The delay was long enough to allow the bulk of the Mareth Line garrison, even though marching on foot, to escape the threatened cut-off and withdraw to the Wadi Akarit position. About 5,000 Italians had been taken prisoner, mainly in the earlier phase of the battle, and 1,000 Germans were captured in the fighting near El Hamma – but their sacrificial effort to cover the coastal corridor of retreat enabled the bulk of the Axis forces to withdraw safely, and with little loss of equipment. A quick switch of thrust-line might have reached the coast and cut them off, but the opportunity was missed. More than a week's pause followed before Montgomery was ready to tackle the enemy's new position.

Meanwhile Patton renewed his attack towards the coast and the enemy's rear, being reinforced for the purpose with the US 9th and 34th Infantry Divisions. While the main thrust was to be from El Guettar towards Gabes, with the 1st and 9th Infantry Divisions opening a path for the 1st Armored, the 34th was to capture the Fondouk Pass, a hundred miles to the north, and thus open a further route into the coastal plain. But the Fondouk attack, made on Marth 27th, was soon checked – by a thinly strung defence – and abandoned next day. The 34th Division then fell back four miles to the west to get out of range and reorganize – a withdrawal that led its opponents to draw the conclusion, in a battlefield report, that: 'The American gives up the fight as soon as he is attacked.'

The main attack, from El Guettar, was delivered on the 28th but also suffered a check, after a small gain of ground in harder fighting. By that time Montgomery had broken through at El Hamma and reached Gabes, so Alexander directed Patton to launch his armoured column towards the coast without waiting until the infantry had cleared its path. The attempt was baulked by the enemy's well-knit chain of anti-tank guns, and after three days of ineffectual effort the infantry were again called on to clear the way – but achieved no better success, despite Patton's prodding. Nevertheless the threat of a breakthrough, into the enemy's rear, had led to the 21st Panzer Division being dispatched to this sector to support the 10th, and that additional distraction of the enemy's meagre armoured reserve was of great help to Montgomery's impending frontal assault on the Wadi Akarit position – for which he had 570 tanks and 1,470 guns.

This was strong by nature, as the flat coastal strip is barely four miles wide, and covered by the deep trough of the Wadi Akarit, while at the point where this Wadi becomes shallow and narrow a range of steep-sided low hills rises from the plain and stretches to the verge of the salt-marsh belt. But the Axis decision to quit the Mareth Line had been taken so late that there had been scant time to fortify the position and extend it in depth. Worse still for the defenders, they were very short of ammunition – having used up most of their limited supply by making their stand prematurely and too far forward.

Montgomery's first idea, as at Mareth, was to pierce the enemy's position on a narrow sector near the coast, and then pass the armour through to exploit the penetration. The 51st (Highland) Division was to make the breach, while the 4th Indian Division under Tuker was to capture the eastern end of the hill-barrier to cover its flank. But Tuker urged that the attack frontage should be widened, and extended west-

ward to capture the dominating heights in the centre – following the
mountain warfare axiom that 'the second highest ground is no good'.
He was confident that his troops had the trained skill in both hill and
night fighting to tackle such a difficult obstacle. Montgomery accepted
the proposal and extended the attack frontage, employing the three
infantry divisions of 30th Corps in the breaching assault. Moreover,
rather than wait a further week for a moonlight period, he took the bold
decision to launch it in the dark, relying on the advantage of obscurity
to outweigh the risk of confusion.

At nightfall on April 5th, the 4th Indian Division started to advance,
and long before dawn on the 6th had penetrated deeply into the hills,
capturing some 4,000 prisoners, mainly Italians. At 4.30 AM, the 50th
and 51st Divisions launched their assault supported by a bombardment
from nearly 400 guns. The 50th was checked on the line of the anti-
tank ditch, but the 51st soon achieved a breach in the enemy's defences,
although not so large as that which the 4th Indian Division had made.
The two-pronged penetration offered opportunity for speedy exploitation by the armoured forces of the 10th Corps, under Horrocks, which
had been posted close behind the front for the purpose.

At 8.45 AM Horrocks came forward to Tuker's headquarters, and an
office note recorded that: 'Commander Fourth Indian Division pointed
out to Commander 10 Corps that we had broken the enemy; that the
way was clear for 10 Corps to go through; that immediate offensive
action would finish the campaign in North Africa. Now was the time to
get the whips out and spare neither men nor machines. Commander 10
Corps spoke to Army commander on the telephone requesting permission to put in 10 Corps to maintain the momentum of the attack.' But
there was an unfortunate delay in starting the move, and a greater one
in starting the exploitation. Alexander's Despatch states that 'at 1200
hours General Montgomery put in 10 Corps'. By that time the German
90th Light Division had counterattacked and ejected the British 51st
from some of the ground it had gained, partially closing the breach.
Then, in the afternoon, when the leading armoured elements of Horrocks's 10th Corps belatedly' began pushing through it, they were
checked by the deployment and counterattack of the 15th Panzer Division, the enemy's only available reserve. Meanwhile nothing was done
that day to use the heavyweight punch of the 10th Corps in exploiting
the gap made by the 4th Indian Division.

Montgomery planned, in his characteristically deliberate way, to
make his breakthrough the following morning, laying on a tremendous
air attack and artillery bombardment to help in driving it through. But

when morning came the enemy had vanished, and his intended knock-out blow turned into another follow-up of an army which had slipped out of his grasp.

But while he had lost his chance of a decisive victory, his opponents had lost their chance of sealing the breach, and maintaining their position on the Wadi Akarit line, because two of their three panzer divisions, the 10th and 21st, had been drawn away in turn to check the American threat to their rear. So on the previous evening, Messe had told Arnim that it was not possible to hold on at Wadi Akarit for another day, in the absence of such reinforcement, and had obtained his agreement for a withdrawal to the Enfidaville position, 150 miles to the north – the next line where the coastal plain was narrow, and also buttressed by a hill-barrier.

The Axis troops had begun withdrawing soon after dark on the 6th, and they reached the Enfidaville position safely on the 11th, although most of them had to march on foot. The leading troops of the Eighth Army, advancing on a two corps front, did not arrive there until two days later, although fully motorized and overwhelmingly strong compared with the weak German rearguards which occasionally deployed to put a brake on their pursuit.

In an effort to intercept the enemy's retreat, Alexander launched the 9th Corps (of the First Army) on an attack to capture the Fondouk Pass and then to thrust fifty miles eastward through Kairouan to the coast town of Sousse, some twenty miles south of Enfidaville. This newly formed corps, commanded by John Crocker, was given the British 6th Armoured Division, an infantry brigade of the 46th Division, and the US 34th Infantry Division, which had 250 tanks. The task of the infantry was to capture the commanding heights on either side of the Fondouk Pass, in order to clear a passage for the armoured drive. The attack, hurriedly mounted, was to start on the night of April 7th–8th. But the troops of the 34th Division were nearly three hours late in starting, and having lost the cloak of darkness were soon halted by the enemy's fire, being all the more inclined to stop and take cover because of the damping experience of the previous attack only ten days before. Their failure to advance enabled the enemy to switch his fire northward to check the brigade of the 46th Division, which had been making better progress towards gaining the higher ground north of the pass. So Crocker decided to throw in his armour to force the passage rather than wait for the infantry to clear it, since the whole point of the attack depended on a quick breakthrough to the coastal plain.

This was delivered next day, April 9th, by the 6th Armoured Division under Major-General Keightley, with a loss of thirty-four tanks (but only sixty-seven men) – a loss which seemed heavy, but was astonishingly light relatively to the difficulties it had to overcome in driving through minefields and running the gauntlet of the fifteen anti-tank guns covering the narrow passage – all of which were knocked out. It was not until the afternoon, however, that the armour got through, so Crocker decided to suspend the exploitation until next morning, and called the units back to lie up for the night in protected leaguer at the mouth of the pass. That decision was a cautious contrast to the boldness of his earlier one. But the minefield had still to be gapped for the passage of the wheeled transport, and reports showed that the German armour withdrawing from the south, under Bayerlein's control, was already approaching Kairouan. The 6th Armoured Division resumed its eastward drive at dawn on April 10th but by the time it reached Kairouan the enemy's retreating columns had already passed safely through this road centre. The small German detachment (of two infantry battalions and an anti-tank company) holding the Fondouk sector had also slipped away, having fulfilled Bayerlein's order that it must keep the 9th Corps in check until the morning of April 10th, to cover the retreat of Messe's army up the coastal corridor. Its successful extrication from such a precarious situation, threatened in front and rear by vastly superior forces, was a remarkable feat.

The two Axis armies had now linked up for the defence of the hundred-mile arc from the north coast to Enfidaville. While this had improved their situation temporaily, the benefit was diminished by the losses they had suffered, particularly in equipment, so that even the shortened line was too long for their shrinking strength in face of the Allies' mounting superiority in numbers and weapon power, now concentrated for the assault on this defensive arc. Moreover, the ground that Arnim's February counterstroke had gained near Medjez el Bab and northward had mostly been recaptured by the British in attacks carried out by Lieutenant-General Allfrey's 5th Corps at the end of March and beginning of April – so that the Allies were well-placed for the delivery of fresh easterly thrusts against Tunis and Bizerta.

Political and psychological considerations strongly influenced the choice of the area for the Allies' coming effort to settle the issue of the campaign by a knock-out blow. In a letter to Alexander on March 23rd, and others that followed, Eisenhower had urged that the main effort should be made in the north, in the First Army's sector, and that Patton's corps should be transferred there to take part in the decisive thrust, so as to serve the needs of American morale. Alexander accepted the suggestion in drafting his plans, and on April 10th directed Anderson to prepare the main attack for delivery about the 22nd. He also bowed to Patton's vigorous protest against being placed under the First Army again, and arranged that the US 2nd Corps should continue to operate separately under his own direction. At the same time he turned down Montgomery's request that the 6th Armoured Division, which had just linked up with the Eighth Army, should be transferred to it – while notifying Montgomery that the Eighth Army's part would become subsidiary, and that he must release one of his two armoured divisions (the 1st) to reinforce the First Army.

On this occasion the interests of policy and strategy coincided. The northern sector provided more scope for exerting the Allies' superior strength, because of the wider avenues of attack and the shorter line of supply, whereas the southern approach by Enfidaville was less promising for effective action, being more cramping to the deployment of armoured forces.

The troops of the US 2nd Corps were brought from the southern to the northern sector of Tunisia on a staging schedule involving the movement of some 2,400 vehicles a day across the British rear arc – a complex feat of staffwork (Omar Bradley now took over command of this corps from Patton, who returned to the task of planning the American part in the invasion of Sicily). The British 9th Corps was also switched northward, in a shorter move, and inserted on the right centre between the British 5th and French 19th Corps – which now adjoined the Eighth Army on the Allied right wing.

Under the 'final plan', issued by Alexander on April 16th, the offensive was to be a converging four-pronged thrust. The Eighth Army was to strike on the night of April 19th, with Horrocks' 10th Corps, through Enfidaville northward towards Hammamet and Tunis with the aim of cutting across the neck of the Cap Bon peninsula and blocking access to it, in order to prevent the rest of the Axis forces withdrawing there for a prolonged stand. This aim called for an advance of at least fifty miles through a very difficult bottleneck area. The French 19th Corps, next in line, was to keep up a threatening pressure and exploit any opportunities arising from the advance of its neighbours. The British 9th Corps, which had one infantry and two armoured divisions, was to strike in the early morning of April 22nd between Pont-du-Fahs and Goubellat, with the aim of opening the way for an armoured breakthrough there. The British 5th Corps on its left, with three infantry divisions and a tank brigade, was to make the main effort and strike at nightfall that same day near Medjez el Bab against the fifteen-mile sector held by two regiments of the German 334th Division. The US 2nd Corps was to launch its attack in the northern sector a day later; this forty-mile stretch was held by the three regiments of the Manteuffel Division and one of the 334th – but their strength was less than 8,000 men compared with the 95,000 of the US 2nd Corps.

The prospects of such a general offensive – delivered almost simultaneously on every sector – looked very favourable. On the Allied side there were now twenty divisions with a combat strength of well over 300,000 men and 1,400 tanks. The total strength of the nine German divisions which formed the backbone of the defence along the hundred-mile arc was estimated, correctly, by the Allied intelligence to be barely 60,000 men, and they had less than 100 tanks altogether – one German report gives the total fit for action as only forty-five. Moreover a spoiling attack that Arnim launched south of Medjez el Bab on the night of April 20th, although it penetrated some five miles in the dark, was repulsed when daylight came – and failed to upset the mounting and delivery of the British attack in this sector.

But the Allied general offensive, though delivered on time, did not go according to plan. In defence the Germans still proved very stubborn, and skilful in utilizing difficult ground to block superior strength. Thus Alexander's 'final' plan miscarried, and had to be recast – becoming the penultimate one.

The Eighth Army's attack at Enfidaville, with three infantry divisions, met tough opposition in the hills bordering the coastal strip, and suffered a costly check – belying the optimistic belief of Montgomery and Horrocks that the enemy could be 'bounced' out of this bottleneck. The Italians here fought as vigorously as the Germans. Farther inland, the massed armour of the British 9th Corps succeeded in penetrating the enemy's front to a depth of eight miles in the Kourzia area northwest of Pont-du-Fahs, but was then brought to a standstill by the intervention of Arnim's only substantial mobile reserve, the depleted 10th Panzer Division, which now had less than a tenth of the attacking force's tank strength (which was 360 fit for action). The main attack, by the British 5th Corps, made slow progress in face of the tenacious resistance of the two German infantry regiments defending this central sector, and after four days' hard fighting was only six to seven miles beyond Medjez el Bab. It was then definitely stopped, and in places pushed back, by the intervention of an improvised panzer brigade composed of most of the remaining tanks of Army Group Afrika. On the northern sector, the US 2nd Corps made little progress during the first two days of its attack, through very rugged country, and then found on April 25th that the enemy had slipped back stealthily to another defence line a few miles farther back. In sum, the Allied offensive had come to a halt everywhere without achieving a definite breach anywhere.

But the Axis forces had strained themselves and their scanty resources to the limit in foiling it. By April 25th their two armies were reduced to about one-quarter of a refill unit of fuel – ie only enough for twenty-five kilometres – while the ammunition remaining was estimated as barely sufficient for three days' further fighting. Scarcely any supplies were now reaching them to replenish the ammunition and fuel on which their hope of parrying thrusts depended. Here lay the decisive factor in the issue of the Allies' next offensive. Food supplies were also becoming desperately short – Arnim later said that 'even without the Allied offensive I should have had to capitulate by the 1st of June at the latest because we had no more to eat'.

At the end of February Rommel and Arnim had reported that at least 140,000 tons of supplies a month would be required to maintain the fighting power of the Axis forces, if the Supreme Command decided to hold on to Tunisia. The authorities in Rome, acutely conscious of the shipping difficulty, put the figure at 120,000 tons, while reckoning that up to a third of the total might be sunk in transit. But in the event only 29,000 tons reached the Axis forces during the month of March, a quarter of it by air. By contrast, the Americans alone brought some 400,000 tons of supplies safely into North African ports that month. In April the Axis supplies dwindled to 23,000 tons, and in the first week of May to a trickle of 2,000 tons. That was the measure of the grip which Allied airpower and seapower (mainly British) aided by excellent intelligence evaluation of the enemy's shipping movements, had established on the trans-Mediterranean supply routes. The figures amply account for the sudden collapse of the Axis forces' resistance – and explain the collapse far more clearly than do any of the Allied leaders' accounts.

Alexander's fresh 'final plan' emerged, indirectly, from the block in the Enfidaville bottleneck. On April 21st, when the failure of the three-division attack there had become painfully plain, Montgomery was driven to suspend it because of the mounting losses – a suspension that had helped Arnim to shift all his remaining armour northward to stop the main British attack from breaking through east of Medjez el Bab, as already related. Montgomery planned to resume his effort on the 29th, concentrating it in the narrow coastal strip, without trying to secure the high ground inland. This directive, though accepted by Horrocks, met with strong objection from the two foremost divisional commanders, Tuker and Freyberg. Their warning arguments were supported by the early check suffered when the fresh attack was delivered. Next day, April 30th, Alexander arrived on the scene to discuss the situation with Montgomery, and then gave orders that the two best available divisions of the Eighth Army should be switched to the First Army for a fresh and reinforced thrust in the Medjez el Bab sector. That alternative course had been urged by Tuker before the abortive Enfidaville attack. It might well have been adopted earlier, for the Enfidaville attack had not even fulfilled the limited object of pinning down the Axis forces there and preventing the reinforcement of the central sector.

The switch, once decided, was quickly put into effect. The two picked divisions, the 4th Indian and 7th Armoured, started on their long north-westward move before dark that same day. For the 7th Armoured, which was lying back in reserve, it entailed a circuitous journey of nearly 300 miles along rough roads, but this was completed in a couple of days – the tanks being carried on transporters. The two divisions were transferred to the 9th Corps, which was entrusted with the decisive stroke, and itself side-stepped northward to concentrate for the purpose behind the sector held by the 5th Corps. Horrocks himself was also included in the transfer, to take over command of the 9th Corps, as Crocker had just been disabled by an accidental injury incurred in demonstrating a new mortar – a personal stroke of ill luck at a moment of great opportunity.

Meanwhile Bradley's US 2nd Corps had resumed its attack in the northern sector on the night of April 26th. In four days of stiff fighting its efforts to advance through this hilly region were baffled by the enemy's obstinate resistance. But persistent pressure strained the enemy's resources so heavily, and produced such an acute shortage of ammunition on his side, that he was compelled to withdraw to a fresh and less easily defensible line east of Mateur. The withdrawal was skilfully carried out during the nights of May 1st and 2nd without interference, but the new line was only fifteen miles from the base-port of Bizerta, so that the defence had now become perilously lacking in depth – as it was, already, in the Medjez el Bab sector facing Tunis.

Such lack of depth for defence made fatal the defenders' extreme shortage of supplies, and this went far to assure the decisiveness of the fresh offensive that was now being mounted by the Allies for launching on May 6th. For once the crust was pierced there would be no possibility of prolonging resistance by elastic defence and manoeuvre in retreat. Although the Axis forces had managed to frustrate the previous attacks they had succeeded at the price of almost exhausting their scanty stocks, being left with only enough ammunition for a brief reply to the attackers' overwhelming fire and only enough fuel for the shortest of countermoves. Moreover they were devoid of air cover as the airfields in Tunisia had become untenable and almost all the remaining aircraft had been withdrawn to Sicily.

The impending blow came as no surprise to the Axis commanders, as they had intercepted Allied radio messages which revealed the switch of large forces from the Eighth Army to the First. But awareness of the blow was of little help in meeting it when they lacked the means.

In Alexander's new plan, 'Vulcan', the breakthrough was to be made by a hammer-blow with the 9th Corps, passing through the 5th, and striking on a very narrow front – less than two miles wide – in the valley south of the Medjerda River. The assault was to be delivered by a massive phalanx composed of the 4th British and 4th Indian Divisions with four supporting battalions of 'infantry' tanks, closely followed by the 6th and 7th Armoured Divisions. The armoured strength comprised more than 470 tanks. After the two infantry divisions had penetrated the defence to a depth of some three miles, the two armoured divisions were to drive through and in their first bound reach the area of St Cyprien, twelve miles from the starting line and halfway to Tunis. Alexander emphasized in his instructions that 'the primary object is to capture Tunis', so as to forestall any rally, and that there must be no pause for 'mopping up localities which the enemy continues to hold'.

As a preliminary to the 9th Corps assault, the 5th Corps was ordered to capture the flanking height of the Djebel Bou Aoukaz on the evening of May 5th – a mission which was achieved after some stiff fighting. After that the chief task of the 5th Corps was 'to keep open the funnel' through which the 9th Corps was thrusting. In the event it proved to be no problem, as the enemy no longer had the means of developing an effective counterattack.

Opening the funnel might have been more difficult if the 9th Corps assault had been launched in daylight as originally intended – in view of the First Army's lack of experience in night attacks. But on Tuker's insistence the plan was altered and zero hour was fixed for 3 AM, so as to gain full benefit from the cloak of obscurity provided by a moonless night. At his urging, too, the customary barrage was replaced by successive concentrations of fire, centrally controlled, on all known enemy strongpoints, and the provision of artillery ammunition was doubled, raising it to a thousand rounds per gun. These concentrated shoots put down a shell on every two yards of front, so that the defences were plastered five times more thickly than by the barrage at Alamein the previous autumn. The paralysing effect of these concentrated shoots, by the 400 guns immediately supporting the assault, was increased and extended by the terrific air attack starting at dawn, which comprised over 200 sorties.

By 9.30 AM the 4th Indian Division had punched a deep hole, at a cost of little more than a hundred casualties, and reported that there was no sign of any serious opposition ahead – telling Corps Headquarters that the armour could now 'go as fast and as far as it liked'. Before 10 AM the leading troops of the 7th Armoured Division had begun to pour through the line gained by the infantry. On the right wing, the British 4th Division was late in starting and slower in advancing, but was helped by the thrust of its left wing neighbour, and reached its objective before noon. The armoured divisions were then at last permitted to drive on. In mid-afternoon, however, they were halted for the night near Massicault – which was barely six miles beyond the start-line of the assault and three miles beyond the line gained by the infantry, while only a quarter of the way to Tunis. This extreme caution is explained in the divisional history of the 7th by the statement that the commander 'considered that it would be wiser to keep each Brigade in the firm positions they both held rather than to loosen the hold of both and complicate the long task of replenishment' – an explanation which shows all too clearly a failure to grasp the elementary principles of exploitation, and to fulfil its spirit. As at Wadi Akarit, Horrocks and the commanders of the armoured divisions were slow to respond to the call of opportunity, and continued to operate at a tempo more characteristic of infantry action than fitted to fulfil the potentialities of mechanized mobility.

There was no need for such caution. The eight-mile sector south of the Medjerda River where the blow was struck, on a two-mile frontage, had been held by two weak infantry battalions and an anti-tank battalion of the 15th Panzer Division, supported by a composite force of less than sixty tanks – almost all that remained of the Axis armour. This very thin shield had been stunned and pulverized by the tremendous concentration of shells and bombs supporting the assault. Moreover lack of fuel had prevented Arnim from bringing northward the unarmoured remainder of the 10th and 21st Panzer Divisions, as had been planned. That fatal lack of fuel had proved more effective in pinning them down than the elaborate deception plan which the British had designed to make it appear that they were again going to strike in the Kourzia sector.

The 6th and 7th Armoured Divisions resumed their advance at dawn, on May 7th, but again showed excessive caution, and were held up until the afternoon by a handful of Germans, with ten tanks and a few guns, at St Cyprien. It was 3.15 PM before the order was given to drive into Tunis. The armoured-cars of the 11th Hussars entered the city half an hour later, and thus fittingly crowned the leading role this regiment had played since the start of the North African campaign nearly three years earlier. The Derbyshire Yeomanry, the armoured-car regiment of the 6th Armoured Division, entered almost simultaneously. They were followed up by tanks and motor-borne infantry to extend and complete the occupation of the city. In the process, the troops suffered more embarrassment and obstruction from the hysterical enthusiasm of the population, pelting them with flowers and kisses, than from the sporadic resistance put up by small pockets of confused and disorganized Germans. A considerable number were taken prisoner that evening, and many more were rounded up next morning, while a much larger proportion sought to escape by fleeing northward or southward from the city. What remained of the fighting formations on the perimeter also retreated in these divergent directions once they were split asunder by the thrust into Tunis.

Meanwhile the US 2nd Corps had resumed its attack in the northern sector to coincide with the British thrust. Progress on May 6th had been slow, and resistance seemed still stiff, but on the next afternoon reconaissance elements of the 9th Infantry Division found the road open and drove into Bizerta at 4.15 PM, the enemy having evacuated the city and withdrawn south-eastward. Formal entry into the city was reserved for the French Corps Franc d'Afrique, which arrived on the 8th. The 1st Armored Division, advancing from Mateur, had suffered checks on the first two days. So had the 1st and 34th Infantry Divisions farther south. But on the 8th the 1st Armored found the defence collapsing and progress easy, as the enemy's ammunition and fuel became exhausted and the British 7th Armoured Division were swinging north from Tunis along the coast in his rear.

Trapped between the British and American spearheads, and without means of resistance or retreat, mass surrenders began. The leading squadron of the 11th Hussars had some 10,000 prisoners on its hands before evening. Early next morning, the 9th, part of another squadron drove on to Porto Farina, near the cape of that name twenty miles east of Bizerta, where it received the surrender of 9,000 more who were crowded on the beach, some of them pathetically trying to build rafts – and were relieved to be able to hand this crowd of prisoners over to the American armoured force which arrived soon afterwards. At 9.30 AM General von Vaerst, commanding the 5th Panzer Army and the northern area, signalled to Arnim: 'Our armour and artillery have been destroyed. Without ammunition and fuel. We shall fight to the last.' The final sentence was a gallant bit of absurdity, for troops cannot fight without ammunition. Vaerst soon learnt that his troops, realizing how nonsensical were such heroic orders, were giving themselves up. So by midday, he agreed to a formal surrender of his remaining troops, which raised the total bag in this area to nearly 40,000.

A much larger part of the Axis forces, when the split was produced, lay in the area south of Tunis. This area was also more defensible by nature, and the Allied commanders expected that the enemy would make a more prolonged stand there. But there, too, the exhaustion of the enemy's ammunition and fuel produced a quick collapse after a short resistance. The collapse was accelerated by a general feeling of hopelessness, since even where some supplies remained the Axis troops were aware that no replenishments were possible – for the same reason that no escape was possible.

Alexander's aim now was to prevent Messe's army, the southerly part of the Axis forces, retreating into the large Cap Bon peninsula and establishing a firm 'last ditch' position there. So the 6th Armoured Division, as soon as Tunis had been captured, was ordered to turn south-east and drive for Hamman Lif, the near corner of the peninsula's baseline, while the 1st Armored Division converged in the same direction. At Hamman Lif the hills came so close to the sea that the flat coastal strip was only 300 yards wide. This narrow defile was held by a German detachment, supported by 88-mm guns withdrawn from airfield defence, and for two days it blocked all efforts to force a passage. But the obstacle was eventually overcome by a well-combined effort. The infantry of the 6th Armoured Division captured the heights overlooking the town, the artillery swept the streets methodically block by block, and a column of tanks was then sent along the beach at the edge of the surf, where they were better shielded from the fire of the one German gun that remained in action. By nightfall on the 10th the drive was extended across the baseline of the peninsula to Hammamet, thus cutting off the enemy's surviving forces. Paralysed by lack of fuel, they had been unable to withdraw to the peninsula. Next day the 6th Armoured Division drove on southward into the rear of the Axis troops who were keeping the British Eighth Army in check near Enfidaville. Although these still had some ammunition in hand, the definite proof that they were trapped and without hope of escape produced their speedy surrender.

By the 13th all the remaining Axis commanders and their troops had submitted. Only a few hundred had escaped by sea or air to Sicily – beyond the 9,000 wounded and sick who had been evacuated since the beginning of April. As to the size of the final bag, there is a lack of certainty. On May 12th Alexander's headquarters reported to Eisenhower that the number of prisoners since May 5th had risen to 100,000 and it was reckoned as likely to reach 130,000 when the count was complete. A later report 'gave the total bag at about 150,000'. But in his postwar Despatch Alexander said that the total was 'a quarter of a million men'. Churchill in his Memoirs gives the same round figure, but qualifies it with the word 'nearly'. Eisenhower gives it as '240,000, of which approximately 125,000 were Germans'. But Army Group Afrika had reported to Rome on May 2nd that its ration strength during the month of April had varied between 170,000 and 180,000 – and that was before the heavy fighting in the last week of the campaign. So it is hard to see how the number of prisoners taken could have exceeded this strength by nearly 50 per cent. Administrative staffs who are responsible for feeding troops do not tend to underestimate their numbers. Here it is worth remark that much larger discrepancies still, between the last known German ration strength and the Allied claims about the number of prisoners captured, were manifest in the final stages of the war.

But whatever may have been the exact number taken in Tunisia it was certainly a very large bag. The most important effect was that it deprived the Axis of the bulk of its battle-tested troops in the Mediterranean theatre which could otherwise have been used to block the Allies' coming invasion of Sicily – the first and crucial phase of their re-entry into Europe.

CHAPTER TWENTY-SIX

Re-entry into Europe – Through Sicily

After the event, the Allies' conquest of Sicily in 1943 looked an easy matter. But actually this initial re-entry into Europe was a hazardous leap, hedged with uncertainties. For its successful outcome it owed much to a series of long-hidden factors. First to the blind pride of Hitler and Mussolini jointly in trying to 'save face' in Africa. Then to Mussolini's jealous fear of his German allies, and reluctance to let them take a leading part in the defence of Italian territory. Then to Hitler's belief, in disagreement with Mussolini, that Sicily was not the Allies' real objective – a mistaken belief that partly arose from a brilliantly subtle ruse 'planted' by the British deception plan.

The first factor counted most of all. One of the greatest ironies in the whole war was the way that Hitler and the German General Staff – who had always feared to embark on overseas expeditions in reach of British seapower – abstained from sending Rommel sufficient forces to follow up his victories, yet in the last lap sent so many troops across to Africa as to forfeit their prospects of defending Europe.

Ironically, too, they were drawn into this fatal folly by their own un-expected success in halting Eisenhower's first drive for Tunis after they had been caught napping by the Anglo-American invasion of French North Africa in the previous November. While the Allies' spearhead was advancing rather cautiously eastward from Algeria, the Germans had quickly reacted to the threat by starting to fly troops across the Mediterranean in the hope of frustrating the Allies' early capture of the ports of Tunis and Bizerta. They succeeded in holding the mountain approaches and producing a prolonged stalemate.

But the success of this forestalling move encouraged Hitler and Mus-solini to believe that they could hold on to Tunisia indefinitely. So they decided to pour in reinforcements on a large enough scale to match Eisenhower's growing strength. The more their commitment increased, the more they felt that they could not withdraw without losing prestige. At the same time the difficulty either of withdrawing or of holding on increased as the Allies' superior naval and air forces began to develop a stranglehold on the straits between Sicily and Tunisia.

The German–Italian bridgehead that was built up in Tunisia kept the Allies at bay throughout the winter, and provided shelter for the remains of Rommel's army at the end of his 2,000-mile retreat from Alamein. Nevertheless, the Allies' early failure to capture Tunisia turned out immensely to their advantage in the long run. For Hitler and Mussolini would not listen to any argument for evacuating the German and Italian troops while there was still time and opportunity to get them away.

In a final effort to convince Hitler of the necessity, Rommel flew to Hitler's headquarters in East Prussia on March 10th, 1943. His journal records how futile it proved: 'I emphasized as strongly as I could that the "African" troops must be re-equipped in Italy to enable them to defend our southern European flank. I even went so far as to give him a guarantee – something which I am normally very reluctant to do – that with these troops, I would beat off any Allied invasion in southern Europe. But it was all hopeless.'*

As the Allied armies closed in upon the bridgehead 'for the kill', the Axis troops had to sit there with sinking spirits, awaiting the blow – and foregoing the chance provided by a spell of misty weather in April that would have helped to screen their embarkation and transportation if they had been allowed to withdraw. They managed to check the Allies' first attempt to crack their defence, April 20th–22nd, but collapsed when their front was penetrated in the next big attack, on May 6th. The complete breakdown that followed was largely due to the shallowness of the bridgehead and the defending troops' acute consciousness that they were fighting with their backs close to a hostile sea.

The complete capture of the eight divisions in Tunisia, including most of Rommel's veterans and the pick of the Italian Army, left Italy and the Italian islands almost naked of defensive covering. These forces would have provided a very strong defence for the Italian gateways into Europe, and the Allies' chances of successful invasion would have been dim. The Allies, however, were not ready to take immediate advantage of the opportunity – although they had decided in January that a landing in Sicily should be the next step, and Tunis had been captured close to the time expected. Fortunately, for them, the opportunity was prolonged by dissension and divergent views in the opposing headquarters.

Here we come to another point of evidence, provided in the first place by General Westphal, who was then Chief of Staff to Field-

* *The Rommel Papers*, p 419.

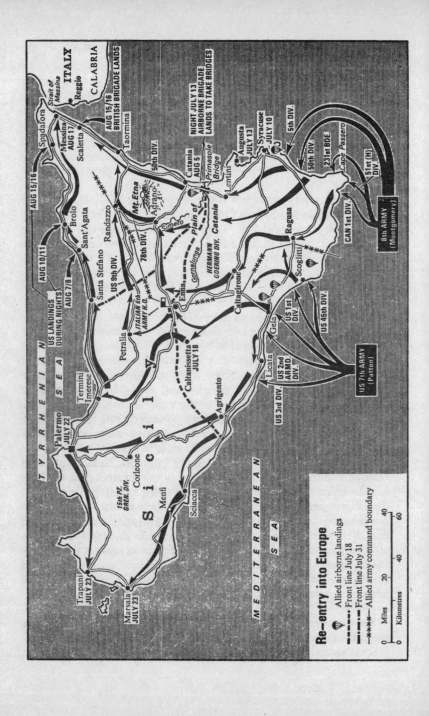

Re-entry into Europe

🪂 Allied airborne landings

----- Front line July 18

—·—·— Front line July 31

✳✳✳✳ Allied army command boundary

	Miles		
0	20	40	60
0	40		
Kilometres			

ITALY
CALABRIA
Strait of Messina
Reggio
Spadafora
Messina AUG 17
Scaletta
Taormina
AUG 15/16
AUG 15/16 BRITISH BRIGADE LANDS
NIGHT JULY 13 AIRBORNE BRIGADE LANDS TO TAKE BRIDGES
Catania AUG 5
Primasole Bridge
Lentini
Augusta JULY 13
Syracuse JULY 10
5th DIV.
50th DIV.
231st BDE
Cape Passero
51st (H) DIV.
8th ARMY (Montgomery)
50th DIV.
Mt. Etna
Adrano
Simeto
Plain of Catania
HERMANN GOERING DIV.
Gornalunga
Ragusa
CAN 1st DIV.
Scoglitti
Caltagirone
78th DIV.
ITALIAN 6th ARMY H.Q.
Enna
Gela
US 1st DIV.
US 45th DIV.
US 7th ARMY (Patton)
AUG 15/16
AUG 10/11
US LANDINGS DURING NIGHTS
AUG 7/8
Brolo
Sant'Agata
Randazzo
Santa Stefano
US 9th DIV.
Petralia
Caltanissetta JULY 18
Licata
US 3rd DIV.
US 2nd ARMD. DIV.
Agrigento
Termini Imerese
TYRRHENIAN SEA
Palermo JULY 22
Corleone
15th PZ. GREN. DIV.
Menfi
Sciacca
S i c i l y
Trapani JULY 23
Marsala JULY 23
MEDITERRANEAN SEA

Marshal Kesselring, the Commander-in-Chief in southern Italy. As Italy had no mobile mechanized forces left, her military chiefs besought the Germans to provide a strong reinforcement of panzer type divisions. At that moment Hitler was moved to meet this urgent need, and sent Mussolini a personal message offering him five divisions. But Mussolini, without telling Kesselring, sent Hitler a reply that he wanted only three – and that meant only one fresh division beyond the two improvised from drafts which had been in transit to Africa. He even expressed the wish that no further German troops should be dispatched.

Mussolini's reluctance to accept this mid-May offer was due to a mixture of pride and fear. He could not bear to let the world, and his own people, see that he was dependent on German aid. As Westphal remarked: 'He wanted Italy to be defended by Italians, and shut his eyes to the fact that the appalling state of his forces made such an idea quite impracticable.' But his further reason was that he did not want to let the Germans acquire a dominating position in Italy. Anxious as he was to keep out the Allies, he was almost as anxious to keep out the Germans.

The new Chief of the Army Staff, General Roatta (previously commanding Sicily) eventually convinced Mussolini that larger German reinforcements were essential for any chance of a successful defence of Italy and its island outposts. So he agreed to further German divisions coming in – subject to the condition that they should be subordinated to the tactical control of Italian commanders.

The Italian garrison of Sicily consisted of only four field divisions and six static coast defence divisions that were poor in equipment and morale. The German drafts in transit to Africa when the collapse occurred were formed into a division and given the title of the '15th Panzergrenadier Division', but it had only one tank unit. The similarly rebuilt 'Hermann Göring' panzer division was sent to Sicily near the end of June. But Mussolini would not allow these two divisions to be constituted as a corps under a German commander. They were placed directly under the Italian army commander, General Guzzoni, and distributed in five groups along the 150 mile diameter of the island as mobile reserves. The senior German liaison officer, Lieutenant-General von Senger und Etterlin, was provided with a small operations staff and a signals company so that he could exercise emergency control.

By the time that Mussolini was willing to accept more German help, Hitler was becoming more dubious about providing it, and also tending to a different view about the danger-point. On the one hand, he suspected that the Italians would throw over Mussolini and make peace – a suspicion that was soon borne out by events – and for that reason hesi-tated to push in more German divisions so deeply that they might be cut off if their allies collapsed or changed sides. On the other hand, he came to think that Mussolini, the Italian High Command, and Kessel-ring were mistaken in their view that the Allies' next move from Africa would be a jump into Sicily. On that point he proved wrong.

Hitler's greatest strategic disadvantage in meeting the Allies' re-entry into Europe lay in the immense stretch of his own conquests – from the west coast of France, on the Atlantic Ocean, to the east coast of Greece, on the Aegean Sea. It was very difficult for him to gauge where the Allies would strike. Their greatest strategic advantage lay in the wide choice of alternative objectives and power of distraction which they enjoyed, through seapower. Hitler, while having always to guard against a cross-Channel stroke from England, had cause to fear that the Anglo-American armies in North Africa might land anywhere on his southern front between Spain and Greece.*

Hitler thought that the Allies were more likely to land in Sardinia than in Sicily. Sardinia would provide an easy stepping stone into Cor-sica, and a well-placed springboard for a jump on to either the French or Italian mainland. At the same time an Allied landing in Greece was expected, and Hitler wished to have reserves kept back so that they could be rushed in that direction.

These ideas were fostered by receiving from Nazi agents in Spain copies of documents found on a 'British officer' whose body had been washed ashore on the Spanish coast. Besides identity papers and per-sonal correspondence, the documents included a private letter – of which the dead man had been the bearer – written by Lieutenant-General Sir Archibald Nye, the Vice-Chief of the Imperial General Staff, to General Alexander. This letter referred to recent official tele-grams about forthcoming operations, and its supplementary comments indicated that the Allies were intending to land in Sardinia and Greece while aiming by their 'cover plan' to convince the enemy that Sicily was their objective.

The corpse and the letter were part of an ingenious deception devised by a section of the British Intelligence service. This was so well worked out that the heads of the German Intelligence service were convinced of its genuineness. Although it did not alter the view of the Italian chiefs and Kesselring that Sicily would be the Allies' next objective, it ap-pears to have made a strong impression on Hitler.

On Hitler's orders the 1st Panzer Division was sent from France to

* For map see p 292.

Greece – to support the three German infantry divisions and the Italian 11th Army there – while the newly formed 90th Panzergrenadier Division reinforced the four Italian divisions in Sardinia. Further reinforcement of that island was hindered by the difficulty of supply, since most of the piers in the few harbours had been destroyed by bombing, but as an additional insurance Hitler moved General Student's 11th Air Corps (of two parachute divisions) down to the south of France, ready to deliver an airborne counterattack against an Allied landing in Sardinia.

Meanwhile, Allied planning proceeded at a slower gait. The decision to land in Sicily had been born of a compromise, and unaccompanied by any conclusion as to further aims. When the American and British Chiefs of Staff met at the Casablanca Conference in January 1943, their initial divergence of views was in contrast to their common title, the 'Combined Chiefs of Staff'. The Americans (Admiral King, General Marshall, and General Arnold) wanted to wind up what was regarded as the Mediterranean diversion, once North Africa was cleared, and get back on the direct line of action against Germany. The British (General Brooke, Admiral Pound, Air Chief Marshal Portal) considered that conditions were not yet ripe for a direct cross-Channel invasion, and that such an attempt in 1943 would end in disaster or futility – an estimate that will hardly be questioned in historical retrospect. But all agreed that some further action must be initiated in order to maintain pressure and draw away German forces from the Russian front. On the British side the Joint Planning Staff advocated a landing in Sardinia, but both the British and the American Chiefs of Staff were inclined to prefer Sicily – which was also Churchill's preference – so that agreement on this line was quickly reached. The most potent argument was that the capture of Sicily would effectively clear the sea passage through the Mediterranean, and thus save a lot of shipping – for, since 1940, most of the troop and supply convoys to Egypt and India had been forced to go the long way round by South Africa.

In coming to the decision, on January 19th, to move against Sicily, the Combined Chiefs defined the object as '(i) Making the Mediterranean line of communications more secure; (ii) diverting German pressure from the Russian front; (iii) intensifying the pressure on Italy.' The question of how it should be exploited was left open. An attempt to decide on the next objective would have revived divergencies of view – but in such matters tactful deferment is apt to result in strategic unreadiness.

Nor was there an emphatic sense of urgency in the planning of the Sicilian stroke. Although it was assumed that the conquest of Tunisia might be completed by the end of April, the Combined Chiefs set the moon period of July as the target date for the landing in Sicily. The British produced an outline plan on January 20th for this 'Operation Husky' – a converging sea approach and invasion by forces coming from the eastern and western Mediterranean respectively. It was agreed that Eisenhower should be the Supreme Commander, while Alexander became his Deputy. (That was a significant acceptance of the United States as the senior partner in the alliance, for the British Commander-in-Chief was the senior in rank and experience, and in this campaign the British would still provide the larger part of the forces.) A special planning staff was formed early in February, with headquarters in Algiers, but its branches were widely separated, and in the case of the air force the separation was not only in space but also in thought – the outcome being that air action during the Sicilian campaign was not closely or well related to the needs of the land and sea forces. Much time passed while the draft plan was being carried to and fro. Eisenhower, Alexander, and the two chosen army commanders, Montgomery and Patton, were too occupied with the last lap of the North African campaign to give adequate attention to the next move. Montgomery did not find time to study the draft plan until late in April, and then called for numerous changes in it. The plan was recast on May 3rd, and final approval of it, by the Combined Chiefs of Staff, was received on May 13th – a week after the collapse of the German–Italian front at Tunis, and the day that the last enemy fragments surrendered.

These delays in the planning were the more regrettable since only one of the ten divisions to lead the invasion of Sicily was engaged in the final stage of the North African campaign, and seven of them were fresh entries. A landing in Sicily soon after the Axis collapse in Africa would have found the island almost naked of defence. The long interval that the enemy was allowed for reinforcing the defence of Sicily might have been longer still but for Churchill who, at the Casablanca Conference and subsequently, urged that the landing should be made in June. He gained the backing of the Combined Chiefs of Staff but the commanders in the Mediterranean were not ready to launch the invasion earlier than July 10th.

The main change that had been made in the plan was that Patton's army (the Western Task Force), instead of landing at the western end of Sicily near Palermo, would land in the south-east close to Montgomery's army, whose landing points would now be more concentrated. In view of the time that had elapsed for the enemy's possible reinforcement, this tighter massing of the invading forces was a sound precaution against the danger of a heavy counterstroke – though in the even it proved an unnecessary precaution. But it forfeited the chance of capturing the port of Palermo at the outset – a forfeit that would have been of serious effect but for the way that the new DUKW amphibious vehicles in conjunction with the LSTs ('Landing Ships, Tank') proved capable of solving the problem of maintaining supply over the beaches. The revised plan also forfeited much of the distracting effect sought in the original one, and thereby helped the enemy to concentrate his dispersed reserves after the landing had taken place, and block the Allies' advance across the mountainous centre of the island. If Patton had landed near Palermo on the north-west coast, he would have been well on the way to the Straits of Messina, the enemy's line of reinforcement or retreat – whereby all the enemy forces in Sicily could have been trapped. In the event, the escape of the German divisions had far-reaching ill effects on the Allies' further moves.

To err on the side of security was, however, a very natural preference in this first bound back into Europe by the Allies – and first big sea-borne assault on a coast held by the enemy. Here it is worth note that the assault landing, by eight divisions simultaneously, was larger in scale even than in Normandy eleven months later. Some 150,000 troops were landed on the first day and the next two days, and the ultimate total was about 478,000 – 250,000 British, 228,000 American. The British landings were made along a forty mile stretch of coast at the south-east corner of the island, and the American along a forty mile stretch of the south coast, with a twenty mile interval between the British left and the American right wing.

The naval side of the operation was planned and conducted under the direction of Admiral Sir Andrew Cunningham. It involved a complex pattern of moves leading up to a landing by night, yet went through from start to finish with a wonderful smoothness that did great credit to the planners and the executants. As an amphibious operation it worked much better than 'Operation Torch', the landings in French North Africa, the previous November, from which much had been learned.

The Eastern Naval Task Force (British), under Vice-Admiral Sir Bertram Ramsay, comprised 795 vessels, while a further 715 landing craft were carried with it for the beaching stage. The 5th and 50th Divisions (and 231st Infantry Brigade) came from the east end of the Mediterranean – from Suez, Alexandria, and Haifa – in ships; they were to land along the southerly stretch of Sicily's east coast between Syracuse and Cape Passero. The 51st Division came from Tunisia, in craft, part of it staging at Malta; it was to land on the south-east corner of Sicily. The 1st Canadian Division, to land just west of the corner, came from Britain in two convoys – the second and faster one, carrying the bulk of the troops, sailed from the Clyde on D – 12 (June 28th). It passed through the mine-protected channel near Bizerta immediately ahead of the American convoys.

The Western Naval Task force (American), under Vice-Admiral H. Kent Hewitt, comprised 580 vessels, while a further 1,124 landing craft were carried with it. The 45th Infantry Division, for the right wing landing at Scoglitti, was brought across the Atlantic in two convoys and, after a brief pause at Oran, picked up its LSTs and smaller craft off Bizerta. The 1st Infantry and 2nd Armored Divisions, for the Gela landing, embarked from Algiers and Oran. The 3rd Infantry Division, for the left wing landing at Licata, embarked at Bizerta and was carried entirely in landing ships and landing craft.

The passages and assembly of the convoys in this vast armada were achieved, under naval and air cover, without any serious interference. Only four ships in convoy and two LSTs were lost – to submarine attack. No appreciable damage was suffered from air attack during the approach, and enemy aircraft were kept so well at bay that most of the convoys were not even sighted. The Allies' air superiority in this theatre was so great – over 4,000 operational aircraft against some 1,500 German and Italian – that the enemy bombers were withdrawn in June to bases in north-central Italy. From July 2nd onward the airfields in Sicily were so heavily and persistently attacked that only a few subsidiary landing strips remained usable when D-day came, and most of the undamaged fighters had retired to the mainland or Sardinia (though the actual number of planes destroyed throughout the campaign was not more than 200, compared with the 1,100 claimed by the Allies).

In the afternoon of July 9th the convoys began to arrive in their assembly areas east and west of Malta, and at the same time the wind rose sharply, stirring up the sea to such a steep pitch as to endanger the smaller craft and threaten to dislocate the landings. Fortunately, it moderated by midnight, though leaving a troublesome swell, and only a small proportion of the assault craft were late in reaching the beaches.

The worst effect was on the airborne drop that preceded the seaborne landings – carried out by parts of the British 1st and American 82nd Airborne Divisions. The first large stroke of this kind that the Allies had attempted, it would have been difficult in any case, because of inexperience and the call to make it at night. The high wind increased the navigational complications for the transport and tow aircraft in reaching their goals, and then combined with the anti-aircraft fire to disturb the descent. The American parachute troops were scattered in small parties over an area fifty miles wide. The British glider troops were also very scattered, and forty-seven of the 134 gliders fell into the sea. Nevertheless the unintendedly wide spread of these airborne troops helped to produce a widespread state of alarm and confusion behind the enemy's front, while some of the parties had a more concrete effect by seizing key bridges and road junctions.

The trouble that the sudden storm caused the attackers was, on balance, more than compensated by the extent to which it disarmed the defence. For although in the afternoon five convoys were sighted advancing northward from Malta, and a series of reports were received before dark, the warnings from the higher command either failed to reach or failed to impress the lower headquarters. While all the German troops in reserve were alerted an hour after the first report, the Italians on the coast tended to assume that the whistling wind and rough sea guaranteed them another night's rest at least – Admiral Cunningham aptly remarked in his Dispatch that the unfavourable conditions had 'the effect of making the weary Italians, who had been alert for many nights, turn thankfully in their beds saying "tonight at any rate they can't come". But they came.'

But the Italians' weariness was more than physical. Most of them were tired of the war, and not many had shared Mussolini's belligerent enthusiasm. Moreover the coast defence troops were mostly Sicilian, the idea behind that choice being that they would be the more inclined to live up to their fighting reputation when defending their own houses. But this assumption did not take account of their long manifest dislike of the Germans, or of their practically minded realization that the harder they fought the less would be left of their homes.

Their reluctance to resist was deepened when daylight came on July 10th, and they could see the tremendous array of ships, filling the sea to the horizon, and the continual flow of landing craft with reinforcements to back up the assault waves that had poured ashore in the early hours.

The beach defences were quickly overrun, and the anguish that many of the assault troops had suffered from seasickness was amply offset by the slightness of their casualties from the enemy's fire on arriving ashore. The first stage of the invasion was summed up by Alexander in two sentences: 'The Italian coastal divisions, whose value had never been rated very high, disintegrated almost without firing a shot and the field divisions, when they were met, were also driven like chaff before the wind. Mass surrenders were frequent.' Thus from the first day onward almost the whole burden of the defence fell on the shoulders of the two scratch German divisions, subsequently reinforced by two more.

There was one dangerous counterattack during the critical period before the invading armies were firmly established ashore. This was delivered by the Hermann Göring Division which, along with a detachment of the new 56-ton Tiger tanks, had been posted around Caltagirone, twenty miles from the coast in the mountain belt overlooking the Gela plain – where the American 1st Infantry Division had landed. Fortunately this punch did not come until the second day. A small group of Italian light tanks of obsolete type made a gallant little counterattack on the first morning, and actually penetrated into the town of Gela before they were driven off, but the main German column was delayed on the way and did not appear on the scene until next morning. Even then only a few of the American tanks had been landed – owing to unloading troubles in the heavy surf and congestion on the beaches. There was also a shortage of anti-tank guns and artillery on shore. The German tanks came down over the plain in converging packets, overran the American outposts, and reached the sand dunes bordering the beaches. It looked as if the invaders might be driven back into the sea, but well-directed naval gunfire helped to break up the attack in the nick of time. A menacing thrust on the left flank of the 45th Division by another German column, with a company of Tigers, was stopped in the same way.

Next day, two battle groups of the 15th Panzergrenadier Division arrived on the American front after a hurried march from the west of Sicily, but by that time the Hermann Göring Division had moved off to the British sector, on a call to stem the extending advance there, which at the time looked the most ominous – as it was already close to the port city of Catania, midway up the east coast, whereas the three American beach-heads were still shallow and not yet linked up.

The British landings had met as little opposition as the American landings, while progress was aided by the absence of any early counterattack. Although there were troubles and delays in the unloading process, this went rather better on the whole than on the western beaches, which were more exposed. Air raids were more frequent, after the first day, but the air cover provided was also better, so that shipping losses were almost as small as on the American sectors. Indeed, to those who had seen the earlier years of the war in the Mediterranean it seemed, as Admiral Cunningham remarked, 'almost magical that great fleets of ships could remain anchored on the enemy's coast ... with only such slight losses from air attack as were incurred'. That degree of immunity was a key factor in the success of the amphibious invasion. But in the next stage its progress suffered a check from a different kind of air action.

The British forces had cleared the whole south-eastern part of the island in the first three days. Then Montgomery 'decided to make a great effort to break through into the Plain of Catania from the Lentini area' and ordered 'a major attack for the night of July 13th'. The key problem was to capture the Primasole bridge over the River Simeto, a few miles south of Catania. A parachute brigade was used for this purpose. Only about half of it was dropped in the right place, but this portion succeeded in securing the bridge intact.

The next phase is epitomized in the account provided by General Student, the Commander of the 11th Air Corps – which comprised the German airborne troops. His two divisions had been stationed by Hitler in the south of France ready to fly to Sardinia if the Allies landed there as Hitler expected. But airborne troops formed a very flexible strategic reserve, easily switched to meet different situations, as Student's story shows:

When the Allies landed in Sicily, on July 10th, I at once proposed to make an immediate airborne counterattack there with both my divisions. But Hitler turned this down – Jodl, in particular, was against it. So the 1st Parachute Division was merely flown [from the south of France] to Italy in the first place – part to Rome and part to Naples – while the 2nd Parachute Division remained at Nîmes with me. The 1st Parachute Division, however, was soon sent on to Sicily – for use as ground troops to reinforce the scanty German forces which were there when the Italian troops began to collapse *en masse*. [Part of] the division was flown by air, in successive lifts, and dropped behind our front in the eastern sector south of Catania. I had wanted them to be dropped behind the Allied front. The first contingent was dropped about 3 kilometres behind our front, and by a strange coincidence it landed almost simultaneously with the British parachute troops who were dropped behind our front to open the bridge across the Simeto river. It overcame these British parachute troops and rescued the bridge from their hands. This was on July 14th.*

The main British forces, when they came up, succeeded after three days' stiff fighting in recapturing the bridge and reopening the way into the plain of Catania. But their attempt to press on northward was

* Liddell Hart: *The Other Side of the Hill*, p 355.

blocked by increasingly strong resistance from the German reserves now concentrating to cover this direct east-coast route to Messina, sixty miles distant, where the north-east corner of Sicily lies close to the toe of Italy.

That frustrated the hope of a quick clearance of Sicily. Montgomery was forced to shift the weight of the Eighth Army westward for a more circuitous push through the hilly interior and round Mount Etna, in combination with an eastward advance by the Seventh Army – which reached the north coast and occupied Palermo on July 22nd, though too late to intercept the eastward withdrawal of the enemy's mobile troops. The new plan brought an important change of role for Patton's army. Its action as shield to the flank of the Eighth Army's intended decisive drive for Messina, and as a distraction to the enemy's concentration, was extended into that of an offensive lever – and, in the end, prime spearhead.

For the new push, planned to start on August 1st, two fresh infantry divisions (the 9th US and 78th British) were brought over from Africa – raising the total to twelve. Meanwhile the Germans were reinforced by 29th Panzergrenadier Division, together with 14th Panzer Corps Headquarters under General Hube, who now took control of the fight. His task would not be to maintain the defence of Sicily, but merely to conduct a delaying action and cover the evacuation of the Axis forces – a decision reached, by Guzzoni and Kesselring independently, soon after Mussolini's overthrow on July 25th, and before the Allies' renewed offensive.

Such a delaying action was aided by the shape as well as by the ruggedness of north-eastern Sicily – a triangle of mountainous country. While the ground favoured the defence and each step back brought a shortening of the front, so that fewer defenders were needed, the Allied armies became increasingly cramped in deploying their full superiority of force. Patton made three attempts to quicken progress by small amphibious leaps – a landing at Sant' Agata on the night of the August 7th/8th, a second at Brolo on the 10th/11th, and a third at Spadafora on the 15th/16th – but in each case they were too late to be effective. Montgomery tried a small one on the 15th/16th, but by then the enemy's rearguard had gone north of it – and most of the enemy troops had already crossed the Straits to the mainland.

The ably organized withdrawal across the Straits was carried out, for the main part, in the course of six days (and seven nights), without suffering any serious interception or loss from the Allied air or sea forces. Nearly 40,000 German troops and over 60,000 Italian were safely evacuated. Although the Italians left behind all except some 200 of their vehicles, the Germans brought away nearly 10,000 vehicles as well as forty-seven tanks, ninety-four guns, and 17,000 tons of supplies and equipment. About 6.30 AM on August 17th the leading American patrol entered Messina, and not long afterwards a British party appeared – to be greeted with gleeful cries of 'Where've you tourists been?'

The success of this well-planned 'get away' gave a rather hollow sound to what Alexander said that day in reporting the completion of the campaign to the Prime Minister: 'By 10 AM this morning, August 17th, 1943, the last German soldier was flung out of Sicily ... It can be assumed that all Italian forces in the island on July 10th have been destroyed, though a few battered units may have escaped to mainland.'

So far as can be gauged from the records, the number of German troops in Sicily was a little over 60,000 and the Italian troops 195,000 (Alexander's estimate at the time was 90,000 German and 315,000 Italian). Of the German troops 5,500 were captured, while 13,500 wounded were evacuated to Italy before the withdrawal, so that the number killed can hardly have been more than a few thousand (the British estimate was 24,000 killed). The British losses were 2,721 killed, 2,183 missing, and 7,939 wounded – a total of 12,843. The American losses were 2,811 killed, 686 missing, and 6,471 wounded – a total of 9,968. Thus, in all, the Allied losses amounted to approximately 22,800. It was not a very heavy cost for the great political and strategic results of the campaign – which caused Mussolini's downfall and Italy's surrender. But the 'bag' of Germans could have been larger, with a consequent smoothing of the path beyond, if the Allies had made fuller use of amphibious outflanking moves. That was Admiral Cunningham's view, and in his Despatch he pointedly remarked that after the opening days

> no use was made by the 8th Army of amphibious opportunities. The small LSIs were kept standing by for the purpose ... and landing craft were available on call ... There were doubtless sound military reasons for making no use of this, what to me appeared, priceless asset of seapower and flexibility of manoeuvre: but it is worth consideration for future occasions whether much time and costly fighting could not be saved by even minor flank moves which must necessarily be unsettling to the enemy.

Much to Kesselring's relief, the Allied High Command had not attempted a landing in Calabria, the 'toe' of Italy, behind the back of his forces from Sicily – to block their withdrawal across the Straits of Messina. He had been anxiously expecting such a stroke throughout the Sicilian campaign, while having no forces available to meet it. In his view, 'a secondary attack on Calabria would have enabled the Sicily landing to be developed into an overwhelming Allied victory'. Until the close of the Sicilian campaign and the successful escape of the four German divisions engaged there, Kesselring had only two German divisions to cover the whole of southern Italy.*

* Cunningham: *Despatch*, p 2082.

CHAPTER TWENTY-SEVEN

The Invasion of Italy – Capitulation and Check

'Nothing succeeds like success' is a very well-known saying, based on an old French proverb. But it often proves true, in a deeper sense, that 'nothing succeeds like failure'. Religious and political movements which reigning authority crushed have frequently been revived and come out on top in the long run after their leaders gained the halo of martyrdom. The crucified Christ became more potent than the living one. Conquering generals have been eclipsed by the conquered – that is shown by the immortal fame of Hannibal, Napoleon, Robert E. Lee, and Rommel.

In the history of nations the same effect can be seen, though in a subtler way. Everyone knows the saying that in a war 'the British only win one battle – the last'. It expresses their characteristic tendency to start with disasters but end with victory. The habit is hazardous, and costly. Yet it happens, ironically, that the final outcome can often be traced to the initial way that the early defeats suffered by the British and their allies, by making the enemy overconfident, have led him to overreach himself.

Moreover, even when the scales have turned, a failure to gain immediate success has at times turned out very advantageously by helping towards fuller success and making final success more sure. That happened twice, most strikingly, in the Mediterranean campaigns of the Second World War.

It was due to the frustration of the Allies' original advance on Tunis, from Algiers, in November 1942, that Hitler and Mussolini were encouraged to send a stream of reinforcements there, across the sea, where the Allies were eventually able to trap them six months later and put two Axis armies in the bag – thus removing the chief obstacle to their own cross-sea jump from Africa into Southern Europe.

The next case of a miscarriage turning out well was the invasion of Italy itself. After the swift capture of Sicily, and the downfall of Mussolini, the second and shorter jump into Italy had looked a compara-

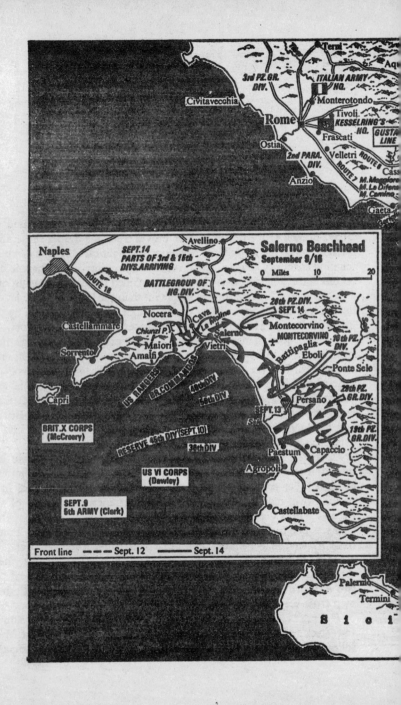

Terni
Aq

3rd PZ. GR. DIV.
ITALIAN ARMY HQ.
Civitavecchia
Monterotondo
Rome
Tivoli
KESSELRING'S HQ.
GUSTA LINE
Ostia
Frascati
2nd PARA. DIV.
Velletri
ROUTE
Cass
Anzio
M. Maggiore
M. Le Difensa
M. Camino
Gaeta

Avellino
Salerno Beachhead
September 9/16
Naples
SEPT. 14 PARTS OF 3rd & 16th DIVS. ARRIVING
0   Miles   10   20
ROUTE 18
BATTLEGROUP OF HG. DIV.
26th PZ. DIV. SEPT. 14
Nocera
Cava
La Padre
Castellammare
Chiunzi P.
Salerno
Montecorvino
MONTECORVINO
16th PZ. DIV.
Maiori
Vietri
Battipaglia
Eboli
Sorrento
Amalfi
Ponte Sele
US RANGERS
BR COMMANDOS
46th DIV
56th DIV
29th PZ. GR. DIV.
Capri
Persano
SEPT. 13
BRIT. X CORPS (McCreery)
RESERVE 45th DIV (SEPT. 10)
36th DIV
19th PZ. GR. DIV.
Paestum
Capaccio
US VI CORPS (Dawley)
Agropoli
SEPT. 9 5th ARMY (Clark)
Castellabate

Front line — — — Sept. 12 ———— Sept. 14

Palermo
Termini
S i c i

The Landings in Southern Italy
Allied advance September 3/December 28, 1943

◄──── Anglo-US attacks
◄════ German counterattacks
1st PARA.DIV. Situation of German units on Sept. 3
──xxx── Allied army command boundary

| 0 | Miles | 50 | | 100 |
| 0 | Kilometres | 50 | 100 | 150 |

AM.OCT.3
SPECIAL SERVICE BDE.
LANDS, FOLLOWED BY
78th DIVISION

...tona DEC.28
...oro

Termoli

T.V

SEPT.22
78th DIV.DISEMBARKS

Foggia
SEPT.27

Barletta

Bari

ADRIATIC
SEA

US VI

Benevento

GR.DIVS.
OCT 1

1st
PARA.DIV.

Melfi

16th PZ.DIV.

...erno

Auletta

Potenza

Matera

Eboli

Polla

SEPT.20

Brindisi
SEPT.11

FRONT LINE
SEPT.14

10th ARMY
(Vietinghoff)

Taranto

A

Lagonegro

Castrovillari

...ALANCHE

HRS, SEPT.9
RMY (Clark)

Belvedere

26th PZ.DIV.

Cariati

SLAPSTICK

SEPT.9
1st AIRBORNE DIV
(8th ARMY) LANDS

29th PZ.GR.DIV.

...HENIAN SEA

Catanzaro
SEPT.10

Pizzo

BRIT.XXX
CORPS

Messina

BRIT.XIII
CORPS

Reggio

...TOWN

RS, SEPT.3
NY
omery) LANDS

*HG—HERMANN GORING

tively easy matter. The prospects were all the brighter because Italy's surrender had been secretly arranged, unknown to the Germans, and was timed for announcement simultaneously with the main Allied landing. At that moment there were only six weak German divisions in the south of Italy, and two divisions near Rome, to cope with the double burden of meeting the Allied invasion and at the same time holding down their own Italian ex-allies.

Field-Marshal Kesselring, however, managed to keep the invaders in check while disarming the Italians, and then brought the Allied armies to a standstill on a line a hundred miles short of Rome. Eight months passed before the Allies succeeded in reaching the Italian capital, and then they were again held up – for a further eight months – before they could break out of the narrow and mountainous peninsula into the plains of northern Italy.

Yet that long postponement, of the end that had seemed so close in September 1943, carried important compensations for the Allies' prospects in general. Hitler had at first intended to extricate his forces from southern Italy, and establish a mountain blocking-line in the north. But Kesselring's unexpectedly successful defence induced Hitler, contrary to Rommel's advice, to pour resources southward with the aim of holding on to as much of Italy as possible, and for as long as possible. That decision was taken at the expense of the resources which Hitler soon needed to meet the more dangerous menace of the two-sided advance on Germany by the Russians from the East and by the Western Allies from Normandy.

Relative to its own strength, the Allied force in Italy absorbed a higher proportion of the Germans' resources than those on other fronts. Moreover, the Italian front was the one where the Germans could afford to yield ground with least risk, while the more they strained their strength to hold an extended front on every side, the more liable they became to a fatal collapse through over-stretch. Such reflections helped to console the Allied troops in Italy, under Alexander, for the prolonged frustration of their own hopes of early victory.

Even so, it should be realized that great expeditions are not launched in the hope of reaching a frustration that may ultimately become profitable. It is not in human nature to desire and seek a failure. So it is worthwhile to explore what happened and the way it did.

The first important factor in the Allies' frustration was their delay in exploiting the opportunity offered by the anti-war coup d'état in Italy which overthrew Mussolini. This took place on July 25th, yet more than six weeks passed before the Allies moved into Italy. The causes of delay were both military and political. At the conference of the Anglo-American service chiefs in Washington at the end of May, the Americans had opposed the idea of going on from Sicily to Italy, lest such a step might interfere with the plans for invading Normandy and defeating the Japanese in the Pacific. It was not until July 20th, when the Italian forces in Sicily had shown their eagerness to surrender, that the American Chiefs of Staff agreed to a follow-up advance into Italy. But that was too late for making ready an immediate follow-up.

The political demand for 'unconditional surrender', formulated by President Roosevelt and Mr Churchill at the Casablanca Conference in January, was also a hindrance. The new Italian Government under Marshal Badoglio was naturally anxious to see if more favourable conditions could be obtained in negotiation with the Allied Governments but found that it was difficult to get in touch with them. The British and American Ministers at the Vatican were an obvious channel, and easily accessible, but proved useless owing to an extraordinary double case of official shortsightedness, as Badoglio's account reveals. 'The British Minister informed us that unfortunately his secret code was very old and almost certainly known to the Germans, and that he could not advise us to use it for a secret communication to his Government. The American chargé d'affaires replied that he had not got a secret code.' So the Italians had to wait until in mid-August they found a plausible pretext for sending an envoy on a visit to Portugal, where he could meet British and American representatives. Even then this roundabout way of negotiation entailed further delay in settling the matter.

Hitler, by contrast, had wasted no time in taking steps to counter the likelihood that the new Italian Government would seek peace and abandon the alliance with Germany. On the day of the coup d'état in Rome, July 25th, Rommel had arrived in Greece to take command there, but just before midnight he received a telephone call telling him that Mussolini had been deposed, and that he was to fly back at once to Hitler's headquarters in the East Prussian forests. Arriving there at noon next day he 'received orders to assemble troops in the Alps and prepare a possible entry into Italy'.

The entry soon began, in a partially disguised way. Fearing that the Italians might make a sudden move to block the Alpine passes with the help of Allied parachute troops, Rommel gave orders on July 30th for the leading Germans to move across the frontier and occupy the passes. This was done under the excuse of safeguarding the supply routes into Italy against sabotage, or paratroop attack. The Italians protested, and for a moment threatened to resist the passage, but hesitated to open fire and precipitate a conflict with their allies. The German infiltration was then extended on the pretext of relieving the Italians of the burden of defending the northern part of their country so that they could reinforce the south, where it was manifest that the Allies were likely to land at any moment. Strategically, this argument was so reasonable that the Italian chiefs could hardly reject it without showing their own intention to change sides. So by the beginning of September eight German divisions under Rommel were established inside Italy's Alpine frontier-wall as a potential support or reinforcement to Kesselring's forces in the south.

Moreover the 2nd Parachute Division, a particularly tough force, was flown from France to Ostia, close to Rome. General Student, the Commander-in-Chief of the German airborne forces, went with it. When interrogated after the war, he said:

The Italian High Command was given no previous warning of its arrival, and was told that the division was intended for the reinforcement of Sicily or Calabria. But my instructions, from Hitler, were that I was to keep it near Rome, and also take under my command the 3rd Panzergrenadier Division, which had moved down there. With these two divisions I was to be ready to disarm the Italian forces around Rome.*

The presence of these divisions nullified the Allies' plan to drop one of their own airborne divisions, the 82nd American (General Matthew Ridgway), on Rome itself to support the Italians in holding the capital. If that reinforcement had come, Kesselring's own headquarters would have been in jeopardy, for it was located at Frascati, barely ten miles south-east of Rome.

Even so, Student's allotted task looked a very difficult one – before the event. Marshal Badoglio had kept five Italian divisions concentrated in the Rome area despite the Germans' efforts to persuade him to send some of these divisions to help in defending the coast in the south. Unless and until they could be disarmed Kesselring would be in the awkward situation of having to face two Anglo-American invading armies with a third hostile army already lying astride the line of supply and retreat of his six German divisions in southern Italy. These had just been formed into what was called the 10th Army, commanded by Vietinghoff, and included four divisions which had escaped from Sicily,

* Liddell Hart interrogation. See also Liddell Hart: *The Other Side of the Hill*, pp 356–7.

badly depleted by the losses they had suffered in that campaign.

On September 3rd, the invasion was opened by Montgomery's Eighth Army crossing the narrow Straits of Messina, from Sicily, and landing on the toe of Italy. That same day the Italian representatives secretly signed the armistice treaty with the Allies. But it was arranged that the fact should be kept quiet until the Allies made their second and principal landing – which was planned to take place on the shin of Italy, at Salerno, south of Naples.

At midnight on September 8th the Anglo-American Fifth Army under General Mark Clark began to disembark in the Gulf of Salerno – a few hours after the BBC had broadcast the official announcement of Italy's capitulation. The Italian leaders had not been expecting the landing to come so soon, and they were warned about the delivery of the broadcast only late in the afternoon. Badoglio complained, with some justification, that he was caught unready to cooperate, before his preparations were complete. But the Italians' state of unreadiness and trepidation had already become so evident to General Maxwell Taylor, who had been sent to Rome secretly by Eisenhower, that Ridgway's intended airborne descent on Rome had been cancelled after Eisenhower had received that morning a warning message from Taylor that the prospects were poor. It was then too late to revert to the original plan of dropping Ridgway's troops along the Volturno River, on the north side of Naples, to block enemy reinforcements from moving southward, to Salerno.

The broadcast announcement of the Italian capitulation also took the Germans by surprise, but their action in Rome was prompt and decisive, despite the simultaneous emergency in the south produced by the landing at Salerno.

The outcome might well have been different if Italian action had matched Italian acting, which had gone a long way to conceal intentions and lull Kesselring's suspicions during the preceding days. A piquant account of this is given in a narrative written by his Chief of Staff, General Westphal:

On September 7th the Italian Minister of Marine, Admiral Count de Courten, called on Field-Marshal Kesselring to inform him that the Italian Fleet would put out on the 8th or 9th from Spezia to seek battle with the British Mediterranean Fleet. The Italian Fleet would conquer or perish, he said, with tears in his eyes. He then described in detail its intended plan of battle.*

* Liddell Hart: *The Other Side of the Hill*, pp 360–61.

These solemn assurances made a convincing impression. The next afternoon Westphal and another general, Toussaint, drove to the head-quarters of the Italian Army at Monterotondo (sixteen miles north-east of Rome).

> Our reception by General Roatta was very cordial. He discussed with me in detail the further joint conduct of operations by the Italian 7th and German 10th Armies in Southern Italy. While we were talking a telephone message came through from Colonel von Waldenburg with the news of the broadcast announcement of the Italian capitulation to the Allies ... General Roatta assured us that it was merely a bad propaganda manoeuvre. The joint struggle, he said, would be con-tinued just as had been arranged between us.*

Westphal was not altogether convinced by these assurances and when he got back to the German headquarters at Frascati late in the evening he found that Kesselring had already signalled to all subordinate com-mands the codeword 'Axis' – the pre-arranged signal which meant that Italy had quitted the Axis and that the appropriate action must be taken to disarm the Italians immediately.

The subordinate commands applied a mixture of persuasion and force according to the situation and their own disposition. In the Rome area, where the potential odds against him were heavy, Student used shock tactics.

> I made an attempt to seize the Italian General Headquarters by dropping on it from the air. This was only a partial success. While thirty generals and a hundred and fifty other officers were captured in one part of the headquarters, another part held out. The Chief of the General Staff had got away, following Badoglio and the King, the night before.†

Instead of trying to overcome Student's couple of divisions, the Ital-ian commanders hastened to withdraw out of reach, falling back east-ward to Tivoli with their forces, and leaving their capital in the hands of the Germans. That also cleared the way for negotiations, in which Kesselring applied a more gentle form of persuasion, proposing that if the Italian troops laid down their arms they should be allowed to go back to their homes immediately. That offer was contrary to Hitler's

* Liddell Hart: *The Other Side of the Hill*, p 359.
† Ibid, p 360.

order that all Italian soldiers should be made prisoners, but it proved more effective at less cost of life and time. The results can be related in Westphal's words:

The situation around Rome calmed down completely when the Commander of the Italian forces accepted in its entirety the German capitulation suggestion. This eliminated the danger to the supply of the 10th Army ...

It was a further relief to us that Rome no longer needed to become a battlefield. In the capitulation agreement, Field-Marshal Kesselring undertook to regard Rome as an open city. He undertook that it should be occupied only by police units, two companies in strength, to guard telephone communications, etc. This undertaking was always observed up to the end of German occupation. Through the capitulations it was now again possible to resume the wireless signals link with OKW [the German Supreme Command] which had been broken off since the 8th. A further consequence of the bloodless elimination of the Italian forces was the possibility of immediately moving reinforcements by road from the Rome area to the 10th Army in the South ... Thus the situation around Rome, after so many initial worries, had been resolved in a manner which one could hardly hope to better.*

Until then, Hitler and his military advisers at OKW had tended to regard Kesselring's army as doomed. Westphal has contributed significant evidence on this score:

... supplies and replacements of personnel, arms, and equipment were almost completely cut off from us from August onward. All demands were at the time brushed aside by OKW with, 'We'll see later on'. This unusually pessimistic attitude probably also played a part in the employment of [Rommel's] Army Group B in Upper Italy. It was told to take into the Apennine position such parts of our forces as had managed to escape the joint attack of the Allies and the Italians.

Field-Marshal Kesselring, similarly, took a grave view of the situation. But in his view it was still capable of being mastered in certain circumstances – the farther south that the expected large-scale landing took place, the better the chances would be. But if the enemy landed by sea and air in the general area of Rome, one could hardly

* Liddell Hart: *The Other Side of the Hill*, pp 360–61.

bank on saving the 10th Army from being cut off. The two divisions we had near Rome were far from sufficient for the double job of eliminating the strong Italian forces and repelling the Allied landing – and in addition keeping open the rear communications of the 10th Army. As early as September 9th it was becoming unpleasantly apparent that the Italian forces were blocking the road to Naples, and thus the supply of the 10th Army. The Army could not have held out against this for long. And so the Commander-in-Chief heaved a sigh of relief when no air landings took place on the airfields round Rome on the 9th and 10th. On both these days we hourly expected such a landing to be made, with the cooperation of the Italian forces. Such an air landing would undoubtedly have given a great stimulus to the Italian troops and to the civil population that was unfavourably disposed towards us.*

Kesselring himself put the matter in a nutshell, saying: 'An air landing on Rome and sea landing nearby, instead of at Salerno, would have automatically caused us to evacuate all the southern half of Italy.'†

Even as it was, the days that followed the Allies' landing at Salerno were a period of intense strain on the Germans, and all the more nerve-racking through lack of information as to what was happening there. Never was the 'fog of war' so thick – that being due to the fact that the Germans were fighting in the country of an ally who had suddenly deserted them. The effect can best be conveyed by again quoting Westphal's account:

The Commander-in-Chief could at first learn very little about the position at Salerno. Telephone communication broke down – as it was on the Italian postal network. It could not be easily restored, as we had not been allowed to examine Italian telephone technique. Wireless communication could not be arranged at first because the signal personnel of the newly formed 10th Army headquarters were not familiar with the peculiar atmospheric conditions in the South.

It was fortunate for the Germans that the main Allied landing came in the area where they had expected it, and where Kesselring could most conveniently concentrate his scanty forces to meet it. The British Eighth Army's advance up the toe of Italy also ran according to expec-

* Liddell Hart: *The Other Side of the Hill*, p 361–2.
† Ibid, p 362–3.

tation, and was too remote to carry an immediate danger to his forces. He benefited much from the Allied commanders' reluctance to venture outside the limits of air cover – and in his calculations was able to reckon on their consistency in observing such conventional limitations. As a result the Allied landings at Salerno – optimistically styled 'Operation Avalanche' – suffered a costly check. Indeed, Mark Clark himself speaks of it as a 'near disaster'.* Only by a narrow margin did the landing force hold off the German counterattack and avoid being driven back into the sea.

In the original planning, Mark Clark had proposed that the landing should be made in the Gulf of Gaeta on the north side of Naples, where the country was more open and there was no mountainous ground as at Salerno to hinder the advance inland from the beaches. But when Tedder, the Allied Air Commander-in-Chief, told him that air support could not be so good if stretched to the Gaeta sector, Clark gave way and agreed to the choice of Salerno.

In some Allied quarters it had been urged that the most effective way to take the Germans off their guard, and throw them off their balance, was to make a landing beyond these limits; and it was argued that a landing on the heel of Italy, in the area of Taranto and Brindisi, would be 'the line of least expectation' while entailing little risk – and promising the early possession of two fine ports.

Such a landing was added to the plan at the last moment, as a subsidiary move, but the Taranto force consisted only of the British 1st Airborne Division, which was hurriedly collected from rest-camps in Tunisia, and rushed across in such naval vessels as were available at short notice. It met no opposition – but arrived without any tanks, and with scarcely any artillery or motor transport. In fact, it lacked the very things it needed to exploit the opportunity it had gained.

From this broad survey of the Allied invasion we come to a closer examination of the course of the operations, which started with the crossing of the narrow Straits of Messina by Montgomery's Eighth Army on September 3rd.

The orders for this landing in Calabria, 'Operation Baytown', were not issued until August 16th, when the last German rearguard was in process of withdrawing from Sicily. Even then, no 'object' was specified in the orders – as Montgomery caustically pointed out in a signal to

* Clark: *Calculated Risk*, p 179.

Alexander on the 19th. In reply, the object was belatedly defined, and he was told:

> Your task is to secure a bridgehead on the toe of Italy, to enable our naval forces to operate through the Straits of Messina.
>
> In the event of the enemy withdrawing from the toe, you will follow him up with such force as you can make available, bearing in mind that the greater the extent to which you can engage enemy forces in the southern tip of Italy, the more assistance will you be giving to *Avalanche* [the Salerno landing].

This was a meagre object, and a rather hazy one, to set the veteran Eighth Army. Montgomery remarks in his memoirs: 'No attempt was made to coordinate my operations with those of the Fifth Army, landing at Salerno...' For the secondary purpose of giving assistance to this army, the landing of the Eighth was made at the most unsuitable place – over 300 miles from Salerno, along a very narrow and mountainous approach, ideally suited to obstruction by the enemy. There were only two good roads up the toe, one skirting the west coast and the other the east coast, so that only two divisions could be employed, with a single brigade heading each, and it was often difficult to deploy more than one battalion on either line of advance. There was thus no need for the enemy to keep large forces in this area, and all the less incentive to do so since he could be sure that the larger part of the Allied forces would be landing elsewhere. Once the Eighth Army was committed to the Calabrian peninsula, any chance of surprise by the Fifth was diminished, as the alternative possibilities with which the enemy had to reckon were reduced. The toe was the worst possible place for creating an effective distraction. The enemy could safely bring his forces back from there, and leave the invasion to suffer from operational cramp.

Despite the unlikelihood of meeting any strong opposition, Montgomery's assault landing on the toe was mounted with his habitual carefulness and thoroughness. Nearly 600 guns were assembled, under the command of the 30th Corps, to provide an overwhelming barrage from the Sicilian shore to cover the crossing of the Straits and the landings on the beaches near Reggio, which were carried out by General Miles Dempsey's 13th Corps. The process of assembling this mass of artillery delayed the assault for days beyond the intended date. The bombardment was further increased by the fire of the 120 naval guns.

During the previous days, Intelligence reports showed that the Germans had left 'not more than two infantry battalions' near the toe; and even these were posted over ten miles back from the beaches, to cover the roads up the peninsula. That information of the enemy's withdrawal caused critical observers to remark that the preparatory barrage was a case of 'using a sledgehammer to crack a nut'. The comment was apt, but not exact – as not even a nut was left to crack. It was a tremendous waste of ammunition.

At 4.30 AM on September 3rd, the two divisions employed in the assault, the 5th British and 1st Canadian, landed on empty beaches, devoid even of mines and barbed wire. A Canadian note jocularly recorded that 'the stiffest resistance of the day came from a puma which had escaped from the Zoological Gardens in Reggio, and was seemingly taking a fancy to the Brigade Commander'. No casualties were suffered among the assaulting infantry, and by evening the toe of the peninsula had been occupied, to a depth of more than five miles, without meeting resistance. Three German stragglers and three thousand Italians had been picked up as prisoners. The Italians readily volunteered to help in unloading the British landing craft. No serious resistance was met in the days that followed, as the invaders pushed up the toe, and there were only brief contacts with enemy rearguards. But numerous demolitions, which the Germans skilfully executed in withdrawing, imposed repeated checks on the Eighth Army's advance. By September 6th, the fourth day, it was barely thirty miles beyond the beaches where it had landed, and it did not reach the toe joint – the narrowest part of the peninsula – until the 10th. That was less than one-third of the distance to Salerno.

Yet according to Montgomery, 'Alexander was most optimistic' when he visited the Eighth Army on September 5th, and brought the news that the Italians had privily signed an armistice two days before. Montgomery remarks that Alexander 'was clearly prepared to base his plans on the Italians doing all they said'. That confidence was questioned by Montgomery – 'I told him my opinion was that when the Germans found out what was going on, they would stamp on the Italians.' Events confirmed that comment, recorded in Montgomery's diary.

Alexander's confidence in the prospects of 'Operation Avalanche' is the more surprising because two weeks before it took place the German military commentator, 'Sertorius', had broadcast a forecast that the Allies' main landing would be in the Naples–Salerno sector, with a subsidiary landing on the Calabrian peninsula.

A week earlier still, on August 18th, Hitler had issued his orders to meet the threat, and these significantly said:

1. Sooner or later the capitulation of Italy before enemy pressure is to be expected.
2. In preparation for this, 10th Army must keep the line of retreat open. Central Italy, especially the Rome area, is to be held until then by OBS.
3. In the coastal area from Naples to Salerno, which at first is the most threatened, a strong group consisting of at least three mobile formations from 10th Army is to be assembled. All no longer mobile elements of the Army are to be moved to this area. At first fully mobile elements may remain between Catanzaro and Castrovillari to take part in mobile operations. Elements of 1 Para Div may be employed for the protection of Foggia. In the case of an enemy landing the area Naples–Salerno must be held. South of the defile of Castrovillari there is only to be delaying action . . .

Kesselring put six of his eight divisions in the south, under General von Vietinghoff's newly formed 10th Army – which established its headquarters at the inland town of Polla, south-east of Salerno. For Hitler had personally told Vietinghoff on the 22nd, to regard Salerno as 'the centre of gravity' (as that Army's war diary records). Kesselring's two other divisions were held in reserve near Rome, ready to seize control of the capital and keep open the 10th Army's line of retreat 'in the event of Italian treachery'. The six divisions in the south comprised two which had newly arrived in Italy, the 16th and 26th Panzer, and the four which had escaped from Sicily. The two of these which were most depleted by losses, the Hermann Göring and the 15th Panzergrenadier, had been brought back to the Naples area to refit, and the 1st Parachute went to Apulia while the 29th Panzergrenadier had been left in the toe of Italy facing Montgomery. To help it keep him in check, the 26th Panzer, which had arrived without any tanks,* was temporarily sent to Calabria. The 16th Panzer Division, the best armed of the batch, was posted to cover the Gulf of Salerno, the most likely sector for a large landing, and it could be quickly reinforced there by the other divisions.

---

* Like most of the German armoured divisions at this period, it had only two tank battalions – one equipped with Panther tanks and one with the lighter Mark IV tanks – and of these the Panther battalion had not been sent to Italy, while the other had been kept near Rome to help in overawing the Italians.

Even so, it comprised only one tank battalion* and only four infantry battalions, although strong in artillery.

That was a slender force to meet the armada which was sailing towards the Gulf of Salerno – with some seven hundred ships and landing craft, carry some 55,000 troops for the initial landing, and a further 115,000 for the follow up.

The landing was to be made by the US 36th Infantry Division on the right, and the British 46th and 56th Divisions on the left, while part of the US 45th Infantry Division provided a flanking reserve. These divisions were grouped respectively under the US 6th Corps (General Dawley) and the British 10th Corps (General R. L. McCreery). The latter was to land on a seven-mile stretch of the beaches just south of Salerno, near the main road to Naples, which crosses the neck of the mountainous Sorrento peninsula through the Cava Gap, by a low but awkward pass. Its early success was thus of key importance, both in opening the way north to the great port of Naples and in blocking the arrival of German reinforcements from the north. To ease its task, two British Commandos and three battalions of American Rangers were employed for the quick capture of this defile and of the Chiunzi Pass on a neighbouring route.

The main British assault convoy sailed from Tripoli on September 6th, and the main American one from Oran the previous evening. Others sailed from Algiers, Bizerta, and the north Sicilian ports of Palermo and Termini. Although their destination was a heavily guarded secret, it was not difficult to deduce or guess in view of the practicable limits of air cover and the need for early capture of a large port, two conditions which here coincided in such a way as to provide a very obvious pointer. The Chinese cook of a water-boat at Tripoli caused some palpitation by his farewell shout 'See you in Naples'.† But he was only echoing what was a matter of common talk among seamen and soldiers. A fostering factor was the unfortunate choice of the titles 'Force N' and 'Force S' for the northern and southern attack forces. Nor was it only a matter of guesswork, for one of the administrative

---

* This battalion had about eighty tanks, of Mark IV type. Its missing Panther battalion had been replaced by an armoured assault-gun battalion, of forty self-propelled pieces – which could be mistaken for tanks on a distant view. Even so, it is difficult to understand how General Mark Clark in his book of war memoirs, *Calculated Risk*, can have arrived at his calculation that the Germans 'originally had probably about six hundred tanks at Salerno' (p 199) – which was nearly eight times the actual number.

† Linklater: *The Campaign in Italy*, p 63.

orders which had a wide circulation mentioned by name a number of places in and around Salerno.

Since the objective was so obvious, a greater handicap was that the army commander, Mark Clark, persisted in counting on surprise to such an extent that he forbade any preliminary naval bombardment of the defences, despite strong arguments from the commander of the naval task force escorting and supporting the landing force, Vice-Admiral H. Kent Hewitt USN – who clearly saw that 'it was fantastic to assume we could obtain tactical surprise'.* But it can be argued, on the other hand, that the advantage of softening up the coast defences might have been offset by a quicker concentration of the enemy's reserves if the intended landing site had been more definitely made clear in this way.

The approach of the convoys, made round the west and north coasts of Sicily, was spotted and reported to the German headquarters early in the afternoon of the 8th, and at 3.30 PM their troops were put on the alert in readiness for the expected landing. At 6.30 PM the announcement of the armistice with Italy was broadcast by Eisenhower on Radio Algiers, and at 7.20 PM repeated by the BBC News. One or other of these broadcasts was heard by the Allied troops on board the convoys. This news, despite warnings from some of their officers that they still had to deal with the Germans, unfortunately gave them the impression that the landings would be a walkover. They were soon disillusioned. So were those Allied planners who had optimistically forecast the capture of Naples by the third day – a goal that was reached only after three weeks of struggle and a narrow escape from disaster.

During the afternoon of the 8th the approaching convoys came under air attack several times, and again after dark, when German bombers flew over them dropping parachute flares, but the armada was fortunate in suffering little damage. Just after midnight the leading transports arrived at the release points, eight to ten miles off shore, and began lowering their landing craft. These reached the beaches at or close to the scheduled H-hour of 3.30 AM. Two hours earlier, a coastal battery taken over by the Germans had opened fire on the landing craft approaching the northern flank, but had been tackled and silenced by the escorting destroyers, and the final stage had been aided by a short but intense bombardment of the beach defences by naval guns and rocket-craft – a new aid which here made its debut. But in the southern sector no such supporting fire was provided as the American divisional commander stuck to the army commander's 'no fire' instructions in the hope

* S. E. Morison: *History of U.S. Naval Operations in World War II*, vol IX, p 249.

that local surprise might still be achieved by a silent landing. The result was that, in the last lap to the beach, the landing craft came under a hail of fire from the shore, and many casualties were suffered by the troops.

As the prospects of a quick advance to Naples turned on the capture of the road northward from Salerno through the mountains, it is appropriate to recount the landings from left to right, starting with the northern flank. Here the American Rangers landed unopposed on a small beach at Maiori and within three hours secured the Chiunzi Pass, while establishing themselves on the ridges overlooking the main Salerno–Naples road. The British Commandos also had an easy landing at Vietri, where the road leaves the coast and starts to mount. But the enemy reacted quickly, delaying the clearance of the town, and the Commandos were then held up just north of it in the low pass of La Molina at the start of the Cava Gap.

The main British landings, on beaches a few miles south of Salerno, met a stiff resistance from the start, and their progress was also adversely affected because part of the 46th Division was put ashore by mistake on the beaches of its right-hand neighbour, the 56th, causing confusion and congestion. Although some of the leading troops pushed two miles inland, they suffered many casualties and fell short of securing the important first day objectives – Salerno harbour, Montecorvino airfield, and the road junctions at Battipaglia and Eboli. Moreover, at the end of the day there was still a seven-mile gap between the British right flank north of the Sele and the American left flank south of that river.

The American landings were made on four beaches close to the famous Greek temples at Paestum. The strain of approaching the shore under heavy fire, without support from their own ships, was followed by running into further curtains of fire after landing, as well as a battering from successive German air attacks on the beaches. It was a severe ordeal for the troops of the 36th Division, who had no previous experience of battle. Fortunately, they were now given good support by naval gunfire, from destroyers which drove in boldly through minefields to aid them, and this proved particularly helpful both here and on the British sector in checking counterthrusts by small groups of German tanks, which were the chief menace to the invaders. By nightfall the American left wing had pushed about five miles inland, to the hill town of Capaccio, but the right wing was still pinned down close to the beaches.

The second day, September 10th, was a quiet one on the American sector, as the 16th Panzer Division had moved most of its meagre strength northwards to the British sector, which was strategically the greater menace to their hold on the Salerno area. The Americans profited by the opportunity to expand their bridgehead, and to land the bulk of the 45th Division, their floating reserve. Meanwhile the British 56th Division had occupied Montecorvino airfield and Battipaglia early in the morning, but was later driven back by vigorous counterattack from two German motor infantry battalions along with some tanks – which produced a local panic, even in part of the Guards Brigade, before the tanks of the Royal Scots Greys came to provide support of a similar kind.

That night the 56th Division mounted a three-brigade attack to capture the dominating heights of Mount Eboli, but it made only slight progress, which included a re-entry into Battipaglia. The 46th Division occupied Salerno and sent a brigade to relieve the Commandos, but did not develop a northward push. On the American sector the fresh 45th Division advanced some ten miles inland up the east bank of the Sele through Persano and came near to reaching the road-centre of Ponte Sele, the apex of the desired beachhead line. But it was checked and then led to withdraw by a counterattack from a German motor infantry battalion and eight tanks, switched back across the river from the British sector. Thus at the end of the third day the four Allied divisions that had landed, with extra units equivalent to a fifth, were still confined in two shallow and separate beachheads while the Germans held both the surrounding heights and the approach routes to the flat coastal strip. Allied hopes of reaching Naples on the third day had vanished. The 16th Panzer Division, barely half of the scale of an Allied division in fighting units, had succeeded in curbing the invasion and gaining time for the arrival of German reinforcements.

The first to arrive were the 29th Panzergrenadier Division, which was already on its way back from Calabria, and a battle-group (with two infantry battalions and some twenty tanks) that the refitting Hermann Göring Division had managed to raise. This battle-group, coming from the Naples area, counterattacked and broke through the British line above the La Molina pass, coming close to Vietri before it was stopped, on the 13th, by the re-entry of the Commandos in to the fight. Even so, the pass was now firmly sealed. It had become all too clear that the British 10th Corps was penned into the very narrow coastal strip near Salerno with the Germans ensconced on the surrounding heights. Meanwhile Mark Clark's initial confidence was being still worse shaken by events in the southern sector. For the 29th Panzergrenadier Division along with part of the 16th Panzer thrust into the gap between the British and Americans. On the evening of September 12th, the British right wing was again driven out of Battipaglia, and suffered heavy loss, particularly in prisoners. On the 13th, the Germans exploited the widened gap between the two Allied corps for a stroke against the American left wing, driving it out of Persano and producing a general withdrawal. In the confusion that ensued, the Germans penetrated the line in several places and at one point came within about half a mile of the beaches.

That evening the situation looked so grim that the unloading of all merchant ships was stopped in the southern sector. Moreover Mark Clark sent Admiral Hewitt an urgent request to prepare for re-embarking Fifth Army Headquarters and to make all available craft ready to evacuate the 6th Corps from the beachhead, and re-land it in the British sector, or alternatively to transfer the 10th Corps southward.* Such a large-scale emergency shift was hardly practicable, and the suggestion drew a horrified protest from McCreery and his naval colleague Commodore Oliver, while it caused consternation in higher quarters when reported to Eisenhower and Alexander. But it helped to produce an accelerated reinforcement of the troops on shore, additional landing craft being provided for the purpose by diverting eighteen LSTs which were *en route* to India. The 82nd Airborne Division was put at Mark Clark's disposal, and in swift response to his emergency call in the afternoon Matt Ridgway managed to drop the first instalment in the southern beachhead that evening. The British 7th Armoured Division began to land in the northern beachhead on the 15th. But by then the crisis had passed, thanks largely to the quicker emergency relief given by Allied seapower and airpower.

On the 14th all available aircraft, of the strategic as well as the tactical air forces, in the Mediterranean theatre were turned onto bombing the German troops and their immediate communications. They carried out more than 1,900 sorties during the day. Even more effective in checking the Germans' drive for the beaches was the hammering they received from naval gunfire. Vietinghoff said in his retrospective account:

The attack this morning pushed on into stiffened resistance; but above all the advancing troops had to endure the most severe heavy fire that had yet been experienced – the naval gunfire from at least 16

* Cunningham of Hyndhope: *A Sailor's Odyssey*, p 569. Only the last of these emergency measures is mentioned in S. E. Morison's *History of U.S. Naval Operations*, vol IX.

to 18 battleships, cruisers and large destroyers lying in the roadstead. With astonishing precision and freedom of manoeuvre these ships shot with very overwhelming effect at every target spotted.

With such powerful support, the American troops succeeded in maintaining the rearward defence line to which they had been withdrawn during the previous night.

There was a lull on the 15th, while the Germans were reorganizing their shell-and-bomb-battered units for a fresh effort, with the aid of some reinforcements. The still tankless 26th Panzer Division had now arrived from Calabria, after slipping away from Montgomery's front as ordered by Vietinghoff on the day of the Salerno landing. Detachments of the 3rd and 15th Panzergrenadier Divisions had also arrived, from Rome and Gaeta respectively. But even with these additions the German strength was the equivalent of only four divisions, with little more than a hundred tanks, whereas by the 16th the Fifth Army had on shore the equivalent of seven divisions, of larger scale, with some 200 tanks. So the Allied Command had no cause for worry except for the possibility of a crack in morale before their manifold superiority took effect. Moreover the Eighth Army was now close at hand, to augment this superiority and threaten the enemy's flank.

Alexander arrived at Clark's headquarters that morning on a visit, having come across from Bizerta in a destroyer, and toured the beachheads. In his characteristically tactful way he squashed the idea of evacuating either of them. A fresh material reinforcement was provided by the arrival about 10 AM of the British battleships *Warspite* and *Valiant*, which had sailed from Malta the previous afternoon, along with six destroyers. They did not come into action until seven hours later, owing to communication delays with forward observers, but then bombarded targets up to a dozen miles inland, and the very heavy shells from their 15-inch guns had a shattering effect both physically and morally.

Another arrival that morning was a group of war correspondents from the Eighth Army. Feeling that its advance to the aid of the Fifth Army was too slow and needlessly cautious, they had gone ahead on their own the previous day in a couple of jeeps, using minor roads and tracks to avoid the blown up bridges on the main road, and came through the fifty-mile stretch of 'enemy country' without meeting any Germans. Twenty-seven hours later the leading reconnaissance unit of the Eighth Army arrived to make touch with the Fifth.

On the morning of the 16th the Germans launched their renewed effort, starting on the British sector, with a thrust from the north towards Salerno and another towards Battipaglia. These thrusts were stopped by the combined effect of artillery fire, naval gunfire, and tanks. This failure and the approach of the Eighth Army led Kesselring to the conclusion that the possibility of throwing the invaders back into the sea had passed. So, that evening, he authorized 'a disengagement on the coastal front', and a gradual retreat northward. The first stage was to be a withdrawal to the line of the Volturno, twenty miles north of Naples – which, he laid down, was to be held until mid-October.

In view of the way that naval gunfire had helped thwart the Germans' counterattack – although largely before the big ships came on the scene – it was some consolation to them that the *Warspite* was disabled that afternoon by a direct hit from one of their new FX 1400 radio-guided gliding bombs. By the same new means they had also delivered a parting kick at the main fleet of their late Italian ally when this sailed from Spezia on September 9th to join the Allied Navies – sinking its flagship, the *Roma*, with one of these guided bombs.

In analysis it is evident that once the German efforts to throw the invaders back into the sea had been curbed, a German withdrawal from Salerno became inevitable. For although Kesselring had striven to exploit the opportunity allowed by what he termed 'Montgomery's very cautious advance', it was very clear that he could not hang on to this stretch of the west coast when the British Eighth Army arrived on the scene and became able to outflank his position by advancing through the interior, after emerging from the narrow Calabrian peninsula. He had far too few troops to cover such a widening front. But the threat did not develop fast enough to endanger or hustle the German withdrawal. For it was not until the afternoon of September 20th that a Canadian spearhead of the Eighth Army drove into Potenza, the main road-centre on the ankle of Italy, fifty miles inland from the Gulf of Salerno. A hundred German paratroops, rushed to Potenza the previous afternoon, had imposed an overnight pause and caused the mounting of a brigade attack, with about thirty times their strength, in order to overcome their resistance – a significant example of the delaying power of skilful defence in a hazy situation. The attack which forced the retreat of this tiny detachment brought the capture of only sixteen Germans, but nearly 2,000 of the Italian inhabitants had been killed in the preliminary air attacks on the town. Canadian patrols pushed on cautiously during the next week to Melfi, forty miles northward, having only fleeting contact with enemy rearguards. Meantime the main body of the Eighth Army had halted, as its supplies were becoming short, while switching its line of supply to Taranto and Brindisi in the south-east corner of Italy.

For the landings here, on Italy's heel, had been achieved without meeting any opposition. Taranto had been among the possible objectives considered in June, after the Combined Chiefs of Staff had instructed Eisenhower to prepare plans for following up the capture of Sicily. But it had been rejected largely because it did not fit the cardinal principle which his staff had immediately laid down, that no opposed landing could be contemplated outside the limit of fighter cover. Taranto, like Naples, was just beyond the 180-mile radius of action of Spitfires operating from airfields in the north-east of Sicily, whereas Salerno was just inside that radius. The Taranto project was only revived when the armistice with Italy was signed on September 3rd. It was then added to the invasion plan as an improvised subsidiary move – code-named 'Operation Slapstick', following information that only a handful of German troops was posted in the heel of Italy, and a belated realization that the port of Naples, even when captured and made usable, would not suffice to maintain an advance up the eastern side of the Apennines as well as up the western side.

Admiral Cunningham, who took the initiative in suggesting this move, told Eisenhower that if the troops were produced for the purpose he would provide ships to carry them. At that moment the British 1st Airborne Division was available in Tunisia, owing to a lack of sufficient transport aircraft for employing it in an airborne role, so it was hurriedly embarked at Bizerta in five cruisers and a minelayer, which sailed for Taranto on the evening of September 8th. The next afternoon, as the convoy approached Taranto, it passed the Italian squadron based on Taranto sailing to surrender at Malta. At dusk the convoy entered the port, and found most of its facilities intact. Two days later the success was extended over the heel by the occupation of Brindisi (to which King Victor Emmanuel and Marshal Badoglio had fled from Rome), and also of Bari, sixty miles farther up the coast – on the back of Italy's ankle. Thus three large ports had been secured in this area, for the maintenance of an advance up the east coast, long before any comparable one had been captured on the west coast – and it was all too clear that the long delay in reaching Naples, from Salerno, would allow the Germans ample time to demolish the port before abandoning it.

But the wonderful opportunity thus presented on the east coast went begging through want of foresight, and inadequate effort subsequently to redeem it. The codename 'Slapstick' became painfully apt. Visualized as merely an operation to secure the ports, the 1st Airborne Division was dispatched without transport vehicles, except for half a dozen jeeps, and remained in this destitute state until the 14th. During these five days a few patrols in jeeps and requisitioned cars had pushed north as far as Bari without finding any enemy troops in the broad coastal belt. For the depleted German 1st Parachute Division had been the only one in this area, and part of it had been called away to the Salerno sector, while the rest had been ordered to withdraw to Foggia, 120 miles north of Taranto, to cover Kesselring's deep eastern flank. Yet even when transport arrived to restore mobility to the British troops they were still held in leash while the planning and preparation for a large-scale advance up the east coast proceeded in a methodical way. Adherence to this cautious habit was the more unfortunate in such a period of far-reaching opportunity as the German 1st Parachute Division was too far back to counterattack, and its entire fighting strength was only 1,300 men, while that of the British was already four times as large, with much larger reinforcements on the way to back up a forward move. But habit prevailed.

The conduct of operations here had been given to the commander of the 5th Corps, General Allfrey – who had been in charge of the too cautious, and abortive, advance on Tunis the previous December – and his task had been defined by Alexander as being 'to secure a base in the Heel of Italy covering the ports of Taranto and Brindisi, and if possible Bari, with a view to a subsequent advance'. Any likelihood of an early thrust beyond these bounds diminished when, on the 13th, Allfrey's Corps was placed under the Eighth Army, for Montgomery could always be counted on to mass his forces and make sure of ample resources before advancing.

On September 22nd, the 78th Division began to disembark at Bari, followed by the 8th Indian Division at Brindisi, while Dempsey's 13th Corps was being brought over to the east coast. But it was not until September 27th that a small mobile force, sent forward from Bari to explore the enemy's situation, occupied Foggia, which the Germans promptly evacuated as soon as the British approached – so that the much desired airfields were captured without a fight. Even then Montgomery adhered to his earlier order that no main bodies were to advance before October 1st, and when his advance began he used only the two divisions of the 13th Corps, keeping the three divisions of the 5th Corps back to ensure 'a firm base' and protect his inland flank.

The German 1st Parachute Division was now holding a line along the Biferno River, covering the small port of Termoli – a very wide front for its slender strength. Montgomery's attack on this line was well designed to crack it open, by a seaborne stroke in its rear. In the early hours of October 3rd, a Special Service brigade was landed beyond Termoli and, with the advantage of night surprise, in driving rain quickly captured the port and town, then linking up with a bridgehead over the river gained by the direct advance. During the next two days two more infantry brigades, of the 78th Division, were brought up by sea, from Barletta to Termoli, to reinforce the bridgehead and continue the advance.

But the German army commander, Vietinghoff, benefiting from the British delay in building their east coast advance, had already (on the 2nd) dispatched the 16th Panzer Division from the Volturno line on the west coast to reinforce the thin screen of paratroops which had been covering the distant left flank of his army's withdrawal. Hurrying across the mountain spine of Italy they arrived near Termoli early on the 5th and promptly launched a counterattack which drove the British back to the edge of the town and came close to cutting their line of communications southward. But the Germans were checked and then pushed back as the 78th Division brought its seaborne reinforcements into action, supported by a stronger body of tanks, British and Canadian.

The Germans then disengaged and withdrew to positions covering the next river line, the Trigno, a dozen miles northward. The impression made by their sharp counterattack led Montgomery to pause for two weeks for a further build-up of his strength and supplies before tackling the Trigno line.

Meanwhile Mark Clark's Fifth Army had been slowly pushing forward from Salerno up the west coast, and trying to hustle the withdrawal of Vietinghoff's German 10th Army. The first stage was the stickiest, as the German right wing held on stubbornly to the hill-barrier north of Salerno to cover the extrication of the left wing as this wheeled back from the southerly coastal stretch around Battipaglia and Paestum. Nearly a week passed after the beginning of that withdrawal before the British 10th Corps, on September 23rd, developed an offensive to force the passage from Salerno to Naples. In this offensive the 10th Corps employed not only the 46th and 56th Divisions but the 7th Armoured Division, and an additional armoured brigade, against the small German force of three to four battalions which was holding the passes. Little progress was made until September 26th, when it was found that the opposing Germans had vanished during the previous night – having fulfilled their mission of gaining time for the wheel-back of their comrades in the south. After that, demolished bridges were the main hindrance to the Allied advance. On the 28th the 10th Corps emerged into the plain at Nocera, but it was not until October 1st that its leading troops entered Naples, twenty miles on.

Meanwhile the American 6th Corps had come up level with the 10th Corps after a slow advance along the demolition-blocked inland roads – during which it had averaged only three miles a day – and entered Benevento on October 2nd. This corps now had a new commander, Major-General John P. Lucas, who had been brought in to replace Dawley.

The Fifth Army had taken three weeks since the landing to reach Naples, its initial objective, at a cost of nearly 12,000 casualties – close on 7,000 British and 5,000 American. That was the penalty paid for choosing a too obvious line of attack and place of landing, at the sacrifice of surprise, on the ground that the Salerno sector was just within the limit of air cover.

Another week passed before the Fifth Army closed up to the line of the Volturno River, to which the Germans had withdrawn. Muddy roads and sodden ground put a brake on the advance as rainy weather had set in during the first week of October, a month earlier than expected. Fifth Army's attack on the Volturno line, held by three German divisions, was launched on the night of October 12th, three nights later than intended. The US 6th Corps gained a bridgehead over the river above Capua, but its development was cramped by the check which the right wing of the British 10th Corps suffered in trying to force a crossing at Capua, on the main road from Naples to Rome. The small crossings which the two other British divisions gained nearer to the coast were curbed by speedy counterattacks. Thus the German forward troops fulfilled Kesselring's order to stay on this river line until the 16th before beginning to withdraw to the next line of defence, fifteen miles northward – a hurriedly improvised line starting near the mouth of the Garigliano River and continuing through the cluster of rugged hills which cover the approach, along Highway 6 and through the Mignano defile, to the upper reaches of the Garigliano and the valleys of its tributaries, the Rapido and the Liri. Kesselring hoped to hold this outpost line while he was fortifying, for a prolonged defence, a carefully planned line along the Garigliano and Rapido, pivoted on the Cassino defile. This slightly rearward positon was called the Gustav, or Winter Line.

Bad weather and demolitions delayed the Fifth Army's attack on the first of these lines for a further three weeks, until November 5th, and then the Germans' resistance proved so tough that after ten days' struggle, with little progress except on the coastal flank, Mark Clark was driven to pull back his weary troops and reorganize them for a stronger effort. This was not ready for launching until the first week of December. The Fifth Army's losses had risen to 22,000 by mid-November – of which nearly 12,000 were Americans.

During these long pauses Hitler's view changed in a way that was of far-reaching effect. Encouraged by the slowness of the Allied advance from Salerno and Bari he had come to feel that it might not be necessary to withdraw to northern Italy, and on October 4th he issued a directive that 'the line Gaeta–Ortona will be held' – promising Kesselring that three divisions from Rommel's Army Group 'B' in northern Italy would be sent to help him in holding on south of Rome as long as possible. Hitler was becoming more inclined to favour Kesselring's case for a prolonged stand, but it was not until November 21st that he definitely committed himself to this course by putting all the German forces in Italy under Kesselring's command. Rommel's army group was dissolved, and its remaining troops were now at Kesselring's disposal. Even so, Kesselring still had to keep part of them in the north to guard and control that large area, while four of the best divisions, three of them armoured, were sent to Russia and replaced by three depleted ones which needed to recuperate.

A smaller but valuable reinforcement came from the arrival of the 90th Panzergrenadier Division. This division had been in Sardinia at the time of the Italian armistice, but had been evacuated to Corsica, across the narrow Strait of Bonifacio, and then successfully carried by air and sea to the Italian mainland at Leghorn, in driblets over a period of two weeks, evading interception by the Allied air and sea forces, whose efforts to interfere were slight and spasmodic. Although the division was not put at Kesselring's disposal until more than six weeks later, he then rushed it southward in time to help in checking the Eighth Army's delayed offensive up the east coast of Italy.

Hitler's decision to place all the German forces in Italy under Kesselring's command, now named Army Group 'C', was taken the morning after Montgomery began a probing attack against the German position along the Sangro River – covering Ortona and the Adriatic extension of the Gustav Line.

After the tough resistance he had met on getting across the Biferno in the first week of October, Montgomery had brought up the 5th Corps to take over the coastal sector and shifted the 13th Corps to the hilly sector inland, where German rearguards were imposing repeated checks on the Canadians' advance. After this regrouping the 5th Corps pushed on to the Trigno (twelve miles beyond the Biferno) and gained a small bridgehead on the night of October 22nd, which it expanded by a larger night attack on the 27th. But it was checked by a combination of mud and fire, so that it did not break into the enemy's main position until the night of November 3rd. The Germans then withdrew to the Sangro, seventeen miles northward.

Another long pause followed, while Montgomery was mounting his attack and bringing up the recently arrived 2nd New Zealand Division, a powerful reinforcement which increased his attacking strength to five divisions and two armoured brigades for the Sangro offensive. Meantime the so-called 76th Panzer Corps opposing the Eighth Army had received the 65th Infantry Division, to take over the coastal sector from the 16th Panzer Division, which was being dispatched to Russia. But beyond this it had only the remnants of the 1st Parachute Division and a battle-group of the 26th Panzer Division, which was now returning bit by bit to the Adriatic side as the Allied Fifth Army's pressure waned.

Montgomery's aim in the Sangro offensive was to smash the Germans' winter line, then drive on twenty miles to Pescara, get astride the east to west highway from there to Rome, and threaten the rear of the German forces which were holding up the Fifth Army. For Alexander still hopefully adhered to his directive of September 21st, two months earlier, which had set the objectives to be attained by the Allied armies, in four successive phases – the first to 'consolidate' the Salerno–Bari line; the second to capture 'the port of Naples and the Foggia airfields'; the third to capture 'Rome, its airfields, and the important road and rail centre of Terni'; and the next having as its objective 'the port of Leghorn and the communications centres of Florence and Arezzo', 150 miles north of Rome. The speedy capture of Rome had been reiterated as the key point of the fresh directive which Alexander issued on November 8th, after receiving a similar one from Eisenhower.

Montgomery's offensive was planned for delivery on November 20th, but the worsening weather and swollen river compelled him to reduce the initial assault to a limited effort which, after several days' fighting, gained a bridgehead about six miles wide and a mile deep. This was maintained under great difficulties until the big attack was launched on the night of the 28th, a week behind schedule. Yet Montgomery still showed complete confidence in the outcome, and in a personal message to his troops on the 25th declared: 'The time has now come to drive the Germans north of Rome ... The Germans are, in fact, in the very condition in which we want them. We will now hit the Germans a colossal crack.' But it seemed ominous that he delivered this message after stepping down from his caravan to stand in the rain under an outsize umbrella.

The attack started well, under cover of a tremendous air and artillery bombardment, backed by a 5 to 1 superiority in numbers. The enemy's 65th Division – a raw and ill-equipped division of mixed nationalities – gave way under the impact, and the ridge beyond the Sangro was cleared by the 30th. But the Germans rallied on retiring to their main line farther back, and were helped by the way that their pursuers complied with Montgomery's oft-repeated emphasis on establishing 'a firm base'. A particularly good opportunity for exploitation went begging at Orsogna on the inland flank during December 2nd and 3rd. Thus time was allowed for the arrival of the rest of the 26th Panzer Division and of the 90th Panzergrenadier Division, which Kesselring brought down from the north. Thus the advance became increasingly sticky. There was always 'one more river, one more river to cross'. It was not until December 10th that the Eighth Army succeeded in crossing the Moro, eight miles beyond the Sangro, and it did not clear Ortona, two miles beyond the Moro, until December 28th. Then it was checked at the Riccio, barely halfway to Pescara, the Pescara River, and the lateral highway to Rome. That was the stalemate situation at the end of the year, when Montgomery handed over command of the Eighth Army to Oliver Leese, and returned to England to take over the 21st Army Group in preparation for the cross-Channel invasion of Normandy.

Meanwhile Mark Clark's renewed offensive west of the Apennines had started on December 2nd. By this time the Fifth Army's strength had risen to the equivalent of ten divisions, but two of these, the British 7th Armoured and the US 82nd Airborne, were being withdrawn to England for the coming cross-Channel attack. Kesselring's strength had also risen, and four divisions now held the front west of the Apennines, with one in reserve.

In the first phase of the renewed offensive the objective was the mountain buttress west of Route 6 and the Mignano gap. The British 10th Corps and the newly arrived US 2nd Corps, under Major-General Geoffrey Keyes, were employed in this attack, supported by over 900 guns, which fired over 4,000 tons of shells onto the German positions in the first two days. The British came near to reaching the 3,000 foot summit of Monte Camino by December 3rd but were driven back by counterattacks and did not secure it until the 6th. That brought them up to the Garigliano river line. Meanwhile the Americans, on their right, had captured Monte La Difensa and Monte Maggiore, which were lower, but closer to the highway through the gap. In the second phase, starting on December 7th, the US 2nd and 6th Corps attacked towards the Rapido on a wider front, hoping to clear the enemy off the mountain buttress east of Highway 6, by a deep thrust on each side of it. But they met increasing resistance, achieving only a few miles 'inching' progress in successive efforts during the next few weeks. By the second week of January this offensive had petered out, while still short of reaching the Rapido and the forward edge of the Gustav Line. The Fifth Army's battle losses had risen to nearly 40,000 – a total far exceeding the enemy's. In addition the Americans alone had suffered a loss of 50,000 in sick during the two months' duration of this bitter winter struggle in the mountains.

The sequel to the invasion of Italy had been very disappointing. In four months the Allied forces had advanced only seventy miles beyond Salerno – mostly in the first few weeks – and were still eighty miles short of Rome. Alexander himself described the process as 'slogging up Italy'. But a more general description that came to be used in the autumn was 'inching'. 'Gnawing' would have been an even more apt term in view of the country's geographical resemblance to a leg.

Even when full allowance is made for the difficulties of the terrain and the bad weather, it becomes evident in examining the campaign that favourable opportunities of faster progress were repeatedly missed through the Allied commanders' heavy emphasis on 'consolidating' each advance and establishing a 'firm base' before pressing on, together with their predominant concern to ensure ample strength and supplies before advancing. Time after time they were 'too late' from fear of having 'too little'.

In comment on the campaign, Kesselring significantly remarked:

The Allied plans showed throughout that the Allied High Command's dominating thought was to make sure of success, a thought that led it to use orthodox methods and material. As a result it was almost always possible for me, despite inadequate means of reconnaissance and scanty reports, to foresee the next strategic or tactical move of my opponent – and thus to take the appropriate counter-measures so far as my resources allowed.*

* Liddell Hart: *The Other Side of the Hill*, p 364.

But the original source of the trouble which the Allies suffered lay in their choice of Salerno and the toe of Italy as their landing sites – a choice which conformed all too closely to the opponent's expectation, from experience of their cautious habit. Kesselring and his Chief of Staff, Westphal – the beneficiaries of that too obvious decision – considered that the Allies had paid heavy strategic forfeit for their desire to ensure tactical security against air attack, and that this was an over-insurance in view of the then scanty strength of the German air force in southern Italy. They felt, too, that the Allied High Command's habit of limiting the scope of its strokes to the limits of constant air-cover had been the defenders' salvation, by simplifying the multiple problems of the defence.

As to the course that the Allies should have taken, Westphal expressed the view that:

> If the forces employed in the landing at Salerno had been used instead at Civitavecchia [thirty miles north of Rome] the results would have been much more decisive ... there were only two German divisions in Rome and ... no others could have been brought up quickly enough to defend it. In conjunction with the five Italian divisions stationed at Rome, a combined sea and air landing would have taken the Italian capital inside seventy-two hours. Quite apart from the political repercussions of such a victory this would have resulted in cutting off at one blow the supplies of the five German divisions retreating from Calabria ... That would have brought all Italy south of the line Rome–Pescara into Allied hands.*

Westphal also considered it was a mistake to land Montgomery's Eighth Army on the toe of Italy, where it had to push up the whole length of the foot, while the greater opportunity on the exposed heel of Italy and along the Adriatic coast went begging:

> The landing of the British Eighth Army should have taken place in full strength in the Taranto sector, where only one parachute division (with only three batteries of divisional artillery!) was stationed. Indeed, it would have been even better to have carried out the landing in the sector Pescara–Ancona ... No resistance to this landing could have been provided from the Rome sector, owing to our lack of available forces. Likewise no appreciable forces could have been brought down rapidly from the Po plain [in northern Italy].†

* Liddell Hart: *The Other Side of the Hill*, pp 364–5.
† Ibid, p 365.

It would also have been impossible to switch Kesselring's forces quickly from the west coast to the south-east coast if the main landing, by the Allied Fifth Army, had been made at Taranto instead of Salerno.

In sum, the Allies failed to profit either initially or subsequently from their greatest advantage, amphibious power – and its neglect became their greatest handicap. The evidence of Kesselring and Westphal supports, and in a wider way, the scathing conclusion which Churchill expressed in a telegram, from Carthage, to the British Chiefs of Staff on December 19th:

the stagnation of the whole campaign on the Italian front is becoming scandalous ... The total neglect to provide amphibious action on the Adriatic side and the failure to strike any similar blow on the west have been disastrous.

None of the landing craft in the Mediterranean have been put to the slightest use [for assault purposes] for three months ... There are few instances, even in this war, of such valuable forces being so completely wasted.*

What he did not see was that the doctrine of war on the Allied side was at fault – from following the cautious banker's principle of 'no advance without security'.

* Churchill: *The Second World War*, vol V, p 380.

CHAPTER TWENTY-EIGHT

The German Ebb in Russia

At the start of 1943 the German armies in the Caucasus looked likely to suffer the same fate as the Stalingrad armies. They were far deeper in the nose of the bag than the latter had been. Yet they had already been made to remain there for more than a month after the Stalingrad encirclement, while winter was deepening and danger extending. It was a grim outlook for the 1st Panzer Army and the 17th Army, composing 'Army Group A' – in command of which General Kleist had succeeded Field-Marshal List.

In the first week of January, the precarious situation of 'Army Group A' was emphasized by the development of multiple enveloping threats. The most direct was where its head stuck into the Caucasus mountains. The Russians struck first at its left cheek near Mozdok, and then at its right cheek near Nalchik, regaining both places. More dangerous was a simultaneous Russian move across the Kalmuk Steppes 200 miles behind its left flank, at the joint between it and 'Army Group Don'. Capturing Elista, the Russians drove down past that end of Lake Manych towards Armavir – through which ran Kleist's communications with Rostov. Most dangerous of all was a sudden surge southward down the Don line, from the Stalingrad direction, towards Rostov itself. One of the Russian spearheads came within fifty miles of that bottleneck.

This alarming news reached Kleist on the same day that he received an emphatic order from Hitler that he was not to withdraw his front in any circumstances. At that moment his 1st Panzer Army stood nearly 400 miles *east* of Rostov. The next day he received a fresh order – to retreat from the Caucasus, bringing all his equipment away with him. That requirement added to the handicap of distance in a race with time.

To leave the Rostov routes clear for the 1st Panzer Army, the 17th Army was ordered to withdraw westwards along the Kuban River towards the Taman peninsula, whence it might if necessary be transported back across the Kerch Straits into the Crimea. That withdrawal was not a long step, and the Russian forces recently besieged in the

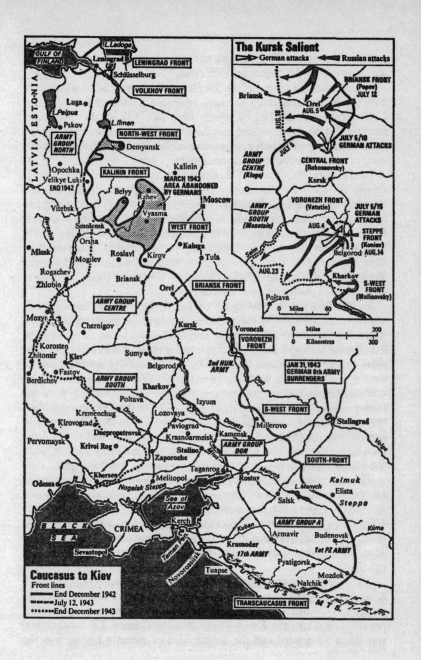

The Kursk Salient

⊐▷ German attacks ◁⊏ Russian attacks

GULF OF FINLAND

I.Ladoga

Leningrad

Schlüsselburg

LENINGRAD FRONT

Briansk

BRIANSK FRONT (Popov) JULY 12

Orel AUG. 5

VOLKHOV FRONT

Luga

I.Peipus

Pskov

L.Ilmen

AUG.18

JULY 5

JULY 5/10 GERMAN ATTACKS

ARMY GROUP NORTH

NORTH-WEST FRONT

Demyansk

ARMY GROUP CENTRE (Kluge)

CENTRAL FRONT (Rokossovsky)

Opochka

Velikye Luki END 1942

KALININ FRONT

Kalinin

Kursk

Vitebsk

MARCH 1943 AREA ABANDONED BY GERMANS

Belyy

Rzhev

Vyasma

Moscow

ARMY GROUP SOUTH (Manstein)

VORONEZH FRONT (Vatutin)

AUG.4

JULY 5/15 GERMAN ATTACKS

Smolensk

Orsha

Minsk

Mogilev

Roslavl

Kirov

WEST FRONT

Kaluga

Tula

Seim

STEPPE FRONT (Koniev)

Belgorod AUG.14

Rogachev

Zhlobin

Briansk

Orel

BRIANSK FRONT

AUG.23

Kharkov

S-WEST FRONT (Malinovsky)

Mozyr

Chernigov

Kursk

Voronezh

VORONEZH FRONT

Poltava

0 Miles 60

Korosten

Zhitomir

Kiev

Sumy

Belgorod

2nd HUN. ARMY

0 Miles 200

Berdichev

Fastov

ARMY GROUP SOUTH

Kharkov

Don

0 Kilometres 300

JAN 31, 1943 GERMAN 6th ARMY SURRENDERS

Poltava

Izyum

S-WEST FRONT

Kremenchug

Lozovaya

Kirovograd

Dnepropetrovsk

Pavlograd

Krasnoarmeisk

Kamensk

Millerovo

Stalingrad

Pervomaysk

Krivoi Rog

Stalino

ARMY GROUP DON

Zaporozhe

Taganrog

SOUTH-FRONT

Odessa

Khersen

Melitopol

Nogaisk Steppe

Rostov

Manych

Kalmuk

L.Manych

Elista

Steppe

Sea of Azov

Salsk

BLACK SEA

CRIMEA

Kerch

ARMY GROUP A

Kuban

Kùma

Armavir

Budenovsk

Sevastopol

Tamen Pen.

Krasnodar

17th ARMY

Pyatigorsk

1st PZ ARMY

Mozdok

Novorossisk

Tuapse

Nalchik

Caucasus to Kiev
Front lines
— End December 1942
═══ July 12, 1943
••••• End December 1943

TRANSCAUCASUS FRONT

CAUCASUS MTS.

coastal strip around Tuapse were not strong enough to exert a dangerous pressure on the retreating 17th Army.

By contrast, the retreat of the 1st Panzer Army was beset with perils,
both direct and indirect. The most dangerous phase was from January
15th until February 1st, by which time the bulk of that army had
reached Rostov. Even so, the continuation of its line of retreat, though
not so narrowly constricted, was menaced by a series of Russian thrusts
ranging over a further two hundred miles.

On January 10th General Rokossovsky had launched a concentric
assault on the encircled German forces at Stalingrad, following the
rejection of a Russian ultimatum to surrender. Paulus's troops were so
enfeebled by hunger, cold, disease, depression, and shortage of ammunition that they were in no state to offer strong or prolonged resistance.
Still less were they capable of breaking out of the ring. Thus the Russians were able to spare part of the investing forces to reinforce the
southward drive to cut off the Germans' Caucasus forces, and more
were released as the ring was contracted.

As this final act at Stalingrad began, Kleist's forces, having withdrawn from the nose of their Caucasus salient, were standing on the
Kuma River, between Pyatigorsk and Budenovsk. Ten days later the
Russian thrust south from Elista reached a point more than a hundred
miles in rear of the Kuma line. But by then Kleist's retreating columns
were nearing Armavir, and thus passing the immediate point of danger.

Nevertheless, farther back an acute danger was developing from the
more powerful Russian drive down both sides of the Don towards Rostov. On the east side the Russians were now close to the Manych River
and the rail junction of Salsk. On the west side they had reached the
Donetz not far from the point where it entered the lower Don. Kleist's
rearguards had still three times as far to go as the Russians before they
could reach Rostov. Moreover, Manstein's exhausted forces, striving to
cover the flank of Kleist's escape-corridor, were now so hard-pressed
that they seemed on the verge of cracking under the strain.

The retreating forces won the race, however, and managed to slip out
of the trap. Ten days later Kleist's rearguards were close to Rostov, and
their would-be interruptors had been baffled. Luckily for the Germans
the desolate snow-covered country had limited even the Russians'
capacity to push on beyond their distant railheads fast enough and in
force enough to close the trap. But its jaws had only been held open by
a narrow margin. Manstein's forces had clung on so long to exposed
positions that their own chances of withdrawal were jeopardized,
and some of Kleist's divisions had to be rushed back to help in

extricating them, as well as reinforcing them.

The German forces from the Caucasus safely crossed the Don at Rostov just as the Stalingrad forces collapsed. Paulus himself and a large section of them surrendered on January 31st. The last remaining fragment surrendered on February 2nd. In all, 92,000 had been taken prisoner since the start of the assault three weeks earlier, while the total loss had been nearly three times that figure. Among those who surrendered were twenty-four generals. Although the German generals on the Eastern Front had been provided with little tubes of poison in case they fell into Russian hands, few seem to have used these until after the failure of the 'Generals' Plot' to assassinate Hitler on July 20th, 1944, when they began to do so rather than risk delivery into the hands of the Gestapo. But 'Stalingrad' henceforth worked like a subtle poison in the minds of the German commanders everywhere, undermining their confidence in the strategy which they were called on to execute. Morally even more than materially, the disaster to that army at Stalingrad had an effect from which the German Army never recovered.

Yet there was justification for Hitler's consoling declaration that the sacrifice of the army at Stalingrad had given the Supreme Command time for, and the possibility of, countermeasures on which depended the fate of the whole Eastern Front. If the army at Stalingrad had surrendered any time during the first seven weeks after its encirclement, a much greater disaster might have overtaken the other German armies. For Manstein's scanty forces could not possibly have withstood the Russian flood that would have poured down the Don to Rostov, and the forces in the Caucasus would have been cut off. Their fate might also have been sealed if the army at Stalingrad had succeeded in breaking out of the trap and retreating westward. Moreover, although its resistance during the last fortnight of January was not strong enough to prevent the Russians pushing down towards Rostov in great strength, it still detained a proportion of their strength sufficient to make a vital difference to the chances of the Caucasus forces reaching Rostov in time to slip through the bottleneck.

Even with this help the retreat from the Caucasus was achieved by the narrowest of margins. In terms of time, space, force, and weather conditions it was an astonishing performance – for which Kleist was made a field-marshal. While the skill and tenacity with which it was conducted deserves due recognition, its greatest significance lies in the proof it provided of the extraordinary resisting power inherent in modern defence so long as commanders and troops keep cool heads and stout hearts.

Further proof came in the weeks that followed. For after the retreating armies had passed safely through the Rostov bottleneck they had still to deal with dangers that were developing far back on their line of retreat. In the middle of January General Vatutin's left wing had resumed its push southward from the central Don to the Donetz behind Rostov. Besides producing the collapse of Millerovo, after that tough obstacle had been by-passed, the Donetz itself was crossed at and east of Kamensk.

In the same week two fresh Russian offensives had been launched. One was far away in the Leningrad sector. This broke the seventeen months' encirclement of that great city, lifting the pressure of the siege. Although it did not go far enough to wipe out the German salient that had projected to Lake Ladoga, across the rear of the city, it cut a hole through to Schlüsselburg along the lake shore – and that strategic tracheotomy created a windpipe through which the garrison and population could breathe more freely.

The other fresh offensive menaced the Germans' breathing space in the south. It was launched on January 12th by General Golikov's armies from the western stretch of the Don below Voronezh, and broke through the front of the 2nd Army and the 2nd Hungarian Army. Within a week it had penetrated a hundred miles – halfway from the Don to Kharkov. General Vatutin's right wing delivered a converging thrust eastward down the corridor between the Don and the Donetz.

In the last week of January the offensive was extended afresh. While attention was focused on the south-westerly drive towards Kharkov, the Russians struck westward from Voronezh on a broad front, upset the local withdrawal that the Germans were making there, and turned this into a widespread reflux. In barely three days the Russians had advanced nearly halfway to Kursk – the springboard from which the enemy had launched his summer offensive.

During the first week of February they threw their right shoulder forward, and drove a wedge deep across the railway and road between Kursk and Orel. Then they drove another wedge across the line between Kursk and Belgorod. Having thus outflanked Kursk on both sides they captured the city on February 7th by a sudden bound forward. In the same way the second wedge they had driven was used as a means to produce the collapse of Belgorod two days later. This gain, in turn, became a threat to the northern flank of Kharkov.

Meanwhile, the apparently direct advance on Kharkov had developed a more south-westerly bias – towards the Sea of Azov and the line of retreat from Rostov. On the 5th Vatutin's forces captured Izyum

– where the Germans had created their decisive flanking leverage in the spring – and exploited their crossing of the Donetz to form a leverage the other way round. After driving a wedge across the railway south of the Donetz, they spread westwards and captured the important rail junction of Lozovaya on the 11th.

These fresh gains undermined the situation of Kharkov itself, which fell into Golikov's hands on the 16th. That was a triumph, yet the more immediate danger to the German situation as a whole came from the Russians continued southward push from the Donetz towards the Sea of Azov. Four days earlier, a mobile force had reached Krasnoarmeisk, on the main line from Rostov back to Dnepropetrovsk. Such a development threatened to cut off the retreat of the armies that had just escaped from the Caucasus trap.

The alternating pattern and rhythm of the Russian offensive had become even more marked than during its earlier stage. It is easy to appreciate what a strain was thus placed on the Germans' resisting power, and their already overstretched resources – taking account of the wideness of the front which they had to cover with a shrinking margin of reserves. The progressive and variable way in which the Russians had played on that weakness provided an illuminating demonstration of the Russians' improved technique and the way they had learnt to exploit their new superiority. Examining the process by which they had captured such an important succession of key places, it can be seen that in each case the capture – even when it followed upon an advance in the immediate neighbourhood – was the sequel to an indirect move which virtually made the place untenable, or at best crippled its strategic value. The effect of that series of indirect leverages can be clearly traced in the pattern of operations. The Red Army Command might be likened to a pianist running his hands up and down the keyboard.

While this alternating rhythm of the Russian offensive was similar to that carried out by Marshal Foch in 1918, it was a more subtle as well as a more speedy application of that strategic method. The striking-point was more deceptive each time, and the process was punctuated by shorter pauses. While the preparatory moves were never directly aimed at the place which they were intended to threaten, the completing moves were often direct in the geographical sense – and thus had a psychological indirectness, because they came from the least expected direction.

But a dramatic change came over the scene in the last fortnight of February. The Russians' advantage began to pass when they wheeled down over the Donetz towards the Sea of Azov and the Dnieper bend, to cut off the southern German armies. The Russians' aim here was now obvious, while it carried them into the same area for which the Germans were making. The next stage thus became a race, the issue of which turned on the question whether the Russians could establish themselves across the Germans' escape-corridor before the latter could arrive and concentrate to check the down stroke.

Unfortunately for the Russians, an early thaw hampered them at this moment, and added to the handicap which ensued from their prolonged advance. When they had planned their winter offensive they had found that the administrative side of the plan did not fit the strategic side, since there was not sufficient transport to carry even half the minimum supplies of petrol, ammunition, and food required for such an extensive range of thrusts. With characteristic boldness they decided that, instead of modifying the plan, they would bank on obtaining the larger part of their necessities from the enemy! That policy succeeded, as a large number of supply depots and dumps were overrun in each breakthrough. But when the enemy's resistance stiffened and such captures became fewer, the Russians became more subject to the transport handicap the farther they advanced beyond their railheads. Thus the law of overstretch came into operation again; this time to the Russians' disadvantage. There were few railways in the Don–Donetz corridor, and these ran at right angles to their line of advance south-westward. By contrast, the east-to-west run of the relatively numerous rail routes south of the Donetz helped the Germans to hasten their assembly at the danger-point. The latter also began to profit by the contraction of their front – now 600 miles shorter than it had been in the autumn.

Brought to a halt by this combination of causes, the Russians were left in a very awkward position. They had driven a large wedge eighty miles beyond the Donetz towards the Dnieper, but stopping thirty miles short of it, at Pavlograd. They had driven a narrow wedge seventy miles beyond the Donetz southwards, to Krasnoarmeisk, across the corridor between that river and the Sea of Azov. The Germans, gathering all their available forces, quickly mounted a three-pointed counterstroke under Manstein's direction. It was designed to take advantage of the irregularity of the Russians' salient position, and particularly of its two projections. A left-hand thrust was delivered from the Dnieper against the south-western tip; a right-hand thrust was made against the south-eastern tip; a central thrust was made into the sagging front between them, towards Lozovaya. Both tips were broken off and German armoured wedges were driven deep into the body of the salient. These counterstrokes in the last week of February developed into a general counteroffensive as the Germans' westward withdrawal from Rostov provided more reinforcements. By the first week of March the German drive had reached the Donetz again on a wide frontage around Izyum, the Russian salient had been almost wiped out, and a large portion of the Russian forces had been cornered south of Kharkov.

If the Germans could have crossed the Donetz quickly, and cut astride the rear of the Russian armies that were advancing west, they might have produced a Russian disaster comparable to their own at Stalingrad. But they were baulked in the attempt, lacking sufficient weight to carry by assault any strongly held obstacle. After this check, the centre of gravity was shifted north-west, where the Germans' enveloping pressure squeezed the Russians out of Kharkov, once again, on March 15th. Four days later a rapid German drive north of Kharkov regained Belgorod. But that was the limit of the Germans' success. Their counteroffensive petered out the following week in the slush of the spring thaw.

While the Germans had been delivering their counteroffensive in the south, they had been falling back in the north. It was the first significant retreat there for more than a year. After the winter campaign of 1941–2, the German front facing Moscow had the shape of a clenched fist, with the Russians lapping round the wrist – where Smolensk lay. In August the Russians had struck hard at the left knuckle, the fortified centre of Rzhev, in an effort to create a diversion in aid of Stalingrad by cracking the enemy's central front. Their offensive had been baffled by the stubborn resistance of Rzhev, though they had cut into its flanks and left the knuckle exposed. A fresh effort in November had increased its exposure, so that it came to look like a peninsula with a narrow isthmus. At the end of the year the Russians attacked from the tip of their own great salient north of the German salient, and captured the junction of Velikye Luki, 150 miles due west of Rzhev, on the line from Moscow to Riga. As a result the danger, not only to Rzhev, but to the whole fist, became more manifest.

A month later the danger was indirectly emphasized by the surrender of the forces at Stalingrad, while the subsequent spreading collapse in the south showed the price of trying to hold overextended fronts. Zeitzler now achieved his only significant piece of persuasion in dealing with Hitler. Much as the Leader hated any withdrawal, and particularly one that would be a step back from Moscow, he was induced to agree that the front must be straightened in that sector, to avoid a collapse and to free reserves. Rzhev was evacuated at the beginning of March, just as a fresh Russian attack was opening, and by the 12th the whole fist was abandoned, including the important communications centre of Vyasma. The Germans withdrew to a straighter line covering Smolensk. The smaller fortified salient of Demyansk, between Velikye Luki and Lake Ilmen, was also abandoned at the beginning of March. (The significance of this step-back was obscured in the West by the way that British and American newspaper maps had for over a year shown a straight line here, with Demyansk well inside the Russian front.)

What the German armies gained by this shortening of the front in the north was, however, more than offset by the fresh extension, and temptation, created by the success of their counteroffensive in the south. It nullified the generals' hope that Hitler might be led to sanction a long step-back to a line where they could consolidate and reorganize well out of reach of the Russians. It provided a new-old set of offensive springboards that looked all too promising to a man whose instincts were predominantly offensive, and whose mind was intensely reluctant to give up the idea that an offensive gamble might still turn the whole situation in his favour.

The success of the counteroffensive had removed any urgent necessity for leaving the Donetz Basin. By standing on his last year's line south of the Donetz, near Taganrog, Hitler could preserve that industrial asset while also preserving the hope of a fresh bid for the Caucasus. By the recent return to the banks of the Donetz farther west, between Kharkov and Izyum, Hitler could picture the development of a fresh flanking leverage there. By recapturing Belgorod and maintaining Orel he had excellent flank positions for a pincer-stroke against the Russians' nearby captured position at and around Kursk. By pinching off that great salient, he would produce a yawning hole in the Russian front, and once his panzer divisions poured through it anything might develop. The Russians' strength was greater than he had reckoned earlier, but their losses had been very heavy. It was only the 'old generals' who deemed their resources inexhaustible. Pursuing this line of thought, biased by his natural inclination, it increasingly appeared to Hitler that a breakthrough at Kursk might again turn the balance in his favour, and provide a solution for all his problems. He found it easy to convince himself that his troubles were due to the Russian winter, and that he could always count on having the advantage in summer. The prospect became his midsummer night's dream.

While the main offensive was to be on the Kursk sector, his summer programme also included the attack on Leningrad that had been twice postponed – it is curious how closely his plan repeated the lines, and points, of the 1942 pattern. A parachute corps of two divisions had now been formed, and this was to be used for a swoop on Leningrad to open the way for the land attack. Hitler was growing more venturesome as his chances faded, for a year before he had hesitated to accept General Student's proposal for an airborne stroke at Stalingrad. But after the Tunisian collapse this corps was dispatched to the south of France, ready to deliver an airborne riposte against the anticipated Allied landing in Sardinia. And then the defeat of the Kursk offensive led to the complete, and final, abandonment of the Leningrad attack.

Opinion among the generals was divided over the Kursk plan. An increasing number of them had come to doubt whether victory in the East was possible, and the doubters this year included such a thruster as Kleist. But he was not directly concerned with the offensive on this occasion. In regrouping during the winter campaign Manstein was placed in charge of the main part of the southern front. The 1st Panzer Army had been transferred to his army group at the beginning of the year, while Kleist was merely left in charge of the Crimea and the Kuban bridgehead. The offensive against the Kursk salient was to be carried out by Manstein's left wing against its southern flank, and by the right wing of Kluge's Army Group Centre against its northern flank. Both these commanders talked beforehand as if they were hopeful of the chances of success. But hope is commonly fostered by professional opportunity. Keen soldiers have a natural inclination to develop faith in a venture of which they are placed in charge, and a natural reluctance to express doubts that would weaken a superior's faith in their powers.

The whole trend of military education also contributed to stifle doubts. While many of the generals would now have favoured a long withdrawal to shake off the Russians, as Rundstedt had advocated more than a year before, the Leader forbade any such step. As the line on which the German armies were standing, at the end of the winter, was not well chosen for defence, the generals were the more inclined to rely on the principle which they had been taught – that 'attack is the best defence'. By attacking they might iron out the defects of the position, and upset the enemy's dispositions for resuming his offensive. So all efforts were concentrated on making a success of the attack without regard to the consequences of failure, and to the way that the expenditure of Germany's newly accumulated reserves would bankrupt any subsequent defence.

The shrinkage of Germany's assets was veiled by a policy of extreme internal secrecy combined with an increased dilution of units and formations. The number of divisions was so nearly maintained at the old level that the falsity of the figure, as an index of strength, was not apparent. By the spring of 1943 they averaged little more than half their establishment in men and weapons, but many divisions were left much below that level while others were brought almost up to establishment. Commanders were kept in such watertight compartments under the security policy that few of them had any clear idea of the general situation, and they were taught that it was healthier not to inquire. But the dilution policy was dictated by other factors besides the camouflage motive.

Hitler was fascinated, and intoxicated, by figures. To his demagogic mind, numbers spelt power. As the division was the standard unit of military measure, he was obsessed with the importance of having the largest possible number of divisions – although his victories in 1940 had essentially been gained by the qualitative superiority of the mechanized fraction of his forces. Before he invaded Russia, he had insisted on the dilution policy in order to produce the maximum number of divisions, and he had subsequently increased the dilution in order to avoid a decrease in that misleading total. The consequence of such dilution was a perilous degree of inflation in the sphere of military economics.

In 1943 the extent of this inflation went far to nullify the advantage furnished by qualitative improvements in the German equipment, notably the production of the new Tiger and Panther tanks. Whenever divisions suffer heavy losses, the spearheads tend to shrink out of proportion to the overheads – since the loss is incurred mainly by the fighting troops. In an armoured division, the highest ratio is normally borne by the tanks and tank-crews, a lower ratio by the infantry component, and the lowest by the administrative troops. It is thus uneconomic in fighting power to maintain divisions, particularly armoured divisions, at a level below their establishment. Unless the wastage is promptly made up, the body remains unprofitably large by comparison with the punch it can produce.

These handicaps of the German Army were accentuated because the Russian Army was now much better qualitatively than in 1942, as well as numerically stronger. Its performance profited from the increasing flow of equipment from the new and expanded factories in the Urals, and from its Western allies. Its tanks were at least as good as those of any other army – most German officers considered them better. While they suffered from a lack of supplementary fittings, such as wireless equipment, they reached a high level of efficiency in performance, endurance, and armament. The Russian artillery was excellent in quality, and there had been a large-scale development of rocket-artillery that was remarkably effective. The Russian rifle was more modern than the German, and capable of a higher rate of fire, while most of the heavier infantry weapons were equally good.

The main deficiency was the motor transport, and that vital need was now being met by an increasing stream of American trucks. Hardly less important for mobility was the quantity of American canned food that was poured in, for it also helped to solve the supply problem that, because of the huge size of Russia's forces and the scarcity of communications, formed the biggest check on her capacity to exert her strength. It would have been a much worse problem if the Russian troops had not been accustomed to live and fight on a lower standard of provisioning than any of the Western armies. While the Red Army never reached an equal level of mobility, it was more mobile than they were relatively to its technical means, because it could operate on a much lower scale of requirements. Its primitiveness was an asset as well as a deficit. Russian soldiers could subsist where others would have starved. Thus the Red Army's spearheads could now attain a deeper penetrative power, through being endowed with more ample resources, while its masses could follow them up, through needing so little in the way of transport and food.

The Red Army had also improved greatly in tactical ability. Whereas 1942 had seen a deterioration, owing to the loss of a high proportion of its best trained troops in 1941, increasing battle-experience had largely repaired this defect by 1943 and given the new formations a better grounding than the old ones had received in prewar training. The improvement began at the top. A drastic elimination of the original leaders had made room for the rapid rise of a generation of dynamic young generals, mostly under forty, who were more professional and less political than their predecessors. The average age of the Russian higher commanders was now nearly twenty years less than the German, and the lowering of the age level brought a heightening of efficiency as well as of activity. The combined effects of fresher leadership and ripening battle-experience were reflected both in the staffwork and the tactical ability of the troops.

The improvement would have been even more effective but for the tendency of the generals, from fear or desire for favour, to continue attacks, pressing attacks unprofitably at points where strong opposition was met. Rather than admit failure, their troops were often hurled again and again at unbreakable obstacles, with mounting cost. Such abortive assaulting is a common tendency in armies because of the combination of a hierarchical system with military discipline, but it was naturally accentuated in the Red Army by Soviet conditions, Russian traditions, and Russia's resources. Under such a system only the best established commanders could venture to exercise a sense of the limits of the possible, while the abundance of human material encouraged lavish expenditure. It was easier to be ruthless in sacrificing men than to risk the wrath of the man above.

On the whole, the vastness of space went far to balance these battering-ram tendencies. There was generally room for manoeuvre, and the Russian High Command had become skilled in choosing soft spots in the enemy's far-stretched front. Since the Red Army had now a general superiority in numbers, the High Command could count on enjoying odds higher than 4 to 1 on any sector where it decided to concentrate for a thrust, and once a breakthrough was made the room for manoeuvre further expanded. Vain frontal assaults, and the wasteful repetition of them, were more common in the north where the German defences were more closely knit and better established. In the south, the Russians had their best commanders and troops, along with the space to exploit their skill.

Nevertheless, the extent to which the Germans still held firm in face of such odds was evidence – even before two years' prolongation of the war confirmed it – that the Russian forces were still a long way from overtaking the German forces' technical superiority. A consciousness of that professional advantage coloured the outlook of both sides in the spring of 1943. It encouraged Hitler, and even his military advisers, in the hope that the scales might still be turned in Germany's favour if the mistakes of the past were avoided. It left a doubt underlying the confidence which the Russian leaders had gained from their winter successes, for they could not forget that the hopes raised by their successes in the previous winter had been dispelled in the summer following. With another summer at hand, they could not feel sure that the issue was certain.

That underlying uncertainty may have accounted for a significant interlude of diplomacy before the battle was joined. In June, Molotov met Ribbentrop at Kirovograd, which was then within the German lines, for a discussion about the possibilities of ending the war. According to German officers who attended as technical advisers, Ribbentrop proposed as a condition of peace that Russia's future frontier should run along the Dnieper, while Molotov would not consider anything less than the restoration of her original frontier; the discussion became hung up on the difficulty of bridging such a gap, and was broken off after a report that it had leaked out to the Western Powers. The issue was then referred back to the judgement of battle.

The opening of the summer campaign was later than in either of the previous years. Over three months' pause occurred after the close of the winter campaign. That prolonged delay was due, in part at least, to the Germans' increasing difficulty in refitting their forces and accumulating the reserves necessary for another offensive. But there was also an increased desire to see the Russians take the offensive lead, and become hooked, so that the German offensive might have the effect of a counterstroke. That desire was disappointed – not so much by Hitler's impatience as by the Russians' decision to adopt a similar angling strategy this time.

The retrospective view of the German leaders was that their offensive might have achieved a great success if the striking forces had been ready in time to launch it six weeks earlier. When their pincer-stroke became hung up in a deep series of minefields, and they found that the Russians had withdrawn their main forces well to the rear, they ascribed their frustration to the fact that the Russians had got wind of their preparations during the interval, and thus been able to make appropriate dispositions. That view overlooked the obviousness of the Kursk salient as an objective. It offered as clear an invitation to a German pincer-stroke as the Germans' adjoining salient round Orel offered to a Russian pincer-stroke. Thus there was little room for doubt as to the site of a stroke by either side, and the main question was which would strike first.

That had been in debate on the Russian side. There, the argument for striking first was that the Russian defence had been overcome two summers running by the German attack; and the confidence generated by the Russians' many offensive successes from Stalingrad onwards made their leaders more eager to take the initiative in the summer. On the other hand, it was pointed out that in 1942 Timoshenko had, in fact, led off with his Kharkov offensive in May, to which the Russian collapse between there and Kursk in June had been a disastrous sequel.

At his first conference with the Russian General Staff at the end of May, the new head of the British Military Mission, Lieutenant-General G. Le Q. Martel, gained the impression that the balance was tilted in favour of initiating the offensive. He frankly said that he thought they were asking for trouble if they launched it while the renewed German panzer forces were still uncommitted, and that the Russians 'would be hit for six if they tried anything of the kind'.

A few days later he was asked about British tactics in North Africa, and 'explained to them that our success at Alamein was largely due to the fact that we had let the Germans smash up, or at any rate blunt, their armoured forces on our defences. When they were committed and had been badly knocked about, then was the time to assume the offensive.' At the next conference he had the impression that the Russian General Staff were inclining to that plan. He took the opportunity to impress on them another lesson of British experience: the importance of holding the 'haunches' on each side of a hostile tank penetration, and using all available reserves to stiffen the flanks of the breach, as an indirect check, rather than to meet the torrent head-on.*

In tracing the origins of any plan it is usually difficult to assess the influences that determined it, even where all the files are open to examination, for documents rarely register the real originating causes. They do not show how ideas are sown, and grow, in the minds of the actual planners. While some who sow ideas are apt to overestimate the effect of their particular seed, those in whose minds they grow are even more inclined to discount the effect, however influential it may have been. That applies with special force in official quarters, and most of all where national pride is concerned. Among allies, it is normal for each to minimize the help received, and maximize the help given, whether material or intangible. It is thus unlikely that history will throw any clearer light on the way that the Russians' plan of 1943 was determined, while it is manifest that their strategic planners had ample experience from their own campaigns to draw the conclusions that were implicit in the plan they came to adopt.

The greater significance lies in the dramatically decisive outcome of following the defensive-offensive method.

The German attack was launched at dawn on July 5th, against the two flanks of the Kursk salient. The straight face of that salient was nearly a hundred miles wide; the southern side was about fifty miles deep; the northern side was over 150 miles, since it coincided with the flank of the Germans' Orel salient which projected in the opposite direction. The main stretch of the salient was held by Rokossovsky's troops, while Vatutin's right wing embraced the southern corner.

Manstein's southern pincer and Kluge's northern pincer were approximately equal in strength, but Manstein had a larger proportion of armour. In all, eighteen panzer and panzergrenadier divisions were committed to this offensive. They formed nearly half of the total force engaged – and nearly the whole of the German armour that was avail-

* See Martel: *An Outspoken Soldier*, pp 211–54.

able on the Eastern Front. Hitler was gambling for high stakes.

The southern pincer penetrated about twenty miles at some points in the first few days – that was not a rapid penetration. The Germans were slowed down by the deep minefields they met, and found that the mass of the defending forces had been withdrawn to the rear, so that their bag of prisoners was disappointingly small. Moreover, the wedges which they drove in were hindered in expansion by the stubborn defence of the haunches. Kluge's pincer on the north made a still more limited penetration and did not succeed in breaching the Russians' main defensive position. After a week of struggle, the panzer divisions were much reduced in strength. Kluge, alarmed by signs of an imminent threat to his own flank, began to pull out his panzer divisions.

At the same moment, July 12th, the Russians launched their offensive – against the northern flank and the nose of the Orel salient. The northern stroke penetrated thirty miles in three days, towards the rear of Orel, while the other advance, which had not so far to go, came within fifteen miles of the city. But four of the panzer divisions which Kluge had disengaged came up just in time to check the Russians' northern wing from establishing itself astride the railway from Orel back to Briansk. After that the offensive became a process of hard pushing, relying on superior weight to force the Germans back. It was a costly effort, but was helped by Rokossovsky's forces changing over to the offensive on the southern flank, from the Kursk salient. The Germans were at last squeezed out of Orel on August 5th. Orel had not only been one of the main and most formidable bastions of the German front since 1941, but while it remained intact a renewal of the menace to Moscow remained possible. Orel's strategic situation had combined with its proved strength to make it a military symbol – and its evacuation was thus as depressing to German confidence as it was stimulating to the Russians.

Meanwhile Vatutin's troops had followed up the Germans' withdrawal from the breach on the southern side of the Kursk salient, to the original line. On August 4th Vatutin launched an attack on that weakened line, and captured Belgorod next day. Exploiting the enemy's exhaustion, he drove eighty miles deep in the next week, wheeling down towards the rear of Kharkov and its communications with Kiev. This scythe-stroke opened up a prospect of dislocating the Germans' whole southern front. Ten days later Koniev's forces, on Vatutin's left, crossed the Donetz south-east of Kharkov and threatened to complete the encirclement of the city. Koniev had created the opening for this threat by audaciously choosing the Liubotin marshes as his point for crossing the Donetz.

If either of the strokes had reached Poltava junction it might not only have trapped the garrison of Kharkov but spread confusion among all the German forces forming the extended right arm along the Donetz. At that moment the 3rd Panzer Corps was almost the only considerable reserve left. With the three SS panzer divisions it had just been sent to meet a threat to the fingers, on the Mius River near Taganrog. It was now rushed back up to the arm, and just sufficed to check the danger round Poltava. This enabled the bulk of the troops at Kharkov to be safely withdrawn before the city fell, on August 23rd. At other points, too, the depleted panzer divisions showed that, though they had little punch left, they were still able to keep a curb on the advancing Russian masses. The crisis was weathered and the situation became stabilized – though not static. The Russians continued to make headway, but at a slow pace. In the six weeks that followed the launching of their offensive they took 25,000 prisoners. It was a small total for such a vast battle, covering many sectors, and an indication that any collapses of the defence had been local and limited.

In the second half of August the Russian offensive was more widely extended. While Popov's forces were advancing gradually from Orel on Briansk, a push towards Smolensk was begun by Eremenko's forces on their right flank. On their left flank a deeper thrust towards the Dnieper near Kiev was developed by Rokossovsky, while Vatutin was also converging thither. In the extreme south, Tolbukhin crossed the Mius River, and forced the abandonment of Taganrog. Then early in September Malinovsky struck south across the Donetz towards Stalino, and this flanking leverage produced a hasty retreat of the Germans from the projecting 'arm' south of the Donetz. Significantly, however, they managed to hold on to the points that immediately covered the flank of their long retreat, and to the railways, until most of their troops were safely out of the trap. Lozovaya junction, in the armpit, was not yielded until the middle of September.

The pattern, and rhythm, of the Russian operations came to appear still closer to Foch's general offensive in 1918 – with its alternating series of strokes at different points, each temporarily suspended when its impetus waned in face of stiffening resistance, each so aimed as to pave the way for the next, and all timed to react on one another. In 1918 it had led the Germans to scurry reserves to the points that were struck while simultaneously restricting their power to move reserves in time to the points that were going to be struck next. It paralysed their freedom of action, while progressively draining their balance of reserves. The Russians were repeating it a quarter of a century later under more favourable conditions and in an improved form.

This is the natural method for an army which is limited in mobility but possesses a general superiority of force. It is all the more suitable when and where the lateral communications are too sparse to make it possible to switch reserves quickly from one sector to another to back up a particular success. As it means breaking into a fresh front each time, the cost of this 'broad' exploitation tends to be higher than with a 'deep' exploitation. It is also less likely to be quickly decisive, but the end may be surer, provided that the army which applies it has an adequate balance of material superiority to maintain the process.

In that offensive process the Russian losses were naturally heavier than the Germans', but the Germans lost more than they could afford, following the costly failure of their own offensive. For them attrition spelt ruin. Hitler's unwillingness to sanction any long step-back retarded their retreat but hastened their exhaustion.

In September the thinning of their front, and the diminution of their reserves, was reflected in an acceleration of the Russians' pace of advance. Skilful commanders such as Vatutin, Koniev, and Rokossovsky, were quick to take advantage of weak spots in the wide front. Their momentum was helped by the ever-increasing flow of American trucks. Before the end of the month the Russians had reached the Dnieper not only at its great easterly bend near Dnepropetrovsk, but along most of its course as far up as the Pripet river, beyond Kiev. Crossings were quickly made at a wide range of points, and bridgeheads established. That was ominous for the Germans' chances of being able to rest and reorganize behind the shelter of that wide river-barrier, which military spokesmen had incautiously described as their 'winter line'. The ease with which crossings had been gained by the Russians was helped by their commanders' skill and boldness in exploiting the potentialities of space. The important bridgehead established around Kremenchug, south-west of Poltava, owed much to Koniev's decision that, instead of concentrating his effort on one line, crossings were to be made at a wide range of points – eighteen altogether on a stretch of sixty miles. The 'unexpectedness' of this calculated dispersion was increased by the way that the crossings were made under cover of fog. Similar methods enabled Vatutin to gain a series of footholds north of Kiev that were subsequently linked up.

The fundamental factor in the situation was, however, that the Germans no longer had enough troops to cover the whole of their front even when thinly spread, and had to rely on counterattack to prevent the expansion of enemy footholds. That was bound to be a precarious policy when their own reserves were so scanty, and the attackers' so numerous.

Three hundred miles to the north of Kiev the Germans abandoned Smolensk on the 25th, and had been squeezed out of Briansk a week earlier. They were falling back slowly on the chain of bastion-towns that stretched along the upper Dnieper – Zhlobin, Rogachev, Mogilev, and Orsha, to Vitebsk on the Dvina.

In the far south they evacuated their bridgehead in the Kuban, and withdrew across the Kerch Straits into the Crimean peninsula, which itself was now in danger of being isolated by the Russian tide on the mainland. Kleist had received orders to bring his forces back from the Kuban to take over the sector between the Sea of Azov and the Dnieper bend at Zaporozhye. The decision was taken a fortnight too late. By the time his troops began to arrive in their new positions in mid-October, the Russians had broken through at Melitopol, and the whole sector was in a state of flux.

After the initial crossings of the Dnieper, that sector was relatively uneventful during the first half of October, while the Russians were bringing up reinforcements, accumulating supplies, and building the bridges to carry them forward. Most of these were pile or trestle bridges, and they were quickly constructed from trees felled near the site of the crossing. The Russians were masters in this art of improvising bridging – like Sherman's troops in the march through Georgia and the Carolinas. Four days was the average time required for a bridge to span this great river, and carry the heaviest transport.

While attention was focused on Kiev, where the storm was expected to break, the next phase opened with a stroke almost midway in the long stretch between the Dnieper bend and Kiev. Koniev suddenly burst out of the Kremenchug bridgehead – south-west of Poltava – and drove a massive wedge southward across the baseline of the great salient. There were few German troops there to meet him at the outset, but Manstein quickly switched reserves thither and slowed him down, thus gaining time to withdraw the imperilled German forces within the bend. These helped to hold up the Russians outside Krivoi Rog, seventy miles south of their jumping-off line and midway across the salient.

But the collapse south of the Dnieper bend was part of the price, since Manstein had been compelled to draw off troops from that sector before Kleist's troops arrived to replace them. Exploiting the penetration at Melitopol, the Russians swept across the Nogaisk Steppe to the lower reaches of the Dnieper, in the first week of November, cutting the exits from the Crimea and isolating the enemy forces that remained there.

Results, however, did not fulfil the optimistic assumptions that a 'million men' had been trapped east of the Dnieper. Only 6,000 prisoners were taken in the two fastest days of the pursuit, and the bulk of the German forces – which was far less than the imagined scale – had time to withdraw across the Dnieper. Altogether only 98,000 were claimed by the Russians during the whole four months since the campaign opened, and over half of these were wounded. A remarkable inconsistency, though few Allied commentators remarked it, was revealed in the simultaneous Russian claim that 900,000 of the enemy had been killed and 1,700,000 wounded in the same period. For in any breakthrough a large part of the wounded usually fall into the attacker's hands, and the more severe the defeat the smaller the proportion that can be evacuated. More remarkable still was Stalin's statement on November 6th that the Germans had lost 4 million men in the past year. If that had been true, or even half true, the war would have been over. It had still a long course to run, but it was running down.

In the last half of October little news came from the Kiev sector, but the Russians were extending their bridgehead north of the city until it formed a wide springboard – wide enough for a powerful outflanking stroke to be mounted. This was launched by Vatutin in the first week of November. It found soft spots in the now widely overstretched frontage, penetrated westward through these, then swung inwards to cut the roads out of Kiev, and took the city from the rear. The Germans once again succeeded in slipping out of the trap, leaving only 6,000 prisoners in the Russians' hands, but they were incapable of stemming the Russians' onrush, as most of the panzer divisions had been drawn southward by Koniev's thrust in the Dnieper bend.

On the day after the capture of Kiev the Russian armoured forces reached Fastov, forty miles to the south-west. That was a stroke at pursuit-pace. After overcoming opposition on that line, they drove on sixty miles in the next five days to capture Zhitomir junction on the one remaining lateral railway east of the Pripet Marshes. Then they spread northward and on the 16th captured Korosten junction. At that moment the German resistance was on the verge of a breakdown, and that might have brought early fulfilment of Stalin's declaration of the 6th that 'victory is near'. For Manstein had no reserves at hand.

In this emergency he told Manteuffel, the dynamic commander of the 7th Panzer Division, to collect such units as he could find to add to his own remnant, and deliver an upper-cut from Berdichev with this scratch force. Daringly handled on a zig-zag course, Manteuffel's light stroke succeeded brilliantly, piercing the Russians' flank and recapturing Zhitomir by a night attack on the 19th, after which it drove on to Korosten. The distribution of the force in a number of small armoured groups, moving wide, had helped to magnify the impression of its strength. They darted between the Russian columns, and cut across their rear, striking at headquarters and signal centres, so that they spread a paralysing confusion along their track.

In an effort to develop the opportunity thus created, Manstein now launched a definite counteroffensive against the still invitingly large Russian salient west of Kiev. He was helped by the arrival of several fresh panzer divisions from the West. The plan was for a pincer-stroke – by an armoured thrust from the north-west aimed at Fastov and a converging thrust from the south. The former was delivered by Balck's panzer corps of three divisions, including Manteuffel's. But Vatutin's advanced troops had now been reinforced by an increasing volume of artillery and anti-tank guns, poured across the Dnieper bridges, as well as by reserve divisions. The German counteroffensive achieved no such striking results as the initial riposte. It looked more dangerous on the map than it was on the ground. For it no longer enjoyed the advantage of surprise to compensate its limited strength, and was further handicapped by bad weather. Early in December it faded out in the mud. During the lull that followed Vatutin massed his armies for a further drive with mounting weight.

The most apt comment on the situation was provided unconsciously by Hitler when, to mark his appreciation of Manteuffel's saving stroke, he invited the latter to spend Christmas with him at Angerburg, and then said – 'As a Christmas present, I'll give you fifty tanks.' That was the best reward Hitler could conceive, and a big one relatively to his resources. For the strongest and best favoured panzer division existing only had a strength of 180 tanks, and few exceeded half that figure.

The northern stretch of the German front had also been subjected to severe and prolonged strain during the autumn. But here repeated Russian offensives had failed to crack the line in front of the upper Dnieper to which the Germans had withdrawn after evacuating Smolensk. The Russians' frustration here was due to the inherent power of modern defence combined with the fact that they had less room for manoeuvre than in the south, and also made their aim too obvious.

In these battles the air forces played an insignificant part, being curbed by snow and ice. This limitation relieved the defence of the overhead pressure that might have multiplied the tremendous odds against them on the ground. While it also restricted the defenders' air reconnaissance the latter were able to deduce the likely direction of the Russians' main thrust-point, and to confirm it by a vigorous use of raiding patrols.

The brunt of the attack was borne by Heinrici's 4th Army, which with ten depleted divisions held the hundred mile front between Orsha and Rogachev. The Russians delivered five offensives against it between October and December, each lasting five or six days, with several re-newed efforts every day. They employed some twenty divisions in the first offensive, when the Germans had just occupied a hastily prepared position comprising a single trench-line. They employed thirty divisions in the next offensive, but by that time the Germans had developed their defences. The subsequent offensives were made with some thirty-six divisions.

The main weight of the Russian assault was concentrated against Orsha, on a frontage of a dozen miles astride the great Moscow–Minsk highway. As a thrust-point it had obvious advantages for supply and potential exploitation. But its obviousness helped the Germans to con-centrate in meeting it. Their defensive methods here are worth study. Heinrici used $3\frac{1}{2}$ divisions on this very narrow sector, leaving $6\frac{1}{2}$ to cover the remainder of his extensive front. He thus had a fairly dense ratio of force to space at the vital point. His artillery was almost intact, and he concentrated a mass of 380 guns to cover the crucial sector. Controlled by a single commander at 4th Army Headquarters, it was able to concentrate its fire at any threatened point of the sector. At the same time the Army Commander made a practice of 'milking' the divisions on the quiet part of his front in order to provide one fresh battal-ion daily, during the battle, for each of the divisions that were heavily engaged. This usually balanced the previous day's loss, while giving the division concerned an intact local reserve that it could use for counter-attack. The drawbacks of mixing formations were diminished by work-ing a system of rotation within the divisions – which now consisted of three regiments, each of two battalions. For the second day of battle the reinforcing battalion would be the sister of the one that was brought in the day before, and was accompanied by the regimental headquarters; after two more days a second completely new regiment would be in the line; and by the sixth day the original division would have been re-lieved altogether and have gone to hold the quiet sector from which the replacement had been drawn unit by unit.

These repeated successes of the defence against numerical odds of over 6 to 1 were a remarkable achievement. They indicated how the war might have been spun out, and the Russians' strength exhausted, if the defensive strategy had matched the tactics. But the prospect was wrecked by Hitler's insistence that no withdrawal was to be made without his permission, and his accompanying reluctance to give such permission. Army commanders who used their discretion were threatened with a court-martial, even in cases where it was a matter of withdrawing a small detachment from a dangerously isolated position. The veto was pressed so hard that juniors were still worse paralysed, and it came to be said that battalion commanders did not dare 'to move a sentry from the window to the door'. With parrot-like reiteration the Supreme Command recited 'every man must fight where he stands'.

That rigid principle had helped to bring the German Army through the nerve-crisis of the first winter in Russia, but it became fatal in the long run – when the German troops had overcome their acute fear of the Russian winter, but were more and more short of the forces with which to fill the Russian spaces. It cramped the essential flexibility of the commanders on the spot in slipping out of reach, regrouping their forces and fulfilling the principle 'reculer pour mieux sauter'.

The disastrous results of rigidity had been registered on the southern front in 1943. In 1944 they were to be repeated in the north, in the very sector where the German defence had previously proved so hard to overcome.

CHAPTER TWENTY-NINE

The Japanese Ebb in the Pacific

The first phase of the war in the Pacific had seen Japan's conquest of the whole western and south-western area of that ocean – all the islands there – and of the adjoining countries in South-east Asia. The second phase had seen Japan's attempt to extend her control to the American and British bases in the Hawaiian Islands and Australia, and her decisive repulse in the naval-air battle of Midway and at Guadalcanal, in the Solomon Islands, on the approach to Australia.

In the third phase the Japanese were on the defensive – as was emphasized by the orders to their commanders in the South-west Pacific that they were 'to retain all positions in the Solomons and New Guinea'. Only in Burma did they pursue offensive operations against the Western Allies, and these were defensive in essence – to forestall and frustrate a British counteroffensive from India. The possibility of effectual action by the Japanese had been annulled by their loss of four fleet carriers at Midway, of two battleships and many smaller craft at Guadalcanal, together with their loss of hundreds of aircraft in both these crucial operations. The Western Allies had regained the advantage; the real question now was whether and how they could use it.

The Japanese offensive plan, and action, had profited greatly by the strategic advantage of Japan's geographical position. They had, and their plan had exploited, this basic advantage both offensively and defensively. For the outcome of their rapid conquests was that they had covered Japan with concentric rings of defence that provided formidable obstacles to any countermove towards Japan that the Western Allies attempted.*

On the map there appeared to be numerous alternatives, but in closer analysis these were few. Examining them from the top of the map downwards, the north Pacific route was ruled out by the lack of ad-

* For maps, see pp 210–11, 370.

equate bases as well as by the frequency of storms and fogs along that route. A counteroffensive from Soviet Russia's position in the Far East was annulled by Stalin's unwillingness to cooperate and engage in a fight against Japan as long as Russia was hard-pressed by the German attack on her western flank. An Allied countermove through China was made impossible by the difficulties of supply, under existing circumstances, as well as by the unreliability of the Chinese. The still more distant route of return through Burma was nullified by the extent to which the British had been driven back – over the Indian frontier – and their all too evident lack of adequate resources for an early comeback.

Thus it soon became clear that any effective counteroffensive must depend on the Americans, and be by a route suitable to them. There were two main alternatives – along a south-western Pacific route from New Guinea to the Philippines, or through the central Pacific. General Douglas MacArthur – as Commander-in-Chief, South-west Pacific – naturally favoured and urged that line of comeback. He argued that it would be the quickest way to deprive Japan of her newly gained southern possessions on which she depended for the raw materials essential to her war effort. In his view, the central Pacific route would be exposed to attack from the cluster of mandated islands that Japan had captured, and in which she had quickly built sea and air bases. Moreover, Australian anxieties would not be allayed by such a remote line of counteroffensive action.

The American Naval chiefs, however, favoured a central Pacific route. They argued that this would enable them to use their large and growing numbers of fast aircraft-carriers more effectively than in the more crowded waters around New Guinea – and would better fulfil their new concept of employing carrier task forces to isolate, and dominate, a group of islands. It would also fit their new idea of a seaborne supply system, instead of having to send their carriers back to port at intervals. They also argued that it would avoid the risk that the southerly route would suffer by being exposed to flank attacks from the Japanese forces lying among the mandated islands, while an advance along the southerly route, being more obvious and predictable, was itself likely to meet tougher and more continuous opposition. A more potent, if more private reason, was that the admirals wanted to keep the bulk of their new carrier strength out of McArthur's control – and his monopolizing tendencies.

Eventually, it was decided at the 'Trident Conference' in Washington in May 1943, to carry out a double-pronged thrust, advancing along both routes, which would keep the Japanese in a state of uncertainty, and keep their forces dispersed, while hindering them from concentrating or switching their reserves from one route to the other. Both routes would eventually converge off the Philippines. That decision fulfilled the aim of threatening alternative objectives, a vital advantage in the strategic concept of indirect approach. But the compound, and compromise, decision did not take sufficient account of the fact, and lesson of history, that such dilemma-producing duality is apt to be more economically attained by taking a single line of advance that threatens alternative objectives – each of which the opponent is anxious to preserve – while itself being a single line of operation.

The two-pronged thrust inevitably required much larger, and thus longer, preparation – in terms of forces, shipping, landing craft, naval bases, and airfields. This prolonged preparatory period gave the Japanese more time to develop their own defensive preparations, and make the American task harder, especially in carrying out land, and landing, operations.

During this lengthy lull, the only operation of any importance was the American expedition to regain the Aleutian Islands, in the Northern Pacific. Strategically, this move was so remote as to carry no promise of effect on the course of the war. It was secondary without being supplementary or diversionary. Its only value was psychological, as a reassurance to the American public, which had been alarmed at the apparent threat to the security of Alaska brought by the seizure of Kiska and Attu by a small Japanese landing force the previous June. But the tonic was purchased by a very large and uneconomic use of the still limited American resources.

An early reaction to the seizure of the two islands had been a naval bombardment of Kiska at the beginning of August; then at the end of that month American troops had landed on the island of Adak, some 200 miles east of Kiska, and built an airfield there to assist an attack on that captured island. In January 1943 they had gone on to re-occupy the island of Amchitka, ninety miles east of Kiska, for the same purpose. But then the local American commanders decided to tackle Attu, the farthest west of the Aleutian island chain, as they had discovered that it was more weakly defended than Kiska. An interruption came at the end of March when the naval blockading force encountered a slightly more powerful Japanese force that was escorting three troop-transports. After a three-hour fight at long range, the Japanese withdrew. No ships were sunk on either side, but the reinforcing transports were turned back.

On May 11th the Americans landed a division on Attu, cloaked by a fog and supported by a bombardment from three battleships. With odds of more than 4 to 1 in its favour this division gradually pushed the Japanese garrison (of about 2,500) back into the mountains in a fortnight's tough fighting, and then the Japanese solved the problem of overcoming them there by launching a suicidal assault on the American positions in which they were wiped out – only twenty-six prisoners being taken. The Americans now concentrated on Kiska. Constant pressure, from air and sea, on this now isolated island led the Japanese to evacuate their garrison (of some 5,000 troops) on the night of July 15th, under cover of the frequent fog. The Americans continued to bombard the island for a further two and a half weeks, and landed a large force of some 34,000 troops – who spent five days in searching the island until they were convinced that it was empty.

Thus the Aleutians were cleared, but the Americans had employed 100,000 troops in all, supported by large naval and air forces, in this trivial task – a flagrant example of bad economy of force, *and* a good example of the distraction that can be caused by diversionary initiative with slight expenditure.

The apparent stalemate in the South-west Pacific continued until the summer of 1943.

Fortunately for the Americans, and their allies, forestalling and frustrating action by the enemy was hindered and hampered by the acute differences of view between the Japanese Army and Navy chiefs. While both were intent on maintaining all the Japanese conquests, they were sharply divided as to the best way of doing so. The Army chiefs favoured land operations in New Guinea, an advanced position which they considered necessary for the security of their captured territory in the Dutch East Indies and the Philippines. The Navy's chiefs wanted priority for the Solomon and Bismarck Islands, as strategic cover for the great naval base at Truk, in the Carolines, 1,000 miles to the north. In the strategic decision the Army, as usual, got its way.

The eventually agreed line of defence was from Santa Isabel and New Georgia in the Solomon Islands, westward of Guadalcanal, to Lae in New Guinea – ie the area west of the Papuan Peninsula. The Navy was to be in charge of the Solomons sector, and the Army of the New Guinea sector.

Army Command at Rabaul, the headquarters of the whole area, directed the operations of the 17th Army in the Solomons and the 18th Army in New Guinea – the 7th Air Division being attached to the former, and the 6th Air Division to the latter. The naval forces comprised the 8th Fleet and the 11th Air Fleet, both being directed by the naval headquarters at Rabaul. The naval forces were light, consisting of cruisers and destroyers, but could be reinforced by heavier ships from Truk.

The Army forces in the theatre were of larger scale – three divisions of the 18th Army in New Guinea, totalling 55,000 troops, and two divisions plus a brigade and other troops of the 17th Army in the Solomons and Bismarcks. Although Japanese air strength had been heavily depleted in the struggle for Guadalcanal, the Army had 170 aircraft and the Navy 240 available. Within six months, it was reckoned, the theatre could be reinforced by from ten to fifteen divisions and upward of 850 aircraft. So there was reason to feel that a holding, or 'containing', strategy was quite possible.

American planning was complicated by the earlier decision to divide this theatre between a Pacific Ocean area and a South-west Pacific area, with the Solomon Islands in the line of division. In the effort to make this more workable the Joint Chiefs of Staff decreed that MacArthur would have strategic command of the whole New Guinea–Solomons part of the theatre, but that Admiral Halsey, C-in-C South Pacific, would have tactical control, while naval forces from Pearl Harbor operating in that area would remain under Admiral Nimitz's Pacific Ocean command.

The American strategic aim was to break down the barrier formed by the Bismarck Archipelago, and capture the main Japanese base at Rabaul. This was to be achieved by alternating strokes on both approach routes – to keep the Japanese 'on the hop'. First, Halsey's forces were to occupy the Russell Islands, just west of Guadalcanal, as an air and naval base. Then two islands in the Trobriand group east of New Guinea would be seized to provide air bases for the Rabaul attack – and intermediate staging-points for switching air forces from one line to the other. In the second phase, Halsey would advance to New Georgia (in the Solomons west of Guadalcanal) and capture the key airfield of Munda, while MacArthur was to capture the Japanese footholds around Lae on the north coast of New Guinea. By then, it was hoped, Halsey would have secured the island of Bougainville, at the west end of the Solomons. In the third phase, McArthur's forces, turning northward, were to cross the sea-gap to New Britain in the Bismarck Archipelago, the great island where Rabaul was situated, at the northern end. Then, in the fourth phase, the Allied attack on Rabaul itself was to be launched. It was a very gradual process, even as planned – the calculation being that the attack on Rabaul would be launched within eight months of the opening moves in the campaign.

MacArthur had seven divisions (three of them Australian) in his South-west Pacific area, and about 1,000 aircraft (a quarter of these Australian) – with two more American divisions to come as well as eight Australian divisions in training. Halsey had seven divisions (two being Marine divisions and one New Zealand), and 1,800 aircraft (of which 700 were US Army planes). The naval strength varied, for while an amphibious force was being built up for each prong of attack, a large number of the warships were on short loan from Nimitz's vast force at Pearl Harbor; at the outset Halsey had six battleships and two carriers as well as many smaller ships. In all, there was now ample strength for success, even though it was not so much as MacArthur wished – he had asked for some twenty-two divisions and forty-five air groups.

During the preliminary or 'stalemate' period, Halsey landed a force on the Russell Islands on February 21st, but found no trace of the Japanese garrison that was believed to be there. Moreover, his naval forces put a stop to the Japanese practice of raiding runs down 'the Slot'. In New Guinea, a Japanese attempt to capture the airfield at Wau, near the Huon Gulf, was foiled by the Australians, who air-lifted a brigade there; and when the Japanese dispatched the bulk of a division thither as reinforcement, the convoy – of eight transports escorted by eight destroyers – was promptly spotted and caught by the Allied air force in New Guinea – losing all its transports and half its destroyers, along with over 3,600 troops (half the total). After this disastrous 'Battle of the Bismarck Sea', the Japanese only ventured to send supplies to their troops in New Guinea by submarines or in barges.

Admiral Yamamoto then sought to retrieve the adverse Japanese situation in the air by sending the carrier aircraft of the 3rd Fleet from Truk to Rabaul in the hope of wearing down the Allies' air strength by constant raids on their bases. But this harassing operation (which began, ominously, on April 1st) actually cost the Japanese almost twice as many planes as the defenders in a fortnight – contrary to the optimistic reports of the attacking pilots. And then Yamamoto himself was ambushed and shot down on a flying visit to Bougainville – of which the US Intelligence had gained advance news. His successor as C-in-C of the Japanese Combined Fleet was Admiral Koga, but he did not prove as formidable as Yamamoto.

The long-planned American offensive was due to open on June 30th – with a three-fold stroke – when General Krueger's US Army force would land on the Kiriwina and Woodlark (or Murua) Islands in the Trobriand group; the New Guinea Force (mainly Australian) under General Herring would land near Salamaua in the Huon Gulf; and the troops under Admiral Halsey would land in New Georgia.

The landing in the Trobriands proved easy, as no opposition was met, and the building of airfields began at once. The fresh New Guinea move started well, and the American landing in support of the Australians met no serious opposition, but the Japanese force in this part (about 6,000) was not pushed back to the outskirts of Salamaua until the middle of August – and the American advance force here was then told to wait for the intended main landings on the Huon Peninsula, prior to the attack on Lae, the main objective. The third-prong stroke, by Halsey's forces against New Georgia, proved still more difficult.

The large island of New Georgia had a Japanese garrison of about 10,000 troops, the formidableness of which was multiplied by the mountainous jungle and wet climate. The obstacle was made worse by the orders of Imperial GHQ that it was to be held as long as possible. Moreover, the difficulties of invasion were increased by the reefs on the north-east coast and the surrounding belt of islands on the south and west.

The American plan was to carry out a three-piece landing. The main one, of divisional scale, was to be made on the west coast island of Rendova, whence it was intended to cross the five-mile straits and land near the important airfield at Munda Point. As soon as this hop had been achieved, a smaller force was to land on the north coast of New Georgia, ten miles from Munda, and thereby cut the Japanese off from seaborne reinforcements. There were also to be three subsidiary landings in the south. The naval covering force comprised five carriers, three battleships, nine cruisers and twenty-nine destroyers, while the air force allotted was about 530 planes.

A coastwatcher's report that the Japanese were moving into the southern part of New Georgia led Halsey to begin the initial landing there on June 21st, instead of waiting until the 30th, but no opposition was met, and the other subsidiary landings in that sector were successfully made on the 30th.

As for the main landing on Rendova Island, the 6,000 American troops employed in it soon overcame its garrison of only 200 Japanese, and the follow-up landings near Munda were made during the first week of July. That week and the next, small Japanese naval forces made several ripostes, as in the Guadalcanal campaign, and managed to inflict considerable damage on the cruisers, while slipping ashore in all some 3,000 troops.

On shore, the inexperienced American division employed in this operation made very slow progress in its jungle advance on Munda after crossing the straits from Rendova – despite immense air, artillery, and naval gun support. Reports on its state of poor morale led to a further one and a half divisions being ordered to New Georgia. By August 5th, however, Munda and the surrounding area were at last captured, although most of the Japanese garrison was able to withdraw to the adjoining northerly island of Kolombangara. Moreover, in further sea actions the American domination of the sky caused the Japanese to suffer disadvantageous naval losses.

By far the most important effect of the Americans' slow progress in New Georgia was that it led Halsey, and other American leaders, to recognize the drawbacks of such a step-by-step advance, and to realize that it gave the enemy ample time to strengthen his next line of defence. Such a process was forfeiting the great advantage of air and naval superiority. So it was now decided that Kolombangara, with its garrison of over 10,000 Japanese, should be sealed off, and left 'to wither on the vine', while the American forces moved on to the large but lightly defended island of Vella Lavella, which the Japanese held with a garrison of only 250 men. (This was a case of planned 'by-passing', and an improvement on what had happened in the Aleutian Islands.) Moreover, to establish an airfield on Vella Lavella would bring them within a hundred miles of Bougainville, the most westerly island of the Solomons.

The landing on Vella Lavella took place on August 15th, even before the occupation of New Georgia was completed. Moreover, the hopes of General Sasaki, the local Japanese commander, that he might maintain a prolonged resistance in Kolombangara, were also annulled by higher level orders to abandon the Central Solomons and fall back to Bougainville. At the end of September and early October, in successive nights, the large garrison of Kolombangara, and the small garrison of Vella Lavella, were evacuated.

In all, the Japanese lost about 2,500 killed in the New Georgia campaign, and seventeen warships, while the Allies lost about 1,000 killed (though many more from sickness) and about six warships. In the air, moreover, the Japanese losses were much heavier.

The Allies' pressure on Salamaua in August had been maintained largely to cloak, and distract Japanese attention from, the preparations for their attack on Lae and the Huon Peninsula – whose ports and airfields were wanted for the coming bound northward into the island of New Britain, as well as to cover their flank during that bound.

In tackling the Huon Peninsula, MacArthur's plan was to combine an amphibious, an airborne, and an overland attack. This three-fold nature made it a complex operation, and he had sufficient resources to rely on one kind had it been desired. On September 5th his amphibious force landed the bulk of the 9th Australian Division just east of Lae. Next day the 503rd US Parachute Regiment was dropped on the disused Nadzab airfield northwest of Lae – the first airborne operation by the Allies in the Pacific – and as soon as this airfield was made unable the 7th Australian Division was flown in by transport aircraft. Meanwhile the overland Australian–American advance on Salamaua was resumed.

The converging attacks met little opposition. For the Japanese Imperial GHQ had realized that their one division in the area was likely to be cut off, and sanctioned the withdrawal of this division across the mountainous peninsula towards Kiari, some fifty miles beyond Lae. So Salamaua was evacuated on September 11th, and Lae on the 15th. But Japanese hopes of holding on to the port of Finschhafen at the tip of the peninsula were frustrated by the landing there on the 22nd of an Australian brigade from the Amphibious Force. Although the Japanese brought another division forward as reinforcement they were gradually pushed back along the coast. Meanwhile the 7th Australian Division was advancing, more quickly, up the Markham River valley from Lae, and early in October reached Dumpu, barely fifty miles from the next important point, and port, Madang – 160 miles north-west of Lae. By the end of 1943 the Allied forces were poised to launch a two-pronged threat, along the coast and through the interior, at Madang – although their progress was behind schedule.

By September, 1943, it was at last clear to Imperial GHQ that its previous optimistic estimates of the situation, and the prospect, would have to be revised. Japan's forces were stretched too thinly over too large an area, and the Americans had recovered from their early defeat in an unexpectedly short time. Both in the air and on the sea they now had the upper hand. It became clear to the Japanese they would have to draw in their horns and shorten their defensive arc. For beyond the pressure this was suffering on its flanks, there was the potential menace from Pearl Harbor, in the centre, where Admiral Nimitz now had the largest number of ships ever amassed since Admiral Jellicoe's Grand Fleet of World War I.

Japan's precarious military situation was accentuated by her weak economic foundations. Her production of aircraft was inadequate to meet America's challenge, and she was proving unable to protect her merchant shipping.

The 'New Operational Policy' laid down by Imperial GHQ in mid-September was based on an estimate of the minimum area essential for the fulfilment of Japan's war aims. In this the minimum, termed the 'absolute national defence sphere', extended from Burma along the Malay barrier to Western New Guinea, and from there to the Carolines, the Marianas, and up to the Kuriles. This contraction of the defensive arc meant that most of New Guinea, and all the Bismarcks (including Rabaul), the Solomons, the Gilberts, and the Marshalls were now considered, and classed, as non-essential – although they were to be held for a further six months. By then, it was hoped, the minimum or 'absolute' area would have been developed into an invulnerable barrier, Japan's aircraft production trebled, and the Combined Fleet built up sufficiently to challenge the US Pacific Fleet in battle once again.

Meanwhile the Japanese forces in the South-west Pacific were called on to hold back an Allied strength now amounting to some twenty divisions, supported by nearly 3,000 aircraft. The Japanese had three divisions in eastern New Guinea, one in New Britain, one in Bougainville, while a sixth was on the way. Yet there were still twenty-six divisions in China, and fifteen in Manchuria – to face the possibility of a Russian invasion – so that in land forces the Japanese weakness lay not in numbers but in distribution.

On the Allied side, the slow progress made MacArthur all the more eager to press on, especially since he knew that the American Joint Chiefs of Staff were now inclined to give priority to the central Pacific drive, as shorter in distance and likely to be shorter in time. His sense of urgency was increased by their expressed view that the capture of Rabaul was not essential and that this strongly defended point might well be by-passed and left isolated. Admiral Halsey, too, was a natural thruster, and his eagerness to expedite his advance through the Solomons was increased by the fact that many of his ships, as well as the 2nd Marine Division, were being recalled to help the central Pacific drive.

THE BOUGAINVILLE CAMPAIGN

This large island, the most westerly of the Solomons, had a Japanese garrison of nearly 40,000 troops, and 20,000 sailors, the bulk in the south of the island. Halsey was by now so reduced in ships and landing craft that he could only land one reinforced division at the outset. Its landing place, shrewdly chosen, was in Empress Augusta Bay on the weakly defended west coast – and with good terrain for building airfields.

After heavy air bombardment of the Japanese air bases on Bougainville, and the preliminary seizure of the islands on the approach to Bougainville, the landings were made on November 1st – to the surprise of the Japanese, who felt sure that the attack would come in the south, where the surf was slighter. Japanese air and naval counterattacks were beaten off, while inflicting much less damage than they suffered themselves. Air attacks on Rabaul by the American carrier forces, as well as by the Allied air force in New Guinea, were also of great effect in nullifying the intervention of the recently reinforced Japanese air strength at Rabaul. A significant lesson for the future was the way that fast carrier forces proved able to operate in areas that were apparently well covered by the Japanese land-based aircraft.

On land, the American troops, reinforced by a further division, gradually expanded their beachheads into a comfortably large bridgehead more than ten miles wide, and by mid-December had 44,000 ashore to hold it. The reaction of the Japanese was slow because they continued to believe that the main American effort would come elsewhere. Even when they came to realize that the Empress Augusta Bay landing was the main threat, their countermoves were further delayed by having to bring their forces back through fifty miles of jungle from the main position in the south. As a consequence they did little until the end of February, and there was a prolonged state of stalemate.

THE CAPTURE OF THE BISMARCKS AND THE ADMIRALTIES

Meanwhile the Allied advance in New Guinea continued. On January 2nd, 1944, MacArthur landed a US force of nearly 7,000 men at Saidor, midway between the Huon Peninsula and Madang, and that force was soon doubled. Thus the weak and weary remains of the Japanese force, of similar size, which was trying to hold on at Sio, just west of the peninsula, had its coastal line of retreat blocked. It only managed to wriggle out of the trap by a long and round-about march through the mountainous jungle, a retreat in which it lost several thousand more men. At the same time the converging Australian pincer was pressing on again from Dumpu in the Markham Valley towards the coast, which it reached on April 13th. On April 24th MacArthur's forces occupied Madang, without meeting serious opposition. For Japanese Imperial GHQ had been driven to accelerate the withdrawal, and order their troops in New Guinea to fall back to Wewak, nearly 200 miles farther to the west.

MacArthur launched his next stroke even before the Huon Peninsula was cleared. On December 15th General Krueger's 'Alamo' force had begun landing on the south-west coast of New Britain near Arawe, and then just after Christmas the bulk of this force of two divisions landed on the western tip near Cape Gloucester, to gain the airfield there. For although the idea of attacking Rabaul had been discarded, MacArthur wanted to obtain two-sided control of the straits as a safeguard to the flank of his continued westward drive in New Guinea. The western end of New Britain, where the Americans landed, was held by a detachment of about 8,000 Japanese troops recently arrived from China, but they were separated by a wide stretch of wild country from Rabaul – 300 miles distant at the other end of this large crescent-shaped island and they could only be given scanty air support as the 7th Air Division had just been moved back to the Celebes area, 2,000 miles farther west. Thus the Japanese force near Cape Gloucester offered little resistance, and soon set out on a long retreat towards Rabaul.

Then at the end of February a reconnaissance force of the dismounted 1st Cavalry Division landed in the Admiralty Islands (250 miles north of Cape Gloucester) – which had several airfields, and room for many more, while there was also a very large sheltered anchorage. The Japanese garrison, of some 4,000, put up a stiffer fight than had been expected, but was overcome after the main part of the US force had landed on March 9th, and taken the Japanese in the rear. By mid-March the Americans had secured their principal objectives, and could start work on converting the Admiralties into a major base – although the remains of the Japanese continued fighting until May, when they were completely wiped out.

Thus Rabaul, with its garrison of more than 100,000 Japanese, was now isolated – and likewise left to 'wither on the vine'. The barrier presented by the Bismarcks had been effectively pierced, with much less loss than would have been incurred in a direct attack.

In Bougainville Island nearly four months passed after the landings before the Japanese commander belatedly came to realize that the American landings on the west coast were their main ones. In March 1944 he brought a force of about 15,000 up there through the jungle and attacked the American beachhead, now held by over 60,000 men. He had estimated the American strength as about 20,000 troops and 10,000 aircraft ground crews – a figure which, even as an estimated total, ought to have made him see that his belated counterattack had a poor chance. In his abortive 1 to 4 assault, starting on March 8th and continued for two weeks, he suffered the loss of over 8,000 – more than half his force – while the American loss was less than 300. After this shattering repulse, what remained of the Japanese garrison, now hopelessly isolated, was also left to wither.

THE CENTRAL PACIFIC ADVANCE

This thrust, like the one through the South-west Pacific, was directed towards the Philippines, and the recovery of America's position there – not direct towards Japan herself. At this stage of the war, the basic idea of the Joint Chiefs of Staff in Washington was that after reconquering the Philippines the American forces would move on to China and there establish large air bases from which the American air force could dominate the sky over Japan and pulverize her power of resistance, as well as cutting off her supplies.

This strategic plan was an underlying factor in American efforts to help the Chinese Nationalists under Chiang Kai-Shek, and sustain their resistance to the Japanese. Likewise it explained American anxiety to see the British resume their advance in Burma and re-open the Burma Road into southern China, so as to send war supplies to Chiang Kai-Shek and give him armed reinforcement.

In the event, the central Pacific advance proceeded so rapidly that Admiral Nimitz's forces were led to switch their line of operation northward, and seize the Mariana Islands, while the development of the new long-range B29 Superfortress bombers made it possible to strike direct at Japan, for the Marianas were less than 1,400 miles from the Japanese mainland. Moreover by the time the Marianas were captured, in October 1944, it had become clear to the American Chiefs of Staff that there was little prospect of Chinese Nationalist help, or of the British reaching southern China, in the near future.

THE CAPTURE OF THE GILBERT ISLANDS

In settling the plan of a central Pacific advance, Admiral King had wanted to start with a thrust at the Marshall Islands, but this idea was discarded for the lack of shipping and of trained troops needed to ensure success. Instead, it was decided to begin by a stroke at the Gilbert Islands, although they were a little farther from America's Hawaiian base at Pearl Harbor, as their capture seemed a less exacting task while it would provide practice in amphibious operations and bomber bases for a subsequent attack on the Marshall Islands. In the Gilberts, the two most westerly islands, Makin and Tarawa, were to be the main objectives.

Nimitz, as overall C-in-C, chose Vice-Admiral Raymond Spruance to command the attacking force. The ground troops, called the 5th Amphibious Corps, were under Major-General Holland Smith of the Marines, while the force that conveyed the troops was put in charge of Rear-Admiral Richard Turner, who had already acquired much experience of such operations in the Solomons. The whole was divided into two attack forces, a northern one to take Makin, with six transports carrying about 7,000 troops of the 27th Division, and a southern one to take Tarawa, with sixteen transports carrying the 2nd Marine Division of over 18,000 men. Besides escort carriers with the transports, the invasion was covered by Rear-Admiral Charles Pownall's Fast Carrier Force, comprising six fleet carriers, five light carriers, and six new battleships, as well as smaller warships. In addition to 850 aircraft in the carriers, there were 150 land-based (Army) bombers.

The most important development here employed was the mobile Service Force to maintain the fleet in operations, and meet all its needs except for major repairs to the larger warships. It had tankers, tenders, tugs, minesweepers, barges, lighters, ammunition ships. Later, hospital ships, barrack ships, a floating drydock, floating cranes, survey ships, pontoon assembly ships and others were added. This floating 'train' greatly increased the range and power of the Navy in amphibious operations.

After preliminary bombing, the attack on the Gilberts, code-named 'Operation Galvanic', began on November 20th, 1943 – which happened to be the anniversary of the epoch-making offensive with massed tanks at Cambrai in 1917. The Gilberts were very weakly defended, as reinforcements promised under Japan's 'New Operational Policy' of September had not yet arrived. On Makin, there was a garrison of only 800, and on the atoll of Apamama, a subsidiary objective, only twenty-

five. But Tarawa had a garrison of over 3,000 and was strongly fortified.

At Makin, the small garrison held out for four days against a US
Army division, which was handicapped by inexperience. Far more
effective was the action of a few 'amphtracks' (amphibious tracked
vehicles that surmount coral reefs), but the landing force had only a few
of these new vehicles.

Tarawa, much more strongly defended and fortified, was given a
heavy naval bombardment (3,000 tons of shells in 2¼ hours) as well as
massive air bombing before being attacked by the 2nd Marine Division,
which had distinguished itself at Guadalcanal. Even so, a third of the
5,000 landed on the first day were knocked out in crossing the 600-yard
strip between the coral reef and the beaches. But the survivors were
indomitable and forced the Japanese to withdraw to two interior strong-
points, and that withdrawal enabled the Marines to spread over the
island and hem in the defending strongpoints. Then on the night of the
22nd the Japanese solved the Marines' still difficult problem by switching over to repeated counterattacks, in which they were wiped out.
After that the remaining islands were soon cleared.

The Navy lost an escort carrier, but on the whole the carrier groups
proved that they could beat off Japanese air attacks both by day and
night, while the Japanese surface warships did not challenge Admiral
Spruance's large fleet.

The American people were shocked by the losses suffered, and the
attack on the Gilberts became a source of violent controversy. But the
experience gained proved valuable in many detailed respects, and led to
important improvements in the technique of amphibious operations.
Rear-Admiral S. E. Morison, the official Naval historian, called it 'the
seed bed of victory in 1945'.

Nimitz and his staff were already busy in planning the next bound, to
the Marshalls, but it was only after the attack on the Gilberts that a key
change was made in the plan, at Nimitz's insistence. Instead of a direct
attack on the nearest, most easterly, islands in the group, they were to
be by-passed, and the next leap made to Kwajalein atoll, 400 miles
farther on. After that, if all went well, Spruance's reserve would be sent
on to seize Eniwetok, at the far end of this 700-mile chain of islands.
The command was organized similarly to that for the attack on the
Gilberts, but two fresh divisions were employed for the assault, which
totalled 54,000 assault troops as well as 31,000 garrison troops to

occupy the conquered territory. On the naval side, there were four carrier groups, which included twelve carriers and eight battleships. Many more 'amphtracks' were used, and these were both armed and armoured, while fighter aircraft and gunboats were equipped with rockets. The preparatory bombardment was to be four times as great as the attack on the Gilberts.

The success of the plan was helped by the way that the Japanese sent such reinforcements as they could provide to the easterly islands of the group, thus being caught unawares by the remodelled American strategy – of indirect approach and by-passing moves.

After a brief return to Pearl Harbor for a rest and refit, the fast carrier forces came back at the end of January 1944, and by sustained sorties (over 6,000 in all) paralysed Japanese air and sea movements throughout the attack on the Marshalls – while destroying some 150 Japanese aircraft.

The first move in the attacks was the capture on January 31st of the undefended island of Majuro, in the easterly chain, which provided a good anchorage for the Americans' supporting Service Force. Then the small islands flanking Kwajalein were captured, and the main attack promptly followed on February 1st. The garrison assisted the process of overcoming it by repeated suicidal counterattacks, charging in the wild and sacrificial 'Banzai' spirit. Although the Japanese garrison had totalled over 8,000 men, of whom some 5,000 were combat troops, only 370 Americans were killed in achieving this victory.

As the Corps reserve (of some 10,000 men) had not been called on, it was sent on to seize Eniwetok. There the Americans would be still a thousand miles short of the Marianas, while less than 700 miles from Truk, the major Japanese base in the Carolines. So as a flank safeguard to the move against Eniwetok a heavy raid on Truk was delivered from nine of the American carriers on the same day as the Eniwetok landings. A further stroke was delivered that night, with the aid of radar to identify the targets, and a third the next morning. Although Admiral Koga had prudently withdrawn most of his Combined Fleet, two cruisers and four destroyers were sunk, as well as twenty-six tankers and freighters. In the air the Japanese suffered much worse, losing over 250 planes, for an American loss of twenty-five. The strategic effects were even more striking, as this shattering triple raid caused the Japanese to withdraw all aircraft from the Bismarcks, leaving Rabaul helpless – thus proving that the central Pacific advance could assist, and not retard, MacArthur's progress in the South-west Pacific.

Above all, the operation showed that carrier forces could cripple a major enemy base without occupying it, and without the help of land-based aircraft.

In these circumstances, the capture of Eniwetok proved easy. The surrounding islands were quickly taken, and even the garrison of the main island was overcome in three days, by a landing force of less than half a division's strength. The building of new airfields in the Marshalls, for American use, then proceeded fast. The Gilberts and the Marshalls had been gained in only just over two months, whereas the Japanese had hoped that this delaying zone could be held for six months, and the key position of Truk in their 'absolute', or essential, barrier zone had been badly impaired.

BURMA, 1943-4

The season's campaign in Burma ran a very different course from expectation, and formed a depressing contrast to the now rapid Allied advance in the Pacific, especially the Central Pacific. For the main feature of the war in Burma was another Japanese offensive – and the only one in the war that saw the Japanese cross the Indian frontier, into southern Assam – whereas the British had been counting on, and planning, an offensive that would clear the invaders out of northern Burma and open the road to China. The great improvement in communications from India, and the growing strength of their forces, had appeared to offer a good prospect.

The Japanese attack was aimed to forestall and dislocate the British offensive, and it came uncomfortably close to tactical success, despite inferior strength, while even its eventual failure had the strategical effect of postponing the British advance until 1945. But once it was foiled, in the spring of 1944, by the tough defence of Imphal and Kohima, both thirty miles inside the Assam border, it soon became evident that the Japanese had exhausted so much of their scanty strength in this last offensive effort that they could offer no strong resistance to the immediate British counteroffensive, nor to the larger scale British offensive that followed in 1945.

In preparation for the campaign the Allies had agreed among themselves that the reoccupation of northern Burma was to be the primary objective, as the shortest way to renew direct touch with China and resume supplies to her over 'the Burma Road' across the mountain barrier. After prolonged discussion, other schemes were put aside –

such as amphibious operations against Akyab, Rangoon, or Sumatra. The British offensive in northern Burma was to be preceded by a renewed attack in Arakan, and a diversionary attack by the Chindits in the north.

At the end of August 1943 a new and unified 'South-East Asia Command' was set up under Admiral Lord Louis Mountbatten, previously Chief of Combined Operations. The respective Service heads under him were Admiral Somerville, General Giffard, and Air Chief Marshal Peirse, while General Stilwell, the American, was to be Deputy 'Sup-

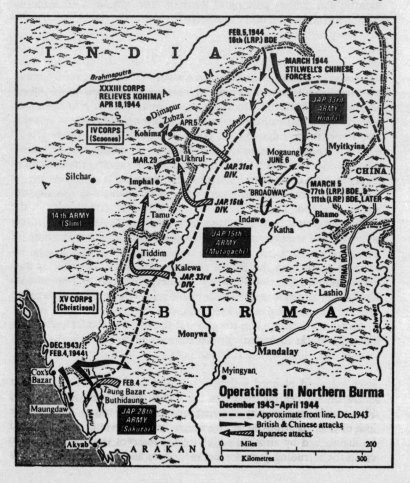

Operations in Northern Burma
December 1943-April 1944
- - - - - Approximate front line. Dec.1943
British & Chinese attacks
Japanese attacks

Miles   200
Kilometres   300

remo' to Mountbatten. The India Command was separated from SEAC, and made responsible for training as distinct from operations; Wavell was 'pushed upstairs' to become Viceroy of India and Auchinleck appointed to succeed him as C-in-C India.

The main part of the army strength under General Giffard (Eleventh Army Group) was the newly formed Fourteenth Army, of which General Slim was given command. It comprised Christison's 15th Corps in Arakan and Scoones's 4th Corps on the central front, in northern Burma, while having operational control of the Chinese divisions in this theatre of war. The naval strength remained small, but the air strength was increased to some sixty-seven squadrons, of which nineteen were American – an effective total of about 850 aircraft.

It was this large increase of Allied strength, and the obvious offensive move that it portended, which spurred the Japanese to embark on a fresh and preventive offensive, into Assam, when they would otherwise have been content to stay on the defensive and consolidate the area, in Burma, they had conquered early in 1942. Wingate's first Chindit foray had made them realize that the Chindwin River was not a secure defensive shield. The object of the Japanese offensive was to foil an Allied offensive in the dry season of 1944 by occupying the Imphal plain and controlling the mountain passes from Assam – not to attempt a far-reaching invasion of India, or a 'march on Delhi'.

The Japanese command system, too, was reorganized during the preparatory period. Under General Kawabe, the top commander in the Burmese theatre, there were three so-called armies (they were barely equivalent to army corps scale) – the 33rd, under General Honda (of two divisions) in the north-east; the 28th, under General Sakurai (of three divisions) on the Arakan front; and the 15th, under General Mutagachi, on the central front, consisting of three divisions and an 'Indian National Division' which had only 9,000 men – little more than half the strength of a normal Japanese division.

Mutagachi's 'army' was to carry out the Imphal offensive, after preliminary attacks in Arakan and Yunnan.

Each side had planned a limited offensive in Arakan before a larger thrust on the central front. On the British side, it provided General Slim with an opportunity of trying out new jungle tactics, based on the idea of creating strongholds into which the troops would withdraw, and be maintained by airborne supply, while reserves were brought up to crush the intruding Japanese between them and the strongholds. This technique was a contrast to the previous practice, and habit, of retreating when outflanked.

By the beginning of 1944 Christison's 15th Corps was gradually advancing southward, in three columns, towards Akyab. But then, early in February, its progress was interrupted when the Japanese launched their planned attack – although with only one of their three divisions in Arakan. Helped by British negligence, they were able to capture Taung Bazar and then, turning south, put the advancing British columns in an awkward situation – until relieved by fresh reinforcements that were flown in. But despite local blunders the value of the new British technique was proved, and the Japanese, running short of food and ammunition, were driven to abandon their counteroffensive, even before the monsoon intervened in June and halted operations.

Wingate's forces had been quiescent since the first Chindit operation had ended, with a withdrawal, in May 1943. But during the interval their strength had been increased from two brigades to six – largely owing to the way that Wingate's ideas and arguments had fired Churchill's imagination, and had come to be regarded favourably by the previously sceptical Chiefs of Staff when he was summoned to attend the Quadrant Conference at Quebec in August 1943. Orde Wingate himself was promoted major-general, and his forces were given an air unit of their own, No. 1 Air Commando – a force much exceeding the scale implied by its official title, being equivalent to eleven squadrons. It was commonly called 'Cochran's Circus' after its young American commander, Philip Cochran.

The later months of 1943 and the early months of 1944 were spent in the specialized training of the newly allotted brigades. Although still called the 3rd Indian Division, as camouflage, the force did not comprise any Indian troops and now amounted to the equivalent of two divisions, the chief new element being provided by the British 70th Division.

Wingate's ideas, too, had changed and developed – from guerrilla 'hit-and-run' tactics to a more concrete and prolonged kind of long-range penetration. His LRP groups were to seize Indaw and the area around it on the Irrawaddy, some 150 miles north of Mandalay – the space between the British 4th Corps and Stilwell's Chinese forces (two divisions) – and disrupt the Japanese communications by establishing a string of strongholds that would be supplied by air. They were to 'fight it out' with the enemy forces, not merely harass them. In essence, the

Chindits would become the spearhead, and the 4th Corps the supporting, and mopping-up force. Wingate visualized, and aimed to have eventually, several LRP divisions operating far ahead of the main army.

The operation was launched on the evening of March 5th, and had an ominous start when many of the sixty-two gliders used by the initial contingent miscarried or crashed on landing at 'Broadway', a spot fifty miles north-east of Indaw, while another chosen site was found to be obstructed by felled tree-trunks and a third soon discarded for various reasons. Nevertheless the construction of an airstrip went ahead at 'Broadway' and the bulk of Mike Calvert's 77th (LRP) Brigade was successfully landed during the next few nights, and was followed by Lentaigne's 111th (LRP) Brigade. By March 13th, some 9,000 men had been put down deep in the enemy's rear. In addition, Bernard Fergusson's 16th (LRP) Brigade had set off on an overland march from Assam early in February, and despite the appalling difficulties of the country was approaching Indaw soon after the middle of March.

Although the Japanese had been taken by surprise, they soon managed to assemble an improvised force under General Hayashi, amounting to the equivalent of a division, to deal with this airborne invasion. Part of it arrived at Indaw by March 18th, and the bulk of it before the end of March. Moreover the Japanese air force in a counterstroke on the 17th destroyed most of the half dozen Spitfires that were now operating from 'Broadway', and after that its air defence depended on fighter patrols flown from the distant airfields around Imphal. Then on March 24th Wingate himself was killed when his plane crashed in the jungle. But even before that tragic accident his over-elaborate yet rather ill-thought out plan was becoming disjointed. On the 26th a direct attack on Indaw by the overland marching 16th (LRP) Brigade, ordered by Wingate, was repulsed by the Japanese in their prepared position, and they also succeeded in countering the threat of the other LRP brigades. Wingate's development of the concept from guerrilla action into long-range penetration of a more concrete kind had not proved a success, although it is true that he was not given the main force backing-up he had intended.

After Wingate's death, Lentaigne was appointed to replace him as commander of the Special Force, and early in April he agreed in discussion with Slim and Mountbatten that the Chindits should be moved northward to assist Stilwell's advance, with the Chinese, as they were not hampering the Japanese thrust to Imphal. Although Stilwell did not welcome their transfer, feeling that they would draw Japanese forces in

his direction, they helped his advance to some extent by capturing
Mogaung - although even then Stilwell's Chinese troops failed in the
effort to reach the enemy's key position at Myitkyina. The northward
move of the Chindits was made just before a fresh Japanese division
arrived on the scene.

The 'preventive' Japanese offensive into Assam, to capture Imphal and
Kohima, had been launched in the middle of March, by three divisions.
Its launch and progress was not affected, contrary to expectation, by the
Chindits' descent into the Irrawaddy valley on its easterly flank and
rear - a threat which was too remote to endanger its own northward line
of advance and communications.

At the end of January, Scoones had broken off the gradual southward
advance of his own 4th Corps, from Imphal, and taken up defensive
positions in view of reports and evidence that the Japanese were regrouping and concentrating on the upper reaches of the Chindwin for
an offensive of their own towards Imphal. Even so, Scoones's three
divisions were still rather scattered, while the southernmost (the 17th)
was by-passed near Tiddim and then found its road of withdrawal to
Imphal blocked. The situation looked so precarious that a fourth British division, just back from Arakan, was hastily made ready for an
emergency switch by air to Imphal, as well as other reinforcements.
The Japanese flanking advance from the Chindwin was also making
progress and hustling the withdrawal of the 20th Division. Then the
British position at Ukhrul, some thirty miles north-east of (and behind)
Imphal, was attacked on March 19th and it became uncomfortably
evident that this Japanese deep-flank thrust was aimed at Kohima,
sixty miles north of Imphal, on the road back across the mountains into
India. The Imphal–Kohima road was actually cut, for a time, on
March 29th. Two more fresh divisions were then sent forward as a
safeguard and stop-gap. In sum, Japanese nimbleness and thrustfulness
had once again thrown their numerically superior opponents off balance
and put them in an awkward plight.

Although the British managed to get back to the Imphal plain, and
had there got more than four divisions defensively deployed, Kohima
was held by only 1,500 troops (under Colonel Hugh Richards). It was
fortunate for the British that the top Japanese commander, General
Kawabe, refused permission to General Mutagachi, the local army
commander, to push on a force to seize Dimapur, thirty miles beyond
Kohima, at the exit from the mountains. Such a coup would have fore-

stalled, and disrupted, any British counteroffensive to relieve Imphal.

In the breathing space thus allowed, Lieutenant-General Montagu Stopford and the leading part of his 33rd Corps was brought forward from India, and on April 2nd he was put in charge of the Dimapur–Kohima area, pending the arrival of the bulk of his corps.

The Japanese attack on Kohima (by their 31st Division) began on the night of the 4th, and it quickly seized the dominating heights, so that by the 6th the small garrison was cut off from the brigade that had been sent to reinforce it, while this brigade in turn was cut off from Dimapur by a road-block at Zubza that the Japanese established behind it.

General Slim, however, ordered a general counteroffensive on the 10th. By the 14th a fresh brigade sent forward by Stopford captured the road-block at Zubza, and on the 18th the two relieving brigades broke through to the tiny and exhausted Kohima garrison just as it was making its last stand. In the next phase, they drove the Japanese off the surrounding heights.

Around Imphal, also, there was hard fighting when two of the British divisions there counterattacked – northward to clear the road to Kohima and north-eastward to recapture Ukhrul and threaten the rear of the Japanese division attacking Kohima. The other two British divisions at Imphal were thrusting southward.

Fortunately for the British they now had almost complete command of the air – the Japanese had less than 200 aircraft in the whole of Burma – and were thus able to keep their large force at Imphal supplied by air during these crucial weeks. (They had about 120,000 men at Imphal even after 35,000 wounded, sick and non-combatants had been flown out.)

In May, Stopford's now reinforced troops cleared the road to Imphal, after driving off the Japanese who were clinging on to their positions around Kohima, and Scoones's troops came close to cornering the Japanese south of Imphal. But the Japanese could have withdrawn comfortably, and without further loss, if Mutagachi had not insisted on pursuing his offensive efforts long after any prospect of success had passed, and in face of the protests of his executive subordinates. In his furious persistence he sacked all three of his divisional commanders – and was subsequently sacked himself.

During July the British 14th Army under Slim continued its counteroffensive and eventually reached the Chindwin. Its progress was delayed by the advent of the monsoon more than by the resistance of the Japanese – now only an exhausted and hungry remnant.

During their excessively prolonged offensive the Japanese losses had amounted to over 50,000 out of the 84,000 troops they had brought into action. The British, handled more carefully, lost less than 17,000 – out of a larger initial strength, and much larger ultimate strength. In all they had employed six divisions and a number of smaller formations, while benefiting greatly from control of the air, whereas the Japanese had only employed three of their divisions plus a so-called division of Indian Nationalists, low in strength and poor in quality. On the other hand, the Japanese had forfeited their advantage in tactical skill by blind conformity to an unrealistic military tradition – and would pay for such folly still more dearly in the next stage of the war.

PART VII

FULL EBB
1944

CHAPTER THIRTY

Capture of Rome and Second Check in Italy

The Allied situation in Italy at the opening of 1944 was disappointing compared with the high hopes that accompanied the landings there in September 1943. Both the invading armies, the Fifth (United States) and the Eighth (British) had lost heavily and become palpably exhausted by their successive frontal attacks up the leg of the Italian peninsula, on the left and right sides respectively of its shin bone – the Apennine mountain range. Their slow, crawling progress up the length of the peninsula had become all too like the battering-ram process of the Allied armies on the Western Front in the First World War. The great disadvantage at which the Germans had been placed in September by their Italian ally's simultaneous capitulation and change of sides, coupled with the triple Anglo-American landings – at Reggio, Taranto, and Salerno – had been retrieved by their speedy reaction. Kesselring's temporarily disjointed and confused forces had met the multiple emergency so well that Hitler was soon able to cancel the initial idea and plan, of abandoning the Italian peninsula and falling back to the north of Italy, in favour of a prolonged defence of the peninsula.

From the autumn of 1943 onward, the most that the Allies could hope to achieve was a negative aim – that of keeping as many German divisions as possible pinned down in Italy, and away from the force available to meet the coming Anglo-American invasion of France, through Normandy, in mid-summer 1944.

The Teheran Conference of the three major Allied Powers in November 1943, and immediately preceding the Anglo-American Conference at Cairo, confirmed this conclusion by the decision that 'Operation Overlord', the cross-Channel attack through Normandy was to have priority, along with 'Anvil', the supplementary landing in the South of France, while the aim in Italy was confined to the capture of Rome and a subsequent advance to the Pisa–Rimini line in the peninsular leg. Exploitation north-eastward into the Balkans was not to be undertaken. Indeed, it does not appear to have been a major point, or consideration, of British policy at this time.

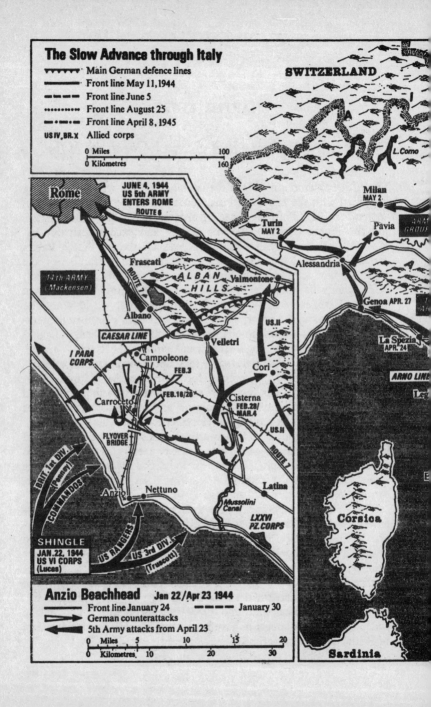

The Slow Advance through Italy

vvvvv Main German defence lines
──────── Front line May 11, 1944
──────── Front line June 5
•••••••• Front line August 25
──•──•── Front line April 8, 1945
US IV, BR. X Allied corps

0 Miles 100
0 Kilometres 160

SWITZERLAND

L. Como

Rome

JUNE 4, 1944
US 5th ARMY
ENTERS ROME
ROUTE 6

Milan
MAY 2

Turin
MAY 2

Pavia

ARMY
GROUP

14th ARMY
(Mackensen)

Frascati

ALBAN
HILLS

Valmontone

Alessandria

A

Genoa APR. 27

Albano

CAESAR LINE

Velletri

US II

Cori

La Spezia
APR. 24

ARNO LINE

I PARA
CORPS

Campoleone

FEB. 3

FEB. 10/20

Cisterna
FEB. 28/
MAR. 4

US II

ROUTE 7

Leg

Carroceto

FLYOVER
BRIDGE

BRIT. 1st DIV.
(Penney)

COMMANDOS

Anzio

Nettuno

Latina

Mussolini
Canal

LXXVI
PZ. CORPS

Corsica

SHINGLE
JAN. 22, 1944
US VI CORPS
(Lucas)

US RANGERS

US 3rd DIV.
(Truscott)

E

Anzio Beachhead   Jan 22/Apr 23 1944

──────── Front line January 24   ── ── ── January 30
▷▷ German counterattacks
◀━━ 5th Army attacks from April 23

0 Miles 5 10 15 20
0 Kilometres 10 20 30

Sardinia

The Argenta Gap

- – – – Front line April 8
- ◄──── Allied attacks April 9

0 ·Miles 30

AUSTRIA

Brenner Pass
MAY 5

Trento

Belluno

Udine

VENETIA

Verona

Padua

Venice
APR. 28

Trieste
MAY 2

Adige

10th ARMY

Argenta

Comacchio
BR.V
Ravenna

Modena

Bologna

US.IV

CAN.I
POL.II

M.Battaglia

BR.
XIII

BR.X

US.II

GOTHIC LINE

Rimini

Coriano Ridge

Conca
Foglia

Pisa

Florence

San
Marino

Pesaro

Arno

Arezzo

Metauro

POL.II
CAN.I
BR.V

Ancona
JULY 18

ADRIATIC

Siena

L.
Trasimene

TRASIMENE LINE

SEA

Perugia

San
Benedetto

Todi

POL.II

YUGO-
SLAVIA

Tiber

Terni

Civita

Pescara

GUSTAV LINE (HITLER LINE)

US.IV

POL.
II.
BR.
V

Civitavecchia
JUNE 7

Rome

US.VI

US II

BR.XIII

BR.X

Valmontone

Arce

Sangro

BR.8th ARMY
(Leese)

Anzio
US.VI

Ceprano

Cassino
BR.XIII
FR.CORPS
US.II
BR.X

POL.II

US 5th ARMY
(Clark)

15th ARMY
GROUP
(Alexander)

Garigliano

Naples

The Argenta Gap (inset)

ARGENTA GAP

Po

Ferrara

Reno

L.
Comacchio

Argenta

Bastia

APR 1
CMDS.&
GDS. BDE.

Bologna

BR.V

Santerno

Senio

Ravenna

R.66

Imola

POL.II

Forli

US.
IV

BR.X

M.Battaglia
BR.XIII

ROUTE 9

(See also map pp 468–9)

In spite of the basic agreement on priority for 'Overlord' and 'Anvil', there was still much underlying disagreement between the American and British leaders over the importance of the campaign in Italy. The British view, as held by Mr Churchill and Sir Alan Brooke, was that the more forces the Allies put into Italy the more German forces they could draw thither, away from Normandy – a view that proved mistaken, but was inspired by Churchill's hope of a great and primarily British success in that theatre of war. The Americans' view, in so far as it differed, was governed by their concern that any reinforcement of the Allied strength in Italy should not subtract from its strength in France which they considered, rightly, the decisive theatre. They recognized more realistically than Churchill, or the British military chiefs, the difficulties of terrain that were likely to hinder any quick success in Italy, and its exploitation. They were also deeply suspicious of a British inclination to focus on Italy as an evasion of an invasion of France, the harder task.

Kesselring now had fifteen divisions in the 10th Army (apart from a further eight with the 14th Army in the north) to hold his front, on what was called the Gustav Line, against a continuation of the Allied offensive. Although most of the German divisions were of weaker strength,* and some badly reduced, they looked capable of holding on against any direct frontal assault by the eighteen Allied divisions which had been landed in Italy by the end of 1943.

So the natural solution was an amphibious landing behind the Gustav Line, and that promised to be all the easier since the Allies had both air and naval superiority. If launched in conjunction with a fresh attack on the Gustav Line, it should be able to lever the Germans out of that line and break their hold south of Rome. Such a plan, named 'Operation Shingle', was already on the stocks, and Churchill, who had been feeling impatient at the slow progress in Italy, gave it fresh impetus. He obtained the necessary shipping at the Cairo–Teheran Conference by agreeing to the American desire for 'Anvil', the South of France landing planned for the summer, and then asking that the assault-craft should remain in the Mediterranean until that time – so that they would be available for the amphibious landing at Anzio, just south of Rome, which was projected for January.

* The strength of the German divisions varied widely, and some that had been engaged in heavy fighting were very shrunk, but even on full establishment they averaged only about two-thirds the size of Allied divisions.

The plan drawn up by Alexander and his staff was well designed in broad outline. The offensive on the existing peninsular front, the Gustav Line, was to be launched by Mark Clark's Fifth Army, about January 20th. The US 2nd Corps was to strike across the Rapido River, and up the Liri valley, as soon as the French Corps on its right and the British 10th Corps on its left had drawn off most of General Senger's 14th Panzer Corps by preliminary thrusts. Once the main advance got going, the seaborne US 6th Corps would be landed at Anzio. It was hoped, and expected, that the German reserve divisions would then be hurrying southward, and would turn back to meet the Allied landing forces at Anzio – while in the confusion, the Fifth Army should be able to break through the Gustav Line and link up with the 6th Corps at Anzio. Even if the German 10th Army was not crushed between the two, the Allied Command hoped that it would have to withdraw to the Rome area to reorganize.

But the plan did not work out. The German troops were not so confused or exhausted as the Allied Command hoped, and they fought with their usual tenacity. On the other hand, the Allied preparations had been rushed and the Fifth Army's offensive was disjointed in delivery.

It started well with a successful assault crossing of the Garigliano River, on the night of January 17th/18th, by McCreery's British 10th Corps on the westerly sector. And this led Kesselring to dispatch a large proportion of his reserves (29th and 90th Panzergrenadier Divisions, and parts of the Hermann Göring Division) to that front. But the attack, on the 20th, of the US 2nd Corps across the Rapido, in the left centre, proved a costly failure – the two leading regiments being largely destroyed. The Liri valley was strongly held, and any attack up it was in full view of Monte Cassino, the formidableness of which position had been underestimated. The Rapido itself had a very fast current and even an unopposed crossing would have been difficult, while in this case the US 36th Division was launched at it after only five days for rest and preparation since its capture of the outlying Monte Trocchio on the approach to the Rapido. The assault attempted by the British 46th Division advancing on its immediate left was also a failure. The Fifth Army's offensive was still proceeding, but looking gloomy, when the seaborne force landed at Anzio on January 22nd.

The Anzio sector offered the only suitable beaches for a landing behind the German flank, unless the Allied planners ventured to choose a site north of Rome – and that would be considerably farther from the main front on the Gustav Line. Even so, Kesselring was taken by sur-

prise, considering a north of Rome landing more dangerous to him
strategically, and had only one unit in the Anzio area when the Allied
landing took place – a battalion of the 29th Panzergrenadier Division
that was in rest there. Fortunately for him the commander of the invading force, Major-General John P. Lucas, who had taken over the
command of the 6th Corps during the last part of the Salerno battle,
was extremely cautious and also deeply pessimistic; he had expressed
his pessimistic views, even before the operation was launched, not only
in his diary but also to his subordinates and allies, including Alexander
himself.

His 6th Corps comprised for the initial landing two infantry divisions, the 1st British and 3rd US, assisted by Commando and Ranger
units, a parachute regiment, and two tank battalions, while they were to
be followed up by the American 1st Armored Division and 45th Infantry Division. That strength would assure not only overwhelming
superiority at the landing places but the prospect of powerful exploitation – which Churchill hoped would quickly reach the Alban Hills
south of Rome and cut the strategically vital Routes 6 and 7, thus
cutting off the German 10th Army in the Gustav Line.

The landings – by the British just north of Anzio, and the Americans
just south of the town – were easily achieved, being almost unopposed.
But the Germans' reaction was rapid and resolute. Their forces in the
Gustav Line were ordered to stand fast, on the defensive, while the
Hermann Göring Division was switched back northward and other
available units rushed down from Rome. Kesselring was told by OKW
that he could call on any of the divisions in northern Italy, and that in
addition he was to be sent two divisions, three independent regiments,
and two heavy tank battalions. For Hitler was anxious, and eager, to
give this Allied seaborne move such a knock as would frighten off the
Allies from further landings in Italy, and from their prospective landings on the coast of France.

Kesselring's re-shuffle of his forces was a remarkable feat. Elements
of eight German divisions were brought to the Anzio sector in the first
eight days. The command set-up was also reorganized at the same time.
Mackensen's 14th Army took over the Anzio sector, controlling the 1st
Parachute Corps and 76th Panzer Corps that now respectively held the
areas north and south of the Allied beachhead. Vietinghoff's 10th Army
was left to hold the Gustav Line, with the 14th Panzer Corps and the
51st Mountain Corps. In all, eight German divisions were assembled
round the Anzio beachhead, seven were under Senger's 14th Panzer
Corps opposing Mark Clark's Allied Fifth Army, and only three were

under the 51st Mountain Corps to check the British Eighth Army on the Adriatic side of Italy – while six divisions were left in northern Italy under General von Zangen. (The British Eighth Army was now commanded by Sir Oliver Leese, with Montgomery's recall to England to take charge of the plans and preparations for the coming Allied invasion of Normandy.)

Churchill's hope of a speedy thrust from Anzio to the Alban Hills was nullified by Lucas' obstinate determination, backed by Mark Clark, to concentrate on consolidating the beachhead before thrusting inland. But in view of the Germans' swift reaction and superior skill, along with the clumsiness of most of the Allied commanders and troops, Lucas' super-caution may have been a blessing in disguise. An inland thrust, in such circumstances, could have been an easy target for flank attacks, and have led to disaster.

While the planned beachhead area was secured by the second day, and the supply problem thereby simplified, the first real attempt to push inland did not start until January 30th – more than a week after the landing. It was soon brought to a halt by the German forces on the spot. Moreover the whole beachhead could now be harassed by German artillery fire, and Allied aircraft, which were operating from the Naples area, were unable to prevent Luftwaffe raids on the crowded shipping around Anzio. So Mark Clark's forces on the Gustav Line, instead of being aided by the Anzio lever, again tried a direct attack to aid the hemmed-in seaborne force at Anzio.

This time the US 2nd Corps sought to overcome the Gustav Line by an attack on Cassino from the north side. On January 24th the American 34th Division led the assault, with the aid of the French on its flank. But it was not until after a week's heavy fighting that it managed to secure a firm bridgehead, and before then Senger had brought more of his reserves into the sector, making this strong defensive position stronger than ever. On February 11th the Americans were withdrawn, heavily depleted and badly exhausted.

After that abortive effort the newly formed New Zealand Corps (Lieutenant-General Bernard Freyberg) was brought up, composed of the 2nd New Zealand and 4th Indian Divisions, both of them veteran divisions that had greatly distinguished themselves in the North African campaign – the 4th Indian, of combined British and Indian units, had been rated by the Germans as the best division there. Freyberg's plan for a converging assault on Cassino offered no real change from the past procedure of costly frontal assaults on well-sited and stubbornly defended German positions. Francis Tuker, commanding the 4th Indian, urged an indirect approach and wider manoeuvre, through the mountains, which the French also favoured, but his influence was diminished by him falling ill. His division was cast to tackle Monte Cassino itself, and after the rejection of his proposals for a wider manoeuvre he asked that the historic monastery, which crowned this height, should be neutralized by a concentrated air bombardment. While there was no evidence that German troops were using the monastery – and ample proof subsequently that they abstained from entering it – the great edifice so dominated the scene as to have a sinister and depressing effect on troops who had to attack the height. The request was granted, after endorsement by Freyberg and Alexander, and on February 15th a tremendous bombing attack was delivered that demolished the famous monastery buildings. The German troops then felt justified in moving into the rubble, which enabled them to establish a still firmer defence.

That night, and the following one, repeated attacks by the 4th Indian Division made no important progress. So on the next night, February 17th/18th, the New Zealand Corps reverted to the original plan. The 4th Indian Division succeeded in capturing the oft-disputed Point 593, but was pushed out by counterattacks from German parachute troops, and the 2nd New Zealand Division was driven out next day from its bridgehead over the Rapido by a counterattack from German tanks.

Pending the arrival of the large reinforcements that OKW had promised, to help in wiping out the Allied bridgehead, Mackensen launched counterattacks to hinder the Allied forces from expanding it. The first, on the night of February 3rd, was against the salient created by the British 1st Division in its abortive push towards Campoleone on January 30th. Fortunately the leading brigade of the British 56th Division had just landed, and the thrust was held. A further and heavy counterattack came on the 7th and although it was held at bay British losses were so heavy that the 1st Division had to be replaced by the US 45th Division, which had now arrived.

By mid-February Mackensen was ready to launch his counterstroke, having now ten divisions surrounding the five Allied divisions in the bridgehead, and a strongly reinforced Luftwaffe to give him good support. 'Goliaths', the new remote-controlled, explosive-filled, miniature tanks, were to be used to cause confusion among the defenders. The build-up had not been affected by the Allied attacks at Cassino, nor was it seriously hindered by Allied airpower.

The German attack on the bridgehead began on February 16th, with probes all along the perimeter, and frequent raids by the Luftwaffe. By evening a gap developed in the sector held by the US 45th Division. It was the opportunity for which the Germans had been waiting – fourteen battalions, led by Hitler's favourite, the Infantry Lehr Regiment, supported by tanks thrust forward on the 17th to expand the gap and push down the Albano–Anzio road. Victory was in sight.

But the amount and mixture of forces crammed on this one road became an internal hindrance while offering a crowded target for the Allied artillery, aircraft, and naval bombardment squadrons. And the 'Goliath' tanks were a failure. However, despite the heavy losses suffered, the weight of the assault pushed the Allied forces back, and on the 18th a renewed assault, reinforced by the 26th Panzer Division, made further progress towards the beaches. But the 56th and 1st British and 45th US Divisions fought desperately, and successfully, to hold the final defence line of the bridgehead. The German thrust was checked at the Carroceto creek, and the assaulting troops wilted under the strain. The Panzergrenadier divisions made their final effort on the 20th, but it was soon brought to a halt. The conduct and success of the defence was helped by the arrival of General Lucian K. Truscott, first as deputy, and then as successor, to Lucas. On the British sector Major-General W. R. C. Penney, commander of the 1st Division, had been wounded, and replaced by Major-General Gerald Templer, who ably coordinated the defence of both this and the 56th Division. —

Galled at the repulse, Hitler ordered a fresh offensive, opening on February 28th, with diversionary attacks and the main thrust, by four divisions, down the Cisterna road. But this was held in check without difficulty by the American 3rd Division, and when, after the first three days, the low cloud cleared, the Allied air forces pulverized the attacking troops. On March 4th Mackensen was compelled, by his losses, to stop the offensive. Five German divisions were left to hold the ring, while the others were withdrawn to rest.

The Allies now embarked on still another attack on Cassino, in order to clear the way for their spring offensive. This time the attack was even more direct than before. The New Zealand Division was to push through the town, and then the 4th Indian was to take over the assault on Monastery Hill. A very heavy bombardment from the ground and the air – 190,000 shells and 1,000 tons of bombs – was used with the aim of paralysing the German troops in the town.

This bombardment was delivered on March 15th, when the weather was clear enough. But the defenders of the sector, a regiment (three battalions) of the élite 1st Parachute Division, not only endured the dual bombardment without flinching but survived it well enough to check the follow-up of the assaulting infantry. They were helped by the mass of rubble created by the bombardment, which blocked the way for the Allied tanks. Although Castle Hill was captured, the 4th Indian Division's further advance up the height was hampered by torrential rain that came down in a deluge to the aid of the defenders. A company of Gurkhas got as far as Hangman's Hill, below the Monastery, but was there isolated. Meanwhile fierce fighting continued in the town. Fresh efforts by both sides proved abortive on the 19th, and the next day Alexander decided that if success was not achieved within thirty-six hours the operation should be abandoned, for losses were becoming heavy. On the 23rd it was definitely broken off, with Freyberg's agreement. So the Third Battle of Cassino ended in disappointment. After that the New Zealand Corps was disbanded, its units being given a rest and then dispersed to other corps, while the Cassino sector was taken over by the British 78th Division and the 1st Guards Brigade of the 6th Armoured Division.

Alexander had proposed on February 22nd that 'Operation Diadem' should be delivered up the Liri valley in conjunction with a break-out and converging thrust from the Anzio bridgehead. It would be broadly similar in pattern to the January offensive, but better planned and co-ordinated, and was to be launched about three weeks before 'Overlord', the cross-Channel attack from England into Normandy, so that it might draw German divisions from France.

The plan devised by Alexander's Chief of Staff, John Harding, concentrated extra punch into the blow by leaving only one corps on the Adriatic side of Italy, and sidestepping the rest of the Eighth Army westward, to take over the Cassino–Liri valley sector. The Fifth Army, including the French, would be in charge not only of the Garigliano sector on the left flank but of the Anzio bridgehead. An accompanying proposal was that 'Operation Anvil', the South of France landing, should be abandoned.

While the British Chiefs agreed to the plan, rather naturally, the American Chiefs of Staff opposed it, as they considered that a landing in the South of France would be a better diversion to help the Normandy invasion. Eisenhower then proposed a compromise, by which the

Italian offensive should be given priority, but planning for 'Anvil' be continued. If, by March 20th, it was clear that a major amphibious operation could not be mounted, most of the shipping in Italian waters should be withdrawn to aid 'Overlord'. The compromise was agreed by the Combined Chiefs of Staff on February 25th.

As the date for a decision approached, General Maitland Wilson – who had been given the new post of Supreme Commander, Mediterranean – heard from Alexander that the spring offensive in Italy could not be mounted before May, and it was emphasized that no troops should be withdrawn for 'Anvil' before the main forces facing the Gustav Line had broken through and linked up with the Anzio force. This meant that, allowing ten weeks for regrouping and preparation, 'Anvil' could not take place before the end of July – nearly two months after the Normandy landing, instead of being a preliminary diversion to help it. So Maitland Wilson and Alexander felt that the circumstances set them free to drop 'Anvil' and concentrate on an effort to complete the Italian campaign decisively. That view accorded with the preference of Churchill and the British Chiefs of Staff. Eisenhower tended to agree with them, if on the somewhat different ground that most of the Mediterranean shipping could now be transferred to 'Overlord'. But the American Chiefs of Staff, while reluctantly accepting a delay in launching 'Anvil' until July, were opposed to its abandonment, and doubted the value of pursuing the offensive in Italy beyond the limits already set. They also doubted its effect in drawing off German divisions from Normandy – in which respect they were soon proved right. A prolonged wrangle ensued, being carried on and up in an interchange of lengthy telegraphic arguments between Mr Churchill and President Roosevelt.

Meanwhile, in Italy, preparations for the spring offensive went forward – this being in the British sphere of command. The move and redeployment of the Eighth Army along with other factors, including shipping shortages, delayed the launching of the offensive until May 11th. The Eighth Army's task was to break through at Cassino while the Fifth Army was to assist it, on the left flank, by thrusting across the Garigliano, and by a break-out from the Anzio bridgehead towards Valmontone on Route 6. At Anzio there were now six Allied divisions facing five German – with four more German divisions in reserve around Rome. On the Gustav Line sixteen Allied divisions (of which four lay close up in readiness for the exploitation) were assembled against six German divisions (with one in reserve). Much the larger part of the Allied strength on this front was concentrated on the stretch from Cassino to the mouth of the Garigliano – a total of twelve divisions (two American, four French, four British and two Polish) for the break-in, with four more close behind to exploit this by a thrust up the Liri valley, in the hope of piercing the Hitler Line, some six miles in the rear, before the Germans could rally on it and build it up.

The nine divisions of the Eighth Army were supported by over 1,000 guns, and they benefited still more by a spell of dry weather which enabled their tanks and other motor vehicles to follow up the advance – in contrast to the mud-bound conditions prevailing in the winter offensive. So the three armoured divisions (the 6th British, 5th Canadian and 6th South African) had better prospects of suitable action than ever before.

In the attack, the Polish Corps (of two divisions) was to tackle Cassino, while the British 13th Corps (of four divisions) advanced on its left, towards St Angelo.

The Allied offensive as a whole on the main front was to be supported by over 2,000 guns, while the Allied air forces in this theatre cooperated by heavy and widespread attacks on the enemy's rail and road network, before turning on to battlefield targets in the final stage. (This 'Operation Strangle', however, did not seriously affect the German communications and supply system, as had been hoped.) Extensive sabotage activities were also mounted, but had disappointing results. As a deception, Allied troops openly rehearsed amphibious landings in the hope of making Kesselring believe that they were to come – particularly near Civitavecchia just north of Rome – but he was already so strongly convinced that the Allies ought to use their seaborne advantage in such a way that these attempts at deception seem to have had no marked effect.

The offensive opened at 11 PM on the night of May 11th with a massive artillery bombardment, promptly followed up by the advance of the infantry. But for the first three days the attack made little progress against stiff resistance on most sectors. The Polish Corps under General Anders suffered heavily in its assault at Cassino despite great determination and skill in using less direct routes of approach. The British 13th Corps also made slow progress, and would have suffered heavy losses but for the way the Poles focused the enemy's attention. The US 2nd Corps on the coast sector likewise gained little ground. But the French Corps, under Juin, which lay between these two, found only one division opposing its four, and made relatively fast progress through the mountainous region beyond the Garigliano, where the Germans had not expected a serious thrust. On the 14th the French broke into the Ausente valley, and the German 71st Division began falling back fast before them. That helped the American 2nd Corps which now began to push faster along the coast road against the German 94th Division. Moreover these two German divisions were now on lines of retreat split by the almost roadless Aurunci Mountains. Juin, seizing the opportunity, sent his mountain-bred Moroccan Goums – a force of divisional strength under Guillaume – into the gap across the mountains to pierce the rearward Hitler Line in the Liri valley before it could be properly manned.

The German right flank, or western wing, was now collapsing, and its prospects of rallying were all the worse because Senger, its able commander, was away on a course when the Allied offensive was launched. Moreover Kesselring, this time, was slow to send reserves southward until he saw how the situation in the north developed, and it was not until the 13th that one division was moved south, to the Liri valley. Although three more soon followed they were sucked into what soon became a whirlpool battle, and arrived too late to stabilize the front. The Germans in the Cassino sector continued to hold on for several days more, although the Canadian Corps was thrown in on the 15th for the exploitation, but on the night of the 17th these indomitable German paratroops at last withdrew – and the Poles entered the long-sought ruins of the monastery next morning, having lost nearly 4,000 men in their gallant efforts.

As most of the scanty German reserves had at last been drawn southward, the time was ripe for the planned break-out from the Anzio bridgehead – which was now reinforced by another American division, the 36th. Ordering this break-out attack for the 23rd, Alexander hoped there would be a strong and rapid thrust to Valmontone, to cut Route 6 – the main inland road – and thus cut off most of the German 10th Army that had been holding the Gustav Line. If that was achieved Rome should fall like a ripe apple. But the prospects were marred by Mark Clark's differing views, and his eagerness that the troops of the Fifth Army should be the first to enter Rome. The US 1st Armored and 3rd Infantry Divisions reached Cori, just beyond the coastal Route 7 – but well short of Route 6 – by the 25th, after a twelve-mile advance, and had linked up with the 2nd Corps that was driving northward along Route 7. Kesselring's one remaining mobile division, the Hermann Göring, was rushing to the scene to stop this thrust – and being badly harassed by Allied air attacks. But at this stage Mark Clark swung his drive direct towards Rome, with four divisions, while only one was allowed to continue towards Valmontone – and this was held up three miles short of Route 6 by the larger part of three German divisions.

Alexander's appeals to Churchill did not succeed in changing the direction of Mark Clark's thrust, and that was slowed down by the Germans' resistance in the 'Caesar Line' defences just south of Rome. Moreover the Eighth Army's armoured divisions had found that their exploiting drive up the Liri valley was not as easy as had been hoped and they failed to pin the retreating German 10th Army against the mountain-spine formed by the Apennines. Instead the Germans were able to slip away to safety by roads running through the mountains, while their escape was helped by the absence of intervention from the Allied forces at Anzio.

Indeed, for a few days the Germans seemed to have a chance of establishing themselves and stabilizing their front on the Caesar Line because of the tough resistance put up, under Senger's direction, on the Arce–Ceprano sector along Route 6, coupled with the size and cum- brousness of the transport tail of the armoured divisions which was striving to drive up that overcrowded road.

But the gloomy prospect of another deadlock was annulled by the success of the US 36th Division on May 30th in capturing Velletri on Route 7, in the Alban Hills, and piercing the Caesar Line. Exploiting the opportunity, Mark Clark ordered a general offensive by the Fifth Army, in which his 2nd Corps took Valmontone and thrust on up Route 6 towards Rome while the bulk of his 6th Corps backed the thrust up Route 7. Under pressure from eleven divisions the comparatively small German forces holding the approaches were forced to give way, and the Americans entered Rome on June 4th. The bridges were found intact, as Kesselring had declared it an 'open city' rather than risk the Holy City's destruction in prolonged fighting.

On June 6th, two days later, the Allies' invasion of Normandy opened – and the campaign in Italy receded into the background. Their spring offensive in Italy, 'Operation Diadem', had cost the Americans 18,000 casualties, the British 14,000, and the French 10,000 by the time it was crowned by the capture of Rome. The German loss was about 10,000 in killed and wounded, but about 20,000 more were taken prisoner in the successive actions.

In comparative absorption of strength – thirty Allied divisions in this theatre against twenty-two German, and about two to one in actual troops – the continuation of the Allied offensive in Italy had not proved a good strategic investment. Nor did it make possible the invasion of Normandy by drawing the German forces away from there. Indeed, it 'did not succeed in preventing the enemy from reinforcing north-west Europe.'* Their strength in the northern part of France (north of the Loire) and in the Low Countries was increased from thirty-five divisions at the beginning of 1944 to forty-one when the Allied cross-Channel invasion was launched in June.

The claim that can more justly be made for the strategic effect of the Italian campaign, as an aid to the success of the Normandy landing, is that without its pressure the German strength on the Channel front could have been increased even more. The scale of the assault and immediate follow-up forces there were limited by the number of landing craft available, so that the Allied forces employed in Italy could not have added to the weight of the Normandy landing during its crucial opening phase. On the other hand, the use in Normandy of the German forces detained in Italy might have been fatal to the prospects of the landing. This is a valid claim which, strangely, many of its British advocates have failed to make in trying to claim too much. But even this claim is subject to a doubt whether a large movement of troops to Normandy would have been possible in face of the Allied interdiction bombing of the railways.

In the political sphere the most notable feature of the period was the abdication of King Victor Emmanuel in favour of his son, and the replacement of Marshal Badoglio as Italy's prime minister by the anti-Fascist Signor Bonomi.

For the Allied armies in Italy the sequel to the long-sought capture of Rome was very disappointing. That was partly due to higher decisions and partly to the Germans' recovery and countermoves.

Although Maitland Wilson had accepted the American view that 'Anvil', even though delayed, was the most effective operation that the Mediterranean Command could undertake to draw German divisions from northern France, and thereby aid the progress of the Normandy advance, Alexander had a different view. On June 6th, two days after the entry in Rome, he set forth his plan for exploiting 'Diadem'. He considered that if his forces were left intact, they would be able to attack the Germans' 'Gothic Line' north of Florence, on the 'thigh' of the Italian peninsula, by August 15th – the same date that Wilson had

* Ehrman: *Grand Strategy*, vol V, p 279.

fixed for 'Anvil', and would be able to break through this barrier-line unless Hitler diverted eight or more divisions to reinforce it. After that he considered that he would soon be able to overrun the north-east of Italy and have a good chance of driving on through the 'Ljubliana Gap', as it was called, into Austria. It was a remarkably optimistic view of the possibilities of speedily overcoming the series of mountain obstacles between Italian Venetia and Vienna, with their many potential delaying positions – and the more optimistic in view of the repeated repulses that the Italians had suffered there during the First World War even in the initial approaches.

But the plan appealed to Churchill and the British Chiefs of Staff, particularly Alan Brooke – as an alternative to the heavy losses, and even catastrophe, they feared in Normandy. In advocating the plan Alexander had better ground in emphasizing the moral value of impressing his troops with the importance of the Italian campaign.

The American Chiefs of Staff, under General Marshall's guidance, opposed this dubious new extension of the offensive in Italy, but Alexander succeeded in winning over Maitland Wilson. Then, however, Eisenhower intervened in favour of 'Anvil'. Once more, Churchill and Roosevelt were brought into the dispute. By July 2nd, the British had to give way, and Wilson was ordered to launch 'Anvil' – now more modestly re-named 'Dragoon' – on August 15th. The decision entailed the departure of the US 6th Corps (with its three divisions), and then of the French Corps (of four divisions) – whose chiefs and members naturally preferred to help in the liberation of their motherland. The Fifth Army was thus reduced to five divisions, and the Army Group lost about 70 per cent of its air support.

Meanwhile Kesselring and his men were already striving with much effect to check the Allies' exploitation of the partial victory they had gained. The German losses in 'Diadem' had been serious, four of the infantry divisions having to be withdrawn to refit, while a further seven had been seriously reduced. But four fresh divisions were on the way, as well as a regiment of heavy tanks. Most of these reinforcements were sent to the 14th Army, which was covering the easier routes of advance. Kesselring's plan was to slow down the Allied advance by a series of delaying actions throughout the summer, and retreat to the strong Gothic Line for the winter. About eighty miles north of Rome there was a natural line of defence near Trasimene, the scene of Hannibal's most skilful trap, which offered a suitable position for the first stand. The skilled demolition work of the German engineers would help to slow down the Allied advance.

This advance began on June 5th, the day after the Americans entered Rome. But it was not pushed very hard at the moment when it could have been most dangerous. Then the French took over the lead in the Fifth Army's sector. Meanwhile the British 13th Corps was pressing up Routes 3 and 4, further inland, but it met increasingly stiff opposition, and came to a standstill along the Trasimene line. The advance in other sectors was also brought to a standstill. Thus in barely a fortnight after the withdrawal from Rome, Kesselring had stabilized the momentarily very dangerous situation.

Moreover he had been told that OKW was sending him four more divisions – which were on or earmarked for the Russian front – as well as drafts to resuscitate his more battered divisions. And this was in addition to the four fresh divisions and one heavy tank regiment that were already arriving. Ironically, this large addition to Kesselring's strength came at a time when Alexander was faced with the depressing fact of having to part with seven of his divisions, and the larger part of his air support as well as much of the logistical elements of the Allied Army Group in Italy.

Kesselring had proved himself a very able commander, and he was now rewarded by good fortune. He had decided to make a stand, on a convenient natural line of defence, just as the Allies' exploiting drive was running out of steam.

The two months of the summer following June 20th were a period of disappointment and frustration for Alexander's armies. Advances were piecemeal and never looked decisive. Battles were a series of isolated actions between individual Allied and German corps, in which the German policy was to hold a position until the Allied corps opposite was seen to be deploying for a massive attack and to slip away to the next obstacle line.

The upshot of Kesselring's rapid regrouping meant that the 14th Panzer Corps, on the west coast, now faced the 2nd US Corps; the 1st Parachute Corps faced the French Corps (not yet withdrawn for 'Anvil'); the 76th Panzer Corps faced both British Corps, the 13th and 10th; while the 51st Mountain Corps faced the Polish 2nd Corps on the Adriatic coast.

By the beginning of July, the Allied centre, hindered by bad weather, was at last pushing through the Trasimene line – but after a few days was again checked, on the Arezzo line. By July 15th the Germans slipped away from that, and gradually retired to the Arno line, from Pisa through Florence and eastward. Here the Allied armies were forced to a prolonged halt, with their goal, the Gothic Line, only a short distance beyond. Some compensation for their frustrations was the Poles' capture of Ancona, on July 18th, and the Americans' capture of Leghorn on the 19th, which shortened their supply lines.

In view of the British desire, especially Alexander's and Churchill's, to press on with the campaign in Italy – despite repeated disappointments and reduced forces – plans went ahead for mounting a great autumn offensive against the Gothic Line. It was hoped that it would still be of value in drawing off German forces from the principal theatres, or, alternatively, that if a collapse occurred on the Western Front this would lead to a German withdrawal from Italy and thereby enable Alexander's forces to exploit a breakthrough in northern Italy by a drive towards Trieste and Vienna.

The previous plan for an attack on the Gothic Line, devised by Alexander's Chief of Staff, Harding, and the Army Group staff, had been based on the idea of a surprise thrust through the centre of the German front, in the Apennines, but on August 4th Oliver Leese, commanding the Eighth Army, persuaded Alexander to adopt a different plan. The basis of this was to switch the Eighth Army back to the Adriatic side, secretly, and for it to break through there towards Rimini. Having thus focused Kesselring's attention on the Adriatic coast, the Fifth Army would strike in the left centre, with Bologna as its objective. Then, when Kesselring reacted to this fresh thrust, the Eighth Army would thrust forward again and break into the Plain of Lombardy, where its armoured forces would have more scope for manoeuvre than they had ever enjoyed since landing in Italy.

Despite the administrative problems it would involve, this new plan was the more welcome since the prospects of the original one were impaired by the removal of the French, with their skilled mountain troops. Leese also considered that the Fifth and Eighth Armies would function better when they were not aiming at the same objective. Alexander was quick to agree with his arguments, and adopt the new plan – which was code-named 'Operation Olive'.

But it had drawbacks which became more evident after the operation was launched. While the Eighth would no longer be faced with a series of mountain ridges it would now have to overcome a series of awkward river crossings that would slow down its advance. By contrast, Kesselring profited from having a good lateral highway for switching his forces, in Route 9 – the trunk road from Rimini westward through Bologna. The planners also seem to have been unduly optimistic about a continuance of dry weather. In any case, the country north of Rimini, although flat, was boggy – and far from suitable for a fast drive by armoured forces.

Alexander's offensive opened well, on August 25th – ten days later than originally promised. The Germans were again taken by surprise – as the move of the British 5th Corps (of five divisions) and the Canadian 1st Corps (of two divisions) into positions of readiness behind the Polish 2nd Corps had not been detected. (The British 10th Corps continued to hold the mountain sector near the centre, while the 13th Corps moved farther westward to support the Fifth Army's coming attack.)

Only two low-grade divisions, although backed by the 1st Parachute Division, held the Adriatic sector – German troop movement at the time was mostly going from east to west. The Polish Corps' advances up the Adriatic had attracted little attention, and it was only on August 29th, after four days' progress by these three Allied corps on a broad front – by which time they had advanced some ten miles, from the Metauro to the Foglia – that the Germans began to react. By next day, parts of two more divisions had arrived on the scene, to help in checking the Allied advance, but they were too late to prevent the Allied thrust reaching the Conca river-line, about seven miles farther on, by September 2nd.

But the Eighth Army's momentum was flagging. The key battle was for the Coriano ridge behind the Ausa – two more rivers further – on September 4th. Here the British advance came to a halt and crumbled. Meanwhile the Germans were getting some reinforcements – and heavy rains came to their aid on September 6th.

Kesselring had ordered a general withdrawal of his other divisions into the Gothic Line positions, which had shortened his front and set free some of his troops for the Adriatic sector. That partial withdrawal opened the crossings of the Arno so that the Fifth Army was now ready to strike. From September 10th onward the US 2nd Corps and British 13th Corps attacked the weakly held but stubbornly defended German positions, and eventually, a week later, broke through the Il Gioga Pass north of Florence. Once again Kesselring seems to have been taken by surprise, as he did not recognize that this was a major offensive until the 20th, ten days from the start, when two divisions were rushed to that sector. By then, however, the Americans' reserve division, the 88th Infantry, was thrusting forward to attack Bologna from the east. Even then, although the Germans had lost the Gothic Line and a rearward key feature in Monte Battaglia, they proved capable of checking the

Allied attacks. In late September Mark Clark was led to revert to the idea of a more direct attack on Bologna.

Meanwhile the Eighth Army was still in difficulties on the Adriatic flank. By September 17th, elements of ten German divisions were on the scene and helping to slow it down. Although the Canadians succeeded in reaching Rimini by the 21st, and thus the Po Valley delta, the Germans fell back to another defence line, the River Uso – the historic Rubicon of ancient times. There were still thirteen rivers to cross in this flat and waterlogged region before the Po itself, and in the effort nearly 500 tanks had been knocked out, bogged, or broken down, while many of the infantry divisions had been reduced to skeletons. So the Germans were able to move a large proportion of their strength to check the Fifth Army.

On October 2nd, Mark Clark's renewed offensive towards Bologna opened, this time along Route 65. All four divisions of his 2nd Corps were thrown in, but the defending Germans fought with such tenacity that during the next three weeks the American advance averaged no more than a mile a day, and on October 27th the offensive was abandoned. By the end of October the Eighth Army advance had also petered out, after only five more rivers had been crossed, and the Po was still fifty miles distant.

The only notable changes of the period were command changes. Kesselring was injured in a motor accident and replaced by Vietinghoff. McCreery replaced Leese – who was being sent to Burma – in command of the Eighth Army. Towards the end of November, Maitland Wilson was sent to Washington, and succeeded by Alexander, while Mark Clark took over the Army Group in Italy.

The Allied situation at the end of 1944 was very disappointing in comparison with the high hopes of the spring, and the summer. Although Alexander still showed optimism about an advance into Austria, the slow crawl up the Italian peninsula made such distant horizons appear increasingly unrealistic. Maitland Wilson himself admitted as much in his report of November 22nd to the British Chiefs of Staff. The disbelief, and discontent, of the Allied troops was manifested in a growing rate of desertions.

A final Allied offensive in 1944 sought to gain Bologna and Ravenna as winter bases. The Canadians, in the Eighth Army, succeeded in capturing Ravenna on December 4th, and their success led the Germans to send three divisions to check the Eighth Army's further progress. That seemed to offer the Fifth Army a better chance. But this was forestalled by an enemy counterattack in the Senio valley on December

26th – prompted by Mussolini with the idea of emulating Hitler's counteroffensive in the Ardennes, and largely carried out by Italians who remained loyal to him. This attack was soon, and easily, stopped. But the Eighth Army was now exhausted, and very short of ammunition, while the Germans were known to have strong reserves near Bologna. So Alexander decided that the Allied armies should go on the defensive, and prepare for a powerful spring offensive.

A further damper to the hopes placed in the Italian campaign was the decision of the Combined Chiefs of Staff to withdraw five more divisions from that theatre to the Western Front, in order to give the Allied armies there more punch for their spring offensive into Germany. As a consequence, the Canadian Corps of two divisions was dispatched thither, although further divisions did not have to go.

CHAPTER THIRTY-ONE

The Liberation of France

Before its launching, the invasion of Normandy looked a most hazardous venture. The Allied troops had to disembark on a coast that the enemy had occupied during four years, with ample time to fortify it, cover it with obstacles and sow it with mines. For the defence, the Germans had fifty-eight divisions in the West, and ten of these were panzer divisions that might swiftly deliver an armoured counterstroke.

The Allies' power to bring into action the large forces now assembled in England was limited by the fact that they had to cross the sea, and by the number of landing craft available. They could disembark only six divisions in the first seaborne lift, together with three airborne, and a week would pass before they could double the number ashore.

So there was cause to feel anxious about the chances of storming what Hitler called the 'Atlantic Wall' – an awesome name – and about the risks of being thrown back in the sea.

Yet, in the event, the first footholds were soon expanded into a large bridgehead, eighty miles wide. The enemy never managed to deliver any dangerous counterstroke before the Allied forces broke out from the bridgehead. The break-out was made in the way and at the place that Field-Marshal Montgomery had originally planned. The whole German position in France then quickly collapsed.

Looking back, the course of the invasion appears wonderfully easy and sure. But appearances are deceptive.

It was an operation that eventually 'went according to plan', but not according to timetable. At the outset the margin between success and failure was narrow. The ultimate triumph has obscured the fact that the Allies were in great danger at the outset, and had a very narrow shave.

The common idea that the invasion had a smooth and sure run was fostered by Montgomery's subsequent emphasis that 'the battle was fought exactly as planned before the invasion', and the fact that the Allied armies reached the Seine within ninety days – the line shown on the forecast map, produced in April, as the line to be gained by 'D+90'.

It was 'Monty's way' to talk as if any operation that he had conducted had always proceeded exactly as he intended, with the certainty and precision of a machine – or of divine providence. That characteristic has often obscured his adaptability to circumstances, and thus, ironically, deprived him of the credit due to him for his combination of flexibility with determination in generalship.

In the original plan, Caen was to be captured the first day of the landing, June 6th. The start was good and the coastal defences were overcome by 9 AM. But Montgomery's account has covered up the fact that the advance inland to Caen did not start until the afternoon. That was due partly to a paralysing traffic jam on the beaches but also to the excessive caution of the commanders on the spot – at a time when there was hardly anything to stop them. When they eventually pushed on towards Caen, the keypoint of the invasion area, a panzer division – the only one in the whole invasion area of Normandy – arrived on the scene and produced a check. A second panzer division came up next day. More than a month passed before Caen was at last secured and cleared, after much heavy fighting.

Montgomery's original intention, also, was that on the British right wing an armoured force would make an immediate drive inland to Villers-Bocage, twenty miles from the coast, and so cut the roads running west and south-west from Caen. But this is not mentioned in his story. The fact is that this push was very slow to get going, although opposition west of Caen was negligible once the coast defences had been penetrated. Prisoners subsequently revealed that until the third day a ten mile stretch of front was covered by one solitary German mobile unit, a reconnaissance battalion. A third panzer division then began to arrive on the scene, and was put in here. Although the British managed to push into Villers-Bocage on the 13th, they were pushed out again. Then a fourth panzer division reinforced the block. Two months passed before Villers-Bocage was finally captured.

The original idea, too, was that the whole of the Cotentin peninsula, along with the port of Cherbourg, would be captured within two weeks, and that the break-out would then be made, by 'D+20', on this western flank. But the advance inland from the American landing points, on this flank, also proved much slower than expected, although the larger part of the German forces, and later-arriving reinforcements, were absorbed in checking the British advance on the eastern flank near Caen – as indeed Montgomery had calculated.

While the break-out ultimately came on the western flank, as Montgomery had planned, it did not come until the end of July – 'D+56'.

It had been clear beforehand that, if the Allies could gain a bridge-

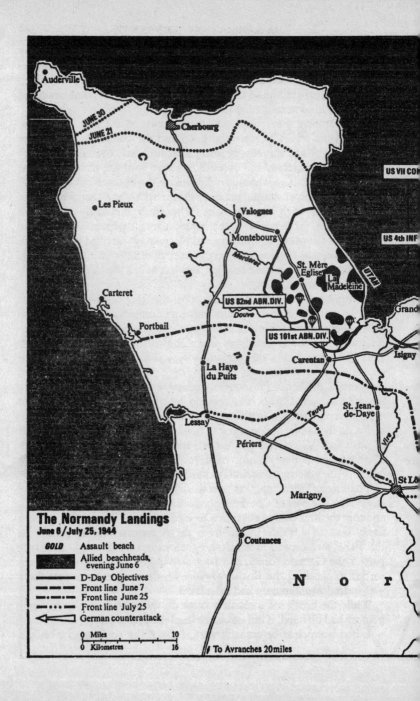

The Normandy Landings map, June 6/July 25, 1944. Labels include: Auderville, Cherbourg, JUNE 30, JUNE 21, Les Pieux, Valognes, Montebourg, Cotentin, Merderet, St. Mère Eglise, La Madeleine, UTAH, US VII CO[R], US 4th INF, Carteret, Portbail, Douve, US 82nd ABN. DIV., US 101st ABN. DIV., Carentan, Isigny, Grand, La Haye du Puits, Lessay, Taute, St. Jean-de-Daye, Vire, Périers, St L[ô], Marigny, Coutances, N o r, To Avranches 20 miles.

The Normandy Landings
June 6/July 25, 1944

GOLD	Assault beach
▬	Allied beachheads, evening June 6
—	D-Day Objectives
– – –	Front line June 7
–·–·–	Front line June 25
·····	Front line July 25
⟵	German counterattack

0 Miles 10
0 Kilometres 16

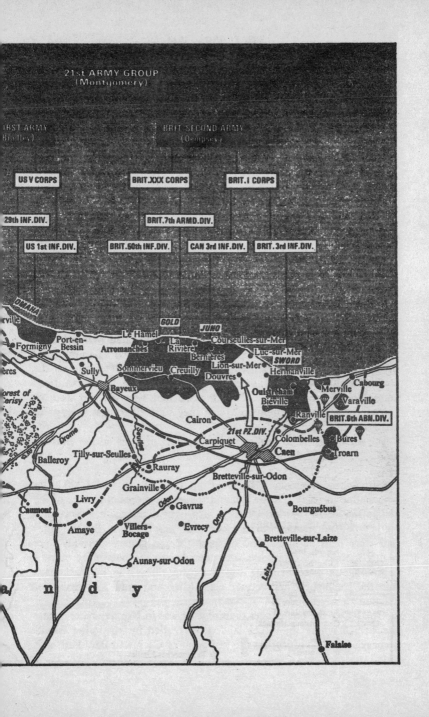

21st ARMY GROUP
(Montgomery)

FIRST ARMY
(Bradley)

BRIT SECOND ARMY
(Dempsey)

US V CORPS	BRIT.XXX CORPS	BRIT.I CORPS
29th INF.DIV.	BRIT.7th ARMD.DIV.	
US 1st INF.DIV.	BRIT.50th INF.DIV.	CAN 3rd INF.DIV.	BRIT. 3rd INF.DIV.

OMAHA

rville

Formigny
Port-en-Bessin
GOLD
Le Hamel
JUNO
Courseulles-sur-Mer
Arromanches
La Rivière
Luc-sur-Mer
Bernières
SWORD
Lion-sur-Mer
res
Sully
Sommervieu
Creully
Douvres
Hermanville
orest of
erisy
Bayeux
Ouistreham
Merville
Cabourg
Biéville
Varaville
Cairon
Ranville
BRIT.6th ABN.DIV.
Drome
21st PZ.DIV.
Colombelles
Bures
Carpiquet
Balleroy
Tilly-sur-Seulles
Caen
Troarn
Rauray
Bretteville-sur-Odon
Grainville
Caumont
Livry
Odon
Gavrus
Bourguébus
Amaye
Villers-Bocage
Evrecy
Orne
Bretteville-sur-Laize
Aunay-sur-Odon
Laize
a   n   d   y
Falaise

head sufficiently wide and deep to build up their strength on the far side of the Channel, their total resources were so much greater than the enemy's that the odds were heavily on a break-out sooner or later. No dam was likely to be strong enough to hold the invading flood in check permanently if the Allies gained enough space to pile up their massed power.

As things turned out the prolongation of the 'Battle of the Bridgehead' worked out to their advantage. It was the proverbial 'blessing in disguise'. For the bulk of the German forces in the West was drawn there, while arriving bit by bit owing to divided views in their High Command and constant hindrance from the vast Allied force that dominated the sky. The panzer divisions, arriving first and used to plug gaps, were ground down first – thus depriving the enemy of the mobile arm he needed when it came to fighting in the open country. The very toughness of the resistance that so much delayed the Allies' break-out ensured them a clear path through France once they broke out.

The Allies would have had no chance of ever getting established ashore but for their complete supremacy in the air. They owed much to the support from naval gunfire, but the decisive factor was the paralysing effect of the Allied air forces, directed by Air Chief Marshal Tedder, Eisenhower's deputy as Supreme Commander. By smashing most of the bridges over the Seine on the east and over the Loire on the south, they turned the Normandy battle-zone into a strategical isolation-zone. The German reserves had to make long detours, and were so constantly harried on the march, that they suffered endless delays and only arrived in driblets.

But almost as much was owed to a conflict of ideas on the German side – between Hitler and his generals, and among the generals themselves.

Initially, the Germans' main handicap was that they had 3,000 miles of coastline to cover – from Holland round the shores of France to the Italian mountain frontier. Of their fifty-eight divisions, half were of a static type, and anchored to sectors of that long coastline. But the other half were field divisions, and of these the ten panzer divisions were highly mobile. That provided the enemy with the possibility of concentrating an overwhelming superiority to throw the invaders back into the sea before they became established and grew too strong for eviction.

On D-Day the one panzer division that was in Normandy, and near the stretch where the Allies landed, succeeded in frustrating Montgomery's hope of capturing the key-point of Caen that day. Part of it actually pierced the British front and drove through to the beach, but the thrust was too small to have a wide effect.

If even the three panzer divisions, out of ten, that were on the scene by the fourth day had been at hand and able to intervene on D-Day the Allied footholds could have been dislodged before they were joined up and consolidated. But any such strong and prompt counterstroke was frustrated by discord in the German Command, both about the probable site of the invasion and the method of meeting it.

Before the event, Hitler's intuition proved better than his generals' calculation in gauging where the Allies would land. After the landing, however, his continual interference and rigid control deprived them of the chance of retrieving the situation, and eventually led to disaster.

Field-Marshal von Rundstedt, the Commander-in-Chief in the West, thought the invasion would come across the narrower part of the Channel, between Calais and Dieppe. His view was based on a conviction that this course was the more correct strategy for the Allies to follow. But it was fostered by a lack of information. Nothing important leaked out from the tight-lipped island where the invasion armies were assembling.

Rundstedt's Chief of Staff, General Blumentritt, later related in interrogation how badly baffled was the German Intelligence:

> Very little reliable news came out of England. [Intelligence] gave us reports of where, broadly, the British and American forces were assembling in Southern England – there were a small number of German agents in England, who reported by wireless transmitting sets what they observed.* But they found out very little beyond that ... nothing we learnt gave us a definite clue where the invasion was actually coming.†

Hitler, however, had a 'hunch' about Normandy. From March onward he sent his generals repeated warnings about the possibility of a landing between Caen and Cherbourg. How did he arrive at that conclusion, which proved correct? General Warlimont, who was on his staff, said that it was inspired by the general lay-out of the troops in England – with the Americans in the south-west – along with his belief that the Allies would seek to capture a big port as early as possible, and that Cherbourg was the most likely for their purpose. His conclusion was strengthened by observers' reports of a big invasion exercise in

* There is virtually no evidence to support this – B.H.L.H.
† Liddell Hart: *The Other Side of the Hill*, pp 391–2.

Devon where the troops disembarked on a stretch of flat and open coastline similar to the intended area in Normandy.

Rommel, who was in executive charge of the forces on the Channel coast, came round to the same view as Hitler. In the last few months he made feverish efforts to hasten the construction of underwater obstacles, bomb-proof bunkers, and minefields, and by June they were much denser than they had been in the spring. But, fortunately for the Allies, he had neither the time nor the resources to develop the defences in Normandy to the state he desired, or even to the state of those east of the Seine.

Rommel also found himself in disagreement with Rundstedt over the method of meeting an invasion. Rundstedt relied on a plan of delivering a powerful counteroffensive to crush the Allies after they had landed. Rommel considered that this would be too late, in face of the Allies' domination of the air and their capacity to delay the German reserves in concentrating for such a counteroffensive.

He felt that the best chance lay in defeating the invaders on the coast, before they were properly ashore. Rommel's staff said that 'he was deeply influenced by the memory of how in Africa he had been nailed down for days on end by an air force not nearly so strong as that he now had to face'.

The actual plan became a compromise between these different ideas – and 'fell between two stools'. Worse still, Hitler insisted on trying to control the battle from remote Berchtesgaden, and kept a tight hand on the use of the reserves.

There was only one panzer division at Rommel's disposal in Normandy, and he had brought this close up behind Caen. So it was able to check the British there on D-Day. He had begged in vain for a second one to place near St Lô – where it would have been close to the beaches where the Americans landed.

On D-Day precious hours were wasted in argument on the German side. The nearest available part of the general reserve was the 1st SS Panzer Corps, which lay north-west of Paris, but Rundstedt could not move it without permission from Hitler's headquarters. Blumentritt stated:

As early as 4 AM I telephoned them on behalf of Field-Marshal von Rundstedt and asked for the release of this Corps – to strengthen Rommel's punch. But Jodl, speaking for Hitler, refused to do so. He doubted whether the landings in Normandy were more than a feint, and was sure that another landing was coming east of the Seine. The battle of argument went on all day until 4 PM, when this Corps was at last released for our use.*

Two other startling facts about the opening day are that Hitler himself did not hear of the landing until very late in the morning, and that Rommel was off the scene. But for these factors, action might have been more prompt and more forceful.

Hitler, like Mr Churchill, had a habit of staying up until long after midnight – a habit very exhausting to his staff, who could not sleep late but were often in a sleepy state when they dealt with affairs in the morning. Jodl, reluctant to disturb Hitler's late morning sleep, took it upon himself to resist Rundstedt's appeal for the release of the reserves.

They might have been released earlier if Rommel had not been absent from Normandy. For, unlike Rundstedt, he often telephoned Hitler direct and still had more influence with him than any other general. But Rommel had left his headquarters the day before on a trip to Germany. As the high wind and rough sea seemed to make invasion unlikely for the moment he had decided to combine a visit to Hitler, to urge the need of more panzer divisions in Normandy, with a visit to his home near Ulm for his wife's birthday. Early next morning, before he could drive on to see Hitler, a telephone call told him that the invasion had begun. He did not get back to his headquarters until the evening – by which time the invaders were well established ashore.

The commander of the army in that part of Normandy was also away – directing an exercise in Britanny. The commander of the panzer corps that lay in reserve had gone on a visit to Belgium. Another key commander is said to have been away spending the night with a girl. Eisenhower's decision to proceed with the landing despite the rough sea turned out greatly to the Allies' advantage.

A strange feature of the weeks that followed was that, although Hitler had correctly guessed the site of the invasion, once it had taken place he became obsessed with the idea that it was only a preliminary to a second and larger landing *east* of the Seine. Hence he was reluctant to let reserves be moved from that area to Normandy. This belief in a second landing was due to the Intelligence Staff's gross overestimate of the number of Allied divisions still available on the other side of the Channel. That was partly due to the British deception plan. But it was also another result of, and testimony to, the way that Britain was 'watertight' against spying.

* Liddell Hart: *The Other Side of the Hill*, p 405.

When the initial countermoves broke down, and had obviously failed to prevent the Allies' continued build-up in the bridgehead, Rundstedt and Rommel soon came to realize the hopelessness of trying to hold on to any line so far west.

Relating the sequel, Blumentritt said:

In desperation, Field-Marshal von Rundstedt begged Hitler to come to France for a talk. He and Rommel together went to meet Hitler at Soissons on June 17th, and tried to make him understand the situation … But Hitler insisted that there must be no withdrawal – 'You must stay where you are.' He would not even agree to allow us any more freedom than before in moving the forces as we thought best … As he would not modify his orders, the troops had to continue clinging on to their cracking line. There was no plan any longer. We were merely trying, without hope, to comply with Hitler's order that the line Caen–Avranches must be held at all costs.*

Hitler swept aside the field-marshals' warnings by assuring them that the new V weapon, the flying bomb, would soon have a decisive effect on the war. The field-marshals then urged that, if this weapon was so effective, it should be turned against the invasion beaches – or, if that was technically difficult, against the invasion ports in southern England. Hitler insisted that the bombardment must be concentrated on London 'so as to convert the English to peace'.

But the flying bombs did not produce the effect that Hitler had hoped, while the Allied pressure in Normandy increased. When asked one day on the telephone from Hitler's HQ: 'What shall we do?' Rundstedt retorted: 'End the war! What else can you do.' Hitler's solution was to sack Rundstedt, and replace him by Kluge, who had been on the Eastern Front.

'Field-Marshal von Kluge was a robust, aggressive type of soldier', Blumentritt remarked. 'At the start he was very cheerful and confident – like all newly appointed commanders … Within a few days he became very sober and quiet. Hitler did not like the changing tone of his reports.'†

On July 17th Rommel was badly injured when his car crashed, after being attacked on the road by Allied planes. Then, three days later, on the 20th, came the attempt to kill Hitler at his headquarters in East Prussia. The conspirators' bomb missed its chief target, but its 'shock

* Liddell Hart: *The Other Side of the Hill*, p 409.
† Ibid, p 413.

wave' had terrific repercussions on the battle in the West at the critical moment. Blumentritt recalled:

When the Gestapo investigated the conspiracy ... they found documents in which Field-Marshal von Kluge's name was mentioned, so he came under grave suspicion. Then another incident made things look worse. Shortly after General Patton's break-out from Normandy, while the decisive battle at Avranches was in progress, Field-Marshal von Kluge was out of touch with his headquarters for more than twelve hours. The reason was that he had gone up to the front, and there been trapped in a heavy artillery bombardment ... Meantime, we had been suffering 'bombardment' from the rear. For the Field-Marshal's prolonged 'absence' excited Hitler's suspicion immediately, in view of the documents that had been found ... Hitler suspected that the Field-Marshal's purpose in going right up to the front was to get in touch with the Allies and negotiate a surrender. The Field-Marshal's eventual return did not calm Hitler. From this date onward the orders which Hitler sent him were worded in a brusque and even insulting language. The Field-Marshal became very worried. He feared that he would be arrested at any moment – and at the same time realized more and more that he could not prove his loyalty by any battlefield success.

All this had a very bad effect on any chance that remained of preventing the Allies from breaking out. In the days of crisis Field-Marshal von Kluge gave only part of his attention to what was happening at the front. He was looking back over his shoulder anxiously – towards Hitler's headquarters.

He was not the only general who was in that state of worry for conspiracy in the plot against Hitler. Fear permeated and paralysed the higher commands in the weeks and months that followed.*

On July 25th the US First Army launched a fresh offensive, 'Cobra', while the recently landed Patton's Third Army was ready to follow it up. The last German reserves had been thrown in to stop the British. On the 31st the American spearhead burst through the front at Avranches. Pouring through the gap, Patton's tanks quickly flooded the open country beyond. On Hitler's orders the remnants of the panzer forces were scraped together, and used in a desperate effort to cut the bottleneck at Avranches. The effort failed – whereat Hitler caustically said: 'It only failed because Kluge didn't want to succeed.' All that

* Liddell Hart: *The Other Side of the Hill*, pp 414–15.

remained of the German armies now tried to escape from the trap in
which they had been kept by Hitler's ban on any timely withdrawal. A
large part were trapped in the 'Falaise Pocket', and the survivors had to
abandon most of their heavy arms and equipment in crossing back over
the Seine.

Kluge was then sacked. On the way home he was found dead in his
car, having swallowed a poison capsule – as his Chief of Staff explained, 'he believed he would be arrested by the Gestapo as soon as he
arrived home'.

It was not only on the German side that stormy recriminations arose
within the High Command. Fortunately those on the Allied side had no
such serious consequences on the issue or to individuals although they
left sore feelings that were of ill effect later.

The biggest 'blow-up' behind the scenes occurred over a near
break-out by the British a fortnight before the Americans actually
burst open the front at Avranches. This British blow, by the Second
Army under Dempsey, was struck on the extreme opposite flank, east of
Caen.

It was the most massive tank attack of the whole campaign, delivered
by three armoured divisions closely concentrated. They had been
stealthily assembled in the small bridgehead over the Orne, and poured
out from it on the morning of July 18th after an immense carpet of
bombs had been dropped, for two hours, by two thousand heavy and
medium bomber aircraft. The Germans on that sector were stunned,
and most of the prisoners taken were so deafened by the roar of the
explosions that they could not be interrogated until at least twenty-four
hours later.

But the defences were deeper than British Intelligence had thought.

Rommel, expecting such a blow, had hurried their deepening and
reinforcement – until, on the eve of the attack, he was himself caught
and knocked out by British aircraft, near the aptly named village of
Sainte Foy de Montgommery. Moreover the enemy had heard the massive rumble of tanks as the British armour moved eastward by night for
the attack. Dietrich, the German Corps commander, said that he was
able to hear them over four miles away, despite diverting noises, by
pressing his ear to the ground – a trick he had learned in Russia.

The brilliant opening prospect faded soon after passing through the
forward layers of the defence. The leading armoured division became
entangled amid the village strongholds behind – instead of by-passing

them. The others were delayed by traffic congestion in getting out of the narrow bridgehead, and the spearhead had come to a halt before they came on the scene. By the afternoon the great opportunity had slipped away.

This miscarriage has long been enshrouded in mystery. Eisenhower in his report spoke of it as an intended 'breakthrough', and as a 'drive ... exploiting in the direction of the Seine basin and Paris'. But all the British histories written after the war declare that it had no such far-reaching aims, and that no breakthrough on this flank was ever contemplated.

They follow Montgomery's own account, which insisted that this operation was merely 'a battle of position', designed to create a 'threat' in aid of the coming American break-out blow 'and secondly to secure ground on which major forces could be poised ready to strike out to the south and south-east, when the American break-out forces thrust eastwards to meet them'.

Eisenhower in his postwar memoirs tactfully glides over the matter by avoiding any mention of this battle, while Churchill makes only the barest reference to it.

Yet anyone behind the scenes at the time was acutely aware of the violent storm that blew up. The air chiefs were very angry, especially Tedder. The state of temper is revealed in the diary of Captain Butcher, Eisenhower's naval aide. 'Around evening Tedder called Ike and said Monty had, in effect, stopped his armor from going further. Ike was mad.' According to Butcher, Tedder next day telephoned Eisenhower from London and conveyed that the British Chiefs of Staffs were ready to sack Montgomery if requested, although this is denied by Tedder in his own account of the affair.*

It was thus natural that on Montgomery's side the immediate reaction to such complaints should have been to assert that the idea of a break-out on this flank had never been in mind. That assertion soon became an article of belief, and has since come to be accepted without question by military chroniclers. Yet it did not tally with the racy note of the code-name given to this attack – 'Operation Goodwood', after the English racecourse. Nor with the term 'broke through' that Montgomery used in his first announcement of the attack on the 18th. Moreover his remark that he was 'well satisfied with the progress made' on the first day seemed hard to reconcile with the absence of a renewed effort of similar scale on the second day. That infuriated the air chiefs, who would not have agreed to divert the heavy bomber armada to the

* Lord Tedder: *With Prejudice*, p 563.

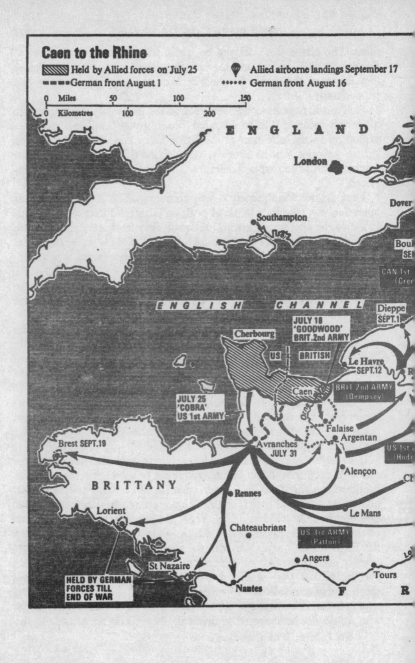

Caen to the Rhine

Held by Allied forces on July 25   Allied airborne landings September 17
===German front August 1   •••••• German front August 16

| 0 | Miles | 50 | 100 | 150 |
| 0 | Kilometres | 100 | 200 |

ENGLAND

London

Dover

Southampton

Boul
SE

CAN 1st
(Crer

ENGLISH CHANNEL

Dieppe
SEPT. 1

Cherbourg

JULY 18
'GOODWOOD'
BRIT. 2nd ARMY

US   BRITISH

Le Havre
SEPT. 12

Caen

BRIT 2nd ARMY
(Dempsey)

JULY 25
'COBRA'
US 1st ARMY

Falaise
Argentan

US 1st
(Hod

Brest SEPT. 19

Avranches
JULY 31

Alençon

BRITTANY

Rennes

Le Mans

Lorient

Châteaubriant

US 3rd ARMY
(Patton)

Angers

Tours

St Nazaire

HELD BY GERMAN
FORCES TILL
END OF WAR

Nantes

F   R

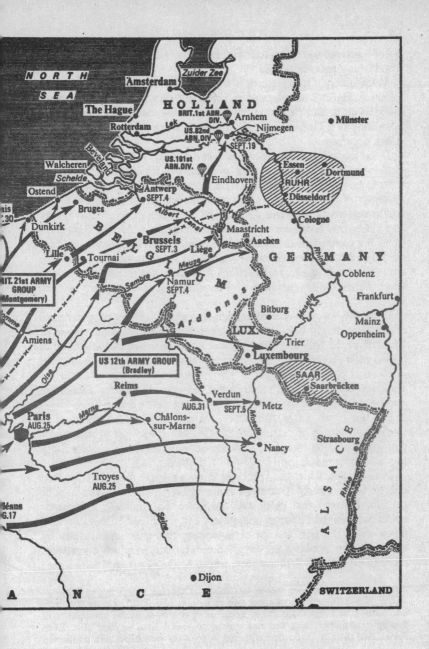

aid of a ground operation had they not believed that the aim of 'Goodwood' was a mass break-out.

Montgomery's later assertion was a half-truth, and did himself an injustice. He had not planned to break out on this flank, and was not banking on it. But he would have been foolish not to reckon with the possibility of a German collapse, under this massive blow, and exploit it if it occurred.

Dempsey, who commanded the Second Army, thought a speedy collapse was likely, and had moved up himself to the armoured corps HQ so as to be ready to exploit it: 'What I had in mind was to seize all the crossings of the Orne from Caen to Argentan' – that would establish a barricade across the German's rear, and trap them more effectively than any American break-out on the Western flank could do. Dempsey's hope of a complete breakthrough was very close to fulfilment at midday on July 18th. In view of his revelation of what he had in mind it is amusing to note the many assertions that there was no idea of trying to reach Falaise – for Argentan, his prospective goal, was nearly twice as far.

Dempsey, too, was shrewd enough to realize that the disappointment of his hopes might be turned to compensating advantage. When one of his staff urged him to protest against press criticism of the failure of 'Goodwood', he replied: 'Don't worry – it will aid our purpose, and act as the best possible cover-plan.' The American break-out on the opposite flank certainly owed much to the way that the enemy's attention had been focused on the threat of a break-out near Caen.

But the break-out at Avranches, far to the west, carried no such immediate chance of cutting off the German forces. Its prospects depended on making a very rapid sweep eastward, or on the enemy clinging onto his position until he could be trapped.

In the event, when the break-out came at Avranches, on July 31st, only a few scattered German battalions lay in the ninety-mile-wide corridor between that point and the Loire. So American spearheads could have driven eastward unopposed. But the Allied High Command threw away the best chance of exploiting this great opportunity by sticking to the outdated pre-invasion programme, in which a westward move to capture the Brittany ports was to be the next step.*

* The break-out at Avranches was made by the US 4th Armored Division under John S. Wood. I had spent two days with him shortly before the invasion and he had impressed me as being more conscious of the possibilities of a deep exploitation and the importance of speed than anyone else. Even Patton had then, in discussion with me, echoed the prevailing view at the top

The diversion to capture the Brittany ports brought no benefit. For the Germans in Brest held out until September 19th – forty-four days after Patton had prematurely announced its capture – while Lorient and St Nazaire remained in the enemy's hands until the end of the war.

Two weeks passed before the American forces pushed eastwards far enough to reach Argentan and come up level with the British left wing – which meanwhile was still held in check just beyond Caen. This caused fresh recriminations. For when Patton was told that he must not drive on northward to close the gap and bar the Germans' escape route, for fear of a collision with the British, he exclaimed on the telephone: 'Let me go on to Falaise and we'll drive the British back into the sea for another Dunkirk.'

It is evident that the German forces would have had ample time to pull back to the Seine, and form a strong defensive barrier-line there, except for Hitler's stubbornly stupid orders that there should be 'no withdrawal'. It was his folly that restored the Allies' lost opportunities and enabled them to liberate France that autumn.

The war could easily have been ended in September 1944. The bulk of the German forces in the West had been thrown into the Normandy battle, and kept there by Hitler's 'no withdrawal' orders until they collapsed – and a large part were trapped. The fragments were incapable of further resistance for the time being, and their retreat – largely on foot – was soon outstripped by the British and American mechanized columns. When the Allies approached the German border at the

---

that the Allied forces must 'go back to 1918 methods' and could not repeat the kind of deep and swift armoured drives that the Germans, especially Guderian and Rommel, had carried out in 1940.

Telling me later what happened after the break-out, Wood said: 'There was no conception of far-reaching directions for armour in the minds of our top people, nor of supplying such thrusts. I was still under the First Army, and it could not react fast enough. When it did react, its orders consisted of sending its two flank armoured divisions back, 180 degrees away from the main enemy, to engage in siege operations against Lorient and Brest. August 4th was that black day. I protested long, loud, and violently – and pushed my tank columns into Châteaubriant (without orders) and my armoured cavalry to the outskirts of Angers and along the Loire, ready to advance (east) on Chartres. I could have been there, in the enemy vitals, in two days. But no! We were forced to adhere to the original plan – with the only armour available, and ready to cut the enemy to pieces. It was one of the colossally stupid decisions of the war.'

beginning of September, after a sweeping drive from Normandy, there was no organized resistance to stop them driving on – into the heart of Germany.*

On September 3rd one spearhead of the British Second Army, the Guards Armoured Division, swept into Brussels – after a seventy-five-mile drive through Belgium from its morning starting point in northern France. Next day the 11th Armoured Division, which had raced level with it, drove on to Antwerp and captured the vast docks undamaged before the surprised German base units there had a chance to carry out any demolitions.

That same day the spearheads of the American First Army captured Namur, on the Meuse.

Four days earlier, on August 31st, the spearheads of Patton's American Third Army had crossed the Meuse at Verdun, a hundred miles to the south. Next day, patrols had pushed on unopposed to the Moselle near Metz, thirty-five miles farther east. There they were barely thirty miles from the great industrial area of the Saar on the German frontier, and less than one hundred miles from the Rhine. But the main bodies could not immediately follow up this advance to the Moselle as they had run out of petrol, and did not move up to the river until September 5th.

By that time the enemy had scraped up five weak divisions, very scantily equipped with anti-tank guns, to hold the Moselle against the six strong American divisions that were spearheading Patton's thrust.

Meanwhile the British had arrived in Antwerp – which, also, was less than one hundred miles from the Rhine at the point of entry into the Ruhr, Germany's greatest industrial area. If the Ruhr was captured Hitler could not maintain the war.

On this flank there was now an immensely wide gap – 100 miles wide – facing the British. No German forces were yet at hand to fill it. Rarely in any war has there been such an opportunity.

When the news of this emergency reached Hitler, in his far distant headquarters on the Eastern front, he put through a telephone call on the afternoon of September 4th to General Student, the chief of the parachute troops, who was in Berlin. Student was ordered to take charge of the open flank, from Antwerp to Maastricht, and form a line

---

* I explored this question immediately after the war, questioning the German generals principally concerned. General Blumentritt, who was Chief of Staff in the West, summed up the situation in a sentence, 'There were no German forces behind the Rhine, and at the end of August our front was wide open.' *The Other Side of the Hill*, p 428.

along the Albert Canal with such garrison troops as could be scraped up from Holland, while rushing there the scattered parachute troop units that were under training in various parts of Germany. These were alerted, mobilized, and entrained as quickly as possible. The newly formed units only received their arms after reaching the de-training stations, and were then immediately marched up to the battle-line. But all these parachute troops only amounted to about 18,000 men – hardly the equivalent of one Allied division.

This collection of oddments was named the 'First Parachute Army', a high-sounding title that covered a multitude of deficiencies. Policemen, sailors, convalescent sick and wounded, as well as boys of sixteen, were hauled in to help fill the thin ranks. Weapons were very short. Moreover the Albert Canal had not been prepared for defence on the northern bank; there were no fortifications, strong-points or trenches.

After the war, General Student said:

The sudden penetration of the British tank forces into Antwerp took the Führer's Headquarters utterly by surprise. At that moment we had no disposable reserves worth mentioning either on the Western Front or within our own country. I took over the command of the right wing of the western front on the Albert Canal on September 4th. At that moment I had only recruit and convalescent units and one coast-defence division from Holland. They were reinforced by a panzer detachment – of merely twenty-five tanks and self-propelled guns.*

At that time, as the captured records reveal, the Germans had barely 100 tanks available for action on the whole Western Front, against more than 2,000 in the Allies' spearheads. The Germans had only 570 serviceable aircraft to support them, whereas the British and American aircraft then operating in the West totalled over 14,000. Thus the Allies had an effective superiority of 20 to 1 in tanks and 25 to 1 in aircraft.

But just as complete victory appeared within easy reach, the Allies' onrush petered out. During the next two weeks, up to September 17th, they made very little further progress.

The British spearhead, after a pause to 'refit, refuel, and rest', resumed its advance on the 7th, and soon secured a crossing over the Albert Canal, east of Antwerp. But in the days that followed it only pushed eighteen miles farther – to the Meuse–Escaut Canal. That short

* Liddell Hart: *The Other Side of the Hill*, p 429.

stretch of swampy heath country was interspersed with small streams, and the German parachutists, fighting with desperate courage, put up a resistance out of all proportion to their slight numbers.

The First American Army came up level with the British, but pushed no deeper. The major part of it ran into the fortified belt and coal-mining area around the city of Aachen – which lies in, and obstructs, this historically famous 'gateway' into Germany. There the Americans became entangled, and bogged down, while wider opportunities slipped away. For when they reached the German frontier the eighty-mile stretch between the Aachen area and the Metz area was covered by a mere eight enemy battalions, strung out across the hilly and wooded country of the Ardennes. The Germans had most effectively used this rough stretch for their surprise armoured thrust into France in 1940. By taking what appeared to be the easier paths into Germany the Allies met greater difficulties.

That was seen in the south as well as in the north. For Patton's Third Army began to cross the Moselle as early as September 5th, yet was little farther forward two weeks later – or, indeed, two months later. It became stuck in its attack on the fortified city of Metz and nearby points – where the Germans had at the outset concentrated more than anywhere else.

By mid-September the Germans had thickened up their defence all along the front, and above all on the most northerly sector, leading to the Ruhr – where the gap had been greatest. That was the more unfortunate since Montgomery was now mounting another big thrust there, to the Rhine at Arnhem, on September 17th. In this he was planning to drop the recently formed First Allied Airborne Army to clear the path for the British Second Army.

This thrust was checked by the enemy before it reached its goal, and a large part of the British 1st Airborne Division, which had been dropped at Arnhem, was there cut off and compelled to surrender after an attempt to hold out until it was relieved which has become legendary for its gallantry. The next month was spent by the American First Army in grinding down the defences of Aachen, while Montgomery brought up the First Canadian Army to clear out the two 'pockets' of Germans – on the coast east of Bruges and in Walcheren island – which commanded the passage up the Schelde estuary to Antwerp, and had thus blocked the use of the port at the time of the Arnhem operation. Clearing these pockets proved a painfully slow process, which was not completed until early in November.

Meanwhile the German build-up along the front covering the Rhine was progressing faster than that of the Allies, despite Germany's inferiority in material resources. In mid-November a general offensive was launched by all six Allied armies on the Western Front. It brought disappointingly small gains, at heavy cost. Only in the extreme south, in Alsace, did the Allies reach the Rhine, and that was of little importance. In the north they were still left nearly thirty miles distant from the stretch of the river covering the vital area of the Ruhr. It was not gained until the spring of 1945.

The price that the Allied armies paid for the missed opportunity in early September was very heavy. Out of three-quarters of a million casualties which they suffered in liberating Western Europe, half a million were after their September check. The cost to the world was much worse – millions of men and women died by military action and in the concentration camps of the Germans with the extension of the war. Moreover, in the longer term, in September the Russian tide had not yet penetrated into Central Europe.

What were the causes of a missed opportunity so catastrophic in its consequences? The British have blamed the Americans, and the Americans have blamed the British. In the middle of August an argument had begun between them as to the course which the Allied armies should pursue after crossing the Seine.

With the swelling stream of reinforcements the Allied forces in Normandy had been divided on August 1st into two army groups, each of two armies. The 21st Army Group, under Montgomery, retained only the British and Canadians, while the Americans formed the 12th Army Group, under Omar Bradley. But Eisenhower, the Supreme Commander, arranged that Montgomery should continue in operational control and 'tactical coordination' of both army groups until Eisenhower moved his own headquarters over to the Continent and took over direct control – which he did on September 1st. The interim arrangement, hazily defined and delicate, was prompted by Eisenhower's spirit of conciliation and consideration for Montgomery's feelings, as well as his appreciation of the latter's greater experience. But the well-meaning compromise resulted in friction, as so often happens.

On August 17th Montgomery had suggested to Bradley that 'after crossing the Seine, 12th and 21st Army Groups should keep together as a solid mass of forty divisions, which would be so strong that it need fear nothing. These forces should advance *northwards*' to Antwerp and Aachen '*with their right flank on the Ardennes*'.*

The wording of this proposal tends to show that Montgomery had

* My italics – B.H.L.H.

not yet realized the extent of the enemy's collapse, or the difficulty of keeping up supplies to such a 'solid mass' – unless it went forward at a slow pace.

Meantime Bradley had been discussing with Patton the idea of an *eastward* thrust past the Saar to the Rhine south of Frankfurt. Bradley wanted this to be the main thrust, using both the American armies along this line. This meant reducing the northward thrust to a secondary role, and naturally did not appeal to Montgomery. Moreover, it would not lead directly to the Ruhr.

Eisenhower was now in the uncomfortable position of being the rope in a tug of war between his chief executives. On August 22nd he considered the differing proposals and next day had a discussion with Montgomery, who urged the importance of concentrating 'on one thrust' and devoting the bulk of the supplies to it. That would mean halting Patton's eastward thrust, just as it was going at top speed. Eisenhower tried to point out the political difficulties. 'The American public would never stand for it.' The British had not yet reached the Lower Seine, whereas Patton's eastward thrust was already over 100 miles beyond them, and less than 200 miles from the Rhine.

Faced with these conflicting arguments, Eisenhower sought an agreeable solution in a compromise. Montgomery's northward thrust into Belgium should be given priority for the moment, and the American First Army was to advance north along with the British to cover and aid their right flank as Montgomery required, in order to ensure the success of his advance. Meantime the bulk of the available supplies and transport should be used to maintain this northern thrust, at the expense of Patton's. But once Antwerp was gained, the Allied armies were to revert to the pre-invasion plan of advancing to the Rhine 'on a broad front both north and south of the Ardennes'.

None of Eisenhower's executives liked the compromise but their complaints were not so loud at the time as they became in later months, and years, when each felt that he had been deprived of victory in consequence of that decision. Patton called it 'the most momentous error of the war'.

On Eisenhower's orders, Patton's Third Army was restricted to 2,000 tons of supplies a day, while 5,000 tons were given to Hodges's First Army. Bradley says that Patton came 'bellowing like a bull' to his headquarters, and roared 'To hell with Hodges and Monty. We'll win your goddam war if you'll keep Third Army going.'

Unwilling to submit to the limitations of supply, Patton told his leading corps to drive on as long as it had any petrol left, 'and then get out and walk'. The advance reached the Meuse before the tanks ran dry, on August 31st. On the previous day Patton's army had received only 32,000 gallons of petrol instead of its current daily requirement of 400,000, and was told that it would not get any more until September 3rd. Meeting Eisenhower at Chartres on the 2nd, Patton burst out: 'My men can eat their belts, but my tanks have gotta have gas.'

After the capture of Antwerp on September 4th, Patton was again given an equal share in supplies with the First Army, for his eastward drive to the Rhine. But he now met much stiffer enemy resistance, and was soon checked on the Moselle. That caused him to complain all the more violently of the way he had been cut short of petrol, for the benefit of Montgomery's thrust, in the crucial last week of August. He felt that 'Ike' had put harmony before strategy and sacrificed the best chance of early victory in his desire to appease 'Monty's insatiable appetite'.

On the other hand, Montgomery regarded Eisenhower's idea of a 'broad front' advance to the Rhine as basically wrong, and was opposed to any diversion of supplies to Patton's diverging eastward thrust while the issue of his own northward thrust hung in the balance. His complaints became stronger, naturally, after his thrust to Arnhem had fallen short, and failed to fulfil his hopes. He felt that Patton's pull with Bradley, and Bradley's with Eisenhower, had been decisive in the tug of war and spoilt the prospects of his own plan.

It is easy to understand Montgomery's disapproval of any effort which made no direct contribution to his own. On the surface there is such obvious justification for his complaint about Eisenhower's decision to resume a two-prong thrust that most British commentators on the war have come to accept it as the main cause through which victory was forfeited. But in closer examination it becomes evident that the effect was relatively small.

For, in fact, Patton received an average of only 2,500 tons of supplies a day during the first half of September – a mere 500 tons more than during the days when his army was halted. That excess was a trifling amount compared with the total daily allotment to the armies engaged in the northern thrust during the crucial period, and barely enough to maintain one additional division. So we must probe deeper for the real causes of failure.

One heavy handicap came from a plan to drop large airborne forces near Tournai, on the Belgian frontier south of Brussels, to aid the northward thrust. The ground forces arrived there before the drop was due to take place, on September 3rd, and it was accordingly cancelled. But the withdrawal of air transport in preparation for it caused a six-day suspension of air supply to the advancing armies that cost them 5,000 tons of supplies. In petrol that would have been equivalent to one-and-a-half million gallons – enough to have carried two armies to the Rhine without pausing, while the enemy were still in chaos.

The responsibility for this superfluous airborne plan, so costly in effect, is not easy to determine. Curiously, both Eisenhower and Montgomery claim the parentage in their postwar accounts. Eisenhower says: 'It appeared to me that a fine chance for launching a profitable airborne attack was developing in the Brussels area, and though there was divided opinion on the wisdom of withdrawing planes from supply work ... I decided to take the chance.' But Montgomery says: 'I had plans ready for an airborne drop in the Tournai area' and refers to it as 'my idea'. In contrast Bradley says: 'I pleaded with Ike to discard the scheme and leave us the aircraft for supply ... "We'll be there before you can pull it, I warned." ' That proved true.

Another factor was that a large proportion of the supply tonnage for the northward thrust was devoted to the replenishment of ammunition that was not needed, so long as the enemy were in a state of collapse, instead of concentrating on maintaining the supply of petrol needed to keep up the pursuit and allow the enemy no chance of rallying.

A third discovery is that the flow of supplies to Montgomery's thrust was seriously reduced at the crucial time because 1,400 British-built three-ton lorries, and all the replacements for this model, were found to have faulty pistons. If these lorries could have been used, a further 800 tons of supplies could have been delivered daily to the Second Army – sufficient to maintain two more divisions.

A fourth point, of still wider significance, is the great handicap caused by the lavishness of the British and American scales of supply. The Allied planning was based on the calculation that 700 tons of supplies a day would be consumed by each division, of which about 520 tons a day would be required in the forward area. The Germans were far more economical, their scale of supply being only about 200 tons a day for a division. Yet they had to reckon with constant interference from the air, and from guerrillas – two serious complications from which the Allies were free.

The self-imposed handicap that the Allies suffered from their extravagant scale of supply was increased by the wastefulness of their troops. One glaring example was over jerricans, which were so important in refuelling. Out of 17½ million jerricans which were sent to

France since the landing, in June, only 2½ million could be traced that autumn!

Another big factor in the failure of the northern thrust was the way that the US First Army became stuck in the fortified and coal-mining web around Aachen – a strategic 'entanglement' which virtually became a vast 'internment camp', as Salonika had been for the Allies in World War I. In analysis it becomes evident that the abortiveness of the US First Army's thrust – to which nearly three-quarters of the American supply tonnage was devoted, at Patton's cost – arose from Montgomery's demand that the bulk of this army should be used north of the Ardennes to cover his right flank. The space between his own line of advance and the Ardennes was so narrow that the US First Army had little room for manoeuvre or chance of by-passing Aachen.

That badly entangled army was unable to give Montgomery any help in the next phase, too, when he launched his mid-September drive for Arnhem. But here the British also paid forfeit for an extraordinary oversight. When the 11th Armoured Division raced into Antwerp on September 4th it had captured the docks intact, but made no effort to secure the bridges over the Albert Canal, in the suburbs, and these were blown up by the time a crossing was attempted two days later – the division then being switched eastwards. The divisional commander had not thought of seizing the bridges immediately he occupied the city, and no one above had thought of giving him orders to do so. It was a multiple lapse – by four commanders, from Montgomery downwards, who were usually both vigorous and careful about important detail.

Moreover, barely twenty miles north of Antwerp is the exit from the Beveland Peninsula, a bottleneck only a few hundred yards wide. During the second and third weeks of September the remains of the German 15th Army, which had been cut off on the Channel coast, were allowed to slip away northward. They were then ferried across the mouth of the Scheldt and escaped through the Beveland bottleneck. Three of the divisions arrived in time to strengthen the enemy's desperately thin front in Holland before Montgomery launched his drive for the Rhine at Arnhem, and helped to check it.

What in the other side's view would have been the Allies' best course? When interrogated, Blumentritt endorsed Montgomery's argument for a concentrated thrust in the north to break through to the Ruhr, and thence to Berlin, saying:

He who holds northern Germany holds Germany. Such a break-through, coupled with air domination, would have torn in pieces the

weak German front and ended the war. Berlin and Prague would
have been occupied ahead of the Russians.*

Blumentritt considered that the Allied forces had been too widely and
evenly spread. He was particularly critical of the attack towards Metz:

> A direct attack on Metz was unnecessary. The Metz fortress area
> could have been masked. In contrast, a swerve northward in the
> direction of Luxembourg and Bitburg would have met with great
> success and caused the collapse of the right flank of our 1st Army
> followed by the collapse of our 7th Army. By such a flank move to
> the north the entire 7th Army could have been cut off before it could
> retreat behind the Rhine.*

General Westphal, who on September 5th replaced Blumentritt as
Chief of Staff on the Western Front, took the view that the choice of
the thrust-point was, in the circumstances, less important than a concentrated effort to drive home any thrust.

> The overall situation in the West was serious in the extreme. A heavy
> defeat anywhere along the front, which was so full of gaps that it did
> not deserve this name, might lead to a catastrophe, if the enemy were
> to exploit his opportunity skilfully. A particular source of danger was
> that not a single bridge over the Rhine had been prepared for demoli-
> tion, an omission which took weeks to repair ... Until the middle of
> October the enemy could have broken through at any point he liked
> with ease, and would then have been able to cross the Rhine and
> thrust deep into Germany almost unhindered.†

Westphal said that in September the most vulnerable part of the
whole Western Front was the Luxembourg sector, leading to the Rhine
at Coblenz. His evidence confirmed what Blumentritt had said about
the effects of a thrust in that part – the long, and thinly defended,
stretch of the Ardennes country between Metz and Aachen.

What are the main conclusions that emerge in the light that has since
been thrown on this crucial period?

Eisenhower's 'broad front' plan of advance on the Rhine, designed
before the invasion of Normandy, would have been a good way to strain
and crack the resistance of a strong and still unbeaten enemy. But it was

---

* Liddell Hart: *The Other Side of the Hill*, p. 428.
† Westphal: *The German Army in the West*, pp 172 and 174.

far less suited to the actual situation, where the enemy had already collapsed, and the issue depended on exploiting their collapse so deeply and rapidly that they would have no chance to rally. That called for a pursuit without pause.

In these circumstances, Montgomery's argument for a single and concentrated thrust was far better in principle. But it becomes evident, when the facts are explored, that the frustration of his thrust in the north was not really due to the diversion of supplies to Patton, as is commonly assumed. A much greater, and compound, handicap came from a series of impediments within his own orbit – the delay in opening up the port of Antwerp, the six-day stoppage of supply by air for a superfluous object; the excessive provision of ammunition and other supplies that subtracted from the transport available for bringing up petrol; the 1,400 defective British lorries; the 'blind-alley' employment of the US First Army on his flank; the neglect to seize the bridges over the Albert Canal before they were blown up, and the crossings manned, by the enemy.

Most fatal of all to the prospect of reaching the Rhine was the pause from September 4th to 7th after reaching Brussels and Antwerp. That is hard to reconcile with Montgomery's declared aim, in his drive from the Seine, 'to keep the enemy on the run straight through to the Rhine, and "bounce" our way across that river before the enemy succeeded in reforming a front to oppose us'. Persistent pace and pressure is the key to success in any deep penetration or pursuit, and even a day's pause may forfeit it.

But throughout the Allied forces there was a general tendency to relax after they drove into Belgium. It was fostered from the top. Eisenhower's inter-Allied Intelligence Staff told him that the Germans could not possibly produce sufficient forces to hold their frontier defence line – and also assured the press 'we'll go right through it'. Eisenhower conveyed these assurances to his subordinate commanders – even as late as September 15th he wrote to Montgomery: 'We shall soon have captured the Ruhr and the Saar and the Frankfurt area, and I would like your views as to what we should do next'. A similar optimism reigned in all quarters. Explaining the omission to seize the bridges over the Albert Canal, the commander of the spearhead corps, General Horrocks, frankly said: 'I did not anticipate at that time any serious resistance on the Albert Canal. It seemed to us that the Germans were totally disorganized.'

John North in his history of the 21st Army Group, based on official sources, has aptly summed up the situation: 'a "war is won" attitude of mind ... prevailed among all ranks.'* In consequence, there was little sense of urgency among commanders during the vital fortnight in September and a very natural inclination among the troops to abstain from pushing hard, and avoid getting killed, when everyone assumed that 'the war is over'.

The best chance of a quick finish was probably lost when the 'gas' was turned off from Patton's tanks in the last week of August, when they were 100 miles nearer to the Rhine, and its bridges, than the British.

Patton had a keener sense than anyone else on the Allied side of the key importance of persistent pace in pursuit. He was ready to exploit in any direction – indeed, on August 23rd he had proposed that his army should drive north instead of east. There was much point in his subsequent comment: 'One does not plan and then try to make circumstances fit those plans. One tries to make plans fit the circumstances. I think the difference between success and failure in high command depends upon its ability, or lack of it, to do just that.'

But the root of all the Allied troubles at this time of supreme opportunity was that none of the top planners had foreseen such a complete collapse of the enemy as occurred in August. They were not prepared, mentally or materially, to exploit it by a rapid long-range thrust.

* North: *The Achievements of 21st Army Group*, p 115.

CHAPTER THIRTY-TWO

The Liberation of Russia

The campaign on the Eastern Front in 1944 was governed by the fact that, as the Russians advanced, the front remained as wide as ever while the German forces were shrinking – with the natural result that the Russian advance continued with little check except from its own supply problem. The course of events provided the clearest possible demonstration of the decisive importance of the ratio between space and force. Moreover, the pauses in the progress were the measure of the space over which the Russian supply lines had to be brought forward.

The main campaign consisted of two great Russian spurts, on alternate wings, each followed by a long pause. The first was in midwinter and the second in midsummer. In the subsidiary campaign that developed with the extension of the southern flank, through central Europe, the pauses were shorter – a difference largely explained by the fact that there the ratio of space to the German forces was greater than in the main theatre, so that the Russian forces needed less of a build-up before tackling each of the successive German defence lines.

The winter offensive saw an opening move similar to that of the autumn, and the similar effect it produced was evidence not so much of the Germans' miscalculation as of their decreasing ability to 'make ends meet'. Early in December 1943 Koniev had developed a fresh outflanking advance to overcome the check at Krivoi Rog in his first attempt to pinch out the Dnieper bend. Striking westward from the Kremenchug bridgehead this time, instead of southward, he penetrated almost to Kirovograd, but was then again checked. But this push, and a converging one from the Cherkassy bridgehead, had absorbed a considerable proportion of the meagre German reserves. Manstein was impaled on the horns of a dilemma. Forbidden by Hitler to take the long step-back that strategy suggested, he was bound to putty up these cracks in the stretch between the Dnieper bend and Kiev, even though this diminished his chances of keeping Vatutin confined within the Kiev salient. Inside that salient the Russian forces were mounting up like a dammed up flood.

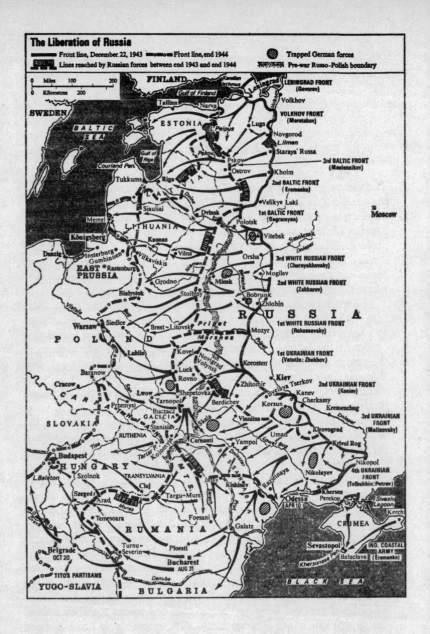

The Liberation of Russia

Front line, December 22, 1943　Front line, end 1944　Trapped German forces
AUG 29 Lines reached by Russian forces between end 1943 and end 1944　Pre-war Russo-Polish boundary

Miles 100 200
Kilometres 200

SWEDEN

FINLAND

BALTIC SEA

Gulf of Finland

Leningrad — **LENINGRAD FRONT** (Govorov)

Tallinn　Narva　Volkhov

VOLKHOV FRONT (Meretskov)

ESTONIA

L.Peipus　Luga

Pskov　Novgorod

L.Ilmen

Staraya Russa

Ostrov

3rd BALTIC FRONT (Maslennikov)

Gulf of Riga

Kholm

Courland Pen.

Tukkums

Riga

2nd BALTIC FRONT (Eremenko)

Velikye Luki

1st BALTIC FRONT (Bagramyan)

Memel

Siauliai　Dvinsk

Polotsk

LATVIA

Vitebsk

Smolensk　Moscow

Königsberg　LITHUANIA

Kaunas

Danzig　Insterburg　Vilkaviskis　Vilna

Gumbinnen

EAST PRUSSIA　Rastenburg

Grodno

Orsha

3rd WHITE RUSSIAN FRONT (Chernyakhovsky)

Mogilev

2nd WHITE RUSSIAN FRONT (Zakharov)

Bialystok　Minsk

Stolbtsy

Bobruisk

Zhlobin

R U S S I A

Warsaw　Siedlce

Brest-Litovsk

Mozyr

1st WHITE RUSSIAN FRONT (Rokossovsky)

P O L A N D

Pripet Marshes

Lublin

Kovel

1st UKRAINIAN FRONT (Vatutin; Zhukhov)

Baranow

Novgrad Volynsk

Luck　Korosten

Cracow　Rovno

Lwow　Shepetovka　Zhitomir　**Kiev**

Przemysl　Tarnopol　Berdichev　Byelaya Tserkov

2nd UKRAINIAN FRONT (Koniev)

Buczacz　Kanev

GALICIA　Korsun　Cherkassy

Kremenchug

SLOVAKIA　Stanislav

Vinnitsa

3rd UKRAINIAN FRONT (Malinovsky)

RUTHENIA　Cernauti

Kolomyja　Uman

Kirovograd

Krivoi Rog

Budapest

Szolnok

Jassy　Kishinev　Nikopol

4th UKRAINIAN FRONT (Tolbukhin; Petrov)

L.Balaton　HUNGARY

TRANSYLVANIA

Nikolayev

Szeged　Cluj　Targu-Mures

Kherson　Perekop

Sivash Lagoon

Arad　Kishinev

Temesoara

Foesani　Odessa APR 10

CRIMEA

Kerch

R U M A N I A　Galatz

Belgrade OCT 20

Turnu-Severin　Ploesti

Sevastopol

IND. COASTAL ARMY (Eremenko)

Bucharest AUG 31

Khersonesa Pen.　Balaclava

TITO'S PARTISANS

YUGO-SLAVIA　B U L G A R I A

Danube

BLACK SEA

Vatutin's new offensive started on Christmas Eve, under cover of a thick early morning fog – like almost every successful attack in the later stages of the First World War. With that help it swamped the German positions on the first day, and, once it had burst out, spread so widely as to nullify countermeasures. Within a week it had regained Zhitomir and Korosten, and at the same time extended southward to lap round the previously untouched strongholds of Berdichev and Byelaya Tserkov.

On January 3rd, 1944, Russian mobile forces, driving westward, captured the junction of Novigrad Volynsk, fifty miles beyond Korosten. Next day they crossed the prewar Polish frontier. On the southern flank Byelaya Tserkov and Berdichev were now abandoned by the Germans, who fell back towards Vinnitsa and the Bug – to cover the main lateral railway from Odessa to Warsaw. Here Manstein collected some reserves, and attempted another counterstroke, but it had little weight behind it, and Vatutin was well prepared to parry it. While it temporarily held up the Russian's advance to the Bug, a check was only imposed here at the price of leaving the way clear for their flankwise spread. From Berdichev and Zhitomir they pushed westward, by-passing a block at Shepetovka, to capture the important Polish communications-centre of Rovno on February 5th. On the same day a flanking drive captured Luck, nearly fifty miles north-west of Rovno and 100 miles beyond the Russian frontier.

More immediately damaging results were produced by the southerly spread of the flood. For here Vatutin's left wing was converging with Koniev's right wing to pinch off the German forces that had been kept, by Hitler's rule of 'no retreat', in the strip between the Russians' Kiev and Cherkassy bridgeheads. These forces, clinging to their forward position near the Dnieper, invited an encirclement that they were not permitted to evade. When the pincers closed behind them on January 28th, elements of six divisions were caught in the trap. Attempts to break through to them eventually succeeded, due to the efforts of the 3rd and 47th Panzer Corps. Of the 60,000 men in the Korsun pocket, 30,000 were extricated without their equipment and 18,000 were left as prisoners or wounded. Stemmermann, the commander of the 11th Corps, was among the killed.

The effort to release their trapped force had been at the cost of the position farther south, in the Dnieper bend. The Germans here were unable to check a stroke which Malinovsky delivered towards the baseline of their Nikopol salient. Nikopol had to be abandoned on February 8th, and although most of the garrison managed to slip away the Germans had forfeited their long lease of that important source of manganese ore. They held on to Krivoi Rog for a fortnight longer, and then evacuated it under threat of a greater encirclement.

The deep bulges which the Russians had made in the southern front, between the Pripet Marshes and the Black Sea, had extended the frontage that the Germans needed to cover, while Hitler's rigid principle had barred any timely step back to shorten the front by straightening it. The increasing toll of losses, especially in the Korsun coup, left gaps they were now powerless to cement. The price of Hitler's principle was thus a much bigger retreat than would have been required two months earlier.

Weakness and the wide spaces produced a feeling of helplessness among the German troops; this feeling was deepened not only by the size of the advancing host but by its apparent immunity from supply problems. It rolled on like a flood, or a nomadic horde. The Russians could live where any Western army would have starved, and continue advancing when any other would have been sitting down to wait for the destroyed communications to be rebuilt. German mobile forces that tried to put a brake on the advance by raiding the Russian communications rarely found any supply columns at which to strike. Their impression was epitomized by one of the boldest of the raiding commanders, Manteuffel:

> The advance of a Russian Army is something that Westerners can't imagine. Behind the tank spearheads rolls on a vast horde, largely mounted on horses. The soldier carries a sack on his back, with dry crusts of bread and raw vegetables collected on the march from the fields and villages. The horses eat the straw from the house roofs – they get very little else. The Russians are accustomed to carry on for as long as three weeks in this primitive way, when advancing.*

The chances of stemming the tide were diminished by the dismissal of Manstein, who was suffering from eye trouble. While that was the immediate reason, it was expedited by friction with Hitler, whose strategy Manstein described as making no sense, and with whom he had argued in terms that the Führer could not stomach. Henceforth the man who was regarded by German soldiers as their best strategist was left on the shelf. Although his sight was restored by an operation, he was only able to use it to follow on the map, in his aptly named place of retirement at Celle, the German Army being led blindly to the abyss.

* Liddell Hart: *The Other Side of the Hill*, p 339.

The beginning of March 1944 saw a new combined manoeuvre, of still wider sweep, in development. Attention was at first focused by a thrust, near the headwaters of the Bug, into the south-eastern corner of Galicia. This was delivered by Marshal Zhukov, who had taken command of the armies west of Kiev in place of Vatutin, when the latter was ambushed and fatally wounded by anti-Soviet partisans. Striking from Shepetovka, Zhukov's forces penetrated thirty miles in a day, and on the 7th were astride the Odessa–Warsaw lateral railway near Tarnopol. This thrust outflanked the defensive line of the Bug before the Germans could fall back to occupy it.

On the other flank of the southern front, Malinovsky was already exploiting the untenable position occupied by the Germans in the lower part of the Dnieper bend – utilizing his newly gained positions near Nikopol and Krivoi Rog to start a scissors-movement. On March 13th he captured the port of Khersen at the mouth of the Dnieper, and cornered part of the German forces in this area. Meanwhile his converging sweep from the north was approaching Nikolayev, at the mouth of the Bug – although the resistance here was so stubborn that the place was not captured until the 28th. Long before then, a more dramatic development on the central stretch, between the sectors of Zhukov and Malinovsky, overshadowed the advances achieved by both.

Masked by these two horns, Koniev had struck from the direction of Uman and reached the Bug on March 12th. Crossings were quickly secured. Losing no time, his armoured forces pressed on towards the Dniester, which in this area was only seventy miles beyond the Bug. Now that the ice was melting, the Dniester, with its fast-flowing stream and steep cliffs, looked a strong line for a stand. But there was no strength available, on the German side, for its defence. The Russian armoured forces reached its banks on the 18th and crossed the river on the heels of the retreating army – over pontoon-bridges at Yampol and neighbouring places. That easy passage was the sequel to their swift advance and their opponents' confusion. Here again, much was due to the way that the Russian armoured forces, under General Rotmistrov's direction, baffled opposition by the new tactics of moving widely deployed, thus nullifying the enemy's attempt to check them by holding keypoints on the main lines of approach.

Any risk to this deep-driven wedge was lessened by a fresh stroke of Zhukov's left wing southward from Tarnopol. This stroke was well timed in delivery, coming immediately after the Germans' counter-attacks near Tarnopol had been foiled by the Russians' quick-knit defence, and in such a way as to exploit the Germans' recoil. It was so aimed as to converge with Koniev's thrust. After a rapid advance to the line of the Dniester, Zhukov's left wing turned down the east bank, rolling up the enemy's flank, and squeezing them in as it closed in towards Koniev's right wing. Such combined and compound leverage carried both a defensive insurance and an extended offensive prospect.

While these flankwise sweeps were widening the breach, and cutting off portions of the opposing army that had started to retreat too late, the Russians were continuing the westward thrusts. Before the end of March, Koniev's spearheads had penetrated to the line of the Prut near Jassy, and Zhukov's had captured the important centres of Kolomyja and Cernauti – where they had forced the crossings of the upper Prut. This advance brought them close to the foothills of the Carpathians, the ramparts of Hungary.

In immediate reaction to this threat, the Germans occupied Hungary. It was obvious that this step was taken in order to secure the mountain-line of the Carpathians. They needed to maintain this barrier, not only to check a Russian irruption into the Central European plains, but as the pivot of any continued defence of the Balkans. The Carpathians, prolonged southward by the Transylvanian Alps, constitute a line of defence of great natural strength. Its apparent length is diminished, in strategical measurement, by the small number of the passes across it – thus facilitating economy of force. Between the Black Sea and the corner of the mountains near Focsani there is a flat stretch of 120 miles, but the eastern half of this is filled by the Danube delta and a chain of lakes, so that the 'danger area' was reduced to the sixty-mile Galatz Gap.

Early in April it looked as if the Germans would soon have to fall back on this rearward line, which was already endangered at the north-eastern corner by the wedge that Zhukov was driving between Tarnopol and Cernauti, towards the Yablonica Pass – more famous as the Tartar Pass. It seemed that Zhukov was going to repeat the torrential descent on Budapest of Sabutai who, leading Jenghiz Khan's Mongols – the forerunners of modern armoured forces – had swept through the Hungarian Plain from the Carpathians to the Danube, in March 1241, covering 180 miles in three days.

On April 1st Zhukov's spearhead reached the entrance to the Tartar Pass. The mountain-barrier is here a much lower and shallower obstacle than farther south, and the height of this pass is only 2,000 feet. Even such an easy climb can form a difficult defile if it is stubbornly defended – because the manoeuvring power of the attacker is cramped. So it proved here. The spearhead failed to penetrate, and there was not sufficient weight behind it to renew the momentum, as supplies could not keep up with such a prolonged advance.

By contrast, the Germans now benefited through having fallen back on the network of communications radiating from Lwow, while their forces had become more concentrated with the retreat into Galicia. The following week, the week before Easter, the Germans launched a stronger counterstroke than they had been able to deliver for a long time. It had a double aim – to paralyse the Russian advance, and to release the eighteen under-strength divisions of the 1st Panzer Army which had been trapped east of the Dniester between the horns of Zhukov and Koniev. This large force had then tried to find a way out to the west past Skala and Buczacz towards Lwow.

The German counterstroke was made along both banks of the Dniester. On the right it cut deeply into the 'Tartar' wedge, recapturing the junction of Delatyn on the railway from Kolomyja to the Pass. On the left it recaptured Buczacz, and opened a path through which the divisions isolated near Skala were able to withdraw. After their extrication the front in southern Poland, between the Pripet Marshes and the Carpathian Mountains, was stabilized along a line well to the east of Lwow. It remained static from April to July.

Koniev's thrust across the Prut – which formed Rumania's frontier – had also been checked just beyond the river. It did not succeed in penetrating into Jassy, which lies only ten miles west of the Prut, though a little farther north it reached the Sereth. Koniev, however, had a more important aim for the moment. His left wing had now wheeled southward down the Dniester against the rear of the enemy forces near the Black Sea – which were largely composed of Rumanian divisions. This flank move of Koniev's was closely combined with Malinovsky's more direct advance from Nikolayev westward on Odessa.

The combined threat presented a very awkward problem for Schörner, who had relieved Kleist in command of the former Army Group A (now 'Army Group South Ukraine') and for Model, who had replaced Manstein as commander of 'Army Group North Ukraine' (formerly Army Group Don and, later, Army Group South). Schörner's difficulties were increased by the poor state and paucity of the communications in his rear, for since the Russian drive to the Carpathians he was separated from the armies in Poland, and dependent on the circuitous lines running back through the Balkans and Hungary.

At the same time the Allied heavy bombers from Italy launched a series of blows at the main railway bottlenecks, beginning with attacks on Budapest, Bucharest, and Ploesti, in the first week of April. This rearward menace developed rather late for immediate effect, but it paid a deferred dividend.

On April 5th Malinovsky's troops reached the junction of Razdelnaya, closing the only unbroken rail route out of Odessa. On the 10th they occupied that great port itself. But most of the enemy forces had slipped away. They only fell back a short distance – to the line of the lower Dniester, whence the front now curved back to Jassy. For Koniev's southward thrust had been checked in the area of Kishinev.

In the first week of May, Koniev launched a heavy attack west of Jassy, down both banks of the Sereth, employing the new Josef Stalin tanks. With their aid the Russians achieved a breakthrough, but Schörner had a fairly strong panzer reserve close at hand, under Manteuffel. This succeeded in curbing the exploitation of the breakthrough, by well-judged defensive tactics, based on the natural advantages of the riposte and the skilful use of mobility to offset an advantage in armour and armament. A big tank battle, in which some five hundred tanks were engaged, ended in a Russian repulse and the renewed stabilization of the front.

That success became the Germans' undoing three months later. For it encouraged Hitler to insist on maintaining the ground they held, not only near Jassy but in the southern part of Bessarabia, between the Prut and the Dniester. It meant that the forces were kept in an exposed position a long way to the east of the Carpathian mountain-barrier and the Galatz Gap. During the interval their rear was crumbling, under pressure of the Rumanian people's desire for peace.

April also saw the liberation of the Crimea. Its occupying forces, half German and half Rumanian, had been gradually reduced by evacuation across the sea, but the attacker's problem was still a difficult one, since no large numbers were required to maintain a formidable barrier at the two narrow approaches. The capture of the Crimea called for a strong and carefully mounted attack. That was Hitler's justification for clinging to it so long after the incoming Russian tide had swept beyond it on the mainland, and in this case he had better ground than elsewhere for sacrificing a detachment, since it produced a large subtraction from the Russians' total in a critical period.

The main attack on the Crimea was launched by Tolbukhin on April 8th, after a preliminary attack designed to make the Germans disclose their battery positions. The frontal assault on the defences of the Perekop Isthmus was assisted by crossing the Sivash Lagoon on its flank, and getting astride its rear. As soon as this manoeuvre had unlocked the northern gate of the Crimea, Eremenko's troops attacked from their foothold on the eastern tip at Kerch. By the 17th these converging sweeps had reached the outskirts of Sevastopol, and taken 37,000 prisoners. The size of this bag was largely due to the German mistake, following Hitler's rigid principle, of trying to make a stand on a second line south of the Perekop Isthmus, instead of falling back immediately to Sevastopol. This enabled Tolbukhin to bring up his tanks, make a breach in an improvised defence line that was much too wide for the forces available, and overrun a large part of these before they could get back to Sevastopol.

The Russians paused to bring up heavy artillery before tackling this fortress – where the defending forces were now insufficient to fill the defences to a reasonable density. Yet Hitler still insisted that Sevastopol must be held at all costs. The assault opened on the night of May 6th, and quickly made a decisive breach on the south-east approaches, between Inkerman and Balaclava. On the 9th, Hitler belatedly reversed his order and promised ships to evacuate the garrison. On the 10th the garrison abandoned Sevastopol and fell back into the Khersonese peninsula, where nearly 30,000 surrendered on the 13th, after only a few handfuls had got away by sea. Most of the prisoners were Germans. Before the offensive opened, the German Command had chosen to evacuate the Rumanians by sea, and rely on their own troops. That policy might have prolonged the defence but for the fatal rigidity of the defensive plan.

On the other flank of the Eastern Front the Russians had also gained ground during the opening months of 1944, though not in equal measure to that in the south. At the start of the year the Germans had still closely enveloped Leningrad. Their front extended past the city to a point about sixty miles to the east, and then turned south along the Volkhov River to Lake Ilmen; on either side of that great lake they held the bastion-towns of Novgorod and Staraya Russa. In mid-January the Russians launched their long expected offensive to break the enemy's grip on Leningrad. Striking from the coast just west of the city, Govorov's forces drove a wedge into the left flank of the German salient, while Meretskov's drove a deeper one into its right flank near Novgorod. The initial penetrations produced the familiar illusion that the German forces were 'trapped', but they achieved an orderly withdrawal, by stages, to the baseline of the salient. The exaggerated anticipations tended to obscure the definite advantages which the Russians had gained by freeing Leningrad, reopening the railway from there to Moscow, and isolating Finland.

At the end of the withdrawal the Germans stood on a line running from the Gulf of Finland near Narva to Pskov. The straightening and shortening of the front much improved the Germans' situation for the moment, and all the more so because the practical reduction of the defensive front was much greater than its map-measure. For three-quarters of the 120 miles stretch between the coast and the new bastion-town of Pskov was filled by the two vast lakes of Peipus and Pskov. At the end of February a sudden stroke by Govorov captured a bridgehead over the Narva River, between the sea and Lake Peipus, but he was then blocked. South of the lakes, too, the Russian advance was held up when it reached Pskov, 120 miles behind Staraya Russa. That was a disappointment to the Red Army, which had hoped to celebrate its 26th birthday by recapturing the city where it was born in battle, against the Germans, on February 23rd, 1918.

The military results of this winter offensive in the north were less important than the political repercussions. Shaken by its sense of isolation, the Finnish Government entered into negotiations for an armistice in the middle of February. In view of the circumstances the Russian conditions were notably moderate – being based on a return to the 1940 basis and frontiers – but the Finns were apprehensive that they might be extended in practice, and asked for more explicit safeguards than the Russians were willing to insert. The Finns also protested that they were not capable of fulfilling the demand that they should disarm German forces in the North of Finland, and were fearful of allowing the Russian forces to march in for the purpose. But although the discussions were broken off in March, it was clearly no more than a postponed decision. Moreover, the Finnish lead in these open negotiations for peace encouraged Germany's other satellites to begin similar approaches in a more covert way. Such a move on the Rumanians' part was stimulated by Stalin's statement that he favoured the idea of restoring Transylvania to Rumania.

Thus the stabilization of the Eastern Front which the Germans achieved in May brought only a superficial improvement of their situation. The attrition of their strength had gone so far that they could benefit little by gaining time, whereas the Russians needed time to mount their next great offensive effort, and negotiators needed time for the completion of their peace efforts. Only an autocrat can change sides overnight. Meanwhile the pressure for peace, as well as the strain upon the enemy's communications, was increased by the progressive extension of Allied bombing attacks in the Balkans. On June 2nd the development of a shuttle-service was inaugurated when American Flying Fortresses landed at newly prepared bases in Russian territory to refuel and re-munition before delivering a second blow on their way back to their own Mediterranean bases. A similar shuttle-service between air bases in England and Russia began on the 21st, the American bombers being escorted the whole way by long-range fighters.

On June 10th the earlier Russian air pressure on the hesitant Finns was reinforced by a land drive through the Karelian isthmus – between Lake Ladoga and the Gulf of Finland. After breaking through successive positions, Marshal Govorov's forces captured Viipuri on the 20th, thus gaining the outlet from the isthmus. Thereupon the Finns offered to accept the Russian terms for an armistice which they had earlier rejected. But Stalin now demanded a symbolical act of capitulation, and at this the Finns baulked. In the meantime Ribbentrop hurried to Helsinki, where he played on the Finns' fears while promising them German reinforcements. His mission was helped by the fact that the Russian advance lost impetus as it stretched farther and entered the lakeland belt behind the 1940 frontier. So the Russo-Finnish war had a further extension, though in a quiescent form. The immediate outcome was that the American Government now broke off relations with Finland, which it had so long maintained, while the Germans continued and increased their commitment there, at a moment when their own front was in desperate need of reserves.

The Russians had reason to be content with this small profit. Their own summer offensive against the Germans was launched on June 23rd – by which time the Anglo-American invasion of Normandy was well established. This, together with the Allied advance beyond Rome, ensured that the Germans were hard-pressed everywhere before the Russians struck. The Russians however profited most of all from Hitler's continued insistence on rigid, instead of elastic, defence.

While Russian preparations were manifest along the whole front between the Carpathians and the Baltic, attention was focused on the sector south of the Pripet Marshes. For here the Russians were already deep into Poland, and it was natural to expect a renewal of their spring drive, which had carried them close to Lwow and momentarily into Kovel. Three months' pause had enabled Zhukov to repair the rail communications behind his vast bulge.

The Russians chose, however, to open their offensive from the most backward 'echelon' of their front – as the German Command had done in 1942. They struck in White Russia, north of the Pripet Marshes –

where the enemy still had a large foothold on their soil.

Their choice was well-calculated. As the northern sector was the least advanced, the Russian communications there were best developed to provide initial momentum for the attack. As this sector had proved so tough in 1943 the German Command would be unlikely to reinforce it at the expense of the more vital, and obviously precarious, position between Kovel and the Carpathians. Although the main stretch of the northerly sector had withstood all attacks during the previous autumn and winter, the Russians had succeeded in driving two wedges into its flanks, near Vitebsk and Zhlobin respectively. These promised them a valuable leverage for a renewed effort. Moreover, once they could get the enemy on the run, a wider leverage on his rear could be developed from their own southern bulge, near Kovel. For here they lay at the western end of the marshland belt that divided the German armies.

Prior to the offensive, the stretch between the Baltic and the Pripet Marshes was reorganized and reinforced. It now held seven handy-sized army groups, or 'fronts'. Govorov's 'Leningrad front' was on the right, and next the '3rd Baltic front' under Maslennikov and the '2nd Baltic front' under Eremenko. These were inactive for the moment. The four which carried out the offensive were, from north to south, the '1st Baltic' under Bagramyan, who had earlier driven in the wedge north of Vitebsk; the '3rd White Russian' under Chernyakhovsky, who at thirty-six was the youngest of all the higher commanders; the '2nd White Russian', under Zakharov; and the '1st White Russian', under Rokossovsky, who had driven in the wedge near Zhlobin. These four groups comprised some 166 divisions.

The weight of the Russian offensive fell on the Germans' Army Group Centre, now commanded by Busch, who had filled Kluge's place when the latter was badly injured in a motor crash. Although the Russian offensive during the winter had failed to break down the defence of the sector, Busch and his principal subordinates knew how narrow the margin had been, and were uneasy about their chances of resisting a renewal of the shock when summer came, with conditions more favourable to the attacker. In anticipation of the blow, they wished to withdraw to the historic line of the Beresina, ninety miles behind their existing front. Such a timely step-back would have thrown the Russian offensive out of gear. But it ran contrary to Hitler's principle, and he would not listen to the arguments for it.

Tippelskirch, who had succeeded Heinrici as commander of the 4th Army, succeeded in damping the shock by a veiled withdrawal of short measure, from his forward positions to the line of the upper Dnieper.

But the benefit was nullified by the way that the Russian plan concentrated on exploiting the wedges on either flank.

On the northern flank, Vitebsk was pinched off by converging thrusts, delivered by Bagramyan's forces between Polotsk and Vitebsk, and by Chernyakhovsky's between Vitebsk and Orsha. Vitebsk fell on the fourth day, and a great gap was made in the front of the 3rd Panzer Army. This opened the way for a southward drive that cut the Moscow–Minsk highway, and threatened the rear of the German 4th Army, which had resisted Zakharov's frontal pressure. Its danger was increased by Rokossovsky's thrust on the other flank, just north of the Pripet Marshes, against the German 9th Army. Breaking through near Zhlobin, which also fell on the fourth day, he crossed the Beresina and by-passed the potential blocking position at Bobruisk. On July 2nd his mobile forces reached Stolbtsy, forty miles west of the still greater communication centre of Minsk, thus cutting both the railway and highway to Warsaw.

Space, exploited by the Russians' increased manoeuvring power, baffled all German attempts to put a check on this sweeping advance which had covered 150 miles in a week since the breakthrough. The value of American supplies to Russia was marked in the way that large numbers of motorized infantry followed on the heels of the tanks, closely backing them up. Meanwhile Chernyakhovsky's forces were converging on Minsk from the north-east, while also threatening the route to Vilna. Between the two horns a reserve force of tanks under Rotmistrov swept down the Moscow–Minsk highway, and drove into Minsk on the 3rd, after covering nearly eighty miles in the last two days.

This great pincer-manoeuvre bore a striking resemblance to the one which the Germans had executed three years earlier, in the opposite direction. As in that case, only a proportion of the enveloped forces succeeded in slipping out of the trap. In the first week nearly 30,000 prisoners were taken in the northerly breakthrough and 24,000 in the southerly. About 100,000 troops were encircled at Minsk, and although the main route back through Minsk had been closed, part of Tippelskirch's 4th Army was extricated by diverting it southward to secondary roads whose use, as supply routes, had been abandoned for some time past owing to the harassing activity of the Russian partisans. Army Group Centre was virtually destroyed and the total loss exceeded 200,000 men.

West of Minsk the retreating Germans made a momentary stand, but no naturally strong line was available, and their reduced forces were inadequate to cover the space, which became wider as the Russian bulge

grew deeper. The Russians could always find room to penetrate between and by-pass the towns to which the enemy clung. Their advance
appeared like a semi-circle of radiating spearpoints – thrusting towards
Dvinsk, Vilna, Grodno, Bialystok, and Brest-Litovsk respectively.
Vilna was entered on the 9th, and fell on the 13th, after the Russian
mobile forces had driven past it on either side. That same day another
spear-point reached Grodno.

By the middle of July the Red Army had not only swept the Germans out of White Russia but overrun half of north-eastern Poland. Its
most westerly forces were deep into Lithuania and not far short of the
East Prussian frontier. Here they were nearly two hundred miles beyond the flank of the German Army Group North, under Friessner,
which was still covering the front gates into the Baltic states. Bagramyan's spear-points, now approaching Dvinsk, were closer to the German
base at Riga than was Friessner's front. Chernyakhovsky, who reached
the Niemen beyond Vilna, was almost as close to the Baltic – along a
line that was much farther west. Thus it looked as if a double barrier
would be established across Friessner's rear before he could retreat.
The difficulties of his situation were increased by an extension of
the Russian offensive northward to the Pskov sector – where the
'3rd Baltic front' under Maslennikov attacked in conjunction with
Eremenko's.

At the same time the strain on the German forces as a whole was
multiplied by a still bigger development. For on July 14th the Russians
launched their long-expected offensive south of the Pripet Marshes,
between Tarnopol and Kovel. It was a two-horned thrust. The right
horn pushed across the Bug towards Lublin and the Vistula – converging with Rokossovsky's drive north of the marshes, which was now
swerving round the southern side of Brest-Litovsk. The left horn drove
through the enemy's front near Luck, and outflanked Lwow from the
north.

This famous city fell to Koniev's forces on July 27th, by which time
his spearheads were already over the river San, seventy miles west of
Lwow. The vastness of Russia's offensive effort was dramatically sig-
nalized by the capture on the same day of Stanislav, in the Carpathian
foothills; Bialystok in northern Poland; Dvinsk, in Latvia; and Siauliai
junction on the railway back from Riga to East Prussia. This last
stroke, the result of a dash by one of Bagramyan's armoured columns,
threatened to seal the fate of the German forces in the north.

Yet even this coup was overshadowed by the deep advance in the
centre, and the danger it carried. For three days earlier, on the 24th,

Rokossovsky's left wing had swept into Lublin, only thirty miles from the Vistula and 100 miles south-east of Warsaw. In that stroke he had exploited the way the German armies were divided by the Pripet, and the confusion caused by the near offensive south of it. On the 26th several of Rokossovsky's mobile columns reached the Vistula, while others were wheeling north towards Warsaw. Next day the Germans abandoned Brest-Litovsk, while that same day one of the Russian columns that had by-passed it reached Siedlce, fifty miles west of it, and barely forty miles from Warsaw.

At Siedlce the Germans imposed a momentary check on the advance. On the Vistula, too, there were signs of stiffening resistance, for although Rokossovsky's troops secured five crossings on the night of the 29th, four were eliminated on the following morning.

But on July 31st the Germans were forced back from Siedlce by outflanking pressure, while one of Rokossovsky's columns reached the outskirts of Praga, the suburb of Warsaw that lies on the east bank of the Vistula. Next morning the German troops began to retreat across the bridges into the city; and the Polish 'underground' leaders were encouraged to give the signal for a rising.

That day also saw striking developments near the Baltic. On Bagramyan's front an armoured column under General Obukhov captured Tukkums junction on the Gulf of Riga, after a fifty mile night advance, and thereby cut the escape-corridor of the Germans' Army Group North. Chernyakhovsky occupied Kaunas, the Lithuanian capital, while his advanced forces, which had pushed ahead, arrived close to the East Prussian frontier at the approach to the Insterburg Gap. On August 2nd Koniev's forces established a fresh and large bridgehead over the Vistula 130 miles south of Warsaw, near Baranow, above the point where the San flows into the Vistula.

It was a moment of universal crisis for the Germans. In the West their front in Normandy was collapsing, and Patton's tanks were pouring through the Avranches breach. Behind the fronts there had been a political earthquake, and its tremors were spreading outwards. For the concerted attempt to kill Hitler, and overthrow the Nazi regime, had taken place on the 20th, and a number of generals were implicated in the plot that had then miscarried. Initial uncertainty as to the outcome, and subsequent fear of retribution, had produced a paralysing confusion in many of the military headquarters.

After the bomb had burst in Hitler's headquarters at Rastenburg, in East Prussia, telegrams had been sent out from there to members of the conspiracy at the various Army Group Headquarters, telling them that

Hitler had been killed. The contradictory report that was broadcast by the German radio service raised doubt of the first message, but naturally resulted in perplexity as to the truth. Moreover, the conspirators' telegram to Friessner's headquarters was accompanied by explicit instructions that the forces in the north were to retreat without delay, and avoid any risk of a second 'Stalingrad'. There, as in the West, the events of July 20th had important repercussions.

But the effect was least in Army Group Centre. That was largely due to its new commander, Model, who had replaced Busch almost immediately after the original breakthrough – when Busch broke down under the combined pressure of the Russians in front and Hitler behind. Model had been merely a divisional commander in the 1941 invasion of Russia, and now at fifty-four was nearly a decade younger than most of the German higher commanders. In his rapid rise he had maintained the same driving energy and ruthlessness that he had shown in handling a panzer division. He was also one of the few generals who dared to argue with Hitler, and the latter preferred his roughness to the caustic manner of Manstein, thus being more ready to allow him a free hand. Profiting by Hitler's unusual tolerance, Model acted on his own judgement in pulling out from awkward positions, and frequently disregarded the instructions he received. It was this insubordinate initiative, even more than the skill shown in conducting the retreat, which accounted for his achievement in extricating the imperilled armies. At the same time, his position and Hitler's way of accepting his decisions naturally heightened his sense of loyalty under his oath to Hitler. After July 20th Model was the first of the military leaders to denounce the plot and proclaim the Army's continued fidelity. Hitler's faith in him was still better justified by the military events that followed.

For a remarkable German rally was seen at the beginning of August, and the Russian entry into Warsaw was deferred until the following year. By nightfall on the 1st most of the city was in the hands of its own people. But just as they were expecting the Russians to cross the river, and come to their help, they heard the sound of the guns fading away, and were left to nurse their perplexity in an ominous silence. Then on the 10th that silence was shattered by a massed bombardment from the air and the ground, inaugurating the Germans' bid to regain control. Inside the city, the Polish underground forces under General Bor fought on stubbornly, but they were soon isolated in three small areas, and no aid reached them from the other side of the river.

It was natural that they should have felt that the Russians had deliberately stood back. It was understandable, too, that the Soviet Government was not keen to see the Poles take the lead in freeing their capital from the Germans, and thus be inspired to adopt a more independent attitude. But although it is difficult to unravel the skeins of this controversy, the much wider extent of the Russian check at this time indicates that military factors could well have been more decisive than political considerations.*

In front of Warsaw the most upsetting factor was the intervention of three fairly strong SS panzer divisions, which had only arrived on July 29th – two from the southern front and one from Italy. The counterstroke which they delivered from the northern flank drove a wedge into the Russians' salient position, forcing a withdrawal. At the same time an attempted Russian advance from the bridgeheads over the Vistula was brought to a halt with the aid of some reinforcements from Germany. By the end of the first week of August the Russians were held up everywhere except for some diminishing progress in the Carpathian foothills and in Lithuania. The wave had spent its force long before it stopped. The later stages of that racing advance had been carried on by wavelets of mobile troops, and Model's scanty reserves sufficed to stop them once he had reached suitable ground for a stand. After advancing up to 450 miles in five weeks – much the longest and fastest advance they had yet achieved – the Russians were suffering the natural consequences of overstretching their communications, and had to bow to that strategic law. They were to stay on the Vistula for nearly six months before they were ready to mount another massive drive.

The second week of August was marked by stiff fighting at many points, with the Germans counterattacking vigorously and the Russians seeking fresh openings, but neither side gained an appreciable advantage. The Vistula front became stabilized. On the East Prussian frontier the Russian advance towards the Insterburg Gap was checked by Manteuffel's panzer division, just brought back from the Rumanian front, which pushed the Russians back from the road-centre of Vilkaviskis. Stalemate set in along that lake- and swamp-filled frontier. Manteuffel was then sent north, and in the later part of August drove through from Tauroggen to Tukkums on the Gulf of Riga, reopening the line of retreat for Army Group North.

The results achieved by such a small armoured force strikingly illu-

---

* Nevertheless, Russia's refusal to allow American bombers from Western Europe to land on Soviet airfields after dropping supplies to the Poles in Warsaw has never been satisfactorily explained. British and Polish pilots flew from Italy and back on such missions, but at such extreme range their efforts, courageous though they were, could hardly affect the issue.

strated the fluid nature of the situation, and the extent to which the difficulties of supply limited the Russians' capacity to consolidate their gains. In such conditions packets of armour weighed far more heavily than masses of infantry, and the course of the campaign was determined by the capacity of either side to produce such packets at the critical points. The story of David and Goliath was repeated many times in its modern form.

The reprieve which the Germans obtained by stabilizing the situation on the main front, between the Carpathians and the Baltic, was offset by the development of a wider threat, along a more indirect line of approach. This was inaugurated by a Russian offensive on the Rumanian front, following political moves which had helped to clear the way for the advance.

On August 20th the troops of the '2nd Ukrainian front' (now Malinovsky) struck south from Jassy down both sides of the Sereth, in the direction of Galatz. It was a threat to the flank and rear of the large salient that still projected into southern Bessarabia. The '3rd Ukrainian front' (now Tolbukhin) attacked it more directly, advancing westwards from the lower Dniester. At the opening they met stiff opposition, and the enemy only gave ground slowly, but the pace soon quickened.

On the 23rd the Rumanian radio announced that Rumania was at peace with the Allies and at war with Germany. Marshal Antonescu had been arrested, and his successor had accepted Russia's terms, involving an immediate change of sides.

Profiting by the general confusion, the Russians swept into Galatz on the 27th, occupied the great Ploesti oilfields on the 30th, and entered Bucharest the next day. The tanks had covered 250 miles in twelve days' driving. In the next six days they covered nearly 200 miles more to reach the Yugo-Slav frontier, at Turnu-Severin on the Danube. A large part of the German forces were trapped in the Bessarabian salient or overrun on the march. The whole of the German 6th Army, totalling twenty divisions, was lost. The defeat was as disastrous in that respect as Stalingrad.

Rumania's capitulation had spurred the Bulgarian Government to sue for peace with Britain and America. For although it had abstained from joining the invasion of Russia, it had reason to be uneasy about the Russians' view of its neutrality. That fear was well justified. Bulgaria's readiness to submit to the Western Allies did not satisfy the Soviet Government, which promptly declared war on Bulgaria, and followed this up with an immediate invasion from the east and north. The invasion was merely a parade, for the Bulgarian Government ordered that no resistance should be offered, and expedited its own declaration of war against Germany.

The way was clear for the Red Army to exploit the widest open flank that had ever been known in modern war. The turning manoeuvre was mainly a problem of logistics, governed by the factors of movement and supply, rather than the enemy's opposition. More than 100,000 Germans had been taken prisoner in the Rumanian trap, and the possibility of filling their place was nullified by the desperate situation in the West, where by the end of September over half a million had been captured on the various fronts.

The autumn saw the gradual development of a great wheel by the armies of the Russian left wing through the vast spaces of south-eastern and central Europe. All that the Germans could do was to put an extra brake on it by holding on to the successive communication-centres as long as possible and destroying the communications when they were compelled to fall back. Their available forces were scanty compared with the space to be covered, but fortunately for them the communications in that region were also scanty, while natural obstacles were plentiful. So the oncoming menace became a movement in slow-time, while the Germans gained time to extricate their forces in Greece and Yugo-Slavia.

They might have imposed a greater delay but for the leverage which the Russians had gained by a dash into the north-western corner of Rumania during the first weeks of confusion produced by her change of sides. Racing round the southern flank of the mountains, a mechanized force had entered this projecting stretch of Rumanian territory, occupying Temesoara (Temesvar) on September 19th and Arad on the 22nd. This carried the Russians across some of the routes north from Belgrade and close to the southern frontier of Hungary, only 100 miles from Budapest. Such a daring advance could only have been risked against an opponent who had no strength for a counterstroke to pinch off the wedge. Even as things were, it could not be exploited until larger forces had been accumulated in the wedge. That was a slower process, yet it proved quicker than the more direct advance through the mountains into Transylvania.

It was not until October 11th that the enemy were ejected from Cluj, the Transylvanian capital, which was 130 miles farther east than Arad. But by then Malinovsky had built up his strength in the wedge, advanced over the Mures into the Hungarian plain, and spread across the routes running back from Transylvania. When Cluj fell to his right wing, the leading columns of his left wing were 170 miles to the west of it, and less than sixty from Budapest. The indirect approach now paid a big dividend.

The following week a fresh leverage was created when the troops of the newly reactivated '4th Ukrainian front' under Petrov burst through the Carpathian passes from the north – on the stretch, from the Tartar Pass to the Lupkov, that was held by the 1st Hungarian Army – and descended into Ruthenia. Petrov then turned westward into Slovakia. In that week, also, the Yugo-Slav capital was liberated as a result of Tolbukhin's advance across the Danube from the southern side of the wedge, carried out in conjunction with Marshal Tito's partisans. The German garrison put up a tough fight but was finally driven out on the 20th. That it had stayed so long was surprising, but stranger still was the fact that considerable German forces had remained in Greece, obedient to Hitler's principle of no voluntary withdrawal. It was the first week of November before they quitted Greece to attempt a Xenophon-like retreat through 600 miles of wild and hostile country.

The liberation of Belgrade and the Russians' arrival in the Hungarian plain marked the completion of the first stage of the great wheel.

Having closed up to the line of the Tisa River on an eighty-mile front, from north of Szolnok to Szeged, Malinovsky launched a powerful drive direct for Budapest on October 30th. He had now assembled over sixty-four divisions, including the Rumanian. His forces had only fifty miles to go. Gradually pushing back the German and Hungarian forces, some of their columns reached the suburbs of Budapest on November 4th, but bad weather put a brake on their attempt to rush the city before the defence consolidated. Like other cities that had been stubbornly defended, Budapest proved a hard nut to crack. At the end of the month the Russians were still blocked there, and had made little progress in efforts to envelop its immediate flanks.

Petrov was also held up in his attempt to push west from Ruthenia into Slovakia and come to the aid of the Slovak partisans. The rugged nature and corridor shape of Slovakia cramped manoeuvre.

Baulked at Budapest, the Russians began a wheel within a wheel. Tolbukhin's forces, totalling some thirty-five divisions, were brought up from Yugo-Slavia, and in the last week of November they launched a wide outflanking manoeuvre from a bridgehead gained near the junction of the Danube and the Drava some 130 miles south of Budapest. By December 4th they had reached Lake Balaton, on the rear flank of the Hungarian capital. At the same time Malinovsky opened a fresh attack north of Budapest as well as a fresh assault on the city defences. But the combined effort was checked, and at the end of the year Budapest was still unconquered. Even after it was isolated by a renewed encircling attack at Christmas, it continued to hold out – until the middle of February.

At the other end of the Eastern Front, the Baltic flank, the autumn campaign had run a somewhat similar course – starting with a collapse and ending in a check. Germany's summer defeats had brought the Finns to bow to the inevitable – almost simultaneously with Rumania and Bulgaria – and early in September they accepted the Russian armistice terms. These included the provision that they were to take action against any German forces which were not out of Finland by the 15th. Following a German attempt to land on the island of Hogland, in the Gulf of Finland, the Finns announced that they were now at war with Germany.

The surrender of Finland cleared the way for a concentrated Russian offensive against the Germans' Army Group North – now commanded by Schörner, in place of Friessner. The forces of two 'fronts' – Govorov's and Maslennikov's – advanced against Schörner's front, while Eremenko's enveloped his flank, and Bagramyan's menaced his rear. It seemed hardly possible the Germans could escape from the bottom of such a deep bottle, especially as the bottleneck was so narrow. But within a week they had fallen back nearly 200 miles to reach the shelter of the Riga defences, without any large numbers being cut off; and Bagramyan's forces had not succeeded in their efforts to cut the bottleneck. Once more events had shown the difficulty of attack on narrow fronts, where the defence enjoys an adequate density.

To retrieve the opportunity, the Russian Command strongly reinforced Bagramyan's group for the purpose of striking towards the Baltic coast south of Riga – from the direction of Siauliai in central Lithuania. This fresh offensive was launched on October 5th. Profiting from the wide front, and the enemy's concentration near Riga, it reached the coast, north and south of Memel, on the 11th. Two days later Schörner abandoned Riga and fell back into Courland – the northwest 'peninsula' province of Latvia. Here, however, his isolated forces succeeded in maintaining a prolonged resistance. So, too, did the closely encircled garrison of Memel. But the Russians had a surplus of strength that could be used to invest these positions. Their problem turned on capacity of supply and space for manoeuvre.

Having cleared their Baltic flank, they now tackled East Prussia, launching a strong offensive here in the middle of October. But defence again scored against direct attack on a cramped front – where the lines of approach were canalized by lakes and marshes. The main thrust was towards the Insterburg Gap, but it was blunted in a big tank battle near Gumbinnen – the scene of the Russians' first illusory success in 1914. Other thrusts, on neighbouring sectors, also failed to penetrate far enough to disrupt the front. By the end of October the offensive petered out, and deadlock reigned.

The Germans' amazing rally in the east, and the West, and also the centre of Europe was striking proof of the combined effect of their contracted front and the attackers' extended communications – as well as of the way the Allies' 'unconditional surrender' policy had helped Hitler to stiffen the Germans' resistance. Moreover, the course of the autumn campaign showed how elastic defence, aptly applied, might spin out time until Germany's new weapons were ready. But Hitler was only prepared to take its course as confirmation of his principle of rigid defence.

Under that conviction he not only refused to allow his commanders in the West to make a timely withdrawal from their Ardennes bulge, but ordered a move to bolster up Budapest that fatally weakened his front in the East.

CHAPTER THIRTY-THREE

The Crescendo of Bombing – the Strategic Air Offensive Against Germany

The theory and doctrine of strategic air attack was developed in England at the end of the First World War and during the years following. It was partly, or even predominantly, a product of the creation on April 1st, 1918, the last year of that war, of the Royal Air Force, as an independent Service – combining the former Army and Navy air arms. The theory was espoused the more ardently by the new, third, Service because it constituted a justification for the existence, and independence, of the Royal Air Force.

Ironically, the theory soon came to be strongly supported by Major-General Hugh Trenchard, who had commanded the Army air arm, the Royal Flying Corps, in France, and in that capacity had opposed the creation of a third, independent Service. In January 1918 he was brought back from France to become the military head of the new Service, as Chief of the Air Staff. Almost immediately, he clashed with the newly appointed Secretary of State for Air, Lord Rothermere, and was replaced as Chief of the Air Staff by Major-General Sir Frederick Sykes, another air pioneer. Trenchard himself was then appointed to command the independent bombing force that had been set up in the autumn, with the aim of bombing Berlin and other targets in Germany, following the raids on London by the German Gotha bombers in 1917–18, which had an effect on the morale and thinking of British military chiefs out of proportion to the damage they caused. But even by the time of the Armistice, in November, 1918, the RAF's bomber force comprised only nine squadrons and had barely begun operations – indeed, only three of the large Handley-Page bombers designed for attacking Germany had been delivered by that time. But Trenchard had become an enthusiastic advocate of independent strategic bombing. This was made very clear when in 1919, after the war ended, he was brought back to London to reassume his post as Chief of the Air Staff, and continued in that office for the next ten years, until 1929. During the interval the theory of air strategy had been considerably developed by

Brigadier-General P. R. C. Groves, who was Sykes's right hand and Director of Flying Operations on the Air Staff.

In America, the idea was taken up ardently by Brigadier-General William Mitchell in the 1920s, but he soon ran into trouble with the older Services, and was driven out, in reaction to his enthusiastic aggressiveness. Not until many years had passed, and a new generation had come into power, did the USA become a leading airpower and exponent of strategic air attack.

A still later generation of historians has come to attribute the theory to an Italian general, Giulio Douhet, who in 1921 wrote a book about the future of air warfare. But his writings, although of interest to study in retrospect, had in Europe at least no influence at all during the formative period.*

The British Air Staff theory and doctrine is summed up in the Official History, *The Strategic Air Offensive against Germany*, written by Sir Charles Webster and Dr Noble Frankland:

> The strategic air offensive is a means of direct attack on the enemy state with the object of depriving it of the means or will to continue the war. It may, in itself, be the instrument of victory or it may be the means by which victory can be won by other forces. It differs from all previous kinds of armed attack in that it alone can be brought to bear immediately, directly and destructively against the heartland of the enemy. Its sphere of activity is, therefore, not only above, but also beyond that of armies or navies.†

Although actual experience gained by the end of the 1914–18 war had been very slight, it was this concept of strategic bombing that enabled the heads of the RAF to uphold its independence against the encroachments of the Army and Navy during the inter-war years, and

---

* I came across a French translation of Douhet's *The Command of the Air*, when on a visit to Paris in 1935, and on returning to England mentioned it to several friends on the Air Staff, but found that none of them had heard of it. Indeed, long before that time, Air Staff doctrine was far more fully developed. A translation in English of Douhet's writings appeared in America only in 1942, and in Britain in 1943. Moreover, it had made little impact in Italy. When I visited the Italian forces in 1927, by official invitation, neither Marshal Balbo, the Air Minister, nor any of the air chiefs under him at that time, even referred to Douhet's writings in conversation, although they were remarkably frank in discussion, and showed keen interest in the new ideas on air strategy that had been developed in England.

† Vol I, p 6.

the repeated efforts of their chiefs, particularly during the first postwar decade, to get it abolished as a separate Service and subordinated to them as before.

Moreover the concept was, as a natural reaction, developed by Trenchard and his devoted assistants in extreme 'pro-bomber' terms. They argued that the Air Force and its activities were absolutely different in kind, and in a different sphere, from those of the Army and Navy. While this helped to bolster the shaky independence of the Air Force, such denigration of the tactical side of the air action proved mistaken. A second argument, arising from the first, was that the best means of air defence was a bombing campaign against the heartland of the enemy – dubious even in theory, it became preposterous in view of the preponderance of air strength that Germany had attained by the late 1930s. The doctrinal intensity with which this argument was pursued led on to a conclusion that was epitomized in the phrase, too readily accepted by Stanley Baldwin when Prime Minister, 'the bomber will always get through'. That was a fallacy to which both the RAF and the USAAF adhered until their severe losses in 1943–4 forced them to recognize that command of the air is the prime prerequisite to an effective strategic bombing offensive.

Another prewar assumption was that air attacks would be made in daylight, and directed against specific military and economic targets, since any other form of bombing would be 'unproductive'. Trenchard did stress the 'morale' effects of bombing on the civil population, and night flying was practised to some extent, but in general there was a tendency in the Air Staff, shared by most of the RAF, to underrate operational difficulties.

In view of the constancy and consistency with which the strategic bombing concept was proclaimed during the inter-war years, future historians will be puzzled to find that when war came in 1939 the RAF possessed no suitable force for strategic bombing. That was not altogether due to the financial stringency and policy of economy that prevailed during the 1920s and early 1930s, but also to RAF misconceptions about the kind of force, and aircraft, needed for the purpose. Even when the obsolescent biplane types began to be replaced after 1933, there were still too many light bombers useless for strategic bombing, while the majority of the newer types – Whitleys, Hampdens, Wellingtons – were not good enough even by the standard of the period. Out of the seventeen heavy bomber squadrons available in 1939 only the six equipped with Wellingtons were reasonably effective. Moreover, the force was handicapped by a shortage of adequately trained aircrew –

largely due to prolonged concentration on light two-seater machines – as well as to a lack of navigational and bombing aids.

Trenchard, who had retired from office as Chief of the Air Staff at the end of 1929, and been elevated to the House of Lords, continued during the next decade to have a great influence in the RAF through his disciples. He, and they, also continued to put bombers first long after it was known that the Luftwaffe had attained a great superiority. The Air Staff's 'Scheme L', drawn up early in 1938, was designed to provide seventy-three bomber squadrons compared with thirty-eight fighter squadrons by the spring of 1940 – a ratio of nearly 2 to 1 (and in number of aircraft actually more). After the Munich crisis of September 1938, the Air Staff's revised 'Scheme M' increased the programme to eighty-five bomber and fifty fighter squadrons – thus raising the 1 to 2 ratio of fighters to bombers to just under 3 to 5.

Trenchard deplored this change, slight though it was, and as late as the following spring argued in the House of Lords that the 2 to 1 ratio of bombers to fighters ought to be maintained, and was the best deterrent to the Luftwaffe. Yet it was obviously chimerical – since the German bombing force was already close on double the strength of the British, while the expansion of a bombing force took much longer than that of a fighter force.

Fortunately a more realistic attitude had begun to take shape in the Air Staff. As early as 1937, Sir Thomas Inskip, the Minister for Co-ordination of Defence, had expressed his doubts, suggesting that it would be better to destroy a German bomber force over England than by bombing it on its aerodromes or in its factories. Then early in 1939 Air Vice-Marshal Richard Peck – who in the 1920s had been the young head of the 'Plans' branch and formulated many of Trenchard's bomber arguments for the Cabinet – was brought back from India, where he had been senior Air Staff Officer for three years, to become Director of Operations. He had come to revise his views in the light of the actual situation, like many of the younger men, and soon after the outbreak of war he convinced the Chief of the Air Staff, Sir Cyril Newall, that it was vital to increase the fighter scale. His arguments were reinforced by the fact that the prospects of effective air defence were now improved by the development of radar for early detection, accompanied by the advent of new and faster types of fighter, the Hurricane and the Spitfire. So in October the order was given to form eighteen more fighter squadrons for the defence of Britain. That decision, speedily implemented, proved of vital importance in turning the scales of the Battle of Britain a year later, in July–September 1940. Without it the air defence of Britain could hardly have held out against the heavy and prolonged attack of the Luftwaffe.

The revival of a more realistic view also led the Cabinet, and the Air Staff, more reluctantly, to agree that in the circumstances of 1939 Britain might be wiser not to initiate strategic bombing, if the Germans refrained – at any rate until her bomber force was much stronger and her fighter force had been built up to a better proportion.

The irony of the situation, and of the Air Staff's planning, is epitomized in the comment of the Official History:

> Since 1918 their strategy had been based on the conception that the next war could not be won without strategic bombing, but when it broke out Bomber Command was incapable of inflicting anything but insignificant damage on the enemy.*

For the reasons outlined above, the RAF abstained from anything more than very restricted action during the Polish campaign and the so-called 'phoney war' period that followed – the dropping of propaganda leaflets over Germany and occasional attacks on naval targets. Moreover the French, who feared bombing reprisals still more, were opposed to Bomber Command operating from French bases, while themselves believing – like the Germans – only in the tactical value of bombers, in cooperation with the Army. The Germans, in contrast to the British, had nursed the belief that the Gotha raids of World War I had been a failure in all respects, and had virtually abandoned the concept of strategic bombing from their planning.

Although the British Air Staff had plans for air attack on German industrial centres in the Ruhr, they were not allowed to put them into practice. That was probably fortunate, as the attacks would have been made in daylight by bombers that were slow and defenceless. Air Chief Marshal Sir Edgar Ludlow-Hewitt, the Commander-in-Chief of RAF Bomber Command from 1937 to 1940, himself thought such an operation would bring only prohibitive losses for results of questionable value. In December 1939 the Wellingtons of RAF Bomber Command suffered severe losses in daylight raids on naval targets, from German fighters directed by a primitive form of radar, without achieving effective bombing results – whereas the less efficient Whitley which had been used for leaflet raids at night suffered no losses at all in operations between mid-November and mid-March. As a consequence of this contrasting experience Bomber Command raids were confined to night-

* Vol I, p 125.

time after April 1940. That showed the fallacy of the Air Staff's pre-war view that daylight bombing would be possible without heavy loss.

Another fallacy, that a specific target could be easily found and hit, was longer in becoming evident – mainly because photographic recon-naissance of results did not become general until 1941, so that undue reliance was placed on crews' reports – which were often wildly in error, as came to be known later.

The bombers and dive-bombers of the Luftwaffe played a dominant part in the April invasion of Norway, as they already had in the Sep-tember invasion of Poland, and were still more dominant in the May invasion of the West, operating in conjunction with the panzer forces. But the RAF remained averse to cooperation with the Army, and still insistent on its doctrine of specifically strategic bombing. Thus Bomber Command had little effect – even less than was possible – on the course of these tremendously crucial campaigns. Some spasmodic attacks on the advancing German Army by the Air Component with the BEF, particularly directed against the Meuse bridges, were costly without being effective. It was not until May 15th that the War Cabinet, now headed by Winston Churchill, authorized the use of Bomber Command to attack east of the Rhine. That night ninety-nine bombers were sent to strike at oil and railway targets in the Ruhr – and this is generally dated as the start of the strategic air offensive against Germany. But Bomber Command overestimated, and long continued to overestimate, the results and effects of this and subsequent strategic bombing attacks.

Air Staff plans for the development of attacks on oil targets in Ger-many were postponed by the urgent threat of the Luftwaffe's attack on England from July onwards, and during this 'Battle of Britain' period Bomber Command was directed to strike at enemy ports, shipping, and barge concentrations, as well as at airframe and aero-engine works – to hinder and weaken German invasion prospects.

Meanwhile the German bombing of Rotterdam on May 14th, and of other cities subsequently, had begun to change the climate of opinion in Britain, and diminish repugnance to the idea of indiscriminate bomb-ing. That change of feeling was much accentuated by the bombs that were dropped by error on London on August 24th. All these cases were, actually, products of misinterpretation – if quite natural ones – as the Luftwaffe was still operating under orders to conform to the old, and longstanding, rules of bombardment, and exceptions hitherto arose from navigational mistakes. But they created a growing desire to hit back at German cities, and indiscriminately. Awareness that Bomber Command now constituted Britain's only offensive weapon in the near future, deepened both the instinct and the desire. Both were particularly evident in Mr Churchill's attitude.

The change of view and attitude in the mind of the Air Staff, however, largely came from operational factors. Their weakening both to operational reality and to Churchill's pressure was shown in their directive of October 30th, 1940, ordering that oil targets be attacked on clear nights, and cities on other nights. That embodied, quite clearly, their acceptance of the idea of indiscriminate, or 'area bombing'.

Both these aims, and views, manifested an excess of optimism. It was as nonsensical to think that Bomber Command could hit the small oil plants in Germany with the poor bombing means available in 1940, as it was to believe that the German people's morale would crack and the Nazi regime be discredited by the bombing of cities.

The gradual accumulation of factual evidence about the effect of specific raids forced the Air Staff to admit their ineffectiveness. Even in April 1941 the theoretical average error of drop was assumed to be 1,000 yards – which meant that small oil plants would usually be untouched. However, the controversy was diverted by the need to throw Bomber Command's resources against German naval bases and submarine bases during the 1941 crisis in the 'Battle of the Atlantic'. Bomber Command's reluctance to help in this sea-crisis showed a combination of shortsightedness and doctrinal rigidity.

In slow modification of, and gradual retreat from, its original position, Bomber Command attempted after July 1941 to strike at 'semi-precise' targets such as the German railway system. These, too, were replaced as targets by large industrial areas when the weather was not clear. But even this modified idea was found to be futile in practice. The Butt report of August 1941, made after careful investigation, indicated that only one-tenth of the bombers in the raids on the Ruhr even found their way to within five miles of their assigned target*, let alone the theoretical 1,000 yards. The mastery of navigation was all too clearly the prime problem of Bomber Command. Operational difficulties, combined with outside pressure, eventually forced the Air Staff to realize: 'that the only target on which the night force could inflict effective damage was a whole German town'.†

As the inaccuracy of British bombing became clearer, increasing emphasis was given by the Air Staff to the effect on the morale of the civil

* Official History, vol I, p 178.
† Ibid, p 233.

population – in a word, to terrorization. Breaking the enemy people's will to fight was becoming as important as breaking the enemy forces' means to fight.

Churchill was becoming increasingly critical of the continued optimism shown by the Air Staff, particularly in their September 2nd plan for breaking Germany with a force expanded to 4,000 bombers, and their confidence that this object could be achieved in six months. Impressed by the Butt report, and others, he pointed out that an increase in accuracy would quadruple the bombing effects, and in a more economical way. He also questioned the Air Staff optimism about German morale and defences, telling Sir Charles Portal, now Chief of the Air Staff:

It is very disputable whether bombing by itself will be a decisive factor in the present war. On the contrary, all that we have learnt since the war began shows that its effects, both physical and moral, are greatly exaggerated.*

He also emphasized, rightly, that German defences were 'very likely' to improve.

Prophetically, he remarked in a minute to Portal that 'a different picture would be presented if the enemy's Air Force were so far reduced as to enable heavy accurate daylight bombing of factories to take place'. That policy was put into practice in 1944, but not before, and then by the Americans.

Churchill's fears, and warning, as to the strengthening and improvement of the German air defence were soon fulfilled. Heavy losses were suffered by Bomber Command in November, especially in a multiple attack by 400 bombers on the 7th, when $12\frac{1}{2}$ per cent of the 169 bombers sent to raid Berlin failed to return, although losses in raids on nearer targets were less expensive.

The sum of experience since the outbreak of war had shown that the long-established concepts of the Air Staff and Bomber Command were badly in error. The results of their bombing in the first two years of the war had proved very disappointing.

The low ebb of Bomber Command lasted until March 1942. During the winter operations were mainly concentrated on the German battle-cruisers, *Scharnhorst* and *Gneisenau*, at Brest – on which some hits

* Official History, vol I, p 182.

were achieved. The initial effect of America's entry into the war in December 1941 was to reduce the prospect of receiving an increase on the small number of bombers coming from American factories. Moreover the reverses that the German armies suffered in Russia that winter, within six months of their June invasion, raised questions about the necessity or value of seeking to win the war by bombing.

The bombing campaign against Germany began to revive in mid-February, when the problem of Brest had resolved itself by the homeward 'Channel Dash' of the battle-cruisers. By this time many of the British bombers were being fitted with 'Gee' – a radio aid to navigation and target identification. A new directive to Bomber Command on February 14th, 1942, emphasized that the bombing campaign was now to 'be focused on the morale of the enemy civil population and in particular, of the industrial workers'. That was to be the 'primary object'.* Thus terrorization became without reservation the definite policy of the British Government, although still disguised in answers to Parliamentary questions.

The new directive was a recognition of operational feasibility. The prevailing thought had been expressed earlier, on July 4th, 1941, by Portal: 'The most suitable object from the economic point of view is not worth pursuing unless it is tactically attainable'.†

This directive was ready for Air Marshal A. T. (later Sir Arthur) Harris when he became Commander-in-Chief, Bomber Command, on February 22nd, 1942 – in succession to Sir Richard Peirse, who had gone out to the Far East as C-in-C of the Allied air forces there shortly after Japan's entry into the war. A forceful personality, Harris gave a stimulating lead to the crews and organization of Bomber Command, but in retrospect many of his views and decisions were shown to be mistaken.

Another support, and encouragement at a time of stress and depression, came from a memorandum which Lord Cherwell (formerly Professor F. A. Lindemann), Churchill's personal adviser on scientific matters, drew up at the end of March. His reassurance to Churchill followed close on a devastating attack early in March on the Renault factory at Billancourt, near Paris, where only 1 out of 235 bombers was lost; it was the first large experiment in using flares as guides.

Later that month came a 'successful' attack on the Baltic town of Lübeck, in which the closely packed town-centre was devastated with incendiary bombs, while in April there were four such attacks on Ros-

* Official History, vol I, p 323.
† Ibid, p 189.

tock. (Most of the damage, however, was suffered by the lovely old houses in the centre of these historic Hanseatic towns, not by the nearby factories.) These towns were in fact beyond the range of Gee, but they were easy to locate, so undue encouragement was drawn from the fact that equipped with Gee, 40 per cent of the bombers found their targets. Nevertheless, Bomber Command's losses over Lübeck were heavy, and eight raids on Essen during these two months met a stronger defence, less favourable conditions of weather, and were much less effective.

On the German side, defences were being built up quickly – with a radar system directing anti-aircraft fire and searchlights, along with a growing number of night-fighters. At the beginning of 1942, only 1 per cent of the bombers was being lost to night-fighters, but by the summer the toll had risen to $3\frac{1}{2}$ per cent – despite the increasing use of diversions and ruses.

'All these plans involved the assumption that the opposing air force could be successfully evaded at night.'* This was the basic fallacy remaining in the minds of Bomber Command, and the Air Staff. They disregarded the basic lesson of experience that a bomber, however well protected – which those of the RAF were not – is bound to be vulnerable to an aircraft designed and created to destroy it. Evasion tactics and all the technical devices produced to aid them would not for long hide, and preserve, the bombers from the ever-growing German air defence system – unless the RAF could gain command of the air.

Such an aim was foreshadowed by the so-called 'Circus' operations which were started early in 1941, and continued in 1942 – daylight penetrations of the Continental coastal area, by bombers and fighters operating in combination, with the object of drawing the Luftwaffe up into the air for Fighter Command's Spitfires to attack. These 'Circuses' had some success, but this was limited by the relatively short range of the British fighters, and when daylight operations were extended farther, losses were severe wherever strong opposition was met, even when the magnificent Lancaster bomber became available. The main effect of the 'Circus' operations was that despite setbacks, they opened the struggle for Allied air superiority along the north coast of France that was important for later invasion purposes.

In 1942 the chief new development came with the much acclaimed '1,000 bomber' raids. By these Harris sought to cut losses by concentration, and produce a greater effect. Although Bomber Command's first-line strength in May 1942 was only 416 aircraft, by using second-line and training squadrons he managed to send 1,046 bombers against

* Official History, vol I, p 350.

Cologne on the night of May 30th. In this attack, 600 acres of the city were devastated – much more than by the 1,346 sorties against Cologne in the previous nine months. The cost was a loss of forty bombers (3·8 per cent). On June 1st the whole available strength of Bomber Command, 956 aircraft, was used against the more difficult target of Essen – but cloud and haze saved that city from serious damage, while thirty-one aircraft were lost (3·2 per cent). The '1,000 bomber' force was then disbanded, but Harris continued to plan for similar raids, and on June 26th a total of 904 bombers, including 102 from Coastal Command, attacked the great port of Bremen and the Focke-Wulf aircraft factory. This time heavy cloud prevailed, and the damage inflicted was relatively slight, whereas the loss rose to nearly 5 per cent, largely among the training squadrons. No more '1,000 bomber' raids were launched until 1944.

These specially enlarged raids, by the public impression they made, certainly helped Harris in his struggle to sustain Bomber Command's claims to priority, and to obtain an authorized increase in his force to fifty operational squadrons. He was also helped by the creation in August 1942 of the Pathfinder force – which, ironically, he had opposed – and by the new navigational aids of Oboe and H2S in December and January respectively.

It is, however, evident in retrospect that the effects of British bombing were still much exaggerated and German industrial damage negligible, in view of the fact that Germany's armaments production increased about 50 per cent in 1942. Oil, which was Germany's weakest point, was scarcely touched, and her aircraft output greatly increased. Ominously, the Luftwaffe day-fighter strength in the West increased that year from 292 to 453, and the night-fighter strength from 162 to 349. By contrast, Britain's loss of bombers had risen to 1,404 in 1942.

The Casablanca Conference in January 1943 laid down the ancillary nature of strategic bombing as forerunner of a land invasion. Then the directive to the Allied Air Forces ordered: 'the progressive destruction and dislocation of the German military, industrial and economic system, and the undermining of the morale of the German people to a point where their capacity for armed resistance is fatally weakened'. This satisfied Harris (who stressed the second part of the directive) and Lieutenant-General Eaker, Commander of the 8th USAAF (who stressed the first part). While the directive laid down a general order of priority targets, it left the tactical choice to the air commanders. Thus, although the British would bomb by night and the Americans by day, the attacks were not complementary except in a general sense.

Nevertheless, the Washington Conference in May 1943 stressed the cooperation expected from (and indeed often achieved by) the two bomber forces; and it also stressed the danger, which was then becoming apparent, to them both from the German fighters. Thus the first objective of 'Point-blank' – the Combined Bombing Offensive – was to be the destruction of the Luftwaffe and the German aircraft industry, which was: 'essential to our progression to the attack of other sources of the enemy war potential'. It was as important in the long run to Bomber Command as to the Americans. Even so, it was a loosely phrased enough document which allowed Harris to continue general area bombing on the German towns, and to avoid facing reality, that the future of the bombers, and 'Operation Overlord', lay in the destruction of the Luftwaffe whose strength had doubled between January and August 1943. However, the great successes of Bomber Command in the raids on the Ruhr and Hamburg tended to obscure this danger.

Although the Pathfinder force was being gradually built up, while Oboe and H2S were now in operation, the opening months of 1943 were a quiet period for Bomber Command compared with 1942. This gave the crews a chance to correct some flaws in the new equipment, and also to acclimatize themselves to the rising number of Lancasters and Mosquitoes that were replacing the old bombers. (Operational strength in general rose from 515 in January 1943 to 947 by March 1944.) The crew problem was met by the large Commonwealth training schemes, especially in Canada, and by the abolition of the post of second pilot in 1942.

All these factors helped in the 'Battle of the Ruhr' – a series of forty-three major raids between March and July 1943, ranging from Stuttgart to Aachen, but mainly focused on the Ruhr. It opened on March 5th, when 442 planes attacked Essen – which was a strongly defended area, as it contained the Krupp works. Essen was hit much harder than before owing to the marking of targets by Pathfinders directed by Oboe, and only fourteen bombers were lost. Essen was again severely hit four times, and also most of the major centres of the Ruhr, during the months that followed. The damage was inflicted mainly by incendiaries, but also by explosive bombs as heavy as 8,000lb. Duisburg, Dortmund, Düsseldorf, Bochum, and Aachen all suffered badly, due to the new Oboe marking system, while 90 per cent of Barmen-Wuppertal was devastated in a single attack, on the night of May 29th. Although the weather often interfered, it was evident that Bomber Command's accuracy had much improved – and strengthened Harris's hand in his arguments about the use of his force.

Even so, Bomber Command was still hardly capable of precise bombing by night – with exceptions such as the breaching of the Möhne and Eder dams in the Ruhr on the night of May 16th by the specially trained 617 Squadron – the 'Dambusters' – led by Wing Commander Guy Gibson. Despite the brilliant success achieved in this 'dams' raid eight of the nineteen Lancasters used in it were lost.

In sum, as the Official History remarks, the 'revolutionary advances in the technique of bombing' demonstrated in the Battle of the Ruhr had made Bomber Command 'into an effective bludgeon but that ... had not yet enabled it to develop the potential of a rapier.'* Moreover, as Oboe was the crucial factor, the results were not promising for anything outside its range.

After the first attack on Essen losses rose rapidly, and averaged 4·7 per cent (872 planes lost) in this entire campaign. Only the high morale of the crews, and continual reinforcements, made it possible for Bomber Command 'to take' such losses, which were approaching danger level.

Significantly the Mosquitoes, whose great speed and altitude made them almost immune to German fighters and flak, suffered very few losses. Oboe would not have worked without such a high-flying aircraft (the transmission left the curvature of the earth at a tangent), and there would otherwise have been no accurate marking for the Lancaster bombers of the main force.

The introduction of Beaufighters as night-time escorts was no solution, as these aircraft were too slow. Moreover, just as the British technical advances were tending to turn night into day for Bomber Command, so did the German countermeasures for the Luftwaffe – and it looked likely that the time would soon come when bombers would be as vulnerable at night as in daylight.

The 'Battle of the Ruhr' was followed by the 'Battle of Hamburg' – a series of thirty-three major attacks on that city and others between July and November, 1943, involving 17,000 bomber sorties. It opened with the great raid on July 24th, by 791 bombers – which included 374 Lancasters. Thanks to the new navigational aids, clear weather and good marking, a vast number of incendiary and explosive bombs hit the centre of Hamburg – and thanks to a new radar-distracting device called Window only twelve bombers were lost. Moreover the 8th USAAF joined in the attack on July 24th and 26th, and Mosquitoes

* Vol II, p 136.

(which themselves could carry a bomb-load of 4,000lb.) kept the city's defences busy on those two nights. On the night of the 27th 787 British bombers renewed their devastating attack, and only seventeen were lost. On the 29th, 777 bombers hit the city again, although with less accuracy, while British losses rose to thirty-three, as the Germans began to adjust themselves to the effect of Window. Bad weather prevented the fourth attack, on August 2nd, from being as successful. In sum, however, the city suffered terrible devastation, and Bomber Command's losses, though rising each time, averaged only 2·8 per cent. Moreover, on July 25th and 30th – in the middle of the 'Battle of Hamburg' – Bomber Command had severely hit Remscheid and the Krupp works at Essen. In the following months its attacks ranged to Mannheim, Frankfurt, Hanover and Kassel, badly damaging all these cities. It also delivered, on the night of August 17th, its famous attack on the flying bomb research and experimental station at Peenemünde on the Baltic coast. This attack was carried out by 597 four-engined bombers, of which forty were lost and thirty-two others damaged, while the effects were not so great as was imagined in London.

Attacks on Berlin during this period had still less effect – owing to bad weather, inability to use Oboe at such a range, and the size of the city affecting H2S. Moreover, German night-fighters had lengthy opportunity to strike during the long flight – a round trip of 1,150 miles – and were directed by radar stations which had now mastered Window to the extent of identifying the main stream of the attack, though not the individual bombers. Of the 123 bombers lost in three raids on Berlin, about eighty fell to the night-fighters. That was a foretaste of the coming 'Battle of Berlin'.

This battle, lasting from November 1943 to March 1944, was encouraged by Churchill – as Berlin raids pleased Stalin. It involved sixteen major attacks on the German capital, while the twelve other major targets included Stuttgart, Frankfurt, and Leipzig. In all, more than 20,000 sorties were flown.

The results of this massive offensive turned out different from those predicted by 'Bomber' Harris. Germany was not brought to her knees, nor Berlin, whereas the British losses became so heavy that the campaign had to be abandoned. The loss rate rose to 5·2 per cent, while the bombing damage did not compare with that inflicted on Hamburg or Essen. The morale of Bomber Command was shaken* which was hardly surprising since 1,047 bombers were lost and a further 1,682 damaged. The presence, or absence, of German night-fighters was

* *Official History*, vol II, pp 195–6.

usually crucial – for example when they were misdirected in meeting the Munich attack of October 7th, Bomber Command lost only 1·2 per cent of the force employed. Usually, the night-fighters were promptly on the scene, and very active – gradually forcing Bomber Command to shift to targets farther south, and to use a greater part of its strength in diversionary raids. The culmination came with the catastrophic Nuremberg raid of March 30th, 1944, when ninety-four bombers were lost, and seventy-one damaged, out of 795 employed.

Already opposition to Harris's strategy had been growing, and the Air Staff were coming to recognize that the policy of selective bombing, that is to say attack upon selected industries such as oil, aircraft, and the like, was better suited to the Casablanca concept that a land invasion of northern Europe was necessary and that it could not be launched unless command of the air was definitely gained.

As the German air defences and production grew the more questioned Harris's views became. He was mainly concerned to get the Americans to join him in attacking Berlin – which was impossible for them by night, as they were untrained for such action, and by late 1943 this would have been suicidal by day. By the beginning of 1944, the Air Staff rejected his notion that he could bring Germany to her knees with Lancasters alone by April, and insisted on selective attacks against German industry, such as the Schweinfurt ball-bearings plant.

The attack of February 25th on these plants, reluctantly agreed by Harris, was probably the first true example of the Combined Bombing Offensive. The threat to the bombing offensive and to the prospects of 'Overlord' produced by the ever-growing Luftwaffe was responsible for the defeat of Harris's views, and the failure of the 'Battle of Berlin' confirmed this trend. Harris himself clearly recognized the defeat when, in April, he called for the 'provision of night-fighter support' for his bombers – as the Americans had done already in seeking long-range fighters to support their daylight operations.

The whole future of Bomber Command's massed attack upon the German cities was in doubt, and the force was fortunate that in April it was switched, as previously planned, to operations against the French railway network in aid of the coming cross-Channel invasion. That both lightened its task and helped to cover up its heavy defeat in the direct offensive against Germany. It was still luckier to find, after the 'Overlord' invasion, that the situation had decisively changed in favour of the Allies.

*   *   *

After 1942 the British strategic air offensive became part of a joint effort; it was no longer independent and unconnected as before. The scheme propounded at the Washington Conference by General H. H. Arnold, the Commanding General of the US Army Air Forces, for setting up a large bombing force in Britain was naturally pleasing to Churchill and the British Chiefs of Staff, and curbed their criticism of the American policy of daylight bombing. The Americans felt sure that if bombers were well-armed and armoured, flew high enough and close together, they could make daylight raids without suffering heavy casualties. It proved a fallacy, like the RAF's belief in evading interference by operating at night.

Early American raids in 1942 were on too small a scale to provide any clear evidence, but when bigger ones at longer range were launched in 1943, losses soon rose high. In the Bremen raid of April 17th, sixteen bombers were lost, and forty-four damaged, out of 115 employed. In the Kiel raid of June 13th, the loss was twenty-two out of the sixty-six B17 Flying Fortresses; in a raid on Hanover in July, twenty-four out of ninety-two; against Berlin on July 28th, twenty-two out of 120. The Americans tried using as escorts Thunderbolt fighters, fitted with extra fuel tanks, but their range was not good enough, and the need for more adequate escort was made still clearer in the autumn, when the series of attacks on the ball-bearings factory at Schweinfurt, to the east of Frankfurt, were made.

In the catastrophic raid of October 14th, a force of 291 Flying Fortresses set out with a strong escort of Thunderbolts, but these could not continue beyond the Aachen area, and when they withdrew the B17s were assailed by wave after wave of German fighters all the way to their target and then back as far as the Channel coast. By the time the American force got back, sixty of its bombers had been shot down, and a further 138 damaged. It was the climax of a terrible week in which the 8th Air Force had lost 148 bombers, with their crews, in four attempts to break through the German defences beyond the existing range of fighter escort. Such an extremely high rate of loss could not be sustained, and the American air chiefs were forced to realize the need for a really long-range fighter escort – a need hitherto discounted, or considered technically impossible.

Fortunately, the right instrument was at hand in the North American Company's Mustang fighter. The British had placed an order for this in 1940, while the Americans rejected it, and its performance was greatly improved by the installation of British Rolls-Royce Merlin engines. With a Packard-Merlin engine tried in the autumn of 1942 the P51B

Mustang was faster at all heights than all the German fighters of the period, and had also superior manoeuvrability. Fitted with long-range fuel tanks, it had a range of nearly 1,500 miles, and thus could give bombers escort for more than 600 miles from base – in fact, to the eastern frontier of Germany. A crash programme of Mustang production was begun after the Schweinfurt disasters, and the first lot went into action with the 8th USAAF in December 1943. By the end of the war in May, 1945, a total of 14,000 Mustangs was produced.

The winter of 1943–4 was a relatively quiet period for the 8th USAAF, as the bombers were temporarily restricted to short-range targets. In December losses were only 3.4 per cent compared with 9.1 per cent in October. The creation of the 15th USAAF to operate from Italy was a further step in the American plan to cripple the German war economy. General Carl Spaatz was appointed to command the two forces.

The early months of 1944 were marked by the ever-increasing flow of Mustangs, and an extension of their range. Moreover they were unleashed to attack the Luftwaffe wherever it could be found, rather than being tied to the bombers – with the aim of attaining an overall command of the air, not merely command of it in the immediate vicinity of the bombers. In this way they forced a fight on the German fighters, with consequent infliction of ever-increasing losses on them. By March, the German fighters showed more and more reluctance to come up and engage the Mustangs. That aggressive action not only enabled the American bombers to pursue their daylight attacks with diminishing interference, and loss, but smoothed the way for 'Overlord'.

Ironically, it also aided the pursuance of Bomber Command's nighttime offensive against Germany. Just as the Luftwaffe became masters of the air by night, it lost command of the air by day – to the Americans. When the British bomber force renewed its strategic offensive against Germany, after being diverted to aid the Normany invasion, the German night-fighter force had become very short of fuel, and also suffered from the loss of its early warning radar system in France – whereas Bomber Command had correspondingly benefited by establishing transmitter stations on the Continent.

The change is reflected in the figures of loss, which were high for Bomber Command's few raids over Germany in May 1944 – and in June rose to 11 per cent in its raids on oil targets. In consequence, about half of the British raids on Germany during August and September were made in daylight, and suffered much reduced losses. By that time, however, even night raids were becoming much cheaper – 3·7 per cent and 2·2 per cent respectively. In September Bomber Command dispatched more than three times as many aircraft on night raids as it had in June 1944, but lost only about two-thirds as many.

The introduction of long-range night-fighters for Bomber Command helped in the trend, but was never a major factor, as the aircraft used were too slow and the task proved too difficult for them. Only thirty-one German night-fighters were destroyed in the period December 1943 to April 1944, and even when more squadrons of better aircraft became available the total claimed from December 1943 to April 1945, the last seventeen months of the war, was only 257 – an average of barely fifteen a month. So neither this nor new radar and radio jamming techniques counted as much as the German loss of oil, territory, and daylight control.

In 1943, a total of 200,000 tons of bombs was dropped on Germany – nearly five times as much as in 1942. Yet German productivity rose to new heights, thanks largely to the reorganization carried out by Albert Speer, the minister put in charge of war production, while 'air raid precaution' measures and the German ability of quick recovery prevented any crisis in either morale or production. The increased output of aircraft, guns, tanks, and submarines contributed to the overall 50 per cent rise of armaments production in 1943.

The Germans were certainly worried by the mass attacks of Bomber Command, for the first time since the war began, and after the great attack on Hamburg in July 1943, Speer is reported to have said gloomily that six more city raids on that scale would bring Germany to her knees. But no such devastation and moral effect was achieved by area-bombing in the raids that followed during the second half of the year, while Speer's brilliant activities in the dispersal of industry annulled his earlier anxieties.

The American selective precision-bombing had more effect for a time, and by August reduced fighter production by some 25 per cent, but after the costly defeat inflicted on the 8th USAAF in October it rose again, and to new high levels early in 1944. While assessments of the damage inflicted had become fairly accurate, the Allies underrated the capability of German productive power, and mistakenly assumed that the evident rise in the Luftwaffe's strength was due to the transfer of aircraft from the Eastern Front.

For Bomber Command, the most significant feature of the period was a development in precision-bombing at night, confined at first to the use of 617 Squadron as a specialist 'marking force' following their dams raid, but becoming more general with improvements in the Pathfinder marking system, the new bomb-sights, and the advent of the 12,000-lb Tallboy 'earthquake' bomb – followed by that of the 22,000-lb Grand Slam.

The most important general effect of the Anglo-American bombing campaign was that it did eventually draw off an increasingly large proportion of Germany's fighter and anti-aircraft force from the Eastern Front to the Western, thus aiding the Russian advance, while also dominating the air by day to an extent that enabled 'Overlord' to go ahead with little interference from the Luftwaffe.

In the final year of the war, from April 1944 to May 1945, the Allies definitely achieved command of the air, thanks mainly to the American onslaught in February–April 1944. But the requirements of 'Overlord' were a major diversion that for several months tended to turn the Combined Bombing Offensive away from German targets to ones which would give direct help to the Allied armies, both before and after the Normandy landing.

This diversion was naturally disagreeable to Sir Arthur Harris and other single-minded bombing enthusiasts, but Sir Charles Portal and the Air Staff showed a more balanced outlook, and recognized that the bomber must play a more auxiliary role in Allied strategy. As the strategic bomber forces were needed to assist the tactical forces, the direction of all of them was placed in mid-April under Sir Arthur Tedder, who had by then been appointed Deputy Supreme Commander to General Eisenhower. Tedder had previously commanded the air forces in the Middle East, and made a great impression there. He saw that the chief immediate effect that the bombing forces could give to 'Overlord' was in paralysing the German transport network. This plan was actually agreed on March 25th, 1944, despite Churchill's worries about French civilian losses and Spaatz's preference for oil targets – a preference shared by Portal.

Spaatz's determination to concentrate on oil targets resulted in the 8th USAAF continuing the attack on Germany in the spring of 1944, while the British Bomber Command spent the months April–June mainly in attacking railway targets in France. (In June, only 8 per cent of its bombs were directed against German targets.) By June, over 65,000 tons of bombs had been cast on the enemy's transport system, together with strikes at coastal batteries, rocket-sites, and similar targets. In retrospect, it can be seen that Tedder's paralysis of the transport, or communications, system was the greatest factor in paving the way for the success of the Normandy invasion. Harris's objections, that Bomber Command was not capable of the precision needed, was disproved as early as March by the effectiveness of the attacks on the French marshalling yards.

The much criticized 'diversion' was beneficial to Bomber Command, as it not only eased the strain on it but was a stimulus to the improvement of bombing. Moreover German fighter opposition over France was much less than in the 'Battle of Berlin' and other attacks on targets in Germany.

The precision of bombing was helped by the innovation in technique developed by Wing Commander Leonard Cheshire in low-level marking of targets by Mosquitoes. First applied in France during April, target after target was destroyed without many bombs overshooting the target and killing French civilians as Churchill had feared. The average bomb error was reduced from 680 yards in March to 285 yards in May.

The success of the 'Communication' attacks before D-Day strengthened Tedder's view that such a campaign should be extended to Germany, with top priority. He felt that a collapse of the German rail system, besides disrupting troop movement – and thus being welcome to the Russians – would also mean the collapse of her economy. It would thus be an alternative to Harris's general area-bombing and to Spaatz's oil campaign. It certainly had a quicker effect on the German Army and on the Luftwaffe than general area-bombing.

The period after the cross-Channel invasion saw the bombers attacking a variety of targets. While the Americans turned mainly to oil and aircraft targets during these months, only 32,000 of the 181,000 tons of bombs dropped by Bomber Command during the period were on targets in Germany.

The trend away from area-bombing became very marked. The British Air Staff embraced the American view that oil targets should be given priority. Already in April the 15th USAAF had reached out from Italy and attacked the Ploesti oilfields in Rumania. On May 12th, the 8th USAAF from England started attacking oil targets in Germany. Although 400 German fighters came up to oppose the 935 American bombers, they were beaten off by a thousand American fighters, and lost sixty-five of their number, against an American loss of forty-six bombers.

This campaign became greater after D-Day, and in June the Air Staff, conscious of Bomber Command's developments in precision-bombing by night, ordered British attacks on oil targets. The Gelsen-kirchen raid on the night of July 9th was fairly successful, though rather costly, but the other raids were less effective because of the weather, while the losses were catastrophic – ninety-three bombers were lost, mainly to night-fighters, out of the 832 dispatched on three nights.

The American attacks continued in full force. On June 16th, over a thousand bombers escorted by nearly 800 fighters were employed, and on the 20th the bombers totalled 1,361. On the next day Berlin was attacked, while another force attacked oil plants and flew on to land in Russia. (After their cool reception there the experiment was discontinued.) American losses were heavy, but an increasing number of oil plants were disabled, with damaging effect on the Luftwaffe's fuel supply. By September this was reduced to 10,000 tons of octane – whereas a monthly minimum of 160,000 tons was needed. By July every major oil plant in Germany had been hit, and the vast number of new aircraft and tanks produced by Speer's efforts were becoming virtually useless for lack of fuel.

While the effective number of German aircraft fell, the Allied air forces grew stronger. Bomber Command's first-line strength in bombers rose from 1,023 in April to 1,513 in December, and to 1,609 in April 1945. The 8th USAAF's strength in bombers rose from 1,049 in April 1944, to 1,826 in December, and 2,085 in April 1945.

Meanwhile Bomber Command had adopted mass day bombing for the first time. Harris's suspiciousness about it was allayed by the lack of opposition it met from the Luftwaffe compared with what was met by night. The first large daylight raid was made against Le Havre in mid-June, and, like those that followed, was escorted by Spitfires. By the end of August Bomber Command was raiding the Ruhr in daylight, and still finding the opposition negligible.

These new circumstances tempted Bomber Command to resume night attacks on German oil plants. These attacks proved more effective and less costly than they had before. The very successful raid of August 29th on the distant target of Königsberg, though not itself an oil target, showed the all-round improvement.

Thus was October 1944 to May 1945 the time of domination by the bombers. Bomber Command dropped more bombs in the last three months of 1944 than during the whole of 1943. The Ruhr alone was battered by over 60,000 tons of high explosives in those months. More-over, as the Official History says, it was a time when the bombers had 'virtual operational omnipotence'.* Under the onslaught, German power of resistance was gradually ground down, and her war economy strangled.

In view of this new capacity for precision bombing, with little opposition, it is questionable whether it was wise, either operationally or morally, for Bomber Command to devote 53 per cent of its bombs in this period to town areas, compared with only 14 per cent to oil plants and 15 per cent to transportation targets. (The corresponding figures for January–May 1945 were 36·6 per cent, 26·2 per cent, and 15·4 per cent – a ratio that was still very questionable.) The ratio in the Ameri-cans' targeting was essentially different. Their idea of aiming to hit Germany's known weak points was more sensible than that of trying to ensure that every bomb hit something, and somehow weaken Germany. It also avoided the increasing moral censure that Harris's policy was to attract.

The final phase suffered overall by a failure to maintain the best priorities. A directive of September 25th, 1944, established oil as the first priority, with communications jointly heading a list of others. Here was a good chance to shorten the war, since Bomber Command was also concentrating on targets in Germany by October – dropping 51,000 tons of bombs there, and suffering losses of less than 1 per cent. Yet two-thirds of the October raids were for general area-bombing, while little was thrown on oil or communications. Thus on November 1st, 1944, the commanders were given a fresh directive setting oil as the first priority, and communications as the second; there were no others to confuse the choice. The two objectives, now relatively easy of attain-ment, would certainly tend to hasten Germany's collapse quicker than area-bombing.

Harris's obstinacy, however, prevented the plan from being properly carried out – he even threatened resignation in resistance to it.

At the beginning of 1945 the outlook became complicated by the Germans' counteroffensive in the Ardennes, the advent of their jet fighters, and Schnorkel submarines. That led to a fresh discussion of priorities. But with the various authorities pulling in different ways, the issue became a compromise – and, as with most compromises, hazy and unsatisfactory.

The most controversial aspect is the deliberate revival of 'terroriza-tion' as a prime aim. It was revived largely to please the Russians. On

* Vol III, p 183.

January 27th, 1945, Harris was given instructions to carry out such blows – which thus became second in priority to oil targets, and ahead of communications and other objectives. As a consequence, the distant city of Dresden was subjected to a devastating attack in mid-February – with the deliberate intention of wreaking havoc among the civil population and refugees – striking at the city centre, not the factories or railways.

By April, worthwhile targets were so few that both area-bombing and precise strategic bombing were abandoned in favour of direct assistance to the armies.

COMPARATIVE TARGET RESULTS IN STRATEGIC BOMBING OFFENSIVE

Even when the torrential bomb-deluge after the summer of 1944 began to reduce German production, Speer's great efforts in dispersal of plant and in improvisation did much to counter the material effects. Morale also kept up in a remarkable way, until after the Dresden attacks in February 1945.

OIL TARGET ATTACKS

Owing to the long immunity of the distant oilfields in Rumania and the increasing development of synthetic plants in Germany, Germany's oil stocks actually reached a peak in May 1944, and only began to shrink in later months.

More than two-thirds of the hydrogenated oil was produced in seven plants, whose vulnerability was manifest, and as the refineries were also vulnerable the effects of the concentrated bomber attacks on these installations in the summer of 1944 quickly began to take effect. April's output of automotive fuels was reduced to half by June, and to a quarter by September. Aircraft fuel production fell to the 10,000 tons of September against a target figure of only 30,000 tons – whereas the Luftwaffe's monthly minimum demand was 160,000 tons. About 90 per cent of the aviation fuel, the most vital need of all, came from the Bergius hydrogenation plants.

As German consumption was increased in meeting 'Overlord' and the Russian advance from the East, the situation became very serious – from May onwards consumption exceeded production. Speer's frantic countermeasures succeeded in achieving some alleviation, and produced a rise in fuel stocks prior to the Ardennes counteroffensive in mid-

December, but not enough to maintain it effectively, and that too prolonged battle went far to exhaust the stocks, in combination with the
Allied oil attacks in December and January. Bomber Command's night
attacks were particularly effective, owing to the much larger bombs that
the Lancasters could now carry, and their new standards of accuracy in
night-bombing.

The attacks on oil targets also greatly cut down German production
of explosives and synthetic rubber, while the shortage of aviation fuel
led to almost the entire cessation of training, and drastic reduction of
combat flying in the Luftwaffe. For example, only fifty night-fighters at
a time could be employed at the end of 1944. Those deficiencies, too,
went far to offset the potential value, and menace, of the new jet-
engined fighters which were now being introduced in the Luftwaffe.

COMMUNICATION TARGET ATTACKS

This objective, a mixture of tactical and strategic, was clearly of
tremendous importance in the success of the Normandy invasion and
the battle there, but its effect is more difficult to assess as the Allied
armies approached the Rhine. The November plan focused on railways
and canals in Western Germany, and particularly around the Ruhr – as
cutting off coal supplies would bring the main part of German industry
to a halt. The effects were very damaging, and much worried Speer in
the autumn of 1944, but the Allied chiefs tended to underrate them in
their own assessments. Divergence of views delayed and diminished
this course of action, and its effects. But in February 1945 a total of
some 8,000–9,000 aircraft were busy in attacking Germany's transport
system. By March it was in ruins and industry starved of fuel. After the
loss of Upper Silesia in February, when the Russian advance captured
that area, Germany had no alternative source of coal supply. Her steel
production, although she still had sufficient iron ore, was not enough to
meet her minimum ammunition requirements. It was then that Speer,
realizing that the position was hopeless, began planning for the period
after the war.

DIRECT ATTACKS

The results of such attacks now became more and more apparent. City
after city was devastated. German industrial production steadily shrank
after its peak month, July 1944. The Krupp works at Essen ceased
production after October. It was often the destruction of electricity,

gas, or water systems that primarily caused the losses in production. Outside the Ruhr, however, the sheer shortage of raw materials, resulting from the breakdown of the transport system, was the main factor in the final collapse of German industry, in 1945.

CONCLUSIONS

The strategic bombing offensive against Germany opened with much hope, but at the outset had very little effect – showing a vast excess of confidence over commonsense. The gradual development of a sense of reality was manifested in the abrupt change from daylight to night bombing, and then in the adoption of the policy of area-bombing – questionable as this was in many respects.

Until 1942 the bombing was merely an inconvenience to Germany, not a danger. It may have given a fillip to the British people's morale, although even this is questionable.

In 1943, thanks to ever-growing American help, the damage inflicted by the bomber forces of the two Allied countries became larger – but had, in fact, no great effect on German production, or on the German people's morale.

A real and decisive change did not come until the spring of 1944, and that was due mainly to the Americans' introduction of adequate long-range fighters to escort bombers.

After rendering great service to 'Overlord', the Allied bombers returned to their attack on German industry with much increased success. In the last nine months of the war they owed much to their new developments in navigation and bombing techniques, as well as to shrinking opposition in the air.

Through indecision, and divergence of views, Allied progress in the air, as on the ground, suffered from lack of concentration. The potential of the Allied air forces was greater than their achievement. In particular, the British pursued area-bombing long after they had any reason, or excuse, for such indiscriminate action.

There is ample evidence to show that the war could have been shortened, several months at least, by better concentration on oil and communications targets. Even so, despite the errors in strategy and disregard for basic morality, the bombing campaign unquestionably played a vital part in the defeat of Hitler's Germany.

CHAPTER THIRTY-FOUR

The Liberation of the South-west Pacific and Burma

The situation in the Pacific at the approach of spring 1944 was that the Central Pacific forces commanded by Admiral Spruance, under the higher direction of Admiral Nimitz, had successively captured the Gilbert and the Marshall Islands, while devastating by air attack the Japanese base of Truk in the Caroline Islands, and thus severely denting what the Japanese had defined as their essential rearward barrier zone of defence. Meanwhile General MacArthur's forces in the South-west Pacific had successively captured most of the Bismarck Archipelago and the Admiralty Islands, piercing that barrier zone, while effectively neutralizing the advanced Japanese base at Rabaul. At the same time MacArthur's forces had considerably extended their westward advance in New Guinea, and were preparing their next big bound, to the Philippines.

THE RECONQUEST OF NEW GUINEA

The continuance of the campaign in New Guinea was marked by a development of the leap-frogging method that had been tried earlier in the Solomon Islands. In four months MacArthur's forces advanced a thousand miles by a series of such hops – from the Madang area to the Vogelkop Peninsula at the western end of New Guinea. The Japanese had hoped to keep their hold on the few suitable coastal points where airfields could be built, but the Allies, unable to outflank these positions on the landward side, utilized their superior air and naval strength to carry out by-passing moves along the coast.

The Japanese strategic situation was weak as the main air and naval forces were kept back to meet Admiral Spruance's next advance in the central Pacific. On the ground, too, the Japanese were dispersed as well as unsupported. The so-called 8th Area Army at Rabaul was left to defend itself, while on the northern coast of New Guinea, the remnants

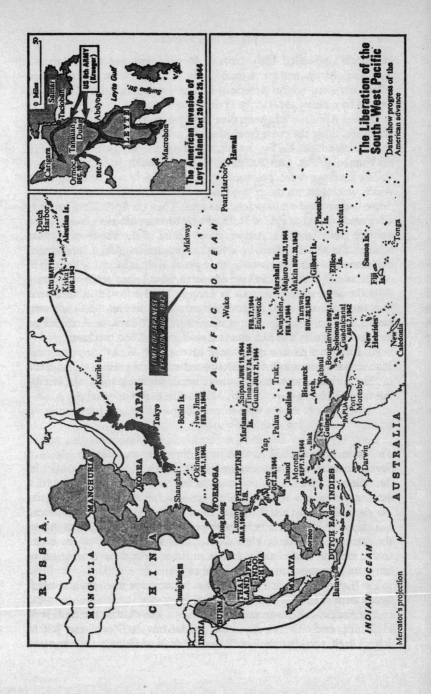

The American Invasion of
Leyte Island Oct 20/Dec 25, 1944

US 6th ARMY
(Kruger)

Leyte Gulf

Surigao Str.

Samar
Tacloban
Abuyog
Dulag
Tanauan
Carigara
Ormoc DEC.10
DEC.7
LEYTE
Macrohon

0 Miles 50

The Liberation of the
South-West Pacific

Dates show progress of the
American advance

RUSSIA

MONGOLIA

MANCHURIA

CHINA

KOREA

JAPAN

Tokyo

Bonin Is.
Iwo Jima
FEB.19,1945

Okinawa
APR.1,1945

FORMOSA

Shanghai

Hong Kong

Chungking

THAI-
LAND
BURMA
INDO
CHINA
MALAYA

INDIA

DUTCH EAST INDIES

Batavia

Borneo

Mindanao

PHILIPPINE
IS.

Luzon
JAN.9,1945

Leyte
OCT.20,1944

Yap.

Palau.

Caroline Is.

Talaud

Morotai
SEPT.15,1944

Biak

Truk.

Marianas
Is.
Saipan JUNE 15,1944
Tinian JULY 24, 1944
Guam JULY 21, 1944

Wake

LIMIT OF JAPANESE
EXPANSION AUG. 1942

Kurile Is.

Attu MAY 1943
Kiska
AUG.1943
Aleutian Is.

Dutch
Harbor

Midway

PACIFIC OCEAN

Pearl Harbor
Hawaii

Marshall Is.
Majuro JAN.31,1944
Makin NOV.20,1943

Kwajalein.
FEB.1,1944
Eniwetok
FEB.17,1944

Gilbert Is.
Tarawa
NOV.20,1943

Phoenix
Is.

Tokelau

Ellice
Is.

Samoa Is.

Fiji
Is.

Tonga

New
Guinea

PAPUA
Port
Moresby

Bismarck
Arch.

New
Britain

Rabaul

Bougainville NOV.1,1943
Solomon Is.
Guadalcanal
AUG.7,1942

New
Hebrides

New
Caledonia

AUSTRALIA

Darwin

INDIAN OCEAN

Mercator's projection

of Adachi's so-called 18th Army at Wewak were put under Anami's 2nd Area Army, making a total of six weak divisions to face fifteen Allied divisions (eight American and seven Australian), which were backed by a heavy superiority in the air and at sea.

During April the 7th Australian Division, and then the 11th, pushed westward along the coast from Madang, while MacArthur was mounting a fresh bound, his biggest yet, to capture the key base of Hollandia, on Humboldt Bay, over 200 miles west of Wewak.

The landings were preceded by a series of heavy bombing raids which destroyed, on the ground, most of the 350 aircraft that the Japanese had scraped up to defend the area. Then on April 22nd landings were made on either side of Hollandia by two amphibious groups, while another group landed at Aitape (about a third of the way from Wewak) to seize the airfields there as a further precaution. Allied Intelligence estimates had put the Japanese strength at Hollandia as 14,000 and at Aitape as 3,500, so to make sure of success MacArthur employed nearly 50,000 troops, mainly from Eichelberger's US 1st Corps, in the operation. Actually the defending forces proved to be even less than estimated, and consisted largely of administrative troops, who offered no serious opposition and fled inland after the initial bombardment.

As a result Adachi's three weak divisions at Wewak were cut off. Rather than make another circuitous and exhausting retreat through the interior he chose to attempt a direct break-out along the coast, but by the time he launched it, in July, MacArthur had reinforced the American lodgement at Aitape with three strong divisions, and the break-out attempt was repelled with heavy loss.

Long before this abortive counterattack the Americans had moved on 120 miles westward to their next objective, the offshore island of Wakde, where the Japanese had built an airfield. In mid-May the Americans landed a force at Toem on the New Guinea coast, and then crossed the narrow strait to Wakde Island – but there the small Japanese garrison put up a stiff though short resistance, while the American coastal advance to Sarmi met more prolonged opposition. Nevertheless the Japanese defence of New Guinea had now become, in the broad sense, sporadic and chaotic. American submarines were causing heavy losses to troopship convoys from China, while the central Pacific threat to the Marianas annulled the hope that further Japanese reinforcements would be sent to New Guinea.

MacArthur's next leap was made barely a month after the capture of Hollandia, and only ten days after the landings at Toem and Wakde Island. It was to capture Biak Island, with its airfields, which was 350 miles west of Hollandia (and 220 miles beyond Wakde). This operation did not go so smoothly. In contrast to the case of Hollandia the Americans greatly underestimated the strength of the garrison, which was over 11,000 men, and although their initial landings of May 27th met little resistance the situation changed when they pushed inland to occupy the airfields. For the Japanese had chosen to avoid any attempt to hold the beaches, where they could be crushed by bombardment from the Allied ships and aircraft, and had posted the bulk of their garrison in caves and entrenched positions on the high ground overlooking the airfields, while their counterattacks with tanks even cut off for a time part of the American infantry. Although MacArthur poured in reinforcements, the clearing of the island became a slow, grinding, process – and was not completed until August. It cost the American ground forces nearly 10,000 casualties; a large proportion, however, was due to disease, and deaths in action were only about 400. It was a foretaste of the problem and the trouble they would meet in their landing at Iwo Jima nine months later, in February 1945.

The effect of the very tough resistance of the Japanese on Biak might have been greater if the High Command, in Japan, had persevered with its belated decision to reinforce Biak. Reversing its earlier decision to concentrate on defending the Marianas, it sent a convoy of troop transports to Biak early in June, covered by a large force of warships and aircraft from the Marianas. But the move was postponed five days owing to a mistaken report that a US carrier force was at Biak, while on the second attempt the Japanese encountered a US cruiser and destroyer group and promptly retreated. The Japanese High Command then sent a stronger covering force, including the giant battleships *Yamato* and *Musashi*, but the very day after its arrival near New Guinea, the US carrier groups of the Central Pacific force began their attacks on the Marianas – and the Japanese naval force was rushed back northward to meet this greater threat. The two-pronged American advance across the Pacific had again proved its alternating value in dislocating the enemy's balance.

By contrast, MacArthur had lost no time when the advance on the Biak airfields was slowed down, and mounted an alternative attack on the nearby island of Noemfoor. This landing was made on July 2nd, after the heavy air and naval bombardment, and all its three airfields were captured by the 6th.

Having no air-strength left, the Japanese on the mainland had already begun to retire to the extreme western tip of the Vogelkop Peninsula. On July 30th MacArthur put a division ashore near Cape Sansapor, and without any preliminary bombing or bombardment, as there were known to be no Japanese troops in that remote stretch of the peninsula. A defensive zone was speedily constructed, and work started on building further airfields there.

The way was now clear for a leap to the Philippines, supported from three groups of airfields at the western end of New Guinea. The remnants of the five Japanese divisions still in New Guinea could be ignored, and were left for the Australians to mop up.

THE CAPTURE OF THE MARIANAS – AND THE BATTLE OF THE PHILIPPINE SEA

The attack on the Marianas, by Admiral Spruance's central Pacific prong, marked the American penetration of Japan's inner ring of defence. From there, the American bombing forces could strike at Japan herself, as well as the Philippines, Formosa and China. At the same time the capture of the Marianas brought a strangling threat to Japan's line of communications with her recently acquired southern empire.

In the Marianas the vital islands were, as elsewhere, those with airfields – Saipan, Tinian, and Guam. They were held by garrisons of, respectively, 32,000, 9,000, and 18,000 troops. The Japanese air strength there was nominally 1,400 planes, but actually much smaller as many had been sent to New Guinea and many more destroyed by the carrier groups of Admiral Mitscher's fast carrier force, which had been striking at the bases from February onward. Even so, the Japanese hoped to have 500 aircraft available if they could obtain some reinforcement from other areas. Their naval forces in the area, under Admiral Ozawa, were organized in three groupings – the main battle fleet of four battleships, with three light carriers, cruisers, and destroyers, under Admiral Kurita; the main carrier force of three fleet carriers, with cruisers and destroyers, under Ozawa himself; and a reserve carrier force under Admiral Joshima of two fleet carriers and one light carrier, with a battleship as well as cruisers and destroyers.

The Japanese had prepared a counter to the American seaborne advance across the Pacific, and hoped to utilize it as a trap for Spruance's forces, whereby his carriers could be smashed. The plan had been drawn up in August 1943 by the Naval Commander-in-Chief, Admiral Koga, but at the end of March 1944 he and his flying-boat had been lost – when withdrawing his headquarters from Truk to Davao in the Philippines – and he had been succeeded by Admiral Toyoda, who took over the counterstroke plan with some alteration. Toyoda's hope, and aim, was to lure the American carrier forces into the waters east of the Philippines, and there 'pincer' them between Ozawa's powerful carrier force and aircraft operating from bases in the mandated islands.

The American invasion armada for the Marianas sailed from the Marshalls on June 9th, the landings on Saipan being planned for the 15th. Two days later Mitscher's carriers began an intensified bombing of the target islands, and by the 13th the US battleships had developed a heavy bombardment of Saipan and Tinian. At the same time Admiral Toyoda ordered 'Operation A-Go' to begin – the long-planned Japanese counter-operation – and that decision caused, as already mentioned, the abandonment of the attempt to reinforce Biak Island and retain a hold in New Guinea.

The American armada comprised three Marine divisions, with an Army division in reserve, closely supported by a naval force of twelve escort carriers, five battleships, and eleven cruisers, while behind these was Admiral Spruance's 5th Fleet, the most powerful fleet in the world, comprising seven battleships, twenty-one cruisers, and sixty-nine destroyers, together with Admiral Mitscher's four carrier groups (fifteen carriers and 956 aircraft). The task of bringing nearly 130,000 troops to the Marianas from Hawaii and Guadalcanal was finely organized and executed.

On the morning of the 15th the first wave of Marines landed on the beaches of Saipan, covered by heavy naval shelling, inshore gunboats and rocket-firing aircraft – 8,000 Marines being put ashore in twenty minutes, which was testimony to their high degree of training. But although the total troops ashore was increased to 20,000 by nightfall, little advance had been made from the beaches owing to the way that the Japanese controlled the heights, and to their fierce counterattacks.

A more distant but still greater threat to the invasion came from the Japanese fleet, with its battleships and carriers – which had been spotted steaming into the Philippine Sea that morning by US submarines. Spruance thereupon cancelled the intended landings on Guam, put his reserve of troops, the 27th Division, ashore at Saipan to speed up the capture of this key island, and cleared the transports away to safer waters. The 5th Fleet assembled some 180 miles west of Tinian, but did not move farther west in case it missed the Japanese fleet.

This defensive positioning proved wise. Up to now Toyoda's plan seemed to be working out well, but for the important difference that the second arm of his pincer was not operating – as Mitscher's carrier planes had wiped out the Japanese air forces on the Marianas. From 8.30 AM on June 19th, Ozawa's carriers delivered four successive strikes – but all of them were detected in advance by the US radar, and hundreds of fighter aircraft flown off to meet them, while Mitscher's carrier-borne bombers again attacked the Japanese island airbases. The outcome of this tremendous battle aloft was the massacre that became known as 'The Great Marianas Turkey Shoot'. The American pilots gained an overwhelming advantage over the less experienced Japanese, who lost 218 aircraft and brought down only twenty-nine American planes. Worse still, two of the Japanese fleet carriers, the *Shokaku* and *Taiho*, both containing many more aircraft, were torpedoed and sunk by American submarines.

Ozawa, believing that his planes had landed on Guam, still hung around the battle area, and was thus spotted by US reconnaissance planes the following afternoon – whereupon Admiral Mitscher launched a strike by 216 of his carrier-borne planes, although knowing that their recovery would have to be in the dark. Three hours after the sighting, his planes delivered their attack, and so effectively that they sank one fleet carrier (and damaged two more, plus two light carriers, a battle-ship, and a heavy cruiser), as well as destroying sixty-five Japanese planes. They lost only twenty of their own planes in action, although a further eighty were lost or crashed on the long night return flight. Many of their crews were saved, however, as Ozawa's ships had fled from the scene, towards Okinawa in the Ryukyu Islands south of Japan.

By that time the Japanese loss of aircraft in the battle had totalled about 480, over three-quarters of their total, and most of their crews were lost. The destruction of such a large proportion of the Japanese planes and carriers was a very serious loss – although by the autumn the planes and carriers were largely replaced. Far worse was the loss of so many pilots, for these could not be replaced. It meant that in any further battle in the near future the Japanese Fleet would be heavily handicapped, and forced to rely mainly on its more traditional armaments.

The Battle of the Philippine Sea thus turned out a very grave Japanese defeat – the American naval historian Admiral S. E. Morison considered it even more important than the subsequent Battle of Leyte Gulf, in October. The way to the Philippines was now wide open, and the land battles in the Marianas were assured of success.

After the sea–air battle the conquest of the Marianas was no longer in doubt, although the resistance on land continued to be tough. The three divisions landed in the south of Saipan pushed their way steadily north, with strong air and naval support, and by June 25th the commanding height of Mount Tapotchau was captured. On July 6th the two top Japanese commanders on Saipan, Admiral Nagumo (the former carrier chief) and General Saito, committed suicide 'in order to encourage the troops in their final attack'. Next day the surviving 3,000 troops virtually did likewise by a vainly suicidal charge against the Americans' lines. The campaign cost the Japanese over 26,000 men, whereas the American casualties were 3,500 dead and 13,000 wounded or sick.

On July 23rd, the two Marine divisions on Saipan were shipped to Tinian, and within a week that island was captured, though mopping-up took longer. Three days before the Tinian landings the force allotted for the Guam invasion, which had been sent away when Ozawa's fleet threatened to interfere, returned to carry out its mission, reinforced by a further Army division. Although Japanese resistance was tough, and helped by an intricate network of cave defences, the island was cleared by August 12th.

The fall of the Marianas, and the shattering naval defeat that preceded it, made the weakening situation of Japan very clear, even though Japanese pride still would not face realities. Very significantly, however, these dramatic events were followed by the resignation of General Tojo's government on July 18th.

Four days later, General Koiso formed a Cabinet dedicated to the task of creating a better defence against the American advance. Although the campaign in China was still to be pursued, the primary concern was the defence of the Philippines – based on a recognition that if this great group of islands was lost, Japan's forces would be fatally affected by lack of oil supplies from the East Indies.

Even as it was, the Japanese situation had become badly handicapped by shortage of fuel supplies. In producing that effect the American submarine sinkings of Japanese oil tankers was a most important strategic factor. The much reduced scale of oil supplies reaching Japan restricted the training programme of aircraft pilots. It led also to the Japanese fleet being kept at Singapore, so as to be near the source of supply – and when the fleet was brought up to intervene it sailed without sufficient oil fuel to take it back.

At this stage of the war it might well have been possible for the United States forces to by-pass the Philippines, and move on in their next bound to Formosa, or to Iwo Jima and Okinawa, as Fleet Admiral King and several other naval chiefs urged. But political considerations, and MacArthur's natural desire for a triumphant return to the Philippines, prevailed against such arguments for by-passing these great islands.*

There were several small objectives whose capture had been considered necessary prior to the invasion of the Philippines. The original scheme had been to capture Morotai Island near the Halmaheras (west of New Guinea), the Palau Islands, Yap Island, the Talaud Islands, and then Mindanao – the great southern island of the Philippines – building advance air and naval bases to aid the main attack on the Philippines. Early in September, however, Admiral Halsey's 3rd Fleet (called the 5th Fleet when Spruance controlled it) found that the defences of the Philippines coast were very weak, and he accordingly proposed that the intermediate stages should be dropped. However, the early parts of this original plan were retained as they were almost under way, and felt to be an extra insurance.

A detachment from MacArthur's forces landed on Morotai Island on September 15th, meeting little opposition, and by October 4th American aircraft were operating from the newly built air base there. On September 15th, also, the Palau Islands were invaded by Admiral Halsey's Central Pacific forces, and were mostly occupied within a few days. That provided them with advanced airfields only 500 miles from Mindanao, more than halfway from Guam.

The two main lines of advance across the Pacific, MacArthur's and Nimitz's, had now converged, and were within direct supporting distance of one another – ready and able to attempt the reconquest of the Philippines.

The Japanese plan for the defence of the Philippines, known as 'SHO-1', was two-fold. On land, it was entrusted to the 14th Area Army under General Yamashita, the conqueror of Malaya in 1941–2, who had for the purpose nine infantry divisions, one armoured division, and three independent brigades, plus the 4th Air Army. His command included in addition the naval forces around Manila, which numbered some 25,000 men capable of land fighting. The key part of the plan, however, was the intended action at sea, and on this the Japanese High Command was now disposed to stake everything. As soon as the location of the American landings was known, the Japanese carrier forces were to lure the American fleet northward, while the American landing forces were to be pinned by Yamashita's troops and 'pincered' by the two Japanese battleship groups. Toyoda calculated that the Americans, who had come to value the carriers above all, would be the more likely to rush after their opposite numbers as they themselves had always used

* For map, see p 643.

battleships as the decoy, and carriers as the striking force.

The plan was influenced by Japan's growing weakness in the air, but buttressed by continued faith in battleships. The admirals' pride and confidence had been unduly heightened by the completion of two colossal battleships, much the biggest in the world – the *Yamato* and *Musashi*. These had a displacement of over 70,000 tons and mounted nine 18-inch guns – they were the only warships in the world to mount so many guns of that size. By comparison the Japanese had done little, far too little, to develop their carrier-force and the aircraft it required. As so often happens in history, they had been slower than their opponents to apply the lesson of their own great successes at the outset of the war.

Accelerating the planned programme by two months, the Americans made their next big bound, to the Philippines, in October. These islands stretch a thousand miles – from Mindanao in the south, as big as Ireland, to Luzon in the north, nearly as big as England. The first thrust was delivered against Leyte, one of the smaller central islands, thus splitting the defence. MacArthur's troops – four divisions of Lieutenant-General Walter Krueger's Sixth Army – began to be landed there on the morning of October 20th by Admiral Kinkaid's 7th Fleet – a convoy and support fleet composed of old battleships and small escort carriers. It was backed and covered by Admiral Halsey's 3rd Fleet – which took up its station, in three groups, a little east of the Philippines. This was the main battle fleet, composed of the newer battleships and of large carriers, all fast.

The invasion had been preceded by a series of air strikes from October 10th on for a week by Mitscher's carrier forces (of Halsey's 3rd Fleet) against Formosa, and to a lesser extent against Luzon and Okinawa, that were of devastating effect and proved of great importance in their influence on subsequent events. On the other hand, the Japanese pilots made such exaggerated claims that their government in official communiqués and broadcasts claimed to have sunk eleven carriers, two battleships, and three cruisers. Actually these American carrier strikes had destroyed over 500 Japanese planes, while losing only seventy-nine of their own – and none of the ships that the Japanese had claimed. Momentary belief in the truth of these claims led the Imperial GHQ to move forward the rest of the forces for the 'SHO-1' operation. The naval forces soon discovered the absurdity of these claims, and withdrew, but the Army's plans were permanently changed in consequence – three of Suzuki's four divisions in the southern part of the Philippines being ordered to stand there instead of being kept ready for use in the north, in Luzon, as Yamashita had intended.

As already mentioned, the Japanese High Command had planned a crushing counterstroke with all available naval forces when and where the thrust came. Two days before the landing on Leyte Island, an uncoded message sent out from one of the American chiefs provided the Japanese with the vital information they required as a guide for their counterstroke.

Toyoda realized that it was a gamble, but the Japanese Navy depended for its fuel supplies on the oil from the captured East Indies, and if the Americans established themselves in the East Indies that line of supply would be cut. When questioned after the war, Toyoda explained his calculations thus:

> If the worst should happen there was a chance that we would lose the entire fleet; but I felt that that chance had to be taken ... should we lose in the Philippine operations, even though the fleet should be left, the shipping lane to the south would be completely cut off so that the fleet, if it should come back to Japanese waters, could not obtain its fuel supply. If it should remain in southern waters, it could not receive supplies of ammunition and arms. There would be no sense in saving the fleet at the expense of the loss of the Philippines.

The decoy was to be provided by Admiral Ozawa's force, coming south from Japan. It included the four aircraft-carriers that remained serviceable and two battleships converted to carriers, but could not act as much more than a decoy since its total of aircraft was down to barely a hundred and most of the pilots lacked experience.

So in this great gamble for victory the Japanese relied on an old-fashioned fleet – of seven battleships, thirteen cruisers, and three light cruisers – which came up from the Singapore area. The commander, Admiral Kurita, sent a detachment to push into Leyte Gulf from the south-west via the Surigao Strait, while he came in with the main force from the north-west, through the San Bernardino Strait. He hoped to crush MacArthur's transports and their escorting warships between his two jaws.

He thought the *Yamato* and *Musashi*, with their 18-inch guns, easily able to pulverize the older American battleships and believed them to be almost unsinkable owing to their armoured decks and much subdivided hulls. Moreover air attack should not be heavy if Halsey's carrier-force was off the scene. It was hoped that this would have been lured away by the time that Kurita broke into the Leyte Gulf – a stroke timed for delivery on October 25th.

But the decoy did not work. On the night of the 23rd Kurita bumped into a couple of American submarines, the *Darter* and the *Dace*, which had been cruising off the coast of Borneo. These promptly hurried northward, keeping ahead of the Japanese fleet by running full speed on the surface under cover of the dark. When first light came they submerged to periscope depth, awaited the oncoming fleet, and then fired their torpedoes at close range – sinking two of the Japanese cruisers and crippling another. Kurita himself was in the leading cruiser, and although he was rescued before it sank – and later transferred to the *Yamato* – it was a shaking experience. Moreover the American admirals had been made aware of the enemy's approach and strength.

When Ozawa heard of Kurita's clash with the submarines, he made haste to reveal his own approach from the north, sending out uncoded signals repeatedly to catch Halsey's attention. But his signals were not picked up by the Americans. Nor was he spotted by any of their reconnaissance planes – as all of them were sent westward to watch for Kurita's approach!

Soon Halsey's carriers launched their bombers and torpedo-bombers in waves against Kurita's fleet. The only interruption to their onslaught came from the relieving attacks of Japanese land-based aircraft from the islands, and also from Ozawa's carriers. These were beaten off and more than 50 per cent of the attacking planes shot down, though the carrier *Princeton* was badly hit and had to be abandoned.

The American naval planes achieved a greater success in their attacks on Kurita's fleet. For the Goliath-like *Musashi* capsized and sank after the fifth attack, in the afternoon – after a total of nineteen hits by torpedoes and seventeen hits by bombs. Although the American pilots reported that three other battleships and three heavy cruisers had been heavily hit, actually only one ship, a heavy cruiser, was too badly damaged to continue. After the fifth onslaught and the sinking of the *Musashi*, however, the Japanese fleet turned about and steamed away to the west.

On getting these reports from his air observers it appeared to Admiral Halsey that Kurita was definitely in retreat. But the fact that no aircraft-carriers had been seen in either part of Kurita's fleet had led Halsey to send out reconnaissance planes on a wider search for them, and about 5 PM Ozawa's force was spotted on its way southward. Thereupon Halsey decided to dash north and smash it at dawn, following his motto 'Whatever we do, we do fast.' To make sure of annihilating Ozawa's force he took the whole of his available fleet, leaving nothing behind to guard San Bernardino Strait.

A quarter of an hour after announcing his decision in a signal to Kinkaid, a report was received from a night reconnaissance plane that Kurita had turned round again and was steaming at high speed towards the Strait. Halsey discounted the report. Now that he saw the opportunity of playing the kind of bold and dashing game he loved he became blind to other possibilities. Early in the war he had been aptly nicknamed 'The Bull'.

Kurita's retreat had been only a temporary expedient to get out of reach of air attack while daylight lasted, with the intention of returning under the cloak of darkness. Apart from the sinking of the *Musashi* none of his bigger ships had been seriously damaged – contrary to what the American pilots had optimistically reported.

At 11 PM, when Halsey had gone 160 miles northward, Kurita's fleet was again spotted by reconnaissance planes – still heading for San Bernardino Strait and now only forty miles away. Halsey could no longer ignore its advance, but discounted the seriousness of the threat, regarding the renewed advance as merely a sacrificial effort on traditional Japanese lines by a badly crippled fleet. He pushed on northward, confidently assuming that Kinkaid's fleet would easily be able to beat off what he supposed to be a much weakened attacker.

So the Japanese bait, though it had not been taken at the intended time, was swallowed in the end.

The situation of Kinkaid's fleet was the more dangerous because he was misled in a double way. The appearance of Kurita's southern detachment, heading for Surigao Strait, had focused Kinkaid's attention in that direction, and he concentrated most of his force there to meet this threat. He assumed that part of Halsey's battle fleet was still covering the more northerly approach through San Bernardino Strait, as it had not been made clear that Halsey had sailed away with the whole fleet. Worse still, Kinkaid did not take the precaution of sending out any reconnaissance to see if any enemy was approaching from that direction.

The attack by the Japanese southern detachment was defeated after a tense night battle – thanks largely to the 'night-sight' provided by the Americans' radar, which was much superior to that of the Japanese Navy. Another Japanese disadvantage was that as their ships came in line ahead through the narrow Surigao Strait, they were exposed to the concentrated fire of Admiral Oldendorf's battleships – which could thus 'cross the T'. The detachment included two battleships, and both were sunk. Almost the whole of the attacking force was wiped out. When daylight came the Strait was empty of the enemy except for bits of floating wreckage and streaks of oil.

But a few minutes after Kinkaid had signalled his congratulations on the victory, another signal came to say that a much larger Japanese force – Kurita's main fleet – had come down from the north-west, through San Bernardino Strait, and was off the east coast of Samar Island assailing the smaller portion of Kinkaid's fleet that had been left there to cover General MacArthur's landing points on Leyte.

This small force, supporting the army's invasion of Leyte Island, comprised six escort-carriers – converted merchant ships – and a handful of destroyers. They fled southward under a hail of heavy shells from the giant *Yamato* and the other three battleships.

After getting this alarming news, Kinkaid sent a signal to Halsey, at 8.30 AM: 'Urgently need fast battleships Leyte Gulf at once.' At 9 AM Kinkaid made another pressing appeal, and this time, in clear, instead of in code. But Halsey continued to steam northward, determined to fulfil his aim of destroying Ozawa's carrier force. He persisted on this course despite Kinkaid's repeated appeals for help – feeling that Kinkaid's carrier-borne aircraft should be able to hold off Kurita's attack until the bulk of Kinkaid's fleet, with its six battleships, came up to the rescue. He did, however, order a small detached force of carriers and cruisers under Admiral John McCain, then in the Caroline Islands, to hasten to Kinkaid's help. But it was 400 miles away – fifty miles farther than he was.

Meantime a brake was put on Kurita's southward onrush by the gallant efforts of the handful of American destroyers that were covering the retreat of the six escort-carriers, as well as of such planes as these still had available. One escort-carrier and three destroyers were sunk, but the rest escaped, though battered.

Just after 9 AM Kurita broke off the chase and turned towards Leyte Gulf, where a mass of American transports and landing craft now lay open to attack. He was then less than thirty miles from the entrance.

Before striking he paused to concentrate his ships, which had become dispersed in the running fight. The turn and pause again created the mistaken idea on the Americans' side that he was retiring – under pressure of their air and destroyer attacks. They were soon disillusioned, and Kinkaid sent another urgent call for Halsey's help: 'Situation again very serious. Escort-carriers again threatened by enemy surface forces. Your assistance badly needed. Escort-carriers retiring to Leyte Gulf.'

This time Halsey responded to the appeal. By now, 11.15 AM, his planes had severely mauled Ozawa's force, and although he dearly wanted to finish it off with his battleships' guns, he curbed his desire and came racing back with his six fast battleships and one of his three carrier groups. But he had gone so far north in pursuit of Ozawa that he could not possibly reach Leyte Gulf until the next morning. Even McCain's carrier force would not arrive near enough to intervene with its planes for several hours still. So the situation at Leyte looked very grim at midday as Kurita's fleet bore in towards the Gulf.

But suddenly Kurita turned back north – and this time for good. What was the cause? A combination of intercepted messages and their effect on his mind. The first was a radio call telling the aircraft of the American escort-carriers to land on Leyte Island. He imagined that this was preparatory to a land-based and more concentrated attack on his ships, whereas it was merely an emergency measure to save them from being sunk with the carriers. A few minutes later he received an intercept report of Kinkaid's 9 AM signal in clear to Halsey. From this he jumped to the mistaken conclusion that Halsey must have been racing south for more than three hours, for Kurita was out of touch with Ozawa and did not know how far north Halsey had gone. Also, he was worried about his lack of air cover.

The crowning effect came from a confused intercept which gave him the impression that part of the American relieving force was only seventy miles north of him and already close to his line of retreat through the San Bernardino Strait. So he decided to abandon his attack on Leyte Gulf and hurry north to tackle this threat before it was reinforced and his line of retreat blocked.

It was one more of the many cases in history which show that battles are apt to be decided more by fancies than by facts. The impression made on the commander's mind often counts much more than any actual blow and its physical effect.

When Kurita reached San Bernardino Strait he found no enemy there, and slipped away through it to the westward. Although he did not reach this bolt-hole until nearly 10 PM – delayed in the process by having to dodge repeated air attacks – that was three hours before Halsey's leading ships arrived there in their race southward.

But the escape of the Japanese battleships, which had achieved so little, was amply compensated by the sinking of all the four Japanese carriers – one, the *Chitose*, about 9.30 AM by Mitscher's first strike, and the other three (*Chiyoda*, *Zuikaku*, and *Zuiho*) in the afternoon, after Halsey with the bulk of his fleet had departed on his belated southward dash.

Regarding as a whole its four separate and distinct actions, the Battle of Leyte Gulf, as it is collectively called, was the largest naval battle of all time. A total of 282 ships was engaged as well as hundreds of aircraft, compared with 250 (with five seaplanes) in the 1916 Battle of Jutland. If the June battle of the Philippine Sea had been in a sense more decisive, through its devastating effects on Japanese naval air strength, the four-piece Battle of Leyte Gulf reaped the harvest and settled the issue. The Japanese ship losses in it were four carriers, three battleships, six heavy cruisers, three light cruisers, and eight destroyers – whereas the Americans lost only one light carrier, two escort carriers and three destroyers.

It is worth mention that this battle also saw the inauguration of a new form of tactics, difficult to counter. For after the American escort-carriers of Kinkaid's 7th Fleet had succeeded in surviving the unexpected and overwhelmingly powerful onslaught of Kurita's 'Centre Force' until Kurita was led to turn about and withdraw through the San Bernardino Strait they were then subjected to the first organized 'Kamikaze' attack – carried out by pilots who had volunteered for a special air corps dedicated to the sacrificial, suicidal mission of crash-diving their planes on to an enemy ship, setting it on fire with their burst fuel-tanks and the explosion of their bombs. In their first essay, however, only one escort-carrier was sunk, although several were damaged.

The major significance of the battle lay in the sinking of Ozawa's four aircraft-carriers. Without any carriers, the six remaining Japanese battleships were helpless, and they made no further positive contribution in the war. Moreover the Japanese Navy was rendered useless. Thus, while Halsey's northward dash had exposed the rest of the American forces to grave dangers, the outcome provided justification. Moreover it showed the hollowness of the battleship bogey, and exposed the folly of the faith that had been placed in such out-of-date monsters. Their only important value in World War II was for shore bombardment – a role for which, ironically, they had in previous generations been considered unsuitable, and too vulnerable.

The Japanese decision to fight for Leyte, and make that the core of their defence of the Philippines, came too late to allow the reinforcements from Luzon, nearly three divisions, to reach the island before the American troops had expanded their footholds. First, striking out from their landing points, they took the nearby airfields at Dulag and Tacloban, on the east coast. Then, stretching out on both flanks, they reached by November 2nd Carigara Bay on the north coast and Abuyog midway down the east coast. Those expanding thrusts not only captured all five Japanese airfields, and threw into confusion the enemy's one division already on the island, but forestalled the plan of Suzuki (35th Army) to concentrate his reinforcing divisions in the Carigara plain.

Krueger intended, next, to carry out a two-fold flanking sweep round both ends of the island's mountain spine, to capture the Japanese main base at Ormoc on the west coast. But torrential rain hampered the work of making the captured airfields serviceable to support the concentric move, and in the interval two Japanese reinforcing divisions were landed at Ormoc by November 9th. More reinforcements followed, despite serious losses in transports and escorts, and by early December the Japanese had brought their troop strength on Leyte up from 15,000 to 60,000. But by that time Krueger's strength had been increased to more than 180,000. To hasten progress he landed one of his fresh divisions on the west coast just south of Ormoc, thus splitting the defence, and three days later, on December 10th, it occupied that base-port with little opposition. After that, the hungry Japanese quickly collapsed and by Christmas organized resistance ceased. Thus, under much worsened circumstances, and with much diminished strength, Yamashita reverted to his own original desire of concentrating his defensive effort on the main island of Luzon.

During the crucial weeks three fast carrier groups of Halsey's 3rd Fleet had stayed close to the Philippines to give continued, and continuous, support to MacArthur's troops, despite suffering increasing Kamikaze attacks. These inflicted a considerable number of damaging hits, and two of the carriers had to be withdrawn for extensive repairs, although it was not until the last week of November that the carriers were released.

As a preliminary to the invasion of Luzon, MacArthur's main objective, he decided to seize the intermediate island of Mindoro in order to establish airfields from which his air force, the 5th USAAF, could cover the seaborne approach to Luzon. It was a risky move as Mindoro was nearly 300 miles from Leyte Gulf, while much closer to the Japanese airfields on Luzon, especially the cluster around Manila. But the garrison of Mindoro was only about a hundred men, and the four abandoned Japanese airstrips were occupied within a few hours of the landing on December 15th – and converted so quickly for American use that US Army planes were being flown in before the end of the month. The ease of the process was much helped by the way that Halsey's fast carrier force pounded the airfields on Luzon and kept an umbrella of fighters over them to prevent the Japanese bombers taking off to attack Mindoro and its sea approaches.

On January 3rd the American armada, assembled from many quarters, sailed from Leyte Gulf – a total of 164 ships, including six battleships and seventeen escort carriers, under Admirals Kinkaid and Oldendorf. On January 9th, it arrived off Lingayen Gulf (110 miles north of Manila) – where the Japanese had begun their invasion of the Philippines nearly four years before. Early on the 10th it began disembarking four divisions of Krueger's Sixth Army (with two more to follow).

Great help was given by the fast carrier force of Halsey's fleet, especially in countering the Kamikaze attacks that were now causing growing damage to ships. After covering the Lingayen Gulf landings, this carrier force made a deep raid into the China Sea, ravaging Japanese bases and shipping in Indo-China, South China, Hong Kong, Formosa, and Okinawa. It was a demonstration of the vulnerability of Japan's southern empire.

Krueger's troops were meanwhile pushing southward from Lingayen Gulf towards Manila against fierce opposition. To help in hastening their progress, and to prevent the Japanese falling back into the Bataan Peninsula, MacArthur landed a further corps close to that peninsula on January 29th. Two days later an airborne division was landed, unopposed, at Nasugbu, some forty miles south of Manila. But by the time it advanced on Manila, Krueger's troops had reached the outskirts of the city, and Yamashita's troops had withdrawn into the mountains.

Manila was still defended, however, by Admiral Iwabachi, commanding the naval base. He refused to obey Yamashita's order making Manila an open city, and fanatically persevered in a house-to-house fight that continued for a further month – and wrecked the city. Not until March 4th was Manila completely cleared. Meanwhile the Bataan Peninsula had been captured, and Corregidor retaken, although the Japanese garrison of this fortress-island held out for ten days. By the middle of March the port of Manila was ready for use by American ships, although the process of mopping up continued in the mountainous part of Luzon as well as in Mindanao and the lesser southern islands.

THE ATTACK ON IWO JIMA

After the capture of the key places in the Philippines the Americans were eager to press on and strike at Japan herself, dropping earlier ideas on MacArthur's part of capturing Formosa or part of China's coast as air bases for the assault on Japan. But the Joint Chiefs of Staff agreed in considering it necessary to take Iwo Jima in the Bonin Islands, midway between Saipan and Tokyo, and Okinawa in the Ryukyus, midway between the south-western end of Japan and Formosa, as strategic stepping stones – close-up island bases to aid the air bombardment of Japan.

Iwo Jima, being regarded as the easier operation, was to be tackled first. Moreover it was wanted as an emergency landing place for the B29 Superfortresses which had been bombing Tokyo from the Marianas since late November, and as a base for the fighter planes escorting them – as no fighters could fly the entire distance.

A volcanic island, only four miles long, Iwo was uninhabited except for its garrison. This had not been large until September, and could not have offered much resistance, but since then the garrison had been increased to some 25,000 men, and General Kuribayashi had developed the defences into a network of excavated caves, well-concealed and connected by deep tunnels. His aim was simply to hold out as long as possible, as there could be no later reinforcement because of the Americans' huge naval-air superiority, and he relied on the sheer defensive strength of his position, eschewing costly and characteristic Japanese counterattacks.

The attack on Iwo Jima was entrusted by Nimitz to Admiral Raymond Spruance, who took over command of the 3rd Fleet from Halsey in the last week of January, 1945 – it was now for the time being renamed the 5th Fleet – and for the land part of the operation he was given three Marine divisions. The preparatory air and sea bombardment was the most prolonged hitherto in the Pacific war, with daily air strikes from December 8th on, day and night bombing from January 3rd on, and a final three days of intense naval bombardment. But all this had disappointingly little effect on the deeply fortified Japanese defences. When the Marines landed on the morning of February 19th, they were met with intense mortar and artillery fire, and for a long time were pinned down on the beaches, suffering 2,500 casualties on that first day out of 30,000 men who were landed.

In the days that followed the Marines slowly fought their way forward, almost yard by yard, with abundant and constant fire-support from air and sea, which was increased when Mitscher's fast carriers were brought back to reinforce, after their great raid on Tokyo. Not until March 26th was the conquest of the island achieved, after over five weeks' bitter fighting, and by then the Marine battle losses had risen to about 26,000 – 30 per cent of the entire landing force. The Japanese had fought so stubbornly that 21,000 had been killed, and barely 200 taken prisoner. The mopping up of pockets continued for more than two months longer, bringing the total of Japanese killed up to over 25,000, while only a thousand were taken prisoner. Before the end of March three airfields were ready for the American planes, and by the end of the war some 2,400 landings by B29 bombers had been made there.

THE BURMA CAMPAIGN – FROM IMPHAL TO THE RECAPTURE OF RANGOON, IN MAY 1945

Although the repulse, at Imphal, of the Japanese offensive in the spring of 1944 was a severe setback, it was not crushing enough to break their hold on Burma. That depended on whether it could be followed up effectively, and for this purpose the British supply system had to be more fully developed.

The task that Mountbatten was set by the Combined Chiefs of Staff directive of June 3rd was to broaden the air-link to China and exploit the development of a land-route, with the forces already allotted to him. Although not specifically mentioned, the reconquest of Burma was expected. The two main plans considered were 'Capital', an overland thrust to recapture north-central Burma, and 'Dracula', an amphibious one to take southern Burma. The latter had the prospect of greater effect, but it depended on outside supplies. In the circumstances General Slim and the Americans preferred the overland plan. So, although preparation for both plans was ordered, the emphasis was on 'Capital'.*

Despite the great improvement of communications from India, and India's development as a major base, it became evident that much more had to be done if an invasion of Burma was to be really, and speedily, effective. Basically, the main problems were logistical, rather than tactical. Notwithstanding the improvement of land communications and inland water transport, the dependence of Slim's Fourteenth Army on air supply remained, and that in turn depended on adequate aid from American cargo aircraft.

* See also map on p 538.

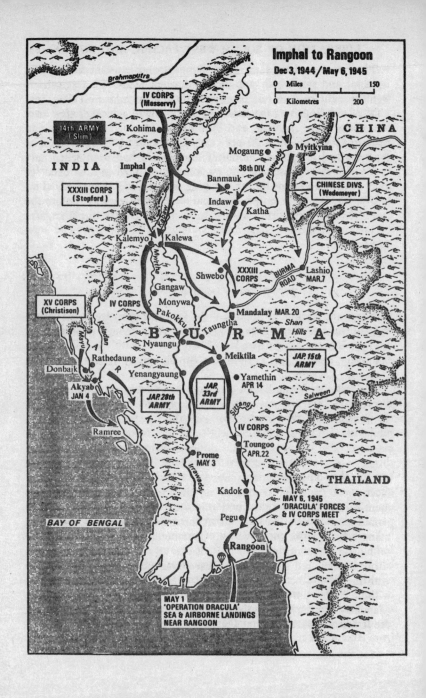

Imphal to Rangoon
Dec 3, 1944 / May 6, 1945

Miles 0 — 150
Kilometres 0 — 200

Brahmaputra

CHINA

14th ARMY (Slim)

Kohima

Mogaung • Myitkyina

INDIA

Imphal

36th DIV.

Banmauk

CHINESE DIVS. (Wedemeyer)

XXXIII CORPS (Stopford)

Indaw • Katha

Chindwin

Kalemyo • Kalewa

Myittha

Shwebo

XXXIII CORPS

BURMA ROAD

Lashio MAR. 7

XV CORPS (Christison)

Gangaw

IV CORPS

Monywa

Pakokku

Mandalay MAR. 20

Shan Hills

B U R M A

Taungtha

Kaladan

Rathedaung

Nyaungu

Meiktila

JAP. 15th ARMY

Donbaik

Yenangyaung

Yamethin APR 14

Salween

Akyab JAN 4

JAP. 28th ARMY

JAP. 33rd ARMY

Ramree

Sittang

IV CORPS

BAY OF BENGAL

Prome MAY 3

Toungoo APR. 22

THAILAND

Irrawaddy

Kadok

Kalok

MAY 6, 1945
'DRACULA' FORCES & IV CORPS MEET

Pegu

Rangoon

MAY 1
'OPERATION DRACULA'
SEA & AIRBORNE LANDINGS
NEAR RANGOON

Thus the second half of 1944 became primarily devoted to such development, and to reorganization in the commands. Among the more significant features, the air supply system was put under an integrated HQ called Combat Cargo Task Force, the Intelligence services were coordinated, and the 'Special Force' units disbanded. Reorganization was facilitated when, in October, Stilwell was recalled from China at the insistence of Chiang Kai-Shek, with whom he had been increasingly at loggerheads. General A. C. Wedemeyer replaced him as Chief of Staff to Chiang Kai-Shek and the Chinese forces. In November General Sir Oliver Leese, who had been commanding the Eighth Army in Italy, was sent out to be C-in-C Allied Land Forces, South-East Asia, under Mountbatten.

In mid-October, when the monsoon rains ceased and the ground dried, Slim began the advance on the central front, 'Operation Capital', concentrating Stopford's 33rd Corps forward, at the southern end of the Kabaw valley, to capture Kalemyo and Kalewa (130 miles south of Imphal), establishing a bridgehead across the Chindwin near Kalewa by mid-December, and then, reinforced by the 4th Corps (now under General Messervy), exploiting south-eastward to Monywa and Mandalay (160 miles beyond Kalewa).

On the other side, the Japanese High Command, facing the greater and near-approaching menace of the American seaborne advance to the Philippines, could spare no reinforcements for General Kimura's Burma Area Army – although telling Kimura that he must hold his ground in order to prevent the Allies opening the Burma Road, or moving on Malaya. The Japanese prospects of fulfilling these defensive tasks were poor, with their strength badly diminished by their own protracted Imphal offensive. On the Central Front four understrength divisions of the Japanese 15th Army, amounting to a total of merely 21,000 troops, faced a possible eight or nine strong divisions, and the only reinforcement could come from the division in south Burma – the use of which would mean uncovering Rangoon. Although some of Slim's forces were being held back for the projected 'Operation Dracula', he could count on having a superior number of divisions, all of larger strength, much stronger armoured support, and clear command of the air. Reckoning with these hard facts, the Japanese recognized that they might have to withdraw from northern Burma, but still hoped to hold a line covering Mandalay and the Yenangyaung oilfields (140 miles to the south, down the Irrawaddy River).

*   *   *

While the British offensive on the Central Front was developing, operations in the two subsidiary areas of Arakan and northern Burma reached a successful conclusion.

The objective of Christison's 15th Corps, as soon as the monsoon ceased, was to clear Arakan, seize Akyab Island for its air bases, and then release troops for the main campaign. For his task Christison had three strong divisions against the two weak divisions of Sakurai's so-called 28th Army. The British advance began on December 11th, and quickly took Donbaik at the tip of the peninsula, on the 23rd, and Rathedaung on the east bank of the Mayu River a week later, while the third of Christison's divisions was clearing the Kaladan valley, farther inland. The lack of opposition was due to the fact that the Japanese were in the process of withdrawing from Arakan. This prompted an acceleration of the plans to take Akyab – which was found abandoned when the British occupied it on January 4th.

The need for further air bases led Christison to plan the capture of Ramree Island, seventy miles farther south, and this was easily secured on the 21st – as the Japanese were now mainly concerned to hold the passes across the mountains to the lower Irrawaddy, and prevent the British breaking into central Burma. Indeed the credit of the campaign largely went to the small Japanese rearguards who held on to the approaches, and the passes, until the end of April, thus enabling Sakurai's depleted army to extricate itself from Arakan. Their tenacious defence was helped, however, by the fact that Christison's corps was now more concerned in planning for 'Dracula', for which a large part of its forces had already been withdrawn.

In China itself the campaign had gone badly for Chiang Kai-Shek's forces during 1944, and that had led to a reversal of the Trident Conference's decision on the priorities for air supplies over the 'Hump', the emphasis now being given to building up the Chinese armies rather than the American strategic air forces in China. Even in the westerly province of Yunnan, an offensive by twelve Chinese divisions was checked by a single Japanese division, although this was outnumbered 7 to 1.

On the northern front in Burma, Stilwell's forces, mostly Chinese, had made little progress during the spring against the three weak divisions of Honda's 33rd Army, in their effort to advance through Myitkyina against the northern flank of the Burma Road. There was an improvement in the autumn, however, after the exhausted Chindits had been replaced by the 36th Indian/British Division, and also, ironically, after the majority of the Chinese divisions had been withdrawn to meet the Japanese offensive in China. A further improvement followed Stilwell's replacement by Wedemeyer, and under him the take-over of the NCAC (Northern Combat Area Command) by General Sultan, another fresh American commander.

In December Sultan's forces, and not least its two remaining Chinese divisions, made quicker progress, and Honda's weak Japanese divisions were forced to retreat – south-westward, towards Mandalay. By mid-January this west-central stretch of the Burma Road was clear of the Japanese. By April the whole of it, from Mandalay to China, was again open.

By mid-November 1944, Stopford's 33rd Corps had established a bridgehead over the Chindwin, and Messervy's 4th Corps then thrust on eastwards into the Shwebo–Mandalay plain – while making contact at Banmauk, north-west of Indaw, with Festing's 36th Division which had by then pushed as far south as Indaw and Katha, on the Irrawaddy. From the lack of opposition it became evident that the Japanese were withdrawing from the Shwebo plain, thus disappointing Slim's hope of encircling and crushing them in relatively open country with his superior armour, artillery, and air force, and were falling back to positions on the Irrawaddy near Mandalay. So Slim recast his plan. While Stopford's 33rd Corps (with the equivalent of four divisions) pressed down on Mandalay from the north to gain crossings there over the Irrawaddy, the 4th Corps (with the equivalent of three divisions) was to advance due south from Kalemyo up the Myittha valley, as stealthily as possible, and then from Gangaw move south-east to gain a crossing over the Lower Irrawaddy near Pakokku, with the aim of creating a strategic barrier near Meiktila across the rear of the Japanese forces holding Mandalay – thus blocking their retreat south to, and supply from, Rangoon. The whole of this encircling plan on the central front depended on the solution of the logistical problems, and especially on adequate air supply.

By the beginning of 1945, while the 4th Corps was preparing for its deep flanking move, Stopford's 33rd Corps continued its southward advance on Mandalay. Shwebo was reached and occupied by January 10th, Monywa (on the Chindwin) by the 22nd, and another of his divisions had already gained crossings over the Irrawaddy fifty to seventy miles north of Mandalay – making a triple line of advance and threat.

Apart from an outlying detachment opposite Mandalay, the Japanese were now all on the east bank of the Irrawaddy.

Slim's new plan worked almost perfectly. Messervy's capture of Kahnla near Pakokku on February 10th was the signal for the operation to start. On the 14th his leading division gained a bridgehead near Nyaunga, south of Pakokku, where the Indian Nationalist troops holding that sector were easily overcome. His striking force under General Cowan, the specially motorized 17th Division plus a tank brigade, then passed through and took Taungtha on the 24th, reaching the outskirts of Meiktila on the 28th. It was momentarily cut off when a Japanese detachment reoccupied Taungtha, but was effectively kept supplied by air, and was thus able to capture Meiktila on March 3rd, after two days' fighting. Cowan then did his best to keep the initiative, and keep the Japanese confused, by a series of aggressive raids in various directions, by small infantry columns with tanks.

The Japanese were in a perilous situation – hard-pressed around Mandalay and with their rear communications being strangled, as well as being heavily outnumbered on the ground and largely without air cover. Nevertheless they fought back fiercely. Repeated attacks on Fort Dufferin, their stronghold in Mandalay, were repulsed, and they staged a desperate counteroffensive in the Meiktila area to clear their communications, two divisions working up from the south while another was hurried down from Mandalay, all now placed under Honda's 33rd Army (which had withdrawn from the Northern Front and the Burma Road). During the middle of March this battle was in a critical stage, but by the end of the month the Japanese counteroffensive had been defeated, and was abandoned. Meanwhile Stopford had at last captured Fort Dufferin, and Mandalay, on the 20th. Realizing the hopelessness of the situation the Japanese 15th Army had given up its attempt to hold Mandalay and retreated southward. Central Burma was now in British hands, and the way to Rangoon was open. The two British corps had suffered some 10,000 casualties in these weeks of struggle, but the Japanese losses were much higher – amounting probably to a third of their already depleted strength. Worse still for the prospects of further resistance was the loss of equipment they suffered, as they had to retreat eastward into the Shan Hills by a long and circuitous route.

While Rangoon now lay open to the British, the city had to be reached quickly because of the approach of the monsoon, coupled with the fact that the American transport aircraft were to be withdrawn from Burma and sent to help China at the beginning of June. Rangoon was more than 300 miles from Meiktila, and the whole supply system, already stretched, of Slim's Fourteenth Army would break down, if a South Burma port was not gained before then, to offset the transfer of the American aircraft and provide Slim's army with an alternative, seaborne, line of supply. So on April 3rd Mountbatten took the decision to order 'Operation Dracula', for early May, as an insurance in case Slim's army did not reach Rangoon in time. It was to be carried out by a division from Christison's corps with a regiment of medium tanks and a Gurkha parachute battalion.

Slim's plans for the exploiting southward advance from Mandalay and Meiktila were that Messervy's 4th Corps would drive down the main road and rail route, while Stopford's 33rd Corps would drive down both banks of the Irrawaddy – the latter depending for supply on inland water transport, while the former continued to have air supply.

The Japanese hoped to hold the Irrawaddy with the troops of their 28th Army arriving from Arakan, and that the remnants of their other two armies would be able to block Messervy. But this proved a vain hope as the remains were not in a fit state to fight. Meanwhile the 5th Division, originally Slim's reserve, pushed ahead, and by April 14th captured Yamethin, nearly forty miles south of Meiktila. Stopford's 33rd Corps also started its advance down the Irrawaddy and on May 3rd its spearhead division reached Prome, midway to Rangoon, while the Japanese 28th Army was kept bottled on the west bank of the Irrawaddy. Messervy's spearhead, after a slow start, pushed on still faster by the main road – reaching Toungoo (level with Prome) on April 22nd, where it headed off the leading remnants of the Japanese 15th Army that were retreating through the Shan Hills. By that time other Japanese remnants were 100 miles behind. A week later Messervy's spearhead reached Kadok, ninety miles from Toungoo and only seventy from Rangoon. Here it met stiffer resistance, as the Japanese were trying to keep open a link to the east, through Thailand. Within a few days the resistance was overcome, but brief as was the check it sufficed to deprive Messervy's men of the honour of liberating Rangoon.

For on May 1st 'Dracula' had been launched – with a parachute landing at the mouth of the Rangoon River and amphibious landings on both banks. Hearing that the Japanese were already evacuating Rangoon, the whole force re-embarked and moved up the river, entering the city next day. Early on May 6th it met Messervy's spearhead driving down from Kadok and Pegu. The liberation of Burma was now virtually complete.

Lack of opposition in the later stages of the campaign was mainly due to the Japanese having withdrawn most of their air force, and naval force, to meet the greater menace of the American advance in the Pacific. Against over 800 Allied combat aircraft (650 bombers and 177 fighters) they could only put up fifty obsolescent planes. Moreover, the success of the spirited British advance as a whole had depended on the American transport aircraft which maintained its supplies.

CHAPTER THIRTY-FIVE

Hitler's Ardennes Counterstroke

On December 15th, 1944, Montgomery wrote a letter to Eisenhower in which he said that he would like to spend Christmas at home before launching the next big offensive on the Rhine. He enclosed an account for £5 for payment of a bet that Eisenhower had made, the year before, that the war would be ended by Christmas, 1944.* That jesting reminder was not very tactful, since only a fortnight earlier – in a letter which 'made Ike hot under the collar' – he had pungently criticized Eisenhower's strategy and its failure to finish off the Germans, and gone on to suggest that Eisenhower should hand over the executive command.†

Showing exemplary patience, Eisenhower chose to take Montgomery's second letter as a joke rather than a jab. Replying on the 16th, he wrote: 'I still have nine days, and while it seems almost certain that you will have an extra five pounds for Christmas, you will not get it until that day.'

Neither of them, nor the commanders under them, reckoned with possible enemy interference in the pursuit of their offensive plans. On this day Montgomery's latest estimate of the situation, sent out to his troops in the 21st Army Group, confidently said: 'The enemy is at present fighting a defensive campaign on all fronts; his situation is such that he cannot stage major offensive operations.' Bradley, commanding the American forces of the 12th Army Group, held the same view.

But that very morning, December 16th, the enemy launched a tremendous offensive which upset the Allied commanders' plans. The blow was delivered against the front of the US First Army in the Ardennes, a hilly and wooded sector where the troops had been thinned out in order to amass the maximum force along the flatter avenues into Germany. Regarding the Ardennes as unsuitable for their attack, the Allies tended to disregard it as a likely line of enemy attack. Yet it was here that the Germans had chosen to stage the Blitzkrieg four years

* Butcher: *My Three Years with Eisenhower*, p 722.
† Ibid, p 718.

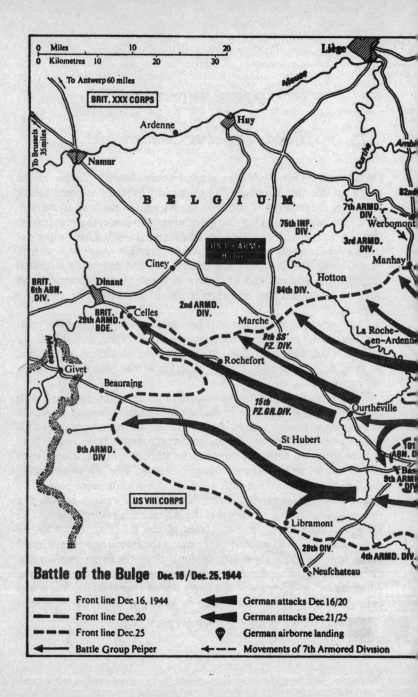

Battle of the Bulge Dec. 16 / Dec. 25, 1944

——— Front line Dec. 16, 1944	◄ German attacks Dec. 16/20
— — Front line Dec. 20	◄ German attacks Dec. 21/25
- - - Front line Dec. 25	◆ German airborne landing
◄—— Battle Group Peiper	◄- - - Movements of 7th Armored Division

Map labels: Liège · To Antwerp 60 miles · BRIT. XXX CORPS · Ardenne · Huy · To Brussels 35 miles · Namur · BELGIUM · 75th INF. DIV. · 7th ARMD. DIV. · Werbomont · 82nd · 3rd ARMD. DIV. · Manhay · U.S. 1 ARMY Hqtrs · Ciney · Hotton · BRIT. 6th ABN. DIV. · Dinant · 84th DIV. · Celles · BRIT. 29th ARMD. BDE. · 2nd ARMD. DIV. · Marche · 9th SS PZ. DIV. · La Roche-en-Ardenne · Rochefort · Givet · Beauraing · 15th PZ.GR.DIV. · Ourtheville · St Hubert · 101 ABN. D · 9th ARMD. DIV · Bas · 9th ARMD. DIV · US VIII CORPS · Libramont · 28th DIV. · 4th ARMD. DIV. · Neufchateau

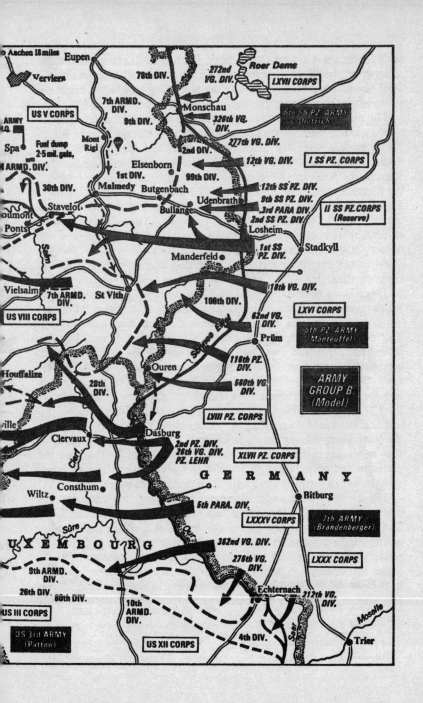

earlier which had shattered the Allied front in 1940 and produced the collapse of the West. It was strange that the Allied commanders of 1944 should have been so blind to the possibility that Hitler might try to repeat the surprise and its success in the same sector.

The news of the attack was slow to reach the higher headquarters in rear, and they were slower still to recognize its menace. It was late in the afternoon when the news came to SHAEF, Eisenhower's head-quarters at Versailles, where he and Bradley were discussing the next steps in the American offensive. Bradley frankly says that he regarded the German stroke merely as 'a spoiling attack',* to hinder his own. Eisenhower says he 'was immediately convinced that this was no local attack',† but the significant fact is that the two divisions which he held in SHAEF reserve were not alerted for moving to the scene until the evening of the next day, the 17th.

By that time the thin Ardennes front – where four divisions (of General Middleton's 8th Corps) were holding an eighty-mile stretch – had been burst wide open by the assault of twenty German divisions, of which seven were armoured, mustering nearly a thousand tanks and armoured assault guns. Bradley, on getting back to his Tactical HQ at Luxembourg, found his puzzled Chief of Staff brooding over the map in the war room, and exclaimed: 'Where in hell has this sonuvabitch gotten all his strength?'** The situation was worse than his HQ yet knew. Panzer spearheads had already penetrated up to twenty miles, and one of them had reached Stavelot. Until then, the Commander of the US First Army, Hodges, had also discounted the German thrust – and at first insisted on pressing on with his own offensive moves against the Roer Dams farther north. It was only on the morning of the 18th that he awoke to the seriousness of the menace on finding that the Germans had passed through Stavelot and were close to his own head-quarters at Spa – which was hurriedly moved back to a safer area.

The Higher Command's slowness in grasping the situation was partly due to the slowness with which information came back to them. This in turn was largely due to the way that German commandos, infiltrating in disguise through the broken front, cut many of the tele-phone wires running back from the front, and also spread confusion.

But that does not explain the Higher Command's seeming blindness to the possibility of a German counterstroke in the Ardennes. Allied Intelligence had known since October that the panzer divisions were

---

* Bradley: *A Soldier's Story*, p 455.
† Eisenhower: *Crusade in Europe*, p 342.
** Bradley: *A Soldier's Story*, p 466.

being withdrawn from the fighting line to refit for fresh action, and that part had been formed into a new 6th SS Panzer Army. By early December it was reported that the HQ of the 5th Panzer Army, after being relieved in the Roer sector west of Cologne, had shifted south to Coblenz. Moreover tank formations had been spotted moving towards the Ardennes, and newly formed infantry divisions had appeared in the line there. Then on December 12th and 13th came reports that two specially famous 'Blitz' divisions, the Grossdeutschland and the 116th Panzer, had arrived in this 'quiet' sector, and on the 14th that bridging equipment was being hauled up to the River Our which covered the southern half of the American front in the Ardennes. As early as December 4th a German soldier captured on this sector had revealed that a big attack was being prepared there, and his account was confirmed by many others taken in the days that followed. They also stated that the attack was due in the week before Christmas.

Why did these increasingly significant signs receive such scant attention? The Intelligence head of the First Army was not on very good terms with the Operational head, nor with the Intelligence head of the Army Group, and was also regarded as an alarmist inclined to cry 'Wolf'.* Moreover, even he failed to draw clear deductions from the facts he had gathered, while the imminently threatened 8th Corps formulated the perilously mistaken conclusion that the change-round of divisions on its front was merely the enemy's way of giving the new ones front-line experience prior to use elsewhere, and 'indicates his desire to have this sector of the front remain quiet and inactive'.

But besides lack of a clear picture of the strength of the attack from Intelligence, the miscalculation of the Allied Higher Commanders seems to have been due to four factors. They had been on the offensive so long that they could hardly imagine the enemy taking the initiative. They were so imbued with the military idea that 'attack is the best defence' as to become dangerously sure that the enemy could not hit back effectively so long as they continued their own attack. They reckoned that even if the enemy attempted a counterstroke it would be only in direct reply to their own direct advance towards Cologne and the industrial centres of the Ruhr. They counted all the more on such orthodoxy and caution on the enemy's side since Hitler had reappointed the veteran Field-Marshal Rundstedt, now in his seventieth year, as Commander-in-Chief in the West.

They proved wrong in all these respects, and the misleading effect of the first three was multiplied by the error of the last assumption. For

* Bradley: *A Soldier's Story*, p 464.

Rundstedt had nothing to do with the counterstroke except in a nominal way, although the Allies called it 'the Rundstedt offensive' – much to his annoyance then and later, since he not only disagreed with this offensive but washed his hands of it, leaving his subordinates to conduct it as best they could, with his HQ acting merely as a post office for Hitler's instructions.

The idea, the decision, and the strategic plan were entirely Hitler's own. It was a brilliant concept and might have proved a brilliant success *if* he had still possessed sufficient resources, as well as forces, to ensure it a reasonable chance of succeeding in its big aims. The sensational opening success was due partly to new tactics developed by the young General Hasso von Manteuffel – whom Hitler had recently promoted from a division to command an army, at forty-seven. But it was due also to the widely paralysing effect of a half-fulfilled brainwave of Hitler's – aimed to open the way to victory over the Allied armies, with their millions of men, by the audacious use of a few hundred men. For its execution he employed another of his discoveries, the thirty-six-year old Otto Skorzeny, whom he had sent the year before on a glider-borne raid to rescue Mussolini from a mountain-top prison.

Hitler's latest brain-wave was given the code-name 'Operation Greif' – the German word for that mythical creature, the Griffin. It was aptly named, for its greatest effect would be in creating a gigantic and alarming hoax behind the Allied lines.

As planned, however, it was a two-wave design that formed a modern version in strategy of the 'Trojan Horse' strategem of Homeric legend. In the first wave a company of English-speaking commando troops, wearing American field jackets over their German uniforms and riding in American jeeps, was to race ahead in little packets as soon as the front was pierced – to cut telephone wires, turn sign posts to misdirect the defender's reserves, hang red ribbons to suggest that roads were mined, and create confusion in any other way they could. Second, a whole panzer brigade in American 'dress' was to drive through and seize the bridges over the Meuse.

This second wave never got going. The Army Group staff failed to provide more than a fraction of the American tanks and trucks required, and the balance had to be made up with camouflaged German vehicles. That thin disguise entailed caution, and no clean breakthrough was made on the northern sector where this brigade was waiting, so its advance was postponed, and eventually abandoned.

But the first wave achieved astounding success – even more than had been expected. Some forty jeeps got through, and got busy on their confusion-spreading task – and all save eight came back safely. The few that fell into American hands caused the most trouble – by immediately creating the impression that many such sabotage bands were roving about behind the American front. One result was to cause an immense hold-up of traffic in the search for them, and hundreds of American soldiers who failed to satisfy questioners were arrested. Bradley himself says:

> ... a half-million GI's played cat and mouse with each other each time they met on the road. Neither rank nor credentials nor protests spared the traveler an inquisition at each intersection he passed. Three times I was ordered to prove my identity by cautious GI's. The first time by identifying Springfield as the capital of Illinois (my questioner held out for Chicago); the second time by locating the guard between the center and tackle on line of scrimmage; the third time by naming the then current spouse of a blonde named Betty Grable. Grable stopped me but the sentry did not. Pleased at having stumped me, he nevertheless passed me on.*

It was harder still for British liaison officers and visiting staff officers who did not know the right answer to such test-questions.

Then on the 19th one of the captured raiders said, when interrogated, that some of the jeep-parties had the mission of killing Eisenhower and other high commanders. It was an unfounded rumour that had circulated in the raiders' training camp before they were told their actual task. But now, when passed on to the Allied headquarters, it produced a security-service panic that spread the network of paralysing precautions right back to Paris – and kept it clamped on for ten days.

Eisenhower's naval aide, Captain Butcher, has a diary note on the 23rd:

> I went out to Versailles and saw Ike today. He is a prisoner of our security police and is thoroughly but helplessly irritated by the restriction on his moves. There are all sorts of guards, some with machine guns, around the house, and he has to travel to and from the office led and at times followed by an armed guard in a jeep.†

Fortunately the Germans also suffered heavily from self-inflicted difficulties, as well as from overstretched resources in straining to fulfil

---

* Bradley: *A Soldier's Story*, pp 467–9.
† Butcher: *My Three Years with Eisenhower*, pp 727–9.

Hitler's excessively ambitious aims. For in the large-scale planning his imagination ran away with him.

The project was well summarized by Manteuffel*:

The plan for the Ardennes offensive was drawn up completely by OKW [Hitler's HQ] and sent to us as a cut and dried 'Führer order'. The object defined was to achieve a decisive victory in the West by throwing in two panzer armies – the 6th under Dietrich, and the 5th under me. The 6th was to strike north-west, cross the Meuse between Liège and Huy, and drive for Antwerp. It had the main role, and main strength. My army was to advance along a more curving line, cross the Meuse between Namur and Dinant, and push towards Brussels – to cover the flank ... The aim of the whole offensive was, by cutting off the British Army from its bases of supply, to force it to evacuate the Continent.†

Hitler imagined that if he produced this second Dunkirk, Britain would virtually drop out of the war, and he would have breathing space to hold up the Russians and produce a stalemate in the East.

The plan was presented to Rundstedt, and the executive Army Group Commander, Field-Marshal Model, at the end of October. Describing his reactions, Rundstedt said:

I was staggered. Hitler had not consulted me about its possibilities. It was obvious to me that the available forces were far too small for such an extremely ambitious plan. Model took the same view of it as I did. In fact, no soldier believed that the aim of reaching Antwerp was really practicable. But I knew by now it was useless to protest to Hitler about the *possibility* of anything. After consultation with Model and Manteuffel I felt that the only hope was to wean Hitler from this fantastic aim by putting forward an alternative proposal that might appeal to him, and would be more practicable. This was for a limited offensive with the aim of pinching off the Allies' salient around Aachen.**

* Soon after the war ended I was able to interrogate a number of the leading German commanders, and discuss operations in detail with them on the map; where suitable I am utilizing striking passages from their accounts, after checking these with other later evidence.

† Liddell Hart: *The Other Side of the Hill,* p 446–7.

** Ibid, p 447.

But Hitler rejected this more modest plan, and insisted on the original design. Preparations were as stealthy as possible. Manteuffel said:

All the divisions of my own 5th Panzer Army were assembled, but kept widely spaced, between Trier and Krefeld – so that spies and the civil population should have no inkling of what was intended. The troops were told that they were being got ready to meet the coming Allied attack on Cologne. Only a very limited number of staff officers were informed of the actual plan.*

The 6th Panzer Army was assembled still farther back, in the area between Hanover and the Weser. Its divisions had been drawn out of the line to recuperate and be re-equipped. Curiously Sepp Dietrich was not informed of the task that was intended for him, nor consulted about the plan he would have to carry out, until much closer to the event. Most of the divisional commanders had only a few days' notice. In the case of Manteuffel's 5th Panzer Army, the move down to the starting line was made in three nights.

The strategic camouflage helped surprise, but a heavy price was paid for the extreme internal secrecy – particularly in the case of the 6th Panzer Army. Commanders who were informed so late had too little time to study their problem, reconnoitre the ground, and make their preparations. As a result many things were overlooked, and numerous hitches occurred when the attack began. Hitler had worked out the plan at his headquarters in detail, with Jodl, and seemed to think that this would suffice for its fulfilment. He paid no attention to local conditions or to the individual problems of his executants. He was equally optimistic about the needs of the forces engaged.

Rundstedt remarked: 'There were no adequate reinforcements, nor supplies of ammunition, and although the number of armoured divisions was high, their strength in tanks was low – it was largely paper strength.'†

---

* Liddell Hart: *The Other Side of the Hill*, p 449.

† That is borne out by the US Official History, by Dr Hugh Cole, which gives the average tank strength of the German armoured divisions as 90 to 100 – only half the American scale. It puts a different complexion on the Allied statement at the time, based on the number of divisions, that this was the most powerful concentration of tanks ever seen in the war.

The worst deficiency of all was motor fuel. Manteuffel said:

Jodl had assured us there would be sufficient petrol to develop our full strength and carry our drive through. This assurance proved completely mistaken. Part of the trouble was that OKW worked on a mathematical and stereotyped calculation of the amount of petrol required to move a division for a hundred kilometres. My experience in Russia had taught me that double this scale was really needed under battlefield conditions. Jodl didn't understand this.

Taking account of the extra difficulties likely to be met in a winter battle in such difficult country as the Ardennes, I told Hitler personally that five times the standard scale of petrol [fuel] supply ought to be provided. Actually, when the offensive was launched, only one and a half times the standard scale had been provided. Worse still, much of it was kept too far back, in large lorry columns on the east bank of the Rhine. Once the foggy weather cleared, and the Allied air forces came into action, its forwarding was badly interrupted.*

The troops, ignorant of all these underlying weaknesses, kept a remarkable trust in Hitler and his assurances of victory. Rundstedt said: 'The morale of the troops taking part was astonishingly high at the start of the offensive. They really believed victory was possible – unlike the higher commanders, who knew the facts.'

Rundstedt receded into the background after Hitler's rejection of the 'smaller' plan, leaving Model and Manteuffel, who had more chance of influencing Hitler, to fight for the technical changes in the plan that were all Hitler would consider. Rundstedt took only a nominal part in the final conference, held on December 12th in his headquarters at Ziegenberg, near Bad Nauheim. Hitler was present, and controlled the proceedings.

As to the technical changes, and tactical improvements, they are most vividly described in Manteuffel's account – which accords with evidence later gathered from documentary and other sources.

When I saw Hitler's orders for the offensive I was astonished to find that these even laid down the method and timing of the attack. The artillery was to open fire at 7.30 AM, and the infantry assault was to be launched at 11 AM. Between these hours the Luftwaffe was to

* Liddell Hart: *The Other Side of the Hill*, pp 450–1.

bomb headquarters and communications. The armoured divisions were not to strike until the breakthrough had been achieved by the infantry mass. The artillery was spread over the whole front of attack.

This seemed to me foolish in several respects, so I immediately worked out a different method, and explained it to Model. Model agreed with it, but remarked sarcastically: 'You'd better argue it out with the Führer.' I replied: 'All right, I'll do that if you'll come with me.' So on December 2nd, the two of us went to see Hitler in Berlin.

I began by saying: 'None of us knows what the weather will be on the day of the attack – are you sure the Luftwaffe can fulfil its part in face of the Allied air superiority?' I reminded Hitler of two occasions in the Vosges earlier where it had proved quite impossible for the armoured divisions to move in daylight. Then I went on: 'All our artillery will do at 7.30 is to wake the Americans – and they will then have three and a half hours to organize their countermeasures before our assault comes.' I pointed out also, that the mass of the German infantry was not so good as it had been, and was hardly capable of making such a deep penetration as was required, especially in such difficult country. For the American defences consisted of a chain of forward defence posts, with their main line of resistance well behind – and that would be harder to pierce.

I proposed to Hitler a number of changes. The first was that the assault should be made at 5.30 AM, under cover of darkness. Of course this would limit the targets for the artillery, but would enable it to concentrate on a number of key targets – such as batteries, ammunition dumps, and headquarters – that had been definitely located.

Secondly, I proposed to form one 'storm battalion' from each infantry division, composed of the most expert officers and men. (I picked the officers myself.) These 'storm battalions' were to advance in the dark at 5.30, without any covering artillery fire, and penetrate between the Americans' forward defence posts. They would avoid fighting if possible until they had penetrated deep.

Searchlights, provided by the flak units, were to light the way for the storm troops' advance by projecting their beams on the clouds, to reflect downwards. I had been much impressed by a demonstration of this kind which I had seen shortly beforehand, and felt that it would be the key to a quick penetration before daylight.

After setting forth my alternative proposals to Hitler, I argued that it was not possible to carry out the offensive in any other way if we were to have a reasonable chance of success. I emphasized: 'At 4 PM it will be dark. So you will only have five hours, after the assault at 11 AM, in which to achieve the breakthrough. It is very doubtful if you can do it in the time. If you adopt my idea, you will gain a further five and a half hours for the purpose. Then when darkness comes I can launch the tanks. They will advance during the night, pass through our infantry, and by dawn the next day they will be able to launch their own attack on the main position, along a cleared approach.'*

According to Manteuffel, Hitler accepted these suggestions without a murmur. That was significant. It would seem that he was willing to listen to suggestions that were made to him by a few generals in whom he had faith – Model was another – but he had an instinctive distrust of most of the senior generals, while his reliance on his own immediate staff was mingled with a realization that they lacked experience of battle conditions.

What these tactical changes did to improve the prospects of the offensive was offset, however, by a reduction of the strength that was to be put into it. For the executive commanders soon had damping news that part of the forces promised them would not be available – owing to the menacing pressure of the Russian attacks in the East.

The result was that the converging attack on Maastricht by the 15th Army, now commanded by Blumentritt, had to be dropped – thus leaving the Allies free to bring reserves down from the north. Moreover the 7th Army, which was to advance as flank cover to the southern wing of the offensive was left with only a few divisions – none of them panzer divisions.

In regard to the planning a number of key points deserve emphasis, and should be borne in mind throughout the narrative of the operations in this Ardennes offensive. The first is the importance of cloudy weather in German planning. The German leaders were well aware that the Allies could, if necessary, throw over 5,000 bombers into the battle, whereas Göring could promise only a thousand aircraft of all kinds for air support – and Hitler, by now wary of Luftwaffe promises, watered the figure down to 800–900 when presenting his plan to Rundstedt. In the event his estimate was fulfilled only on one day, and that when the ground battle had already been decided.

* Liddell Hart: *The Other Side of the Hill*, pp 451–3.

A second factor was that, after the July Plot, no German general could, or would, categorically oppose Hitler's plans, however foolhardy these were; the most they could secure was to persuade him to accept technical and tactical modifications, and here he was susceptible only to suggestions from those generals in whom he had special trust.

Other important factors were the whittling away of the strength originally promised, the role proposed for the flanking armies; the effect of the American attacks in November around Aachen in absorbing divisions originally earmarked for the German counteroffensive; the postponement of this counteroffensive from November to December, when conditions were less suitable; and the many differences of an adverse nature between the 1940 and the 1944 Blitzkreig.

Much depended on a quick advance of Dietrich's 6th SS Panzer Army which was nearest the Meuse on the key sector. Airborne troops could have been most valuable for opening the way here, but they had largely been used up in defensive ground fighting. A mere thousand parachutists were scraped up, barely a week before the offensive, and formed a battalion under Colonel von der Heydte. On getting in touch with the Luftwaffe command, von der Heydte found that more than half the crews of the aircraft allotted had no experience of parachute operations, and that necessary equipment was lacking.

The task eventually assigned to the parachute troops was, not to seize one of the awkward defiles ahead of the panzer advance, but to land on Mont Rigi near the Malmedy–Eupen–Verviers crossroads, and create a flank block to delay Allied reinforcements from the north. But on the evening before the attack the promised transport did not arrive to take the companies to the airfields, and the drop was postponed until the next night – when the ground attack had already started. Then, only a third of the aircraft managed to reach the correct dropping zone, and as von der Heydte had only been able to collect a couple of hundred men he could not gain the crossroads and establish a blocking position. For several days he harassed the roads with small raiding parties, and then, as there was no sign of Dietrich's forces arriving to relieve him, he tried to push eastwards to meet him, but was captured on the way.

Dietrich's right-hand punch was blocked early by the Americans' tough defence of Monschau. His left-hand punch burst through and, bypassing Malmedy, gained a crossing over the Amblève beyond Stavelot on the 18th – after a thirty-mile advance from the starting line. But it was checked in this narrow defile, and then cornered by an American countermove. Fresh efforts failed, in face of the Americans' rising strength as reserves were hurried to the scene, and the 6th Panzer Army's attack fizzled out.

On Manteuffel's front the offensive had a good· start. In his own words :

My storm battalions infiltrated rapidly into the American front – like rain-drops. At 4 o'clock in the afternoon the tanks advanced, and pressed forward in the dark with the help of 'artificial moonlight'.*

But after crossing the River Our they had to get through another awkward defile at Clervaux on the Clerf. These obstacles, combined with winter conditions, caused delay.

Resistance tended to melt whenever the tanks arrived in force, but the difficulties of movement offset the slightness of the resistance in this early stage.†

On the 18th, the Germans came close to Bastogne – after an advance of nearly thirty miles, but their attempt to rush this key road-centre on the 19th was checked.**

Eisenhower's two reserve divisions had at last been released, and were rushed to the front on the 18th. But they were then at Reims, a hundred miles away – and, worse still, the one intended for Bastogne (the 101st Airborne) was mistakenly sent north, through a staff error. But thanks to a traffic jam and a chance inquiry of a police sergeant, it turned aside on a southerly circuit, and thus came into Bastogne on the crucial morning of the 19th. Its fortunate arrival cemented the defence.

During the next two days successive German thrusts were foiled. So Manteuffel decided to by-pass Bastogne, and push on to the Meuse. But by now Allied reserves were gathering on all sides in a strength much exceeding that which the Germans had put into the offensive. Two of Patton's corps wheeled northward to the relief of Bastogne, and counter-attacked up the roads to Bastogne. Although temporarily held in check this counter-menace caused an increasing subtraction from the forces that Manteuffel could spare for his own advance.

The days of opportunity had passed. Manteuffel's swerving thrust

* Liddell Hart: *The Other Side of the Hill*, p 459.
† Ibid, p 460.
** Not entirely by the defenders – for a spearhead commander confessed to me in later discussion that at this vital moment he dallied with a young American nurse, 'blonde and beautiful', who held him spellbound in a village his troops had overrun. Battles are not always decided in the way that the military textbooks teach!

towards the Meuse caused alarm at Allied headquarters, but it was too late to be really serious. According to plan, Bastogne was to have been gained on the second day, whereas it was not reached until the third, and not by-passed until the sixth day. A 'small finger' came within four miles of the Meuse at Dinant on the 24th, but that was the utmost limit of progress, and the finger was soon cut off.

Mud and fuel shortage had been important brakes on the advance – owing to lack of fuel only half the artillery could be brought into action. While the foggy weather of the opening days had favoured the German infiltration by keeping the Allied air forces on the ground, this cloak of obscurity disappeared on the 23rd, and the scanty resources of the Luftwaffe proved incapable of shielding the ground forces from a terrible pummelling. That multiplied the toll for time lost. But Hitler was also paying forfeit for choosing to give the principal role to his northern wing, the 6th SS Panzer Army – in which his favoured Waffen SS were predominant – regardless of the fact that the ground there was much more cramped, while the Allies' forces were thicker, and reserves closer.

In the first week, the offensive had fallen far short of what was hoped, and the quickened progress at the start of the second week was illusory – for it only amounted to a deeper intrusion between the main road-centres, which the Americans were now firmly holding.

After this broad outline of operations, it is desirable to deal in more detail with some of the key phases of the battle on the different sectors.

In Dietrich's 6th SS Panzer Army – which had the main role but a relatively cramped front – the plan was for three infantry divisions to punch a hole on either side of Udenbrath, and then to swing north-west to form a hard shoulder facing north (reinforced by the two other infantry divisions), while the four armoured divisions drove through the gap, two by two, and made a dash for the great city and communication centre of Liège. These consisted entirely of the Waffen SS, the 1st, 12th, 2nd, and 9th SS Panzer Divisions, forming the 1st and 2nd SS Panzer Corps. They had about 500 tanks, including ninety Mark VIs, Tigers. It deserves mention that Dietrich himself had wished to make the breakthrough with two of his panzer divisions, but had been overruled by Model – who considered that the sector was too difficult for tanks, in such a task.

This sector was held by the US 99th Infantry Division, the most southerly of General Gerow's 5th Corps, and was about twenty miles wide – as were those of the divisions of Middleton's 8th Corps south of it. That was a lot to be allotted to any division – and showed how little any German attack was foreseen.

The bombardment opened at 5.30 AM, but the German infantry on this sector did not start advancing until about 7 AM, on December 16th. Individual posts were overwhelmed one by one, but many put up a great fight against heavy odds, inflicting heavy casualties on the Germans – and delaying the advance of their armoured divisions. Although the Germans were able to push westward on the next two days the tough American defence of the key Berg–Butgenbach–Elsenborn area prevented the Germans capturing the north shoulder as they had planned, and it remained in American hands for future use. Day after day, the defenders were to resist heavy German attacks. That was a great performance on the part of Leonard Gerow's US 5th Corps – which had hitherto been engaged in the American offensive on the Aachen sector, but been switched back, and south, in the emergency. (This repulse did much to damage the credit of the SS troops, and to cause Hitler's decision, on the 20th, to switch the main role in the offensive to Manteuffel's 5th Panzer Army.)

On Manteuffel's Army front, a quick breakthrough had been achieved on the right wing – nearest Dietrich's front. This sector, in the Schnee Eifel, was just over twenty miles wide, and held by the newly arrived US 106th Division along with the 14th Cavalry Group. It covered the approaches to the important road centre of St Vith. The remarkable feature here was that the attackers lacked any such overwhelming strength as had been deployed in the north – it comprised mainly the two infantry divisions of Lucht's German 66th Corps, with a brigade of tanks. But it succeeded, by the 17th, in surrounding two regiments of the 106th Division in a pincer movement, and forced the surrender of at least 7,000 men, probably 8,000–9,000. That was a tribute to the way that Manteuffel's new tactics had been applied. It was on Manteuffel's front that assault detachments were already inside the American positions before the barrage opened. By the verdict of the American Official History, the Schnee Eifel battle was 'the most serious reverse suffered by American arms during the operations of 1944–45 in the European theater.'

Farther south on Manteuffel's front the main thrust was delivered on the right by Krüger's 58th Panzer Corps and on the left by Lüttwitz's 47th Panzer Corps. The 58th, after crossing the River Our, drove towards Houffalize, with the further aim of gaining a bridgehead over the Meuse between Ardenne and Namur. The 47th, after crossing the Our, was to capture the key road-centre of Bastogne, and drive on to gain crossings over the Meuse south of Namur.

American outposts, of the 28th Division, had imposed some delay on the Germans in crossing the Our, but could not halt them, and by the second night, that of the 17th, they were approaching both Houffalize and Bastogne, and the lateral road between these two road centres – which they needed in order to deploy fully and develop their westward sweep.

In the extreme south, Brandenberger's German 7th Army of four divisions (three infantry and one parachute) had the task of offensively protecting Manteuffel's thrust by advancing through Neufchateau towards Mézières. All of its divisions managed to cross the Our, and the 5th Parachute Division on the inner flank thrust forward as far as Wiltz, a dozen miles westward, in three days. But the right wing of the 28th Division only gave ground slowly, while the other two divisions of Middleton's 8th Corps, the 9th Armored and the 4th Division, checked the attack after it had gone three to four miles. By the 19th it was clear that the southern shoulder of the German attack frontage was now firmly held. It was clear, too, that it would soon be reinforced by Patton's 3rd Army, wheeling north from the Saar, and on that day the German 80th Corps went on the defensive.

Manteuffel had appealed for a mechanized division to be given to his neighbour, the 7th Army, to enable it to keep with his own left wing, but it had been refused by Hitler himself. That refusal may have been crucial.

On the northern front, Dietrich's front, the panzer thrust only got going on the 17th, when the élite 1st SS Panzer Division drove forward in an effort to outflank Liège from the south, now that its path had been cleared. The leading column, 'Battle Group Peiper' – which had most of the division's 100 tanks – pressed on almost undisturbed in its drive to seize the Meuse crossings at Huy. On the way it achieved notoriety by massacring, with machine-gun fire, several batches of unarmed American prisoners, as well as of Belgian civilians. (Peiper claimed at his post-war trial that this was done in fulfilment of an order by Hitler that the thrust should be preceded 'by a wave of terror'. Peiper's unit, however, was the only one in the whole offensive that acted in this brutal way.) Peiper's battle-group halted for the night on the outskirts of Stavelot, still forty-two miles from the Meuse – although there was little reason why it should not have taken the vital bridge there, and the great fuel dump just north – which held over 2½ million gallons. Both were scantily guarded at that moment. The US First Army HQ at Spa, the inland watering place, was also close by. American reinforcements reached the area overnight and next day Peiper was kept at bay by a barrier of burning fuel, and then at Trois Ponts, three miles beyond, the bridges were blown in his face. Peiper then tried a detour down the flanking valley, but was checked, and held in check, at Stoumont only half a dozen miles beyond. Meanwhile he also learnt that his advance was isolated, and well ahead of the rest of the 6th Panzer Army.

To the south, on Manteuffel's front, the pressure increased on the key road-centres of St Vith and Bastogne – possession of which might be decisive for the prospects of the offensive. The first attacks on St Vith (twelve miles behind the front on the opening day) were made on December 17th, but only in small strength. By next day the bulk of the reinforcing US 7th Armored Division arrived on the scene. On the 18th the outlying villages fell one after the other as the German assault built up, and it was this pressure that prevented any relief of the two trapped regiments of the 106th Division. Moreover, panzer columns were out-flanking St Vith both from the north and the south, and had to be pushed back, while a German panzer brigade was moving forward to reinforce the attack.

By the 18th, Lüttwitz's 47th Panzer Corps was closing on Bastogne with two armoured divisions (the 2nd and Panzer Lehr) and the 26th Volksgrenadier Division. But reinforcements (a combat command from the US 9th Armored Division and engineer battalions) had arrived to help the defence. A struggle for each village, and transport confusion on the German side, slowed down the attack in time for the 101st Airborne Division, from Eisenhower's strategic reserve, to reach Bastogne on the morning of the 19th, a crucial moment. (It was temporarily commanded by Brigadier Anthony C. McAuliffe, as its usual commander, Major-General Maxwell D. Taylor, was away on leave in America.) The fierce defence of Bastogne, in which the American engineers particularly distinguished themselves, made it impossible for the Germans to rush the town, and the panzer columns swung past on either side – they had already created a gap on the north of the town – leaving the 26th Volksgrenadier Division with a panzer battle-group to reduce this road-centre. Thus Bastogne was cut off on December 20th.

It had been only on the morning of the 17th that Eisenhower and his principal subordinate commanders had begun to accept that a full-scale German offensive was under way – and it was not until the 19th that they were sure beyond doubt. Bradley ordered the 10th Armored Division northward and confirmed the initiative of Lieutenant-General William Simpson (of the 9th Army) in sending the 7th Armored Division southward, to follow the 30th Division. Thus over 60,000 fresh troops were moving to the threatened area, and 180,000 more were diverted thither in the next eight days.

The 30th Division (Major-General Leland S. Hobbs), out at rest near Aachen, was at first told to move to Eupen, then diverted to Malmedy, and then sent farther west to stop Peiper's panzer battlegroup. Part of Stavelot was retaken, with the help of fighter-bombers, and Peiper's links with the rest of the 6th Panzer Army were cut, while he was meeting increasingly strong opposition at Stoumont. By the 19th he was desperately short of fuel while the arrival of the 82nd Airborne Division and armoured reinforcements turned the balance against him. Meanwhile the bulk of the two SS Panzer Corps were still stuck far in rear. There were insufficient roads for them to advance and deploy their mass of tanks and transport. (Peiper's battle-group, ringed in and out of fuel, eventually began on the 24th to make its way back on foot, abandoning its tanks and other vehicles.)

Farther south, on Manteuffel's front, the elements of the US 3rd and 7th Armored Divisions had moved to bar the German advance westward from the St Vith area. The defenders of this town came under tremendous pressure from a strong attack directed by Manteuffel, and were soon forced out with heavy losses. Fortunately for them, a vast traffic jam hindered a quick exploitation, by the 66th Corps, and enabled the remnants of the US 106th Division and 7th Armored Division to slip away to safer positions: That helped to hinder any long-range exploitation of the gap by a rapid advance towards the Meuse in this sector.

When the front was split open Eisenhower was prompted on the 20th to put Montgomery in charge of all the forces on the north side of the breach, including both the 1st and 9th US Armies, and Montgomery had brought up his own reserve corps, the 30th (of four divisions), to guard the Meuse bridges.

His confident air was a great asset but the effect would have been better if he had not, as one of his own officers remarked, 'strode into Hodges' HQ like Christ come to cleanse the temple'. He aroused much wider resentment when at a Press conference later he conveyed the impression that his personal 'handling' of the battle had saved the American forces from collapse. He also spoke of having 'employed the whole available power of the British Group of Armies' and having 'finally put it into battle with a bang'. That statement caused the more irritation because on the southern flank Patton had been counterattacking since December 22nd – and relieved Bastogne on the 26th – whereas Montgomery had insisted that he must 'tidy up' the position first, and did not begin the counterthrust from the north until January 3rd, while keeping his British reserves out of the battle until then.

On the day of the regrouping of the Allied front, December 20th, the northern side of the breach was put in charge of Major-General J. Lawton Collins, whose US 7th Corps had previously been engaged in the American offensive towards the River Roer, and the Rhine. Montgomery made it clear that he wanted Collins – whose nickname was 'Lightning Joe' – and no one else for this crucial task. He was given for his new role the picked 2nd and 3rd Armored Divisions along with the 75th and 84th Infantry Divisions to mount a counterattack southward against Manteuffel's advancing spearheads.

At Bastogne the situation was, and continued, critical. Repeated attacks forced the defenders back, but they were never overwhelmed. On the 22nd Lüttwitz sent in a 'white flag' party calling on the beleaguered garrison to surrender on honourable terms, but merely got McAuliffe's cryptic reply 'Nuts!' – which has since become legendary. The subordinate commander on this sector, in trying to make it intelligible to the Germans, could only express it as 'Go to hell!'

Next day, the welcome advent of fine weather allowed the first supply drop by air, and many Allied air attacks on the German position. Meanwhile Patton's forces were moving up from the south. Even so, the situation was still precarious, for on the 24th, Christmas Eve, the perimeter was reduced to sixteen miles. But Lüttwitz's troops were also receiving few reinforcements or supplies, while being increasingly pounded by the Allied air forces. On Christmas Day, the Germans made an all-out effort, but their newly arrived tanks suffered heavily and the defence was unbroken. Moreover the US 4th Armored Division (now commanded by Major-General Hugh J. Gaffey), from Patton's 3rd Army, had fought its way up from the south, and made contact with the garrison at 4.45 PM on the 26th. The siege was raised.

Although the German 7th Army had initially made some progress in its attempt to cover Manteuffel's advancing left flank, its own weakness exposed it to a counterstroke from the south. By the 19th Patton had been told to abandon his own offensive through the Saar, and concentrate on wiping out the bulge Manteuffel had made, using two of his corps for the purpose. By the 24th his 12th Corps was pushing back the divisions of the German 7th Army, and eliminating the southern 'shoulder' they had tried to create.

Farther west the US 3rd Corps (4th Armored with 26th and 80th Infantry Divisions) concentrated on the relief of Bastogne. The famous 4th Armored was on its toes to carry out Patton's order of the 22nd, 'Drive like hell'. But the ground favoured the defence, and the main opposition came from the tough paratroops, fighting on foot, of the 5th Parachute Division. They had to be prised out of every village and wood. Reconnaissance found, however, less opposition on the Neufchateau–Bastogne road, and on the 25th the thrust was switched to the north-east axis instead of direct. Next day some of the few remaining Sherman tanks of the 4th Armored got through to the southern defences of Bastogne.

Meanwhile Manteuffel's panzer divisions, by-passing Bastogne, had been pushing on towards the Meuse, in the stretch south of Namur. To cover the crossings while fresh American forces were moving up, Horrocks's British 30th Corps had moved on to the east, as well as the west, bank of the river around Givet and Dinant, while American engineers stood ready to blow the bridges.

Hitler, having shortened his sights, now had his vision focused on the Meuse. He released the 9th Panzer and 15th Panzergrenadier Divisions from his OKW reserve to help Manteuffel in clearing the Marche–Celles area in the approaches to Dinant. Thus both sides were planning an offensive for Christmas Day, yet were too heavily engaged with each other to carry it out. But Collins's troops were slowly gaining ground; on Christmas morning his forces (helped by the British 29th Armoured Brigade) regained the village of Celles, barely five miles from the Meuse and Dinant – the highwater mark of the German advance. Numerous isolated pockets were mopped up later by infantry, or wiped out by air attack. From December 23rd on the panzer forces were severely harassed from the air, and by the 26th they were forbidden to try moving by day. The belated arrival of the 9th Panzer Division on Christmas evening failed to overcome the sturdy defence of the US 2nd Armored Division. By the 26th the Germans were falling back – and the Meuse was recognized as unattainable.

Dietrich's 6th Panzer Army had been told to make a fresh effort in support of Manteuffel's thrust, converging south-west towards it, but although it brought its panzer divisions into action it made little progress against American defences that were now strongly reinforced, and readily backed by instantaneous fighter-bomber assaults. The 2nd SS Panzer Division made an initial penetration that caused alarm and confusion, but suffered heavy loss in a prolonged fight for the village of Manhay (twelve miles s uth-west of Trois Ponts). In sum, the 6th

Panzer Army's offensive had produced nothing but exhaustion.

Long before the main counteroffensive opened the Germans had abandoned their northern push, and failed in a final effort on the southern wing. This last bid had followed Hitler's belated decision to switch his weight there and back up the 5th Panzer Army's thrust. But the chance had gone. Bitterly, Manteuffel said: 'It was not until the 26th that the rest of the reserves were given to me – and then they could not be moved. They were at a standstill for lack of petrol – stranded over a stretch of a hundred miles – just when they were needed.'* The irony of this situation was that on the 19th the Germans had come within a quarter of a mile of the huge fuel dump near Stavelot, containing some 2,500,000 gallons – a hundred times larger than the largest of the dumps they actually captured.

> We had hardly begun this new push before the Allied counteroffensive developed. I telephoned Jodl and asked him to tell the Führer that I was going to withdraw my advanced forces out of the nose of the salient we had made ... But Hitler forbade this step back. So instead of withdrawing in time, we were driven back bit by bit under pressure of the Allied attacks, suffering needlessly ... Our losses were much heavier in this later stage than they had been earlier, owing to Hitler's policy of 'no withdrawal'. It spelt bankruptcy, because we could not afford such losses.†

Rundstedt endorsed this verdict: 'I wanted to stop the offensive at an early stage, when it was plain that it could not attain its aim, but Hitler furiously insisted that it must go on. It was Stalingrad No. 2.'†

The Allies had come near disaster at the start of the Ardennes battle through neglecting their defensive flank. But in the end it was Hitler who carried to the extreme the military belief that 'attack is the best defence'. It proved the 'worst defence' – wrecking Germany's chances of any further serious resistance.

* Liddell Hart: *The Other Side of The Hill*, p 463.
† Ibid, p 464.

PART VIII

FINALE
1945

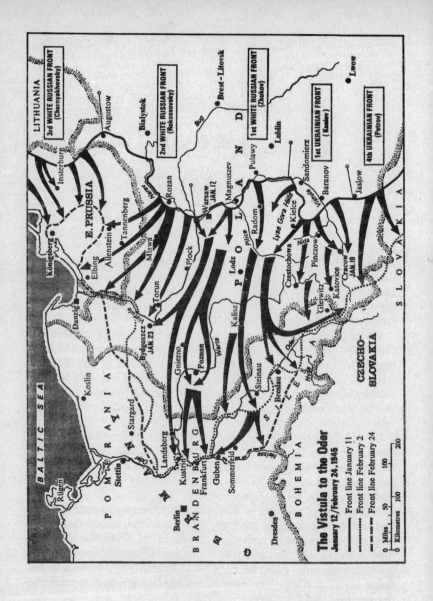

The Vistula to the Oder
January 12/February 24, 1945

Front line January 11
Front line February 2
Front line February 24

0   50   100   200 Miles
0   50   100   200 Kilometres

LITHUANIA

3rd WHITE RUSSIAN FRONT
(Chernyakhovsky)

2nd WHITE RUSSIAN FRONT
(Rokossovsky)

1st WHITE RUSSIAN FRONT
(Zhukov)

1st UKRAINIAN FRONT
(Koniev)

4th UKRAINIAN FRONT
(Petrov)

BALTIC SEA

Rügen

Stettin

Köslin

Danzig

Königsberg

Insterburg

E. PRUSSIA

Elbing

Allenstein

Tannenberg

Augustow

Bialystok

Brest – Litovsk

Lublin

Lwow

P   O   M   E   R   A   N   I   A

Stargard

Berlin

BRANDENBURG

Landsberg

Kustrin

Frankfurt

Guben

Sommerfeld

Dresden

BOHEMIA

CZECHO-
SLOVAKIA

Mlawa

Plock

Torun

Bydgoszcz
JAN. 23

Gniezno

Poznan

Kalisz

Steinau

Breslau

S   I   L   E   S   I   A

Gleiwitz

Katovice

Cracow
JAN. 19

Pinczow

Czestochowa

Kielce

Lysa Gora Hills

Lodz

Radom

Rozan

Warsaw
JAN. 17

Magnuszev

Pulawy

Sandomierz

Baranov

Jaslow

SLOVAKIA

P   O   L   A   N   D

Nida

Warta

Oder

Neisse

Pilica

Bug

Vistula

CHAPTER THIRTY-SIX

The Sweep from Vistula to Oder

Stalin had notified the Western Allies that he would launch a fresh offensive from the Vistula line about the middle of January, to coincide with their intended attack on the Rhine line – now delayed by the dislocation caused by the Ardennes counteroffensive. No great expectations were built on the Russian offensive by high quarters in the West. Some of the Russian reservations about weather conditions, the continued withholding of adequate information about the Russian forces, and the prolonged standstill since the Russians' arrival on the Vistula at the end of July had contributed to a revival of the tendency to underestimate what the Russians could do.

Before the end of December ominous reports were received by Guderian – who, in this desperately late period of the war, had been made Chief of the General Staff. Gehlen, the head of the 'Foreign Armies East' section of Army Intelligence, reported that 225 Russian infantry divisions and twenty-two armoured corps had been identified on the front between the Baltic Sea and the Carpathians, assembled ready to attack.

But when Guderian presented this ominous report of the massive Russian preparations, Hitler refused to believe it, and exclaimed: 'It's the biggest imposture since Jenghiz Khan! Who is responsible for producing all this rubbish?' Hitler preferred to rely on the reports of Himmler and the SS Intelligence service.

Hitler rejected the idea of stopping the Ardennes counteroffensive and transferring troops to the Eastern Front, on the ground that it was of prime importance to keep the initiative in the West which he had 'now regained'. At the same time he refused Guderian's renewed request that the army group (of twenty-six divisions) now isolated in the Baltic States should be evacuated by sea and brought back to reinforce the gateways into Germany.

As a crowning blow, Guderian found, on getting back to his own HQ, that while he had been travelling Hitler had taken advantage of his absence and ordered two panzer divisions from Poland to go south to

Hungary for an attempt to relieve Budapest. That left Guderian with a mobile reserve of only twelve to back up the fifty weak infantry divisions that were stretched out in holding the main front – 700 miles long.

Western doubts of the Russians' capabilities were magnified by news of the German counteroffensive towards Budapest. Impressions of its potentiality were increased by the shock that the Western Allies had themselves suffered in the recent counteroffensive. For several days the attack towards encircled Budapest made ominous progress. Starting near Komorn, forty miles west of the city, it penetrated more than half the distance that separated it from the besieged garrison. But then persistence in face of stiffening opposition made it a costly failure.

The indirect cost was still heavier. The resisting power of this fresh 'hedgehog' had encouraged Hitler's characteristic tendency to insist on staying too long. When as a result his forces there had been encircled, his anxiety to avert a second 'Stalingrad' had prompted him to a step that led him into deeper trouble, for although the two precious panzer divisions held ready to meet the expected Russian winter offensive in Poland had been taken away on the eve of the New Year to form a spearhead for the attempt to relieve Budapest, yet Hitler would not permit any compensating withdrawal from the Vistula line prior to the delivery of the Russian blow. That weakened line was compelled to stand the full shock of it, instead of being allowed to damp the shock by a timely step-back. Once again the psychological assets of the policy of holding 'at all costs' were outweighed by its strategical debits, and entailed bankruptcy.

The Russian High Command was now well prepared to exploit the fundamental weaknesses of the German situation. With due realization of the decisive importance of sustained momentum, and the handicap of overstretched communications, it held its hand until the railways behind the new front had been repaired and converted from the normal Continental gauge to its own broad gauge track. Abundant supplies were accumulated at the railheads. The primary objective was the capture of Upper Silesia, the one important industrial area of Germany which remained intact and was sheltered from Allied bombing. This objective called for an advance of just over a hundred miles from the Baranov bridgehead on the Vistula in southern Poland. But Stalin and Vasilevsky, his Chief of Staff, had wider and deeper aims in the grand design which they had framed. They had their eyes on the Oder, and beyond that on Berlin – nearly 300 miles from their positions near Warsaw. By extending the scope of their offensive they would profit by the wide space for manoeuvre. More important than their numerical superiority of nearly five to one was their increased manoeuvring power. The mounting stream of American trucks had now enabled them to motorize a much larger proportion of their infantry brigades, and thus, with the increasing production of their own tanks, to multiply the number of armoured and mobile corps for exploiting a breakthrough. At the same time, the growing number of Stalin tanks strengthened their punch. These monsters mounted a 122-mm gun, compared with the 88-mm gun of the Tiger. They were also more thickly armoured than the Tiger, though not as thickly as the 'King Tiger'.

Before the new campaign started the 'fronts' were reorganized, and Russia's three outstanding offensive leaders were used to command the main drives. While Koniev remained in charge of the '1st Ukrainian front' in southern Poland, in the central sector Zhukov took over the '1st White Russian front' from Rokossovsky, who was transferred to command of the '2nd White Russian front' on the Narev north of Warsaw.

The Russian offensive was launched at 10 AM on January 12th, 1945, by Koniev's forces, from the Baranov bridgehead (which was some thirty miles wide and deep). Ten armies (including two tank armies) were deployed, comprising some seventy divisions supported by two air armies.

At the start, the speed of the penetration was handicapped by the way that fog hung over the battlefield and kept the air forces on the ground. But the fog helped to cloak the assaulting troops, and the mass of well-handled artillery steadily pulverized the defence, so that on the third day the attack had broken through to Pinczow – twenty miles from the jumping off line – and crossed the Nida on a broad front. Then the phase of exploitation began. Pouring through the gap, the armoured corps spread over the Polish plain in an expanding torrent. For the moment the widening of the breach was more significant than its deepening. Kielce was taken on the 15th by a column that was sweeping north-westward round the end of the Lysa Gora hills, and thus threatening the rear of the German forces facing Zhukov's front.

On the 14th, Zhukov had launched an offensive from his bridgeheads around Magnuszev and Pulawy. His right wing wheeled north towards the rear of Warsaw, while his left wing took Radom on the 16th. That day Koniev's spearheads crossed the Pilica River – only thirty miles from the Silesian frontier. Meanwhile Rokossovsky's forces had struck, also on the 14th, from their two bridgeheads over the Narev and broken through the defences covering the southern approach to East Prussia.

The breach was 200 miles wide, and altogether a flood of nearly 200 divisions (including the reserves) was now rolling westward.

On the 17th Warsaw fell to Zhukov's forces, which had swept round it on both flanks, and his armoured spearheads had penetrated west almost as far as Lodz. Koniev's advanced forces captured the city of Czestochowa, close to the Silesian frontier, and farther south they passed the flank of Cracow.

On the 19th Koniev's right wing reached the Silesian frontier, while his left wing captured Cracow by an enveloping attack. Zhukov's forces captured Lodz, and Rokossovsky's reached the southern gateway into East Prussia, near Mlawa. Chernyakhovsky's and Petrov's forces had made advances on the two extreme flanks. Thus at the end of the first week the offensive had been carried 100 miles deep, and its frontage widened to nearly 400 miles.

In a belated effort to cover the approaches to Silesia, seven German divisions were rushed north from the front in Slovakia. Heinrici, who commanded there, had actually suggested before the storm broke that he could spare part of his strength to provide reserves for the Vistula line, but such a redistribution ran contrary both to Hitler's principle that 'every man must fight where he stands', and to his habit of conducting the campaign in compartments. After the front in Slovakia had been almost stripped, it was still maintained for several weeks – showing that its original strength had been in excess of the need. But the arrival of seven extra divisions on the north side of the Carpathians now counted for less than a couple would have meant before the Russian offensive opened. For the breach had become too wide to be filled.

Most of western Poland is so open that it gives the attacker a natural advantage, easy to exploit if he possesses the superiority of strength or mobility to profit by the wide spaces. The Germans had thus profited in 1939. Now, themselves on the defensive, they were short of both strength and mobility. As an exponent of mechanized warfare, Guderian had realized that rigid defence was vain and that the only chance of checking a breakthrough lay in the counter-manoeuvre of armoured reserves. But he had been compelled both to stay on the Vistula and to see a portion of his scanty armour dispatched to Budapest just before the attack. By throwing in part of the remainder near Kielce, time was gained for the extrication of the enveloped forces in the Vistula bend; consequently the Russian bag of prisoners – 25,000 – in the first week of the offensive was remarkably small for such an immense breakthrough. But the German Army's growing deficiency in the means of mobility, for rapid retreat, was reflected in the fact that the bag was more than trebled in the second week – rising to 86,000. The Russians' increased mobility was similarly reflected in their continued strides.

The hasty evacuation of the civil population from the towns inside Germany's borders was a sign that the pace of the Russian advance had upset all calculations, and hustled the German forces out of intermediate positions which they had hoped to hold.

On January 20th Koniev's forces penetrated the Silesian frontier and established themselves on German soil. More ominous still was Rokossovsky's arrival on the historic field of Tannenberg, across the southern frontier of East Prussia. This time there was to be no repetition of the Russians' 1914 reverse, and next day his spearheads reached Allenstein junction, severing the main rail artery of East Prussia, while Chernyakhovsky, advancing from the east, captured Insterburg. Continuing his uppercut, Rokossovsky reached the Gulf of Danzig near Elbing on the 26th, thus isolating all the German forces in East Prussia. These fell back into Königsberg, where they were invested.

Four days earlier, Koniev had reached the Oder on a forty-mile front, north of the industrial area of Upper Silesia. By the end of the second week of the offensive his right wing was across the Upper Oder at numerous points along a sixty-mile stretch south of Breslau – which was 180 miles from its starting line. Other columns had enveloped the Silesian capital from the north. Behind this line of spearheads other troops had wheeled south to capture Gleiwitz junction and isolate the industrial area of Upper Silesia. The whole area was criss-crossed with trenches, barbed wire, and anti-tank ditches, studded with pillboxes, but the forces to hold this potential fortress zone were lacking. Those that were available, or arriving, were impeded by the flood of civilian refugees. The roads were jammed with wrecked vehicles and abandoned chattels. Exploiting the confusion, the Russian columns were able to enter by the back door when the front was barred. German air reports vividly described the Russian advance as looking like an immense octopus weaving long tentacles among the Silesian towns. They spoke of seeing apparently endless columns of trucks, laden with supplies and reinforcements, stretching far to the east.

Even more striking in measure, and deadly in prospect, was Zhukov's sweeping advance in the centre. Executing an oblique manoeuvre, he had shifted the mass of his armoured forces to his right. They drove down the corridor between the Vistula and the Warta, profiting by this unexpected turn to penetrate the chain of lakes east of Gniezno, at the narrowest part of the corridor, before the passages could be manned. Their drive carried them across the rear of the famous Vistula fortress

of Torun, and into Bydgoszcz (Bromberg) on the 23rd. Other armoured columns were closing on the still greater communication centre of
Poznan. Here they met stiffer resistance. By-passing the fortress, they
drove on to the west and north-west; by the end of the week they had
reached the frontiers of Brandenburg and Pomerania – 220 miles from
Warsaw and barely 100 miles from Berlin. At the same time Zhukov's
left wing, after crossing the Warta and capturing Kalisz, had come up
level with Koniev's right wing.

The third week opened with the occupation of Katovice and other
big industrial towns in Upper Silesia by Koniev's left wing, while his
right wing gained a fresh bridgehead over the Oder at Steinau, forty
miles north-west of Breslau. Zhukov's advanced forces crossed the
frontiers of Brandenburg and Pomerania on the 30th, and then overcame the resistance which the Germans put up on the line of the Oder,
which was frozen. On the 31st Landsberg was captured, while Zhukov's
tank spearheads, thrusting past it, reached the Lower Oder near Kustrin – forty miles from the outskirts of Berlin. A space of only 380
miles now separated the Russians from the forward positions of their
Western Allies.

But the law of overstretch was at last coming to the Germans' aid, in
diminishing the pressure that the Russians could develop on the Oder,
and multiplying the resisting power of the mixture of regular and
Volkssturm 'Home Guard' troops which the German Command had
scraped together to hold that line. The stubborn defence of Poznan
helped to block the routes by which the Russians could bring up supplies and reinforcements to their advanced forces. A thaw in the first
week of February also imposed a brake by turning the roads into quag-
mires, while it unfroze the Oder, thus increasing its effect as an obstacle. Although Zhukov's forces had closed up to the river on a broad
front by the end of the first week of February, and gained crossings near
Kustrin and Frankfurt-an-der-Oder, they had not sufficient weight to
exploit these, and were then penned into shallow bridgeheads.

Koniev now sought to develop a flanking leverage, and oblique approach to Berlin. Extending their bridgeheads north of Breslau, his
forces burst out to the west on February 9th, and then wheeled north-
west in a wide-fronted sweep down the left bank of the Oder. On the
13th they reached Sommerfeld, eighty miles from Berlin (that same
day Budapest at last fell, having yielded 110,000 prisoners altogether).
Two days later, and a further twenty miles on, they reached the Neisse,
near its junction with the Oder, and thus came up level with Zhukov's
advanced forces.

But the Germans' defence also benefited, once more, from being driven back to the straight, shorter line formed by the Lower Oder and the Neisse. On that line their front was only a fraction of its former width – less than 200 miles from the Baltic to the Bohemian mountain-frontier. That great reduction of the space to be covered went far to balance their loss of strength, enabling them to recover a more reasonable ratio of force to space than they had ever enjoyed since the scales turned against them. Behind the Russian front Breslau still held out, and thereby put a rear-wheel brake on Koniev's progress, just as Poznan – which at last fell on the 23rd – had earlier hampered Zhukov's.

Koniev was checked on the Neisse, while Zhukov's more direct advance was still blocked on the lower Oder. By the third week of February the front in the East was stabilized, with the aid of German reinforcements brought from the West and from the interior. The Russians were held up on that line until the issue had been finally decided by the collapse on the Rhine.

It was the crisis produced by the Russian menace, however, which had led to the Germans' fateful decision that the defence of the Rhine must be sacrificed to the needs of the Oder, in order to keep the Russians at bay. More important than the actual number of divisions switched from the West to the East was the diversion eastward of the bulk of the reinforcements that could be scraped up to fill the depleted ranks. The way was thus eased for the Anglo-American offensive to reach the Rhine and cross it.

CHAPTER THIRTY-SEVEN

The Collapse of Hitler's Hold on Italy

While the German winter position looked on the map unpleasantly similar to that of the year before, and almost as formidable, even though 200 miles farther north, there were many favourable factors.* By the end of 1944 the Allies were through the Gothic Line, there was no such naturally strong or well-fortified position ahead, and they were in a much better 'jumping-off' position for their spring offensive in 1945. Moreover, there were other important factors that made the Allied armies relatively far more powerful.

In March, on the eve of their spring offensive, they comprised seventeen divisions, and now had six Italian combat groups. The Germans had twenty-three divisions, and four so-called Italian divisions which Mussolini had managed to raise in northern Italy since his own rescue by the Germans (these, really, were little larger than combat groups). But any such comparison by number of divisions gives an essentially false picture of the balance. The Allied fighting strength included six independent armoured brigades and four independent infantry brigades – the equivalent of three to four more divisions.

A count of the number of men comes nearer the truth. The Fifth and Eighth Armies totalled some 536,000, besides 70,000 Italians. The Germans totalled 491,000, and 108,000 Italians, but of the Germans 45,000 were police or anti-aircraft personnel. The figures of fighting troops and weapons were a still better way of comparison. For example, when the Eighth Army opened the offensive in April it enjoyed odds of approximately 2 to 1 in fighting troops (57,000 against 29,000), 2 to 1 in artillery (1,220 pieces against 665), and over 3 to 1 in armoured vehicles (1,320 against 400).

In addition, the Allies benefited from the help of some 60,000 partisans, who were producing much confusion behind the German lines and forcing the Germans to divert troops from the front to curb their activities.

* For map, see pp 548–9.

Still more important was the Allies' now absolute command of the air. Their strategic bombing campaign was having such a paralysing effect that German divisions could only have been moved out of Italy to other theatres with great difficulty, even if Hitler had ordered it. Along with it was the Germans' increasing shortage of fuel for their mechanized and motorized formations, a shortage which was now becoming so acute that they could neither move quickly to close gaps, as they had done previously, nor carry out a delaying 'manoeuvre in retreat'. But Hitler was more unwilling than ever to sanction any strategic withdrawal even while there was a possibility of attempting it.

The three months' pause since the close of the Allies' autumn offensive had brought a great change in the spirit and outlook of their troops. They had seen the arrival of new weapons in abundance – amphibious tanks, 'Kangaroo' armoured personnel carriers, 'Fantails' (tracked landing vehicles), heavier-gunned Sherman and Churchill tanks, flame-throwing tanks, and 'tank-dozers'. There was also plenty of new bridging equipment, and huge reserves of ammunition.

On the German side, Field-Marshal Kesselring had returned from convalescence in January, but in March he was called to the Western Front on being appointed to succeed Field-Marshal von Rundstedt as Commander-in-Chief there. Vietinghoff now definitely replaced him as C-in-C of Army Group C in Italy. Herr now took command of the German 10th Army which held the eastern part of the front, with the 1st Parachute Corps (of five divisions) and the 76th Panzer Corps (of four.) Senger, commanding the 14th Army, held the western part – which was wider, as it included the Bologna sector – with the 51st Mountain Corps (of four divisions) holding the line towards Genoa and the Mediterranean, while the 14th Panzer Corps (of three divisions) covered Bologna. There were only three divisions in Army Group reserve, as two were posted in rear of the Adriatic flank, and two near Genoa, to guard against amphibious landings behind the front. For the time being, also, the three divisions in Army Group reserve were being used to guard against these same contingencies.

On the Allied side, in Mark Clark's Army Group (entitled the 15th) the right wing, facing the German 10th Army, was formed by the Eighth Army under McCreery, and comprised the British 5th Corps (of four divisions); the Polish Corps (of two divisions); the British 10th Corps, now almost a skeleton consisting of two Italian combat groups, the Jewish Brigade, and the Lovat Scouts; and the British 13th Corps which was really the 10th Indian Division. The 6th Armoured Division was in Army reserve. To the west was the Fifth Army, now com-

manded by Truscott, which comprised the American 2nd Corps (of
four divisions), and 4th Corps (of three divisions), with two more
divisions in Army reserve. They included two armoured divisions,
the 1st US and the 6th South African.

The aim, and primary problem, of the Allied planners was to overrun
and wipe out the German forces before they could escape over the River
Po. This could best be achieved by armoured forces in the flat stretch of
some thirty miles, between the courses of the lower Reno and the Po.
(In the early part of January, when there was a spell of dry weather, the
Eighth Army had closed up to the Senio, which runs into the lower
Reno near the Adriatic.) It was hoped that the Eighth Army, by seizing
the Bastia–Argenta area just west of Lake Comacchio, would be able
to open the way into the plain. The Fifth Army was to attack a few
days later, thrusting northward near Bologna. The combined thrusts
should cut off the Germans' retreat, and trap them. The Allied offensive was to be launched on April 9th.

The Eighth Army's plan was complex, but ably conceived and designed. Simulated preparations for a landing north of the Po were to
keep Vietinghoff looking, and most of his reserve poised, in that direction. To strengthen the impression, Commandos and the 24th Guards
Brigade, at the beginning of April, seized the spit of sand separating
Lake Comacchio from the sea, and a few days later the Special Boat
Service occupied the small islands in that vast inland stretch of water.

The main attack was to be delivered, across the Senio, by the British
5th Corps and the Polish Corps. The former was to break through well
up the Senio, hoping to catch the Germans off balance, and there part
of it would wheel right against the flank of the Bastia–Argenta corridor (which had come to be called the Argenta Gap) just west of Lake
Comacchio, while another part drove north-westward toward the rear of
Bologna, to cut off that city from the north. The Poles were to thrust
along Route 9, the Via Emilia, more directly towards Bologna. The
56th Division on the right wing (of the 5th Corps) was given the task of
storming the Argenta Gap by a combination of direct assault and a
flanking manoeuvre by the 'Fantails' across Lake Comacchio.

The left wing of the Eighth Army, consisting of the skeletonized
10th and 13th Corps, was to start thrusting northward, past Monte
Battaglia, until squeezed out by the converging advance of the Poles
and Americans; the 13th would then join 6th Armoured Division in the
exploitation of success.

After the preliminary operations on the sandspit and Lake Comacchio had focused Vietinghoff's attention on the coastal sector, a massive bombardment was launched in the afternoon of April 9th by some 800 heavy bombers and 1,000 medium or fighter bombers, while 1,500 guns put down a series of five concentrations, each of forty-two minutes' duration with ten minute intervals – for which reason they were called 'false alarm' bombardments. Then at dusk the infantry advanced, while the Tactical air forces kept the Germans pinned down. The defenders were stunned by this storm of bombs and shells, while the flame-throwing tanks that accompanied the infantry proved a terrifying addition. By the 12th General Keightley's 5th Corps had crossed the Santerno and was pressing on. Although opposition became stiffer as the Germans recovered from the initial shock, the Bastia Bridge was captured on the 14th, before its demolition was completed. (The 'Fantails' had been disappointing on Lake Comacchio, where the water was shallow and the bottom soft, but proved much more effective in the flooded area round the Argenta Gap.) Even so, it was the 18th before the British were right through the Argenta Gap. The Poles met even stiffer opposition from the German 1st Parachute Division before they succeeded in overcoming its outstandingly formidable troops.

The start of the US Fifth Army's attack was delayed until April 14th by bad weather, particularly bad flying weather for its supporting aircraft – and it had to overcome several remaining mountain ridges before it could get through to the plains and Bologna. On the 15th its progress was aided by the dropping of 2,300 tons of bombs – a record for the campaign. But for two days more the Germans of the 14th Army put up a tough resistance; and it was not until the 17th that the 10th Mountain Division of the US 4th Corps achieved a breakthrough, and raced on towards the vital lateral highway, Route 9. But within two days the whole front was collapsing, and the Americans had reached the outskirts of Bologna, while their exploitation forces were sweeping on to the Po.

Most of Vietinghoff's forces had been committed to the front line, and he had few reserves – and less fuel – to check an Allied penetration. It was no longer possible to stabilize the front or to extricate his forces, and the only hope of saving them was by retreat – a long retreat. But Hitler had already rejected General Herr's proposals for an elastic defence, by tactical withdrawals from one river to the next – which might have stultified the British Eighth Army's offensive. On April 14th, just before the American offensive was launched, Vietinghoff appealed for permission to retire to the Po before it was too late. His appeal was rejected, but on the 20th he took the responsibility of ordering such a retreat himself.

By then it was far too late. The Allies' three armoured divisions, in two sweeping moves, had cut off and surrounded most of the opposing forces. Although many Germans managed to escape by swimming that broad river, they were in no condition to establish a new line. On the 27th the British crossed the Adige and penetrated the Venetian Line covering Venice and Padua.

The Americans, moving still faster, took Verona a day earlier. The day before that, April 25th, a general uprising of the partisans took place, and Germans everywhere came under attack from them. All the Alpine passes were blocked by April 28th – the day on which Mussolini and his mistress, Claretta Petacci, were caught and shot by a band of partisans near Lake Como. German troops were now surrendering everywhere, and the Allied pursuit met little opposition anywhere after April 25th. By the 29th the New Zealanders reached Venice and by May 2nd were at Trieste – where the main concern was not the Germans but the Yugo-Slavs.

Background negotiations for a surrender had, in fact, begun as early as February, initiated by General Karl Wolff, the head of the SS in Italy, and handled on the other side by Allen W. Dulles, head of the American OSS (Office of Strategic Services) in Switzerland – using Italian and Swiss intermediaries initially, and then face to face. Wolff's motives seem to have been a mixture of wishing to avoid further senseless damage in Italy and the desire to repel Communism by aligning with the Western Powers – motives that many Germans shared. Wolff's importance, besides his control of SS policy, lay in the fact that he was in charge of the regions behind the front, and could thus nullify Hitler's idea of creating an Alpine redoubt for a final stand.

The talks were complicated and delayed on the German side by Vietinghoff being appointed to take over from Kesselring, on the Allied side by Russian demands to participate, and on both sides by the mutual suspicion and caution which accompanies such background negotiations. Although the discussions in March were promising, Karl Wolff's activities were frozen early in April by Himmler. Thus although Vietinghoff by April 8th was considering a way of surrender, this could not be achieved in time to avert the Allies' spring offensive.

At a meeting on April 23rd, however, Vietinghoff and Wolff decided, in agreement, to disregard orders from Berlin for continued resistance, and to negotiate a surrender. By the 25th Wolff had ordered the SS not to resist the partisan take-over – and Marshal Graziani was manifesting a desire for surrender on the part of the Italian Fascist forces. At 2 PM on April 29th, German envoys signed a document providing for an unconditional surrender on May 2nd at 12 noon (2 PM Italian time). Despite a last minute intervention by Kesselring this duly went into effect on that date – six days before the German surrender in the West. Although military success had assured the Allies of victory, this channel smoothed the way to a quicker ending of the war, thereby curtailing loss of life and destruction.

CHAPTER THIRTY-EIGHT

The Collapse of Germany

Hitler had stripped his Western Front, and diverted the major part of his remaining forces and resources to hold the line of the Oder against the Russians, in the belief that the Western Allies were incapable of resuming the offensive after the supposedly crippling blow of his Ardennes counteroffensive coupled with V-weapon flying-bomb and rocket bombardment of the Antwerp base. So most of the available equipment coming out from the German factories or repair shops was sent eastward. Yet at that very time the Western Allies were building up overwhelming strength for an assault on the Rhine. In this massive effort the main striking role was assigned to Montgomery, the US Ninth Army being employed under him in addition to his own two, the First Canadian and Second British Armies. This decision was strongly resented by most of the American generals who felt that Eisenhower was yielding to the demands of Montgomery and the British at the expense of their own prospects.

Indignation spurred them to more vigorous efforts on their sectors to show what they could do, and in the event these efforts achieved striking results, as the strength put into them, though smaller than what Montgomery was amassing, much exceeded what the Germans had left to oppose them.

On March 7th the tanks of Patton's US Third Army broke through the weak German defences in the Eifel (the German end of the rugged Ardennes), and reached the Rhine near Coblenz after a sixty-mile drive in three days. For the moment they were blocked, as the Rhine bridges had been blown up before they arrived. But a little farther north, a small armoured spearhead of the neighbouring US First Army had found a gap and raced through it so quickly that the bridge at Remagen, near Bonn, was reached and brilliantly captured before it could be blown. Reserves were rushed up and secured a vital bridgehead.

When the news reached Bradley, the army group commander, he was quick to grasp the opportunity thus presented of dislocating the enemy's Rhine line – exultantly exclaiming on the telephone: 'Hot dog, this will

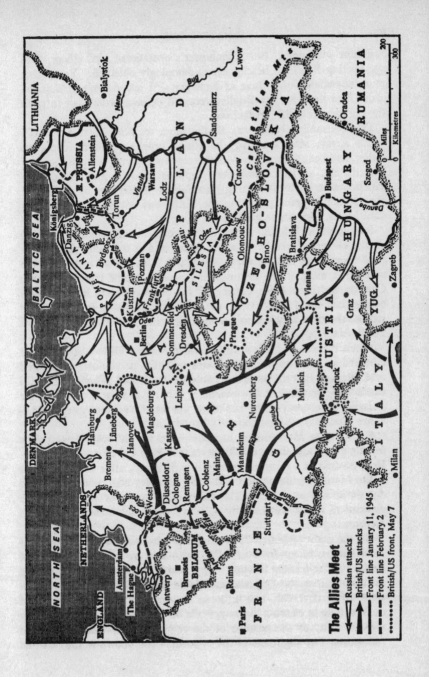

The Allies Meet

▷ Russian attacks
➤ British/US attacks
—·—· Front line January 11, 1945
——— Front line February 2
········ British/US front, May 7

bust him wide open.' But Eisenhower's operational staff officer, who was visiting Bradley's headquarters, dampingly objected: 'You're not going anywhere down there at Remagen – it just doesn't fit into the plan.' And the next day Bradley received definite orders not to push any big force into this bridgehead.

This restraining order was all the more resented because the US Ninth Army, after reaching the Rhine near Dusseldorf four days earlier, had been stopped by Montgomery from trying to cross the river immediately, as its commander, Simpson, desired and urged. Impatience with such plan-fitting restraints increased day by day, since Montgomery's grand attack on the Rhine was not timed for delivery until March 24th, three weeks later.

So Patton, with Bradley's fervent approval, swung southward to roll up the German forces west of the Rhine and at the same time seek a good spot for an early crossing. By March 21st, Patton had swept the west bank clear of the enemy along a seventy-mile stretch between Coblenz and Mannheim, cutting off the German forces in that sector before they could withdraw to the Rhine. Next night, Patton's troops crossed the river almost unopposed at Oppenheim, between Mainz and Mannheim.

When the news of this surprise stroke reached Hitler, he called for immediate countermeasures, but was told that no resources remained available, and that the most that could be dispatched to help fill the gap was a mere handful of five machines just repaired at a tank depot a hundred miles away. 'The cupboard was bare', and the American advance beyond the Rhine became a procession.

By this time Montgomery had completed his elaborate preparations for the grand assault on the Rhine near Wesel, 150 miles downstream. Here he had concentrated twenty-five divisions, after a quarter of a million tons of ammunition and other supplies had been amassed in dumps on the west bank. The thirty-mile stretch of river where he planned to attack was held by only five weak and exhausted German divisions.

On the night of March 23rd the attack was launched after a tremendous bombardment by over 3,000 guns and by successive waves of bombers. The leading infantry, supported by swimming tanks, crossed the river and established bridgeheads on the east, meeting little resistance. After daybreak, two airborne divisions were dropped ahead of them to help in clearing the way, while behind them bridges were being rapidly built for the passage of the reinforcing divisions, tanks and transports. The slightness of the opposition was shown in the fact that the US Ninth Army, which furnished half the assaulting infantry, had barely forty men killed. British losses were also very slight, and stubborn resistance was met only at one point, the riverside village of Rees, where a battalion of German parachutists held out for three days.

By the 28th the bridgehead had been extended to a depth of over twenty miles on a frontage of thirty. But Montgomery, still wary of the German Army's power of resistance, did not sanction a general advance eastward until he had built up a force of twenty divisions and 1,500 tanks in the bridgehead.

When the advance developed, much the most serious hindrance came from the heaps of rubble created by the excessive bombing efforts of the Allied air forces, which had thereby blocked the routes of advance far more effectively than the enemy could. For the dominant desire of the Germans now, both troops and people, was to see the British and American armies sweep eastward as rapidly as possible to reach Berlin and occupy as much of the country as possible before the Russians overcame the Oder line. Few of them were inclined to assist Hitler's purpose of obstruction by self destruction.

On the eve of the Rhine crossing Hitler had issued an order declaring that 'the battle should be conducted without consideration for our own population'. His regional commissioners were instructed to destroy 'all industrial plants, all the main electricity works, waterworks, gas works' together with 'all food and cloth stores' in order to create 'a desert' in the Allies' path.

But his own Minister of War Production, Albert Speer, at once protested against this drastic order. To these protests Hitler retorted: 'If the war is lost, the German nation will also perish. So there is no need to consider what the people require for continued existence.'

Appalled at such callousness, Speer was shaken out of his loyalty to Hitler. He went behind Hitler's back to the army and industrial chiefs, and persuaded them, without much difficulty, to evade executing Hitler's decree.

But as the end drew near, Hitler's illusions continued to grow, and he counted on some miracle to bring salvation almost until the last hour. He liked to read, or have read to him, the chapter from Carlyle's *History of Frederick the Great*, which related how Frederick was saved at the blackest hour, when his armies were on the verge of collapse, by the death of the Empress of Russia, which led to the break-up of the opposing alliance. Hitler also studied horoscopes which had predicted that disaster in April would be redeemed by a sudden change of fortune, bringing a satisfactory peace by August.

At midnight on April 12th, the news reached Hitler that President Roosevelt had died suddenly. Goebbels telephoned him, and said: 'My Führer, I congratulate you. Fate has laid low your greatest enemy. God has not abandoned us.' This was the 'miracle', it seemed, for which Hitler had been waiting – a repetition of the death of the Empress of Russia at the critical moment of the Seven Years War in the eighteenth century. So Hitler became convinced that what Mr Churchill called the 'Grand Alliance' between the Eastern and Western powers would now break up through the clash of their rival interests.

But the hope was not fulfilled and Hitler was driven a fortnight later to take his own life, as Frederick the Great had been about to do, just when his 'miracle' had come to save his fortunes and his life.

Early in March Zhukov had enlarged his bridgehead over the Oder, but did not succeed in breaking out. Russian progress on the far flanks continued, and Vienna was entered in the middle of April. Meanwhile the German front in the west had collapsed, and the Allied armies there were driving eastward from the Rhine with little opposition. They reached the Elbe, sixty miles from Berlin, on April 11th. Here they halted. On the 16th Zhukov resumed the offensive, in conjunction with Koniev, who forced the crossing of the Neisse.

This time the Russians burst out of their bridgeheads, and within a week were driving into the suburbs of Berlin – where Hitler chose to remain for the final battle. By the 25th the city had been completely isolated by the encircling armies of Zhukov and Koniev, and on the 27th Koniev's forces joined hands with the Americans on the Elbe. But in Berlin itself desperate street-by-street resistance was put up by the Germans, and was not completely overcome until the war itself ended, after Hitler's suicide, with Germany's unconditional surrender.

The War in Europe came to an end officially at midnight on May 8th, 1945, but in reality that was merely the final formal recognition of a finish which had taken place piecemeal during the previous week. On May 2nd all fighting had ceased on the southern front in Italy, where the surrender document had actually been signed three days earlier still. On May 4th a similar surrender was signed, at Montgomery's headquarters on Luneberg Heath, by representatives of the German forces in North-west Europe. On May 7th a further surrender document covering all the German forces, was signed at Eisenhower's headquarters in Reims – a larger ceremonial finish carried out in the presence of Russian as well as American, British, and French representatives.

These formalities of surrender were a quick sequel to the death of Hitler. On April 30th, the day after his marriage to the devoted Eva Braun, he had committed suicide along with her in the ruins of the Chancellery at Berlin – when the advancing Russians were reported to be close at hand – and their bodies were hurriedly cremated in the garden in accord with his instructions.

The first of the three official acts of surrender by the German forces was the most significant, for the Italian front armistice was signed while Hitler still lived, and in disregard of his authority. Moreover it was the conclusion to 'backstairs' surrender moves which had started on that front nearly two months before – early in March. The enemy leaders in Germany had been too close to Hitler's dominating presence to venture on such a move, although for a long time past they had been talking privately about its urgent necessity.

Many of them had lost hope after the Western Allies' landing in Normandy the previous summer. Almost all of them were empty of both hope and will by February 1945, after the repulse of their Western counteroffensive in the Ardennes and the Russian surge forward into eastern Germany. They were kept in the fight mostly by fear – fear of breaking their soldier's oath of loyalty to Hitler, fear of his wrath, and fear of being hanged by him for disobedience, reinforced by fear of the punishment which the Allies ominously threatened to deal out after victory on terms of 'unconditional surrender'.

In the months that followed, the war was prolonged almost entirely by Hitler's relentless determination. It might have been ended more quickly if the Western Allies had been less relentless in their demand for 'unconditional surrender' and more aware of its effect on the German mind. A relaxation of that forbidding attitude, and any reasonable assurance about the subsequent treatment of the Germans, would most probably have brought such a swelling stream of surrenders, led by the higher military leaders, that the front would have speedily collapsed, and the Nazi regime with it, so that Hitler would have lost all power to persist in the struggle.

CHAPTER THIRTY-NINE

The Collapse of Japan

Two cumulative factors in the defeat of Japan were, in nature and effect, forms of attrition – strangling pressure. One was by sea – or, more precisely, undersea; the other was by air. The former was the first to become of decisive effect.*

The Japanese empire was basically a sea empire, and even more dependent on oversea supplies than the British empire. Her war-making capacity depended on large seaborne imports of oil, iron ore, bauxite, coking coal, nickel, manganese, aluminium, tin, cobalt, lead, phosphate, graphite and potash, cotton, salt, and rubber. Moreover, for her food supplies she had to import most of her sugar and soya beans, as well as 20 per cent of her wheat and 17 per cent of her rice.

Yet Japan entered the war with a merchant marine totalling barely 6 million gross tons – considerably less than one third of Britain's at the outset in 1939 (approximately 9,500 ships totalling over 21 million tons). Moreover, Japan, despite the lessons of the war during the two years' interval and her expansionist plans, had done little to organize shipping protection – no convoy system and no escort-carriers. She only made a serious effort to retrieve these omissions after her shipping had been heavily reduced.

The outcome was that Japan's shipping became an easy target for the American submarines. In the early period of the war in the Pacific the defectiveness of the American torpedoes lessened the effect, but after these defects had been corrected the submarine attack became a massacre. Whereas the Japanese submarines concentrated their attack on warships – and later had to be used for carrying supplies to by-passed island garrisons – the American submarines were largely directed against merchant ships. In 1943 they sank 296, totalling 1,335,000 gross tons, and in 1944 their campaign became still more damaging – in October alone they sank 321,000 tons of shipping. Moreover their

* For maps, see pp 210–11 and 643.

effect was the greater through being directed primarily against Japanese tankers. As a result, the main Japanese fleet was kept at Singapore in order to be near to the oil-producing areas, while at home the training of aircraft pilots was restricted by shortage of fuel for adequate practice flights.

The American submarines also inflicted heavy loss on Japanese warships, amounting to nearly a third of those that were sunk. In the Battle of the Philippine Sea they sank two Japanese fleet carriers, the *Taiho* and *Shokaku*, while in the later months of 1944 they sank or permanently disabled three more carriers, as well as nearly forty destroyers.

By the time the American submarines were operating from Subic Bay in Luzon, most of Japan's merchant marine had been eliminated, and good targets became so rare that part of the submarine force was employed in picking up the crews of bombers which had to make forced landings in the sea when returning from air raids on Japan.

In sum, the contribution of the US submarine force was immense, and not least towards stopping Japanese efforts to send troop reinforcements and supplies to the cut-off garrisons overseas. The greatest effect was in sinking 60 per cent of the 8 million tons of Japanese shipping lost in the war. That was the most important factor in Japan's final collapse – decisive in the way it exploited her economic weakness and dependence on overseas supplies.

OKINAWA – THE INNER GATEWAY TO JAPAN

The final preparations for the amphibious attack on Okinawa, named 'Operation Iceberg', was in progress before the capture of Iwo Jima was complete, and D-day for the landings was timed for April 1st – barely six weeks after the landings on Iwo Jima. It was a large island, the largest of the Ryukyu group, being sixty miles long and averaging eight miles wide – large enough to provide an army ar.d naval base for an invasion of Japan. It lay exactly midway between Formosa and Japan, 340 miles from each, and 360 miles from the coast of China, so that a force established on Okinawa threatened all three objectives, while aircraft based there could dominate the approaches to all three.

The island was rugged and forested except in parts of the south where the airfields lay – and even there the limestone ridges were easy for excavation. It thus had a natural defensive strength. This was greatly increased by the build-up of the garrison, General Ushijima's 32nd Army, to somewhere around 77,000 combat troops and 20,000 service troops – a total of nearly 100,000 – and an abundance of artillery, light and heavy, well-sited in fortified caves. For the Japanese high command were determined to defend Okinawa with all the force they could provide, and the tactics adopted were an obstinate defence-in-depth of the interior, as on Iwo Jima, without wasting strength in a fight on the beaches where the American warships could pound and pulverize the Japanese troops. But for counteroffensive action Imperial GHQ had conserved and assembled over 2,000 aircraft on airfields in Japan and Formosa, and planned to use Kamikaze tactics on a greater scale than ever before.

The American High Command realized that Okinawa would be a very tough nut to crack, calling for a great superiority of force, and thus involving tremendous logistical problems. It planned to land there the recently formed Tenth Army, under Lieutenant-General Simon B. Buckner, employing five divisions and a total of 116,000 men in the intial landings, with two more for the follow-up, and an eighth in reserve. In all the assault force (of three Marine and four Army divisions) amounted to some 170,000 combat troops and 115,000 service troops. Besides overcoming the powerful Japanese garrison, they would have to control a population of nearly half a million.

In an effort to reduce the counteroffensive air threat, Admiral Mitscher's fast carrier group carried out a series of raids on Japan (March 18th–21st) a week before the landing, and shot down some 160 aircraft as well as destroying many on the ground – but at the cost of having three of its carriers (*Wasp*, *Yorktown*, and *Franklin*) badly damaged by Kamikaze attacks. The following week the B29 Superfortresses from Guam were diverted from their massive attacks on the Japanese cities to blasting the airfields in Kyushu (the southern main island of Japan). Another important preliminary was the occupation of the Kerama Retto group of islands, fifteen miles west of Okinawa, for use as a forward fleet base and anchorage – an idea urged by Admiral Kelly Turner. An American division occupied the group on March 27th, meeting little opposition, and next day tankers arrived there to bring the roadstead into use. The British Pacific Fleet (two battleships, four carriers, six cruisers, and fifteen destroyers) under Admiral Sir Bruce Fraser, which had arrived on the scene in mid-March, covered the area south-west of Okinawa.

On April 1st, which was Easter Sunday, the main landings took place, starting at 8.30 AM, after an intense three-hour preparatory bombardment from sea and air. That same day, Admiral Turner took command of all forces in Okinawa waters. The landings were made on the western coast in its southern part, where a short advance would cut off the southerly end of the island. They met no opposition at all, and by 11 AM the two airfields in the five-mile stretch of the landings were occupied without the enemy even showing themselves – much to the astonishment of the invaders. By evening the American beachhead had been expanded to a width of nine miles, and over 60,000 troops had been put ashore safely. By April 3rd they had crossed the island, and next day the beachhead was extended to fifteen miles. It was only after the 4th, when the Americans began driving south, that they began to meet stiffening resistance – from the two-and-a-half Japanese divisions in that southern part of the island.

In the air, however, the Japanese had been active from the start, and from April 6th onward Kamikaze attacks intensified – nearly 700 aircraft, of which half were Kamikaze, being sent to Okinawa on the 6th and 7th. Most of them were shot down, but thirteen American destroyers were sunk or damaged.

April 6th was also marked by the Japanese navy's most notable 'suicide' action, when the giant battleship *Yamato* was dispatched to the scene, with a small naval escort – but no air cover, and only sufficient fuel for the outward journey. Its approach was quickly spotted, and kept under constant watch while Mitscher's carriers were preparing a strike by 280 aircraft. At 12.30 PM on the 7th it was violently attacked with torpedoes and bombs, and after two hours' sustained onslaught it sank, with immense loss of life. Like-the *Tirpitz*, it never had a chance to fire its great guns against enemy battleships, and its fate provided further confirmation that the battleship era was past.

The land campaign was more protracted. On April 13th the Japanese in the south of the island began a small counteroffensive, but this was easily repulsed. Meanwhile the 6th Marine Division had been pushing northward easily until it reached the rocky and forest-covered Motobu Peninsula, where it was temporarily held up. But the Japanese force here consisted of only two battalions, and their formidable position was overcome on the 17th by a cleverly planned stratagem. Although scattered groups continued resistance until May 6th, the balance was heavily in favour of the Americans, some 2,500 Japanese being killed, on a count of dead bodies, for a Marine loss of less than a tenth of that number. Moreover, a Marine detachment had reached the northern tip of Okinawa on April 13th, without opposition. The neighbouring small islands were also captured during this period, with little trouble, except on Ie Shima.

On April 19th, General Hodge's 24th Corps launched an attack, with three Army divisions, on the Japanese positions in the south of Okinawa. But an intense preparatory bombardment – from sea, air, and land – had little effect on the Japanese cave-defences. Gains were slight and casualties large, even after the 1st and 6th Marine Divisions were brought into the front line. At the beginning of May, however, the local Japanese commanders, with characteristic dislike of defensive action, profitable though it had proved, decided to launch a counteroffensive, in conjunction with a fresh wave of Kamikaze attacks. Despite a penetration at one point, they were beaten off with very heavy losses – some 5,000 killed. That somewhat eased the way for the resumed American offensive, on May 10th, but the following week its progress was halted by prolonged heavy rains.

During the interval, the Japanese withdrew from the Shuri area, covering Naha, the capital, to positions still further south. Early in June the Americans pressed on despite the mud, and by the middle of the month the Japanese were pushed back into the extreme south of the island. Here their strongly held position along the Yaeju–Dake escarpment was broken on the 17th, largely through the use of flamethrowers. Ushijima and his staff committed suicide, as did many other Japanese, but no less than 7,400 surrendered during the mopping-up phase that followed – a significant change.

The total Japanese loss was estimated as 110,000, including Okinawans recruited into the Japanese Army, while the Americans' loss was 49,000 (of whom 12,500 were killed) – their heaviest campaign loss of the war in the Pacific.

During the three months' campaign on Okinawa, the Japanese aircraft made ten massed Kamikaze attacks – which they called 'Kikusui' (floating chrysanthemum). These totalled over 1,500 individual Kamikaze attacks, with almost as many similar suicidal attacks by other aircraft. Altogether thirty-four naval craft were sunk, and 368 damaged, mostly by Kamikazes. This painful experience caused much foreboding as to what would happen in an invasion of Japan, and thus contributed to the decision, in July, to use the atomic bomb.

MOPPING-UP – IN THE PACIFIC AND BURMA

The pace of the dual American advance had been greatly accelerated by the adoption of a by-passing strategy – attacking and capturing only the points on either route that were needed as strategic stepping stones to Japan and as means to gain strategic control of the Pacific. But when the forces arrived close to Japan, and were preparing for the final spring, it was considered desirable by the Chiefs of Staff to clear their rear by wiping out the isolated garrisons of the main islands that had been left behind in the by-passing advance. So the penultimate phase of the war saw a wide range of mopping-up operations in different areas. More certainly necessary was the clearance of south-central Burma, following Slim's swift drive to Rangoon, and before launching South East Asia Command's projected amphibious move to recapture Singapore and the Dutch East Indies.

BURMA*

When Slim reached Rangoon, early in May 1945, there were still some 60,000 Japanese troops in his wake, west of the Salween, and it was important to prevent them escaping eastward into Thailand as well as to stop them causing fresh trouble in the area that had been overrun in Slim's drive to Rangoon. So part of General Messervy's 4th Corps was sent back to hold the crossings of the Sittang, and another part to meet Stopford's 33rd Corps, which was pushing down the Irrawaddy. During May, Stopford succeeded in breaking up two attempts by the remains of Sakurai's 28th Army from Arakan to cross the Irrawaddy eastward, but many small fragments managed to find their way across, and about 17,000 reached the Pegu Yomas area between the Irrawaddy and the Sittang. A diversionary attack to help them by the remains of Honda's 33rd Army was a failure, so after mid-July Sakurai's troops tried to slip through Messervy's guard-screen by splitting up into numerous little groups, of a few hundred men apiece. But most of these little groups were caught and crushed; less than 6,000 men succeeded in reaching the east bank of the Sittang, then in full flood, and were unfit for further fighting.

NEW GUINEA – NEW BRITAIN – BOUGAINVILLE†

In MacArthur's leap-frogging advance along the north coast of New Guinea, during the first half of 1944, he had by-passed several Japanese garrisons and when the Americans passed on to the Philippines they left behind them the remnants of five enemy divisions. Large numbers of Japanese troops were also left stranded in the islands of New Britain and Bougainville. In a directive of July 12th to General Sir Thomas Blamey, the Australian Commander-in-Chief, MacArthur entrusted

* For maps, see pp 538 and 662.
† For maps, see pp 370 and 643.

responsibility to him, as from the autumn, for 'the continued neutraliza-
tion' of the remaining Japanese in those areas. Blamey chose to in-
terpret the directive in a more offensively minded way – although he
had only four divisions available, of which three were militia, after two
Australian Imperial Forces divisions had been earmarked for the
Philippines campaign.

The 6th Australian Division was sent to Aitape, and from there was
to drive eastward in December and destroy Adachi's three weak divisions around Wewak (totalling about 35,000 men) – which were under-
armed, under-nourished, and disease-ridden, as well as isolated. The
100-mile advance through very difficult country strained the Australian
transport system, and the spirit of the troops was damped both by
disease and realization that there was no real strategic need for the
operation. Progress was very slow, and Wewak was not captured until
May, six months later, while remaining Japanese were still holding out
in the interior when the end of the war came in August 1945. The
Japanese strength had diminished by a fifth in that time; the Australians had lost barely 1,500 in battle, but their casualties from sickness
were over 16,000.

To New Britain, in the Bismarcks, the 5th Australian Division had
been sent – and its commander (Major-General A. N. Ramsay) showed
more sense. By the time it arrived in November, the Americans had
gained control of five-sixths of that big island, but the remainder was
held by nearly 70,000 Japanese, mostly concentrated in their long-
standing base at Rabaul. After making a short advance to the neck of
the island, the Australians were content to patrol this short line – and
let the large Japanese garrison 'wither on the vine'. Thereby it was
neutralized at minimum cost, until the end of the war brought its surrender.

Bougainville, at the western end of the Solomons, was the largest
island of that group. Thither was sent General Savige's 2nd Corps,
with the 3rd Australian Division and two extra brigades. Here again
there was no real need for offensive action, as the Japanese, mostly
concentrated around Buin in the south of the island, were amply occupied in growing vegetables and in fishing to eke out their scanty food-
stuffs. But Savige launched an offensive early in 1945. This made slow
progress, as it stirred up the Japanese to fight hard in defence of their
food-producing area, and after six months it was broken off by heavy
floods. The Australian troops, as on New Guinea, showed little enthusiasm for what they felt, rightly, was a needless effort.

BORNEO

The initiative for the recapture of Borneo came mainly from the Americans, who wished to cut off the Japanese oil and rubber supplies, and also to provide the British with an advanced fleet base at Brunei Bay. The British Chiefs of Staff did not favour the idea, as they wanted a base in the Philippines, while the Pacific Fleet was already committed to the Okinawa area, and they did not wish to bring it back southward. So the operation was carried out by the Australian 1st Corps (of two divisions) under Lieutenant-General Sir Leslie Morshead, with the protective aid of the US Seventh Fleet. The island of Tarakan, off the north-east coast, was seized on May 1st, 1945, and Brunei Bay on the west coast was captured without serious opposition on June 10th. From there the Australian troops advanced down that coast into Sarawak. At the beginning of July, after a prolonged bombardment, the oil centre of Balikpapan on the south-east coast was attacked and captured, after some tough resistance – in what proved to be the last large amphibious operation of the war.

By that time British preparations for the recapture of Singapore were well advanced, but were nullified by Japan's surrender in August. So when Mountbatten arrived at Singapore on September 12th it was merely to receive the general capitulation of Japan's forces in Southeast Asia which had already been signed in a preliminary agreement at Rangoon on August 27th. It brought the surrender of three-quarters of a million Japanese.

THE PHILIPPINES*

Although the Americans had gained strategic control of the Philippines within five months of their first landing, at Leyte, in October, large Japanese forces were still there in March. On Luzon alone, later evidence shows them to have been about 170,000 – a much bigger figure than the Americans estimated at the time. The largest groups were in the north of Luzon under Yamashita himself, but some 50,000 under General Yokoyama were in the mountains near Manila, the capital, and controlling the water-supply of that city. Early moves to evict them were checked and the Japanese even took the offensive against General Griswold's 14th Corps, which had been given the task of destroying them. In mid-March General Hall's 11th Corps was brought in to take over the advance and by the end of May had captured the two main dams at

* For maps, see pp 222 and 643.

Awa and Ipo. By then Yokoyama's strength had been halved, largely by hunger and disease, and it soon broke up into disorganized groups that were pursued and harassed by Filipino guerrillas as well as by the American troops. For every man killed in action, ten perished from starvation and disease. At the end of the war barely 7,000 survived to surrender.

Meanwhile, General Krueger's forces cleared the passages through the Visayan Sea, thus shortening the shipping route from Leyte to Luzon, and subsequently started a drive to clear the southern part of Luzon. Other forces cleared the islands south of Leyte, and established a lodgment on Mindanao – where over 40,000 Japanese troops had been placed because of the Imperial GHQ view that it would be a primary objective for the American invasion. By the summer the Japanese forces in all these areas had withdrawn into the mountains, where they dwindled rapidly from hunger and disease.

The last stage of the process was the American drive against Yamashita's forces in the north of Luzon. It was launched on April 27th by three American divisions, soon reinforced by a fourth, but met increasing difficulties as it pressed into the mountains, where Yamashita had concentrated over 50,000 troops – more than double what the Americans had estimated. He was still holding out when the war ended in mid-August, and he surrendered with 40,000 remaining troops, as well as a further 10,000 in other parts of northern Luzon. The strategic necessity for this costly mopping-up campaign is very doubtful.

THE AMERICAN STRATEGIC AIR OFFENSIVE

The air offensive against Japan did not become really effective until it could be launched from the Marianas – which were captured, chiefly for that purpose, in the summer of 1944.

Its chief instrument was the Boeing B29 Superfortress, the largest bomber of the Second World War, which could carry a bomb-load of up to 17,000lb (7¾ tons), fly at speeds approaching 350 mph, and at altitudes of over 35,000 feet. It had a range of over 4,000 miles, and was well-protected by armour-plate, as well as by some thirteen machine guns that it carried.

In mid-June 1944 the steel town of Yawata, on Kyushu, was bombed by some fifty B29s based on China and India, but this and subsequent attacks did little damage – only about 800 tons of bombs were dropped on Japan from that direction in the second half of 1944, and the B29s of the 20th Bomber Command required so much of the air supply over the 'Hump' to maintain them in China, for results so poor, that they were withdrawn early in 1945.

But the first air-strip in the Marianas, at Saipan, was ready for use by the end of October 1944, and then received the first wing (112 machines) of the 21st Bomber Command. A month later, on November 24th, 111 B29s took off from there to bomb a Tokyo aircraft factory. It was the first attack on Tokyo since Colonel Doolittle's raid in April 1942. It inaugurated the new offensive, and although less than a quarter of the bombers found their target, only two of them were lost – despite the 125 Japanese fighters that were sent up to engage them.

During the next three months the B29s continued with their daylight precision-bombing, based on their experience in Europe, but the effects were disappointing – although it forced the Japanese to begin dispersing their air factories and other industries. But by March 1945 the number of B29s in the Marianas was trebled, and General Curtis LeMay, who had taken command there, decided to switch them onto night time low-level area-bombing – in order to exploit Japanese weaknesses in night defence, allow a greater bomb-load to be carried, ease the strain on engines, and be more effective in hitting the numerous small industrial targets.

More important still, LeMay decided that the B29s were to carry incendiary bombs instead of explosive bombs – each B29 could carry forty clusters of thirty-eight incendiaries apiece, which could burn an area of approximately sixteen acres. The results of the change were horrifyingly effective. On March 9th, 279 B29s – each carrying 6–8 tons of incendiaries – devastated Tokyo. Nearly sixteen square miles, a quarter of the total area of the city, was burnt out, over 267,000 buildings being destroyed. The civilian casualties were approximately 185,000 – whereas the American attackers lost only fourteen aircraft. In the next nine days the cities of Osaka, Kobe, and Nagoya were similarly devastated. By the 19th these attacks ceased, as the Americans had run out of incendiaries – in those ten days they had dropped nearly 10,000 tons of them.

But the devastation was soon resumed, and increased – in July the tonnage dropped was three times what it had been in March. In addition, thousands of mines were dropped to block Japanese coastal traffic. Over $1\frac{1}{4}$ million tons of shipping were sunk, and the traffic was brought almost to a halt. Japanese opposition in the air had become negligible.

The effects were tremendous. Civilian morale declined badly after the Tokyo fire-raid, and still more when LeMay began dropping pamphlet warnings of his next targets. Over $8\frac{1}{2}$ million people fled into the countryside, causing war production to sag – at a time when Japan's war economy was almost at the end of its tether. For production in the oil-refining industry had declined by 83 per cent, in aircraft engines by 75 per cent, in airframes by 60 per cent, and in electronics equipment by 70 per cent. More than 600 major war factories had been destroyed or badly damaged by bombing.

Beyond all this was the fact that the bombing campaign had brought home to Japan's people that their forces could no longer protect them, and that surrender, even unconditional, had become unavoidable. The atomic bombs in August merely confirmed what most of the Japanese people, except for military fanatics, had already come to realize.

THE ATOMIC BOMB AND JAPAN'S SURRENDER

Winston Churchill in the last volume of his war memoirs relates how on July 14th, 1945 – when he was at the Potsdam Conference with President Truman and Stalin – he was handed a sheet of paper with the cryptic message: 'Babies satisfactorily born.' Mr Stimson, the US Secretary of War, explained its meaning – that the experimental test of the atomic bomb, on the previous day, had proved successful. 'The President invited me to confer with him forthwith. He had with him General Marshall and Admiral Leahy.'

Churchill's account of the sequel is of such far-reaching significance that the main passage deserves to be quoted at length:

We seemed suddenly to have become possessed of a merciful abridgment of the slaughter in the East and of a far happier prospect in Europe. I have no doubt that these thoughts were present in the minds of my American friends. At any rate, there never was a moment's discussion as to whether the atomic bomb should be used or not. To avert a vast, indefinite butchery, to bring the war to an end, to give peace to the world, to lay healing hands upon its tortured peoples by a manifestation of overwhelming power at the cost of a few explosions, seemed, after all our toils and perils, a miracle of deliverance.

British consent in principle to the use of the weapon had been given on July 4th, before the test had taken place. The final decision now lay in the main with President Truman, who had the weapon; but I never doubted what it would be, nor have I ever doubted since that he was right. The historic fact remains, and must be judged in the after-time, that the decision whether or not to use the atomic bomb to compel the surrender of Japan was never even an issue. There was unanimous, automatic, unquestioned agreement around our table; nor did I ever hear the slightest suggestion that we should do otherwise.*

But later, Churchill himself raises his doubts about the case for using the atomic bomb, when he says:

It would be a mistake to suppose that the fate of Japan was settled by the atomic bomb. Her defeat was certain before the first bomb fell, and was brought about by overwhelming maritime power. This alone had made it possible to seize ocean bases from which to launch the final attack and force her metropolitan Army to capitulate without striking a blow. Her shipping had been destroyed.†

Churchill also mentions that at Potsdam, three weeks before the bomb was dropped, he was told privately by Stalin of a message from the Japanese Ambassador in Moscow expressing Japan's desire for peace – and adds that in passing on this news to President Truman he suggested that the Allies' demand for 'unconditional surrender' might be somewhat modified to ease the way for the Japanese to surrender.

But these Japanese peace-seeking approaches had started much earlier, and were already better known to the American authorities than Churchill indicated or was perhaps aware. Just before Christmas 1944, the American Intelligence in Washington received a report from a well-informed diplomatic agent in Japan that a peace party was emerging, and gaining ground there. The agent predicted that General Koiso's Government – which in July had replaced the Government under General Tojo that had led Japan into the war – would soon be succeeded by a peace-seeking Government under Admiral Suzuki which would initiate negotiations, with the Emperor's backing. This prediction was fulfilled in April.

On April 1st the Americans landed on Okinawa, one of the Ryukyu islands, midway between Formosa and Japan. The shock of that news, coupled with the Russians' ominous notice of terminating their neutrality pact with Japan, precipitated the fall of Koiso's Cabinet, on April 5th, and Suzuki then became Prime Minister.

But although the heads of the peace party were now predominant in the Government they were at a loss how to proceed. Already in Feb-

* Churchill: *The Second World War*, vol VI, p 553.
† Ibid, p 559.

ruary, following the Emperor Hirohito's initiative, approaches had been made to Russia begging her 'as a neutral' to act as an intermediary in arranging peace between Japan and the Western Allies. These approaches were made, first, through the Russian Ambassador in Tokyo, and then through the Japanese Ambassador in Moscow. But nothing developed. The Russians had not passed on any word of the approach.

Three months passed before a hint of it came. This was at the end of May, when Mr Harry Hopkins, as the President's personal envoy, flew to Moscow for discussions with Stalin about the future. In their third meeting Stalin brought up the question of Japan. At the Yalta Conference in February he had undertaken to join in the war against Japan on condition of getting the Kurile Islands, the whole of Sakhalin, and a controlling position in Manchuria. Stalin now informed Hopkins that his reinforced armies in the Far East would be deployed by August 8th for attack on the Japanese front in Manchuria. He went on to say that if the Allies stuck to their demand for 'unconditional surrender' the Japanese would fight to the bitter end, whereas a modification of it would encourage them to yield – and the Allies could then impose their will and obtain substantially the same results. He also emphasized that Russia expected to be given a share in the actual occupation of Japan. It was in the course of this discussion that he revealed that 'peace feelers' were being 'put out by certain elements in Japan' – but did not make it clear that they were official approaches through the ambassadors.

Long before the end of the struggle on Okinawa, the issue was certain. It was also evident that once the island was captured, the Americans would soon be able to intensify their air bombardment of Japan itself, as the airfields there were within less that 400 miles of Japan – barely a quarter of the distance from the Marianas.

The hopelessness of the situation was plain to any strategical mind, and particularly to a naval mind such as Suzuki's, whose anti-war views had led to his life being threatened by the military extremists as far back as 1936. But he and his peace-seeking Cabinet were entangled in a knotty problem. Eager as they were for peace, acceptance of the Allies' demand for 'unconditional surrender' would appear like a betrayal of the forces in the field, so willing to fight to the death; these forces, who still held the lives of thousands of near-starved Allied civilian and military prisoners in pawn, might refuse to obey a 'cease fire' order if the terms were abjectly humiliating – above all, if there was any demand for the removal of the Emperor, who in their eyes was not only their sovereign but also divine.

It was the Emperor himself who moved to cut the knot. On June 20th he summoned to a conference the six members of the inner Cabinet, the Supreme War Direction Council, and there told them: 'You will consider the question of ending the war as soon as possible.' All six members of the Council were in agreement on this score, but while the Prime Minister, the Foreign Minister and the Navy Minister were prepared to make unconditional surrender, the other three – the Army Minister and Army and Navy Chiefs of Staff – argued for continued resistance until some mitigating conditions were obtained. Eventually it was decided that Prince Konoye should be sent on a mission to Moscow to negotiate for peace – and the Emperor privately gave him instructions to secure peace at any price. As a preliminary, the Japanese Foreign Office officially notified Moscow on July 13th that 'the Emperor is desirous of peace'.

The message reached Stalin just as he was setting off for the Potsdam Conference. He sent a chilly reply that the proposal was not definite enough for him to take action, or agree to receiving the mission. This time, however, he told Churchill of the approach, and it was of this that Churchill told Truman, adding his own tentative suggestion that it might be wise to modify the rigid demand for 'unconditional surrender'.

A fortnight later the Japanese Government sent a further message to Stalin, trying to make still clearer the purpose of the mission, but received a similar negative reply. Meantime Churchill's Government had been defeated at the General Election in Britain, so that Attlee and Bevin had replaced Churchill and Eden at Potsdam when, on July 28th, Stalin told the Conference of this further approach.

The Americans, however, were already aware of Japan's desire to end the war, for their Intelligence service had intercepted the cipher messages from the Japanese Foreign Minister to the Japanese Ambassador in Moscow.

But President Truman and most of his chief advisers – particularly Mr Stimson and General Marshall, the US Army's Chief of Staff – were now as intent on using the atomic bomb to accelerate Japan's collapse as Stalin was on entering the war against Japan before it ended, in order to gain an advantageous position in the Far East.

There were some who felt more doubts than Churchill records. Among them was Admiral Leahy, Chief of Staff to President Roosevelt and President Truman successively, who recoiled from the idea of employing such a weapon against the civilian population: 'My own feeling was that, in being the first to use it, we had adopted an ethical standard common to the barbarians of the Dark Age. I was not taught to make war in that fashion, and wars cannot be won by destroying women and children.' The year before, he had protested to Roosevelt against a proposal to use bacteriological weapons.

The atomic scientists themselves were divided in their views. Dr Vannevar Bush had played a leading part in gaining Roosevelt's and Stimson's support for the atomic weapon, while Lord Cherwell (formerly Professor Lindemann), Churchill's personal adviser on scientific matters, was also a leading advocate of it. It was thus not surprising that when Stimson appointed a Committee under Bush in the spring of 1945 to consider the question of using the weapon against Japan, it strongly recommended that the bomb should be used as soon as possible, and without any advance warning of its nature – for fear that the bomb might prove 'a dud', as Stimson later explained.

In contrast, another group of atomic scientists headed by Professor James Franck presented a report to Stimson soon afterwards, in the later part of June, expressing different conclusions: 'The military advantages and the saving of American lives achieved by the sudden use of atomic bombs against Japan may be outweighed by a wave of horror and repulsion spreading over the rest of the world ... If the United States were to be the first to release this new means of indiscrimate destruction on mankind, she would sacrifice public support throughout the world, precipitate the race for armaments, and prejudice the possibility of reaching an international agreement on the future control of such weapons ... We believe that these considerations make the use of nuclear bombs for an early attack against Japan inadvisable.'

But the scientists who were closest to the statesmen's ears had a better chance of gaining attention, and their eager arguments prevailed in the decision – aided by the enthusiasm which they had already excited in the statesmen about the atomic bomb, as a quick and easy way of finishing the war. Five possible targets were suggested by the military advisers for the two bombs that had been produced, and of these the cities of Hiroshima and Nagasaki were chosen, after consideration of the list by President Truman and Mr Stimson, as combining military installations with 'houses and other buildings most susceptible to damage'.

So on August 6th the first atomic bomb was dropped on Hiroshima, destroying most of the city and killing some 80,000 people – a quarter of its inhabitants. Three days later the second bomb was dropped on Nagasaki. The news of the dropping of the Hiroshima bomb reached President Truman as he was returning by sea from the Potsdam Conference. According to those present he exultantly exclaimed: 'This is the greatest thing in history.'

The effect on the Japanese Government, however, was much less than was imagined on the Western side at the time. It did not shake the three members of the Council of six who had been opposed to surrendering unconditionally, and they still insisted that some assurance about the future must first be obtained, particularly as to the maintenance of the 'Emperor's sovereign position'. As for the people of Japan, they did not know until after the war what had happened at Hiroshima and Nagasaki.

Russia's declaration of war on August 8th, and immediate drive into Manchuria next day, seems to have been almost as effective in hastening the issue, and the Emperor's influence still more so. For at a meeting of the inner Cabinet in his presence, on the 9th, he pointed out the hopelessness of the situation so clearly, and declared himself so strongly in favour of immediate peace, that the three opponents of it became more inclined to yield and agreed to holding a Gozenkaigi – a meeting of 'elder statesmen', at which the Emperor himself could make the final decision. Meantime the Government announced by radio its willingness to surrender provided that the Emperor's sovereignty was respected – a point about which the Allies' Potsdam Declaration of July 26th had been ominously silent. After some discussion President Truman agreed to this proviso, a notable modification of 'unconditional surrender'.

Even then there was much division of opinion at the Gozenkaigi, on August 14th, but the Emperor resolved the issue, saying decisively: 'If nobody else has any opinion to express, we would express our own. We demand that you will agree to it. We see only one way left for Japan to save herself. That is the reason we have made this determination to endure the unendurable and suffer the insufferable.' Japan's surrender was then announced by radio.

The use of the atomic bomb was not really needed to produce this result. With nine-tenths of Japan's shipping sunk or disabled, her air and sea forces crippled, her industries wrecked, and her people's food supplies shrinking fast, her collapse was already certain – as Churchill said.

The US Strategic Bombing Survey report emphasized this point, while adding: 'The time lapse between military impotence and political acceptance of the inevitable might have been shorter had the political structure of Japan permitted a more rapid and decisive determination of national policies. Nevertheless, it seems clear that, even without the atomic bombing attacks, air supremacy could have exerted sufficient pressure to bring about unconditional surrender and obviate the need for invasion.' Admiral King, the US Naval Commander-in-Chief, stated that the naval blockade alone would have 'starved the Japanese into submission' – through lack of oil, rice, and other essential materials – 'had we been willing to wait'.

Admiral Leahy's judgement is even more emphatic about the needlessness of the atomic bomb: 'The use of this barbaric weapon at Hiroshima and Nagasaki was of no material assistance in our war against Japan. The Japanese were already defeated and ready to surrender because of the effective sea blockade and the successful bombing with conventional weapons.'

Why, then, was the bomb used? Were there any impelling motives beyond the instinctive desire to cut short the loss of American and British lives at the earliest possible moment? Two reasons have emerged. One is revealed by Churchill himself in the account of his conference with President Truman on July 18th, following the news of the successful trial of the atomic bomb, and the thoughts that immediately came into their minds, among these being:

> ... we should not need the Russians. The end of the Japanese war no longer depended upon the pouring in of their armies ... We had no need to ask favours of them. A few days later I minuted to Mr Eden: 'It is quite clear that the United States do not at the present time desire Russian participation in the war against Japan.'*

Stalin's demand at Potsdam to share in the occupation of Japan was very embarrassing, and the US Government were anxious to avoid such a contingency. The atomic bomb might help to solve the problem. The Russians were due to enter the war on August 6th – two days later.

The second reason for its precipitate use, at Hiroshima and Nagasaki, was revealed by Admiral Leahy: 'the scientists and others wanted to make this test because of the vast sums that had been spent on the project' – two billion dollars. One of the higher officers concerned in the atomic operation, the code-name of which was the 'Manhattan District Project', put the point still more clearly:

> The bomb simply had to be a success – so much money had been expended on it. Had it failed, how could we have explained the huge expenditure? Think of the public outcry there would have been ... As time grew shorter, certain people in Washington tried to persuade

* Churchill: *The Second World War*, vol VI, p 553.

General Groves, director of the Manhattan Project, to get out before it was too late, for he knew he would be left holding the bag if we failed. The relief to everyone concerned when the bomb was finished and dropped was enormous.

A generation later, however, it is all too clear that the hasty dropping of the atomic bomb has not been a relief to the rest of mankind.

On September 2nd, 1945, the representatives of Japan signed the 'instrument of surrender' on board the United States' battleship *Missouri* in Tokyo Bay. The Second World War was thus ended six years and one day after it had been started by Hitler's attack on Poland – and four months after Germany's surrender. It was a formal ending, a ceremony to seal the victors' satisfaction. For the real ending had come on August 14th, when the Emperor had announced Japan's surrender on the terms laid down by the Allies, and fighting had ceased – a week after the dropping of the first atomic bomb. But even that frightful stroke, wiping out the city of Hiroshima to demonstrate the overwhelming power of the new weapon, had done no more than hasten the moment of surrender. This surrender was already sure, and there was no real need to use such a weapon – under whose dark shadow the world has lived ever since.

PART IX

EPILOGUE

CHAPTER FORTY

Epilogue

KEY FACTORS AND TURNING POINTS

This catastrophic conflict, which ended by opening Russia's path into the heart of Europe, was aptly called by Mr Churchill 'the unnecessary war'. In striving to avert it, and curb Hitler, a basic weakness in the policy of Britain and France was their lack of an understanding of strategical factors. Through this they slid into war at the moment most unfavourable to them, and then precipitated an avoidable disaster of far-reaching consequences. Britain survived by what appeared to be a miracle – but really because Hitler made the same mistakes that aggressive dictators have repeatedly made throughout history.

THE VITAL PREWAR PHASE

In retrospect it has become clear that the first fatal step, for both sides, was the German re-entry into the Rhineland in 1936. For Hitler, this move carried a two-fold strategic advantage – it provided cover for Germany's key industrial vital area in the Ruhr, and it provided him with a potential springboard into France.

Why was this move not checked? Primarily, because France and Britain were anxious to avoid any risk of armed conflict that might develop into war. The reluctance to act was increased because the German re-entry into the Rhineland appeared to be merely an effort to rectify an injustice, even though done in the wrong way. The British, particularly, being politically-minded, tended to regard it more as a political than as a military step – failing to see its strategic implications.

In his 1938 moves Hitler again drew strategic advantage from political factors – the German and Austrian people's desire for union, the strong feeling in Germany about Czech treatment of the Sudeten Germans; and again there was a widespread feeling in the Western coun-

Post-War Europe

NORWAY

Oslo

DENMARK

Copenhagen

EIRE

NORTH SEA

GREAT BRITAIN

London

HOLLAND

Hamburg

Bremen

Amsterdam

The Hague

Hanovere

Brussels

Cologne

Bonn

BELGIUM

LUX.

(West)

FRANCE

Paris

Nuremberg

Rhine

Danube

Munich

EAST GERMANY
(Soviet Zone)

Tegeler See

TEGEL

East

BRANDENBURG GATE

West

Havel

Berlin

GATOW

TEMPEL HOF

Spree

Berlin

Wannsee

Teltow Can.

Berne

SWITZ.

Milan

ITALY

Venice

tries that there was a measure of justice in Germany's case on both issues.

But Hitler's march into Austria in March laid bare the southern flank of Czecho-Slovakia – which to him was an obstacle in the development of his plans for eastward expansion. In September he secured – by the threat of war and the resultant Munich agreement – not merely the return of the Sudetenland but the strategic paralysis of Czecho-Slovakia.

In March 1939 Hitler occupied the remainder of Czecho-Slovakia, and thereby enveloped the flank of Poland – the last of a series of 'bloodless' manoeuvres. This step of his was followed by a fatally rash move on the British Government's part – the guarantee suddenly offered to Poland and Rumania, each of them strategically isolated, without first securing any assurance from Russia, the only power which could give them effective support.

By their timing, these guarantees were bound to act as a provocation; and, as we now know, until he was met by this challenging gesture Hitler had no immediate intention of attacking Poland. By their placing, in parts of Europe inaccessible to the forces of Britain and France, they provided an almost irresistible temptation. Thereby the Western powers undermined the essential basis of the only type of strategy which their now inferior strength made practicable for them. For instead of being able to check aggression by presenting a strong front to any attack in the West, they gave Hitler an easy chance of breaking a weak front and thus gaining an initial triumph.

The only chance of avoiding war now lay in securing the support of Russia, the only power that could give Poland direct support and thus provide a deterrent to Hitler. However, despite the urgency of the situation, the British Government's steps were dilatory and half-hearted. But beyond their own hesitations were the objections of the Polish Government, and the other small powers in eastern Europe, to accepting military support from Russia – since these feared that reinforcement by her armies would be equivalent to invasion.

Very different was Hitler's response to the new situation created by British backing of Poland. Britain's violent reaction and redoubled armament measures shook him, but the effect was opposite to that intended. His solution was coloured by his historically derived picture of the British. Regarding them as cool-headed and rational, with their emotions controlled by their head, he felt that they would not dream of entering a war on behalf of Poland unless they could obtain Russia's support. So, swallowing his hatred and fear of 'Bolshevism', he bent his efforts and energies towards conciliating Russia and securing her abstention. It was a turnabout more startling than Chamberlain's – and as fatal in its consequences.

On August 23rd Ribbentrop flew to Moscow, and the pact was signed. It was accompanied by a secret agreement under which Poland was to be partitioned between Germany and Russia.

This pact made war certain – in the intense state of feeling that had been created by Hitler's rapid series of aggressive moves. The British, having pledged themselves to support Poland, felt that they could not stand aside without losing their honour – and without opening Hitler's way to wider conquest. And Hitler would not draw back from his purpose in Poland, even when he came to see that it involved a general war.

Thus the train of European civilization rushed into the long, dark tunnel from which it only emerged after six exhausting years had passed. Even then, the bright sunlight of victory proved illusory.

THE FIRST PHASE OF THE WAR

On Friday, September 1st, 1939, the German armies invaded Poland. On Sunday, the 3rd, the British Government declared war on Germany, in fulfilment of the guarantee it had earlier given to Poland. Six hours later the French Government, more reluctantly, followed the British lead.

Within less than a month Poland had been overrun. Within nine months most of Western Europe had been submerged by the spreading flood of war.

Could Poland have held out longer? Could France and Britain have done more than they did to take the German pressure off Poland? On the face of the figures of armed strength, as now known, the answer to both questions would, at first sight, seem to be 'yes'.

The German Army was far from being ready for war in 1939. The Poles and French together had the equivalent of 150 divisions, including thirty-five reserve divisions, and from which some had to be kept for French oversea commitments, against the German total of ninety-eight divisions, of which thirty-six were in an untrained state. Out of the forty divisions which the Germans left to defend their western frontier, only four were active divisions, fully trained and equipped. But Hitler's strategy had placed France in a situation where she could only relieve pressure on Poland by developing a quick attack – a form of action for which her Army was unfitted. Her old-fashioned mobilization plan was slow in producing the required weight of forces, and her offensive plans dependent on a mass of heavy artillery which was not ready until the sixteenth day. By that time the Polish Army's resistance was collapsing.

Poland was badly handicapped by her strategic situation – the country being placed like a 'tongue' between Germany's jaws, and Polish strategy made the situation worse by placing the bulk of the forces near the tip of the tongue. Moreover, these forces were out of date in equipment and ideas, still placing faith in a large mass of horsed cavalry – which proved helpless against the German tanks.

The Germans at that time had only six armoured and four mechanized divisions ready, but thanks to General Guderian's enthusiasm, and Hitler's backing, they had gone farther than any other army in adopting the new idea of high-speed mechanized warfare that had been conceived twenty years earlier by the British pioneers of this new kind and tempo of action. The Germans had also developed a much stronger air force than any of the other countries, whereas not only the Poles, but the French also, were badly lacking airpower, even to support and cover their armies.

Thus Poland saw the first triumphant demonstration of the new Blitzkrieg technique, by the Germans, while the Western allies of Poland were still in process of preparing for war on customary lines. On September 17th the Red Army advanced across Poland's eastern frontier, a blow in the back that sealed her fate, as she had scarcely any troops left to oppose this second invasion.

The rapid overrunning of Poland was followed by a six months' lull – christened the 'Phoney War' by onlookers who were deceived by the surface appearance of calm. A truer name would have been the 'Winter of Illusion'. For the leaders, as well as the public, in the Western countries spent the time in framing fanciful plans for attacking Germany's flanks – and talked about them all too openly.

In reality, there was no prospect of France and Britain ever being able, alone, to develop the strength required to overcome Germany. Their best hope, now that Germany and Russia faced each other on a common border, was that friction would develop between these two mutually distrustful confederates, and draw Hitler's explosive force eastward, instead of westward. That happened a year later, and might well have happened earlier if the Western Allies had not been impatient – as is the way of democracies.

Their loud and threatening talk of attacking Germany's flanks spurred Hitler to forestall them. His first stroke was to occupy Norway. The captured records of his conferences show that until early in 1940, he still considered 'the maintenance of Norway's neutrality to be the best course' for Germany, but that in February he came to the conclusion that 'the English intended to land there, and I want to be there before them'. A small German invading force arrived there on April 9th, upsetting the British plans for gaining control of that neutral area – and captured the chief ports while the Norwegians' attention was absorbed by the British naval advance into Norwegian waters.

Hitler's next stroke was against France and the Low Countries on May 10th. He had started to prepare it the previous autumn, when the Allies rejected the peace offer he made after defeating Poland – feeling that to knock out France offered the best chance of making Britain agree to peace. But bad weather and the doubts of his generals had caused repeated postponements from November onwards. Then on January 10th a German staff officer who was flying to Bonn with papers about the plan missed his way in a snowstorm, and landed in Belgium. This miscarriage caused the offensive to be put off until May, and it was radically recast meanwhile. That turned out very unfortunately for the Allies, and temporarily very lucky for Hitler, while changing the whole outlook of the war.

For the old plan, with the main advance going through the canal-lined area of central Belgium, would in fact have led to a head-on collision with the best part of the Franco-British forces, and so would probably have ended in failure – shaking Hitler's prestige. But the new plan, suggested by Manstein, took the Allies completely by surprise and threw them off their balance, with disastrous results. For while they were pushing forward into Belgium, to meet the Germans' opening assault there and in Holland, the mass of the German tanks – seven panzer divisions – drove through the hilly and wooded Ardennes, which the Allied High Command considered impassable to tanks. Crossing the Meuse with little opposition, they broke through the weak hinge of the Allied front, and then swept on westward to the Channel coast behind the backs of the Allies' armies in Belgium, cutting their communications. This decided the issue – before the bulk of the German infantry had even come into action. The British Army barely managed to escape by sea from Dunkirk. The Belgians and a large part of the French were forced to surrender. The consequences were irreparable. For when the Germans struck southward, the week after Dunkirk, the remaining French armies proved incapable of withstanding them.

Yet never was a world-shaking disaster more easily preventable. The panzer thrust could have been stopped long before reaching the Channel by a concentrated counterstroke with similar forces. But the French, though having more and better tanks than their enemy, had strung them out in small packets in the 1918 way.

The thrust could have been stopped earlier, on the Meuse if the French had not rushed into Belgium leaving their hinge so weak, or had moved reserves there sooner. But the French Command had not only regarded the Ardennes as impassable to tanks but reckoned that any attack on the Meuse would be a set-piece assault in the 1918 style, and would take nearly a week to prepare after arrival there, thus allowing the French ample time to bring up reserves. But the panzer forces reached the river early on May 13th and stormed the crossings that afternoon. A 'tank-time' pace of action bowled over an out-of-date 'slow-motion'.

But this Blitzkrieg pace was only possible because the Allied leaders had not grasped the new technique, and so did not know how to counter it. The thrust could have been stopped before it even reached the Meuse if the approaches had been well covered with minefields. It could have been stopped even if the mines were lacking – by the simple expedient of felling the trees along the forest roads which led to the Meuse. The loss of time in clearing them would have been fatal to the German chances.*

After the fall of France, there was a popular tendency to ascribe it to the poor state of French morale, and to assume that the fall was inevitable. That is a fallacy, a case of 'putting the cart before the horse'. The collapse of French morale only occurred after the military breakthrough – which could so easily have been prevented. By 1942 all armies had learned how to check a Blitzkrieg attack – but a lot would have been saved if they had learned before the war.

THE SECOND PHASE OF THE WAR

Britain was now the only remaining active opponent of Nazi Germany. But she was left in the most perilous situation, militarily naked while menacingly enveloped by a 2,000-mile stretch of enemy coastline.

Her army had only reached Dunkirk and avoided capture through Hitler's strange action in halting his panzer forces for two days when they were a bare ten miles from the last remaining escape-port, then

* A French friend of mine, then in charge of a sector on the Meuse, begged the High Command for permission to do this, but was told that the roads must be kept clear for the advance of the French cavalry. These cavalry duly pushed into the Ardennes, but came out more rapidly and routed, with the German tanks on their heels.

almost unguarded – a halt order inspired by a complex of motives, including Göring's vainglorious desire that the Luftwaffe should take the final trick.

Even though the bulk of the British Army had got away safely, it had lost most of its arms. While the survivors of the sixteen divisions that came back were being reorganized, there was only one properly armed division to defend the country, and the Fleet was kept in the far north out of reach of the Luftwaffe. If the Germans had landed in England any time during the month after the fall of France there would have been little chance of resisting them.

But Hitler and his Service chiefs had made no preparations to invade England – nor even worked out any plans for such an obviously essential follow-up to their defeat of France. He let the vital month slip away in hopeful expectation that Britain would agree to make peace. Even when disillusioned on that score, the German preparations were half-hearted. When the Luftwaffe failed to drive the RAF out of the sky in the 'Battle of Britain', the Army and Navy chiefs were in fact glad of the excuse thus provided for suspending the invasion. More remarkable was Hitler's own readiness to accept excuses for its suspension.

The records of his private talks show that it was partly due to a reluctance to destroy Britain and the British Empire, which he regarded as a stabilizing element in the world, and still hoped to secure as a partner. But beyond this reluctance there was a fresh impulse. Hitler's mind was again turning eastward. This was the key factor that proved decisive in preserving Britain.

Had Hitler concentrated on defeating Britain, her doom would have been almost certain. For although he had missed the best chance of conquering her by invasion, he could have developed such a stranglehold, by combined air and submarine pressure, as to ensure her gradual starvation and ultimate collapse.

Hitler, however, felt that he could not venture to concentrate his resources on that sea-and-air effort while the Russian Army stood poised on his eastern border, as a threat to Germany on land. So he argued that the only way to make Germany's rear secure was to attack and defeat Russia. His suspicion of Russia's intentions was all the more intense because hatred of Russian-style Communism had so long been his deepest emotion.

He also persuaded himself that Britain would agree to peace once she could no longer hope for Russian intervention in the war. Indeed, he imagined that Britain would have made peace already if Russia were not inciting her to fight on. When, on July 21st, Hitler held his first conference to discuss the hastily drafted plans for invading England, he revealed the turn of his mind, saying: 'Stalin is flirting with Britain to keep her in the war and tie us down, with a view to gain time and take what he wants, knowing he could not get it once peace breaks out.' From this came the further conclusion: 'Our attention must be turned to tackling the Russian problem.'

Planning was initiated immediately, though it was not until early in 1941 that he took the definite decision. The invasion was launched on June 22nd – a day ahead of Napoleon's date. The panzer forces quickly overran the Soviet armies that were immediately available and within less than a month had driven 450 miles into Russia – three-quarters of the way to Moscow. But the Germans never reached there.

What were the key factors in their failure? The autumn mud and snow were the obvious ones. But more fundamental was the Germans' miscalculation of the reserves that Stalin could bring up from the depths of Russia. They reckoned on meeting 200 divisions, and by mid-August had beaten these. But by then a further 160 had appeared on the scene. By the time these in turn had been overcome, autumn had arrived, and when the Germans pushed on towards Moscow in the mud, they again found fresh armies blocking the route. Another basic factor was Russia's continued primitiveness, despite all the technical progress achieved since the Soviet Revolution. It was not only a matter of the extraordinary endurance of her soldiers and people, but the primitiveness of her roads. If her road system had been developed comparably to that of the West, she would have been overrun almost as quickly as France. Even as it was, however, the invasion might have succeeded if the panzer forces had driven right on for Moscow in the summer, without waiting for the infantry – as Guderian had urged, only to be overruled on this occasion by Hitler and the older heads of the army.

The winter in Russia proved a terrible strain and drain on the German forces – and they never fully recovered from it. Yet it is evident that Hitler still had quite a good chance of victory in 1942, as the Red Army was seriously short of equipment, while Stalin's grip on it had been shaken by the heavy initial defeats. Hitler's new offensive swept quickly through to the edge of the Caucasus oilfields – on which Russia's military machine depended. But Hitler split his forces between the double objectives of the Caucasus and Stalingrad. Narrowly checked here, he wore down his army in repeated bull-headed efforts to capture the 'City of Stalin', becoming obsessed with that symbol of defiance. Forbidding any withdrawal when winter came, he doomed the army attacking it to encirclement and capture when Russia's newly raised armies arrived on the scene late in the year.

The disaster at Stalingrad left the Germans with a far longer front than they could hold with their depleted strength. Withdrawal was the only saving course, as the generals urged, but Hitler obstinately refused to sanction it. Deaf to all arguments, he constantly insisted on 'No retreat'. That parrot-cry could not stem the tide, and merely ensured that each eventual retreat would be enforced by a heavy defeat, at higher cost because it was delayed too long.

Hitler's forces were suffering, increasingly, the consequences of strategic overstretch – which had proved the ruin of Napoleon. The strain was all the worse because in 1940 the war had been extended to the Mediterranean – by Mussolini plunging into the war to take advantage of France's downfall and Britain's weakness. That had offered the British a chance for counterattack, in an area where seapower could exert its influence. Churchill was quick to seize the chance – in part, too quick. Britain's mechanized force in Egypt, though small, soon smashed the out-of-date Italian army in North Africa, besides conquering Italian East Africa. It could have driven on to Tripoli, but was halted in order that a force could be landed in Greece – a premature and ill-prepared move that was easily repulsed by the Germans. But the Italian breakdown in North Africa led Hitler to send German reinforcements there, under Rommel. However, having his eyes fixed on Russia, Hitler sent only enough to bolster up the Italians, and never made a strong effort to seize the eastern, central, and western gates of the Mediterranean – Suez, Malta, and Gibraltar.

So in effect he merely opened up a fresh drain on Germany's strength, which ultimately offset the success of Rommel's counter-thrusts in postponing for over two years the clearance of North Africa. The Germans were now stretched out along both sides of the Mediterranean, and the whole coastline of western Europe, while trying to hold a perilously wide front in the depths of Russia.

The natural consequences of such general overstretch were postponed, and the war prolonged, by Japan's entry into the war – in December 1941. But this proved more fatal to Hitler's prospects in the long run, because it brought America's weight into the war. The temporary effect of the Japanese surprise stroke at Pearl Harbor, which crippled the US Pacific Fleet, enabled the Japanese to overrun the Allied positions in the South-west Pacific – Malaya, Burma, the Philippines, and the Dutch East Indies. But in this rapid expansion they became stretched out far beyond their basic capacity for holding their gains. For Japan was a small island state, with limited industrial power.

THE THIRD PHASE OF THE WAR

Once America's strength developed, and Russia survived to develop hers, the defeat of the Axis powers – Germany, Italy, and Japan – became certain, as their combined military potential was so much smaller. The only uncertainties were – how long it would take, and how complete it would be. The most that the aggressors, turned defenders, could hope for was to obtain better terms of peace by spinning out time until the 'giants' became weary or quarrelled. But the chances of such prolonged resistance depended on shortening fronts. None of the Axis leaders could bear to 'lose face' by voluntary withdrawal, and so clung on to every position until it collapsed.

There was no real turning point in this third phase of the war, but only an incoming tide.

The tide flowed more easily in Russia and in the Pacific, because in these areas an ever-growing superiority of force was combined with ample space for manoeuvre. In southern and western Europe the tide met more checks because space was more cramped.

The Anglo-American forces' first bound back into Europe – in July 1943 – was eased by the way that Hitler and Mussolini poured troops across the sea into Tunisia in the hope of holding a bridgehead there to block the converging advance of the Allied armies from Egypt and Algeria. Tunisia turned into a trap, and the capture of the whole German–Italian army there left Sicily almost denuded of defence. But when the Allies pushed on from Sicily into Italy – in September 1943 – their advance up that narrow and mountainous peninsula became sticky and slow.

On June 6th, 1944, the main Allied armies, which had been built up in England for a cross-Channel invasion, landed in Normandy. Here success was certain if they could firmly establish themselves ashore in a bridgehead big enough to build up their massed strength and swamp the German's barricading line. For once they broke out, the whole width of France would be open for the manoeuvre of their armies, which were fully mechanized, whereas the bulk of the German forces were not.

The Germans' defence was thus doomed to eventual collapse unless they could throw the invaders back in the sea in the first few days. But in the event the move-up of their panzer reserves was fatally delayed by the paralysing interference of the Allied air forces, which had a 30 to 1 superiority over the Luftwaffe in this theatre.

Even if the invasion of Normandy had been repulsed on the beaches, the Allies' now tremendous air superiority, applied direct against Germany, would have made her collapse certain. Until 1944 the strategic air offensive had fallen far short of the claims made for it, as an alternative to land invasion, and its effects had been greatly overestimated. The indiscriminate bombing of cities had not seriously diminished munitions production, while failing to break the will of the opposing peoples and compel them to surrender, as expected. For collectively they were too firmly under the grip of their tyrannical leaders, and individuals cannot surrender to bombers in the sky. But in 1944-5 airpower was better directed – applied with ever-increasing precision and crippling effect to the key centres of war production that were vital to the enemy's power of resistance. In the Far East, too, the master key of airpower made the collapse of Japan certain, without any need for the atom bomb.

The main obstacle in the Allies' path, once the tide had turned, was a self-raised barrier – their leaders' unwise and short-sighted demand for 'unconditional surrender'. It was the greatest help to Hitler, in preserving his grip on the German people, and likewise to the War Party in Japan. If the Allied leaders had been wise enough to provide some assurance as to their peace terms, Hitler's grip on the German people would have been loosened long before 1945. Three years earlier, envoys of the widespread anti-Nazi movement in Germany made known to the Allied leaders their plans for overthrowing Hitler, and the names of the many leading soldiers who were prepared to join such a revolt, provided that they were given some assurance about the Allied peace terms. But then, and later, no indication or assurance was given them, so that it naturally became difficult for them to gain support for a 'leap in the dark'.

Thus 'the unnecessary war' was unnecessarily prolonged, and millions more lives needlessly sacrificed, while the ultimate peace merely produced a fresh menace and the looming fear of another war. For the unnecessary prolongation of the Second World War, in pursuit of the opponents' 'unconditional surrender', proved of profit only to Stalin – by opening the way for Communist domination of central Europe.

Books Referred to in the Text

Where British and American publishers are given, the first mentioned is the edition from which I have taken any quotations, and the page numbers of any reference may be valid for that edition only. I would like to thank the authors, publishers and other copyright holders concerned for permission to make quotations from some of these works.

Bradley, Omar N.: *A Soldier's Story of the Allied Campaigns from Tunis to the Elbe*. London, Eyre & Spottiswoode, 1951; New York, H. Holt & Co, 1951.

Butcher, Captain Harry C.: *My Three Years with Eisenhower*. New York, Simon & Schuster, 1946; London, Heinemann, 1946.

Churchill, Winston S.: *The War Speeches of Winston S. Churchill* (compiled by Charles Eade, 3 vols). London, Cassell, 1952; Boston, Houghton Mifflin, 1953.

Churchill, Winston S.: *The Second World War* (6 vols). London, Cassell, 1948–54: Boston, Houghton, Mifflin, 1948–54.

    Vol I: *The Gathering Storm* (9th edition, 1967).
    Vol II: *Their Finest Hour* (9th edition, 1967).
    Vol III: *The Grand Alliance* (5th edition, 1968).
    Vol IV: *The Hinge of Fate* (4th edition, 2nd impression, 1968).
    Vol V: *Closing the Ring* (4th edition, 2nd impression, 1968).
    Vol VI: *Triumph and Tragedy* (2nd edition, 1954).

Clark, General Mark: *Calculated Risk*. London, Harrap, 1951; New York, Harper, 1950.

Cunningham, Admiral Lord: *A Sailor's Odyssey*. London, Hutchinson, 1951.

Douhet, Giulio: *The Command of the Air*. London, Faber, 1943; New York, Coward-McCann, 1942.

Eisenhower, Dwight D.: *Crusade in Europe*. New York, Doubleday, 1948; London, Heinemann, 1949.

Feiling, Keith: *The Life of Neville Chamberlain*. London, Macmillan, 1946.

Halder, General Franz: *Diaries*. Privately printed. Copyright © Infantry Journal Inc. (USA), 1950.

Kippenberger, Major-General Sir Howard: *Infantry Brigadier*. London (and New York), Oxford University Press, 1949.

Liddell Hart, Captain B. H.: *The Defence of Britain*. London, Faber, 1939.

> *The Other Side of the Hill*. London, Cassell, 1951.
> (See my list of books, following the Index. *The Other Side of the Hill* in its 1951 edition has not been published in the United States. The considerably smaller 1948 edition was published in New York by Morrow in 1948 as *The German Generals Talk*.)
> *The Tanks: The History of the Royal Tank Regiment and its Predecessors* etc. (2 vols). London, Cassell, 1959; New York, Praeger, 1959.

Linklater, Eric: *The Campaign in Italy*. London, HMSO, 1951.

Martel, Lt-General Sir Gifford: *An Outspoken Soldier*. London, Sifton Praed, 1949.

North, John: *North-West Europe 1944-5. The Achievements of 21st Army Group*. London, HMSO, 1953.

Rommel, Field-Marshal Erwin: *The Rommel Papers* (ed B. H. Liddell Hart). London, Collins, 1953; New York, Harcourt, Brace, 1953.

Schmidt, H. W.: *With Rommel in the Desert*. London, Harrap, 1951.

Seaton, Lt-Colonel Albert: *The Russo-German War, 1941-45*. London, Arthur Barker, 1970; New York, Praeger, 1970.

Tedder, Marshal of the Royal Air Force Lord: *With Prejudice*. London, Cassell, 1966; Boston, Little, Brown, 1967.

Westphal, General Siegfried: *The German Army in the West*. London, Cassell, 1951.

OFFICIAL HISTORIES

Great Britain

Roskill, Captain S. W.: *The War at Sea*. Vol I. London, HMSO, 1954.

Ehrman, John: *Grand Strategy*. Vol V. London, HMSO, 1956.

Woodburn Kirby, Major-General S.: *The War Against Japan*. Vol I. London. HMSO, 1957.

Playfair, Major-General ISO, and others: *The Mediterranean and the Middle East*. Vol III. London, HMSO, 1960.

Webster, Sir Charles, and Frankland, Noble: *The Strategic Air Offensive Against Germany, 1939-1945*.

> Vol I: *Preparation*. London, HMSO, 1961.
> Vol II: *Endeavour*. London, HMSO, 1961.
> Vol III: *Victory*. London, HMSO, 1961.

United States

United States Army in World War II

Cole, H. M.: *The European Theater of Operations: The Lorraine Campaign*. Washington DC, Historical Division, Department of the Army, 1950.

Matloff, Maurice, and Snell, Edwin M.: *The War Department: Strategic Planning for Coalition Warfare, 1941–1942*. Washington, DC, Office of the Chief of Military History, Department of the Army, 1953.

Howe, George F.: *The Mediterranean Theater of Operations: Northwest Africa: Seizing the Initiative in the West*. Washington, DC, Office of the Chief of Military History, Department of the Army, 1957.

History of United States Naval Operations in World War II

Morison, S. E.: Vol IX: *Sicily–Salerno–Anzio, January 1943–June 1944*. Boston. Little, Brown, 1954.

DISPATCHES

Supplement to The London Gazette, February 3rd 1948.
   Despatch submitted ... by ... Field-Marshal the Viscount Alexander of Tunis, KG, GCB, GCMG, CSI, DSO, MC.
Supplement to The London Gazette, April 25th 1950.
   Despatch submitted ... by Admiral of the Fleet Sir Andrew B. Cunningham, GCB, DSO.

Index

SUBJECT

Absolute national defence sphere of Japan, 530

Admiralty, caution of, in regard to Norway, 56, 66–7; and German landings in Norway, 64–6; and evacuation from Dunkirk, 84; demands anti-aircraft guns, 104; opposes sending more tanks through Mediterranean, 185*n.*

Aerial torpedoes, British development of, 221

Air attack(s), on Dunkirk beaches, 85; on British fighter airfields, 102, 105–6, 107, 109; provokes retaliation, 109; vulnerability of capital ships to, 221, 225, 235–6; on merchant shipping, 387, 393, 398, 721; preliminary to 'Overlord', 561, 572, 633, 635–6, 640, 744; long-distance, on Balkan targets, 601–2, 605; 'suicide', 657–9, 714–16. *See also* Bombardment, preliminary; Incendiary raids; Strategic air offensive, etc.

Air defence, use of bombers considered best for, 619; fighters for, 620; improved German, 624, 630

Air Defence of Great Britain, 103–4

Air Force, British. *See* Royal Air Force

Air Force, German. *See* Luftwaffe

Air Force, Japanese, in 1941, 218; attacks Philippines, 230–31; on Marianas, 646–8; loss of pilots at, 648; difficulties in training of new pilots, 649; Kamikaze tactics of, 657–9, 714–16

   Army, in Malaya, 238; fighter groups, kept at home, 360; in Solomons and New Guinea (6th and 7th Divisions), 525, 532; in Philippines (4th Air Army), 650

   Navy, at Formosa (11th Air Fleet), 218; attacks at Pearl Harbor, 221, 224, 225; at Midway battle, 363–8; losses in, off Guadalcanal, 377–8; at Rabaul (11th Air Fleet), 525

Air Force, Polish, 30

Air Force, Russian, bombs Kleist's army, 264

Air Force, United States Army, raids Tokyo, 359–60, 660–61, 721–2; on Guadalcanal, 377; strategic daylight raids of, on Germany, 628, 632–4, 638, 641; long-range fighter escorts of, 632–3, 641; losses in, in German raids, 632–3, 637; attacks oil targets, 636–8; strategic raids of, on Japan, 721–2, 745

   5th, 658

   8th, 627, 629, 632, 634–7

   10th, 379

   15th, 633, 636

   20th, 720

   21st, 721

   Navy, at Midway battle, 365–7; raids Japan, 714. *See also* Aircraft carriers, US

Air supply: of advancing tanks, 167; of German troops in bastion-towns of Russia, 252–3; of China, 379; Chindits dependent on, 383–4; stoppage of, in Burma, due to withdrawal of transport planes, 590, 593; to Warsaw, hampered by Russia, 611*n.*; of army in Burma, 661, 665, 666, 667, 668

night-time, 635, 637; aided by low-level marking of targets by Mosquitoes, 636; daylight American, on Japan, 721

Promotion, effect of, on producing compliance, 255

Propaganda, ineffective Allied, during phoney war, 38n., 39; of Goebbels to German people, 39; anti-German, to Russian Army, 151; leaflets, dropping of, 621

Radar, *British*, RAF, 101, 620; German bombing of stations, 105–6; German ways of evading, 107–8; assists detection of submarines, 393; new 10-centimetre, 401–2, 406; distracting device, 629

German, 105; directing anti-aircraft fire and searchlight systems, 629; masters 'Window', 630; loses French early warning system, 633

United States, on Hawaii, 225; detects carrier strikes off Marianas, 648; 'night-sight' provided by, at Leyte Gulf, 654

Radio: German, used to demoralize Poland, 30; poor equipment of German fighters, 98; control of British fighters, 101; breakdowns, British and German, in desert, 200; intelligence, German, 401

Radio station at Algiers, taken over by collaborators, 340

Railways, bombing of, before 'Overlord', 561, 631, 635; Allied bombing of Balkan, 601–2; bombing of German, 622–3, 635; Russians repair, and alter gauge, behind Vistula line, 694

Rangers, American, at Salerno, 481, 483; at Anzio, 552

Rearmament, British, 10, 23; French, 23; German, 15

Reconnaissance aircraft, British Coastal Command, 395; German, in Battle of Atlantic, 407; US, at Battle of Philippine Sea, 648; at Battle of Leyte Gulf, 654

Refugees, German, in Silesia, 697

Reserves, method of draining opponent's balance of, 514–15

Rifle, Russian, qualities of, 509

Roads, wheeled vehicles useless without, 165; primitiveness of Russian, 169–70, 177, 742; felling trees over, could have stopped German tanks, 740

Rocket bombardment of Antwerp, 706

Rocket-artillery, Russian, 509

Rocket-carrying aircraft, US, 647

Rocket-craft, 482

Royal Air Force, strength of, in 1939, 18; over Dunkirk, 85; strength of, during Battle of Britain, 98, 100, 101; flying training schools of, 99, 628; pilot wastage in, 99, 108; defence system of, 101; Germans overestimate losses and underestimate production in, 101–2, 107; in N Africa removed to Greece, 125; in Burma, 244; prevents supplies reaching Rommel, 311; created an independent Service, 617; espouses concept of strategic air attack, 617–19, 622; has no strategic bombing force in 1939, 619, 621; averse to co-operation with Army, 622

BOMBER COMMAND: bombers transferred to, from Coastal Command, 399; sinks *Tirpitz*, 408; incapable in 1939 of carrying out strategic bombing, 619, 621; small-scale action of, early in war, 621–2; confined to night-raiding, 621–2, 628; starts strategic bombing, 622; inaccuracy of, in hitting specific targets, 622; navigation the prime problem of, 623; losses in, on raids on Germany, 624, 626–31, 633–4, 637; new directives on 'primary objective' of, 625, 628; diversions and ruses of, to escape night-fighters, 626; combines with Fighter Command in 'Circus' operations, 626; growth in operational strength of, 628; improved accuracy of, 628, 636; 'dam-busting' operation of, 629; shaken morale of, 630; diverted to attacks on French railways, 631,

Searchlight: batteries for air defence, 103–4, 112; Leigh Light in convoying aircraft, 393; system, German radar-directed, 626; use of in lighting opening of Ardennes offensive, 679, 682

Service Force, mobile US, 534, 536

Shipping, German air attacks on, in Channel, 105; British, for 'Torch' landings, 328; problem in planning recovery of Burma, 378; American protection of, in Atlantic, 396; refitting of British, in US yards, 396; sunk by submarines, 411; Axis, in Mediterranean, Allied toll of, 445; losses in Japanese, 712–13, 721. *See also* Convoys; Merchant Shipping

Shuttle-service: of air-raids on E. Europe, 605; of air supplies to Warsaw forbidden by Russia, 611n.

'Snowflake' illumination of sea, 393

Space and force, ratio between, on Eastern front, 275–6, 595, 699

Special Boat Service, 702

Spying, Britain 'watertight' against, 573, 575

Strategic advantages to Hitler of his political moves, 733, 736

Strategic air offensive, *against Germany*, 617–41, 745; theory and doctrine of, 617–20; pre-war assumptions regarding, 619; against specific targets, 619, 621–2, 631, 639–40; against civil populations, 619, 623–4, 640; Germans abandon concept of, 621; over-estimation of results and effects of, 621–4, 627; start of British offensive, 623; indiscriminate, 622–4, 628–31, 638–9, 745; '1000 bomber raids', 626–7; directives on, from Casablanca and Washington Conferences, 627–8; stepped up in 1943, 628–30; does not achieve its aim, 631; joint effort at, 632–3; resumed, after 'Overlord', 633, 636–9; important effects of, 635; trend away from area-bombing in, 635, 636; failure to maintain best priorities in, 638; deliberate revival of 'terrorization', 638–9; comparative target results in, 639–41; conclusions, 641; effect on army in Italy, 701; *against Japanese*, 720–22, 745

Strategic Bombing Survey, US, 727–8

Strategic penetration, deep, Guderian fired by idea of, 71; Guderian carries out, in France, 79–80; Guderian seeks to carry out, in Russia, 167; of Rommel, 198–202, 277, 290–91; Allied failure to use, in 'Overlord', 582–3n.; persistent pace and pressure essential to, 593

Strategy, Japanese errors in, at Midway, 365, 367; defensive, on upper Dnieper front, 519–20

Street fighting, in Stalingrad, 270; in Manila, 659; in Berlin, 710

Submarines, *British*, off Norway, 61; cut off Rommel's supplies in Mediterranean, 311; midget, attack *Tirpitz*, 408

German. See U-boats

Italian 398, 401, 403, 411; in Atlantic, 392

Japanese, 411; used at Pearl Harbor, 225–6; in battle of Midway, 363; reinforcements and supplies carried by, 377, 712; concentrate attacks on warships, 712

United States, attack Japanese troopship convoys, 644; sink carriers, off Marianas, 648; sink Japanese oil tankers, 649; sink cruisers approaching Philippines, 653; sink Japanese merchant ships and tankers, 712–13; part played by, in defeat of Japan, 713

Suicide: attacks by Japanese troops, 535–6, 649; naval action at Okinawa, 715. *See also* Kamikaze attacks

Supplies: Rommel misses British dumps, 199–200; British loss of, in North Africa, 279, 288, 291; to Rommel, lost in Mediterranean, 311–12; minimal, to Axis forces in Tunisia, 445; Russians depend on capture of, 504; Russian ability to survive on less than other armies, 509; restricted, for Patton's Army, 588–9; deficiencies in, hampering

Index

GENERAL

Petsamo, Russia seeks frontier adjust-
ments near, 47; cut off by Russia,
48; plan for Allied landing at, 59
Philippine Islands, Japanese attacks
on, 212, 231-3; US reinforcements to, 216; US and Philippine
troops in, 217, 231-3; US aircraft
in, 218; original plans regarding,
Japanese and US, 219-20; US
decision to hold, 220, 231; timing
of attack on, 224; fall of, 231-3,
358; attacking Japan through, 522-
3, 533; Japanese defence of, 524,
650-51; Allies poised for attack on,
646, 648, 650-51; Japanese naval
HQ moved to, 646; defence of, a
Japanese priority, 649; possibility
of by-passing, 649; landings on,
651, 655; capture of, 658-9;
mopping-up operations in, 719-20
Philippine Sea, Battle of, 646-8, 657,
713
Phillips, Admiral Sir Tom, 235-6
'Phoney War', 36-45, 738
Pile, Lieut-General Sir Frederick,
103, 105n., 112
Pilica, River, 31-2, 695
Pinczow, 695
Plate, River, *Admiral Graf Spee*
scuttled in, 387
Platt, Major-General William, 128, 133
Ploesti oilfields, Allied air attacks on,
601, 636; Russia occupies, 612
'Plum' hill-gap, 436-7
Plymouth, air raids on, 115
Po, River, 702-3; delta of, 566
'Point-blank, Operation' (Combined
Bomber Offensive), 628
Poland, Anglo-French guarantee to,
3, 11-15, 736; German invasion of,
3, 16, 30-31, 737; partitioning of, 3,
14, 34, 737; Russian domination of,
3; joins Germany in pillaging
Czecho-Slovakia, 10, 15; collapse
of, 20, 33; German demands on, 10,
12; Russian help needed for protection of, 11-12, 736; buffer
between Russia and Germany, 14;
illusions about strength of, 16-17;
overrunning of, 29-35, 738; Allies'

inability to help, 34-5, 737; offers
conditions favourable for Blitzkrieg, 50; German army groups in,
138; rain causes impassable roads
in, 140; Hitler transfers troops
from West to, 150; encirclement of
Russian salient in, 168; Russian
troops facing Germans in S, 172;
Russians pursue Germans into, 597,
605, 608; stabilization of front in
S., 601; panzer groups sent from, to
relieve Budapest, 693-4; Russian
advance over plain of, 695-6;
Hitler envelops flank of, in taking
Czecho-Slovakia, 736
Polish Corridor, 10, 31
Polish Guarantee, 3, 11-15, 16, 736-7
Polish 'underground', rising of, in
Warsaw, 610
Polla, 480
Polotsk, 607
Poltava, 514, 515-16
Pomerania, 698
Pont-du-Fahs, 356, 429, 443-4
Ponte Sele, 484
Popov, Lieut-General M. M., 514
Porajorpi, 48
Port Arthur, 209, 227-8
Port Lyautey airfield, 335
Port Moresby, Japanese plan to take,
360; Australia within reach of air
strike from, 360, 369; invading
force turned back from, 363, 369;
Japanese overland attempt to take,
369, 371; air support to Guadal-
canal from, 373
Port Sudan, 128
Portal, Air Chief Marshal Sir Charles,
457, 624, 635
Portland, 105; Bill, 95, 409
Porto Farina, 449
Portsmouth, 95, 105; air attack on
Dockyard, 109
Portugal, Italy negotiates with Allies
through, 471
Potenza, 487
Potsdam: Conference, 722-3, 725,
728; Declaration, 727
Pound, Admiral of the Fleet Sir
Dudley, 457

FURTHER READING IN THE BOOKS OF
CAPTAIN SIR BASIL LIDDELL HART

Memoirs
THE LIDDELL HART MEMOIRS, 2 vols. (London, Cassell, 1965: New York, Putnam, 1965)

The Conduct of War (and general history of wars)
STRATEGY – THE INDIRECT APPROACH (London, Faber, latest edition 1954 – enlarged from *The Decisive Wars of History*, 1929)
THOUGHTS ON WAR, 1919–39 (London, Faber, 1944 – contains the collected essence of the author's military thought)
THE REVOLUTION IN WARFARE (London, Faber, 1946; Yale University Press, 1947)
THE GHOST OF NAPOLEON (London, Faber, 1933; Yale University Press, 1933)

The Theory of Mechanized War (in particular)
PARIS, OR THE FUTURE OF WAR (London, Kegan, Paul, 1925 – in the 'Today and Tomorrow' series; New York, E. P. Dutton & Co., 1925)
THE RE-MAKING OF MODERN ARMIES (London, John Murray, 1927)
WHEN BRITAIN GOES TO WAR (London, Faber, 1935 – enlarged from *The British Way in Warfare*, 1932; also Penguin, 1942, with additional chapters, and under the original title. In America THE BRITISH WAY IN WARFARE, New York, Macmillan, 1933)
THE FUTURE OF INFANTRY (London, Faber, 1933; Harrisburg, Military Service Publishing Co., 1936)
DYNAMIC DEFENCE (London, Faber, 1940)
THE CURRENT OF WAR (London, Hutchinson, 1941 – in particular Chapters I–VI. The rest of the book is a commentary on the 1939–40 campaign)
THE TANKS – THE HISTORY OF THE ROYAL TANK REGIMENT AND ITS PREDECESSORS (etc.) 1914–45, 2 vols. (London, Cassell, 1959; New York, Praeger, 1959)

Other Books on the Theory and Future of War
EUROPE IN ARMS (London, Faber, 1937)
THE DEFENCE OF BRITAIN (London, Faber, 1939)
THIS EXPANDING WAR (London, Faber, 1942 – partly a commentary on the 1941–42 campaigns)

DEFENCE OF THE WEST (London, Cassell, 1950)
DETERRENT OR DEFENCE (London, Stevens, 1960)

Infantry Tactics
NEW METHODS OF INFANTRY TRAINING (Cambridge, 1918)
SCIENCE OF INFANTRY TACTICS (Beccles, Clowes, 1921, 1923, 1926)

Historical Biography – with a bearing on future warfare
T. E. LAWRENCE – IN ARABIA AND AFTER (London, Cape, 1934. In
  America COLONEL LAWRENCE: THE MAN BEHIND THE LEGEND, New
  York, Dodd, Mead, 1934)
FOCH (London, Eyre & Spottiswoode, 1931; also Penguin)
SHERMAN (London, Eyre & Spottiswoode, 1929. In America SHERMAN:
  SOLDIER, REALIST, AMERICAN, New York, Dodd, Mead, 1929)
GREAT CAPTAINS UNVEILED (London, Blackwood, 1927; Boston, Little,
  Brown, 1928)
A GREATER THAN NAPOLEON – SCIPIO AFRICANUS (London, Blackwood,
  1926: Boston, Little, Brown, 1927)

World War I (1914–18)
A HISTORY OF THE FIRST WORLD WAR (London, Cassell, 1970. Originally
  published as *A History of the World War, 1914–1918*, London, Faber,
  1934. Enlarged from *The Real War 1914–1918*, London, Faber, 1930;
  Boston, Little, Brown)
THE WAR IN OUTLINE, 1914–1918 (London, Faber, 1936)
REPUTATIONS: TEN YEARS AFTER (London, John Murray, 1928; Boston,
  Little, Brown, 1928)
THROUGH THE FOG OF WAR (London, Faber, 1938; New York, Random
  House, 1938)

World War II (1939–45)
THE OTHER SIDE OF THE HILL (London, Cassell, 1951 – enlarged by
  some 60 per cent from the original edition of 1948 which alone was
  published in America, New York, Morrow, as THE GERMAN GENERALS
  TALK, 1948)
A HISTORY OF THE SECOND WORLD WAR (London, Cassell, 1970; New
  York, Putnam's, 1970)

General
WHY DON'T WE LEARN FROM HISTORY? (London, Allen & Unwin, 1944)

Contributions
THE STRATEGY OF CIVILIAN DEFENCE (ed. Adam Roberts. London, Faber,
  1967. In America CIVILIAN RESISTANCE AS A NATIONAL DEFENSE,
  Harrisburg, Stackpole, 1967)
CHURCHILL – FOUR FACES AND THE MAN (London, Allen Lane The

Penguin Press, 1969. In America, CHURCHILL REVISED: A CRITICAL ASSESSMENT, New York, Dial, 1969)

Edited Books

THE ROMMEL PAPERS (London, Collins, 1953; New York, Harcourt, Brace, 1953)

THE LETTERS OF PRIVATE WHEELER (Napoleonic Wars) (London, Michael Joseph, 1951)

THE SOVIET ARMY (London, Weidenfeld & Nicolson, 1956. In America THE RED ARMY, Harcourt, Brace, 1956)

Sir Basil Liddell Hart
History of the First World War £12.00

First published in 1930, Liddell Hart's classic history of the First World War is the work of a leading military analyst, but also of a compassionate and uniquely original thinker. Sir Basil Liddell Hart was the author of more than thirty books and a world renowned lecturer in strategy and tactics; a man of whom *The Economist* said: 'he is not simply a prophet and critic but a historian of great rank'.

'The most influential British military writer of his time' THE SPECTATOR

'Brilliant . . . the best one-volume history of the First World War ever likely to be written' NAVAL REVIEW

'It was always his special talent to be able to express military situations in telling and limpid phrases which would stick in the reader's mind' THE DAILY TELEGRAPH

All Pan Books are available at your local bookshop or newsagent, or can be ordered direct from the publisher. Indicate the number of copies required and fill in the form below.

Send to: Macmillan General Books C.S.
                Book Service By Post
                PO Box 29, Douglas I-O-M
                IM99 1BQ

or phone: 01624 675137, quoting title, author and credit card number.

or fax: 01624 670923, quoting title, author, and credit card number.

or Internet: http://www.bookpost.co.uk

Please enclose a remittance* to the value of the cover price plus 75 pence per book for post and packing. Overseas customers please allow £1.00 per copy for post and packing.

*Payment may be made in sterling by UK personal cheque, Eurocheque, postal order, sterling draft or international money order, made payable to Book Service By Post.

Alternatively by Access/Visa/MasterCard

Card No.   ☐☐☐☐☐☐☐☐☐☐☐☐☐☐☐☐☐☐

Expiry Date   ☐☐☐☐☐☐☐☐☐☐☐☐☐☐☐☐☐☐

Signature   _____

Applicable only in the UK and BFPO addresses.

While every effort is made to keep prices low, it is sometimes necessary to increase prices at short notice. Pan Books reserve the right to show on covers and charge new retail prices which may differ from those advertised in the text or elsewhere.

NAME AND ADDRESS IN BLOCK CAPITAL LETTERS PLEASE

Name _____

Address _____

_____

_____

_____

8/95

Please allow 28 days for delivery.
Please tick box if you do not wish to receive any additional information. ☐